Praise for

Making Better Bui

MW01008489

Making Better Buildings is essential reading for home builders, owner-builders, or anyone interested in hiring a contractor to build their green dream home. This book is full of useful, up-to-date, cutting edge information and is amazingly thorough and easy to read. It will help readers make the best decisions possible regarding energy efficiency, cost, durability, health, embodied energy, labor requirements, and so on. Quite possibly the most valuable book ever published on green building!

— Dan Chiras, Ph.D., director, The Evergreen Institute (www.evergreeninstitute.org) and author,
The Natural House, The New Ecological Home and *The Solar House*

Comparing contemporary building technologies based on criteria such as *embodied energy* or *energy efficiency* is a huge job — a job that holds most contractors and owner-builders back from making informed choices. Chris Magwood has saved us all thousands of research hours with *Making Better Buildings*. This book is not only a tool for the builders of today, but is a marvelous textbook for the young, emerging building professionals of tomorrow.

— Emily Niehaus, Founding Director of Community Rebuilds

At last: clarity! There are more and more people all over the world who are discovering the joy and satisfaction of building for themselves with natural materials. Very few, however, are also able to teach, communicate and inspire those around them. Of that precious few, Chris Magwood is at the top of the list; his delight and mastery of the subject hums in every page. Whether you want a broad overview, or access to high-quality, practical information on specific subjects, this is the book for you.

— Bruce King, PE, Director, Ecological Building Network

If you're drilling deep into sustainable building and want more than superficial details, let Chris Magwood be your guide. *Making Better Buildings* will help builders and homeowners quantify the green building process, and better understand the impact of their decisions.

— Scott Gibson, Green Building Advisor

Chris Magwood's new book is exciting news for builders and homeowners everywhere! This includes people who haven't even heard yet of the ideas that Chris lays out with such accessible knowledge and clarity. As one of the most knowledgeable and experienced ecological builders in North America, practicality and efficiency is one of his prime concerns. As one of the leading natural builders in the world, his affordable ideas are offered for all scales, within his broad and creative vision.

— Mark Lakeman, Communitecture Architecture & Planning, and cofounder,
The City Repair Project, Portland, OR

Based on Chris Magwood's considerable experience of sustainable buildings systems, this book provides invaluable guidance for builders, designers and those thinking of building their own home. Stripping away the hype, the book provides a rational and balanced assessment of alternative options for the major components of a building. It is particularly valuable since it includes a wide range of criteria such as cost, durability, code compliance and labour intensiveness together with environmental criteria, which make it a highly useful decision support tool for many sustainable building projects. Also, we are encouraged to get beyond the bickering about different systems at the "micro" level and to focus on the bigger picture, "macro" issues, when choosing building components and systems which will lead to significant change.

— Professor Mark Gorgolewski, Ryerson University

Making Better Buildings belongs in the library of every designer or builder in the green building business and should be read by every owner planning a new home. This is not simply green building — this is the future of construction! Chris Magwood has clearly described the pros and cons of the most viable natural building techniques and places them in context to create a tool that is timeless. All of the systems reviewed have the promise of significantly reducing the environmental footprint of construction.

— Jeff Ruppert, P.E., structural and civil engineer, and publisher, *The Last Straw Journal*

Ever wondered about the many shades of green in Green Building?
The book you hold in your hand not only walks you through the vast array of techniques, written by one of the worlds most experienced green builders and educators, it also provides you with all the information necessary to compose the shade of green which suits you best. The information gathered here about issues such as techniques, embodied energy, health aspects are unique in the world, and is guaranteed to make this book the leading reference book for environmentally concerned building planners for years to come. Excellent work.

— Max Vittrup Jensen, consultant, and director, PermaLot Centre of Natural Building

We're often asked to recommend books to guide people along the path to building their own natural home. The list of books is quite short, but with *Making Better Buildings* it just got one important book longer.

— Oliver Swann, naturalhomes.org

This book is a must read for anyone trying to demystify the myriad of green building options. Chris Magwood packs this book with scientific data plus his unique hands-on experience. The result will leave every reader with a clear understanding of the benefits and challenges for a variety of super eco-friendly building methods."

— Sigi Koko, natural builder, and founder, Down to Earth Design www.buildnaturally.com

Chris Magwood offers a refreshingly objective analysis of technologies from foundations to finishes, informed by a very clear set of criteria that allows the designer or builder to compare and select the correct choice for their project. Where other books offer biased opinions, cursory overviews, or limited perspectives on building options, *Making Better Buildings* presents detail-rich, data-driven, experience-verified, field-tested solutions for every building component. This book is an invaluable resource for every building professional and motivated prospective owner seeking a trust-worthy source for information to help inform their practice. The name says it all!

—Jacob Deva Racusin, author, *The Natural Building Companion* and co-owner,
New Frameworks Natural Building

Someday all buildings will be built sustainably; *Making Better Buildings* provides an expert compass for getting there. A must for any sustainable building library.

—Martin Hammer, architect, lead author of the Strawbale Construction appendix for the
2015 International Residential Code, and co-director, Builders Without Borders

It's a tall task to make the complex set of green building choices accessible and interesting – and Chris Magwood has done it well. As a teacher, and a systems and building consultant, I'd say this book ranks up there as one of the top three green building reference books. And it's the only one that covers the variety of building systems from foundation to roof so well, with enough building science, rationale and hints of philosophy to keep it beside your desk rather than the bookshelf.

—Gord Baird, Eco-Sense (ecosenseliving.wordpress.com)

If you're about to embark on building a new home, whether you're a professional or homeowner, this manual will help you discover the materials most suitable for your location and budget, and that do less damage to the environment than many standard materials.

—Cathy Rust, BE CGreen (becgreen.ca)

A Comparative Guide to

SUSTAINABLE CONSTRUCTION

for **HOMEOWNERS** and **CONTRACTORS**

Chris Magwood

MAKING BETTER BUILDINGS

new society
PUBLISHERS

Cover design by Diane McIntosh. All cover images by Daniel Earle.

All interior photos by Chris Magwood, unless otherwise noted.

Printed in Canada. First printing March 2014.

New Society Publishers acknowledges the financial support of the Government of Canada through the Canada Book Fund (CBF) for our publishing activities.

Paperback ISBN: 978-0-86571-706-0
eISBN: 978-1-55092-515-9

Inquiries regarding requests to reprint all or part of *Making Better Buildings* should be addressed to New Society Publishers at the address below.

To order directly from the publishers, please call toll-free (North America) 1-800-567-6772, or order online at www.newsociety.com

Any other inquiries can be directed by mail to:

New Society Publishers
P.O. Box 189, Gabriola Island, BC V0R 1X0, Canada
(250) 247-9737

New Society Publishers' mission is to publish books that contribute in fundamental ways to building an ecologically sustainable and just society, and to do so with the least possible impact on the environment, in a manner that models this vision. We are committed to doing this not just through education, but through action. The interior pages of our bound books are printed on Forest Stewardship Council®-registered acid-free paper that is **100% post-consumer recycled** (100% old growth forest-free), processed chlorine-free, and printed with vegetable-based, low-VOC inks, with covers produced using FSC®-registered stock. New Society also works to reduce its carbon footprint, and purchases carbon offsets based on an annual audit to ensure a carbon neutral footprint. For further information, or to browse our full list of books and purchase securely, visit our website at: www.newsociety.com

Library and Archives Canada Cataloguing in Publication

Magwood, Chris, author

Making better buildings : a comparative guide to sustainable construction for homeowners and contractors / Chris Magwood.

Includes index.
Issued in print and electronic formats.
ISBN 978-0-86571-706-0 (pbk.).--ISBN 978-1-55092-515-9 (ebook)

1. Sustainable construction. 2. Sustainable buildings--Design and construction. 3. Building--Environmental aspects. 4. Materials--Environmental aspects. I. Title.

TH880.M34 2014   720.47   C2013-908082-1
                                         C2013-908138-0

This one's for Jen

Books for Wiser Living
recommended by *Mother Earth News*

Today, more than ever before, our society is seeking ways to live more conscientiously. To help bring you the very best inspiration and information about greener, more sustainable lifestyles, *Mother Earth News* is recommending select books from New Society Publishers. For more than 30 years, *Mother Earth News* has been North America's "Original Guide to Living Wisely," creating books and magazines for people with a passion for self-reliance and a desire to live in harmony with nature. Across the countryside and in our cities, New Society Publishers and *Mother Earth News* are leading the way to a wiser, more sustainable world. For more information, please visit MotherEarthNews.com.

Contents

There is a basket of fresh bread on your head,
and yet you go door to door asking for crusts.

— Rumi

Thanks

THIS BOOK WOULDN'T EXIST if not for all the amazing builders and designers who have spent lifetimes figuring out the best way to do so many different things. Some I've learned from through the amazing buildings they left behind. Some I've learned from through their books and articles. Others I've been lucky to meet and work with. The sustainable building community is amazingly supportive, collegial, open-source and adventurous. I am so lucky to be a part of it at this exciting time in its development. I hope you all see your names all over this work, even though I can't write them all down here!

I'd like to give personal thanks to:

- Jen Feigin, who never fails to show me that there's always a better way to do things, and a way to have fun doing it.
- Emma and Julie Bowen, who accompanied me as I started down this path and who made it possible for me to find my passion and pursue it.
- Sandy Zabludofsky and Gary Magwood, who always just go for it and work hard to make things work.

- Greg Magwood, for all the kung fu movies and a lifetime of companionship.
- Tina Therrien and Pete Mack, for making an adventure of making a living at making buildings.
- Barb Bolin and Ted Brandon, for bravely giving me the opportunity to teach other people how to make better buildings.
- Tom Rijven, for showing me that a good builder has good instincts, and trusts them.
- David Eisenberg, for being exactly the kind of role model I always seem to need.
- All the people who have participated in courses and workshops with me, because I've always learned as much from you as you have from me. It has been a privilege to make buildings with you all.
- All the clients who have trusted me to share their dreams (and budgets). It has been a privilege to do the work with you and then stand back and see you inhabit it.

Author's note

A HOUSE TODAY IS NOT WHAT A HOUSE USED TO BE. Our modern homes are no more similar to homes of the past than the modern automobile is to the horse. They may share the same purpose, but they achieve it in radically different ways.

A lot of advocates for sustainable building see a logical connection between the low-energy, locally sourced, affordable and sustainable homes of the past and their modern intent to make low-energy, locally-sourced, affordable and sustainable homes, and bemoan the fact that modern construction does not share these goals. This glorifying of the past is understandable, but the comparison is not realistic. Nobody used to the comforts of modern living would feel any glory whatsoever living in the conditions that even the best "non-modern" house would have offered its occupants.

The fact that we expect a higher degree of comfort than our "sustainable" forbears (who, like modern humans, were probably busy non-sustainably over-harvesting and over-using their natural resources; not many human societies have been "sustainable" in their activities) might cause us to conclude that there is no way we can maintain our current level of comfort in a sustainable way. The good news is this is not necessarily the case. What we've learned about making comfortable buildings in the last half century can be successfully married with what our ancestors learned about building with local, natural materials. Today, a smart, well-intentioned builder could

make an amazingly efficient and comfortable modern building out of local materials as basic as earth, clay, timber, straw and stone. It would be as comfortable and "creature-friendly" as most modern homes (minus the overt luxuries), have a negligible energy and carbon footprint and maybe even be healthier to live in.

How we live in our homes has changed just as much as how we make them. Our expectation that a home is a place that does not need our engagement, attention, care, maintenance and love was not the case for our ancestors, and should not be the case in a sustainable world. In fact, a sustainable world is not possible unless we change this expectation.

To a large degree, it is only our unwillingness to give meaningful attention and care to our buildings that makes them unsustainable. It is possible to make a highly energy-efficient and comfortable building in a completely sustainable way if people are willing, able and interested in actively operating and maintaining their homes. A perfect example is the enormous difference between the environmental impacts of vinyl siding and a homemade earthen plaster. The practical difference for a homeowner is that vinyl will need no maintenance (unless it warps, cracks, gets struck and broken, fades, etc) for twentyish years, after which it must be replaced with all new material, while the earthen plaster will require a small amount of manual labor to apply a bit of the same earth from which it originated every five to ten years. Yet the vinyl has a devastating ecological footprint, from the extraction of crude oil to the high levels of air and water pollution created at every stage of its production to the off-gassing that occurs over the material's lifetime to its disposal in a landfill at the end of that life span. The use of such products supports an economy and culture that is at odds with a healthy planet. The clay plaster has almost no impact on the planet.

The trade-offs in terms of our time and attention are surprisingly low, and may even come to be considered an improvement should we reach a day where we are no longer tied to full-time employment in order to make payments on a high-impact, "maintenance-free" house.

I became a sustainable builder not as a career decision but because I wanted a home my family and I could afford and live in comfortably without having to work full time to pay for it all. With many fewer helpful resources than exist today (no Internet!), a family of non-builders was able to design, construct, inhabit and love a home that had a radically lower impact on the planet than all its conventional counterparts. The "sacrifices" we made had nothing to do with our physical comfort but lots to do with things like washing dishes by hand, giving up the blow-dryer, cutting and splitting firewood, keeping track of water levels in a storage tank, not watching a lot of television and turning out lights in rooms when we weren't in them. Not dramatic sacrifices, but the results for the planet — and our family — were very dramatic.

Adjusting our expectations about maintenance and participation in the operation of our homes would make the job of making sustainable buildings entirely feasible today. Currently, the struggle for sustainable builders has little to do with actually making extremely sustainable and comfortable buildings, but convincing people that the small lifestyle changes required to inhabit such homes are worthwhile.

The building world is approaching very interesting times. The status quo is clearly no longer sustainable or feasible, but will we change our expectations of what a home is and can do for us, or will we pursue ever more expensive technologies that only a few can afford?

Human beings are extremely good at finding comfort in the face of any conditions. We are already capable of making functional, low- or no-energy homes with sustainable materials; imagine how much better we could make those homes once we set our minds to it. If the same amount of R&D went into making amazing human-powered tools and devices as goes into making the remarkable power tools and devices we currently use, we would quickly develop no-energy solutions that were affordable and easy to use; perhaps a single, bicycle-driven device that can pump large volumes of water, generate electricity and turn the laundry machine…maybe all at once! For a civilization that has figured out how to make automobiles and nuclear reactors, the hurdles to creating sustainable tools for creature comfort are not stumbling blocks. We just need to really want to get over them.

This book attempts to chart a path in a more sustainable direction, though that path has many variations. From its pages you should be able to select off-the-shelf building materials and solutions and make a home that is substantially more sustainable than current convention. You can also select materials and solutions to assemble your own comfortable, no-energy, lovely home, a home that will have negligible impacts on the environment, require no fossil fuel support and be healthy, beautiful and affordable. It doesn't matter which variation of this path you take; just heading in this direction is an important, life-changing and possibly society-changing decision. Congratulations for considering it, and I hope this book helps you find your own path to a more sustainable life.

Foreword

By David Eisenberg

BUILDING BOOKS TEND TO REPRESENT A KIND OF SNAPSHOT IN TIME. The constantly evolving nature of building materials, systems and technology, and the range of environments and designs in which they are used, makes a level of obsolescence a common fate for many such books. I know this well, having co-authored an early best-selling book on straw bale construction, now woefully out-of-date in many respects but still selling two decades later, mostly as an ebook.

Technical books can transcend this tendency. They can do so by presenting current, clear, relevant information coupled with the insight and understanding necessary to guide the reader in how to find, think about and apply the most up-to-date and specifically relevant information. The reader then can bring their own, now better-informed, judgment to bear on the decisions they have to make. Good technical books don't just provide information but ways of understanding relationships and information *in the context* of a given time, place and project.

This book, *Making Better Buildings,* makes an unusually valuable contribution to the process of actually making better buildings by doing just that. It makes available in straightforward language and usable form the type of information that people need to design and build more sustainable houses. There are no easy, pat answers to the questions about what is best, greenest, most sustainable, safest, etc ... it *always* depends. It is an excellent guide for making better decisions based on a more comprehensive understanding of the particular things achieving your particular goals will depend upon.

To undertake the daunting and ambitious task of creating a book such as this, it would be a blessing for the author to have a healthy mixture of intelligence, curiosity, confidence, competence, actual experience, diligence, skepticism, humility and a good and durable sense of humor. Luckily for us all, Chris Magwood is just such a person.

The contents of this book are drawn from Chris's building experience and research, his observations and analyses and his willingness to openly explore possibilities with others pursuing better buildings. This includes what Chris has learned through leading and teaching the full design and construction process of actual high-performance buildings with ever-changing groups of students, year after year. Chris has thoughtfully woven this wealth of practical knowledge together with an honest and evenhanded presentation of pros and cons, knowns and unknowns and the views of supporters and critics for a wide range of the materials and systems with which more sustainable buildings can be built today.

A strength of this book is that it even enables the reader to make better decisions about topics it does not cover directly. Once informed by an underlying awareness of concerns, impacts, costs and benefits, and the upstream and downstream consequences of various choices, a person cannot help but begin to see all materials, systems and processes in a new way. Lumber or steel or concrete or clay or bales of straw or plastic foam insulation cease to be just inert materials to be chosen strictly on the basis of their initial cost, availability or single-criteria performance factors, or their ability to gain easy code approval. Instead the building, and the whole design and building process, literally take on lives of their own. Considerations stretch far away from the building site to the origins and impacts of those materials, and across time through their whole life cycle in the building and beyond.

Yes, learning to consider all these things appears to make the process more challenging and complex, rather than simpler. But of course it has never been simple, and those approaches that seem to make it simple do so by masking important information from view during the decision-making process. This is mainly how we've created so many of the very problems that we are now trying to solve by building more sustainable buildings. Those of us who have embraced the reality that our choices and actions matter because of their unseen and unknown effects find personal value in aligning our way of working with our intention to design and build buildings that create the most good with the least harm over the longest time — not just for ourselves but also for future generations.

I've had the distinct pleasure of knowing Chris since September 2000, when we met at the Second Nebraska International Straw Bale Construction Conference. I have watched him grow into a leadership role, far beyond straw bale construction to natural building and on to teaching and writing and generously sharing what he is constantly learning. He is clearly an adherent of an old motto of mine — that the way to subvert the dominant paradigm is to have more fun than they do — and, especially, to make sure they know it.

— David Eisenberg

David Eisenberg co-founded and has led the nonprofit Development Center for Appropriate Technology (DCAT) since 1992. He has served two terms on the U.S. Green Building Council Board of Directors, founded and chaired the USGBC Code Committee for ten years, and served on the ICC committee that drafted the International Green Construction Code (IGCC). He has written for Building Safety Journal *(the magazine of the International Code Council), co-authored* The Straw Bale House, *and has published dozens of articles, forewords, book chapters and papers.*

Introduction: Thinking about sustainable building

THERE IS A REMARKABLE PARADOX when it comes to introducing new technologies, in construction or any other field. We expect new ideas or technologies to live up to unrealistically high standards, while at the same time we accept as normal many existing ideas or technologies that are inherently deeply flawed.

It is a commendable tendency to try to be "objective" about new ideas and weigh as much evidence as we have at hand in deciding whether or not we think they are worthy. But we tend to be much less than objective about the ideas and technologies we use on a daily basis. Because they are normal to us, we rarely examine them in any meaningful way. A certain degree of inevitability is attributed to the ideas we've normalized; we don't see them as choices in the same way we see new ideas as choices.

There are countless examples of this paradox in everything we do. In the building world, we find a great example in the use of milled lumber as our prime residential building material. Wood has every flaw imaginable for a building material. It burns; it rots; it's insect food; it warps, twists and cracks; it's a great medium for growing mold; its structural properties vary greatly by species, milling, drying and storing practices; it's often grown far from where it's needed; it's heavy; it's dimensionally unstable as climatic conditions change....

And yet it has come to serve us very well as a building material. We used a natural material that was available to us and figured out how to deal with all its "micro-flaws." In the end, we've normalized it and built an entire successful industry around an entirely flawed material! But if we introduce a new material that has even a small number of the flaws inherent in wood, we find ourselves up against naysayers who can only see the flaws and not the possibilities for being able to work with them.

There is no such thing as an idea or technology with no flaws. Recognizing this simple point is key to being able to consider new ideas fairly. There is an experiment I perform at public talks: I ask the audience how many of them have had to deal with a toilet backup at some point in their lives. The show of hands is almost guaranteed to be unanimous. Then I ask that same audience if they think the flush toilet is a bad, flawed idea that "doesn't work"; very few say Yes. And this despite having to regularly deal with some very unpleasant consequences due to an inherent flaw in the technology. We accept the micro-flaw of an occasional toilet backup as a reasonable trade-off for the convenience of using a flush toilet. However, I hear frequently that composting toilets "don't work" based on second-hand reports of a single incidence of the composter smelling or not composting properly. There's the paradox: the "normal" technology fails disgustingly at a rate of 100 percent, and yet the "alternative" is the one that gets branded as something that "doesn't work." In truth, both systems have some inherent flaws, and both will fail on occasion.

We've just learned to accept the micro-flaws of one and reject the micro-flaws of the other.

Every technology that we examine in this book has a number of micro-flaws, as do those conventional technologies they might replace. This book does not attempt to gloss over any micro-flaws. But the comparisons between sustainable technologies and their conventional counterparts do not and cannot stop at the level of micro-flaws. Sustainable building strives to address the larger and much more important macro-flaws in our approach to building.

It is at the macro level that all of the materials in this book have their advantages over conventional practices. To continue the comparison between flush toilets and composting toilets, we can see that both can be practically functional but also have some micro-flaws. On the macro level, however, the flush toilet is part of a system that sees billions of gallons of untreated or partially treated sewage enter our streams, rivers, lakes and oceans, while using vast amounts of clean potable water and a very expensive public infrastructure. Meanwhile, composting toilets can turn human "waste" into a valuable fertilizer with minimal infrastructure and little to no fresh water usage. It is at this macro level that we should be assessing our building technologies. In this case, the advantages of the composting toilet should be very clear.

If we can start making wise choices at the macro level, we can trust ourselves to figure out how to minimize the micro-flaws of any technology. We humans are incredibly good at refining ideas and techniques. Through repetition, we gain insights that allow us to make the process better and better each time we use it. We're good at doing things better, but we're not very good at doing better things. Doing better things means looking beyond the micro-flaws and basing our choices on minimizing impacts at the macro level.

One of the challenges in adopting any new technology is figuring out where we are on the learning curve, and at what point on that curve we feel comfortable jumping on board. Some of the systems presented here are quite well developed, with installation and maintenance instructions that are very complete and manufacturer and installer warranties that back them up. Others are relative newcomers (at least in the modern context) and the instruction manuals are literally being written and refined right now. We may not know the very best way to use some of these systems until a lot more early adopters have trial-and-errored their way to some kind of standardized practice.

This book is about making better buildings. Better buildings don't wreck the planet. Better buildings do not waste resources. Better buildings are healthy places for their occupants. Better buildings are better at the macro level. The micro stuff we will figure out, as we always have done.

How this book works

THE PAST DECADE HAS SEEN AN INCREDIBLE shift in awareness about the environmental impacts of our built environment. The notion of building sustainably has moved from the rumblings and experimentation of a few fringe activists to a pervasive notion that has an entire industry questioning its priorities and methodologies.

As the building industry reorganizes itself, the first round of changes we are witnessing is the "green building revolution." Green building brings a wide range of improvements to the ways in which we currently make our buildings. It is an important early step in changing a massive, multi-faceted industry, and the inroads made by green building advocates have already brought about remarkable changes in a very short time.

As huge a shift as the green building revolution continues to be, sustainable building activists are attempting to thoroughly reconsider and reinvent how we use materials and energy. The move to more realistically sustainable building will be as remarkable a change as the steel-and-concrete revolution of the early twentieth century.

In the twentieth century, cheap energy dramatically reorganized the building industry. For most of human history, manual labor had been used to convert local raw materials into buildings. The harvesting, processing and crafting of materials into buildings was done regionally, and it was the work of a great number of people in every city, town and village to provide these services. With cheap fossil fuel energy, the economic scale tipped radically in favor of mechanized processes. Materials are now harvested more intensively, transported to centralized factories to be processed, and then transported as building products to distributors, sub-distributors and retailers. Local trades purchase these products and assemble them into buildings using as little manual labor as possible. The occupants of buildings have become far removed from the process of designing and constructing, and therefore know little about what goes into making a building.

Cheap fossil fuel has enabled our society to build more, faster and bigger than anyone could have conceived a century ago. The merits of this growth are endlessly debatable, but we have collectively learned a lot about how to build quickly, efficiently and well. This book is written with the recognition that this era — with all its good and bad points — is coming to an end. The timing and nature of that end are also debatable, but what interests us is, what comes next?

There is no way to predict the direction any major revolution in ideas will take. There are, however, some visible signposts that can be followed in a direction that makes sense from our current vantage point. We aren't forecasting what kinds of new materials might be developed in the future—all of the building materials and systems covered in this book are being used to make buildings right now. Every material and system we examine is currently being

RDM DESIGN SOLUTIONS
www.rdmdesignsolutions.com

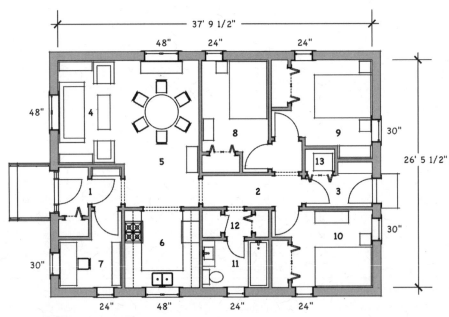

37' 9 1/2"

48"   24"   24"

48"

4

8   9

13

30"

26' 5 1/2"

1   2   3

30"

5

6   12   10

7   11

30"

24"   48"   24"   24"

LEGEND

1 – Front Entry	50 SF	6 – Kitchen	81 SF
2 – Hallways	60 SF	7 – Office/Den	55 SF
3 – Rear Entry	35 SF	8 – Bedroom	104 SF
4 – Living	96 SF	9 – Bedroom	122 SF
5 – Dining	153 SF	10– Bedroom	108 SF

11– Bathroom	44 SF
12– Linen&Mech	25 SF
13– Laundry	10 SF
**– Walls	55 SF

- All Doorways 34" Except: Bathroom 24"; Closets (Varies)

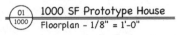

01
1000

1000 SF Prototype House
Floorplan – 1/8" = 1'-0"

used to make code-approved buildings that can meet modern standards of comfort, climate control and structural stability, yet with substantially lowered environmental impacts.

In this time of transition it can be difficult to assess new technologies and ideas, and that's where this book's approach attempts to be useful. We recognize that some of the systems examined in this book lend themselves very well to existing approaches to building and are only ever so slightly outside the mainstream. Others are much further from conventional approaches. We are not setting materials or systems against each other in a competitive manner; instead, we're attempting to objectively apply a well-rounded set of criteria to each one. Our criteria are:

Environmental impacts — What effects do the harvesting, manufacturing, transportation and use of this material have on our ecosystem?

Embodied energy — How much energy is required to harvest, process, transport and install this material?

Waste — What happens to the leftover material at the end of a project?

Energy efficiency — What impacts will the use of this material have on the energy efficiency of the finished building?

Material costs — What are the costs of acquiring and installing this material, based on current quotes for a sample home?

Labor input — How much labor is required to acquire and install this material based on current quotes for a sample home?

Ease of construction for homeowners — What level of skill is required for a homeowner to successfully install this material?

Sourcing/Availability — How widely available is this material, and where can it be obtained?

Durability — How long will this material last given appropriate conditions?

Code compliance — Is this material currently compliant with building code prescriptions and, if not, how is it treated/accepted as an alternative method?

Indoor air quality — What impact does the use of this material have on the indoor air quality in the finished building?

Future development — Does this material lend itself to significant improvements and therefore more widespread use in the near future?

All of these criteria are very important to a sustainable way of building, but not every one will have the same degree of importance for you as a designer, builder or homeowner.

There are no prescriptions, no "winners" in this book. In the end it will be up to you to weigh the information presented and make decisions according to your own needs. A builder looking for the lowest-cost options will find different answers than somebody looking for the highest indoor air quality or best energy efficiency.

Every building system summarized here is worthy of a book, and we point to those resources at the end of each section. There is no way to fully explain the intricacies and nuances of every system, and in attempting to summarize them we will certainly offend those who have devoted entire careers to a building method we explain and rate in just a few pages. Our intent is not to provide a "how-to" guide for any of these materials or systems, or a scientifically definitive rating. Instead we provide an attempt at an even-handed, objective comparison of the relative merits of systems that are all good choices. If there was a bad option, it wasn't included. If there were just one choice that trumped all others, we'd all be building that way. There isn't, and we don't. In the comparison charts, a low score is not a bad thing; it just places that material/technology on a spectrum compared to other viable options. Compared to many conventional building options, these choices are all at the same positive end of the spectrum.

Where we use hard figures to quantify certain criteria, we are doing so based on a theoretical building, so that we are comparing identical scenarios across the board. Our theoretical building is a 1,000-square-foot (93-m3) bungalow with a simple hip roof, and the floor plans and elevation are presented. Obviously, your building project is unlikely to match this exact description, but the figures may be extrapolated and used as reasonable guidelines for your project.

This book can provide options, but it is up to each designer/builder to fully understand their own project goals. While this may seem obvious, it is surprising how often a building project moves forward without a comprehensive set of goals. Without well-defined and clearly stated goals it can be difficult to make the choices that face every builder. Why pick one design, material or system over another? Especially when sustainability is a priority, it is important to be clear about goals.

The list of criteria used to rate materials in this book represents a set of goals, and each builder must decide which of these ranks highest for a particular project. It's not enough to simply want "the best building possible." What will make it the best building for you? Designing a building means making compromises between competing factors. You are unlikely to create the most energy-efficient, least environmentally impactful, cheapest, easiest, fastest, most durable, most code-compliant, most recyclable building with the highest possible indoor air quality. You will be able to do reasonably well in some of these aspects, and very well in others. It's best to know in advance which ones you prioritize, and why. Making a building is a time-, resource- and finance-intensive endeavor; you'll want to complete it with the fewest regrets and mistakes possible, and the only way to do that is to start with clear goals.

This book recognizes the extraordinary number of decisions that must be made when planning to build sustainably, and aims to help you with those choices. There is no one way to build sustainably, and it's our hope that the information presented here allows you to bring your needs, climatic conditions, skills and environmental commitment together to make a better building.

Resources for alternative and natural building

Racusin, Jacob Deva, and Ace McArleton. *The Natural Building Companion: A Comprehensive Guide to Integrative Design and Construction.* White River Junction, VT: Chelsea Green, 2012. Print.

Nunan, Jon. *The Complete Guide to Alternative Home Building Materials & Methods: Including Sod, Compressed Earth, Plaster, Straw, Beer Cans, Bottles, Cordwood, and Many Other Low-Cost Materials.* Ocala, FL: Atlantic, 2010. Print.

Kennedy, Joseph F. *The Art of Natural Building: Design, Construction, Resources.* Gabriola Island, BC: New Society, 2002. Print.

Elizabeth, Lynne, and Cassandra Adams. *Alternative Construction: Contemporary Natural Building Methods.* New York: Wiley, 2000. Print.

Chiras, Daniel D. *The Natural House: A Complete Guide to Healthy, Energy-Efficient, Environmental Homes.* White River Junction, VT: Chelsea Green, 2000. Print.

Pearson, David. *The Natural House Book: Creating a Healthy, Harmonious, and Ecologically Sound Home Environment.* New York: Simon & Schuster, 1989. Print.

Woolley, Tom. *Natural Building: A Guide to Materials and Techniques.* Ramsbury: Crowood, 2006. Print.

Snell, Clarke. *The Good House Book: A Common-Sense Guide to Alternative Homebuilding.* New York: Lark, 2004. Print.

Snell, Clarke, and Tim Callahan. *Building Green: A Complete How-To Guide to Alternative Building Methods: Earth Plaster, Straw Bale, Cordwood, Cob, Living Roofs.* New York: Lark, 2005. Print.

Chiras, Daniel D. *The New Ecological Home: The Complete Guide to Green Building Options.* White River Junction, VT: Chelsea Green, 2004. Print.

1

Foundations

A BUILDING'S FOUNDATION IS EXTREMELY IM-
PORTANT to its longevity and performance.
As such, it is often the one element where homeowners and builders will tend to choose the "tried
and true" techniques and avoid "experimentation."

This is unfortunate, because the "tried and true"
methods and materials typically involve the highest environmental impacts and often the lowest
energy efficiency. Most North American homes use
vast amounts of concrete in their foundations, and
concrete is a perfect example of the kind of energy-intensive building material that has led us to our current
environmental state. The production of the portland
cement that is the "glue" in concrete requires using
large quantities of fuel to heat limestone to very high
temperatures to change its chemical composition. In
the process the carbon dioxide trapped in the stone
is released into the atmosphere (along with additional CO_2 released by the fuel used to heat the rock).
Cement manufacture is one of the world's leading
sources of greenhouse gas emissions.

Widespread and prodigious use of concrete is
only possible when vast amounts of cheap energy
can be used to quarry, heat, process and transport
the material. Every rise in energy costs will be re-
flected in a rise in concrete costs. Where once this

material was the cheap, obvious answer when building foundations, it is becoming less so all the time.

In the attempt to make concrete foundations more
energy efficient, concrete is often combined with
foam insulations. These insulations also have dramatic
environmental impacts. If we can eliminate concrete
use in foundations, we also tend to eliminate foams
(though not always). In the following discussions
about more sustainable foundation materials, careful thought must also be applied to the insulating of
these foundations, and insulation options will be addressed for each system examined.

In considering more sustainable foundation systems, a builder is forced to consider a number of
challenges to typical expectations. In much of North
America, foundations have been twinned with conditioned, subgrade living space: the basement. In
many markets, having a basement is so normal that
it can be hard to convince a homeowner to imagine
a house without one. It is difficult to create a sustainable basement and — unless the home is in the
driest, best draining of soils — impossible to create
a basement that doesn't rely on several layers of petrochemical products to stay dry.

As you will see in this section, there are many
ways to create stable, long-lasting foundations that

1

have reasonable environmental impacts. Most of them, however, do not make basement foundations and those that do come with significant labor requirements. The fact of the matter is that building large, conditioned basements has been a privilege of having cheap energy at our disposal. We are nearing the end of commanding that privilege.

There is one great benefit to moving away from conditioned basement foundations: cost. The cost savings that can be realized by using a sustainable, grade-based foundation are substantial, and can be used to lower the price of the entire project or traded off against sustainable materials or systems that would otherwise drive up the overall cost. It is possible to build with higher-cost renewable energy systems at a competitive cost due to savings on the foundation.

There is no doubt that the most skepticism and wariness about sustainable technologies will happen here, at the foundation. As with any change, the underlying assumption — the "foundation" — is the hardest to change. Yet this is the place that most needs changing.

Building science basics for foundations

A foundation transfers loads from the building to the ground and anchors the building to the ground. To adequately perform this role, a foundation must have enough compressive and shear strength to handle all gravity loads (the weight of roof, walls, floors) and imposed loads (occupants, furniture, snow, rain, wind, earthquakes) placed on the building and prevent the building from moving on the ground.

In areas with cold climates, the foundation must provide stability even when frost has penetrated the soil surrounding the building. When soils containing water freeze, they can expand up to 10 percent in volume and exert pressures upward of 100,000 pounds

per square inch, enough to lift or shift a building. When frozen soils thaw, they can become supersaturated with water, resulting in dramatically reduced bearing capacity, enough to cause a building to sink. There are two basic strategies for achieving frost protection for a foundation:

Footings below frost depth. This strategy involves digging into undisturbed soil to a depth lower than the expected frost depth. Building codes will prescribe frost depths regionally. The foundation then becomes a wall that rests on this sub-frost footing and extends to a suitable height above grade to start the floor/walls of the building. *Frost walls, basements* and *piers* fall into this category.

Shallow, frost-protected foundations. This strategy involves installing an insulation blanket horizontally around the perimeter of the building to prevent frost from entering the soil beneath the footings. The footing can be at grade or just below grade, minimizing the amount of excavation and material required to build the foundation. *Grade beams* and *slabs* fall into this category.

Many of the materials examined in this chapter can be used for either kind of foundation, but some can only be used for one or the other.

The foundation also separates the building from the ground, and this separation must include keeping ground moisture from rising into the building and surface moisture from getting into or under the building.

The foundation must also keep out insects, rodents and other unwanted guests trying to enter the walls or the living space. These pests will vary by region, as will the strategies for keeping them out.

A foundation can play an important role in the energy efficiency of the building. A properly insulated foundation thermally protects all edges of the building. Where floors and/or walls attach to the foundation, preventing thermal bridging and unwanted air movement is particularly important. Strategies for achieving a well-sealed, well-insulated foundation will change depending on materials used and climatic conditions. Don't fall prey to the common mistake of assuming that "heat rises" and therefore it's not important to insulate around and under foundations. Heated air rises, it's true, but heat energy moves effectively in any direction by radiation and conduction. A warm building in contact with colder soils will continuously transfer heat to the ground, which has an almost infinite capacity to absorb that heat. If you don't want to attempt to heat the entire mass of the Earth's crust, insulate your foundation adequately!

Durability is of exceptional importance when it comes to foundations. All the other components of a building can be repaired, restored or replaced as they age. Foundations can also be fixed, but it's rarely easy and usually expensive to do so. If a foundation has a short life span, the building above it is usually condemned to the same short life span. All of the various building science aspects of the foundation will have an impact on its life span, as will the nature of the materials used.

No foundation can be considered sustainable unless it combines adequate strategies for meeting all of these building science objectives and does so with materials that can last a long time in a demanding environment.

Earthbag (or flexible form rammed earth) foundations

What the cheerleaders say...	What the detractors say...
Extremely low environmental impact	Bags won't last
Widely available materials	Too labor intensive
Simple technology, simple tools	Foundation will be leaky
Excellent thermal mass	Low energy performance

Earthbag foundation. (David Elfstrom)

Applications for this foundation system

- Perimeter beams
- Frost walls, including full basement walls
- Piers
- *Can also be used as exterior and interior walls above grade*

Basic materials

- Woven polypropylene bags (grain or feed bags) or continuous polypropylene tubing
- Soil, typically from site excavation, containing a good mix of gravel, sand, clay and silt
- Amendments for soil mixture, if necessary. Can be graded gravel, sand, road base, portland cement, hydrated or hydraulic lime, blast furnace slag or fly ash

- Barbed wire
- Tampers, manual and/or mechanical
- Many different bag stands or chutes have been custom made to facilitate the bag loading process. None are commercially available, but most can be made quickly and easily with available materials.

How the system works

The more descriptive term for earthbag construction is "flexible form rammed earth," which gives a more accurate impression of how the system works. Woven polypropylene bags or continuous tubes are filled with a gravel-based mixture that will tamp well and solidly. As the mixture in the bag is tamped, it flattens until the bag reaches its maximum stretch, at which point it firmly contains the material and allows for tamping to a high density. The bags or tubes can be laid out in straight lines, using string lines, but can also conform to any building shape.

The fill material that is rammed in the earthbags varies widely by region, builder and code/engineering requirements. A high proportion of aggregate is always used, with the binders ranging from indigenous clay soil to hydraulic agents like hydraulic lime,

fly ash, blast furnace slag or portland cement. The compacted mix creates a stable long-lasting mass that does not rely on the bag for containment once it has been compressed and cured or dried to full strength.

Earthbag foundations can be made with fill mixes that rely on the bags for long-term containment of the materials, usually graded gravel or, less frequently, sand. The bags have a long life span when buried, and backfill around them will both protect the bags from degrading in sunlight and provide additional restraint for the materials should the bags fail.

The bags and tubing come in a wide range of widths, from 9–24 inches (230–600 mm), so a foundation can be designed according to the stability and strength requirements of any building. A double wythe system can also be designed, using two rows of narrow bags to create an inner and outer foundation wall for wide wall systems and to allow for internal insulation strategies.

The construction methodology is the same regardless of bag size or fill type. The mix is created, moistened to the correct degree and placed into the bag or tube. When the bag contains the correct amount of mix it is tamped vigorously, manually or mechanically. The tamping process subjects the mix to a force greater than the force that will be placed on the foundation by the building loads.

The foundation wall is built up in a number of courses. The thickness of each course depends on bag size, amount of fill and degree of compaction. Typical earthbag courses range from 4–8 inches (100–200 mm) in thickness.

Between each course of earthbag, a strand or two of barbed wire is typically used to prevent the bags from sliding on top of one another in any direction. Multi-pointed wire (three or preferably four barbs) ensures that every knot is making good contact with both bags. The wire is treated like rebar in concrete, with continuous corners and overlapped joints.

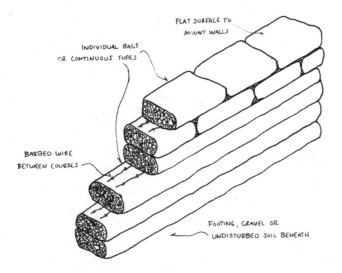

FLAT SURFACE TO MOUNT WALLS

INDIVIDUAL BAGS OR CONTINUOUS TUBES

BARBED WIRE BETWEEN COURSES

FOOTING, GRAVEL OR UNDISTURBED SOIL BENEATH

Walls will sometimes be installed directly on the earthbag (with a suitable moisture break), or wooden sill plates or a thin concrete beam can be used.

With practice, an experienced crew can build courses of earthbag quite quickly and with a high degree of level and plumbness and a consistent compaction.

Tips for a successful earthbag foundation

1. Placement of materials to be mixed should facilitate easy delivery to all points of the foundation.
2. Don't lay string lines directly on the foundation lines, as the bags will nudge the string constantly. Instead, lay out lines that are a couple inches wider than the foundation and measure into the bags.
3. A sturdy loading stand will make the job much faster. The resources listed below describe various loading stand options.
4. A practiced team can move quickly and create a very level surface. As you are learning, don't worry about every course being perfectly level. In the end, only the top course matters and you can make corrections on successive courses. A transit or laser level makes the job much more accurate.
5. Fill a sample bag to determine the height of each course to plan the number of courses and quantity of bag material required.
6. Secure the bag material well in advance to ensure supply and sizing.

Pros and cons

ENVIRONMENTAL IMPACTS: *Low*

Bags:

Harvesting — *High.* Polypropylene (PP) is a resin of the polyolefin family derived from crude oil and natural gas. Impacts include significant habitat destruction and air and water pollution.

Manufacturing — *Moderate to High.* Polypropylene is among the least energy-intensive plastics to manufacture, and a growing percentage of PP is derived from recycled sources. Impacts include significant air and water pollution. Weaving PP strands into bags is a moderately intensive mechanical process with no significant impacts.

Transportation — *Moderate.* Sample house uses 26.25 kg of bag material:

0.04 MJ per km by 15 ton truck
0.025 MJ per km by 35 ton truck
0.0065 MJ per km by rail
0.0042 MJ per km by ocean freighter

The majority of bag production is in Asia, ensuring that most bags used in North America have relatively high transportation distances. Quantity of material required is low, mitigating impacts.

Installation — *Negligible.*

Fill:

Harvesting — *Negligible to High.* Site soil fill will have negligible impacts.

Aggregate and virgin hydraulic binders (if required) are mechanically extracted from quarries and can have low to high impacts on habitat and ground and surface water contamination and flow.

Manufacturing — *Negligible to High.* Site soil fill will have negligible impacts.

Aggregate is mechanically crushed and has moderate impacts for fuel use for machinery and dust dispersion.

Virgin hydraulic binders like lime and portland cement are fired at extremely high temperatures and have high impacts, including fossil fuel use, air and water pollution and greenhouse gas emissions.

Recycled hydraulic binders like fly ash and blast furnace slag are the by-products of industrial processes that have high impacts, but these can be mitigated to some degree by diverting these materials from landfill.

Transportation — *Negligible to High.* Sample house uses 15,616 kg of fill material:

> 23.4 MJ per km by 15 ton truck
> 14.7 MJ per km by 35 ton truck

Site soil will require no transportatiozn. Locally obtained soils will have negligible to low impacts.

Aggregate is typically sourced nearby the project site, and will have low to moderate impacts depending on distance traveled.

Hydraulic binders are often sourced nearby the project site, but may have to travel long distances.

Installation — *Negligible.*

WASTE: *NEGLIGIBLE TO LOW*

Biodegradable/Compostable — All natural soil material.

Recyclable — Polypropylene bag material, barbed wire offcuts.

Landfill — Cement and/or lime containers.

ENERGY EFFICIENCY: *VERY LOW*

A rammed earth foundation has very little thermal resistance. In cold climates, it will need to be properly insulated in order to contribute to an energy-efficient building. Insulation strategies can vary depending on the style of foundation, the climate and the type of insulation used. If the design for the building has accounted for potential heat loss through the earthbag foundation it can easily be part of a well-designed, thermally appropriate structure in a wide range of climates.

In some areas, insulative aggregate may be available in the form of pumice, volcanic rock or other "expanded" minerals. Depending on the type of aggregate and the loads imposed on the foundation, high percentages of these aggregates can result in a foundation with reasonable strength and thermal characteristics.

Earthbag Foundation Embodied Energy

Wall type: 1220x200mm (4ft x 8in) wall, 10 courses of earthbag	Material embodied energy from I.C.E. in MJ/kg	Weight to volume ratio of material*	Volume of material in sample 1000sf/92.9m² building	Sample building embodied energy	Material embodied carbon from I.C.E. in kgCO$_2$e/kg	Sample building embodied carbon	Notes
Lowest Impact							
Recycled bags	0	6.56kg/100m @ 0.3m bag width	400m 26.24 kg	0 MJ	0	0kg	No embodied energy for repurposed materials.
Rammed earth soil fill from site	0.45	1600kg/m³	9.76m³ 15,616 kg	0 MJ	0.024	0kg	No embodied energy for site materials.
Recycled barbed wire	36	0.085kg/m	360m 30.6 kg	0 MJ	3.02	0kg	No embodied energy for repurposed materials.
Totals				**0 MJ**		**0kg**	
Highest Impact							
Virgin bag or tube	99.2 (polypropylene film)	6.56 kg/100m @ 0.3m bag width	400m 26.24 kg	2603 MJ	3.43	90kg	
8% cement stabilized soil	0.83	1600 kg/m³	9.76 m³ 15,616kg	12,961 MJ	0.084	1311 kg	
Barbed wire	36 (wire – virgin)	0.085 kg/m	360m 30.6 kg	1,101 MJ	3.02	92 kg	
Totals				**16,665 MJ**		**1,493 kg**	Figures do not include parging, waterproofing or insulating of foundation.

Transportation: Soil transportation by 35 ton truck would equate to 14.7 MJ per kilometer of travel to the building site   *Typically from engineeringtoolbox.com

MATERIAL COSTS: *LOW*

Soil, aggregate, bags and barbed wire are all relatively inexpensive. Site preparation costs are similar to other comparable foundations.

LABOR INPUT: *HIGH TO VERY HIGH*

Those used to the mechanical mixing and placement of concrete into formwork may find the amount of physical effort involved with earthbag daunting. However, a large part of the labor required to build concrete foundations is in the construction and removal of the formwork that holds the liquid concrete. Because the bags are the formwork for earthbag, this labor-intensive step is eliminated. Once lines are laid for the foundation, earthbag construction begins immediately. When compared this way, the labor balance becomes much more favorable. As there are currently no mechanical means for filling bags or tubes with mix, all work is manual.

SKILL LEVEL REQUIRED FOR HOMEOWNERS: *NEGLIGIBLE TO LOW*

Earthbag building is very simple in practice, and the skills required can be picked up relatively quickly. The process is quite forgiving, as it's possible to correct for errors on a subsequent course. Only the final course needs to be completely level, and most crews will have the methodology developed by then.

It definitely helps to have at least one experienced earthbagger on a crew to get started. One person can usually direct an entire crew until everybody understands the process. If nobody has previous experience, it's worth looking into workshops or other training opportunities before commencing with a foundation.

Health Warnings — Powdered binders are high in silica content, and are dangerous to breathe. Wear proper breathing protection.

SOURCING/AVAILABILITY: *EASY TO DIFFICULT*

Obtaining large quantities of bags/tubes can be difficult. Farm co-ops or grain and feed stores will have new bags, and their customers will have used bags. Bag printers will sometimes have misprinted bags that are given away or sold below cost. Bag manufacturers and printers will have rolls of tube, and may be willing to sell full rolls. Otherwise, rolls of tube will have to come direct from the manufacturer in Asia, or their North American distributor.

Fill materials are typically easy to source. Grades of aggregate will vary by region, but easily tamped mixtures are required for many purposes and are available everywhere. The road-building industry relies heavily on compacted aggregates for road base, and finding out what is being used locally for this purpose can help determine what you should be using in your earthbag mix.

Virgin binders are available from masonry supply stores and well-stocked building supply yards. Recycled binders like slag or fly ash may be easily available, or may require extra effort to obtain. If a local concrete batching plant is adding recycled binders to their mixes, they should be willing to sell the binder in bulk.

Barbed wire is easy to obtain from farm, fencing or hardware stores. The barbs should be at least three- and preferably four-point, but never two-point.

DURABILITY: *HIGH TO VERY HIGH*

The durability of earthbag foundations has not been proven by the test of time. As a relatively recent form of construction, there aren't any historical examples upon which to base durability parameters.

However, rammed earth construction without the poly bags as formwork has a long history of durability. In climates where rammed earth has proven to be viable, earthbag using a soil mixture can be expected to have a similar or longer life span.

Where soil mixtures are not deemed durable enough, the addition of binders creates a concrete-like material inside the bags and this can be expected to share high durability expectations with other concrete materials.

In an area where rammed earth has little history, and even where the materials in the bag lack sufficient binder or are soil-based, an earthbag foundation can be expected to be quite durable as long as the bag material is protected from UV radiation. Polypropylene has shown itself to be very persistent when buried and the bags should maintain their integrity for a long time, continuing to contain the fill for decades or even centuries.

CODE COMPLIANCE: *NOT AN ACCEPTED SOLUTION IN ANY CODES*

Alternative compliance applications will need to be based on accurate load calculations and engineering principles, along with the small amount of study data that currently exists. Soils engineering principles and data are highly applicable and can provide the basis for justification. A mixture that is adequately tamped and has a good degree of internal cohesion can be shown to be feasible in most conditions. It is highly advisable to discuss the earthbag option with code officials and find out whether or not they are willing to consider it, and under what conditions, *before* proceeding with plans to use an earthbag foundation.

It may seem obvious, but it can be worth pointing out to code officials that all buildings with concrete foundations sit on a bed of tamped gravel beneath the footings, so codes already accept the use of restrained, tamped fill for structural purposes.

INDOOR AIR QUALITY

Earthbag foundations will have no direct impact on indoor air quality. A well-built foundation can help

Earthbag Foundation Ratings

	Best							Worst			Notes
	1	2	3	4	5	6	7	8	9	10	
Environmental Impacts											All materials can be from site and recycled. Bag material high impact, but used in low quantities. Addition of insulation will raise impacts.
Embodied Energy											Use of cement-stabilized earth will raise EE dramatically. Addition of insulation will raise EE.
Waste Generated											
Energy Efficiency											System requires addition of insulation to provide energy efficiency.
Material Costs											Addition of insulation will raise costs.
Labor Inputs											
Skill Level Required by Homeowner											
Sourcing and Availability											Bag/tube material requires direct sourcing from manufacturer.
Durability and Longevity											Untested, but rammed earth mixes have historical durability precedent.
Building Code Compliance											Structural engineering and/or alternative compliance required.
Indoor Air Quality											Foundation will not typically affect IAQ, but if used as a wall system, impacts are low.

keep the floors and walls of the building dry and prevent other IAQ issues.

FUTURE DEVELOPMENT

Simplicity, low cost and effectiveness make earthbags attractive. Earthbag foundations are relative newcomers to construction, though their use in civil engineering projects and flood control provides some performance basis. There is a lot of room for the development of earthbag foundations into a more refined, more widely accepted system.

New research is ongoing into the strengths of different mixes, which should help with code compliance issues. As the system becomes more widely used, new tools and techniques are sure to be developed that will streamline the process. Mixing and pouring concrete foundations used to involve large amounts of labor input that have, over time, been replaced with mechanical devices. The same could easily happen to earthbag foundations, making them even more attractive than they already are.

Resources for further research

Geiger, Owen. "Earthbag Building: Earthbag Building Guide." *Earthbag Building: Earthbag Building Guide.* N.p., n.d. Web. 13 Apr. 2013.

Hunter, Kaki, and Donald Kiffmeyer. *Earthbag Building: The Tools, Tricks and Techniques.* Gabriola Island, BC: New Society, 2004. Print.

Wojciechowska, Paulina. *Building with Earth: A Guide to Flexible-form Earthbag Construction.* White River Junction, VT: Chelsea Green, 2001. Print.

Khalili, Nader, and Iliona Outram. *Emergency Sandbag Shelter and Eco-village: Manual—How to Build Your Own with Superadobe/Earthbag.* Hesperia, CA: Cal-Earth, 2008. Print.

Khalili, Nader. *Ceramic Houses and Earth Architecture: How to Build Your Own.* Hesperia, CA: Cal-Earth, 1990. Print.

Dry stone and mortared stone foundations

What the cheerleaders say...	What the detractors say...
Historically proven durability	Too labor intensive
Extremely low environmental impact	Foundation will be leaky
Widely available materials	Poor energy performance
Simple technology, simple tools	Expensive to import stone
Excellent thermal mass	
Aesthetically pleasing	

Applications for this foundation system

- Perimeter beams
- Frost walls, including full basement walls
- Piers

Basic materials

- Stone. Can be available fieldstone, cut stone or rubble. Dry stone walls are best built with stone that has a flat profile.
- Mortar. Can be typical masonry cement or traditional lime mortars.

How the system works

Mortared stone foundations. Stone is gathered to the building site and laid up by choosing stones of appropriate sizes to form courses and staggered joints between courses. Mortar is placed between courses and between the ends of each stone, so that each adjacent face of stone in the wall is embedded in mortar. A mortar cap typically provides a flat, level surface for the sill plates/walls.

Mortared stone foundations can be used for perimeter beam, frost wall and basement style foundations, as well as piers. In basement scenarios, proper drainage and moisture protection must be used as water can penetrate mortar joints and pass into the building.

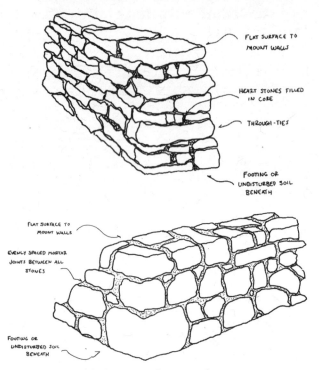

FLAT SURFACE TO MOUNT WALLS

HEART STONES FILLED IN CORE

THROUGH-TIES

FOOTING OR UNDISTURBED SOIL BENEATH

FLAT SURFACE TO MOUNT WALLS

EVENLY SPACED MORTAR JOINTS BETWEEN ALL STONES

FOOTING OR UNDISTURBED SOIL BENEATH

of the quick setting speeds of portland cement. Depending on the lime/cement ratio and the type of stone being used, these mortars can be harder than the stone itself and can lead to stress fractures in the stone rather than the mortar joint. They are somewhat less permeable, but not to a degree that is generally harmful to the wall.

Straight cement mortars are harder to work with and make mortar joints that are much harder than most stone. They are not permeable. Despite their quick setting times, they are not recommended for use in stone foundation walls.

Anchor bolts for walls in a mortared stone foundation can be embedded in the mortar joints between stones, making attachment of a wide range of wall types very straightforward.

Dry-stacked foundations. Stone is gathered to the building site and laid up by choosing successive stones that fit together as tightly as possible. Foundation walls often use a row of larger stones on the inside and outside edge of the foundation. Between these two rows, smaller stones are used as heart-stones to pack and stabilize the spaces between the larger stones. With careful attention to hearting, the foundation walls will be very stable.

Dry-stacked foundations challenge many basic modern assumptions about building. We tend to expect our buildings to be well glued together. However, dry stone advocates are quick to point out that there is an inherent strength in the basic stability and lifelong flexibility of this kind of foundation. Dry-stacked walls can handle a remarkable amount of shifting without giving up any structural strength. Lab testing has shown them to be sufficiently strong to handle moderate earthquake activity. History has shown them to be long-lasting, as they don't tend to retain water so do not go through damaging freeze/thaw cycles like their mortared counterparts. Shifting due to frost heave or settlement under the

In cold climates where insulation strategies are required, mortared stone walls can be insulated from the interior and/or exterior sides, or they can be built as double wythe walls with insulation between the two walls.

There are three choices for mortar in a stone wall: lime, lime/cement or cement. Traditionally, lime mortars were used with stone. These mortars have a long, proven history in conjunction with natural stone. They are "softer" than mortars containing cement, which can allow the stones in the wall to shift slightly without damaging either stone or mortar. Lime mortar is also highly vapor-permeable, which can allow the wall to dry through the mortar joints. Lime mortars take a long time to harden and can limit the speed at which a wall can be laid up.

Lime/cement mortars are the most common modern choice. They retain some of the workability associated with lime mortars but have the advantage foundation is likewise accommodated without any inherent damage to the stability of the wall.

Dry-stacked walls are suitable for perimeter beam or frost wall applications. Because they do not prevent water from migrating through the wall, they cannot be used as basement walls. Piers are possible with dry-stack stone, but need to be wide enough to offer proper stability.

Attaching walls to a dry stone foundation requires adaptation from standard practices. Some natural wall systems (cob, cordwood, straw bale) can be placed directly onto a dry stone foundation, but framed walls will need to be anchored to the stone in some way. This can be achieved by drilling anchors into the larger stones and/or using strapping that runs beneath the stone wall and over the sill plate of the framed wall.

Tips for a successful stone foundation

1. Ensure you have an adequate supply of stone. Mixing different types/sources of stone is not usually recommended, and importing stone can be expensive, so don't start unless you know you have enough to finish the job.
2. Have your stone assessed by somebody knowledgeable, especially if you are site harvesting. There are some kinds of stone that look suitable for building but have properties that are not well suited for foundations.
3. Learn proper stone-laying technique before starting the foundation. There are many tricks to making a structurally sound stone wall, whether dry-stacked or mortared.
4. Ensure you have adequate time to build the foundation. Stone foundations are labor intensive and are not built quickly.
5. Properly separate the walls above from the foundation below. Moisture can "wick" through certain kinds of stone and most kinds of mortar joints, and must be prevented from entering the

Foundation stone.

bottom of the wall. A slate cap was a traditional way of preventing rising moisture issues, or there are modern sealants/barriers that can be used.
6. Provide excellent drainage around the stone foundation. Excessive wetting, especially in freeze/thaw conditions, are hard on mortared stone foundations. And because dry-stack foundations don't keep moisture out, proper precautions must be taken to keep water out from under the building.

Pros and cons

Environmental impacts: *Negligible to Moderate*

Harvesting — *Negligible to Moderate.* Site-harvested stone has negligible impacts. Quarried stone is mechanically harvested and impacts can include habitat destruction and surface and groundwater contamination.

Mortar ingredients extracted from quarries mechanically can have low to high impacts on habitat destruction and ground and surface water contamination and flow.

Manufacturing — *Negligible to High.* Site-harvested stone has negligible to low impacts, depending on the amount and type of cutting/shaping required. Quarried stone is split and/or cut to the desired size and shape using low-impact mechanical equipment.

Mortar ingredients (lime and/or portland cement) are fired at extremely high temperatures and have high impacts including fossil fuel use, air and water pollution and greenhouse gas emissions.

Transportation — *Negligible to High.* Sample house uses 24,790 kg of stone material:

> 37.2 MJ per km by 15 ton truck
> 23.3 MJ per km by 35 ton truck

Installation — *Negligible.*

WASTE: *NEGLIGIBLE*

Biodegradable/Compostable — All leftover stone can be left in the environment.
Landfill — Cement and/or lime bags.

ENERGY EFFICIENCY: *VERY LOW*

A stone foundation has very little thermal resistance. In cold climates, stone foundations will need to be properly insulated in order to contribute to an energy-efficient building. Insulation strategies can vary depending on the style of foundation, the climate and the builder's choices for insulation in adjacent components of the building. As long as the building design has accounted for potential heat loss through the stone foundation and includes a sufficient insulation strategy, this style of foundation can be part of a well-designed, thermally appropriate structure in a wide range of climates.

MATERIAL COSTS: *NEGLIGIBLE TO MODERATE*
LABOR INPUT: *VERY HIGH*

Stone is heavy. A foundation requires a lot of stone. Adding these two factors together results in high labor inputs. The more machinery used to harvest and transport the stone, the less human labor will be needed. However, paying operators for the machinery can still result in fairly high labor costs.

Health Warning: Dust from stone and mortar mixes is high in silica. Wear adequate breathing protection.

SKILL LEVEL REQUIRED: *MODERATE TO HIGH*

Stonemasonry is a well-established trade with a long history. A good mason can create stone foundation

Stone Foundation Embodied Energy

Wall type: 1220x200mm (4ft x 8in) wall	Material embodied energy from I.C.E. in MJ/kg	Weight to volume ratio of material*	Volume of material in sample 1000sf/92.9m² building	Sample building embodied energy	Material embodied carbon from I.C.E. in kgCO₂e/kg	Sample building embodied carbon	Notes
Lowest Impact							
Site harvested, dry-stacked	1.5 (limestone)	2723 kg/m³	9.76 m³ 24,790.4 kg	0 MJ	0.09	0 kg	No embodied energy for site harvested materials. Assumes all manual labour.
Totals				**0 MJ**		**0 kg**	
Highest Impact							
Quarried stone	1.5 (limestone)	2723 kg/m³	7.32 m³ 19,932.4 kg	29,899 MJ	0.09	1794 kg	EE figures range from 1.0 for sandstone to 11.0 for granite.
Mortar 1:1:6 (cement/lime/sand)	1.11	2162kg/m³	2.44 m³ 5275.3 kg	5,855 MJ	0.174	918 kg	Assumes 25% mortar content in wall.
Totals				**35,754 MJ**		**2,712 kg**	Figures do not include parging, waterproofing or insulating of foundation.

Transportation: Stone transportation by 35 ton truck would equate to 18.7 MJ per kilometer of travel to the building site. *Typically from engineeringtoolbox.com walls that are beautiful, strong and durable in an efficient manner. However, with some training and practice it is possible for an amateur to create a dry-stacked or mortared foundation that is completely serviceable, if not as aesthetically pleasing as one built by a professional. It is definitely not advisable to attempt a stone foundation without any training at all, and if the finished look of the foundation is of primary importance, hiring a mason is a good idea. Owner-builders can offer to provide labor for the mason; having a helper who moves the stone and mixes mortar will minimize the mason's time on-site and keep costs lower.

SOURCING/AVAILABILITY: *EASY TO MODERATE*

Viable stone for foundations is widely available but not necessarily easy to source. Site stone must have the right properties and exist in enough quantity to do the job. Local quarries and masonry supply outlets may have locally harvested options.

DURABILITY: *HIGH TO VERY HIGH*

Well-built stone foundations are among the most durable options available. They have a long history of performance in a wide variety of climates and building types. While older stone basement walls tended to be leaky, such moisture issues can be addressed by not having a basement and using the wall as a frost wall or perimeter beam only, or by using modern drainage and waterproofing techniques for basements.

CODE COMPLIANCE

Despite their historical precedents, most codes do not recognize mortared or dry stone as an accepted solution. Mortared stone has sufficient supporting data and history for a successful alternative

Stone Foundation Ratings

	Best					Worst					Notes
	1	2	3	4	5	6	7	8	9	10	
Environmental Impacts	▓	▓	▓	▓	▓						Source of stone and quantity of mortar have large effect on impacts. Addition of insulation will raise impacts.
Embodied Energy	▓	▓	▓	▓	▓	▓	▓	▓	▓		Source of stone and quantity of mortar have large impact on EE. Addition of insulation will raise EE.
Waste Generated	▓	▓									
Energy Efficiency								▓			System requires addition of insulation to provide energy efficiency.
Material Costs	▓	▓	▓	▓							Source of stone has large impact on cost. Addition of insulation will raise costs.
Labor Inputs								▓			
Skill Level Required by Homeowner	▓	▓	▓	▓	▓	▓					
Sourcing and Availability	▓	▓	▓	▓							
Durability and Longevity	▓										
Building Code Compliance	▓	▓	▓	▓	▓	▓	▓				Due to historic precedent, some jurisdictions may accept stone foundations, but not an accepted solution.
Indoor Air Quality	▓	▓	▓								Foundation will not typically affect IAQ, but if used as a wall system, impacts are low.

compliance application. Dry-stacked walls will be more difficult to justify due to the reliance on workmanship to achieve a high-quality wall.

A structural engineer should be able to provide the calculations and support required to get either type of foundation wall accepted.

INDOOR AIR QUALITY

Stone foundation walls will have little direct impact on indoor air quality. By keeping the floors and walls of the building dry they can help to prevent other IAQ issues.

FUTURE DEVELOPMENT

Stone foundations (and mortars) have a long history and it is unlikely that the state of the art will experience dramatic advances or changes. As you inquire about stone for foundations, be aware that many people will discourage you from this option. Stone foundations have associations with older homes in which the foundations experience issues (after a hundred years or so). A well-built, properly drained stone foundation should be able to avoid these issues, but convincing others of this may be difficult.

Resources for further research

Gallagher, A. Robert., Joe Piazza, and Sean Malone. *Building Dry-Stack Stone Walls*. Atglen, PA: Schiffer, 2008. Print.

McRaven, Charles. *Building with Stone*. Pownal, VT: Storey Communications, 1989. Print.

Long, Charles K. *The Stonebuilder's Primer: A Step-by-Step Guide for Owner-Builders*. Willowdale, Ont.: Firefly, 1998. Print.

Cramb, Ian. *The Art of the Stonemason*. White Hall, VA: Betterway Publications, 1992. Print.

McRaven, Charles. *Stonework: Techniques and Projects*. Pownal, VT: Storey, 1997. Print.

McRaven, Charles. *Building Stone Walls*. Pownal, VT: Storey, 1999. Print.

Flynn, Brenda. *The Complete Guide to Building with Rocks and Stone: Stonework Projects and Techniques Explained Simply*. Ocala, FL: Atlantic Group, 2011. Print.

Rammed earth tires (earthships)

What the cheerleaders say...	What the detractors say...
Get paid for your building materials	Too labor intensive
Using an abundant waste material	Slow to construct
Owner-builder friendly	Tires off-gas and/or leach toxins
Strong and durable	Round tires awkward shape for sealing/insulating

Applications for this foundation system

- Perimeter beams
- Frost walls
- Basement walls
- Piers

Basic materials

- Used car and/or truck tires
- Soil suitable for creating rammed earth
- Cob or mortar to fill gaps and plaster

How the system works

Tire walls — Discarded automobile and truck tires are used as permanent formwork for a rammed earth mixture. Tires of a similar diameter and width are laid side by side along the line of the foundation and filled with a soil mixture with good compressive qualities. The mixture is first distributed around the rim of the tire and compressed, typically using a sledgehammer to pound the mixture into the sidewalls. When the sides are filled, the center area of the tire receives mix that is rammed into place.

After a course of tires has been filled and tamped, the next course is laid on top with the joints between tires staggered from the course below. Using tires of the same size will help keep the foundation level as successive courses are added.

When the wall is built to its full height, the indentations where tires meet are packed with a low-cost filler to make the surface of the wall relatively straight and flush. Crushed aluminum cans or glass bottles are sometimes used in this role, but in places where these are recycled this may not be the best choice. A cob mixture with lots of straw can serve this purpose, or rocks can be mortared in with a clay or cob mix.

The finished wall can be insulated and waterproofed in a number of ways, depending on the type of wall and local conditions and codes.

The rammed earth inside the tires will wick ground moisture upwards into the wall, so a barrier of some kind will be needed to separate the wall system from the foundation or the ground. Walls can be attached by bolting sill plates or using strapping to loop beneath the tires and over the sill.

Earthships — Rammed earth tires as a building material were popularized in a form of home construction dubbed earthship. In these structures, rammed earth tires form a subgrade retaining wall for a building that is built into a berm or hillside. The tires form both foundation and wall, typically on the northerly, bermed side of the structure; on the south side they are usually only used as a foundation and knee wall, with a heavily glazed area above. Since the use of tires is so strongly associated with earthship construction, many people are not aware that tires can be used as a foundation system in other forms of construction.

Tire piers — A rammed earth tire pier foundation is built from a stack of tires laid one on top of the other. The first tire is laid on a level gravel bed below the frost line and additional tires stacked and tamped to the desired height above grade. A grid of such piers can be used to support a floor system or a grade beam. A concrete cap is often poured in the top tire to provide a solid anchor for the floor system. Alternatively, a strapping system can be wrapped under the pier to attach the floor system.

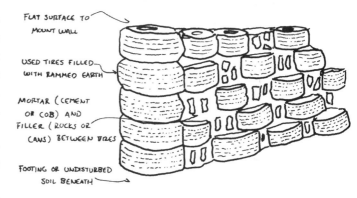

FLAT SURFACE TO MOUNT WALL

USED TIRES FILLED WITH RAMMED EARTH

MORTAR (CEMENT OR COB) AND FILLER (ROCKS OR CANS) BETWEEN TIRES

FOOTING OR UNDISTURBED SOIL BENEATH

Tips for a successful tire foundation:

1. Calculate the number of tires you'll need and source them early. Be sure you can collect enough tires of a similar size. Though used tires are abundant, if you need hundreds you may have to go to multiple sources.

2. Check with local regulations regarding storage of tires. In many municipalities, it is illegal to have more than a small number of tires on a property. This may require bringing tires to site in batches.

3. Ensure that your soil has suitable compaction qualities. In the best-case scenario the excavated site soil is compactable. Very rocky or very sandy soil can be problematic. Because the tire form stays in place, the soil does not need to be able to harden as it would in a traditional rammed earth wall.

4. Assess the amount of time it will take to build the tire foundation properly. If all the work is being done manually, this can be one of the most labor-intensive styles of foundation.

5. Plan for proper drainage around the foundation. It can be difficult to waterproof a tire foundation and sufficient drainage will help the foundation stay dry.

6. Insulation details must suit the unevenness and width of the tire foundation.

Rammed earth tire. (CHESTER RENNIE)

7. If the wall above is much narrower than the tire foundation, plan for details where the floor meets the wide foundation and/or where the width will leave a ledge on the outside edge of the wall.
8. Plan for proper moisture barriers and attachment systems for walls/roofs mounting to the tire walls.

Pros and cons

ENVIRONMENTAL IMPACTS: *NEGLIGIBLE TO LOW*

Harvesting — *Negligible to Low.* Petrochemicals for the rubber and steel for the belting both have high impacts, including habitat destruction and air and water pollution, but as a recycled material these impacts are mitigated.

Site soil has negligible impacts.

Manufacturing — *Negligible to Low.* Recycling the tire as a building material mitigates high impacts from tire manufacturing.

Site soil has negligible impacts.

Transportation — *Negligible to Moderate.* Sample house uses 4,680 kg of tires:

> 7 MJ per km by 15 ton truck
> 4.4 MJ per km by 35 ton truck

Sample house uses 35,200 kg of fill material:

> 52.8 MJ per km by 15 ton truck
> 33 MJ per km by 35 ton truck

Tires and fill material are high-volume materials to transport and impacts will rise proportionally with distance traveled.

Installation — *Negligible to Moderate.* Potential leachate toxicants from the tires entering soil and/or groundwater around the foundation may be a concern. No recognized data exists for tire foundations, as studies tend to focus on different end-uses for old tires, like track and paving compounds, playground surfaces and fish habitat. In most studies, zinc, heavy metals and vulcanization and rubber chemicals from tires are shown to leach into soils and water. What is unclear is the quantity of leachate and the effect on soil, water and living organisms. In a successful foundation the tires are typically separated from the backfill by a waterproofing membrane, which will greatly reduce contact and potential leaching.

WASTE: *NEGLIGIBLE*

Biodegradable/Compostable — Soil fill, aggregate.
Recyclable — Remaining tires may be recyclable.
Landfill — Remaining tires, if no recycling program exists.

ENERGY EFFICIENCY: *VERY LOW*

A rammed earth tire foundation has little thermal resistance. In areas where insulating foundations is crucial, a strategy to add insulation to the inside and/or outside edge of a tire foundation will be important. With a proper insulation strategy in place, a tire foundation can be part of an energy-efficient building. The width of tires and the uneven face of the foundation can provide challenges in the use of interior or exterior insulation layers.

MATERIAL COSTS: *VERY LOW*

In some cases, people building with tires have been paid to take the tires they have used. This is one of the only examples of cost-negative construction materials! However, do not count on this being the case as recycling programs grow more common.

LABOR INPUT: *VERY HIGH*

Tire foundations require a lot of labor. Individual tires are no more difficult to handle and place than any other foundation material, but the placing and tamping of the soil mixture is very laborious. The soil must be placed and compressed into the sidewall of the tire, requiring careful placement of the dirt and a ramming technique that involves applying force toward the outside edge of the tire. This does not lend itself well to mechanical placement and tamping of the dirt. The effort required to tamp sideways (usually with a sledgehammer) is higher than tamping downwards.

A typical tire holds about 140 kg (300 lb) of soil, and experienced builders report that it takes 10–45 minutes (depending on soil conditions, height of wall and other factors) for a pair of workers to fill and tamp each tire. Beginners can take an hour or more per tire.

If the construction crew is also gathering and transporting the tires, this can add significantly to the labor requirements.

Mechanical equipment can lower the amount of manual labor involved, but the need to carefully place the dirt in each tire ensures that there will still be a high amount of labor input.

Health Warning: Sand, silt, clay and dust can be harmful to your lungs. Wear adequate respirators when dealing with dusty materials. It is also

Rammed Earth Tire Foundation Embodied Energy

Wall type: 1300mm (4ft) x 1 tire width	Material embodied energy from I.C.E. in MJ/kg	Weight to volume ratio of material*	Volume of material in sample 1000sf/92.9m² building	Sample building embodied energy	Material embodied carbon from I.C.E. in kgCO₂e/kg	Sample building embodied carbon	Notes
Lowest Impact							
Tires, diverted from landfill	1100 MJ per tire**	9 kg/tire	520 tires 4680 kg	0 MJ	0	0 kg	**Figure averaged from several sources, not included in ICE database. No embodied energy for repurposed materials.
Rammed earth from site soil	0.45 (rammed soil)	1600 kg/m³	22 m³ 35,200 kg	0 MJ	0.024	0 kg	No embodied energy for site harvested materials.
Totals				**0 MJ**		**0 kg**	
Highest Impact							
Tires, diverted from landfill	1100 MJ per tire**	9 kg/tire	520 tires 4680 kg	0 MJ	0	0 kg	No embodied energy for repurposed materials.
Rammed earth soil stabilized with 8% cement	0.83	1600 kg/m³	22 m³ 35,200 kg	29,216 MJ	0.084	2,957 kg	
Totals				**29,216 MJ**		**2,957 kg**	Does not include waterproofing or parging.

Transportation: Tire transportation by 35 ton truck would equate to 4.4 MJ per kilometer of travel to the building site.
Soil transportation by 15 ton truck would equate to 52.8 MJ per kilometer of travel to the building site. *Typically from engineeringtoolbox.com

advisable to wear gloves and respirators while handling tires.

SKILL LEVEL REQUIRED: *EASY*

A tire foundation is quite easy to build. As with any type of foundation, the layout is critical. Beyond the layout lines, people with little or no construction experience can learn the actual mixing, filling and tamping of the tires very quickly. Builders with a lot of experience will likely make a better, more consistent foundation more quickly. However, a dedicated group of amateurs can quickly come up to speed and within a short time could be moving as quickly and accurately as the pros.

It definitely helps to have at least one experienced tire builder on a crew. One person can usually direct an entire crew until everybody gets the pacing and methodology. If nobody has previous experience, it's worth looking into workshops or other training opportunities before commencing with a foundation.

SOURCING/AVAILABILITY: *EASY TO MODERATE*

Tires are an abundant waste product almost everywhere in the world. In theory, used tires are easy to find and access. However, some regions have instituted strict regulations about used tire handling and storage, often in conjunction with tire recycling programs. In these locations there are still lots of tires around, but they may be more difficult to obtain. Check into availability and local regulations about buying, selling and storing tires before committing to this type of foundation.

The dirt for placing in the tires should be widely available, and the wide range of acceptable soil types should mean that soils from the building site are viable. Inspect site soils prior to construction; if not suitable it should be possible to locate useful soil nearby.

DURABILITY: *HIGH TO VERY HIGH*

The elements of a tire foundation are both very durable. Tires are a persistent waste specifically because they do not break down quickly. UV radiation does break them down slowly, but hidden from the sun they have a very long lifetime. Best estimates range from hundreds to thousands of years. The rammed earth in the tires has an immeasurable durability. Examples of tire foundations are at most a few decades old, but there is no reason to think that these foundations won't be among the most durable it is possible to build.

CODE COMPLIANCE

Tire foundations are not an accepted solution in any codes. Alternative compliance will need to be based on a structural engineer's calculations, as very little study has been done on tire foundations.

It is highly advisable to discuss the tire foundation option with code officials and find out whether or not they are willing to consider it, and under what conditions, before proceeding with plans to use tires.

INDOOR AIR QUALITY

Tire foundations will have little direct impact on indoor air quality. By keeping the floors and walls of the building dry they can help to prevent other IAQ issues.

When used as the walls of a building, there are concerns about off-gassing of compounds from the tires. No scientific studies have been performed to date, and advocates point to the fact that tires are sealed behind plaster or other interior wall skin to alleviate concern. Detractors question the effectiveness of the barriers.

FUTURE DEVELOPMENT

Tire foundations have not had much mainstream acceptance, due in large part to the labor intensity of the system. There are ways in which the system could become more mechanized, particularly in the filling and tamping of the dirt into the tires. Pneumatic devices already used in other styles of construction have been adapted to this use, though they aren't commercially available.

Tire foundations would need a much wider acceptance before significant advancements are made in material availability and mechanization. Until then, owner-builders and custom contractors aiming for the highest standards in recycled materials will continue to use tire foundations.

In recent years, government-sponsored tire recycling programs have grown in number. Choosing to reuse old tires to build foundations seems like a reasonable way of repurposing this waste material, but builders may find themselves in competition with mandatory recycling programs in some areas.

Resources for further research

Reynolds, Michael E. *Earthship: How to Build Your Own*. Taos, NM: Solar Survival Architecture, 1990. Print.

Reynolds, Michael E. *Earthship: Evolution beyond Economics*. Taos, NM: Solar Survival Architecture, 1993. Print.

Reynolds, Michael E. *Earthship: Systems and Components*. Taos, NM: Solar Survival, 1991. Print.

Reynolds, Michael E. *Earthship: Engineering Evaluation of Rammed-Earth Tire Construction*. S.l.: S.n., 1993. Print.

McConkey, Robert. *The Complete Guide to Building Affordable Earth-Sheltered Homes: Everything You Need to Know Explained Simply*. Ocala, FL: Atlantic, 2011. Print.

Reynolds, Michael. *Comfort in Any Climate*. Taos, NM: Solar Survival, 2000. Print.

Hewitt, Mischa, and Kevin Telfer. *Earthships in Europe*. Watford, UK: IHS BRE Press, 2012. Print.

Rammed Earth Tire Foundation Ratings

	Best 1	2	3	4	5	6	7	Worst 8	9	10	Notes
Environmental Impacts	▓	▓	▓								Addition of insulation and waterproofing will raise impacts.
Embodied Energy	▓	▓	▓	▓	▓	▓	▓	▓			Cement stabilization of rammed earth will have a large affect on EE. Addition of insulation will raise impacts.
Waste Generated	▓										
Energy Efficiency								▓			System requires addition of insulation to provide energy efficiency.
Material Costs	▓										Addition of insulation will raise costs.
Labor Inputs							▓	▓			
Skill Level Required by Homeowner	▓	▓	▓	▓							
Sourcing and Availability	▓	▓	▓	▓							Tires must be sourced outside regular building supply chain.
Durability and Longevity	▓	▓	▓								Untested, but rammed earth mixes and tires have high durability precedent.
Building Code Compliance						▓	▓				
Indoor Air Quality					▓	▓					Foundation will not typically affect IAQ, but if used as a wall system, impacts are questionable due to off-gassing from tires.

Helical pier, screwpile and screw pier foundations

What the cheerleaders say...	What the detractors say...
Fast, "instant" foundation	Expensive
Extremely low site impact	Requires specialized machinery to install
Cost-effective installation	Lifespan questionable
Low embodied energy	Encourages development in sensitive areas
Functions in difficult soil conditions	

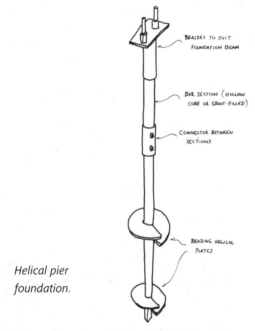

BRACKET TO SUIT FOUNDATION BEAM

BAR SECTION (HOLLOW CORE OR GROUT-FILLED)

CONNECTOR BETWEEN SECTIONS

BEARING HELICAL PLATES

Helical pier foundation.

Applications for this foundation system

- Piers
- Perimeter beams
- Frost walls
- Basement walls
- Slabs

Basic materials

- Galvanized steel shafts and helices
- Connectors for beams
- Torque equipment (manual or hydraulic)

How the system works

A galvanized steel shaft (round or square section tubing) with screw-like flanges is twisted into the ground until the torque required to turn it indicates proper bearing capacity of the soil. Depending on soil conditions and loads, this can happen just below the frost line or hundreds of feet down. For deep piers, the screw is driven down in sections with additional steel shafts added as required. A desired amount of the steel shaft is left above grade and a cap appropriate to the style of foundation is placed or welded on top. The lack of excavation and site disturbance can reduce impacts on the local ecosystem.

Helical piers can be used directly as footings for timber or steel posts or to support beams for a raised floor deck. They can also support concrete perimeter beams, concrete slabs or underpin basement wall footings in areas where the surface soils do not provide adequate bearing capacity.

The piers can be driven into most types of ground, though solid rock requires pre-drilling and will be considerably more expensive. Stony soils can work, as the screws tend to push rocks out of their way. Occasionally, a pier being driven into stony soil may hit a boulder it cannot shift or penetrate — in these cases the pier is extracted and slightly relocated or driven at an angle to avoid the obstacle. These occurrences can be hard to predict and will add unexpected cost to the installation.

Most pier companies provide engineering services to calculate building loads and create a pier layout that matches the building's requirements and the soil conditions. Installations with no unexpected conditions are quite fast and require no excavation, leaving sites with little or no disturbance of the topsoil or subsoil.

Tips for a successful helical pier foundation

1. Consult the pier company early in the planning process. Small changes in pier placement and loads can sometimes make large differences in cost. Different sizes of pier shafts and helices have different costs; costs will vary with fewer, larger piers or more, smaller piers.
2. Perform a geotechnical investigation of your site before committing to helical piers. There will be a cost for this, but the information is valuable. A geotech report will give the pier company accurate information for specifying loads and sizing piers and help avoid any surprises during the installation.
3. Ensure that the bracketry for the piers is compatible with your posts and/or beams. Custom bracketry can add considerable extra cost.
4. Check with your building department regarding their requirements for helical pier installations. The engineering that is done by the pier company should satisfy all code requirements, but as an unusual residential foundation system it is best to bring the idea to the building department early in the process.

Pros and cons

ENVIRONMENTAL IMPACTS

Harvesting — *High.* The steel and zinc are extracted in an intensive mining process, with impacts that include habitat destruction, ground and surface water contamination and dangerous/unhealthy working conditions. The use of recycled content can mitigate these impacts.

Manufacturing — *High.* Steel and zinc are produced using very high heat input, requiring heavy use of fossil fuels. Impacts include air pollution, water contamination and dangerous/unhealthy working conditions. Recycled content is subject to

Helical piers. (KELLY JACOBSEN)

the same intensity of production and does not mitigate impacts.

Transportation — *High.* Sample building uses 175.5 – 487.5 kg of material:

> 0.26 – 0.75 MJ per km by 15 ton truck
> 0.16 – 0.46 MJ per km by 35 ton truck

It can be difficult to track all stages of steel production as there are multiple stages of extraction and manufacture involved which are often international in scope. Components of helical piers may have traveled internationally prior to site of final manufacturing.

Installation — *Negligible.* The use of helical pier foundations can eliminate the need for excavation of the building site, mitigating one of the highest impacts on the local ecosystem. The use of hydraulic equipment to drive piers will typically have lower impacts than excavation.

WASTE: *VERY LOW*

Recyclable — Metal pier offcuts, fasteners.

ENERGY EFFICIENCY: *N/A*

Helical piers in residential construction are used to support structural elements and are typically outside the building enclosure. As such, they don't have a direct impact on energy efficiency.

Piers are often used to build raised floor decks, in which the floor of the building is elevated above grade and the bottom side of the floor system is exposed to the air. When decoupled from the ground, the underside of a floor system is exposed to greater fluctuations in temperature in cold climates and an insulation strategy must be chosen to deal with this exposure. In such cases, the floor insulation should be at least as thick as the walls, and the same attention must be paid to avoiding thermal bridging and air leakage.

MATERIAL COSTS: *MODERATE TO HIGH*

Helical piers themselves are not particularly expensive, but the complete costs of a helical pier foundation must include geotechnical analysis of soils, pier engineering and installation, all of which will depend on regional conditions and competition.

If soil conditions would require a large volume of fill for a foundation, helical piers will compare favorably. The speed at which they can be installed and the fact that installation is not weather-dependent can save money in many cases. A builder can also save because making access roads for excavators and gravel/cement delivery adds costs to the entire project that may be eliminated by switching to piers.

LABOR INPUT: *LOW*

Beyond laying out the pier locations, there is little labor for an owner or builder to contribute to a helical pier installation. Most pier installers send a team of two or three to a residential installation, and a full day is typically all that is required.

SKILL LEVEL REQUIRED FOR THE HOMEOWNER: *N/A*

Since the supplier does most pier installations, the owner or contractor needs no experience or skill. The owner can do the pier layout as most pier foundations have simple grid layouts that do not require a great deal of skill to create.

SOURCING/AVAILABILITY: *MODERATE*

There are numerous pier manufacturers in North America, and suppliers/installers who work regionally with their products. This type of foundation is moderately easy to source and widely available.

Steel Pier Foundation Embodied Energy

Foundation type: 2.4m (7.5ft) grid, 15 piers to 1.3m (4ft) depth, standard beam brackets	Material embodied energy from I.C.E. in MJ/kg	Weight to volume ratio of material*	Volume of material in sample 1000sf/92.9m² building	Sample building embodied energy	Material embodied carbon from I.C.E. in kgCO$_2$e/kg	Sample building embodied carbon	Notes
Lowest Impact							
Lightweight pier, 3.8cm (1.5 inch) diameter	20.1 (General steel, average recycled content)	9 kg/m	19.5 m 175.5 kg	3,528 MJ	1.46	256 kg	Pier weight from averaged industry figures.
Totals				3,528 MJ		256 kg	
Highest Impact							
Heavy duty pier, 6cm (2.5 inch) diameter	20.1 (General steel, average recycled content)	25 kg/m	19.5 m 487.5 kg	9,799 MJ	1.46	712 kg	Pier weight from averaged industry figures.
Totals				9,799 MJ		712 kg	No impacts considered for beams.

Transportation: Pier transportation by 15 ton truck would equate to 0.26 – 0.73 MJ per kilometer of travel to the building site. *Typically from engineeringtoolbox.com

DURABILITY: *HIGH*

Some buildings (mostly lighthouses) built with cast iron screw piles in the mid-1800s are still standing today. This gives some indication that the life span of galvanized screw piles should be considerable. Corrosion will eventually destroy the piers, but it is reasonable to measure assumed life span in centuries, not decades.

CODE COMPLIANCE

Residential building codes do not typically address the use of helical piers as a prescriptive solution. However, building departments will likely be familiar with this system from commercial construction. The engineering support supplied by installer should suffice for approval in most jurisdictions.

INDOOR AIR QUALITY

Screw pier foundations will have little direct impact on indoor air quality. By keeping the floors and walls of the building dry they can help to prevent other IAQ issues.

FUTURE DEVELOPMENT

Screw pile technology was introduced in the 1830s and the basic premise and design have not changed much since. Developments in metallurgy (in particular, hot-dip galvanizing) have ensured higher strengths and longer life span. Experimental piers using carbon fiber and other composites have seen some use, and may become more commercially viable in the future. Such piers may have longer life spans and higher strength, as well as lower shipping costs due to reduced weight.

Resources for further research

Perko, Howard A. *Helical Piles: A Practical Guide to Design and Installation*. Hoboken, NJ: Wiley, 2009. Print.

Steel Pier Foundation Ratings

	Best							Worst			Notes
	1	2	3	4	5	6	7	8	9	10	
Environmental Impacts							▓	▓			High carbon emissions and harvesting impacts. Addition of floor framing and insulation will affect impacts.
Embodied Energy	▓	▓	▓								Addition of floor framing and insulation will affect EE.
Waste Generated	▓										
Energy Efficiency					N/A						Pier foundations make not direct impact on energy efficiency, but require insulation of floor deck system.
Material Costs				▓	▓	▓					Addition of floor framing and insulation will raise costs.
Labor Inputs	▓										
Skill Level Required by Homeowner					N/A						Installations provided by professionals.
Sourcing and Availability	▓	▓	▓	▓							Providers do not typically serve residential clientele, but are widespread.
Durability and Longevity				▓	▓	▓	▓	▓			Quality of steel and galvanizing will impact lifespan, as will soil type/conditions.
Building Code Compliance	▓										Systems are pre-engineered.
Indoor Air Quality					N/A						Pier systems are entirely outside the building enclosure.

Wooden piers

What the cheerleaders say...	What the detractors say...
Inexpensive	Short lifespan
Fast installation time	Code approval may be difficult
Widely available	
Simple to create	

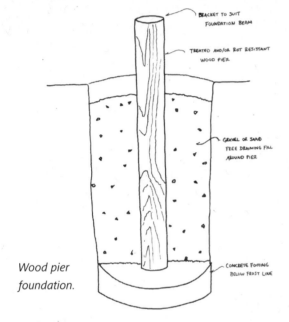

Wood pier foundation.

Labels on diagram: BRACKET TO SUIT FOUNDATION BEAM; TREATED AND/OR ROT RESISTANT WOOD PIER; GRAVEL OR SAND FREE DRAINING FILL AROUND PIER; CONCRETE FOOTING BELOW FROST LINE

Applications for this foundation system

- Piers

Basic materials

- Large timbers, either milled or round
- Treatment for the wood below grade

How the system works

Wooden members of an appropriate size are used to support a floor deck above grade. Typically, a hole is drilled. or excavated to a depth below the frost line and a gravel base and/or concrete footing are placed to receive the pier. The excavation around the wooden pier is then backfilled with a well-draining sand/gravel mixture and tamped in lifts to locate and secure the pier.

The tops of the piers are trimmed to the desired height above grade and prepared to support the floor beams. Attachments between pier and beam can range from traditional timber-framing joinery to notch-and-bolt systems to welded metal plates. These choices will be dictated by budget, skill level and engineering and code requirements.

Tips for a successful wood pier foundation

1. Carefully consider the intended use and desired life span of the building. Wooden piers are not the most durable choice, but not every building needs to endure longer than a few generations. As long as the life span matches expectations, the choice can be appropriate.
2. Choose an appropriate, locally available, rot-resistant wood species. Remember that imported species may not be resistant to rot and pests in another ecosystem.
3. Inspect soil conditions thoroughly. Dry, well-draining soils are preferable, though historically wooden piers have also been used in areas where the soils are continuously wet. Wood will usually last better when it is constantly dry or constantly wet.
4. Provide a well-draining base for the pier. A bed of tamped gravel may be adequate. A drainage tile system should be used in areas with intermittent water saturation of the soils.
5. Backfill around the pier with a well-draining fill.
6. Consider lining the sides of the excavation prior to backfilling. Use a material like landscape fabric or used carpeting that will prevent the surrounding soil from migrating into the backfill and coming into contact with the pier.

7. Use joinery between piers and beams that will facilitate the least complicated replacement of piers. Bolts and metal plates that allow for horizontal extraction will be easier to undo in the future than notched joinery that requires the beam to be lifted over a tenon.

Pros and cons

Environmental impacts

Harvesting — *Negligible to Low.* Site-harvested timber can have negligible impacts. Locally harvested timber is available in many regions and if sustainable forestry practices are used impacts can be very low. Use of third-party certified timber can help to ensure that impacts are minimal.

Manufacturing — *Negligible.* Large round timber can be used without any process beyond bark removal. Squared timbers require a minimal amount of mechanical processing. Use of third-party certified timber can help to ensure that impacts are minimal.

Transportation — *Negligible to High.* Sample building uses 418.5 – 697.5 kg of wooden piers:

> 0.63 – 1.05 MJ per km by 15 ton truck
> 0.4 – 0.66 MJ per km by 35 ton truck

Sample building uses 1920 – 4080 kg of concrete:

> 2.88 – 6.12 MJ per km by 15 ton truck
> 1.8 – 3.84 MJ per km by 35 ton truck

Timber is a heavy and high-volume material to transport and impacts will rise proportionally with distance traveled. Widespread regional production can help to minimize transportation requirements.

Installation — *Negligible.* The use of timber pier foundations can eliminate the need for intensive excavation of the building site, mitigating one of the highest impacts on the local ecosystem.

Waste: *Negligible*

Biodegradable/Compostable — All untreated wood offcuts.

Wood pier. (David Elfstrom)

Recyclable — Metal fasteners.
Landfill — Wood offcuts with treatments, containers for treatment materials.

Energy efficiency: *N/A*

Wooden piers are typically outside the building enclosure. As such, they don't have a direct impact on energy efficiency.

Piers are often used to build raised floor decks, in which the floor of the building is elevated above grade and the bottom side of the floor system is exposed to the air. When decoupled from the ground, the underside of a floor system is exposed to greater fluctuations in temperature in cold climates and an insulation strategy must be chosen to deal with this exposure. In such cases, the floor insulation should be at least as thick as the walls, and the same attention must be paid to avoiding thermal bridging and air leakage.

Material costs: *Very Low*

If metal bracketry and fasteners are being used to connect piers to beams, these may end up being the most expensive element. The use of off-the-shelf bracketry will help keep these costs lower than specialty or custom-welded brackets.

LABOR INPUT: *VERY LOW*

The majority of the labor involved in a wooden pier foundation is in the excavation and backfilling. Using a natural preservation method will add time to the process. Hand-cut joinery will usually be more labor intensive than bracketry.

SKILL LEVEL REQUIRED: *EASY TO MODERATE*

Most forms of joinery used to attach piers to beams are straightforward and well within the abilities of most owner-builders. Grid layouts for pier placement are also straightforward.

SOURCING/AVAILABILITY: *EASY*

Timbers suitable for piers are locally available in most regions. Check for availability of off-the-shelf bracketry for joining piers to beams. Local welders will be able to fabricate suitable brackets, and in some cases these may be easier and less expensive to source than commercially sourced components.

DURABILITY: *LOW*

In most vernacular traditions, buildings with very low embodied energy and materials that were easily reused or compostable served their purpose and were not expected to endure forever. A building made with all natural and recycled materials and largely human embodied energy has little "environmental debt" to repay, so longevity is not as important on a planetary scale as with other, more intensive buildings. If longevity becomes a personal choice rather than an environmental one, it is up to the owner or builder to decide.

Wood in contact with soil is very prone to rot failure, so the key to viable wood pier foundations

Wooden Pier Foundation Embodied Energy

Foundation type: 2.4m (7.5ft) grid, 15 piers to 1.3m (4ft) depth	Material embodied energy from I.C.E. in MJ/kg	Weight to volume ratio of material*	Volume of material in sample 1000sf/92.9m² building	Sample building embodied energy	Material embodied carbon from I.C.E. in kgCO$_2$e/kg	Sample building embodied carbon	Notes
Lowest Impact							
Softwood timber 250mm (10 inch) diameter	2.5 (kiln dried softwood)	450 kg/m³	0.93 m³ 418.5 kg	1,046 MJ	0.2	84 kg	EE figure averaged from multiple sources. ICE figure disproportionately high at 7.4.
Concrete footings 450x450x250mm (18x18x10 inch) with 50% slag content	0.62	2400 kg/m³	0.8 m³ 1920 kg	1,190 MJ	0.077	148 kg	
Totals				**2,236 MJ**		**232 kg**	
Highest Impact							
Hardwood timber 250mm (10 inch) diameter	3.2 (kiln dried hardwood)	750 kg/m³	0.93 m³ 697.5 kg	2,232 MJ	0.24	167 kg	EE figure averaged from multiple sources. ICE figure disproportionately high at 10.4.
Concrete footings 600x600x300mm (24x24x12 inch), no admixtures	0.74 (20/25mPa concrete)	2400 kg/m³	1.7 m³ 4080 kg	3,019 MJ	0.107	437 kg	
Totals				**5,251 MJ**		**604 kg**	Figures do not include bracketry or beams.

Transportation: Pier transportation by 15 ton truck would equate to 0.63 – 1.05 MJ per kilometer of travel to the building site. *Typically from engineeringtoolbox.com is reducing the chance of short-term susceptibility to rot. Choosing a naturally rot-resistant wood is the first step in designing a wood pier foundation. Cypress, redwood, cedar, locust and white oak are among the available species that are appropriate. Methods of preserving or treating the wood should also be considered; there are many, from very natural to highly toxic.

No method of treating wood will guarantee a long life span below grade, but in the right conditions it may help to achieve a life span that is adequate for the intended purpose of the building. Clay/mud coatings, charring, creosote and chemical pressure-treating are among the treatments that have, in some cases, helped wood last longer below grade. New methods of heat-treating and silica impregnation show promise.

The most vulnerable portion of a wooden pier is the junction with grade, which will see frequent wetting and drying cycles and be most susceptible to damage from fungi, insects and even animals like porcupines. Protection for this area can include wide overhangs from the floor system above and a generous circumference of gravel fill around the pier to encourage quick drainage and discourage plant growth.

Even well-built wooden piers will have the shortest life span of any foundation mentioned in this book. In excellent conditions, that life span may be as much as two or three generations. For some builders/buildings, this may be adequate. Replacement of the piers — with new wooden piers or another kind of foundation — is possible. The higher the floor deck from the ground, the easier this will be.

CODE COMPLIANCE

Pole barn construction is an acceptable solution in many code jurisdictions, though typically for

Wooden Pier Foundation Ratings

	Best						Worst				Notes
	1	2	3	4	5	6	7	8	9	10	
Environmental Impacts											Addition of floor framing and insulation will raise impacts.
Embodied Energy											Addition of floor framing and insulation will raise EE.
Waste Generated											
Energy Efficiency					N/A						Pier foundations make no direct impact on energy efficiency, but require insulation of floor deck system.
Material Costs											Addition of floor framing and insulation will raise costs.
Labor Inputs											Type of footings and joinery will affect labour.
Skill Level Required by Homeowner											
Sourcing and Availability											
Durability and Longevity											Type of wood, treatments and soil conditions will have impacts on lifespan.
Building Code Compliance											Wood piers are accepted solutions for pole barns, but will likely require alternative compliance for residential use.
Indoor Air Quality					N/A						Pier systems are entirely outside the building enclosure.

agricultural use and not residential. Where wooden piers are proposed as an alternative solution, a structural engineer's approval may be required. It is likely that code officials will require piers to be treated in an "approved" manner, which is unlikely to include any of the natural treatment options. These will need to be discussed with code officials in advance of construction.

INDOOR AIR QUALITY

Timber pier foundations will have little direct impact on indoor air quality. By keeping the floors and walls of the building dry they can help to prevent other IAQ issues.

FUTURE DEVELOPMENT

A number of recent developments have been made in treating wood to prevent rot. Heat treatment, glass impregnation, sodium silicate-based preservatives and wood acetylation can all prolong the life span of wood in contact with soil and/or water. In some jurisdictions, one or more of these methods may already be recognized. Check with local code officials about their willingness to accept wood treated in any of these ways. These treatments can have effects on the nature of the wood, the ways in which it can be cut and fastened and its structural properties.

A lot of research is taking place on inhibiting rot and extending the desirable properties of wood, and it is worth exploring new developments that may make wooden piers a more attractive option by extending the potential life span of this type of foundation.

Poured concrete foundations

What the cheerleaders say...	What the detractors say...
Durable	High carbon footprint
Adaptable	High embodied energy
Widely available	Extensive formwork required
Affordable	

Applications for this foundation system

- Piers
- Perimeter beams
- Frost walls (not covered in this book due to high environmental impacts)
- Basement walls (not covered in this book due to high environmental impacts)
- Slabs (not covered in this book due to high environmental impacts)

Basic materials

- Portland cement
- Other binders to offset portland cement use (can include fly ash, blast furnace slag and other pozzolans)
- Aggregate
- Water
- Steel reinforcing (rebar and/or mesh)

How the system works

Concrete has many ideal characteristics for use in buildings. It is durable, strong and can be poured as a liquid into any container where it will set. The raw materials are abundant and widespread. If it weren't for the very high environmental impacts in terms of energy input and carbon output, concrete would be ideal.

Concrete is being included in this book because there are foundations that use reasonable and responsible amounts of concrete to achieve results that are consistent with a sustainable approach to building. To make piers or a perimeter beam, concrete usage and its attendant environmental impacts can be minimized in comparison to conventional usage.

Piers — A tubular formwork is placed into the excavated soil, backfilled, and then filled with wet concrete. While the concrete is still wet, an appropriate bracket is placed at the top of the pier to make a connection with the foundation beam.

Formwork for concrete piers comes in several varieties. Cardboard-based tubes are the most popular. These are installed on top of a previously formed footing at the base of the excavation, or can be attached to plastic forms that create a wide footing and allow the pier and footing to be poured at the same time. Plastic footing cones are also cast with footing and pier as one unit and are typically made of recycled plastic. Fabric forms are another option. These use the tensile strength of woven fabric (material varies by manufacturer) to create tubular forms that are placed, braced and then "inflated" with concrete. They offer the advantage of less material use and lower shipping and handling costs because they can be rolled tightly as opposed to being handled as large tubes.

Most concrete piers are reinforced with rebar in the center of the pour. A pair of bars crossed in the footing and a single bar in the center of the pier is typical.

Perimeter beams — A perimeter beam is a grade-based foundation in which a structural beam is cast from concrete to match the width of the walls above.

For narrow wall systems, it may be necessary to use a footing that is wider than the wall above. For thick wall systems, it is possible to cast the perimeter beam as two narrower beams or to displace concrete in the center of the beam using hollow builder's tubes or other means of creating a void. The perimeter beam will require some amount of rebar reinforcement as specified by codes or a structural engineer.

As a grade-based foundation, perimeter beams will require some means of protection against frost issues in colder climates. This can be achieved using a rubble trench (*see rubble trench section page 48) below the perimeter beam that is deeper than the frost line, or by employing an insulated frost skirt around the foundation. A frost skirt creates a

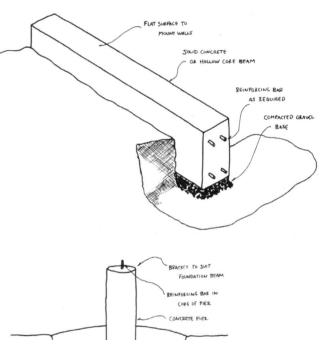

FLAT SURFACE TO MOUNT WALLS

SOLID CONCRETE OR HOLLOW CORE BEAM

REINFORCING BAR AS REQUIRED

COMPACTED GRAVEL BASE

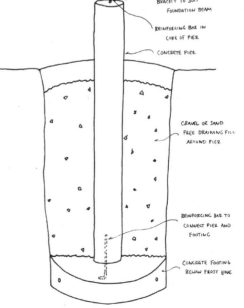

BRACKET TO SUIT FOUNDATION BEAM

REINFORCING BAR IN CORE OF PIER

CONCRETE PIER

GRAVEL OR SAND FREE DRAINING FILL AROUND PIER

REINFORCING BAR TO CONNECT PIER AND FOOTING

CONCRETE FOOTING BELOW FROST LINE

Concrete pier.

shallow, frost-protected foundation (SFPF) and is a widely accepted means of preventing frost from penetrating into soil under a foundation without excavating below the frost line.

Tips for a successful concrete foundation:

1. Use the highest percentage of portland cement replacement possible for the given application. Blast furnace slag and fly ash are commonly available and can displace a high percentage of virgin cement content, lowering the environmental impact of concrete use.

2. Do not over-build. There is a tendency with concrete design to use more than is structurally necessary. Ensure that the design meets the structural needs with enough concrete and rebar without adding more "just for good measure."

3. Discuss measures for displacing concrete with a structural engineer. Creating voids is one strategy; adding stone or chunks of old concrete is another. Both are feasible in many applications.

4. Consider the formwork strategy that will be used from an environmental point of view. Single-use forms or those that have a reasonable chance of being ruined will add to the environmental cost of the foundation.

5. Be sure to specify the correct concrete mix. It is important to know the proper strength rating (usually expressed as an MPa or PSI figure) and the need for special admixtures (air entraining, high early strength, etc) when ordering concrete. Suitable concrete mixes may be specified in building codes or determined by a structural engineer. Local concrete batching plants can also supply useful information about mixes.

6. Mixing your own concrete on-site may not be cheaper or more environmentally sound than ordering ready-mix to be delivered. All the materials will still need to be delivered to your site, so the transportation impacts are the same. If you are using a small gas-powered mixer, chances are the emissions are worse than the larger machinery used at a batching plant. Hand-mixed concrete must be produced quickly enough to suffice for larger monolithic pours like a perimeter beam.

Pros and cons

ENVIRONMENTAL IMPACTS

Harvesting — *Moderate to High.* Limestone and aggregate mechanically extracted from quarries and can have moderate to high impacts on habitat destruction and ground and surface water contamination and flow.

Steel for reinforcement is a high-impact resource to extract.

Manufacturing — *High.* The creation of portland cement is high intensity, with limestone being heated in kilns to very high sustained temperatures.

Fuels used include natural gas, oil, coal and landfill waste, in large quantities, with impacts including significant air pollution and very significant greenhouse gas emissions due to CO_2 being driven out of the stone.

Steel for reinforcement is a very high-impact material to manufacture.

Transportation — *Low to High*. Sample pier foundation uses 3,336 – 6,312 kg of concrete:

> 5 – 9.5 MJ per km by 15 ton truck
> 3.14 – 5.93 MJ per km by 35 ton truck

Sample grade beam foundation uses 5,760 – 15,528 kg of concrete:

> 8.64 – 23.3 MJ per km by 15 ton truck
> 5.4 – 14.6 MJ per km by 35 ton truck

Concrete perimeter beam.

Concrete Pier Foundation Embodied Energy

Foundation type: 2.4m (7.5ft) grid, 15 piers to 1.3m (4ft) depth	Material embodied energy from I.C.E. in MJ/kg	Weight to volume ratio of material*	Volume of material in sample 1000sf/92.9m² building	Sample building embodied energy	Material embodied carbon from I.C.E. in kgCO₂e/kg	Sample building embodied carbon	Notes
Lowest Impact							
200mm (8 inch) diameter pier, 50% slag content	0.62 (20/25mPa, blast furnace slag at 50%)	2400 kg/m³	0.59 m³ 1416 kg	878 MJ	0.077	109 kg	
450x450x250mm (18x18x10 inch) footing, 50% slag content	0.62 (20/25mPa, blast furnace slag at 50%)	2400 kg/m³	0.8 m³ 1920 kg	1,190 MJ	0.077	148 kg	
Reinforcing bar 12mm (½ inch) in footing and pier	17.4 (Bar and rod, average recycled content)	1 kg/m	32 m 32 kg	557 MJ	1.4	45 kg	
Totals				**2,625 MJ**		**302 kg**	
Highest Impact							
250mm (10 inch) diameter piers, no admixtures	0.74 (20/25mPa, general)	2400 kg/m³	0.93 m³ 2232 kg	1,652 MJ	0.107	239 kg	
600x600x300mm (24x24x12 inch) footing, no admixtures	0.74 (20/25mPa, general)	2400 kg/m³	1.7 m³ 4080 kg	3,019 MJ	0.107	437 kg	
Reinforcing bar 12mm (½ inch) in footing and pier	17.4 (Bar and rod, average recycled content)	1 kg/m	32 m 32 kg	557 MJ	1.4	45 kg	
Totals				**5,228 MJ**		**721 kg**	No brackets or floor beams included.

Transportation: Concrete transportation by 15 ton truck would equate to 5–9.5 MJ per kilometer of travel to the building site. *Typically from engineeringtoolbox.com

Cement and aggregate are heavy, high-volume materials and impacts will rise proportionally with distance traveled.

Installation — *Negligible to Moderate.* If formwork is sacrificial, impacts can be significant.

WASTE: *LOW*

Biodegradable/Compostable — Extra concrete is often broken up and left in the environment. To minimize leftover concrete waste, specify the use of a site-mix truck that adds water to dry ingredients in the spout. This ensures that only the amount needed is mixed, as opposed to ready-mix trucks that add water at the batching plant and must dump all leftover material on-site.

Recyclable — Metal reinforcing bar.

Landfill — Cement bags (if site mixing).

Wooden formwork is sometimes treated as waste, but can usually be re-used or recycled into the building.

ENERGY EFFICIENCY: *PIERS — N/A*
PERIMETER BEAM — *VERY LOW*

A concrete perimeter beam foundation has little thermal resistance. In areas where an insulated foundation is important, a strategy to add insulation to the inside and/or outside edge of a concrete foundation will be important. With a proper insulation strategy in place, a concrete foundation can be part of an energy-efficient building.

Concrete piers are typically outside the building enclosure. As such, they don't have a direct impact on energy efficiency.

Piers are often used to build raised floor decks, in which the floor of the building is elevated above grade and the bottom side of the floor system is exposed to the air. When decoupled from the ground, the underside of a floor system is exposed to greater fluctuations in temperature in cold climates and an insulation strategy must be chosen to deal with this

Concrete Perimeter Beam Foundation Embodied Energy

Wall type: perimeter beam	Material embodied energy from I.C.E. in MJ/kg	Weight to volume ratio of material*	Volume of material in sample 1000sf/92.9m² building	Sample building embodied energy	Material embodied carbon from I.C.E. in kgCO₂e/kg	Sample building embodied carbon	Notes
Lowest Impact							
200x300mm (8x12 inch) beam, 50% slag content concrete	0.62 (20/25mPa with blast furnace slag at 50%)	2400 kg/m³	2.4 m³ 5760 kg	3,571 MJ	0.077	444 kg	
2 runs of 12mm (½ inch) steel reinforcing bar	17.4 (Bar and rod, average recycled content)	1 kg/m	85 m 85 kg	1,479 MJ	1.4	119 kg	Parging, waterproofing and insulating of foundation not included.
Totals				**5,050 MJ**		**563 kg**	
Highest Impact							
400x400mm (16x16 inch) beam, no admixture	0.74 (20/25mPa, general)	2400 kg/m³	6.47 m³ 15,528 kg	11,490 MJ	0.107	1,661 kg	
4 runs of 12mm (½ inch) steel reinforcing bar	17.4 (Bar and rod, average recycled content)	1 kg/m	170 m 170 kg	2,958 MJ	1.4	238 kg	
Totals				**14,448 MJ**		**1,899 kg**	Parging, waterproofing and insulating of foundation not included.

Transportation: Concrete transportation by 15 ton truck would equate to 8.6–23.3 MJ per kilometer of travel to the building site.   *Typically from engineeringtoolbox.com exposure. In such cases, the floor insulation should be at least as thick as the walls, and the same attention must be paid to avoiding thermal bridging and air infiltration or leakage.

MATERIAL COSTS: *PIERS — LOW*
PERIMETER BEAM — *MODERATE*

The popularity of concrete as a building material has a good deal to do with its relatively low cost. However, as energy prices rise, so does the price of concrete, which has gone up an average of 6–12 percent annually since the mid-1990s. This trend is unlikely to change and the rising cost of concrete foundations is one of the key reasons for rising residential housing costs.

Builders should be sure to include the cost of formwork into the foundation price. In some cases, wooden formwork can be stripped from the foundation and reused elsewhere in the building. Pier formwork is always single-use.

LABOR INPUT: *PIERS — LOW TO MODERATE*
PERIMETER BEAM — *MODERATE TO HIGH*

Concrete is a form-based building system, and the labor input required is directly related to the type and complexity of the formwork being used.

In the case of perimeter beams, the formwork is likely to be site-built from lumber and plywood and requires carpentry skills to create strong, accurate forms. The more complicated the shape of the building, the more labor will be expended on creating forms.

Piers will not typically require as much labor. If separate footings are being formed and poured prior to setting the piers there will be more labor involved than using all-in-one pier forms with a footing included.

Mixing concrete on site involves considerable labor. Heavy ingredients must be lifted or shoveled into a mixer, poured into a wheelbarrow and delivered to the forms.

SKILL LEVEL REQUIRED FOR HOMEOWNERS: *EASY TO DIFFICULT*

A basic perimeter beam foundation requires adequate, accurate formwork and simple screeding and troweling skills to finish the top surface. Creating accurate formwork requires an ability to read plans and translate the drawings into a formwork that will place the concrete in the right position. The biggest mistake made by inexperienced form builders is underestimating the force that will be applied to the forms by wet concrete. Forms must be extremely well braced, cross-tied with wires and staked to the ground in order not to distort when filled.

Concrete foundations typically require some arrangement of metal rebar reinforcement, and cutting, bending and tying the bar is another skill set to learn.

While many new builders can and do form and pour their own concrete foundations, it's no fluke that most professional contractors hire out concrete work to experienced crews. Experienced concrete contractors employ a great many tricks and techniques. The more concrete being poured, the more valuable that experience.

SOURCING/AVAILABILITY: *EASY*

Most populated regions will have concrete batching plants within a short radius of any building site, and the batchers should be able to create any mix required for a residential project.

Substitute binders like fly ash or blast furnace slag are becoming more widely available. Since these materials cost less than virgin portland cement, many batching plants use a portion of these binders in their mixes to keep costs down. There is typically a hesitation from batchers to supply mixes with very high percentages of alternative binders, but if local code officials and/or structural engineers will allow the use of higher than normal quantities of fly ash or slag, the batching plant should be willing to deliver such a mix.

DURABILITY: *HIGH TO VERY HIGH*

Concrete is a very durable material, capable of performing structurally below and above grade for at least a hundred years.

CODE COMPLIANCE

As a foundation material, concrete is an acceptable solution in all codes. Less conventional approaches, like perimeter beams, may not be formally described but will typically be accepted based on performance evaluation or the approval of a structural engineer. Codes will typically specify concrete strength and the quantity of rebar reinforcement required.

INDOOR AIR QUALITY

Concrete perimeter beams and piers will have little direct impact on indoor air quality. By keeping the floors and walls of the building dry they can help to prevent other IAQ issues.

FUTURE DEVELOPMENT

A great deal of research is being applied to making "greener" concrete. Effort has been made to optimize regular portland cement by increasing the limestone content and crushing the limestone and clinker to a smaller size, producing a "particle packing effect" that restores strength usually lost with higher limestone content.

Developments in the use of recycled binders like fly ash and slag are an improvement the industry is starting to adopt more widely. The science for replacing portland cement with these binders is well developed, but industry uptake of the materials has

Concrete Pier Foundation Ratings

	Best					Worst					Notes
	1	2	3	4	5	6	7	8	9	10	
Environmental Impacts							▓				High carbon emissions. Addition of floor framing and insulation will raise impacts.
Embodied Energy		▓									Addition of floor framing and insulation will raise EE.
Waste Generated		▓									
Energy Efficiency					N/A						Pier foundations make no direct impact on energy efficiency, but require insulation of floor deck system.
Material Costs		▓									Addition of floor framing and insulation will raise costs.
Labor Inputs	▓										Type of formwork and footings will affect labor.
Skill Level Required by Homeowner	▓										
Sourcing and Availability	▓										
Durability and Longevity	▓										
Building Code Compliance	▓										
Indoor Air Quality					N/A						Pier systems are entirely outside the building enclosure.

been slow. Cost has been one of the main factors driving the industry toward the use of alternative binders. It must be kept in mind, however, that the existing alternative binders are by-products of industrial processes that are just as energy-intensive and polluting as cement production. Making use of these by-products offsets the need to make virgin cement, but it does not mean that the alternative binders aren't still consuming large amounts of energy and producing large amounts of pollutants.

The use of recycled aggregate (often crushed concrete from demolitions) is a growing way to offset some of the environmental impacts of concrete. As aggregate represents the majority of the volume of concrete, reducing the amount of virgin quarried material is a very worthy goal. In urban areas, the demand for aggregate quarries results in severe environmental degradation and the destruction of habitat in areas adjacent to cities. Reducing the need

for new aggregate would have very positive impacts. However, aggregate does not represent a high proportion of the embodied energy or carbon output of concrete. Recycling of old concrete into aggregate for new concrete is not widespread, but as the cost of quarrying virgin aggregate rises along with the costs of disposing of old concrete, it is likely to find more market share.

Efforts are being made to find new ways to make concrete, but most are in early, experimental phases. A process for capturing CO_2 from industrial chimneys and injecting it into ready-mix concrete is showing promise, by reducing the amount of portland cement required. This method is currently reaching the market.

Another process using carbon-rich fume gases from natural gas-fired power plants in combination with seawater is showing some promise in creating calcium carbonate cement that could offset portland

Concrete Perimeter Beam Ratings

	Best 1 2 3 4 5 6	Worst 7 8 9 10	Notes
Environmental Impacts		8	High carbon emissions and harvesting impacts. Addition of insulation will raise impacts.
Embodied Energy	3		Addition of insulation will raise EE.
Waste Generated	3		Sacrificial forms can raise waste levels significantly.
Energy Efficiency		9	System requires addition of insulation to provide energy efficiency.
Material Costs	5		Addition of insulation will raise costs.
Labor Inputs		8	Formwork represents high percentage of labor input.
Skill Level Required by Homeowner		8	Formwork can be complicated.
Sourcing and Availability	1		
Durability and Longevity	1		
Building Code Compliance	1		
Indoor Air Quality	1		Foundation will not typically affect IAQ, but if used as a wall system, impacts are low.

cement production. The process can also be used to create a calcium carbonate aggregate to replace quarried aggregate, which has a greater volume in concrete. By sequestering carbon from fossil fuel burning, this material has great environmental potential in either form.

Work is being undertaken at labs around the world to find "green" concrete. As the most widely used building material on the planet, the rewards for finding an environmentally friendly version are significant. There is likely to be a number of innovative, "greener" concretes introduced in the coming years. It remains to be seen whether or not this useful but environmentally destructive material can be significantly improved or if the improvements will only be minimal.

Resources for further research

Fine Homebuilding (COR). *Foundations and Concrete Work: Revised and Updated.* N.p.: Ingram, 2012. Print.

Arnold, Rick. *Working with Concrete.* Newtown, CT: Taunton, 2003. Print.

Kelsey, John. *Masonry: The DIY Guide to Working with Concrete, Brick, Block, and Stone.* East Petersburg: Fox Chapel, 2012. Print.

Lightweight concrete masonry units (CMUs)

What the cheerleaders say...	What the detractors say...
Easier installation than heavy CMUs	Uses polluting portland cement
Better thermal properties	Lightweight aggregates can also be energy intensive
Less material intensive than poured concrete	Requires a full insulation strategy

Applications for this foundation system
- Perimeter beams
- Piers
- Frost walls

Basic materials
- Portland cement
- Aggregate
- Lightweight aggregates, including expanded shale, expanded clay and expanded recycled glass
- Alternative binders, including fly ash and blast furnace slag
- Mortar

How the system works

Lightweight CMUs are visually similar to typical heavy- or medium-weight blocks, but are typically 30–40 percent lighter for the same size block. The lower weight is achieved by using lightweight aggregates in place of standard sand and gravel. These aggregates are still mineral-based, but are expanded through the use of heat.

Concrete blocks are precast off-site and brought to the building site cured. Each block has one to three hollow cores, depending on block size and style. Individual blocks are laid up end to end in courses, with the blocks staggered on each course so a full block on each course spans the joint between blocks on the previous course. All joints are mortared.

Once fully built, rebar and a concrete grout are poured into a select number of the hollow cores. These concrete columns add strength to the mortar joints between the blocks.

For basement walls, the finished block is typically parged using a lime-cement mortar to help seal the joints from water penetration. Other waterproofing membranes or sealants may be applied over the parging.

Tips for a successful lightweight CMU foundation

CMU foundations are a very conventional approach and as such the information required to successfully build with them is widely available and is not detailed here.

Pros and cons

ENVIRONMENTAL IMPACTS

Harvesting — *Moderate to High.* Limestone and aggregate are mechanically extracted from quarries and can have moderate to high impacts on habitat destruction and ground and surface water contamination and flow.

Steel for reinforcement is a high-impact resource to extract.

Manufacturing — *High.* The creation of portland cement is a high-intensity process, with limestone being heated in kilns to very high sustained temperatures. Fuels used include natural gas, oil, landfill waste and coal, in large quantities, with impacts including significant air pollution and very significant greenhouse gas emissions.

Aggregate is produced in mechanical crushers with relatively low impacts.

Lightweight aggregate is produced under high-heat conditions, with similar impacts to portland cement except for lower greenhouse gas emissions.

Steel for reinforcement is a very high-impact material to manufacture.

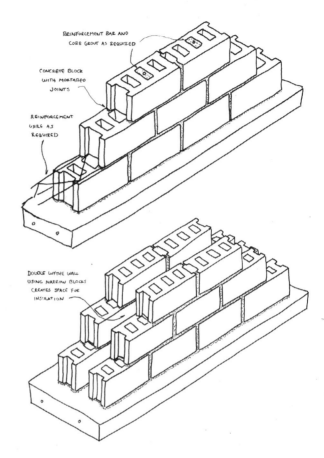

Transportation — *Low to High.* Sample foundation uses 22,863 – 34,013 kg of block, concrete and mortar

21.5 – 32 MJ per km by 35 ton truck

Cement and aggregate are heavy, high-volume materials and impacts will rise proportionally with distance traveled, both in production and site delivery.

Installation — *Negligible to Moderate.* Leftover block can be used elsewhere; leftover mortar must be disposed.

WASTE

Biodegradable/Compostable — CMU offcuts.

Recyclable — Metal reinforcement bar.
Landfill — Mortar bags.

ENERGY EFFICIENCY: *VERY LOW*

The aggregate used in lightweight CMUs gives the blocks a slightly higher thermal resistance than standard concrete blocks or poured concrete. However, this higher R-value does not translate into meaningful cold climate performance and a similar amount of additional insulation will be required as with any foundation to create a properly energy-efficient foundation.

One advantage of CMUs is the ability to affordably build double-wythe foundation walls, which can be particularly advantageous when supporting wider wall systems. When using two walls of narrow

CMU Foundation Embodied Energy

Wall type: 1.3m (4ft) perimeter wall, 12 mPa block	Material embodied energy from I.C.E. in MJ/kg	Weight to volume ratio of material*	Volume of material in sample 1000sf/92.9m² building	Sample building embodied energy	Material embodied carbon from I.C.E. in kgCO₂e/kg	Sample building embodied carbon	Notes
Lowest Impact							
200x200x400mm (8x8x16 inch) lightweight CMU block	0.72 (Block — 12 mPa)	16.15 kg/block	576 blocks 9,302 kg	6,697 MJ	0.088	819 kg	
Mortar 9.5mm (⅜ inch) joints	1.11 (Mortar 1:1:6 cement/lime/sand mix)	2162 kg/m³	3351 kg	3,720 MJ	0.174	583 kg	
Core fill every fourth block, 50% slag content	0.62	2400 kg/m³	1.02 m³ 2448 kg	1,518 MJ	0.077	188 kg	
Reinforcing bar, every fourth block	17.4 (Bar and rod, average recycled content)	1 kg/m	30 m 30 kg	522 MJ	1.4	42 kg	
400x200mm (16x8 inch) footing, 50% slag cement	0.62	2400 kg/m³	3.23 m 7,762.6 kg	4,813 MJ	0.077	598 kg	
Totals				**17,270 MJ**		**2,230 kg**	
Highest Impact							
200x200x400mm (8x8x16 inch) lightweight CMU block	0.72 (Block – 12 mPa)	16.15 kg/block	576 blocks 9,302 kg	6,697 MJ	0.088	819 kg	
Mortar 9.5mm (⅜ inch) joints	1.11 (Mortar 1:1:6 cement/lime/sand mix)	2162 kg/m³	3351 kg	3,720 MJ	0.174	583 kg	
Core fill every block, no admixtures	0.74 (20/25 mPa, general)	2400 kg/m³	4.05 m³ 9720 kg	7,193 MJ	0.107	1,040 kg	
Reinforcing bar, every block	17.4 (Bar and rod, average recycled content)	1 kg/m	234 m 234 kg	4,072 MJ	1.4	328 kg	
400x300mm (16x12 inch) footing, 50% slag cement	0.62	2400 kg/m³	4.85 m 11,640 kg	7,217 MJ	0.077	896 kg	
Totals				**28,899 MJ**		**3,666 kg**	Does not include parging, waterproofing or insulating of foundation.

Transportation: Block transportation by 15 ton truck would equate to 14 MJ per kilometer of travel to the building site. Concrete transportation by 15 ton truck would equate to 21–32 MJ per kilometer of travel to the building site. *Typically from engineeringtoolbox.com

CMU, a builder can insulate the gap between the walls, rather than adding insulation to the interior and/or exterior. This can help create a continuous insulation layer from the foundation up through the wall, and can allow a builder to choose from a wider range of insulations.

MATERIAL COSTS: *HIGH*

Lightweight CMU is less common than the heavyweight version and often costs more per block. The combination of poured footing, reinforcing bar, mortar and block adds up to a significant amount of material, leading to high costs.

LABOR INPUT: *HIGH*

CMU foundations require a similar amount of labor as poured concrete foundations. As no formwork is required (except to pour a footing at the base of the wall), this labor-intensive element is skipped. The movement of blocks and mortar on-site represents the highest amount of labor for a block project, and

can be handled by unskilled labor. Typically, a single laborer serves a single block layer.

SKILL LEVEL REQUIRED: *MODERATE TO DIFFICULT*

A lightweight CMU foundation requires a good deal of unskilled labor to move and deliver blocks and mix and move mortar. The skills required to lay a serviceable block wall can be learned and performed by most owner-builders. Practicing on a smaller project is a good way to determine if you want to tackle the entire foundation, or hire it out to a professional.

SOURCING/AVAILABILITY: *EASY*

Lightweight CMUs are available from most masonry supply outlets, but are not as common as heavy- and medium-weight blocks. It may be necessary to special order the light blocks.

DURABILITY: *HIGH TO VERY HIGH*

A well-built block foundation with an appropriate number of reinforced, grouted cores will be a

CMU Foundation Ratings

	Best						Worst				Notes
	1	2	3	4	5	6	7	8	9	10	
Environmental Impacts								███			High carbon emissions. Addition of insulation will raise impacts.
Embodied Energy						███					Addition of insulation will raise impacts.
Waste Generated	██										
Energy Efficiency								███			System requires addition of insulation to provide energy efficiency.
Material Costs							███				Addition of insulation will raise costs.
Labor Inputs							███				
Skill Level Required by Homeowner					███						
Sourcing and Availability	█										
Durability and Longevity	██										Quality of installation will affect lifespan.
Building Code Compliance	█										
Indoor Air Quality	██										Foundation will not typically affect IAQ, but if used as a wall system, impacts are low.

long-lasting foundation, capable of a century or more of service. The quality of the mortar joints will affect durability.

CODE COMPLIANCE

Lightweight CMU foundations are an accepted solution in most jurisdictions and if designed to code specifications should face no hurdles for permitting.

INDOOR AIR QUALITY

Lightweight CMUs will have little direct impact on indoor air quality. By keeping the floors and walls of the building dry they can help to prevent other IAQ issues.

FUTURE DEVELOPMENT

Standards for block sizing and installation are well developed and unlikely to change significantly.

Lightweight CMUs are gaining wider acceptance in the masonry industry. Some producers are using recycled glass aggregate, and many are using portland cement replacements like fly ash and blast furnace slag in their blocks. The development of very lightweight blocks would lower environmental impacts and increase thermal performance.

CMUs will benefit from any advances made in the "greening" of cement materials and production outlined on page 34.

Resources for further research

The Complete Guide to Masonry and Stonework: Includes Decorative Concrete Treatments. Chanhassen, MN: Creative, 2006. Print.

Autoclaved aerated concrete blocks

What the cheerleaders say...	What the detractors say...
Structural and insulative	Not widely available
Fast and simple installation	Few production facilities can mean excessive transportation
Reduced material use	Susceptible to water and freeze/ thaw damage
Stable and durable	Expensive

Applications for this foundation system

- Perimeter beams
- Frost walls
- Basement walls

Basic materials

- Cement
- Quartz sand
- Aluminum powder

How the system works

Autoclaved aerated concrete blocks (AAC, sometimes called "autoclaved cellular concrete" or "autoclaved lightweight concrete") are cement-based blocks that are light enough to have reasonable thermal properties while maintaining enough strength to be structural. Unlike typical concrete, quartz sand is the only aggregate and the cement is mixed with aluminum powder, causing a chemical reaction that creates hydrogen. These hydrogen bubbles aerate the mix, creating up to 80 percent void space in the mix. The mixes can be designed to have specific densities for particular uses. The formed, wet mix is steam-pressure hardened (autoclaved) for up to twelve hours, giving it its structural properties.

The combination of structural and insulative properties is highly desirable, as most foundation materials require a separate insulation element to achieve thermal resistance.

Cast off-site using the process described above, the blocks are laid on a poured concrete footing. A thin-bed mortar (similar to tile thin-set) is then used to bond them together, with joints staggered between courses. At the top of the wall, a special U-shaped block is laid, which becomes the form for a concrete and rebar bond beam around wall. The wall is then waterproofed in accordance with site conditions and local code requirements.

Tips for a successful AAC foundation

AAC manufacturers provide installation instructions for their blocks, according to published standards, and are not detailed here.

Pros and cons

ENVIRONMENTAL IMPACTS

Harvesting — *Moderate.* Limestone and aggregate are mechanically extracted from quarries and can have moderate to high impacts on habitat destruction and ground and surface water contamination and flow. AAC blocks use a much lower quantity of material than other masonry units, with air displacing up to 80 percent of the total volume of the blocks.
Manufacturing — *High.* The creation of portland cement is a high-intensity process, with limestone being heated in kilns to very high sustained temperatures. Fuels used include natural gas, oil, coal and landfill waste, in large quantities, with impacts including significant air pollution and very significant greenhouse gas emissions.

The autoclaving process used to make AAC subjects the blocks to temperatures of 190°C (375°F) and pressures of 8–12 bars for up to 12 hours, with impacts including high fossil fuel use and air pollution.

Waste and trimmings at the factory are immediately recycled into new blocks, resulting in little to no waste generation from manufacturing.

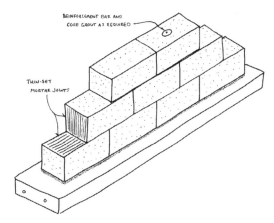

The polymer-modified mortar contains petrochemicals that have numerous impacts.
Transportation — *Moderate to High.* Sample building uses 3,880 – 7,760 kg of AAC:

> 5.82 – 11.64 MJ per km by 15 ton truck
> 3.65 – 7.3 MJ per km by 35 ton truck

Sample building uses 7,800 kg of concrete:

> 11.7 MJ per km by 15 ton truck
> 7.3 MJ per km by 35 ton truck

Blocks are manufactured at a small number of centralized plants and shipped across the continent. They are a high-volume material and impacts will rise proportionally with distance traveled.

WASTE: *LOW TO MODERATE*

Biodegradable/Compostable — AAC offcuts.
Recyclable — Metal reinforcing bar.
Landfill — Bags or pails for adhesives and mortars.

ENERGY EFFICIENCY: *MODERATE TO HIGH*

AAC blocks are among the few foundation options that offer reasonable thermal performance without the addition of an insulation layer. The blocks range from R-0.8 to R-1.25 per inch, depending on the density. Typical block widths for foundations will range from 8–12 inches, resulting in R-values of 6.5–15.

Narrow AAC blocks can be used to make double wythe foundations, allowing any additional insulation to be placed between the blocks. This arrangement makes possible the use of a wider range of insulations, some of which have lower environmental impacts and costs than conventional foam insulations.

MATERIAL COSTS: *MODERATE TO VERY HIGH*

The ingredients of AAC blocks are not high-cost materials, but the manufacturing energy adds significant cost. If the blocks were in wider production, economies of scale would likely reduce the price significantly, but as a specialty product they are currently very high.

The fact that an AAC foundation may not require any further insulation can make it much more competitive with other options when full cost analysis is performed.

LABOR INPUT: *MODERATE TO HIGH*

Cast off-site, AAC blocks do not require any manufacturing labor on-site. The placement and mortaring of delivered blocks, as well as coring and installation of required rebar, constitutes the labor input. A poured concrete footing beneath the blocks is common practice.

SKILL LEVEL REQUIRED FOR THE HOMEOWNER: *MODERATE*

AAC blocks are typically laid using a thin bed mortar that makes the process more like gluing the blocks together than setting them in a mortar bed as with

AAC Block Foundation Embodied Energy

Wall type: 1.3 m (4 ft) perimeter wall	Material embodied energy from I.C.E. in MJ/kg	Weight to volume ratio of material*	Volume of material in sample 1000sf/92.9m² building	Sample building embodied energy	Material embodied carbon from I.C.E. in kgCO₂e/kg	Sample building embodied carbon	Notes
Lowest Impact							
200x200x600mm (8x8x24 inch) lightweight block, 400 kg/m³	3.5 (AAC)	400 kg/m³	9.7 m³ 3880 kg	13,580 MJ	0.375	1,455 kg	Blocks have ~R-16 insulation value.
Mortar, 6mm (¼ inch)	1.11	2162 kg/m³	0.3 m³ 648.6 kg	720 MJ	0.174	113 kg	
Concrete footing, 400x200mm (16x8 inch), 50% slag content	0.62 (20/25 mPa, with 50% blast furnace slag)	2400 kg/m³	3.25 m³ 7800 kg	4,836 MJ	0.077	600 kg	Does not include parging or waterproofing.
Totals				19,136 MJ		2,168 kg	
Highest Impact							
200x200x600mm (8x8x24 inch) heavy block, 800 kg/m³	3.5 (AAC)	800 kg/m³	9.7 m³ 7760 kg	27,160 MJ	0.375	2,910 kg	Blocks have ~R-6.5 insulation value.
Mortar, 6mm (¼ inch)	1.11	2162 kg/m³	0.3 m³ 648.6 kg	720 MJ	0.174	113 kg	
Concrete footing, 400x200mm (16x8 inch), no admixtures	0.74	2400 kg/m³	3.25 m³ 7800 kg	5,772 MJ	0.107	835 kg	
Totals				33,652 MJ		3,858 kg	Does not include parging or waterproofing.

Transportation: Block transportation by 35 ton truck would equate to 3.6–7.3 MJ per kilometer of travel to the building site. *Typically from engineeringtoolbox.com conventional masonry. This method can lend itself more easily to inexperienced builders than many other foundation materials.

SOURCING/AVAILABILITY: *MODERATE TO DIFFICULT*

AAC is not very common in North America, with only a handful of plants producing blocks for the whole continent. Availability will vary regionally, with the blocks being a special order item in areas further from production facilities.

DURABILITY: *HIGH TO VERY HIGH*

This material has been in use for over seventy years, and by most reports and studies it has shown itself to be very durable. The steam curing process brings the cement to a full cure in the factory, so it is not susceptible to the same types of potentially problematic site conditions (water quality, temperature, soil conditions) that can alter the curing of site-poured concrete.

The porous nature of the material means water can penetrate the blocks, and freeze/thaw damage can occur. The blocks are typically protected in the same way as other masonry foundations, by parging and/or waterproofing membranes. Where adequately protected, freeze/thaw issues have not proven problematic.

CODE COMPLIANCE

Acceptance of AAC will vary regionally. In some areas it is an acceptable solution, and is used structurally for buildings up to six stories in height. Manufacturers typically have very thorough studies and reports that can be used to show code equivalency where the material is less common.

INDOOR AIR QUALITY

AAC will have little direct impact on indoor air quality. The greatest impact will be in helping to keep the floors and walls of the building dry and preventing

AAC Foundation Ratings

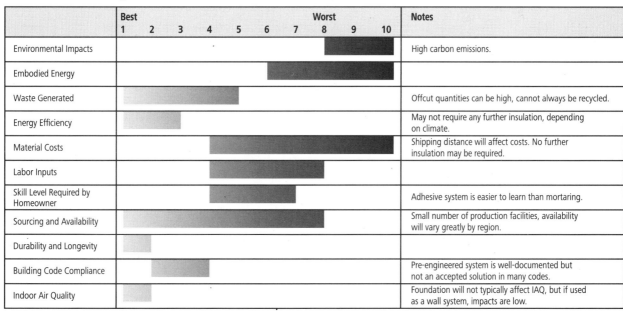

	Best 1 2 3 4 5 6	Worst 7 8 9 10	Notes
Environmental Impacts			High carbon emissions.
Embodied Energy			
Waste Generated			Offcut quantities can be high, cannot always be recycled.
Energy Efficiency			May not require any further insulation, depending on climate.
Material Costs			Shipping distance will affect costs. No further insulation may be required.
Labor Inputs			
Skill Level Required by Homeowner			Adhesive system is easier to learn than mortaring.
Sourcing and Availability			Small number of production facilities, availability will vary greatly by region.
Durability and Longevity			
Building Code Compliance			Pre-engineered system is well-documented but not an accepted solution in many codes.
Indoor Air Quality			Foundation will not typically affect IAQ, but if used as a wall system, impacts are low.

IAQ issues. However, AAC is also used for wall and floor systems, and has excellent indoor air quality ratings in those applications.

FUTURE DEVELOPMENT

AAC is widely used in Europe where masonry units make up a much larger proportion of buildings. It is likely to see growing market share in North America, as its combination of structural strength and insulative value lowers material and labor costs and improves performance, especially in temperate climates where no additional insulation is required. The reduction in raw material consumption also work in favor of this material as it lightens the transportation burden to and from the factory.

Resources for further research

Winter, Nicholas B. *Understanding Cement: An Introduction to Cement Production, Cement Hydration and Deleterious Processes in Concrete.* Woodbridge, Suffolk: WHD Microanalysis Consultants, 2009. Print.

King, Bruce. *Making Better Concrete: Guidelines to Using Fly Ash for Higher Quality, Eco-Friendly Structures.* San Rafael, CA: Green Building, 2005. Print.

Durisol and Faswall insulated concrete forms (ICF)

What the cheerleaders say...	What the detractors say...
Use waste wood	High cement and rebar usage
Provide reasonable thermal performance without using foam insulation	Thermal performance may require additional insulation
Easy and fast to build	High cost
Simple to parge, plaster or drywall	

Applications for this foundation system

- Perimeter beams
- Frost walls
- Basement walls

Basic materials

- Cement binder
- Wood fiber
- Rock wool insulation
- Poured concrete
- Rebar

How the system works

There are many kinds of insulated concrete forms (ICFs), and the majority of market share is held by ICFs made of foam insulation. Durisol and Faswall ICFs, however, are made from cement-bonded wood fiber.

As with all ICFs, Durisol and Faswall blocks are made from a relatively lightweight insulative material with hollow cores. Blocks are dry-stacked in running bond on a poured concrete footing. Rebar is placed horizontally between alternate courses and vertically in every core. Concrete is poured into the cores of the completed wall forms in a single lift.

The wood fiber content is "mineralized" by removing the sugars from the wood and rendering it inert before it is bound with portland cement.

Blocks are available to create a variety of different finished wall widths and insulation values.

Tips for a successful ICF foundation

Durisol and Faswall provide installation instructions for their blocks, according to published standards, so these are not detailed here.

Pros and cons
ENVIRONMENTAL IMPACTS

Harvesting — *Moderate.* Limestone for portland cement is mechanically extracted from quarries and can have moderate to high impacts including habitat destruction and ground and surface water contamination.

The wood fiber is reclaimed waste wood from other industrial sources. Its impacts are mitigated because it is being reused.

Manufacturing — *Moderate to High.* The creation of portland cement is a high-intensity process, with limestone being heated in kilns to very high sustained temperatures. Fuels used include natural gas, oil, land-fill waste and coal, in large quantities, with impacts including significant air pollution and very significant greenhouse gas emissions. Portland cement makes up about 15 percent of the block by volume.

The wood is mineralized in a water bath, and heat is applied to dry the mineralized wood, requiring the use of fossil fuels. Mineralized wood makes up about 85 percent of the block by volume.

Transportation — *Moderate to High.* Sample building uses 4,160 kg of ICF blocks:

> 6.24 MJ per km by 15 ton truck
> 3.9 MJ per km by 35 ton truck

Sample building uses 19,032 kg of concrete:

> 17.9 MJ per km by 35 ton truck

Blocks are manufactured at a small number of centralized plants and shipped across the continent.

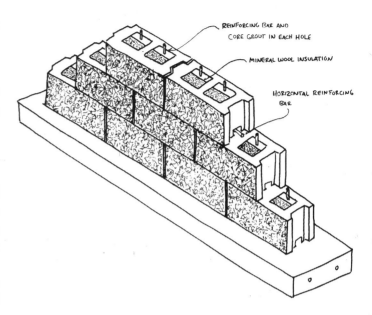

REINFORCING BAR AND CORE GROUT IN EACH HOLE

MINERAL WOOL INSULATION

HORIZONTAL REINFORCING BAR

They are a high-volume, heavy material and impacts rise proportionally with distance traveled.

WASTE: *MODERATE*

Recyclable — Metal reinforcement bar.
Landfill — Block offcuts, insulation offcuts, mortar bags/pails.

ENERGY EFFICIENCY: *HIGH*

Durisol and Faswall foundations can have a reasonable level of thermal performance, ranging from R-8 to R-28, depending on block thickness. The lightweight wood/concrete mix contributes to this performance, but it is largely achieved via mineral wool insulation inserts built into the blocks.

MATERIAL COSTS: *HIGH*

ICF blocks are a relatively high cost option, but the cost includes the highest level of insulation available from a foundation material in this book. Compared on a whole-system basis, the cost would be similar to many other options.

LABOR INPUT: *MODERATE*

The lightweight blocks are laid dry in a straightforward stacking process. The blocks can be cut and shaped with standard carpentry tools. Each block is 60 cm (24 inches) long and 30 cm (12 inches) high, resulting in a relatively fast stacking process.

SKILL LEVEL REQUIRED BY THE HOMEOWNER: *MODERATE*

Placed on a level footing, no special skills are required to build this type of form wall. After the first course, no mortar or glue is used between blocks. Most owner-builders can competently build a Durisol or Faswall foundation, though bracing the walls and managing the concrete pour can present challenges.

SOURCING/AVAILABILITY: *EASY TO MODERATE*

Durisol and Faswall are not very common in North America, with only a handful of plants producing blocks. Availability varies regionally, with the blocks being a special order item in areas further from

production facilities. Check with the manufacturer for distributors in your local area.

DURABILITY: *HIGH*

There is a seventy-year history of cement-bonded wood fiber being used to build foundations, and reports and studies generally point to excellent performance in the field. Life span can be over a hundred years.

CODE COMPLIANCE

Cement-bonded wood fiber ICFs are not an approved solution in most codes, but as they use reinforced concrete and have well-documented standards from the manufacturer, they are likely to be accepted as an alternative solution.

INDOOR AIR QUALITY

As a foundation system, Durisol or Faswall blocks will have little direct impact on indoor air quality. The greatest impact on IAQ will be their role in helping to keep the floors and walls of the building

ICF (Durisol/Faswall) Foundation Embodied Energy

Wall type: 1.3m (4ft) perimeter wall, R-28 block	Material embodied energy from I.C.E. in MJ/kg	Weight to volume ratio of material*	Volume of material in sample 1000sf/92.9m² building	Sample building embodied energy	Material embodied carbon from I.C.E. in kgCO2e/kg	Sample building embodied carbon	Notes
355x300x600mm (14x12x24 inch) block	875 MJ/m³	81.53 kg/m³	260 blocks 0.0267 m³/block 6.9 m³ 16 kg/block 4160 kg	6,038 MJ	1.77	1013 kg	EE figure from manufacturer, not ICE Block includes ~R-28 insulation value.
Mineral wool insulation insert	16.6 (Mineral wool)	64 kg/m³	5.17 m³ 331 kg	5,493 MJ	1.28	424 kg	
Reinforcing bar, every core and every other horizontal row	17.4 (Bar and rod, average recycled content)	1 kg/m	245 m 245 kg	4,263 MJ	1.4	343 kg	
Concrete fill	0.62 (20/25 mPa, blast furnace slag 50%)	2400 kg/m³	4.68 m³ 11,232 kg	6,964 MJ	0.077	865 kg	
400x200mm (16x8 inch) concrete footing, 50% slag	0.62 (20/25 mPa, blast furnace slag 50%)	2400 kg/m³	3.25 m³ 7800 kg	4,836 MJ	0.077	601 kg	
Totals				**27,594 MJ**		**3,246 kg**	Does not include parging or waterproofing.

Transportation: Block transportation by 35 ton truck would equate to 3.9 MJ per kilometer of travel to the building site. *Typically from engineeringtoolbox.com high and dry. However, these blocks are also used for wall systems, and have excellent indoor air quality ratings in those applications.

FUTURE DEVELOPMENT

Versions of this product have been in production and use since 1934. The basic product and construction process have not undergone much change in that time. The use of high-compression mineral wool insulation has added a higher degree of energy efficiency. Advancements in ecological cement production or replacement would have positive impacts on the blocks and the concrete used to fill them.

Resources for further research

"Durisol Materials." *Durisol Building Systems Inc RSS.* N.p., n.d. Web. 20 Apr. 2013.

"Faswall® Green Building System. *ShelterWorks Ltd.* N.p., n.d. Web. 20 Apr. 2013.

Durisol ICF.

Insulated Concrete Form Foundation Ratings

	Best 1	2	3	4	5	6	7	Worst 8	9	10	Notes
Environmental Impacts											High carbon emissions. Does not require any further insulation.
Embodied Energy											Does not require any further insulation.
Waste Generated											
Energy Efficiency											Does not require any further insulation.
Material Costs											Does not require any further insulation.
Labor Inputs											
Skill Level Required by Homeowner											Dry stacking is easier to learn than mortaring.
Sourcing and Availability											Manufacturing is regional.
Durability and Longevity											
Building Code Compliance											System is pre-engineered and well documented, but not an accepted solution.
Indoor Air Quality											Foundation will not typically affect IAQ, but if used as a wall system, impacts are low.

What about rubble trenches?

What the cheerleaders say...	What the detractors say...
Low environmental impact	Potentially unstable
Excellent drainage	Only suitable where footing height is above water table
Easy and fast to build	Only suitable in stable soils
Long-lasting	

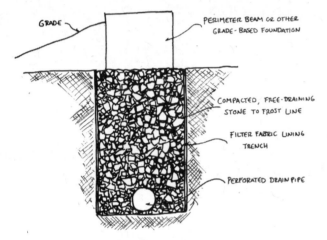

If you have done much research into sustainable building, chances are you've come across mention of rubble trench foundations as a low-impact alternative to conventional foundations. So why is the rubble trench not featured in this book?

A rubble trench is a way of connecting a wall system to stable, frost-free ground without building a solid (usually concrete) wall. With this technique, a trench is dug to the depth of the frost line around the perimeter of the building, as with any continuous foundation. Rather than building a wall (concrete, earthbag, tire, ICF, CMU or AAC) from the base of the trench up to the base of the walls, the trench is filled with compacted, well-draining stone with a continuous weeping tile at the base. The stone will typically have lower environmental impacts than the materials used to build a solid wall, or at the very least be less labor-intensive than building a full wall. Yet it will offer more than adequate compressive strength to transfer building loads to the frost-free ground at the bottom of the trench.

However, as it is not prudent or practical to put walls directly on the stone of the rubble trench, it is not truly a foundation until another material is placed on the trench. This means that a rubble trench is always used in conjunction with another foundation system, typically a perimeter beam made from any of the materials discussed in this book. A rubble trench cannot be used to create habitable space below grade, so is not applicable for basement foundations.

With the caveat that rubble trenches are not foundations but only part of a foundation system, here is an overview of them.

Applications for this foundation system
- Can be used to support perimeter beam foundations

Basic materials
- Compacted, crushed stone (no fines, wide range of particle sizes up to 10 cm / 4 inches)

How the system works
A trench is dug to the depth of the frost line and the width of the perimeter beam required for the building. A weeping tile is laid at the bottom of the trench and sloped to drain to daylight or to a dry well. The sides of the trench are lined with geotextile fabric (or used carpet) to prevent the rubble from migrating into the adjacent soil. Well-graded stone that is free of fines is placed in the trench and compacted in successive lifts, usually every foot (30 cm). The stone is brought to the height of the surrounding grade and tamped level. It is now ready for a perimeter beam of some description to be built on top of the rubble trench.

Tips for a successful rubble trench

1. Check the stability of the soil before committing to a rubble trench. If the sides of the trench collapse, it will need to be re-excavated and enough stone imported to fill the collapsed area.
2. Be sure that the water table is below the level of the rubble trench. This system cheats frost

Hempcrete and Poraver for foundations

Hempcrete is a mixture of lime and chopped hemp stalks most commonly used as infill wall insulation (see wall insulation chapter on page 109).

The density of hempcrete can be altered to provide a consistency very similar to that of Durisol and Faswall, and it can be used for foundations in a similar way. Hempcrete can be casted into blocks or installed monolithically and allowed to cure in place.

The high silica content in the hemp stalks lends itself to a mineralization process in the mix, giving similar high-durability results without the need for a separate mineralization process. This makes it a more accessible version of the type of block described here, able to be made by homeowners on-site with locally available materials in regions where hemp is grown commercially.

Poraver is an expanded glass bead manufactured from recycled glass and typically used as a lightweight aggregate in concrete block manufacturing. It resembles perlite in weight and characteristics. It has recently seen some limited use for both subgrade insulation material and foundations.

During the manufacturing process for Poraver, kaolin clay is used in the kilns that fire the glass beads (to prevent them from sticking to one another while molten). This fired kaolin by-product is combined with hydrated lime and used as a pozzolan to create the binder used to create the insulation or foundation material.

A block, wall or slab of Poraver resembles autoclaved aerated concrete (AAC), but can be poured or cast on site, making the benefits of a material that is both insulative and structural available to builders who do not live within a reasonable distance of an AAC production facility.

These types of materials that combine both insulative and structural properties offer a great deal of promise, simplifying foundation design and construction and eliminating the need for combinations of concrete and petrochemical foam insulation, which currently dominate the market for foundations.

Hempcrete foundation.

Poraver foundation.

because the rubble is well-draining and will not trap water that can freeze and cause the building above to shift. If the rubble trench fills with ground water above the frost line, it will be unstable.

3. Line the walls of the trench with a material that will not hold water but will stop the stone in the trench from migrating into the soil and cause the foundation to sink. Geotextile fabric, used carpet and drainboard insulations have all been used successfully.
4. Compact the gravel in lifts to ensure an even compaction. If too much stone is added to the trench before tamping, the lower levels may not pack down and will be prone to shifting or settling over time.
5. Take time to carefully level the top of the rubble trench. The material being used for the perimeter beam is likely to be more expensive and time-consuming to make level.

Pros and cons
ENVIRONMENTAL IMPACTS

Harvesting — *Moderate.* Aggregate is mechanically extracted from quarries and can have moderate to high impacts on habitat destruction and ground and surface water contamination and flow.

In some areas, it may be possible to obtain "urbanite," which is recycled crushed concrete from building or road demolition. If the urbanite can be properly graded so it contains the right distribution of particle sizes to compact well and remain free-draining, then this would be an ideal, low-impact way to create a rubble trench.

Manufacturing — *Moderate.* Aggregate is crushed in a relatively low-impact mechanical process.

Transportation — *Moderate.* Sample building uses 48,946 kg of rubble:

46 MJ per km by 35 ton truck

Aggregate is heavy, but is rarely transported long distances. Impacts increase proportionally with distance traveled.

Installation — *Negligible.* One of the best environmental advantages a rubble trench can offer is the ability to support a building on frost-free ground without the use of manufactured insulation, as would be required if the same perimeter beam was being used in a shallow, frost-protected foundation. The higher the embodied energy and environmental impacts of the insulation that would be used, the better the rubble trench will be in comparison.

WASTE: *NEGLIGIBLE*

Biodegradable/Compostable — All unused stone.
Landfill — Geotextile fabric offcuts (if used).

ENERGY EFFICIENCY

A rubble trench is a sub-foundation and as such it won't have a direct impact on the energy efficiency of the building. If an appropriate insulation strategy

Rubble Trench Foundation Embodied Energy

Wall type: 1300x600mm (4x2 ft) trench	Material embodied energy from I.C.E. in MJ/kg	Weight to volume ratio of material*	Volume of material in sample 1000sf/92.9m² building	Sample building embodied energy	Material embodied carbon from I.C.E. in kgCO₂e/kg	Sample building embodied carbon	Notes
25-100mm (1-4 inch) rubble	0.083 (Gravel or crushed rock)	1682 kg/m³	29.1 m³ 48,946 kg	4,063 MJ	0.0052	255 kg	Does not include trench lining. Can be used carpet for 0 EE, or geotextile fabric.

Transportation: Stone transportation by 35 ton truck would equate to 46 MJ per kilometer of travel to the building site. *Typically from engineeringtoolbox.com is employed for the portion of the foundation that is in direct contact with the building enclosure, the rubble trench will not be an important factor in the overall energy efficiency of the building.

MATERIAL COSTS: *LOW*

Aggregate is typically a low cost material, and even in the relatively high quantities used in a rubble trench, the overall cost remains low.

LABOR INPUT: *MODERATE*

Typically, the crushed stone is delivered by truck and placed by excavator, which keeps labor input to a minimum. Because the stone needs to be placed in lifts and compacted several times, the excavator will have to work more slowly than if the trench was being filled from top to bottom in one lift. Mechanical tampers work efficiently and can be operated by one person. It is possible to coordinate the work so one side of the trench is being compacted while more stone is being placed on the other.

SKILL LEVEL REQUIRED FOR THE HOMEOWNER: *EASY*

A skilled excavator will be able to place stone accurately and quickly with minimal damage to the sides of the trench. Stone can also be shoveled manually. The tamper operator does not need experience in order to compact each lift.

SOURCING/AVAILABILITY: *EASY*

Graded, crushed stone is widely available across much of the continent, but will vary regionally in price and trucking distance. Stone that is used locally to build roads, railways and other infrastructure will be appropriate for a rubble trench.

Graded, crushed concrete may be available and this recycled resource would be a good option to pursue.

Rubble Trench Foundation Ratings

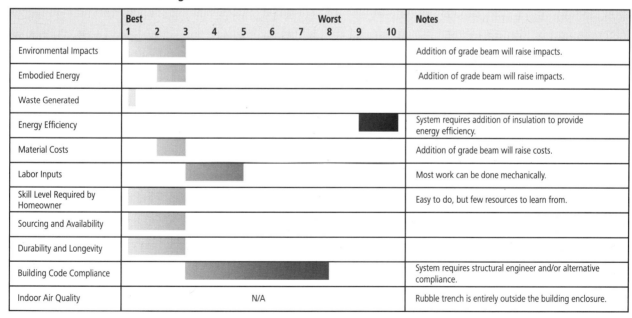

	Best 1	2	3	4	5	6	7	Worst 8	9	10	Notes
Environmental Impacts											Addition of grade beam will raise impacts.
Embodied Energy											Addition of grade beam will raise impacts.
Waste Generated											
Energy Efficiency											System requires addition of insulation to provide energy efficiency.
Material Costs											Addition of grade beam will raise costs.
Labor Inputs											Most work can be done mechanically.
Skill Level Required by Homeowner											Easy to do, but few resources to learn from.
Sourcing and Availability											
Durability and Longevity											
Building Code Compliance											System requires structural engineer and/or alternative compliance.
Indoor Air Quality				N/A							Rubble trench is entirely outside the building enclosure.

DURABILITY: *HIGH TO VERY HIGH*

Three factors will affect durability of a rubble trench: the type of soil surrounding the trench, the degree of compaction and drainage. If the surrounding soils and the barrier used to separate soil and rubble can prevent the migration of soil into the stone, there shouldn't be any significant settling. Adequately tamped and properly drained, there is little that can go wrong with a rubble trench, as it can't crack, break or decompose.

CODE COMPLIANCE

Rubble trenches are not an approved solution in any codes, but the practice of using compacted crushed stone to bear the weight of buildings, roads, bridges and other major constructions is familiar to engineers and building officials alike. It should be possible to have a rubble trench approved with adequate documentation and/or a structural engineer's approval.

INDOOR AIR QUALITY

As a sub-foundation, a rubble trench will have no direct impact on indoor air quality. The greatest impact on IAQ will be their role in helping to keep the floors and walls of the building high and dry.

FUTURE DEVELOPMENT

There is little advancement to be made on the basic technology and materials for a rubble trench. The recycling of old concrete may become more common, and this would allow rubble trenches to be made without the use of virgin, quarried stone.

Resources for further research

Koko, Sigi. "Rubble Trench Foundations — A Brief Overview." *Building Safety Journal* 1.3 (2003): n. pag. Print.

Velonis, Elias. "Rubble Trench Foundations: A Simple Effective Foundation System for Residential Structures," *The Best of Fine Homebuilding.* Newtown, CT: Taunton Press, 1997.

Combination foundations

None of the foundation options discussed in this chapter need to be used in isolation. It is entirely feasible to meet the needs of a particular project by using combinations of different foundation strategies. Combinations are used to match building loads and needs with site conditions, costs and design of space.

Common combinations include the use of partial basement foundations to create space below the building for services, mechanical systems and/ or cold storage. A section of basement foundation can be combined with frost walls, piers or slabs. Pier foundations are often mixed with other systems for additions or to create sections of a building on sharply sloped ground.

When combining foundation styles, it is important to ensure that differential settling will not be problematic and that the places where unlike materials meet are detailed for adequate structural and thermal performance.

What's not included in this chapter

There are foundation materials that are feasible to use, but do not meet the sustainability standards for inclusion in this book. Drawing such lines is always controversial, and there will be green building advocates and practitioners who see this as folly. However, we will present our opinion on these materials and readers who disagree will find ample information in other sources to work with.

Foam insulated concrete forms

Foam ICFs are similar to the cement-bonded wood fiber ICFs detailed earlier in this chapter, except the forms are made from one of three different kinds of foam insulation: expanded polystyrene, extruded polystyrene or polyurethane foam.

Measuring the impacts of foam insulation will reveal high embodied energy figures and carbon outputs, but these alone are not really reason enough to ignore this category of products. As the foam industry is quick to point out, there is a degree of energy savings from using these products (though the same savings are available with similar amounts of other insulators) that can render the embodied energy moot over time. The deeper issue is not measured by straight energy analysis, or even life cycle analysis as it is typically carried out. Neither of these approaches take into account the full impact of the petrochemical industry that produce these products. The full "chain of custody" for foam products needs to address the environmentally disastrous processes of oil exploration, extraction, shipping and pipelining, refining and processing that finally result in supposedly benign foam insulation. Numerous dangerous and environmentally persistent chemicals are key ingredients in creating these materials, and even if they are not proven to be dangerous at the final point of use, their manufacture, storage and use have widespread environmental implications. Human history has taught us nothing if it hasn't shown us that we are hopelessly unable to "contain" the dangerous chemicals we create and use.

Foam used in buildings is also treated with flame retardants (otherwise the foam is too dangerous to use in a building) that are proving themselves to be dangerous to soil, water and the human nervous system.

Foam ICFs combine all the suspect characteristics of petrochemical insulation with high-impact concrete and rebar usage. This combination of materials will also prove very difficult to disassemble and separate at the end of its life, meaning it's most likely headed for landfill and not recycling. The whole system is just too dubious in its environmental impacts to recommend in any way, especially when the existing alternatives are every bit as feasible and practical.

Pressure-treated wood foundations

Pressure-treated wood foundations are built just like above-grades, using wooden studs, sill plates and top plates and sheathing the wall in structural plywood on the exterior, except that all the lumber and plywood is pressure-treated to help prevent rot and insect infestation below grade. This can be an affordable, quick and low embodied energy way to build a basement foundation. It has two major drawbacks: the toxicity and environmental side effects of the pressure-treating process and the inherent dangers of putting a material below grade that nature intends to decay in that position.

While the copper-arsenate pressure-treating formulations of the past have now been outlawed because of their toxicity, their replacements use even higher quantities of copper. Copper is a limited resource with highly problematic mining techniques as a major side effect, and its presence in soils and groundwater can create toxicity issues around the building.

Pressure-treatment processes can help wood to remain sound below grade, but it requires great diligence to ensure that the treatment process is intact on all cuts made to the wood, and penetrations made by fasteners can be problematic. Used above grade, wood building materials have an opportunity to undergo natural drying processes that help make them viable. Wood that gets wet below grade is likely to stay wet for a long time, increasing chances of rot and mold, even with pressure-treated surfaces.

Why do we recommend wooden pier foundations (with warnings about possible life span issues) but not pressure-treated wood foundations? It is relatively easy to replace piers because the entire beam and floor system are exposed above grade. Bracing the building and replacing piers can be done quite simply, and so if the piers are on a 30–60-year replacement cycle it is feasible to maintain such a building over the long term. But a rotting foundation wall that is buried under the building is much harder and more expensive to deal with, and so problems are more likely to cause the demise of the building or require costly and disruptive repairs.

There are new wood treatment systems making their way onto the market that have significantly fewer environmental issues and offer the promise of long-term protection from rot and infestation. At this time, none of the new treatments are applied to plywood and have not been tested for use as a foundation material.

Concrete slab foundations

The number of "green" homes built on giant concrete slabs may indicate that they should be among the options given in this chapter. However, the sheer amount of concrete and rebar that go into a typical slab make them very resource intensive. Most slabs are made to be structural, and this means they have a thickened edge around the perimeter of the building and an extensive rebar and/or mesh grid throughout. Often this thickened edge will use as much or more concrete than building a narrow concrete frost wall, and definitely more reinforcing bar.

Another issue that makes a slab foundation difficult to endorse is the amount of foam insulation that typically accompanies a slab, and the weakness of that insulation around the perimeter of the slab where heat loss is at its most dramatic. In most slab construction the outside edge is insulated with foam, but the quantity tends to be minimal as the addition of a wide foam (or other insulation) band around the foundation can create awkward details at the base of the wall. The insulation is rarely seamless between foundation and wall at this junction and creates a large thermal bridge.

As with the other options "excluded" here, it is certainly feasible to build a home on a slab, and to make efforts to use more responsible concrete and insulation. However, given all the excellent solutions available that do not have the inherent environmental problems of slabs, our advice to those trying to meet high sustainability goals is to avoid pouring a slab.

Chapter title page photo credits. Top left to right.
1 & 2. Chris Magwood 3. Daniel Earle
4. Kelly Jacobsen

2

Walls

WALLS SERVE MULTIPLE FUNCTIONS IN A BUILDING. They are key elements of the structure, they support the windows and doorways that physically define a space, they are a very important part of the building's energy efficiency and they dominate the visual aesthetics. It is no wonder that many people come to define their home by the kind of walls it has.

There are many practical measures by which the walls are not as important. They represent only a fraction of the overall cost and construction schedule of a building, and a similar fraction of the total embodied energy. For the many owner-builders who define their projects by the type of walls they are going to use, it can come as a surprise to find out how much time and money is spent on the rest of the building, and what a comparatively small part of the project the walls turn out to be. They are important, to be sure, but no more important than all the other building elements.

Discussing and dissecting wall options is difficult because there are so many possibilities. The multiple functions of structure, environmental separation and aesthetics have multiple options for achieving each function.

Some common wall systems — such as timber frames or stud frames — are only structural elements and do not inherently include a particular insulation strategy or aesthetic finish. Other wall systems — such as straw bale, cob and cordwood — can be a structural system or infill insulation within another structural element and can have many different aesthetic finishes in either case. In the sections of this chapter a range of possibilities are shown, based on combinations of wall structure and wall insulation.

Building science basics for walls

Structurally, a wall transfers loads from the roof and upper floors to the foundation, including gravity loads and the live loads imposed by wind, snow, rain, seismic activity and occupant activity. Thermally, a wall provides insulation from differences in temperature between inside and outside and barriers against air movement from either side. Walls must also deal with moisture loads from either side, including precipitation and differences in humidity between interior and exterior. The wall is also the mounting point for windows and doors, critical seams that will have a large impact on the overall thermal performance of the building regardless of their type, size or style.

Wall structures can be divided into three basic categories:

Monolithic walls — These systems form a wall in which loads are distributed evenly along the length of the wall. Monolithic walls can be made from materials that are poured or formed into a continuous mass (rammed earth, cob, concrete) or materials that are stacked and bonded such that they form a continuous mass (adobe or compressed earth blocks, CMU). Straw bale walls are a hybrid kind of monolithic wall, in which the bales are stacked like blocks but are not rigid enough to offer the full structural capabilities required, but with a plaster skin bonded to the interior and exterior face the plaster skins become a pair of monolithic walls tied to one another.

Skeletal walls — These systems form a wall made of individual posts carrying beams on which the loads of the roof/floors are distributed. In timber frames (which use traditional wood-to-wood joinery) or post-and-beam frames (which use metal plates/bracket joinery) the posts and beams are of large dimensions and are designed to be spaced far apart. Lightweight framing systems use a greater number of smaller vertical posts (studs) to support less substantial beams (top plates). Skeletal walls require bracing to handle shear loads (loads imposed in any direction except straight down). Large-dimension frames often use built-in triangulation to provide bracing, and lightweight framing systems often use continuous sheathing.

Hybrid walls — The proliferation of natural wall systems over the past few decades has created a subcategory of walls, in which skeletal walls are used as a structure in conjunction with monolithic infill systems. In the best-case scenarios, these systems are combined in such a way that the advantages of skeletal systems (quick construction times, the ability to support a roof prior to completing the full wall system, widespread code acceptance) and the shear strength, low embodied energy and thermal properties of the infill system are optimized. In the worst-case scenarios, one or both elements are overbuilt and redundancies and complications can raise costs, labor time and waste.

In many buildings, hybrids will be created due to design decisions. A monolithic wall with large window openings will rely on skeletal frames of some sort to form and span the large openings. In some buildings with monolithic exterior walls, skeletal interior walls may be an integral structural component.

In residential, low-rise construction all three categories of wall are structurally viable. Choices will have more to do with material selection, thermal properties and code compliance issues than with structural properties.

Wall thermal properties will be determined by the combination of the structural system with an insulation material. For skeletal and hybrid walls there will be two (or more) distinct materials providing structure and insulation. For monolithic walls, it may be the same material or it may also be a combination of materials, depending on the inherent thermal properties of the structural material.

Many builders are obsessed with R-values when it comes to thinking about thermal properties. The R-value measures the resistance of a particular material to the flow of heat energy. R-values are usually given as a "per-inch" figure, or as an overall figure for a particular thickness of insulation, and the higher the number the better the thermal resistance. Insulations can also be rated by a U-value, which measures the ability of a material to conduct heat energy. In the case of U-values, the lower the number the better the insulation. The U-value is the inverse of the R-value; divide either value by 1 to convert one form of measurement to the other. For example, a material with an R-value of 2 will have a U-value of 0.5, reached by dividing 1 by 2.

Understanding how R- and U-values work is key to choosing adequate amounts of insulation for a building. Metric values measure the number of degrees Kelvin required to transfer one watt of energy through one square meter of the material. In imperial measurements, U-factor is a measure of British thermal units (Btu) per hour, per square foot of material, per degree Fahrenheit of temperature difference between the two sides of the material.

From this understanding, two important considerations are made clear. First, diminishing returns are achieved with each successive doubling of the insulating layer. At a certain point, the financial and material costs of adding more insulation do not translate into significant performance improvements. Though highly debatable, in regions with extreme heat and cold, this point is often thought to be around R-40 to R-60 for walls. Second, the measure of R-value and U-value are laboratory figures that are not dynamic and do not represent fluctuating real-world conditions. Standard test practices have a base temperature of 24°C (+/–3°C) / 75°F (+/–5°F), and the temperature differential between the two sides of the test wall must be 22°C (+/–3°C) / 72°F (+/–5°F)[1]. This means that testing is performed at temperatures above 0°C (32°F), and at temperature differentials substantially less than the 50°C (122°F) often experienced in colder climate zones. This form of testing also concentrates exclusively on the conductive transference of heat, and does not take into account radiant and convective heat flows.

Building science teaches us that thermal resistance is only part of the overall thermal performance of a wall system. Often, builders become obsessed with R-values to the exclusion of other considerations. But R-value alone is not an adequate predictor of the thermal performance of a building enclosure. So what else is going on in a wall system that we should understand?

Airtightness is a major factor. Imagine a home with an excellent R-value and an open window on a cold winter or hot summer day. Whatever effect the insulation might provide is short-circuited by the direct exchange of air between inside and outside through the open window. The comfortable, indoor conditions quickly change due to that air exchange. While a wide-open window may seem like an exaggeration being used to make a point, the truth is that almost all older homes and a shocking number of new homes have an equivalent leakage area (EqLA) the size of a large open window. The EqLA is measured by depressurizing a building using a sealed fan in a doorway (a blower door test) and monitoring the pressure difference between inside and outside. The depressurized building will allow balancing air to make its way inside, and the quantity of incoming air can be translated into the EqLA. Just because you don't see an open window doesn't mean your building is not leaking like somebody forgot to close one.

Of all the elements of a building, walls are the most difficult to make airtight. They are bordered on all sides by junctions with floor, foundation, ceiling and other walls, and punctured frequently with openings for doors and windows. Penetrations for electrical and plumbing services riddle many walls. If proper attention is not paid to proper air sealing from the interior and exterior, even the best-insulated walls will not keep a building warm. The "open windows" must first be well and properly closed. Methods for building properly airtight walls exist for all of the materials and systems profiled in this chapter. This book is not a how-to manual intended to guide you with specific advice about air sealing for each type of wall, but there is adequate information in the Resources for Further Research section at the end of this chapter to ensure that the wall is built and detailed properly. Only by building a properly airtight wall will you see the real benefits of the insulative values described for each wall type.

Another form of short-circuit that can affect energy efficiency is thermal bridging. Assuming that a wall is both well insulated and well sealed, heat energy can still be transferred from one side to the other by non-insulating materials that touch the inside and outside surfaces. Skeletal frame members are the main culprits when it comes to thermal bridging. If insulation is placed between framing members, there is significantly less insulation at each stud, sill plate and top plate. Thermal bridges can also occur at window and door openings, where insulation is interrupted. Here, framing members often bridge from inside to outside.

A final thermal consideration is the moisture level within the wall system. Heat will be conducted more easily through a material as the moisture content of that material rises. If the insulation in a wall cavity has elevated levels of humidity or is actually moist or wet, the rated R-value will be subverted by the added conductivity of the water. While rot and mold are key concerns with damp walls, there can be a measurable drop in thermal performance even if there is not enough moisture to create these issues.

All successful wall systems will have four "principle control layers"[2]:

Water control layer — This element of the building controls the entrance of water into the building enclosure. The exterior cladding of the building is the typical water control layer.
Air control layer — This element controls the flow of air through the building enclosure. The air control layer may be a distinct element in some wall systems, or the role may be performed by a structural and/or thermal component.

Vapor control layer — This element controls the flow of water vapor through the building enclosure. Water vapor will move from one side of the wall to the other side depending on differential humidity levels. Just as heat always moves from warm to cold, water vapor moves from areas of high concentration to low. The vapor control layer may be a distinct element in some wall systems, or the role may be performed by a structural and/or thermal component.
Thermal control layer — This element controls the flow of heat energy through the building enclosure.

These layers are a good way to "dissect" a wall assembly and will be used throughout this chapter to identify the elements of various wall systems.

Of the four principle control layers, it is the vapor control layer that is least understood, and worthy of further examination. This layer is a relatively recent addition to wall assemblies. Three factors came together in the past few decades to make it a necessity: increasing airtightness, increasing levels of insulation and greater use of manufactured building materials. In older, less airtight buildings, excessive humidity on either side of the wall was able to move toward equilibrium via direct air exchange through leaks and holes in the building enclosure. Reducing the number of leaks does not reduce nature's need to balance moisture levels, and water vapor will attempt to diffuse through the building enclosure, molecule by molecule, passing through the building materials themselves. As vapor moves through the enclosure, it often meets a progressively cooler environment, and at some point in its travels it may reach its dew point. At the dew point, water vapor becomes liquid water. This liquid water can accumulate in insulation materials and on framing and sheathing materials, and if it can't dry out in a reasonable amount of time can lead to rot and mold on wood and degradation of most insulation. Materials that are not permeable to migrating moisture can retard drying and lead to further accumulations of water.

As these moisture problems manifested in modern homes, the initial solution was to build in a vapor barrier on the warm side of the wall (interior in the north, exterior in the south). The plastic sheeting used for this purpose has a very low perm rating, and keeps moisture from diffusing into the enclosure. But notice that the term being used here to describe this layer is vapor *control* layer, not vapor *barrier*. A layer can control vapor diffusion without being a complete barrier. Many of the wall systems used by natural builders operate on the principle that an airtight vapor control layer (often in the form of a continuous plaster skin) can greatly reduce the amount of vapor entering the enclosure, and if that enclosure has an equally permeable vapor control layer on both sides and an insulation material that has suitable moisture storage capacity, then the plastic vapor barrier is not necessary. In fact, it is likely to be detrimental.

In practice, the use of plastic vapor barriers in wood frame construction, if done properly, can be an effective vapor control layer. However, so is using a permeable wall strategy. Permeable wall systems bring together low-tech natural builders and leading building scientists in agreement, but they are only slowly being accepted in the broader construction industry.

Wall systems are the most numerous and variable of all the choices a designer will face in creating a sustainable building. The good news is that all of the choices offer excellent potential if well planned and well executed. Weighing the options carefully will ensure that your finished project meets all your cost, energy efficiency, environmental impact and aesthetic goals.

Notes

1. ASTM C518 and ASTM C177.
2. Building Science Incorporated, *Insight* 024, October 2009.

Wood frame construction

What the cheerleaders say...	What the detractors say...
Time-tested	Intensive wood use
Resource efficient	Wasteful offcuts
Affordable	Reliance on metal fasteners
Quick and easy to build	
Code-approved	

Wood frame wall.
(Daniel Earle)

Applications for this wall system

- Exterior and interior walls

Basic materials

Structural:

- Dimensional lumber (2x4, 2x6) studs, sills, top plates and lintels
- Structural sheathing or bracing
- Control layers:
  - **Water Control** — Vertical or horizontal cladding (wood, engineered wood, steel), stucco/plaster, brick and stone
  - **Air Control** — Sealed structural sheathing, house wraps, plaster
  - **Vapor Control** — Sheet barriers, sealed sheathing (gasketed drywall) and plaster
  - **Thermal Control** — Natural infill insulations (straw bale, straw/clay, hempcrete, woodchip/clay), manufactured batt insulations (cotton,

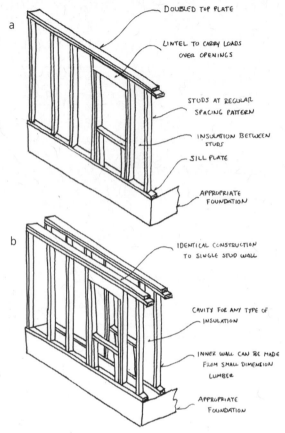

a

DOUBLED TOP PLATE

LINTEL TO CARRY LOADS
OVER OPENINGS

STUDS AT REGULAR
SPACING PATTERN

INSULATION BETWEEN
STUDS

SILL PLATE

APPROPRIATE
FOUNDATION

b

IDENTICAL CONSTRUCTION
TO SINGLE STUD WALL

CAVITY FOR ANY TYPE OF
INSULATION

INNER WALL CAN BE MADE
FROM SMALL DIMENSION
LUMBER

APPROPRIATE
FOUNDATION

a. Single frame wall.

b. Double frame wall.

"Advanced framing" uses similar frame layouts, but the building is designed so roof rafters or trusses and openings line up with regular 24-inch centers. In this way, doubled studs and doubled top plates can be eliminated, saving a good deal of lumber. This technique has been well documented and promoted but not widely adopted. Detractors note that a wall built in this manner does not have much redundancy built in, which can hinder future repurposing of the building.

Double stud walls are becoming more common as the need to add extra insulation and avoid thermal bridging is recognized. In this system, two frames are built for each wall, one for the exterior side and one for the interior, with a gap separating them. While this may seem more lumber-intensive at first glance, a double stud frame with 2x4 exterior wall and 2x3 interior wall uses the same amount of wood as one 2x6 wall while offering superior thermal performance.

Frame walls and double frame walls can be built at unconventional spacing to accommodate different insulation types, such as straw bale, inside each stud cavity.

Frame walls are typically built lying down on the floor deck/foundation and raised in place, relying on temporary bracing until all walls are erected and fastened. The frames are not stable until permanent sheathing or bracing is in place.

hemp, wool, mineral wool, fiberglass), wet-blown cellulose, Air Krete

How the system works

Wood frame construction uses a system of regularly spaced wooden posts or "studs" supported by a horizontal sill plate and topped with a single or double horizontal top plate to create a lightweight wall frame. There are many variations to the basic framing system: studs are typically placed at 16-inch or 24-inch centers and made from 2x4 or 2x6. Openings in the wall are built using lintel beams to transfer loads to a pair of doubled studs on either side of the opening.

Tips for successful walls

1. There are many excellent guides to wood frame construction. Consult these resources in the planning stage to optimize frame design and layout.
2. Ensure that wall frames are built to best suit the sheathing and insulation intended for use. For manufactured sheet materials (OSB, plywood, drywall), proper stud layout and wall heights will result in efficient use and minimal cutting of these materials. For alternative insulations,

be sure to create layouts that similarly optimize efficiency.

3. Both the designer and builder need to thoroughly understand all four control layers and how they will intersect at corners, openings and junctions with roof and foundation.
4. Use properly sized, galvanized fasteners in the recommended patterns.
5. Create complete framing drawings so that the arrangement of studs is clear and easy to follow. This can allow for efficient ordering and use of materials on-site.

Pros and cons

ENVIRONMENTAL IMPACTS

Harvesting — *Negligible to High.* Wood harvested from the building site or the local region can have negligible impacts. Unmanaged forestry can have impacts that include significant habitat destruction, soil erosion and ground water contamination. Third-party certification can help to ensure that impacts are minimized.

Metal fasteners may seem like a small component, but dozens of kilograms can go into a frame wall. Ore for steel production is mined in an intensive process with impacts including habitat destruction and soil and water contamination.

Manufacturing — *Negligible to Moderate.* The sawing and planing of structural lumber is a relatively low-impact mechanical process.

Processing raw ore into nails and screws is a multi-stage and intensive process requiring multiple infusions of high heat and fossil fuel use with impacts including air and water pollution.

Wood Frame Walls Embodied Energy

Wall type: 2.4 m (8 ft) tall, typical code compliant framing	Material embodied energy from I.C.E. in MJ/kg	Weight to volume ratio of material*	Volume of material in sample 1000sf/92.9m² building	Sample building embodied energy	Material embodied carbon from I.C.E. in kgCO₂e/kg	Sample building embodied carbon	Notes
Lowest Impact							
2x4 @ 600mm (24 inch) centers	2.5**	450 kg/m³ (spruce lumber)	352 m (1154 ft) of 2x4 24 m (80 ft) of 2x6 1.32 m³ 594 kg	1485 MJ	0.2	119 kg	**EE figure averaged from multiple sources. ICE figure disproportionately high at 7.4.
Nails	20.1 (General steel, average recycled content)		20 kg (44 lb)	402 MJ	1.46	29 kg	
Totals				**1887 MJ**		**148 kg**	Does not include insulation or sheathing.
Highest Impact							
2x6 @ 400mm (16 inch) centers	2.5**	450 kg/m³ (spruce lumber)	459 m (1506 ft) of 2x6 2.44 m³ 1098 kg	2745 MJ	0.2	220 kg	** EE figure averaged from multiple sources. ICE figure disproportionately high at 7.4.
Nails	20.1 (General steel, average recycled content)		25 kg (55 lb)	503 MJ	1.46	37 kg	
Totals				**3248 MJ**		**257 kg**	Does not include insulation or sheathing. Double stud walls using 2x4 exterior and 2x3 interior would use almost identical amount of wood and EE as a single 2x6 wall.

Transportation: Wood transportation by 15 ton truck would equate to 0.9–1.65 MJ per kilometer of travel to the building site. *Typically from engineeringtoolbox.com

Transportation — *Negligible to High.* Sample building uses 594 – 1,098 kg of lumber:

> 0.9 – 1.65 MJ per km by 15 ton truck
> 0.56 – 1.03 MJ per km by 35 ton truck

Timber is a heavy and high-volume material and accrues significant impacts proportional to distance traveled. In most regions it is possible to source lumber a reasonable distance from the building site.

Installation — *Negligible to Moderate.* The number of offcuts from a wood frame wall can be quite high. Careful cut lists and ordering can minimize this waste.

WASTE: *LOW TO MODERATE*

Biodegradable/Compostable — Wood offcuts.
Recyclable — Metal fasteners.
Landfill — Wood offcuts with impregnated fasteners, lumber tarps.

ENERGY EFFICIENCY

Frame walls can have widely varying levels of energy efficiency, depending on the control layers and stud layouts used. In the worst-case scenario, a thin single frame wall with plenty of thermal bridges and minimal insulation is poorly built and leaky, resulting in very poor thermal performance. In the best-case scenario a double stud wall (or single wall with adequate thermal control to prevent bridging) with excellent insulation is built airtight and offers remarkable thermal performance. Whole assembly R-values could range from as low as 9 to as high as 40 or more.

Almost any thermal control material can be used in a frame wall, which is one of the key strengths of this option. Many insulation products are designed specifically to fit into stud walls at a variety of spacings and most natural insulations are easily adapted to the frame. The specific ratings of each of these materials will have implications for overall energy efficiency and must inform the design to ensure adequate thickness and detailing. Each insulation material will have specific installation requirements that will have implications for energy efficiency. Key considerations for all insulations are tightness of fit around the frame and prevention of settling at the top of the wall, as these will lessen the insulative value and create air pockets where convection loops can create thermal short circuits.

MATERIAL COSTS: *LOW*

Used in relatively small quantities, framing lumber is a low cost component of a wall system. The cost of sheathing and insulating a frame wall must be considered in addition to the basic costs of framing.

LABOR INPUT: *MODERATE*

The construction of wood frame walls is quite fast and relatively simple. Double frame walls will double the labor time. The majority of the labor for a frame wall system will go into the installation of the control layers and not the framing itself.

SKILL LEVEL REQUIRED FOR THE HOMEOWNER: *MODERATE*

Basic framing can be done by most first-time builders with adequate framing drawings and elementary carpentry skills. Training is widely available for beginning framers. Skill levels will vary for the rest of the control layers; consider the skills required to complete the entire system and not just the carpentry element.

SOURCING/AVAILABILITY: *EASY*

Framing lumber is widely available. Third-party certified lumber is beginning to find more market share, but the staff at many lumber stores do not seem to understand the certification programs well and obtaining certified lumber may require some effort on the builder's behalf.

Locally milled lumber will require some research to obtain, and orders may need to be placed well in advance at smaller mills. Where codes require all framing lumber to be graded, a grader may need to be hired to approve lumber from smaller mills.

DURABILITY: *MODERATE TO HIGH*

The majority of North American housing stock is wood framed, and the basic system can claim a pretty good history of durability. It is the control layers that will ultimately influence the durability of the wall. The water control layer (siding or sheathing) will determine the degree to which water is excluded from the outside, and the vapor control layer will have the same impact from the interior. There is more than enough knowledge and precedent surrounding all types of control layers with frame walls to be able to do the right thing and have the best possible durability wood frame walls can offer.

CODE COMPLIANCE

All North American building codes accept wood frame wall construction, and most prescriptive standards are based around this system. If you are building with typical stud spacings and lumber sizes and using commercial insulation products there should be no problem with approvals. The use of framing on unconventional centers may raise concerns with some building departments. Unconventional frames may need the approval of a structural engineer. However, documentation for wood frame walls makes this type of engineering relatively simple.

Some control layer strategies might require alternative compliance pathways, as they are unlikely to be formally recognized in codes. Natural insulations and plasters will probably receive the most resistance; however, if the structure meets prescribed standards many code officials are less hesitant about alternative insulations.

Wood Frame Walls Ratings

	Best 1–10		Notes
Environmental Impacts	▓ (2–5)		Addition of sheathing and insulation will raise impacts.
Embodied Energy	▓ (1)		Addition of sheathing and insulation will raise EE.
Waste Generated	▓ (2–5)		Good planning can minimize offcut waste.
Energy Efficiency	N/A		System requires addition of sheathing and insulation to provide energy efficiency.
Material Costs	▓ (1)		Addition of sheathing and insulation will raise costs.
Labor Inputs	▓ (2–6)		
Skill Level Required by Homeowner	▓ (3–6)		Many available resources to help.
Sourcing and Availability	▓ (1)		
Durability and Longevity	▓ (1–5)		Wood frame walls are susceptible to deterioration under poor conditions, but have a good overall performance record.
Building Code Compliance	▓ (1)		
Indoor Air Quality	▓ (1–5)		Sheathing and insulation choices will have a large impact on IAQ.

If the frame wall strategy uses a combination of wood frame and structural insulations/plasters, the whole system may require structural engineering.

INDOOR AIR QUALITY: *MODERATE TO HIGH*

The control layers and finishes will determine the impact of the wall system on IAQ. Frame wall systems with permeable control layers are less likely to have moisture problems than non-permeable. However, as long as adequate mechanical ventilation/ dehumidification is used, a home with non-permeable walls should not experience problematic moisture levels.

Wood sawdust and most insulation materials create a lot of particulate during construction, and the home must be thoroughly cleaned to remove dust and debris prior to occupation or these dusts can be problematic in the finished home.

Natural insulations, plasters and paints will tend to have the lowest impact on IAQ, and manufactured

Waste Wood Columns

The number of short offcuts generated while building a wood frame can be quite high. Most builders end up throwing short offcuts away, or using them as firewood. But these leftovers can be used in a different way to make viable frames for buildings, especially buildings with wide, well-insulated walls.

Waste wood columns use stacks of offcuts laid in perpendicular layers to create structural posts that match the desired width of the wall. Dimensional lumber, timber ends and even forestry slash can be assembled in this way. Individual pieces are nailed together, and the voids between the pieces can be filled with a number of different insulation materials. The columns are covered with whatever type of sheathing that is being used on the wall system.

Such columns are a low-cost and sustainable way to create a stable frame for a building.

Waste wood columns. (DAVID ELFSTROM)

materials and petrochemical paints the highest. The fewer chemical compounds in the materials and finishes, the less IAQ issues there are likely to be.

See Chapter 7: Surface Finishing Materials, for details on each wall finishing option.

FUTURE DEVELOPMENT

Frame wall systems have had the benefit of decades of study, refinement and codification. Structurally, there is little to improve upon in the future. The increased acceptance and availability of certified wood will have a positive effect on frame construction in the upcoming years.

The understanding of control layers and how to best select and install appropriate layers will be the most important development in frame wall construction. In particular, the acceptance of permeable wall systems will make the use of low-impact natural materials more widely acceptable.

Frame wall construction is unlikely to be replaced as the most widely used building system for residential construction. Refinements to improve performance and environmental responsibility are being actively pursued by the industry and will be gradually accepted in codes.

Resources for further research

Burrows, John. *Canadian Wood-Frame House Construction*. Ottawa, ON: Canada Mortgage and Housing Corporation, 2006. Print.

Thallon, Rob. *Graphic Guide to Frame Construction: Details for Builders and Designers*. Newtown, CT: Taunton, 2000. Print.

Newman, Morton. *Design and Construction of Wood-Framed Buildings*. New York: McGraw-Hill, 1995. Print.

Simpson, Scot. *Complete Book of Framing: An Illustrated Guide for Residential Construction*. Kingston, MA: RSMeans, 2007. Print.

Tollefson, Chris, Fred P. Gale, and David Haley. *Setting the Standard: Certification, Governance, and the Forest Stewardship Council*. Vancouver, BC: UBC Press, 2008. Print.

Wood certification programs: fsc.org and fsccanada.org; sfiprogram.org; pefccanada.org

Straw bale walls

What the cheerleaders say...	What the detractors say...
Annually renewable local resource	Walls will burn easily
Affordable and easy to build	Bales will get eaten by rodents and insects
Excellent insulation value	Labor intensive to build
Permeable wall system	Walls prone to rotting
Great aesthetic potential (deep window sills and rounded openings)	

Straw bale walls.

Applications for straw bale walls

- Exterior load-bearing walls
- Exterior infill insulation
- Interior walls

Basic materials

- Rectangular straw bales (2- or 3-string)
- Interior and exterior plaster (earthen, lime or lime-cement)
- Plaster reinforcement mesh (if required)
- Infill applications require a structural frame (light wood frame, post and beam, timber frame)

- Control layers:
  - **Water** — Plaster is the most common water control layer for bale walls, but it is not ideally suited for climates or locations with high precipitation levels. As a water control layer, most plasters benefit from the use of potassium silicate paints or siloxane treatments, both permeable but water-resistant finishes. Rainscreen sidings of wood, brick or stone are also viable water control layers and are recommended in wet areas or for highly exposed walls.
  - **Air** — Plaster is the air control layer. Seamless on the walls, it is an effective barrier against the movement of air on the interior and exterior. Careful detailing is required where plaster meets other materials to ensure continuous air control or the wall system can be leaky.
  - **Vapor** — Plaster is the vapor control layer. By preventing gross air movement through the wall (when well detailed), vapor is reduced to the small amounts diffusing directly through the thick plaster skin. Unless this vapor meets a barrier on its path through the wall, it will diffuse out of the wall system.
  - **Thermal** — Densely packed bales of straw act as the thermal control layer. A straw bale traps a great deal of air in small pockets between individual straws, and each hollow straw also traps air, creating reasonable thermal control. The quantity of straw in a regular bale creates a thick wall with excellent thermal control properties.

How the system works

Rectangular straw bales are stacked in courses, often in running bond, to form the insulated core of a wall, and the inside and outside face of the bales are coated in a thick plaster. The combination of rigid plaster bonded to semi-rigid bales creates a structural insulated panel (SIP) in which the structural properties of the combined components are greater than the sum of the individual parts.

The most basic form of straw bale wall is a load-bearing (or Nebraska-style) wall, in which the plastered straw panel bears the weight of floors and roof above, typically using some form of wooden top plate or beam at the top of the wall to transfer loads and provide attachment points. Structurally, these walls are similar to other commercially produced SIPs, with a thin structural skin (the plaster) integrally bonded to a dense insulative core (the bale). The skin handles all the gravity and live loads and is reinforced by the bale so that loads travel through the skins vertically to the foundation without buckling the plaster.

Window and door openings are typically created using wooden frames, often built identically to code-approved frame walls. Wooden sill plates and wooden top plates are used at the top and bottom of the wall, though the details of these can vary widely in different designs.

TOP PLATE ASSEMBLY TO BEAR ROOF

WOOD FRAMING FOR OPENINGS

STACKED STRAW BALES

PLASTER SKIN INSIDE + OUT

SILL PLATES

APPROPRIATE FOUNDATION

Load-bearing straw bale walls usually incorporate some form of pre-compression/tie-down system to connect the foundation to the roof plate to prevent uplift and to allow builders to settle and level the walls prior to plastering. Early thought about straw bale walls viewed pre-compression as a critical step to prevent further settling of the wall after plastering, and high amounts of compressive force were applied through wires or straps. However, structural testing has shown that the plaster skins handle the loads and the bales themselves are not subjected to further compression from gravity or live loads once plastered. Most builders now pre-compress only to provide a level, stable wall that is rigid enough for plastering.

The plaster materials for straw bale walls range from earthen plasters made from site soils to clay plasters made from processed bagged clays, to lime plaster (both hydrated and hydraulic limes, or hybrid mixes of both) to lime-cement (mortar) plasters. Different admixtures can be employed in each type of plaster, as can different types of reinforcing fibers. Each plaster type has advocates and detractors, advantages and disadvantages (see Plasters in Chapter 4: Sheathing and Cladding Materials). However, enough successful, long-lasting straw bale walls have been built using all of these plasters that it is clear they are all viable options. Base your choice on cost, climate conditions, availability, builder preference, code compliance and environmental impacts.

The use of plaster reinforcement mesh is another variable in straw bale wall construction. Some builders cover the full walls in mesh (plastic or metal) inside and out, while others mesh only at junctions with other materials, and still others do not use any mesh at all.

The wide variety of options in straw bale construction are rendered somewhat manageable by the numerous and reliable books about this type of building. A builder wishing to determine the best straw bale wall system for a project will be able to do so using the resources at the end of this section.

Tips for successful walls

1. Understanding plasters is key to understanding and building good straw bale walls. Most builders focus on the straw bales and consider the plaster as an afterthought. The plaster is the primary structural element as well as the air and vapor control and the aesthetic finish. It also costs at least as much and likely more than the bales, in both price and labor input. Choosing the right type of plaster, the right plasterers (if you are hiring) and the right plastering details will be the most important steps in a successful straw bale wall.

2. Consider the bale as your basic building module and try to design so the bales need as little modification as possible to be installed. For infill situations in particular, labor will be greatly reduced if wall heights work out evenly with courses of bales, so the bales fit tightly at the top of the wall without the need to trim or stuff loose straw. Do not rely on "standard" bale dimensions to determine heights; if at all possible measure the actual bales that will be used, or bales made in the same baling machine. Notching bales around framework is also very labor intensive, and framing designs that reduce or eliminate notching will be much easier to build.

3. Stuffing the gaps at joints between bales is crucial for thermal performance. Everywhere two bales meet, the builder must pack straw or, even better, a straw/light clay mixture, otherwise there will be many areas of poor insulation and convection loops that will short-circuit the thermal performance. In framed walls, similar care must be taken to stuff tightly where bales meet framing members.

4. The plaster is the continuous air and vapor control layer, so particular attention must be paid to areas where this continuity is interrupted. Plaster seams at the top and bottom of the wall, at window and door openings and at framing members that protrude from the wall should be detailed with an additional air control layer that "backs up" the gaps that will inevitably open up when the plaster shrinks. Bale walls without these types of additional barriers at seams will either be very leaky or rely on plenty of caulking to maintain thermal performance.

5. Straw bale walls are a permeable wall system. Avoid using continuous barriers under the plaster and don't use impermeable paints on the plaster surfaces.

6. If using plaster as the water control layer on the exterior in wet climates, ensure that generous roof overhangs are part of the design strategy. For two-story buildings and gable ends, consider using skirt roofs or porches to provide protection.

7. Ensure that bales are at least 30–45 cm (12–18 inches) above grade and 4 cm (1½ inches) above finished floor height to protect against water entry.

8. Despite what you may read in older resources, don't drive rebar stakes into bales between courses, and if you choose to use a mesh over the straw, do not use chicken wire but a purpose-made plastic or metal mesh.

9. If possible, inspect bales before taking delivery to ensure they are dry, tightly bound and evenly sized. Have a strategy for keeping bales dry on-site and until they are fully plastered.

Pros and cons

ENVIRONMENTAL IMPACTS

Harvesting — *Low to Moderate*. Straw is the stem of cereal grain plants. The plants are grown to maturity and the seed heads cut off for processing. The remaining straw is cut close to the ground and gathered into a baling machine that compacts the straw and ties it into rectangular (or round) bales. Baling is a low-impact mechanical process.

Impacts from straw occur prior to harvest, and can include the application of pesticides, herbicides and chemical fertilizers to the soil and the crop. Impacts can include air pollution and water contamination. Farming practices can have widely varying impacts. These impacts are mitigated because straw is a by-product of harvesting the grain crop.

Raw materials for metal and plastic mesh are harvested in high-impact processes that can result in habitat destruction, air and water pollution.

Manufacturing — *Negligible*. Once baled, the straw requires no further processing.

Metal and plastic meshes require intensive high-heat manufacturing processes, with impacts that include high fossil fuel use, air and water pollution.

Transportation — *Negligible to High*. Sample building uses 3,570 – 4,920 kg of straw bales:

> 5.36 – 7.4 MJ per kilometer by 15 ton truck
> 3.35 – 4.6 MJ per km by 35 ton truck

Straw bales are a high-volume material, and impacts accrue proportional to distance traveled. In many regions, straw can be sourced locally.

Installation — *Negligible*.

For impacts of different plasters, see Environmental Impacts in Chapter 4: Sheathing and Cladding Materials.

WASTE: *LOW*

Biodegradable/Compostable — All leftover straw (unless contaminated with other site waste), wood offcuts.

Recyclable — Polypropylene twine offcuts, metal and plastic mesh.

ENERGY EFFICIENCY

R- value : 1.8–2.8 per inch
(R-value: 25–50 for typical wall thicknesses)

Properly designed and detailed, a straw bale wall can offer excellent thermal performance. Testing of straw bale walls has resulted in widely differing R-value figures, ranging from R-20 to R-55. The middle ground of R-30–35 has become the accepted figure for two-string bales, putting the walls well above code requirements in most jurisdictions. The typical lack of thermal bridging in straw bale wall systems helps them to perform well in practice.

Overall energy efficiency will have as much to do with air leakage as R-value, and here straw bale walls can vary greatly. As mentioned above, proper air sealing at all plaster junctions and openings will ensure the walls perform to expected levels. Extremely leaky bale walls will not perform to levels anticipated by the high R-value alone.

MATERIAL COSTS: *LOW TO HIGH*

Straw bale is often promoted as a "cheap" way to build. If only the cost of the bales is counted, this is true. However, the bales are only one part of the wall

Straw Bale Wall Embodied Energy

Wall type: Exterior walls 2.4 m (8ft high)	Material embodied energy from I.C.E. in MJ/kg	Weight to volume ratio of material*	Volume of material in sample 1000sf/92.9m² building	Sample building embodied energy	Material embodied carbon from I.C.E. in kgCO₂e/kg	Sample building embodied carbon	Notes
Lowest Impact							
Bales on edge, load bearing, earth plaster							
Straw bales, two-string, 350x450x800mm (14x18x32 inch)	0.24	120 kg/m³	225 bales 29.75 m³ 3570 kg	857 MJ	0.01	36 kg	
2x4 wood framing for openings, sills, top plates	2.5	450 kg/m³ (spruce lumber)	325 m (1066 ft) 1.1 m³ 495 kg	1,238 MJ	0.2	99 kg	
Clay plaster (1 clay: 3 sand)	0.083 (Aggregate, General)	1089 kg/m³	Interior and exterior, 325 m² (3500 sf) 6.2 m³ 6752 kg	560 MJ	0.0052	35 kg	
Totals				**2655 MJ**		**170 kg**	
Highest Impact							
Bales on flat, frame walls (double stud), lime/cement plaster							
Straw bales, two-string, 350x450x800mm (14x18x32 inch)	0.24	120 kg/m³	310 bales 41 m³ 4920 kg	1181 MJ	0.01	49 kg	
2x4 wood framing @ 800mm (32 inch) centers	2.5	450 kg/m³ (spruce lumber)	434 m (1424 ft) 1.47 m³ 661.5 kg	1,654 MJ	0.2	132 kg	
Plaster (1 lime: 1 cement: 6 sand)	1.11 (Mortar 1:1:6)	2370 kg/m³	Interior and exterior, 325 m² (3500 sf) 6.2 m³ 14,694 kg	16,310 MJ	0.174	2,557 kg	
Totals				**19,145 MJ**		**2,738 kg**	Both bale wall options include insulation and sheathing.

Transportation: Bale transportation by 35 ton truck would equate to 3.4–4.6 MJ per kilometer of travel to the building site.
Plaster transportation by 35 ton truck would equate to 6.3–13.8 MJ per kilometer of travel to the building site. *Typically from engineeringtoolbox.com

system. Plaster is the other significant component, and will add to costs. The more highly refined the plaster ingredients, the higher the costs. Framing systems or the lumber required to build load-bearing walls are an additional cost, as is mesh to whatever degree it is used.

LABOR INPUT: *MODERATE TO HIGH*

What advantage straw bale has in lower material costs it often loses in higher labor input, especially when many bales need to be modified and extensive meshing is required. If the owner is paying for labor, the lower material costs will typically balance out higher labor costs and straw bale walls will end up being as expensive as other wall types. Plastering will likely represent a higher portion of labor input than bale installation. An owner might decide to undertake either the bale raising or the plastering, and hire out the other work.

SKILL LEVEL REQUIRED FOR THE HOMEOWNER: *EASY TO DIFFICULT*

The sales pitch for straw bale walls says that the system is easy and suitable for novice builders. While it is true that stacking one bale on top of another is straightforward, there is a lot more to a successful straw bale wall. The carpentry involved requires the same skill as building frame walls. The preparation of stacked bales for plastering is a unique skill set and difficult to learn other than via direct experience. Plastering is a complex task involving the mixing, applying, curing and finishing of materials that often have limited working times. This is not to say that a first-time owner-builder cannot build a straw bale wall system, but it is no less difficult a task than any other form of building. A workshop or other hands-on training or experience is a worthwhile investment.

SOURCING/AVAILABILITY: *MODERATE*

Plentiful straw is harvested in most regions, but this doesn't mean the material is always easy to access. A builder will usually need to make a direct connection with a farmer or a straw broker, as there are typically no retail outlets for the sale of straw. Local farm co-ops, feed stores and garden centers are good places to start the hunt for straw, as are classified ads in small town newspapers and online buy-and-sell listings.

The materials for most types of plaster are easy to source. Sand is widely available, and lime-cement mortar mixes are common at building and masonry supply stores. Soils suitable for earthen plasters may be available locally, and checking with excavators will be the best way to find clayey soils. Bagged clays are most easily sourced at pottery supply outlets.

DURABILITY: *MODERATE TO HIGH*

The oldest straw bale walls have withstood the harsh Nebraskan climate for a hundred years, demonstrating the durability of the system. As with any wall system, durability will be a direct result of the effectiveness of the control layers. Straw bale walls that stay dry, and have the ability to dry out if they do get wet, will enjoy long lives. If the walls get wet and stay wet they have the same propensity for decay as wood-based walls.

CODE COMPLIANCE

Several American states have adopted codes or standards for straw bale walls, and as of press time a straw bale chapter for the American International Building Code has received preliminary approval. Of all the "alternative" wall systems, straw bale has been the subject of the most testing programs. Good documentation about structural capacities, moisture behavior and thermal properties has been generated at many institutions and in many countries, making alternative compliance relatively easy to demonstrate.

It is common practice to adopt a code-approved or a code-compliant framing system with straw bale walls to give building officials a degree of comfort with this wall system. However, load-bearing walls have been the subjects of most of the testing and as such it should be possible to make a strong case for their acceptance.

INDOOR AIR QUALITY: *MODERATE TO HIGH*

Straw bale walls are generally considered to have attributes that lend themselves to good indoor air quality. The permeability of the wall system makes it less likely that high indoor humidity will lead to mold, as excess moisture is taken up by the plaster and the straw rather than condensing on the wall surface. The plaster and the straw are inert and do not have off-gassing issues.

If finishes are applied over the plaster, then the attributes of the finish will need to be considered. A straw bale wall painted with a toxic paint is no better or worse than any wall with the same treatment. Kept in its raw state or treated with nontoxic finishes, a plastered straw bale wall should have no ill effect on IAQ.

FUTURE DEVELOPMENT

Straw bale walls are at an interesting stage of development. They have moved beyond the infancy of many alternative wall systems and could be said to be in their "adolescence." There is still a lot of experimentation going on with straw bale walls, and every builder and designer has their own variation. Over time, it is likely that a few different systems will show themselves to be ideal uses of the material and offer the lowest costs and labor inputs for the best results. In the immediate future, builders should not think that all straw bale walls are equal, but do plenty of research into particular approaches and speak to other owners and builders about what has and has not worked.

Straw Bale Wall Ratings

	Best 1	2	3	4	5	6	Worst 7	8	9	10	Notes
Environmental Impacts											Impacts are largely due to plaster material choices, with cement-based plasters raising impacts significantly.
Embodied Energy											EE figures range widely, largely due to plaster material choices, with cement-based plasters raising figures significantly.
Waste Generated											Straw waste can be high in volume, but is compostable.
Energy Efficiency											
Material Costs											Plaster and framing choices will have a large impact on costs.
Labor Inputs											A design that favors easy bale installation and plastering will lower labor inputs.
Skill Level Required by Homeowner											Plaster and framing choices will have a large impact on skill level required.
Sourcing and Availability											Availability of appropriate bales will vary regionally.
Durability and Longevity											Straw bale walls are susceptible to deterioration under poor conditions, but have a good overall performance record.
Building Code Compliance											Straw bale walls are not an accepted solution in any codes, but alternative compliance pathways are common.
Indoor Air Quality											Plaster finishes will typically have excellent IAQ properties, but can be affected by rare mold/moisture issues in damp straw walls.

Straw bale walls are an extremely promising system, with good thermal qualities and low embodied energy. It is up to all builders using bale walls to ensure that they do everything possible to meet this promise and contribute to the development of this wall type.

Resources for further research

Magwood, Chris, Peter Mack, and Tina Therrien. *More Straw Bale Building: A Complete Guide to Designing and Building with Straw.* Gabriola Island, BC: New Society, 2005. Print.

King, Bruce. *Design of Straw Bale Buildings: The State of the Art.* San Rafael, CA: Green Building, 2006. Print.

The Straw Bale Alternative Solutions Resource. Victoria, BC: ASRi, 2013. Print.

Corum, Nathaniel. *Building a Straw Bale House: The Red Feather Construction Handbook.* New York: Princeton Architectural Press, 2005. Print.

Lacinski, Paul, and Michel Bergeron. *Serious Straw Bale: A Home Construction Guide for All Climates.* White River Junction, VT: Chelsea Green, 2000. Print.

Magwood, Chris, and Chris Walker. *Straw Bale Details: A Manual for Designers and Builders.* Gabriola Island, BC: New Society, 2001. Print.

Straw bale SIPs

In the past decade, numerous versions of prefabricated straw bale wall panels have been developed around the world. Though they vary in execution, they share a similar principle: the advantages of straw bale construction are best realized when the walls are assembled and plastered off-site and in a horizontal position. This approach combines the low material costs of straw bale walls with dramatically lower labor costs, and allows straw bale walls to compete with conventional options like wood frame construction in terms of overall cost while maintaining all the environmental and thermal performance advantages of bale wall systems.

A prefabricated straw bale wall system is much like other structural insulated panels (SIPs) on the market, offering ease of installation and excellent thermal performance, but without the higher costs and higher environmental impacts of foam-based SIPs.

The panels are created using forms. The wooden top and bottom plates of the form stay with the wall when it is transported and installed. The sides may be an integral ☞

SIP formwork with plaster in bottom.

Bales being "buttered" in plaster.

part of the wall, or be removed after installation. The plaster for one side of the wall is placed wet into the form and the bales are inserted into the wet plaster. The exposed side of the bales are then coated with plaster, using the formwork as a screed to create a square, level wall surface. In this way, the plaster is applied in one horizontal coat, rather than two or three coats in a vertical position.

There are numerous ways of fastening the panels to different foundations, roofs and to one another, depending on the manufacturer's system.

Straw bale SIPs realize the potential of combining natural building methods and materials with a more industrialized production methodology to provide building products that have minimal environmental impacts while meeting the expectations of modern house-building professionals.

Buttered bales inserted in wet plaster in form.

Top layer of plaster screeded.

Walls lifted from delivery truck by crane.

SIP panel guided into place and fastened.

SIP panels installed.

Round straw bale columns

The majority of straw in North America is baled into large rounds rather than the small rectangular bales used to make straw bale walls. The large round bales have a density far greater than the small rectangles, and this makes them well suited to act as structural columns.

Such columns were tested at Queen's University in Kingston, Ontario, in 2007, and were shown to be able to have a working strength in excess of 120 kN (27,000 Lbs).

Round bale columns were used to create the load-bearing elements of a performing arts center building in Madoc, Ontario, in 2008. The octagonal building used a stack of three bales, each 1.2 m wide x 1.2 m high (4 ft x 4 ft), for a total column height of 3.6 m (12 ft), at each of the eight points. A wooden roof beam joined the columns at the top. ☞

PHOTOGRAPHS
COURTESY OF
CHESTER RENNIE

The completed roof of the building was lowered onto the columns using a crane, and caused no measurable deflection of the columns. The walls between the columns were infilled with rectangular straw bales and the entire structure coated with earthen plaster.

The round bale structural columns proved to be very fast to build and very inexpensive. This structural system could have widespread applications for large buildings, where it would significantly lower costs, construction time and environmental impacts.

Round bales can be produced at diameters ranging from 70–120 cm (28–48 inches), with the smaller diameters being more adaptable to conventional construction methods.

Cob walls

What the cheerleaders say...	What the detractors say...
Affordable	Slow construction
Accessible materials	Little insulation value
Easy and intuitive	Difficult to achieve code compliance
Good thermal mass	
Creative, artistic potential	

Applications for cob walls

- Load-bearing and infill exterior walls
- Interior walls
- Built-in furniture, benches
- Decorative elements

Basic materials

- Soil with adequate clay content
- Sand/aggregate
- Straw
- Plasters for finish
- Framing lumber, if used as infill
- Control layers:
  - **Water** — Plaster is the most common material for this layer, though any kind of rainscreen siding can be used.
  - **Air** — The cob wall itself controls air movement, as it is solid and continuous. If well detailed at intersections with floor, ceiling and openings, it is possible to build an airtight wall with no additional control layers.
  - **Vapor** — The cob regulates vapor movement and is a permeable wall system. If gross air leakage is controlled, then vapor will need to diffuse through the wall system. Cob has a large storage capacity for moisture and high perm ratings.
  - **Thermal** — In most cob construction, the mud/straw mix is relied upon for thermal control. Thermal performance rises with higher

straw content, but in general cob does not perform well thermally (see sidebar page 81). An additional thermal control layer can be added in the middle of a cob wall or on either side of the wall, using a range of different insulation materials.

How the system works

A soil with clay content of 10–40 percent and a good distribution of sand and silt is moistened and thoroughly mixed with chopped straw or other natural fiber. The resulting mix is hand-formed into walls that can bear the weight of floors/roofs using a ring beam, usually made of wood or concrete. Cob can also be used as an infill in a wide variety of frames, including light wood frames, post and beam and timber frames.

Window and door openings are typically created using wooden frames, often built identically to openings in code-approved frame walls, though the details of these can vary widely.

The actual percentages of clay, sand, silt and straw in a cob mix will vary with soil types, region and builder preference. Cob mixtures are very forgiving,

with a wide range of mix percentages resulting in feasible walls. There are many resources available to help a builder test and assess cob mixes.

Hand-formed walls are built in "lifts," with cob being added around the walls until the point where the weight of additional wet cob might cause deformation. Straw, sticks and finger holes are used to ensure adequate mechanical bond between lifts. Once built, the wall is monolithic.

Cob walls are not typically made with any sort of formwork, though it is possible to use forms for a more uniform wall surface.

The finished cob walls are usually treated with one or more coats of earthen plaster, which bonds directly to the cob wall surface. The plaster mixtures are very similar to the cob, using the same basic ingredients in slightly different ratios. Lime plasters are occasionally used for their ability to last longer when exposed to precipitation, but may be prone to delaminating from the cob. Plasters with cement content are rarely used because they have much lower permeability than the cob and can trap moisture in the wall.

Cob walls have a long and proven history in a wide range of geographical locations. The addition of insulation adds a complexity that detracts from the simple efficiency of cob, so the material is not as widely used in colder locations. In general, it is used for small, simple and artistic homes, cottages and cabins, though there are numerous large cob structures as well.

Tips for successful walls

1. Find out if site soils are appropriate for making cob. Soils with too much clay can be amended with additional sand and those that are naturally too sandy can have bagged clay or imported local clay soils added. Because cob mixtures are feasible with a wide range of clay/sand/silt

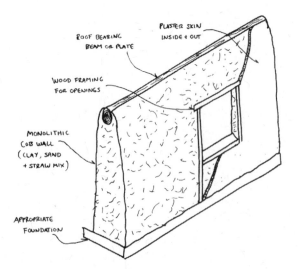

PLASTER SKIN
INSIDE + OUT

ROOF BEARING
BEAM OR PLATE

WOOD FRAMING
FOR OPENINGS

MONOLITHIC
COB WALL
(CLAY, SAND
+ STRAW MIX)

APPROPRIATE
FOUNDATION

ratios, there is usually a way to make local soils work.

2. Create a mixing system that is appropriate to the size of the walls being built. "Cob stomping" — the mixing of cob using bare feet on a tarp — can be fun and is often the image associated with cob construction, but it is not a fast way to mix cob. For larger projects or those with time restraints, a more mechanized system will be useful. Check Resources section at the end of this chapter for tips on mixing in a variety of ways including animals, mortar mixers, tractors and backhoes.

3. As a hand-sculpted, freeform construction style, cob walls lend themselves to creative, curvy designs. This is very liberating from a design point of view, but remember that doors, windows and a roof will need to fit the walls and these elements must be adapted to rounded shapes. Make sure that your plans account for how these elements will interact with the cob walls.

4. Make walls of an appropriate thickness. The taller and straighter the walls, the wider they will need to be. It is common for cob walls to taper from a wider base to a narrower top. Check resources for guidelines about wall thickness.

5. Cob walls can take a long time to build and then a long time to dry out thoroughly. Projects in cold climates or climates with a long rainy season need to be timed to leave adequate drying time before completion of finishes and occupancy.

6. In wet or cold climates, proper detailing needs to be addressed at the foundation, tops of walls and around openings to ensure proper drainage planes, air sealing and protection from rising damp.

7. Cob invites community, so make sure you include others in a cob wall project. As a

Mixing cob by hand. (DANIEL EARLE)

user-friendly, safe and fun way to build, a cob wall-raising is a memorable event to be shared with friends and family.

Pros and cons

ENVIRONMENTAL IMPACTS

Harvesting — *Negligible to Moderate.* Site soil can be harvested with negligible impacts. Amending materials like sand and clay have low to moderate impacts including habitat destruction and water contamination from quarrying. Straw is harvested with low to moderate impacts including water contamination from crop spraying.

Manufacturing — *Negligible to Low.* Cob can be mixed without the use of machinery, resulting in negligible impacts. The use of mechanical mixing equipment has relatively low impacts.

Transportation — *Negligible to Low.* Sample building uses 54,014 kg of soil:

50.8 MJ per km by 35 ton truck

Site soil requires no transportation. Soil, sand and clay are heavy materials and accrue impacts proportional to distance traveled. In most regions these materials can be sourced very close to the building site.

Installation — *Negligible.*

WASTE: *VERY LOW*

Biodegradable/Compostable — All cob ingredients.

ENERGY EFFICIENCY: *LOW*
R-value: 0.3 to 0.9 per inch

Cob does not offer a lot of thermal resistance. It is a massive material, and as such works well in climates where thermal mass is an appropriate strategy for maintaining comfortable temperatures (see Thermal Mass vs. Insulation sidebar page 81). The addition of straw in the mix helps add some insulation value compared to solid earth, but the cob will lose its structural integrity if enough straw is added to provide reasonable thermal performance for northern climates, and will have transformed into light clay/straw (see section page 106) and require a structural frame. Energy efficiency, then, depends on the climate. In the right climate, cob alone can work. In cold climates, additional insulation will need to be added and the energy efficiency will depend on the values of that insulation and the effectiveness of the other control layers.

Cob Wall Embodied Energy

Wall type: Solid cob wall, 300mm (12 in) thick, 2.4m (8ft) high	Material embodied energy from I.C.E. in MJ/kg	Weight to volume ratio of material*	Volume of material in sample 1000sf/92.9m² building	Sample building embodied energy	Material embodied carbon from I.C.E. in kgCO₂e/kg	Sample building embodied carbon	Notes
Lowest Impact							
Load bearing cob, wood framed openings and beam							
Clay/sand harvested on site	0	1089 kg/m³	49.6 m³ 54,014 kg	0 MJ		0	No EE for site harvested materials.
Straw	0.24	120 kg/m³	6.3 m³ 756 kg	181 MJ	0.01	8 kg	
2x4 framing	2.5	450 kg/m³ (spruce lumber)	325 m (1066 ft) 1.1 m³, 495 kg	1,238 MJ	0.2	99 kg	
Totals				**1,419 MJ**		**107 kg**	Does not include plaster/ sheathing or insulation.
Highest Impact							
Standard frame walls with cob infill							
Clay/sand	0.083 (Aggregate, general)	1089 kg/m³	49.6 m³ 54,014 kg	4,483 MJ	0.0052	281 kg	
Straw	0.24	120 kg/m³	6.3 m³ 756 kg	181 MJ	0.01	8 kg	
2x4 framing @ 600mm (24 inch) centers	2.5	450 kg/m³ (spruce lumber)	458 m (1500 ft) 1.55 m³ 697.5 kg	1,744 MJ	0.2	140 kg	
Totals				**6,408 MJ**		**429 kg**	Does not include plaster/ sheathing or insulation.

Transportation: Clay soil transportation by 35 ton truck would equate to 50 MJ per kilometer of travel to the building site. *Typically from engineeringtoolbox.com

MATERIAL COSTS: *LOW*

The basic materials for a cob wall can be very inexpensive, especially if site soils are most or all of the mix. Lumber for framing openings will be an additional cost, and if a skeletal frame of any kind is being used this too will contribute costs. Costs for an insulation layer, if necessary, will depend on the type of insulation used.

LABOR INPUT: *HIGH*

Cob walls are hand-built, and that means lots of manual labor. If the mix is being stomped by foot, the amount of labor increases further. Machine mixes will save on this time. Typically, cob walls are built with many hands so a lot of labor can be accomplished in a relatively short amount of time. This work is usually volunteer-based, as it would be costly to have to pay for the labor input a cob wall system requires.

SKILL LEVEL REQUIRED FOR THE HOMEOWNER: *LOW TO MODERATE*

With forgiving mixes and free-form hand-placement of the wall material, cob is among the most straightforward and beginner-friendly building systems. It is common for new builders to learn while helping others build walls, and then pass on the knowledge to those who helped them build their walls. An experienced cob builder will have time- and labor-saving knowledge and understand detailing for durability, but this information is available through resources for beginners.

SOURCING/AVAILABILITY: *EASY*

If the site soils are appropriate for cob, then sourcing is easy. Even if sand or clay need to be imported, they are widely available from masonry supply and pottery supply outlets. Straw can be obtained directly from local farms or farm supply stores, and may require some effort to obtain. Lumber can come from local sawmills with some research, or easily from building supply stores.

DURABILITY: *MODERATE TO HIGH*

Cob structures have lasted centuries in many different parts of the world. The cob mix is susceptible to long-term erosion from rain, but it is also infinitely repairable. A good roof overhang and proper elevation above grade are the easiest way to ensure minimal exposure to precipitation. A plaster finish can prevent the cob from being damaged by driving rains. If the plaster is well maintained, the cob itself should never see inclement conditions. There are paints and treatments that can be used on the earthen plasters to help them be more durable in wet conditions (see Chapter 7: Surface Finishing Materials), reducing regular maintenance requirements.

CODE COMPLIANCE

Cob is not currently an acceptable solution in any building codes. Many cob buildings are unpermitted, and are often small enough to fall into the legally unpermitted category. In the past decade, there have been a few examples of cob buildings being permitted through alternative compliance mechanisms, and these set a good precedent for builders wishing to attempt permitted cob structures.

INDOOR AIR QUALITY: *MODERATE TO HIGH*

Clay walls have hygroscopic qualities that enable them to store vast amounts of moisture, rather than having moisture condense on the wall surface and potentially cause mold issues. Other desirable IAQ qualities are attributed to clay walls, including an ability to absorb toxins from the air and a negative ion nature that helps balance positive ion charge (static electricity) and can potentially reduce airborne dust and allergen particles.

Because cob is made from unprocessed site soils, the contents of the soil end up in the walls. If soils were contaminated in any way or release radon gas, this would be problematic. If you have any concerns about the soil, testing is recommended.

FUTURE DEVELOPMENT

Cob is a low-tech building system, and the majority of its advocates appreciate the simplicity. Cob mixes could certainly be produced commercially, but there is currently little drive to develop or use such systems. Part of the appeal of cob is that it is made and used today in the same way it was made and used centuries ago.

Positive movement toward testing and code compliance is likely to occur over the next decade or two, as interest in low-impact building makes cob an attractive choice.

The development of insulation strategies that combine well with cob will help to make these walls more applicable in cold climates.

Resources for further research

Weismann, Adam, and Katy Bryce. *Building with Cob: A Step-by-Step Guide.* Totnes, Devon: Green, 2006. Print.

Evans, Ianto, Linda Smiley, and Michael Smith. *The Hand-Sculpted House: A Philosophical and Practical Guide to Building a Cob Cottage.* White River Junction, VT: Chelsea Green, 2002. Print.

Bee, Becky. *The Cob Builders Handbook: You Can Hand-Sculpt Your Own Home.* Murphy, OR: Groundworks, 1997. Print.

Schofield, Jane, and Jill Smallcombe. *Cob Buildings: A Practical Guide.* Crediton, Devon: Black Dog, 2004. Print.

Cob Wall Ratings

	Best 1	2	3	4	5	6	7	Worst 8	9	10	Notes
Environmental Impacts											
Embodied Energy											Addition of insulation will raise EE.
Waste Generated											
Energy Efficiency											Additional insulation required in heating and cooling climates.
Material Costs											Addition of insulation will raise costs.
Labor Inputs											Mechanization of mixing has a large impact on labor input.
Skill Level Required by Homeowner											Amount and extensiveness of framing required will affect skill level required.
Sourcing and Availability											Materials are abundant, but sourcing may be non-conventional.
Durability and Longevity											Cob walls are susceptible to deterioration under poor conditions, but have a good overall performance record.
Building Code Compliance											Cob walls are not an accepted solution in any codes. Alternative compliance pathways are beginning to be developed.
Indoor Air Quality											Cob walls will typically have excellent IAQ properties, but can be affected by rare mold/moisture issues.

Cordwood or stackwall

What the cheerleaders say...	What the detractors say...
Use of abundant resource	Difficult to seal/insulate
Easy to build	Slow to construct
Affordable	Wide wall footprint
Aesthetic appeal	

Applications for cordwood/stackwall

- Load-bearing and infill exterior walls
- Interior walls
- Built-in furniture, benches
- Decorative elements

Basic materials

- Lengths of small diameter and/or split softwood, debarked
- Mortar, either cement or clay based
- Loose-fill insulation
- Control layers:
  - **Water** — Typical cordwood walls leave the ends of the wood exposed on the exterior face, and the matrix of wood ends and mortar are the only water control layer, and are not ideally suited to the task. While the mortar and wood have a reasonable amount of water storage capacity, it is possible to saturate the wall in

Thermal Mass vs. Insulation

There is a lot of "debate" about the effectiveness of thermal mass as an insulation strategy. The subject can be confusing, with disparate claims being made about "effective R-values" or "mass enhanced R-value."

The truth is, thermal mass is *not* insulation. Insulation limits or restricts the flow of heat; thermal mass freely and easily absorbs and releases heat. The confusion between thermal mass and insulation can arise because, under certain conditions, the *thermal performance* of a massive material can lend itself well to occupant comfort. If the climate is such that average daytime temperatures are at or above comfortable range and average nighttime temperatures are at or below it, massive walls will absorb daytime heat slowly without raising indoor temperatures above the level of comfort and then lose that heat to the cooler night air on both sides of the wall. In such a scenario, thermal insulation would prevent this gradual accumulation and discharge of heat. Thermal mass is an entirely adequate strategy for achieving a comfortable living temperature in temperate climates with moderate and regular diurnal temperature swings.

However, if temperatures remain below or above comfortable levels for longer periods of time, massive walls will cool down or warm up and stay cold or hot, influencing the indoor temperature severely. A wall with high thermal mass that is many degrees colder or hotter than the desired indoor temperature will require equally massive inputs of heat or cold to moderate room temperature. In this scenario, a builder needs to use a thermal control layer that is resistant to the flow of heat: insulation.

A combination of thermal mass and insulation is really an ideal arrangement, especially if the thermal mass is on the interior side of the insulation. In such a scenario, the thermal mass is able to absorb and release excess heat (from solar gain, occupant loads, wood-fired heat sources that burn hot and then go out) while transmitting very little of that heat to the outdoors thanks to the insulation. Hot climates will find this system beneficial in the other direction, with massive walls absorbing daytime heat without transmitting it indoors and releasing that heat during the cooler nights. A lot of North American locations experience both conditions, depending on the season, and will benefit from wall systems that have mass on both sides of an insulated core.

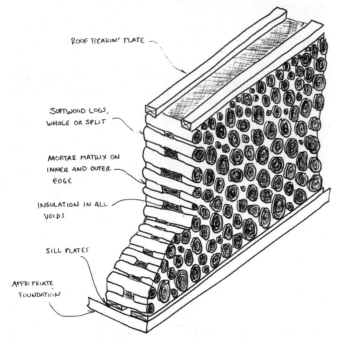

ROOF BEARING PLATE

SOFTWOOD LOGS, WHOLE OR SPLIT

MORTAR MATRIX ON INNER AND OUTER EDGE

INSULATION IN ALL VOIDS

SILL PLATES

APPROPRIATE FOUNDATION

the loose-fill insulation packed in the spaces between each piece of wood. The wood is a thermal bridge spanning from the inside to the outside of the wall system, but if left long enough (typically 60 cm / 24 inches) softwood will have a reasonable R-value. The areas of loose-fill insulation will have higher thermal resistance. Some cordwood walls are built using two separated walls of cordwood with a continuous thermal control layer between them, providing a more consistent R-value.

How the system works

Lengths of dry wood are laid across the wall and embedded in mortar strips at the inner and outer edge of the wall, with each successive row of wood centered in the gap between pieces on the previous row. The wood must be dry, preferably rot-resistant softwood. Lighter, airier softwoods have better thermal performance and shrink and expand less, and are therefore less likely to pull away from the mortar than hardwood. The wood is debarked and usually split to avoid the checking cracks that inevitably occur in round wood.

Load-bearing cordwood walls use columns of crossed courses of wood and mortar at each corner to provide stability. These are built first, and have tie-pieces that key into the walls. Many load-bearing cordwood structures are built round to take advantage of the inherent stability of round walls and avoid the need for corner supports.

Infill cordwood walls use a skeletal frame (light wood frame, post and beam, timber frame) and the cordwood is built between the framing members. The frame provides stability and containment for the cordwood at the corners.

Light wood frames are typically used to form window and door openings in the cordwood wall,

heavy rainfall events, creating the potential for water damage. If the wall is plastered or otherwise sheathed, this layer creates a much more effective water control layer.

- **Air** — Left unplastered, cordwood walls do not have an effective air control layer as differential expansion and contraction between the wood and the mortar can result in gaps developing. Joints between wood and mortar are sometimes caulked to help control airflow through the wall. A plaster skin can act as an effective air control layer.
- **Vapor** — Vapor movement is not regulated in a cordwood wall, unless all joints between wood and mortar are thoroughly caulked or a plaster skin is added over the surface of the wall. In a well-sealed wall, vapour diffusion is adequate to handle typical conditions.
- **Thermal** — Two distinct thermal materials are at work: the lengths of cordwood and

and wooden or concrete beams form a top plate to secure the roof.

There are two different forms of cordwood construction, either of which can be load-bearing or infill:

Throughwall — Pieces of wood traverse the wall from inside to outside. Mortar is used at the inner and outer edges of the wall and thermal insulation is placed in the voids between wood and mortar. In this method, the wood is an integral part of the thermal performance as it bridges from inside to out. For infill scenarios, it is possible to use an insulative mortar (clay/sawdust, hempcrete or similar variation) that is laid continuously from inside to out.

Mortar-Insulation-Mortar (M-I-M) —Two separate walls of cordwood are built with a continuous insulated space between them. Built in this manner, the wood and mortar are not key components of the thermal performance, which is supplied by the chosen insulation.

Tips for successful walls

1. Choosing appropriate wood is key to a good cordwood wall. Softwood is the best choice, and the lightest and most rot-resistant local softwood is ideal. Wood should be thoroughly dry (not to the touch, but measured to be consistent with ambient humidity), debarked and preferably split. The biggest issue with cordwood walls is swelling and shrinking of the wood, and moisture content is the main cause of excessive movement.

2. Plan a cordwood wall that is appropriate for your climate. In colder climates, the M-I-M approach will be the most thermally appropriate.

3. Choose a mortar that best suits the type of cordwood construction and the climate. Pure masonry mortars are strong (good for

Cordwood wall.

load-bearing) but brittle and less permeable and offer little thermal resistance. Lightweight mortars are more flexible and have better thermal performance but may not have the same strength. Mortars can be based on cement, lime or clay binders depending on required strength, durability and environmental impact.

4. Consider plastering cordwood walls. Although the aesthetics of cordwood are a key attraction to the system, its performance and durability are significantly enhanced if the walls are plastered.

5. Choose insulation materials that are not prone to settling. Especially when placed in a matrix of spaces in a cordwood wall, many loose-fill insulations will settle over time and leave gaps in the thermal control layer.

6. Ensure that the foundation chosen for a cordwood wall is wide enough to support the wall and that both foundation and soils below are designed for the weight of a cordwood wall system.

7. Consider cutting cordwood to length with a chop saw or fine-tooth handsaw rather than a chainsaw. This leaves a much cleaner cut that is less prone to water intake and a better surface if applying sealants.

Pros and cons

ENVIRONMENTAL IMPACTS

Harvesting — *Negligible to Low.* Cordwood is typically sourced from wood stock that is not suitable for milling into lumber. Deadfall, logging slash and forestry thinnings are all minimal-impact sources. Trees felled to be sawn into cordwood are low-impact.

Mortar ingredients can have a range of impacts, from negligible for site soils to moderate for manufactured mortars that have quarried ingredients. Quarrying can cause habitat destruction and water contamination.

Manufacturing — *Negligible.* Cordwood requires no processing after being harvested.

Mortar ingredients can have a range of impacts, especially cement- and/or lime-based mortars, which are fired at extremely high temperatures and have high impacts including fossil fuel use, air and water pollution and greenhouse gas emissions. Site-sourced clay mortars have negligible impacts.

Transportation — *Negligible to Low.* Sample building uses 26,775 kg of wood:

25.2 MJ per km by 35 ton truck

Suitable cordwood should be able to be sourced locally. As a heavy and high-volume material, impacts will accrue with distance traveled.

Installation — *Negligible.*

WASTE: *LOW*

Biodegradable/Compostable — Wood offcuts, natural insulation materials.

Landfill — Manufactured insulation offcuts, cement and/or lime bags.

ENERGY EFFICIENCY
R-value: 1 per inch

The inherent leakiness of a system with so many joints between unlike materials has to be addressed, or else no amount of insulation and/or thermal mass will be effective. The cracks that open up between each piece of wood and the mortar surrounding it are inevitable. Using dry, light wood and flexible mortar can minimize gaps, but will not eliminate them. These gaps can be caulked, but this is a lengthy and inevitably flawed process. Plastering the wall on the inside and outside will provide excellent air sealing at the cost of altering the aesthetics. The M-I-M approach affords the builder an opportunity to use air barriers on the inside faces of the two cordwood walls. There can be some logistics involved in applying plaster or using sheet barriers in such a narrow space, but a wall that has all the advantages and aesthetics of cordwood with reasonable energy efficiency will reward these efforts.

The type of insulation chosen for a cordwood wall and the method of installation also have a great impact on energy efficiency. Throughwall designs require the use of loose-fill insulations that must be installed around a matrix of wood, which leaves lots of potential for uneven quantities of insulation and/or gaps. The settling of loose-fill insulations can also affect long-term efficiency as gaps in the insulation layer open up after the wall is sealed and can no longer be monitored. M-I-M designs are appropriate for batt, sheet and sprayed insulations, which can be more stable over time than loose-fill.

MATERIAL COSTS: *LOW TO MODERATE*

Cordwood can be a low-cost construction method, depending on the source of the wood and the mortar and insulation choices. Many options exist for entirely local and minimally processed materials, which can help keep costs low.

LABOR INPUT: *HIGH*

There is a significant amount of labor involved in a cordwood wall. The more energy-efficient the wall the more labor will be needed, especially when two separate walls must be laid up, air barriers put in place and insulation installed. Even a throughwall is labor intensive, as each piece of wood needs to be cut, placed and mortared.

Owners who put their own labor into the construction make most cordwood buildings. It would be costly to hire professionals to build one, though there are some cordwood building companies in the market.

Clay mortars save labor because they can be mixed in large batches and kept over a long period of time, unlike cement-based mortars, which have to be mixed in small batches, requiring cleaning of mixing equipment and tools with each batch.

SKILL LEVEL REQUIRED FOR THE HOMEOWNER: *MODERATE*

Cordwood is definitely approachable for novice builders. There are many good how-to resources available, and the basic skills are fairly easy to learn. It can take practice and a good eye to make an aesthetically pleasing cordwood wall with a good

Cordwood Wall Embodied Energy

Wall type: 600mm (24 in) wide wall, 60% wood, 40% mortar surface area, 2.4m (8ft) tall	Material embodied energy from I.C.E. in MJ/kg	Weight to volume ratio of material*	Volume of material in sample 1000sf/92.9m² building	Sample building embodied energy	Material embodied carbon from I.C.E. in kgCO₂e/kg	Sample building embodied carbon	Notes
Lowest Impact							
Site harvested wood with site harvested clay mortar and sawdust insulation							
Wood	0	450 kg/m³ (spruce lumber)	59.5 m³ 26,775 kg	0	0	0	No EE attributed for site harvested materials.
Clay mortar	0	1089 kg/m³	9.9 m³ 10781 kg	0	0	0	
Sawdust insulation	0.94**	210 kg/m³	29.7 m³ 6237 kg	5,863 MJ	–	–	**No figure in ICE. Figure from averaged industry figures for mill waste. No carbon figure available.
Totals				**5,863 MJ**			
Highest Impact							
Wood harvested off site with cement mortar and mineral wood insulation							
Wood	0.6***	450 kg/m³ (spruce lumber)	59.5 m³ 26,775 kg	16,065 MJ	–	–	***No figure in ICE. Figure from average of air dried softwood results.
Mortar (1 lime:1 cement:6 sand)	1.11 (Mortar 1:1:6)	2370 kg/m³	9.9 m³ 23463 kg	26,044 MJ	0.174	4,083 kg	
Mineral wool insulation	16.6 (Mineral wool)	32 kg/m³	29.7 m³ 950.4 kg	15,777 MJ	1.28	1,217 kg	
Totals				**57,886 MJ**		**5,300 kg**	Both cordwood wall options include insulation, no sheathing required.

Transportation: Wood transportation by 35 ton truck would equate to 25.2 MJ per kilometer of travel to the building site. Mortar transportation by 35 ton truck would equate to 22 MJ per kilometer of travel to the building site. *Typically from engineeringtoolbox.com distribution of wood sizes and shapes and even mortar lines.

SOURCING/AVAILABILITY: *EASY TO MODERATE*

In regions with plentiful softwood forests, the wood will be relatively easy to source. Cordwood is one of the few building materials where used or scrap material is as easy to source as virgin material. A typical construction site will often throw out enough dimensional lumber scraps to make a large cordwood wall, and even areas without natural timber stands are likely to have a lot of frame wall construction producing a lot of "waste."

Mortar materials are easy to source, and insulation availability will depend on type, regional availability and distribution.

DURABILITY: *MODERATE TO HIGH*

In northern Europe and throughout North America there are examples of cordwood buildings that have been standing for 150 to 200 years. Well-built and properly maintained, cordwood can offer a long life span. The exposed end grain of the cordwood is more prone to moisture and pest infiltration than the side grain that is usually exposed; a plaster coating over the cordwood will offer a good deal of protection on both counts. A variety of wood sealants can also be used as a protective layer. If kept reasonably dry and adequately protected from insects, the basic elements of the wall have reasonable durability and proven history.

CODE COMPLIANCE

Cordwood is not an accepted solution in any building codes, but a reasonable amount of testing has been done and some excellent code guidelines have been created, which should make approvals under alternative compliance rules feasible. As an infill wall system, the code compliance of the frame will tend

Cordwood Wall Ratings

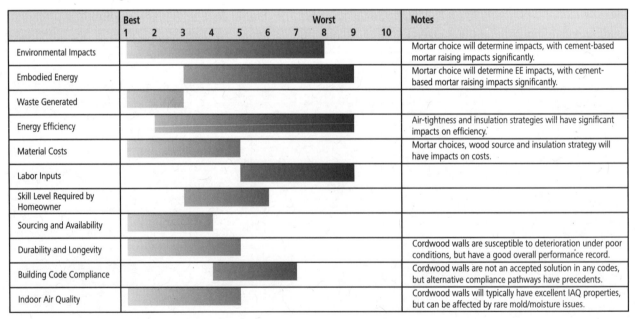

	Best 1	2	3	4	5	6	7	Worst 8	9	10	Notes
Environmental Impacts											Mortar choice will determine impacts, with cement-based mortar raising impacts significantly.
Embodied Energy											Mortar choice will determine EE impacts, with cement-based mortar raising impacts significantly.
Waste Generated											
Energy Efficiency											Air-tightness and insulation strategies will have significant impacts on efficiency.
Material Costs											Mortar choices, wood source and insulation strategy will have impacts on costs.
Labor Inputs											
Skill Level Required by Homeowner											
Sourcing and Availability											
Durability and Longevity											Cordwood walls are susceptible to deterioration under poor conditions, but have a good overall performance record.
Building Code Compliance											Cordwood walls are not an accepted solution in any codes, but alternative compliance pathways have precedents.
Indoor Air Quality											Cordwood walls will typically have excellent IAQ properties, but can be affected by rare mold/moisture issues.

to simplify approvals. Load-bearing walls will likely require the input of a structural engineer. In jurisdictions where cordwood is a historical building method, approvals are likely to be easier because code officials will be familiar with the system and its proven history.

INDOOR AIR QUALITY: *MODERATE TO HIGH*

The wood and mortar matrix of the interior wall surface have some inherently good properties for indoor air quality. Both are vapor-permeable, giving the system a lower likelihood of condensation on the interior wall surfaces, which lowers the chances of mold development. The wood and mortar are fairly benign materials, though certain softwoods (cedar, in particular) can cause allergic reactions in some people. The rough surface of the wall can also trap and accumulate a lot of dust, and will need maintenance to keep from raising dust count in the air.

Many cordwood builders apply caulking to all the wood/mortar joints, and most caulking is not good for indoor air quality, off-gassing a variety of harmful compounds. If you do choose to caulk, make sure that the product conforms to high indoor air quality standards.

A plaster coating on the cordwood will bring to IAQ all the qualities of the plaster and eliminate the need for caulking and the dust collection issue.

FUTURE DEVELOPMENT

Cordwood is a historically proven method of building, and the basic system is unlikely to undergo major changes or transformations. Experiments with different insulation strategies and mortars are likely to continue, but results may only influence regional approaches to the technique.

The most meaningful developments will come with more testing and greater acceptance in building codes. As a building method best suited to owner-building, there is not a strong push from professional builders to move code acceptance forward. There are, however, some dedicated builders and researchers whose efforts are moving the system closer to codification.

Resources for further research

Flatau, Richard C., and Alan Stankevitz. *Cordwood and the Code: A Building Permit Guide*. Merrill, WI: Cordwood Construction, 2005. Print.

Roy, Robert L. *Cordwood Building: The State of the Art*. Gabriola Island, BC: New Society, 2003. Print.

Flatau, Richard C. *Cordwood Construction: A Log End View*. Merrill, WI: Flatau, 1997. Print.

Rammed earth walls

What the cheerleaders say...	What the detractors say...
Low environmental impacts	Costly labor input
Widely available material	Complicated form work
Excellent thermal mass	Requires insulation in most climates
Time-proven technique	

Applications for rammed earth wall systems

- Load-bearing wall systems
- Interior walls
- Built-in furniture, benches
- Decorative elements

Basic materials

- Earth
- Stabilizer (cement or lime where required)
- Insulation (where required)
- Water-resistant finish (where required)
- Control layers:
  - **Water** — The finished rammed earth is typically the water control layer. It is possible to use vapor-permeable, water-resistant finishes

on the rammed earth surface or to include water-resistant additives in the earth mix before ramming. Additional cladding over the rammed earth is feasible but rarely done.
- **Air and vapor** — Solid, continuous and dense, rammed earth is an effective air and vapor control layer.
- **Thermal** — A rammed earth wall requires an additional thermal control layer in hot or cold climates (see Thermal Mass vs. Insulation sidebar). This layer can be on the interior, exterior or center of the wall, and is typically a rigid insulation.

How the system works

A lightly moistened earth mix with a relatively low clay content (10–30 percent is common) is placed into forms in lifts, then tamped heavily to achieve a desired level of compaction. The soil mix varies by region and builder, but it is common to "stabilize" the mix with a small amount (3–9 percent) of portland cement or other hydraulic binder.

The walls are built up in continuous lifts to full height. Often they are built in sections, so that formwork is not needed continuously around the building.

Window and door openings are usually created using a wooden "volume displacement box" or VDB. These VDBs hold the place of the window or door as tamping occurs around them. Once the wall is complete the VDB is removed, leaving a well-formed opening in the wall.

For large openings, lintels of wood, concrete or steel can be used above the opening; these are often buried in the rammed earth so they cannot be seen in the finished wall.

Electrical wiring and switch boxes (or conduits to receive them) are placed in the formwork before adding earth and tamping, and are formed right into

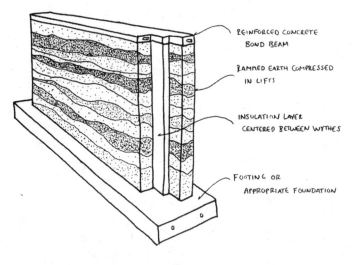

REINFORCED CONCRETE
BOND BEAM

RAMMED EARTH COMPRESSED
IN LIFTS

INSULATION LAYER
CENTERED BETWEEN WYTHES

FOOTING OR
APPROPRIATE FOUNDATION

the wall. Surface mounting after construction is also possible.

At the top of a rammed earth wall is a bond beam made of poured concrete, wood or steel. The beam is fastened to the top of the wall to provide a continuous attachment point for a roof. The method of fastening will depend on expected wind and seismic loads.

In hot or cold climates, insulation is part of a rammed earth wall system. The insulation can be a continuous wrap on the interior or exterior of the wall, but more commonly it is centered in the wall. Types of insulation used will vary with climate, availability, compressive strength and environmental factors.

Rammed earth walls are usually left exposed to provide the finished surface. A variety of sealants can be used on the raw earth to leave it visible but add protection from water. Plasters and others sidings are rarely used but are possible finishes.

Tips for successful walls

1. Formwork is the key to building with rammed earth, and the better the formwork the faster and more accurate the construction. Forms must be able to withstand the considerable forces of ramming the earth within and be able to be assembled and disassembled with a minimum of effort. Formwork that is reusable can help keep costs down. Check with experienced builders to see what formwork systems are being used successfully.
2. Soils used for rammed earth must be very well mixed and not too wet. An even distribution of clay and any additional binders (cement, slag, lime, fly ash) is crucial to final wall strength. Rammed earth mixes do not benefit from the plasticity that water adds, and require plenty of mechanical mixing to achieve best results instead.

3. Test potential soils before using. The makeup of the soil is critical to the performance of the wall. A lot of soil is required to make a rammed earth wall, and changes in its composition will mean that mixes may need to change too. Compact samples of the earth and use reliable sources to determine whether or not you will need stabilizers, and which ones are most appropriate for the soil type.
4. Plan mechanical systems and wall openings carefully, as modifying rammed earth walls is time-consuming. If services are to be run within the walls, consider using conduit so that you can make changes and repairs without opening the wall.
5. Avoid finishes that will reduce or eliminate the permeability of the rammed earth wall.
6. If you are building your own home, consider buying the equipment you will need to dig, mix and tamp the earth. It can be much less costly to buy used equipment and re-sell it at the end of a project than to rent it for a long period of time.

Pros and cons

ENVIRONMENTAL IMPACTS

Harvesting — *Negligible to Moderate.* Site soil can be harvested with negligible impacts. Amending materials like sand and cement have low to moderate impacts including habitat destruction and water contamination from quarrying.

Steel for reinforcing bar is extracted in a high-impact manner, with effects including habitat destruction and ground water contamination.

Manufacturing — *Negligible to Moderate.* Soil can be extracted and processed with negligible to low impacts.

Portland cement, if used, is fired at extremely high temperatures and has high impacts including fossil fuel use, air and water pollution and greenhouse gas emissions.

Steel reinforcement bar is made in a high-heat process that uses a lot of fossil fuel, and has impacts that include air and water pollution.

Transportation — *Negligible to Moderate*. Sample building uses 79,410 – 105,666 kg of rammed earth:

74.6 – 99.3 MJ per km by 35 ton truck

Soil, cement and steel are heavy materials, and accrue significant impacts proportional to distance traveled.

Installation — *Negligible to Moderate*. The process of ramming the soil mixture can be done manually with negligible impact. More often, hydraulic machinery is used, with moderate impacts depending on power source.

WASTE: *LOW*

Biodegradable/Compostable — All leftover earth materials.

Recyclable — Metal reinforcement bar.

Landfill — Manufactured insulation offcuts, cement bags.

ENERGY EFFICIENCY: *LOW TO HIGH*

A rammed earth wall has a lot of thermal mass and can easily be an airtight wall system, but it has no inherent insulation value (see Thermal Mass vs. Insulation sidebar). The overall energy efficiency of a rammed earth wall system will depend on the insulation strategy. Insulation can be placed on either the interior or exterior of the wall or a double wythe system can have insulation in the middle of the wall.

Rammed Earth Wall Embodied Energy

Wall type: 2.4 m (8ft) high	Material embodied energy from I.C.E. in MJ/kg	Weight to volume ratio of material*	Volume of material in sample 1000sf/92.9m² building	Sample building embodied energy	Material embodied carbon from I.C.E. in kgCO$_2$e/kg	Sample building embodied carbon	Notes
Lowest Impact							
Solid rammed earth wall, 300mm (12in), no stabilizers							
Rammed earth	0.083 (Aggregate, general)	1601 kg/m³	49.6 m³ 79,410 kg	6,591 MJ	0.0052	413 kg	
Totals				**6,591 MJ**		**413 kg**	Does not include insulation.
Highest Impact							
Double wythes 200mm (8in) each, 150mm (6in) rigid foam insulation between wythes							
Rammed earth with 5% cement stabilizer	0.68 (Cement stabilized soil @ 5%)	1601 kg/m³	66 m³ 105,666 kg	71,853 MJ	0.024	2,536 kg	
Reinforcing bar	17.4 (Bar and rod, average recycled content)	1 kg/m	156 m 156 kg	2,714 MJ	1.4	218 kg	
Rigid foam insulation	88.6 (Expanded polystyrene)	24.8 kg/m³	24.8 m³ 615 kg	15,252 MJ	3.29	2,023 kg	
Totals				**89,819 MJ**		**4,777 kg**	

Transportation: Earth transportation by 35 ton truck would equate to 74.6–99.3 MJ per kilometer of travel to the building site. *Typically from engineeringtoolbox.com

Insulation on either side of the wall will force a builder to create a finished surface over the insulation, which adds cost and complexity to the wall system and isolates all of the available thermal mass on one side or the other. Core insulation is more effective and leaves the rammed earth as the finish on both sides, but complicates the forming and tamping process and limits choice of insulation to materials that can resist the compressive forces of the tamping process.

MATERIAL COSTS: *NEGLIGIBLE TO MODERATE*

Components for good rammed earth may be sourced on site at negligible cost, but pre-mixed versions with Portland cement stabilizers may be moderately expensive. The addition of rigid foam insulation between two wythes of rammed earth will raise costs considerably.

LABOR INPUT: *HIGH TO VERY HIGH*

Rammed earth construction is labor intensive. The use of machinery can reduce the amount of labor involved in excavating, mixing and tamping earth, but even machine time can be extensive. Building, erecting and disassembling formwork takes a lot of time regardless of tamping method. However, when used as the finished wall surface, a rammed earth wall eliminates the need for steps often required to sheath and finish other walls.

SKILL LEVEL REQUIRED FOR THE HOMEOWNER: *MODERATE*

Mixing and tamping soil does not require prior experience, but the creation and use of formwork does, as does the operation of excavation and dirt-moving machinery. A first-time builder will want some training or experience prior to undertaking a major rammed earth project.

SOURCING/AVAILABILITY: *EASY TO MODERATE*

Soils suitable for rammed earth construction are widely available, as are the ingredients for amending soils that are not inherently suitable. The equipment used for excavating and tamping earth is common to other more conventional construction activities and should be easy to source.

Insulation materials will vary in availability depending on type and location.

DURABILITY: *MODERATE TO HIGH*

Rammed earth buildings have a long history in many parts of the world, with some examples lasting well over a thousand years. Erosion and/or spalling caused by excessive wetting are the main causes of failure. Creating adequate roof overhangs and site drainage can control this. Water repellents are sometimes mixed into the rammed earth or applied over exposed surfaces. These must not affect the strength of the mix or overly reduce permeability. Plasters and other forms of siding can also prevent moisture damage.

Rammed earth, like all soil-based construction types, can be repaired quite easily if damaged, by the addition of new soil mix.

CODE COMPLIANCE

Rammed earth construction is an accepted solution in some building codes, in regions where the technique has historical precedent. A good deal of testing and modeling of rammed earth walls has been done around the world, and the available data is usually sufficient to justify the use of rammed earth as a load-bearing wall for one- and two-story structures. A structural engineer may be needed to approve drawings to obtain a permit.

INDOOR AIR QUALITY

Uncontaminated earth is generally agreed to have no inherently dangerous elements and is consistent with the aims of high indoor air quality.

Soil contamination, from natural sources like radon or synthetic sources like petrochemicals, is possible, and it is wise to inspect and/or test soils carefully before using them to build a house.

FUTURE DEVELOPMENT

Code development for rammed earth is moving forward in several countries, including the US and Australia. Widespread code acceptance is likely to encourage more rammed earth construction.

As the basics of rammed earth construction have remained the same for thousands of years, revolutionary developments in technique are unlikely. However, processes to reduce labor input for formwork and soil mixing and tamping are likely to be streamlined, making the system more affordable.

Resources for further research

Walker, Peter. Rammed Earth: Design and Construction Guidelines. Watford, UK: BRE hop, 2005. Print.

Easton, David. The Rammed Earth House. White River Junction, VT: Chelsea Green, 1996. Print.

Minke, Gernot. Earth Construction Handbook: The Building Material Earth in Modern Architecture. Southampton, UK: WIT, 2000. Print.

Rael, Ronald. Earth Architecture. New York: Princeton Architectural Press, 2009. Print.

Morton, Tom. Earth Masonry: Design and Construction Guidelines. Bracknell, UK: IHS BRE, 2008. Print.

Jaquin, Paul, and Charles Augarde. Earth Building: History, Science and Conservation. Bracknell, UK: IHS BRE, 2012. Print.

Keefe, Laurence. Earth Building: Methods and Materials, Repair and Conservation. London: Taylor & Francis, 2005. Print.

McHenry, Paul Graham. Adobe and Rammed Earth Buildings: Design and Construction. Tucson, AZ: University of Arizona, 1989. Print.

Rammed Earth Wall Ratings

	Best 1–Worst 10 (rating)	Notes
Environmental Impacts	1–6	Insulation strategy and use of cement stabilization will alter impacts.
Embodied Energy	1–10	Cement stabilization and insulation strategy will alter EE significantly.
Waste Generated	1	
Energy Efficiency	1–8	Insulation strategy will affect efficiency significantly.
Material Costs	1–5	Source of rammed earth material and insulation strategy will affect costs significantly.
Labor Inputs	7–10	Degree of mechanization will affect labor impacts.
Skill Level Required by Homeowner	3–6	Amount and complexity of formwork required will affect skill level required.
Sourcing and Availability	1–4	
Durability and Longevity	1–4	Rammed earth walls are susceptible to deterioration under poor conditions, but have a good overall performance record.
Building Code Compliance	2–6	Rammed earth walls are not an accepted solution in most codes, but alternative compliance pathways are common.
Indoor Air Quality	1–3	Rammed earth walls will typically have excellent IAQ properties, but can be affected by rare mold/moisture issues.

Compressed earth block (CEB) walls

What the cheerleaders say...	What the detractors say...
Abundant raw materials	Prone to moisture degradation
Simple to build	No insulation value
Low embodied energy	Limited availability
Affordable	

Applications for compressed earth block wall systems

- Load-bearing exterior walls
- Infill walls
- Interior walls
- Decorative interior elements

Basic materials

- Earth
- Stabilizer (cement or lime where required)
- Mortar or slip
- Insulation (where required)
- Water-resistant finish (where required)
- Control layers:
  - **Water** — The finished earth block is typically the water control layer. It is possible to use vapor-permeable, water-resistant finishes on the rammed earth surface or to include water-resistant additives in the earth mix before ramming. It is also possible to use additional cladding over the blocks, but this is rarely done.
  - **Air and vapor** — Solid and dense, CEB is an effective air and vapor control layer when laid in continuous, gap-free mortar or slip beds.
  - **Thermal** — A CEB wall requires an additional thermal control layer in hot or cold climates (see Thermal Mass vs. Insulation sidebar). This layer can be on the interior, exterior or center of the wall.

How the system works

Compressed earth blocks are masonry units made from rammed earth. As with monolithic rammed earth, a moist soil mix with relatively low clay content (10–30 percent is common) is rammed into block forms under high pressure to achieve a desired level of compaction. The soil mix varies by region and builder, but it is common to "stabilize" the mix with 5–10 percent of portland cement or other hydraulic binder.

Block presses can be simple machines that use leverage and human effort or purpose-made hydraulic presses that include soil-mixing capability. Blocks are typically given time to air dry/cure before being used in a wall.

Once pressed, CEBs are laid up in a running bond similar to other masonry units. Mortars can be clay based, rather than using more conventional lime or cement mixes. Conventional mortaring techniques are common with joints ranging from 6–20 mm (¼–¾ inch). Some builders elect to brush on a thick clay slip rather than lay an actual mortar bed. Blocks are set onto the wet slip and slid into place.

All the conventions of block and bricklaying apply to building with CEBs. Window and door

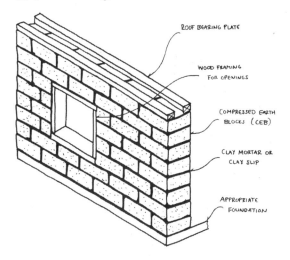

ROOF BEARING PLATE

WOOD FRAMING FOR OPENINGS

COMPRESSED EARTH BLOCKS (CEB)

CLAY MORTAR OR CLAY SLIP

APPROPRIATE FOUNDATION

Compressed earthblock. (CHESTER RENNIE)

openings use wooden, concrete or steel lintels. At the top of the wall, a wooden, concrete or steel beam system is used to provide rigidity and a fastening point for the roof.

CEB walls require insulation in most climates. This can be applied on the interior or exterior wall, or a double wythe system can be insulated in the core.

Tips for successful walls

1. Soils used for CEBs must be very well mixed. Even distribution of clay and any additional binders (cement, slag, lime, fly ash) is crucial to final wall strength. With most other earthen building systems, the mix is made very wet, which aids in thorough mixing. But CEB mixes do not benefit from the plasticity that water

adds, and require plenty of mechanical mixing to achieve best results instead.

2. Test potential soils well before using. The make-up of the soil is critical to the performance of the wall. A lot of soil is required to make a CEB wall, and changes in its composition will mean that mixes must change too. Make sample blocks and use reliable sources to determine whether or not you will need stabilizers, and which ones are most appropriate for the soil type.

3. Consistent sizing of blocks is important if they are going to be attached using slip instead of mortar. The slip doesn't provide enough thickness to make up differences in heights between inconsistent blocks. If blocks are not the same heights, using a mortar joint will help prevent stress points and cracking.

4. Following the conventions of brick/block laying will provide the best results. Though the material in earth blocks is unique, the proper techniques for building are common to all masonry units.

Pros and cons

ENVIRONMENTAL IMPACTS

Harvesting — *Negligible to Low.* Site soils will have negligible impacts. Regionally sourced soil will have minimal impacts from the machinery used for excavation and handling.

If hydraulic binders are used, they are mechanically extracted from quarries and can have low to high impacts on habitat and ground and surface water contamination and flow.

Manufacturing — *Negligible to Low.* Human-powered presses will have negligible impacts. Hydraulic presses will have impacts from the fossil fuel use of the machinery.

Hydraulic binders like lime and portland cement are fired at extremely high temperatures and have high impacts including fossil fuel use, air and water pollution and greenhouse gas emissions.

Transportation — *Negligible to High.* Sample building uses 52,833 kg of rammed earth:

49.7 MJ per km by 35 ton truck

Many CEB manufacturers bring equipment to a site and use native soil, resulting in negligible impacts. Blocks are a heavy and high-volume material and accrue impacts proportional to distance traveled. CEB tends to be used regionally, with little long distance shipping.

Installation — *Negligible.*

WASTE: *LOW*

Biodegradable/Compostable — Unmodified soil ingredients, block offcuts, natural insulation materials.
Landfill — Cement bags, manufactured insulation offcuts.

ENERGY EFFICIENCY: *LOW*

An earth block wall has a lot of thermal mass and can easily be an airtight wall system, but it has no inherent insulation value (see Thermal Mass vs. Insulation sidebar). The overall energy efficiency of a CEB wall system will be dependent on the insulation strategy. Insulation can be placed on either the interior or exterior of the wall or a double wythe system can have insulation in the center of the wall.

Insulation on either side of the wall will force a builder to create a finished surface over the insulation, which adds cost and complexity to the wall system and isolates all of the available thermal mass on one side or the other. Core insulation is more effective and leaves the blocks exposed as the finish on both sides. Unlike rammed earth walls, core insulation can be added after the walls are built, leaving many more options for the builder, including loose-fill insulation types poured between the wythes.

MATERIAL COSTS: *LOW TO MODERATE*

The basic soil mixture for blocks may be found on site or close to the building site for no or little cost. Pre-manufactured blocks can range widely in price

Compressed Earth Block (CEB) Embodied Energy

Wall type	Material embodied energy from I.C.E. in MJ/kg	Weight to volume ratio of material*	Volume of material in sample 1000sf/92.9m² building	Sample building embodied energy	Material embodied carbon from I.C.E. in kgCO₂e/kg	Sample building embodied carbon	Notes
Lowest Impact							
Rammed earth soil	0.083 (Aggregate, general)	1601 kg/m³	33 m³ 52,833 kg	4,385 MJ	0.0052	275 kg	
Wood frame openings and beam	2.5	450 kg/m³	1.1 m³ 495 kg	1,238 MJ	0.2	99 kg	
Totals				5,623 MJ		374 kg	Does not include plaster or insulation.
Highest Impact							
Rammed earth with 5% cement stabilizer	0.68 (Cement stabilized soil @ 5%)	1601 kg/m³	33 m³ 52,833 kg	35,926 MJ	0.061	3,223 kg	
Wood frame openings and beam	2.5	450 kg/m³	1.1 m³ 495 kg	1,238 MJ	0.2	99 kg	
Totals				37,164 MJ		3,322 kg	Does not include plaster or insulation.

Transportation: Soil/block transportation by 35 ton truck would equate to 49.7 MJ per kilometer of travel to the building site. *Typically from engineeringtoolbox.com depending on the economies of scale, with costs ranging from $1–4 per block regionally.

LABOR INPUT: *MODERATE TO HIGH*

There are two distinct labor phases in CEB construction. Making the blocks requires excavation, movement, mixing and compressing of soil. The more mechanization in this process, the less labor required. It is also possible to purchase ready-made blocks from a supplier in some regions, which eliminates this portion of the labor from the on-site inputs of the builder. For builders who don't want to learn about soil mixes and block making but wish to use rammed earth material, CEBs make rammed earth available as a product.

Laying up CEBs requires the same labor input as any masonry unit construction.

SKILL LEVEL REQUIRED FOR THE HOMEOWNER: *MODERATE*

The operation of a low-tech, manual earth block press can be learned quickly. Experimentation and research can help a novice arrive at an appropriate soil mixture.

Purpose-made block pressing machines are expensive and complicated, and this type of production is usually left to professional producers.

The laying of CEBs requires the same skill sets required for any masonry unit construction. A newcomer can learn to lay blocks, and many avenues for such training exist and would be recommended prior to tackling an entire wall system. Working with clay mortar is more forgiving than with hydraulic mortars, as working times are greatly extended.

SOURCING/AVAILABILITY: *EASY TO DIFFICULT*

Soils suitable for making earth blocks are widely available, as are the ingredients needed to amend less ideal soils.

A manual block press can be built using very basic and widely available materials. Hydraulic block presses are made by only a few companies and will need to be imported to most regions.

CEB producers are common in some regions and much less so in others. Blocks are not likely to be sold at conventional building supply stores, even in areas where they are commercially produced. Research will need to be done to locate suppliers.

DURABILITY: *MODERATE TO HIGH*

Though compressed earth blocks do not have quite the same long history as rammed earth walls, the basic material is the same and will have very similar properties. CEBs are susceptible to degradation from wetting and freeze-thaw cycles. Blocks with stabilizers may be less vulnerable. Permeable paints and coatings can improve water resistance, as can plasters and other protective siding options. Adequate roof overhangs and proper site drainage can limit the amount of exposure to precipitation, helping durability.

Earth blocks are quite easy to repair, as new earth mix can be plastered over weathered blocks to restore appearance.

CODE COMPLIANCE

Commercially produced CEBs have consistent strength properties that suit codification. In some regions, CEBs are an accepted solution, and where this is not the case there are a wide range of test documents that can simplify alternative compliance applications. Because masonry unit construction is familiar and code-recognized in all jurisdictions, building officials are likely to understand the principles of the system and therefore be receptive to its use. A structural engineer's approval may be required to validate test results and apply them to a particular design.

INDOOR AIR QUALITY: *MODERATE TO HIGH*

Uncontaminated earth is generally agreed to have no inherently dangerous elements and is consistent with the aims of high indoor air quality.

Soil contamination, from natural sources like radon or synthetic sources like petrochemicals, is possible, and it is wise to inspect and/or test soils before using them to build a house.

FUTURE DEVELOPMENT

CEB construction lends itself well to more widespread acceptance and use. The building process and appearance of bricks and concrete blocks is familiar, and the switch to a raw earth version takes less adaptation than other alternatives. Block presses are well-developed machines with a proven history and lend themselves to mass production of blocks. Most regions have a large enough pool of masons capable of building CEB walls to meet growing demand.

Codification of CEB construction is made simpler by the manufacturing process, which can eliminate many of the variables that make other natural building systems hard to regulate.

Resources for further research

Galer, Titane, Hubert Guillaud, Thierry Joffroy, Claire Norton, and Oscar Salaza. *Compressed Earth Blocks: A Publication of Deutsches Zentrum Für Entwicklungstechnologien — GATE, a Division of the Deutsche Gesellschaft Für Technische Zusammenarbeit (GTZ) GmbH in Coordination with the Building Advisory Service and Information Network — BASIN.* Braunschweig, Germany: Vieweg, 1995. Print.

Rael, Ronald. *Earth Architecture.* New York: Princeton Architectural Press, 2009. Print.

Morton, Tom. *Earth Masonry: Design and Construction Guidelines.* Bracknell, UK: IHS BRE, 2008. Print.

Jaquin, Paul, and Charles Augarde. *Earth Building: History, Science and Conservation.* Bracknell, UK: IHS BRE, 2012. Print.

Keefe, Laurence. *Earth Building: Methods and Materials, Repair and Conservation.* London: Taylor & Francis, 2005. Print.

Compressed Earth Block Wall Ratings

	Best 1 — Worst 10	Notes
Environmental Impacts	(1–3)	Addition of insulation will raise impacts.
Embodied Energy	(2–7)	Addition of insulation and cement stabilization will raise EE.
Waste Generated	(1–1.5)	
Energy Efficiency	(7–9)	Additional insulation is required for efficiency.
Material Costs	(1–3)	Use of double wall system and/or insulation will raise costs.
Labor Inputs	(5–8)	Degree of mechanization in block production will affect labor inputs.
Skill Level Required By Homeowner	(1–3)	
Sourcing and Availability	(1–6)	Manufactured blocks are available regionally.
Durability and Longevity	(1–3.5)	CEB walls are susceptible to deterioration under poor conditions, but have a good overall performance record.
Building Code Compliance	(1–4)	CEB walls are an accepted solution in some regions, and alternative compliance pathways have precedents.
Indoor Air Quality	(1–3.5)	CEB walls will typically have excellent IAQ properties, but can be affected by rare mold/moisture issues.

Adobe block walls

What the cheerleaders say...	What the detractors say...
Abundant raw material	Time-consuming
Easy to build	Not durable
Low embodied energy	Not insulated
Affordable	

Applications for adobe walls

- Load-bearing exterior walls
- Infill walls
- Interior walls
- Decorative interior elements

Basic materials

- Soils with fairly high clay content (25%–40%)
- Straw or other natural fiber
- Block forms (quick release preferable)
- Mortar or slip
- Insulation (where required)
- Water-resistant finish (where required)

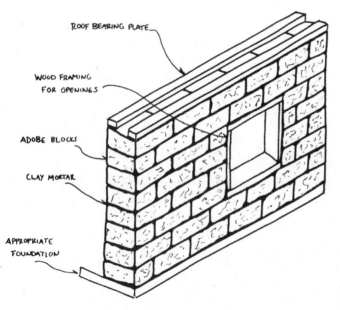

ROOF BEARING PLATE

WOOD FRAMING FOR OPENINGS

ADOBE BLOCKS

CLAY MORTAR

APPROPRIATE FOUNDATION

- Control layers:
  - **Water** — The finished adobe block is typically the water control layer. It is possible to use vapor-permeable, water-resistant finishes on the surface or to include water-resistant additives to the earth mix before forming. It is also possible to use additional cladding over the adobe, but this is rarely done.
  - **Air and Vapor** — Solid and dense, adobe is an effective air control layer when laid in continuous, gap-free mortar or slip beds. The earthen walls are vapor-permeable.
  - **Thermal** — An adobe wall requires an additional thermal control layer in hot or cold climates (see Thermal Mass vs. Insulation sidebar). This layer can be on the interior, exterior of a single wall or center of a double wythe wall.

How the system works

A soil with clay content of 25–40 percent and a good distribution of sand and silt is moistened and thoroughly mixed with chopped straw or other natural fiber. The resulting mix is placed into block forms, released from the forms and allowed to fully dry.

Once dried, adobe blocks are laid up in a running bond similar to other masonry techniques. Mortars can be clay based, rather than using more conventional lime or cement mixes. Conventional mortaring techniques are used with joints ranging from 6–20 mm (¼–¾ inch).

All of the conventions of block and bricklaying apply to building with adobe block. Window and door openings use wooden, concrete or steel lintels. At the top of the wall, a wooden, concrete or steel beam system is used to provide rigidity and a fastening point for the roof.

Adobe walls require insulation in many climates. Insulation can be applied on the interior or exterior wall, or a double wythe system can be insulated in the core.

Recently, some have experimented with "pour-in-place" systems where block forms are placed where needed on the wall, filled and the forms removed immediately. With a stiff mix, this can work well and reduce waiting time and block handling, as well as eliminating the need for mortaring dry blocks together. In this way, the system becomes a hybrid between adobe and cob.

Tips for successful walls

1. The construction of good block forms is important for adobe walls. Filling and releasing forms is done repeatedly while making adobe blocks, and a streamlined process using forms that allows quick release of material will increase productivity.

2. Soil with too much clay can be amended with additional sand and soils that are naturally too sandy can have bagged clay or imported clay soils added. Because adobe mixtures are feasible with a wide range of clay/sand/silt ratios, there is usually a way to make local soils work.

3. Create a mixing system that is appropriate to the size of the walls being built. For larger projects or those with time restraints, a more mechanized system will be useful. Check resources for tips on mixing in a variety of ways including animals, mortar mixers, tractors and backhoes.

4. Adobe walls can take a long time to build and then a long time to dry out thoroughly. Projects in cold climates or climates with a long rainy season need to be timed to leave adequate drying time before completion of finishes and occupancy.

Adobe Block Wall Embodied Energy

Wall type: 200mm (8in) by 2.4m (8ft)	Material embodied energy from I.C.E. in MJ/kg	Weight to volume ratio of material*	Volume of material in sample 1000sf/92.9m² building	Sample building embodied energy	Material embodied carbon from I.C.E. in kgCO₂e/kg	Sample building embodied carbon	Notes
Lowest Impact							
Site harvested soil, air dried							
Adobe soil	0	1401 kg/m³	33 m³ 46,233 kg	0	0	0	No EE attributed for site harvested material.
Straw	0.24 (Straw)	120 kg/m³	6.3 m³ 756 kg	181 MJ	0.01	8 kg	
Wood frame for openings and beam	2.5	450 kg/m³ (spruce lumber)	1.1 m³ 495 kg	1,238 MJ	0.2	99 kg	
Totals				**1,419 MJ**		**107 kg**	Does not include plaster or insulation.
Highest Impact							
Manufactured block	0.083 (Aggregate, general)	1401 kg/m³	33 m³ 46,233 kg	3,837 MJ	0.0052	240 kg	
Straw	0.24 (Straw)	120 kg/m³	6.3 m³ 756 kg	181 MJ	0.01	8 kg	
Wood frame for openings and beam	2.5	450 kg/m³ (spruce lumber)	1.1 m³ 495 kg	1,238 MJ	0.2	99 kg	
Totals				**5,256 MJ**		**347 kg**	Does not include plaster or insulation.

Transportation: Soil/block transportation by 35 ton truck would equate to 43.5 MJ per kilometer of travel to the building site. *Typically from engineeringtoolbox.com

Pros and cons

ENVIRONMENTAL IMPACTS

Harvesting — *Negligible to Low.* Site soils will have negligible impacts. Regionally sourced soil will have minimal impacts from the machinery used for excavation and handling.

Manufacturing — *Negligible to Low.* Human-powered processes will have negligible impacts. Mechanical mixers will have low impacts from the fossil fuel use of the machinery.

Transportation — *Negligible to Moderate.* Sample building uses 46,233 kg of adobe soil:

> 43.5 MJ per km by 35 ton truck

Adobe blocks are typically made on the construction site. As a heavy material, impacts accrue proportional to distance traveled if blocks are made off-site.

Installation — *Negligible.*

WASTE: *NEGLIGIBLE*

Biodegradable/Compostable — All unmodified soil and straw, block offcuts.

ENERGY EFFICIENCY: *LOW*

An adobe wall has a lot of thermal mass and can easily be an airtight wall system, but it has no inherent insulation value (see Thermal Mass vs. Insulation sidebar). The overall energy efficiency of an adobe wall system will depend on the insulation strategy. Insulation can be placed on either the interior or exterior of the wall or a double wythe system can have insulation in the middle of the wall.

Insulation on either side of the wall will force a builder to create a finished surface over the insulation, which adds cost and complexity to the wall system and isolates all of the available thermal mass on one side or the other. Core insulation is more effective and leaves the blocks exposed as the finish on both sides. Unlike rammed earth walls, core insulation can be added after the walls are built, leaving many more options for the builder, including loose-fill insulation types poured between the wythes.

MATERIAL COSTS: *LOW TO MODERATE*

Site harvested soils and local straw can make for very low material costs. If soil must be imported or if blocks are purchased from a manufacturer costs will rise, but in either case adobe block is typically a low cost material. Long shipping distances can add significantly to the cost.

LABOR INPUT: *MODERATE TO HIGH*

There are two stages to the creation of most adobe wall systems. The manufacture of the blocks requires labor to create the forms, make mix, place it in forms and release. The process of mortaring up the blocks requires mixing mortar, moving blocks and placing them on the wall.

The pour-in-place system reduces some of this labor and makes the process a single stage.

SKILL LEVEL REQUIRED FOR THE HOMEOWNER: *EASY TO MODERATE*

Newcomers can undertake the production of blocks with a bit of training or experience in mixing and pouring adobe. The block laying process using clay mortars is much more forgiving than using conventional cement-based mortars and can also be done by those with little previous experience, as long as the basic premises of masonry construction are followed.

SOURCING/AVAILABILITY: *EASY TO MODERATE*

In some regions, especially in the American Southwest, demand for adobe bricks is such that there are commercial production facilities and blocks may be purchased ready-made. However, in most parts of North America, adobe is a site-made material and will not be able to be sourced as a building product.

DURABILITY: *MODERATE TO HIGH*

Adobe is a material with a long, proven history. It shares with other earthen building techniques vulnerability to deterioration due to exposure to water. But when kept relatively dry by the use of generous roof overhangs, good foundations and smart building details, adobe buildings can last for centuries. Adobe walls are straightforward to repair by applying more wet mix to any worn or problematic areas.

Plasters and other protective sidings can reduce the potential for damage from precipitation.

CODE COMPLIANCE

There is acceptance of adobe construction in some codes, including some prescriptive standards used regionally. Sufficient testing of adobe walls exists to inform the design of a wall system by a structural engineer where codes are not in place.

INDOOR AIR QUALITY: *MODERATE TO HIGH*

Uncontaminated earth is generally agreed to have no inherently dangerous elements and is consistent with the aims of high indoor air quality.

Soil contamination, from natural sources like radon or synthetic sources like petrochemicals, is possible, and it is wise to inspect and/or test soils carefully before using them to build a house.

FUTURE DEVELOPMENT

Adobe block construction has a long history and the building method is basic and well understood, so the technique and materials are unlikely to change significantly. Mixing equipment and mechanized production already exist and are in use in some

Adobe Wall Ratings

	Best 1 2 3 4 5 6 7 Worst 8 9 10	Notes
Environmental Impacts	▓ (to ~3)	Addition of insulation will raise impacts.
Embodied Energy	▓ (to ~3)	Addition of insulation will raise EE.
Waste Generated	▓ (to ~1)	
Energy Efficiency	▓ (7 to 10)	Insulation is required to achieve energy efficiency.
Material Costs	▓ (to ~4)	Addition of insulation will raise costs.
Labor Inputs	▓ (5 to 10)	Degree of mechanization in block production will affect labor inputs.
Skill Level Required by Homeowner	▓ (to ~4)	
Sourcing and Availability	▓ (to ~4)	Block availability will vary regionally.
Durability and Longevity	▓ (to ~4)	Adobe walls are susceptible to deterioration under poor conditions, but have a good overall performance record.
Building Code Compliance	▓ (to ~5)	Adobe walls are an accepted solution in some regions, and alternative compliance pathways have precedents.
Indoor Air Quality	▓ (to ~4)	Adobe will typically have excellent IAQ properties, but can be affected by rare mold/moisture issues.

areas, and it is likely that this will spread as interest in affordable, low-impact construction grows. High transportation costs for heavy materials create conditions for regionalized production, rather than large, central factories. The long drying times for adobe blocks mean that production requires climates with warm temperatures and infrequent rain. Creating large, indoor facilities and/or the use of fossil fuels to create ideal drying conditions would add cost and complexity to an otherwise simple process. However, costs would be much lower than for fired brick, so it is feasible that production facilities could develop in areas outside historic adobe regions.

Resources for further research

Schroder, Lisa, and Vince Ogletree. *Adobe Homes for All Climates: Simple, Affordable, and Earthquake-Resistant Natural Building Techniques*. White River Junction, VT: Chelsea Green, 2010. Print.

McHenry, Paul Graham. *Adobe and Rammed Earth Buildings: Design and Construction*. Tucson, AZ: University of Arizona, 1989. Print.

Byrne, Michael, Dottie Larson, and Amy Haskell. *New Adobe Home*. Layton, UT: Gibbs Smith, 2009. Print.

McHenry, Paul Graham, Jr. *Adobe: Build It Yourself, 2nd Revised Edition*. Tucson, AZ: University of Arizona, 1985. Print.

Sanchez, Laura, and Al Sanchez. *Adobe Houses for Today: Flexible Plans for Your Adobe Home*. Santa Fe, NM: Sunstone, 2001. Print.

Van Hall, Michael. *The Cheap-Ass Curmudgeon's Guide to Dirt: Hand Building with Adobe, Papercrete, Paper-Adobe and More*. Tucson, AZ: Cheap-Ass, 2009. Print.

Foundations as walls

Many of the foundation systems described in the previous chapter can also be used as above-grade walls. There can be some advantages to having one continuous material extending from footings to roof, potentially creating less seams and thermal bridges. The foundations that also work as walls nearly all require the addition of an adequate amount of thermal insulation to suit the climate.

Refer to the foundation chapter for detailed consideration of these options:

- Earthbag
- Stone
- Rammed earth tires
- Lightweight CMU
- Aerated autoclaved concrete (AAC)
- Durisol/Faswall insulated concrete forms (ICF)

The resource sections for each of these materials will supply information on using these materials and techniques for walls as well as for foundations. The ratings used in Chapter 1: Foundations will be the same for use in walls.

Infill insulations

Numerous types of infill insulation materials can be used in conjunction with many of the wall and roof systems covered in this book. These materials cannot be used structurally (though a few have some structural significance within a wall). They are placed, formed, sprayed or stuffed into cavities in a structural wall.

———— ∾∾ ————

Cotton batt insulation

What the cheerleaders say...	What the detractors say...
Nontoxic	Difficult to cut
Made from recycled denim	Expensive
Simple to install	Limited distribution
Code-approved	

Applications for cotton batt insulation

- Wall insulation
- Ceiling insulation
- Raised floor insulation

Basic materials

- Post-industrial recycled cotton
- Boron-based fire retardant

Pros and cons

ENVIRONMENTAL IMPACTS

Harvesting — *Low.* Cotton batt insulation is made from offcuts produced by the clothing industry, in particular from denim jean manufacturing.

Manufacturing — *Moderate.* The shredding and binding of the cotton requires numerous mechanical processes that have low or moderate impacts related to the energy use of the machinery.

Transportation — *Low to High.* Sample building uses 1,023 kg of cotton insulation:

1.5 MJ per km by 15 ton truck
0.96 MJ per km by 35 ton truck

There are currently few production facilities in North America. Insulation batts are a high-volume material and accrue impacts proportional to distance traveled.

Installation — *Negligible.* The insulation batts are formed without the use of glues and carry no health warnings on their labels.

0

000# Cotton batt insulation

WASTE: *MODERATE*

Recyclable — Plastic packaging.
Landfill — Insulation offcuts.

ENERGY EFFICIENCY: *HIGH*

R-value: ~3.7 (RSI-0.65) per inch

Cotton insulation has a fairly high R-value, but must be properly installed to avoid settling and voids around framing members and other obstacles in the

Cotton batt.

wall. The material is vapor-permeable and has a high amount of moisture storage capacity, but requires a separate air control layer.

MATERIAL COSTS: *MODERATE TO HIGH*

Cotton batt insulation is not widely distributed, and costs are higher than other batt products with wider distribution.

LABOR INPUT: *LOW TO MODERATE*

Cotton batts have similar installation times as other batt insulations. Cutting of the cotton batts can be more difficult and time-consuming than comparable materials, but batts come with pre-cut lines that assist with resizing.

SKILL LEVEL REQUIRED FOR THE HOMEOWNER: *LOW*

The installation of batt insulation is very straightforward, but care must be taken to ensure a tight fit in all cavities with no gaps or voids, to ensure full thermal value.

SOURCING/AVAILABILITY: *LOW TO MODERATE*

Cotton batts are not commonly available at all building supply stores, but distribution has widened

Cotton Batt Insulation Embodied Energy

Insulation value: Walls = R-30 Ceiling = R-50	Material embodied energy from I.C.E. in MJ/kg	Weight to volume ratio of material*	Volume of material in sample 1000sf/92.9m² building	Sample building embodied energy	Material embodied carbon from I.C.E. in kgCO₂e/kg	Sample building embodied carbon	Notes
Walls @ 200mm (8 in)	27.1** (Miscellaneous – Cotton padding)	31 kg/m³	33 m³ 1023 kg	27,723 MJ	1.28	1,309 kg	**ICE figure for cotton padding, no specific figure given for insulation. Figure assumes virgin cotton, but most products made with high recycled content.
Ceiling @ 350mm (14 in)	27.1	31 kg/m³	33 m³ 1023 kg	27,723 MJ	1.28	1,309 kg	
Totals				**55,446 MJ**		**2,618 kg**	

Transportation: Batt transportation by 35 ton truck would equate to 2 MJ per kilometer of travel to the building site. *Typically from engineeringtoolbox.com

104 *Making Better Buildings*

considerably in the past few years and will likely continue to expand to meet growing demand.

DURABILITY: *MODERATE TO HIGH*

Kept reasonably dry, this insulation will have a long life span. Cotton could provide a food source for mold in overly moist conditions, but the boron added as a fire retardant also has anti-fungal properties.

CODE COMPLIANCE

All applicable code standards for batt insulation are met or exceeded.

INDOOR AIR QUALITY: *HIGH*

Batt insulation is usually contained behind an air or vapor control barrier and a wall finish, and does not directly affect IAQ. Cotton insulation does release some dust during installation, but does not contain any known carcinogens or off-gassing binders and the fibers themselves are not considered dangerous.

FUTURE DEVELOPMENT

Cotton insulation is likely to grow in popularity as it is compatible with conventional building methods but has lower embodied energy and minimal health risks compared to conventional batts. More manufacturing facilities and better distribution will accompany greater demand.

Resources for further research

Bynum, Richard T. *Insulation Handbook.* New York: McGraw-Hill, 2001. Print.

Cotton Batt Insulation Ratings

	Best 1	2	3	4	5	6	Worst 7	8	9	10	Notes All insulations require wall/roof structure
Environmental Impacts			▓	▓							Agricultural impacts vary and are difficult to assess. Most cotton insulation is from recycled sources.
Embodied Energy							▓				Figures difficult to assess.
Waste Generated	▓	▓									
Energy Efficiency	▓										
Material Costs				▓	▓						
Labor Inputs	▓	▓	▓								Similar to all batt insulation.
Skill Level Required by Homeowner	▓										
Sourcing and Availability	▓	▓	▓	▓							Production is regional.
Durability and Longevity	▓	▓	▓								Under good conditions material has excellent properties.
Building Code Compliance	▓	▓									Accepted solution in some regions, thorough alternative compliance documentation exists.
Indoor Air Quality	▓	▓									Generally no off-gassing glues or binders.

Straw/clay, straw light clay or slipstraw insulation

What the cheerleaders say...	What the detractors say...
Natural, abundant materials	Long drying times
Ideal moisture-handling characteristics	Labor intensive
Affordable	Comparatively low insulation value

Applications for slipstraw insulation

- Infill insulation in frame structures

Basic materials

- Straw
- Clay slip
- Borax (as an anti-fungal, if required)
- Temporary wooden formwork

How the system works

Loose straw is tossed with a runny clay slip until lightly coated. The straw/clay mixture is then placed in the wall cavity between temporary form boards. The insulation is lightly tamped in lifts as it is built up in the cavity. Slip forms can be moved up the wall as straw/clay is added. The material is stable in the wall immediately after tamping.

The finished insulation is left exposed on both sides of the wall in order to dry. The straw/clay provides a dense, flat surface and makes an ideal substrate for plasters. Sheet barriers and more conventional siding and wall covering can also be used.

Tips for successful installation

1. There are plans for simple, homemade straw/clay mixing devices that are low-cost and increase productivity dramatically. Even for a single building, it is well worth the time to construct a mixer.
2. Work out accurate systems for measuring quantities of straw and clay slip for mixing. An overly wet mixture compacts a lot when tamped, lowering insulation values and increasing drying times.
3. Allow sufficient time in the building schedule for drying. This process can take up to one week per 2.5 cm (1 inch) of wall thickness, depending on weather conditions. This can require scheduling adjustments for builders unused to such long drying times.
4. As the insulation value of the material depends on the degree of compaction that occurs when the straw/clay is tamped into the forms, ensure consistent installation procedures throughout the process, especially when larger crews are involved.
5. Use hex-head screws to secure formwork. Forms are moved frequently and typical screw heads get covered in clay and can be hard to locate and use.

Straw clay. (KELLY JACOBSEN)

Pros and cons

ENVIRONMENTAL IMPACTS

Harvesting — *Negligible to Moderate.* Clay harvested from the site will have negligible impacts. Clay and straw harvested locally will have low impacts. Bagged clay is mechanically extracted from pits and dried using fossil fuel heat, and will have moderate impacts, including air and water pollution.

Manufacturing — *Negligible.*

Transportation — *Negligible.* Sample building uses 7,920 kg of straw:

> 11.9 MJ per km by 15 ton truck

Sample building uses 581 kg of clay soil:

> 0.9 MJ per km by 15 ton truck

Installation — *Low.* Formwork may be reused elsewhere in the building.

WASTE: *NEGLIGIBLE*

Biodegradable / Compostable — All soil and straw.

ENERGY EFFICIENCY

R-value: Depends on density of material. Tested per-inch values range from:

- R 0.9 at 705 kg/m³ to R 1.9 at 164 kg/m³ (Forest Products Lab results)
- R 0.69 at 700 kg/m³ to R 1.44 at 300 kg/m³ (Gernot Minke)

Where insulation value is a critical design factor, sample mixtures can be created, dried and weighed to estimate the R-value.

Straw/clay is not an air control layer, and will require a sheathing material to achieve insulation values.

MATERIAL COSTS: *LOW*

Both straw and clay soil are low-cost components, and though volumes required are high, costs are relatively low.

LABOR INPUT: *HIGH*

There are three components to the labor input for slipstraw insulation:

- Mixing the material involves making slip from water and clay soil, and then tossing the straw with the slip.
- Creating and moving formwork. Type of formwork will depend on framing style of the walls.
- Tamping slipstraw into wall cavities.

Straw/Clay Insulation Embodied Energy

Insulation: Walls to R-30	Material embodied energy from I.C.E. in MJ/kg	Weight to volume ratio of material*	Volume of material in sample 1000sf/92.9m² building	Sample building embodied energy	Material embodied carbon from I.C.E. in kgCO₂e/kg	Sample building embodied carbon	Notes
Walls @ 400 mm (16 in) @ 164 kg/m³							
Straw	0.24	120 kg/m³	66m³ 7920 kg	1,901 MJ	0.01	79 kg	
Clay	0.083 (Aggregate, general)	44 kg/m³	13.2 m³ 581 kg	48 MJ	0.024	14 kg	Assumes 20% clay content by volume.
Totals				**1,949 MJ**		**93 kg**	

Transportation: Straw transportation by 15 ton truck would equate to 11.8 MJ per kilometer of travel to the building site. Clay transportation by 15 ton truck would equate to 0.9 MJ per kilometer of travel to the building site. *Typically from engineeringtoolbox.com

Each of these phases is fairly labor intensive, resulting in a system with significant embedded labor time.

SKILL LEVEL REQUIRED FOR THE HOMEOWNER: *MODERATE*

Slipstraw mixing and placing is well within the capabilities of novice builders, as long as they take care to create consistent mixes and tamp evenly. Requiring only basic carpentry skills, formwork can be built by beginners.

SOURCING/AVAILABILITY: *EASY TO MODERATE*

The ingredients for straw/clay insulation are widely available in most regions. Straw must typically be sourced directly from farms or straw brokers. Clay for slip making can be found in some site soils or obtained in bagged form from pottery supply

outlets. Materials for formwork (typically plywood or planks) can be sourced via building supply stores. A simple straw/clay tumbler can be built or adapted from recycled or found materials.

DURABILITY: *MODERATE TO HIGH*

Straw/clay insulation has lasted for hundreds of years in a number of different climates. Clay coatings have a beneficial effect on straw, wood and other natural fibers. The hydrophilic clay can help moderate the moisture content of the straw and restrict the likelihood of mold growth. Fire resistance of straw is dramatically increased when lightly coated in clay.

CODE COMPLIANCE

Straw/clay is not prescribed in any North American building codes. Some lab testing of the material has been carried out, but results vary widely and have not

Straw Clay Insulation Ratings

	Best							Worst			Notes
	1	2	3	4	5	6	7	8	9	10	**All insulations require wall/roof structure**
Environmental Impacts	▮										Addition of plaster or sheathing will increase impacts.
Embodied Energy	▮										Addition of plaster or sheathing will increase EE.
Waste Generated	▮										
Energy Efficiency				▮▮▮▮							Density of mixture impacts efficiency and can be difficult to control.
Material Costs	▮										
Labor Inputs							▮▮▮				Degree of mechanization and complexity of formwork impact labor inputs.
Skill Level Required by Homeowner				▮▮							Degree of mechanization and complexity of formwork impact skill level required. Accuracy required for consistent density.
Sourcing and Availability	▮▮▮										Widely available materials, but not conventionally sourced.
Durability and Longevity	▮▮▮										Straw/clay walls are susceptible to deterioration under poor conditions, but have a good overall performance record.
Building Code Compliance					▮▮▮						Not an accepted solution in any codes. Some documentation exists to assist with alternative compliance pathways.
Indoor Air Quality	▮▮▮										Inadequate drying time can result in mold concerns. Properly dry, IAQ is excellent.

originated in certified laboratories. The variability of the mixtures means that it is difficult to accurately quantify insulation value, fire resistance and other elements of code requirements. The time-proven history of straw/clay, however, speaks to its viability, and many code-approved buildings have been able to use straw/clay insulation based on existing test figures and engineer or architect's approval.

INDOOR AIR QUALITY: *MODERATE TO HIGH*

Both straw and clay have excellent moisture handling and storage capabilities, and the straw/clay mix has not shown itself to be prone to mold growth (as long as adequate drying times have been allotted). In conjunction with a natural plaster finish, the material can contribute to a building with very good IAQ.

FUTURE DEVELOPMENT

Straw/clay does not readily lend itself to large-scale production, and is likely to remain a choice of dedicated owner-builders and professionals committed to its strengths as a natural insulation. While bulk mixing of the material would be easy to achieve, the long drying times required do not mesh well with typical construction schedules. It is likely that further testing of the material will make it easier to justify its use, but the choice to do so will remain that of the enthusiast.

Resources for further research

Baker-Laporte, Paula, and Robert Laporte. *Econest: Creating Sustainable Sanctuaries of Clay, Straw, and Timber.* Salt Lake City, UT: Gibbs Smith, 2005. Print.

Thornton, J. *Initial Material Characterization of Straw Light Clay.* Ottawa, ON: Canada Mortgage and Housing Corporation, 2004. Print.

Minke, Gernot. *Building with Earth: Design and Technology of a Sustainable Architecture.* Basel, Switzerland: Birkhäuser, 2012. Print.

Hempcrete insulation

What the cheerleaders say...	What the detractors say...
Carbon neutral insulation system	Long drying times
Mold and moisture resistant	Material difficult to source
Airtight and vapor-permeable	Expensive
Renewable and abundant source materials	Labor intensive
	Relatively low R-value

Hempcrete insulation.

Applications for hempcrete insulation

- Infill insulation in frame walls

Basic materials

- Hemp hurd or shiv
- Lime
- Setting agents (cement, hydraulic lime or other pozzolans) if required/desired

How the system works

The hurd or shiv of the hemp plant is the woody core left over once the fiber has been stripped away. This hurd is lightly coated with hydrated (and sometimes hydraulic) lime and water and the resulting mix is placed into formwork on the wall. Slip forms can be moved up the wall as hempcrete is added. The material is stable in the wall immediately after tamping. Purpose-built machinery has also been developed to spray hempcrete into wall cavities, but this method is not yet common in North America.

The finished insulation is left exposed on both sides of the wall in order to dry. The hempcrete provides a dense, flat surface and makes an ideal substrate for plasters. Sheet barriers and more conventional siding and wall covering can also be used.

Tips for successful installation

1. Hempcrete can be difficult to mix with typical on-site mixing equipment. The dry nature of the mix combined with the small, lightweight hurd does not work well in conventional cement mixers or mortar mixers. Mixers that actively stir rather than tumble will work faster and with fewer problems.
2. Work out accurate systems for measuring quantities of hemp, lime and water. An overly wet mixture compacts a lot when tamped, lowering insulation values and increasing drying times.
3. Allow sufficient time in the building schedule for drying. This process can take up to one week per 2.5 cm (1 inch) of thickness, depending on weather conditions. This can require scheduling adjustments for builders unused to such long drying times. The addition of a portion of portland cement, hydraulic lime or other hydraulic binder can reduce drying times but will also increase the density of the finished insulation.
4. As the insulation value of the material depends on the degree of compaction that occurs when the hempcrete is tamped into the forms, ensure consistent installation procedures throughout the process, especially when larger crews are involved.
5. Use hex-head screws to secure formwork. Forms are moved frequently and typical screw heads get covered in lime and can be hard to locate and use.

Pros and cons

ENVIRONMENTAL IMPACTS

Harvesting — *Low to Moderate.* Hemp tends to be a low-impact crop, as it typically requires little, if any, pesticide or herbicide. It does often require large inputs of fertilizer when grown commercially, but yields of hemp straw per acre tend to be much higher than with other grain straw.

Lime and hydraulic binders are mechanically extracted from quarries and can have low to high impacts on habitat and ground and surface water contamination and flow.

Manufacturing — *Moderate to High.* Hemp stalks require mechanical cutting and shredding, with relatively low impacts.

The production of lime is very energy intensive, requiring burning of limestone at high temperatures. Unlike portland cement, lime recombines with CO_2 from the atmosphere while curing, leaving a lower carbon footprint than other binders.

Transportation — *Moderate to High.* Sample building uses 9,075 kg of hempcrete:

> 13.6 MJ per km by 15 ton truck
> 8.5 MJ per km by 35 ton truck
> 1.45 MJ per km by ocean freighter

Hemp is not widely grown in North America and may have to travel long distances. It is a lightweight material, offsetting some transportation effects. Lime is a heavy material and accrues impacts proportional to distance traveled. Premixed hempcrete products are currently imported from Europe. **Installation — *Negligible.***

WASTE: *LOW TO MODERATE*

Biodegradable/Compostable — Unmodified hemp.

Landfill — Lime and other admixture bags, hempcrete offcuts.

ENERGY EFFICIENCY

R-value: 0.9–2.5 per inch

The density of the mixture and the degree of compaction in the cavity will result in a wide potential range of R-values for hempcrete. Laboratory tests of premixed hempcrete products have given results in the range indicated, but it is possible for those values to be lower or higher in a given installation due to variable tamping density. Claims of extremely high R-values for hempcrete are not based on lab testing protocols but on notions of "mass enhanced R-value," which attempts to blend thermal resistance and thermal mass qualities. While it is true that *in situ* thermal performance can be different from measured R-value, the same is true of any insulation/wall system. Thermal resistance cannot be improved by thermal mass (see page 81).

MATERIAL COSTS: *MODERATE TO HIGH*

Chopped hemp is not widely available in North America, and specialty processing leads to high costs. Commercial hempcrete mixtures are available from Europe, but shipping costs and limited distribution raise costs.

LABOR INPUT: *HIGH*

There are two stages to the labor input for hempcrete. Mixing requires the thorough blending of water and lime (plus any admixtures) with hemp. Conventional mixing machinery is not intended for the lightweight, dry consistency of hempcrete, and finding an adequate mixing strategy is key to keeping labor input as low as possible. The material can be mixed by hand using hoe, shovel or rake, but this is slow, hard work. Pan mixers are well suited to this kind of material, but can be difficult to source.

Packing hempcrete into wall cavities is typically done manually. The material is lightweight and easy to pour into place by bucket or shovel. It is then tamped to give it cohesion. The majority of the labor is involved with making and moving the formwork used to contain the hempcrete.

Hempcrete can be installed using purpose-made sprayers if the project is in a region serviced by an equipped installer.

Hempcrete Insulation Embodied Energy

Insulation: Walls = R-30	Material embodied energy from I.C.E. in MJ/kg	Weight to volume ratio of material*	Volume of material in sample 1000sf/92.9m² building	Sample building embodied energy	Material embodied carbon from I.C.E. in kgCO₂e/kg	Sample building embodied carbon	Notes
Walls @ 400mm (16 in)	2.0**	275 kg/m³***	33 m³ 9075 kg	18,150 MJ	–	–	**EE figure from renuables.co.uk ***Weight/volume ratio from Tradical Hemcrete.
Totals				18,150 MJ		N/A	Comparable carbon figures not available. Industry figures are not weighted equivalently to other materials.

Transportation: Hempcrete transportation by 35 ton truck would equate to 8.5 MJ per kilometer of travel to the building site. Hempcrete transportation by ocean freight would equate to 1.5 MJ per kilometer of travel to the building site. *Typically from engineeringtoolbox.com

SKILL LEVEL REQUIRED FOR THE HOMEOWNER: *MODERATE*

Newcomers with some practice and careful formulation and control of tamping procedures can do the mixing and placing of hempcrete. Formwork requires basic carpentry skills. Spray applications will require a hired professional.

SOURCING/AVAILABILITY: *MODERATE TO DIFFICULT*

Hempcrete is available commercially in some regions as a do-it-yourself mix or it can be professionally installed. Commercial brands of hempcrete are often imported into North America from Europe and must be sourced outside of conventional building supply stores. The raw ingredients to make hempcrete are also available in some regions. Laws restricting the growing of industrial hemp in the US limit availability of local production, but Canadian sources are legal and can be imported into the US.

Hydrated lime is available at most masonry supply and building supply stores. Hydraulic lime, if desired, is typically imported from Europe and will require specialty sourcing.

DURABILITY: *HIGH*

The lime in combination with the high-silica hemp hurd is a very durable material. The lime mineralizes the hemp over time, making it much less susceptible to moisture damage and mold growth than other plant-fiber insulation. Protected by cladding or plasters on both sides of the wall, hempcrete can be expected to last hundreds of years.

CODE COMPLIANCE

Commercial varieties of hempcrete have undergone sufficient lab testing to gain code approval in the UK and Europe. These test results can be used in North America to show code equivalency, but at this

Hempcrete Insulation Ratings

	Best 1 2 3 4 5	Worst 6 7 8 9 10	Notes — All insulations require wall/roof structure
Environmental Impacts			Agricultural practices can vary and are difficult to assess.
Embodied Energy			Lime component requires significant energy inputs.
Waste Generated			Sacrificial forms will impact waste quantity.
Energy Efficiency			
Material Costs			Source of hemp and lime will affect costs.
Labor Inputs			Degree of mechanization and complexity of formwork required will impact labor input.
Skill Level Required by Homeowner			Complexity of formwork required will affect skill level required.
Sourcing and Availability			Production is regional in Canada. Hemp is not grown in the USA.
Durability and Longevity			
Building Code Compliance			European standards exist and may be used for alternative compliance pathways.
Indoor Air Quality			

time no codes recognize hempcrete as an accepted solution.

INDOOR AIR QUALITY: *HIGH*

Lime and mineralized hemp have excellent moisture handling capabilities and the high pH of the mixture is antifungal; both qualities lend themselves to high indoor air quality. There are no off-gassing glues or binders in most hempcrete mixes, though commercial blends should be vetted prior to ordering.

FUTURE DEVELOPMENT

The commercialization of hempcrete in Europe is due in many respects to European support for industrial hemp production. It is legal to grow hemp in Canada, but the hemp industry has been slow getting established and does not currently support production of commercial hempcrete. The growing of industrial hemp is still illegal in most of the US, so development of hempcrete is dependent on lawmakers changing current restrictions.

If European hempcrete products prove popular, greater distribution of them in North America will likely follow. This will increase access and awareness and may drive regulatory changes that will encourage regional production.

Resources for further research

Allin, Steve. *Building with Hemp*. Kenmare, Ireland: Seed, 2012. Print.

Bevan, Rachel, and Tom Woolley. *Hemp Lime Construction: A Guide to Building with Hemp Lime Composites*. London: IHS BRE, 2008. Print.

Hemp batt insulation

What the cheerleaders say...	What the detractors say...
Annually renewable resource	Expensive
Nontoxic, non irritating	Difficult to cut
Insect and vermin resistant	Commercial products mostly imported from Europe
Good hydroscopic properties	

Applications for hemp batt insulation

- Wall insulation
- Ceiling insulation
- Raised floor insulation

Basic materials

- Hemp fiber
- Recycled cotton and/or polyester fiber
- Boron (fire retardant)

How the system works

Hemp fiber, sometimes combined with cotton or polyester fiber, is spun into insulation batts in a range of sizes to fit common stud cavity dimensions.

Pros and cons

ENVIRONMENTAL IMPACTS

Harvesting — *Low.* A fast-growing bio-fiber plant, hemp can have high production yields from less-than-ideal soils. Little in the way of herbicides or pesticides is required for hemp production, though fertilizer use can be high.

Manufacturing — *Low.* Processing energy input is lower than many other insulation products. Additional fibers (cotton or polyester) are typically sourced from waste streams.

Transportation — *Low to High.* Sample building uses 1,320 kg of hemp batt:

> 2 MJ per km by 15 ton truck
> 1.25 MJ per km by 35 ton truck

0.2 MJ per km by ocean freighter

Production of hemp batts in North America is limited and batts are often imported from Europe. Impacts accrue with distance traveled, though it is a lightweight material.

Installation - *Negligible*

WASTE: *LOW*

Recyclable — Plastic packaging.
Landfill — Insulation offcuts. The addition of polyester fibers in most brands prevents the material from being fully biodegradable.

Hemp batt insulation.

ENERGY EFFICIENCY: *HIGH*

R-value: 3.7 per inch

Hemp batts have similar thermal resistance as other forms of batt insulation. As with any batt, proper installation is key to real thermal performance. Gaps and voids in the insulation near framing members, the top of the wall and around obstacles like electrical boxes will reduce overall thermal performance.

MATERIAL COSTS: *HIGH*

Limited availability keeps costs high, though the material has the potential to be cost competitive if large scale production were started in North America.

LABOR INPUT: *LOW TO MODERATE*

Installation of hemp batts will be comparable to other batt materials. Hemp fibers are very strong, and cutting the batts can be more difficult than other insulations, which adds labour time.

SKILL LEVEL REQUIRED FOR THE HOMEOWNER: *LOW*

Batt insulation can be successfully installed with very little experience, as long as care is taken to

Hemp Batt Insulation Embodied Energy

Insulation: Walls = R-30 Ceiling = R-50	Material embodied energy from I.C.E. in MJ/kg	Weight to volume ratio of material*	Volume of material in sample 1000sf/92.9m² building	Sample building embodied energy	Material embodied carbon from I.C.E. in kgCO2e/kg	Sample building embodied carbon	Notes
Lowest Impact							
Walls @ 200mm (8in)	10.5**	40 kg/m³	33 m³ 1320 kg	13,860 MJ	–	–	**EE figure from renuables.co.uk, at low end of range.
Ceiling @ 340mm (13.5 in)	10.5	40 kg/m³	32 m³ 1280 kg	13,440 MJ			
Highest Impact							
Walls @ 200mm (8 in)	33**	40 kg/m³	33 m³ 1320 kg	43,560 MJ	–	–	**EE figure from renuables.co.uk, at high end of range.
Ceiling @ 340mm (13.5 in)	33	40 kg/m³	32 m³ 1320 kg	42,240 MJ	–	–	Carbon figures not available.

Transportation: Hemp batt transportation by 15 ton truck would equate to 4 MJ per kilometer of travel to the building site. Hemp batt transportation by ocean freight would equate to 0.4 MJ per kilometer of travel to the building site. *Typically from engineeringtoolbox.com ensure tight fits in all cavities and to avoid voids or gaps.

SOURCING/AVAILABILITY: *MODERATE TO DIFFICULT*

Hemp batts are not widely available in North America. A few small Canadian producers augment a supply that is otherwise currently imported from Europe. The products are not available at most building supply stores and require user sourcing.

DURABILITY: *HIGH*

Hemp is naturally resistant to insects and rodents. Kept reasonably dry, it offers a long life span.

CODE COMPLIANCE

Producers of hemp batts have certified their products to applicable code standards. Hemp batts imported into the US from Canada or Europe may not have met all the standards required by local codes, but it should be possible to show equivalency.

INDOOR AIR QUALITY: *HIGH*

Hemp batts have no glues or binders that off-gas and the fire retardants are usually boron-based and do not have hazardous side effects. Hemp batts could provide a food source for mold growth, but kept reasonably dry they should not be an impediment to good indoor air quality.

FUTURE DEVELOPMENT

Hemp products in North America are unlikely to reach a wider market until US restrictions against the growing of industrial hemp are changed. Until then, imported hemp products will continue to have higher prices and poor distribution. The potential exists for this type of product to be produced regionally in many parts of the continent and for prices and availability to be competitive with all other insulation materials.

Hemp Batt Insulation Ratings

	Best							Worst			Notes
	1	2	3	4	5	6	7	8	9	10	**All insulations require wall/roof structure**
Environmental Impacts	▓	▓	▓	▓							Figures and sources limited. Agricultural practices can vary.
Embodied Energy						▓	▓				Figures and sources limited and wide-ranging.
Waste Generated	▓	▓									
Energy Efficiency	▓										
Material Costs						▓	▓	▓			
Labor Inputs	▓	▓	▓								
Skill Level Required by Homeowner	▓										
Sourcing and Availability			▓	▓	▓	▓	▓	▓	▓	▓	Production is limited and regional.
Durability and Longevity	▓	▓									
Building Code Compliance			▓	▓	▓						European standards exist and may be used for alternative compliance pathways.
Indoor Air Quality	▓	▓									

Perlite loose-fill insulation

What the cheerleaders say...	What the detractors say...
Durable	Asbestos concerns
High insulation value	Dusty installation
Non-settling	Difficult to source
Easy to install	Energy intensive manufacturing

Applications for perlite insulation

- Loose-fill insulation for wall cavities
- Loose-fill insulation under slab floors
- Loose-fill attic insulation

Basic materials

- Expanded, siliceous rock
- Silicon treatment for water resistance

How the system works

Perlite is a volcanic glass quarried in many parts of the world. When the crushed ore is heated it expands

Perlite.

from four to twenty times its original volume. It has been dubbed "popcorn rock." The expanded perlite is graded to a variety of particle sizes. In the forms most suitable for building insulation, the density of the material ranges from 32–150 kg/m³ (2–9 lb/ft³).

The insulation is poured into open wall cavities, attic spaces or onto grade before slab floors are poured. In walls and attics, perlite insulation does not settle after installation. For use under slab floors, the compressive strength of the perlite would have to be deemed suitable to handle live and dead loads.

Most of the perlite used for building insulation is treated with silicon to help prevent water uptake. While the cellular structure of perlite is closed, there is a lot of porous surface area on each piece of perlite that the silicon treatment is intended to reduce.

Tips for successful installation

1. Obtain a perlite product intended for building insulation purposes. Most perlite is produced for agricultural use, and while the two share many similar properties, perlite is properly graded and treated specifically for use as insulation. Agricultural versions may have a lot of fine particles that are not as well suited for thermal resistance and will not be treated to prevent moisture infiltration.
2. Do not install on windy days! Perlite beads are very lightweight and can easily become airborne. Cover insulated areas immediately after installation to prevent the beads from blowing away.

Pros and cons

ENVIRONMENTAL IMPACTS

Harvesting — *Moderate to High*. Perlite is a naturally occurring siliceous rock that is quarried in many parts of the world. Ecosystem impacts will vary with quarrying practice and governing legislation, but open-pit quarries have impacts including habitat destruction and ground and surface water contamination.

Manufacturing — High. The raw perlite ore must be heated to temperatures of 800–1200°C (1500–2200°F) to vaporize the 2–6 percent embedded water in the rock and cause it to expand. This is a fuel-intensive process with impacts including high fossil fuel use and air pollution.

Transportation – Moderate to High. Sample building uses 930–7,425 kg of perlite:

0.9 – 7 MJ per km by 35 ton truck

Perlite is produced regionally, and transportation impacts will rise with distance traveled.

Installation — Moderate. Perlite is often very dusty, and being lightweight and loose a significant amount of material can be blown from the job site resulting in messy installations.

WASTE: *MODERATE*

Biodegradable/Compostable — Leftover perlite can be left in the environment.

Recyclable — Plastic packaging materials.

ENERGY EFFICIENCY: *MODERATE TO HIGH*

R-values range from 2.5/inch at densities near 150 kg/m^3 up to 4.0/inch at 30 kg/m^3.

Perlite does not prevent the free movement of air and must therefore be used in conjunction with an air control layer of some kind to prevent unwanted heat loss.

MATERIAL COSTS: *MODERATE TO HIGH*

Perlite is not a common residential insulation material, and costs can be high depending on sourcing, packaging and distribution.

LABOR INPUT: *MODERATE TO HIGH*

Perlite is poured from relatively small bags into cavities. The bags are not heavy and the process is very simple as long as the cavity being filled is easily accessible and nothing prevents the free flow of perlite throughout the area to be insulated. Containment must be provided on all sides of the cavity.

Health Warning: Perlite is high in silica dust.

SKILL LEVEL REQUIRED FOR THE HOMEOWNER: *LOW*

Insulating with perlite requires no previous experience or special skills.

Perlite Insulation Embodied Energy

Insulation: Walls @ R-30 Ceiling @ R-50	Material embodied energy from I.C.E. in MJ/kg	Weight to volume ratio of material*	Volume of material in sample 1000sf/92.9m² building	Sample building embodied energy	Material embodied carbon from I.C.E. in kgCO₂e/kg	Sample building embodied carbon	Notes
Lowest Impact							
Walls at R-4/inch, 190mm (7.5 in)	10	30 kg/m³	31 m³ 930 kg	9,300 MJ	0.52	484 kg	
Ceiling at R-4/inch, 320mm (12.5 in)	10	30 kg/m³	29.5 m³ 885 kg	8,850 MJ	0.52	460 kg	
Highest Impact							
Walls at R-2.5/inch, 300mm (12 in)	10	150 kg/m³	49.5 m³ 7425 kg	74,250 MJ	0.52	3,861 kg	
Ceiling at R-2.5/inch, 500mm (20 in)	10	150 kg/m³	47 m³ 7050 kg	70,500 MJ	0.52	3,666 kg	

Transportation: Perlite transportation by 35 ton truck would equate to 1.7–13.6 MJ per kilometer of travel to the building site. *Typically from engineeringtoolbox.com

SOURCING/AVAILABILITY: *MODERATE TO DIFFICULT*

Masonry supply outlets often carry perlite for insulating the cores of CMU walls, and this type of perlite would be appropriate for most insulating purposes. In regions where this practice is not common, perlite can be difficult to source.

DURABILITY: *HIGH*

Perlite is not susceptible to decay or decomposition, and is not affected by the presence of water (other than loss of insulation value). It is fireproof and not a food source for insects or rodents. A long life span can be expected.

CODE COMPLIANCE

Code standards exist for the use of perlite as loose-fill insulation in masonry construction, and these standards should be applicable for similar uses in other wall and roof systems. The use of perlite beneath floor slabs may require the approval of a structural engineer.

INDOOR AIR QUALITY: *MODERATE TO HIGH*

Perlite is often wrongly associated with vermiculite, another type of expanded mineral insulation that can contain asbestos. Perlite does not contain asbestos.

The dust from perlite has high silica content, and is therefore dangerous to breathe during construction. Contained within a wall with an effective air control layer on both sides, this material should not affect indoor air quality, but care must be taken to ensure all cavities are well sealed from the interior space.

Perlite does not support mold growth and is chemically stable.

FUTURE DEVELOPMENT

The concrete industry has long used perlite aggregate in the manufacture of lightweight concrete

Perlite Insulation Ratings

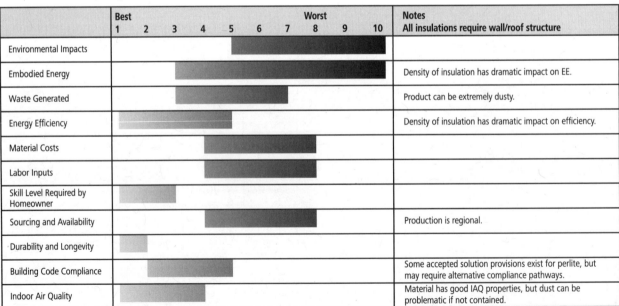

	Best 1	2	3	4	5	6	7	Worst 8	9	10	Notes — All insulations require wall/roof structure
Environmental Impacts											
Embodied Energy											Density of insulation has dramatic impact on EE.
Waste Generated											Product can be extremely dusty.
Energy Efficiency											Density of insulation has dramatic impact on efficiency.
Material Costs											
Labor Inputs											
Skill Level Required by Homeowner											
Sourcing and Availability											Production is regional.
Durability and Longevity											
Building Code Compliance											Some accepted solution provisions exist for perlite, but may require alternative compliance pathways.
Indoor Air Quality											Material has good IAQ properties, but dust can be problematic if not contained.

materials, and the increasing interest in structural/insulated concrete will likely cause an increase in perlite production. Several types of insulation boards also use perlite, and this use is also likely to increase. It is difficult to know if loose-fill perlite will increase in popularity. It has many good characteristics to recommend it, and more energy-efficient buildings are starting to use double-wall systems that are easy to insulate with loose-fill. On-site handling will always remain an issue to overcome, as the material tends to become airborne and spread. At this time, there doesn't seem to be any trend toward more use of perlite insulation as loose fill.

Mineral wool insulation

What the cheerleaders say...	What the detractors say...
Recycled industrial by-product	Off-gassing binders
Not susceptible to water damage	Potentially carcinogenic
Affordable	Post-use disposal issues
Good fire ratings	

Applications for mineral wool insulation

- Wall and roof insulation (batt)
- Loose-fill insulation (blown applications)
- Wall cladding (board)
- Roof and sub-slab insulation (rigid board)

Basic materials

- Most mineral wools are made from mining tailings or slag, though almost any stone can be used
- Binders (vary by manufacturer)
- Oils for dust suppression (varies by manufacturer)

How the system works

Molten rock is spun (using a process similar to making cotton candy) and the resulting fine fibers are intertwined and layered and held together using a binder. Mineral wool can be formed at a variety of densities for different insulation uses.

Tips for successful installations

Batt and rigid board installations must be free of voids and gaps to achieve maximum thermal performance. Manufacturers will provide specifications for installation.

Pros and cons

ENVIRONMENTAL IMPACTS

Harvesting — *Moderate.* The mining of ore is a high-impact process, but as a recycled product the impacts are mitigated.

Manufacturing — *High*. To make mineral wool, rock must be heated to approximately 1600°C (2900°F), an energy intensive process with high fuel usage and emissions. The chemical binders used to form the insulation into batts and boards have wide-ranging impacts throughout their life cycle.

Transportation — *Low to High*. Sample building uses 930 kg of mineral wool:

> 1.4 MJ per km by 15 ton truck
> 0.9 MJ per km by 35 ton truck

North American production is regional. Impacts accrue proportional to distance traveled, though the material is lightweight.

Installation — *Moderate*. Products carry carcinogen warnings on the label, and dust and offcuts can proliferate in the environment.

WASTE: *LOW*

Recyclable — Plastic packaging.
Landfill — Insulation offcuts.

ENERGY EFFICIENCY

R-value: 3.7–4.5 per inch

A wide variety of mineral wool products are available at different densities and thicknesses, and thermal properties vary with density.

All mineral wool insulation requires an air control layer on both sides of the insulation. Gaps and voids in the insulation due to improper installation will lower the thermal performance.

MATERIAL COSTS: *MODERATE*

Market penetration of mineral wool batts has increased dramatically over the past decade, and costs are often competitive with mainstream insulation choices like fiberglass.

LABOR INPUT: *LOW TO MODERATE*

The installation of mineral wool products is similar to that of any batt or board style of insulation.

Health Warning: Mineral wool fibers and formaldehyde binders are both considered carcinogenic. Material will cause skin irritation.

SKILL LEVEL REQUIRED FOR THE HOMEOWNER: *LOW*

Batt and board insulation can be successfully installed with very little experience, as long as care is taken to ensure tight fits in all cavities and to avoid voids or gaps.

SOURCING/AVAILABILITY: *EASY*

Mineral wool products can be sourced through many building supply stores, though availability will vary by region.

DURABILITY: *HIGH*

Mineral wool is not affected by moisture and offers

Mineral Wool Insulation Embodied Energy

Insulation: Walls @ R-30 Ceiling @ R-50	Material embodied energy from I.C.E. in MJ/kg	Weight to volume ratio of material*	Volume of material in sample 1000sf/92.9m² building	Sample building embodied energy	Material embodied carbon from I.C.E. in kgCO₂e/kg	Sample building embodied carbon	Notes
Walls @ 190mm (7.5 in)	16.6	30 kg/m³	31 m³ 930 kg	15,438 MJ	1.28	1,190 kg	
Ceiling @ 320mm (12.5 in)	16.6	30 kg/m³	29.5 m³ 885 kg	14,691 MJ	1.28	1,133 kg	

Transportation: Mineral wool batt transportation by 35 ton truck would equate to 1.7 MJ per kilometer of travel to the building site. *Typically from engineeringtoolbox.com no food value to insects and rodents. It can be expected to have a long life span.

CODE COMPLIANCE

Mineral wool products are produced to meet all building code standards.

INDOOR AIR QUALITY: *LOW TO MODERATE*

During installation, mineral wool particulate is dangerous. To the degree that particulate is sealed in the wall, there should be little evidence of it in the air of the finished home. Many mineral wool products use formaldehyde binders, which off-gas throughout their life span.

FUTURE DEVELOPMENT

Mineral wool products have been in use for many decades. Future developments are likely to include the use of non-off-gassing binders.

Cementitious foam insulation

What the cheerleaders say...	What the detractors say...
High insulation value, free of voids	Expensive
Inert and healthy	Friable (crushable)
Fire resistant	Limited installers
No dangerous blowing or foaming agents	

Applications for cementitious foam insulation

- Wall and roof insulation
- Floor insulation for wood framed floors

Basic materials

- Magnesium oxychloride cement

How the system works

Cementitious foam (or silicate foam) insulation is made of magnesium oxide (extracted from seawater)

Mineral Wool Insulation Ratings

	Best 1 2 3 4 5 6	Worst 7 8 9 10	Notes All insulations require wall/roof structure
Environmental Impacts			By-product of mining industry which has high impacts.
Embodied Energy			Recycled source material, but requires high energy input to spin mineral wool.
Waste Generated			
Energy Efficiency			
Material Costs			
Labor Inputs			
Skill Level Required By Homeowner			
Sourcing and Availability			Produced regionally, but widely distributed.
Durability and Longevity			
Building Code Compliance			
Indoor Air Quality			Products currently contain formaldehyde and carcinogen warnings.

plus calcium (from ceramic talc) and silicate. In its wet form the material resembles shaving cream, and it is pumped at low pressures into the area to be insulated. The material does not expand or contract after installation. It sets within an hour and dries over the course of several days. In framed walls or ceilings, one side of the frame is fully sheathed and the insulation applied in the stud cavity. In retrofit situations, the foam can be pumped into closed wall cavities.

Tips for successful walls

Licensed installers apply cementitious foams and will provide instructions for proper preparations prior to installation.

Pros and cons

ENVIRONMENTAL IMPACTS

Harvesting — *Moderate to High.* Magnesite mining has impacts including habitat destruction and water contamination. Magnesium chloride-rich brine and seawater harvesting have minimal impacts.

Manufacturing — *Moderate.* Magnesium oxide cements are made at lower temperatures than portland cement, requiring less input energy to make. This type of cement also recombines with some of the carbon dioxide driven out of the ore during firing, creating a lower carbon footprint than portland cement. As with any foam material, the quantities of raw material required are quite small as the finished product is mostly air pockets.

There are no chemical foaming agents or petro-chemicals involved in creating cementitious foam.

Transportation — *Low to High.* Sample building uses 1,023 kg of cementitious foam:

1.5 MJ per km by 15 ton truck

Impacts accrue proportional to distance traveled. Use of regional installers will keep distances low.

Installation — *Negligible to Low.* The material is not toxic at any stage of its creation or application. Once cured, it is very stable and does not off-gas. Trimmings can be crushed to very small quantities.

WASTE: *LOW*

Compostable — Leftover cement foam can be crushed and left in the environment.

Recyclable — Metal barrels for raw ingredients.

ENERGY EFFICIENCY: *HIGH*

R value: 3.9–4.3 per inch

Cementitious foam can provide an effective air control layer without the use of sheet barriers. Voids in the insulation will create flaws in the air control layer, but in new construction applications it is easy to avoid gaps and voids because the material does not shrink or swell. In typical installations, a separate air and/or vapor control layer is used.

Cementitious Foam Insulation Embodied Energy

Insulation: Walls = R-30 Ceiling = R-50	Material embodied energy from I.C.E. in MJ/kg	Weight to volume ratio of material*	Volume of material in sample 1000sf/92.9m² building	Sample building embodied energy	Material embodied carbon from I.C.E. in kgCO₂e/kg	Sample building embodied carbon	Notes
Lowest Impact							
Walls @ 190mm (7.5 in)	3.0**	33 kg/m³	31 m³ 1023 kg	3,069 MJ	–	N/A	**Figure averaged from multiple industry sources.
Ceiling @ 320mm (12.5 in)	3.0	33 kg/m³	29.5 m³ 973.5 kg	2,726 MJ	–	N/A	

Transportation: Cementitious foam transportation by 35 ton truck would equate to 1.9 MJ per kilometer of travel to the building site. *Typically from engineeringtoolbox.com

MATERIAL COSTS: HIGH

Limited market penetration results in relatively high costs. Costs will likely come down as more competitors enter the market.

LABOR INPUT: *MODERATE*

Licensed installers apply cementitious foams. The process requires a light mesh installed on vertical walls to contain the foam on the open side of the wall. Install times are comparable to other spray foam systems.

SKILL LEVEL REQUIRED FOR THE HOMEOWNER

A licensed installer is required.

SOURCING/AVAILABILITY: *MODERATE TO DIFFICULT*

Cementitious foam insulation is a relative newcomer to the insulation market. The number of installers is growing, but distribution is uneven across the continent. Check with manufacturers for their distributors and installers closest to you.

DURABILITY: *MODERATE TO HIGH*

Cementitious foam is a very stable material and is not susceptible to rot, mold, decay or pest infestation. The hardened foam is very friable, which means it crumbles easily. Once installed and sealed, little should cause this to happen, but some concern has been expressed about potential damage caused by heavy vibration.

The material is not transferrable or reusable.

CODE COMPLIANCE

Cementitious foams are not recognized in most building codes, but proprietary brands of the material have undergone all the testing required for insulation materials and are expected to be accepted

Cementitious Foam Insulation Ratings

	Best 1 2 3 4 5 6 7 Worst 8 9 10	Notes All insulations require wall/roof structure
Environmental Impacts		Magnesium cement has lower impacts than Portland cement.
Embodied Energy		
Waste Generated		
Energy Efficiency		
Material Costs		
Labor Inputs		Netting formwork required on open walls.
Skill Level Required by Homeowner	N/A	Installation requires professional.
Sourcing and Availability		Recent entry into marketplace, not yet available widely.
Durability and Longevity		Concerns about friability, but no demonstrable failures.
Building Code Compliance		Not an accepted solution in any codes, but standards exist for alternative compliance pathways.
Indoor Air Quality		

in the near future. It should be straightforward to show compliance with codes.

INDOOR AIR QUALITY: *HIGH*

Cementitious foams have many characteristics that make them a good choice for high indoor air quality. The material is vapor-permeable, reducing the chances of trapped moisture causing mold. The material itself is resistant to mold, non-allergenic and does not off-gas. No dust or toxic gas is generated during the installation or *in situ.*

FUTURE DEVELOPMENT

Limited distribution of cementitious foams causes prices to be higher than other insulations, but as the material gains more market share based on its strengths costs should become more competitive. The benefits of this type of insulation — especially for the chemically sensitive — are likely to drive demand.

Wool batt insulation

What the cheerleaders say...	What the detractors say...
Natural, renewable material	Expensive
Excellent moisture properties	Not widely available
Low embodied energy	Vulnerable to insects
Safe, nontoxic	

Applications for wool batt insulation
• Wall and roof insulation

Basic materials
• Sheep's wool
• Poly fibers (in some products)

How the system works

Sheep's wool fibers are formed into batts or rolls in standard dimensions. Some wool insulation is held together mechanically (by interweaving of the fibers) while others use polyester strands interwoven with the wool. It is installed like any other batt product.

Tips for successful walls

1. Batt insulations require careful installation to prevent gaps and voids.
2. An effective air control layer must be used with batt insulations.

Pros and cons

ENVIRONMENTAL IMPACTS

Harvesting — *Low to Moderate.* The raising of sheep can have varying environmental impacts, usually as a result of overgrazing. However, responsible farming techniques can create positive effects from grazing. Some wool insulation companies offer information on their wool sources, and this would be useful if trying to ensure minimal impacts. Most wool batts are made from fiber that would otherwise be considered waste.

Some wool manufacturers use a high percentage of recycled wool. Sometimes this is post-consumer material or material recycled from manufacturer waste.

Manufacturing — *Low to Moderate.* Relatively low-impact mechanical processes are used to form the batts. A lot of water can be used to wash the wool; check with manufacturers to see if water recycling is used.

Transportation — *Low to High.* Sample building uses 825 kg of wool batt:

> 1.2 MJ per km by 15 ton truck
> 0.78 MJ per km by 35 ton truck
> 0.13 MJ per km by ocean freighter

Production is limited in North America, and many brands are imported from Europe. Impacts accrue proportional with distance traveled, though the material is lightweight.

Installation — *Negligible.*

Waste: *Low*

Biodegradable/Compostable — Pure wool products.

Recyclable — Plastic packaging.

Landfill — Insulation offcuts. Certain wool insulations are spun with polyester fiber. Polyester content discounts claims that the wool insulation is biodegradable at the end of its useful life.

ENERGY EFFICIENCY: *HIGH*

R-value: 3.2–3.9 per inch

All wool insulation requires an air control layer on both sides of the insulation. Gaps and voids in the insulation due to improper installation will lower the thermal performance.

Recycled wool.

Wool Batt Insulation Embodied Energy

Insulation: Walls = R-30 Ceiling = R-50	Material embodied energy from I.C.E. in MJ/kg	Weight to volume ratio of material*	Volume of material in sample 1000sf/92.9m² building	Sample building embodied energy	Material embodied carbon from I.C.E. in kgCO₂e/kg	Sample building embodied carbon	Notes
Lowest Impact							
Walls @ 200mm (8 in)	12	25 kg/m³	33 m³ 825 kg	9,900 MJ	–	N/A	EE figure from renuables.co.uk for wool with recycled content.
Ceiling @ 340mm (13.5 in)	12	25 kg/m³	32 m³ 800 kg	9,600 MJ	–	N/A	
Highest Impact							
Walls @ 200mm (8 in)	20.9	25 kg/m³	33 m³ 825 kg	17,242 MJ	–	N/A	
Ceiling @ 340mm (13.5 in)	20.9	25 kg/m³	32 m³ 800 kg	16,720 MJ	–	N/A	

Transportation: Wool batt transportation by 35 ton truck would equate to 1.5 MJ per kilometer of travel to the building site. Wool batt transportation by ocean freight would equate to 0.25 MJ per kilometer of travel to the building site. *Typically from engineeringtoolbox.com

The ability of wool fibers to absorb a great deal of moisture without losing insulation value means that real-world performance may be better than insulations that work best dry.

MATERIAL COSTS: *HIGH*

Limited production and market penetration result in high costs. Quantity of raw material and ease of production could result in lower costs if additional production facilities are developed.

LABOR INPUT: *LOW TO MODERATE*

The installation of sheep's wool products is similar to that of any batt or board style of insulation.

SKILL LEVEL REQUIRED FOR THE HOMEOWNER: *EASY*

Batt and board insulation can be successfully installed with very little experience, as long as care is taken to ensure tight fits in all cavities and to avoid voids or gaps.

SOURCING/AVAILABILITY: *MODERATE TO DIFFICULT*

Wool insulation is not readily available from conventional building supply outlets. There is some manufacturing capacity in North America, but most orders will need to be placed directly with the manufacturer. A high percentage of wool insulation is imported from the UK and Europe.

DURABILITY: *MODERATE TO HIGH*

Wool batts should have a life span similar to other batt insulations. Insects (moths, in particular) can eat the wool insulation. The wool is typically treated with borax or other additives to discourage insect activity. The use of wool insulation in Europe for several decades indicates that durability issues are not problematic.

Wool Batt Insulation Ratings

	Best 1	2	3	4	5	6	Worst 7	8	9	10	Notes — All insulations require wall/roof structure
Environmental Impacts											Figures and sources limited. Farming practices can vary widely.
Embodied Energy											Figures and sources limited and wide-ranging.
Waste Generated											
Energy Efficiency											
Material Costs											
Labor Inputs											
Skill Level Required by Homeowner											
Sourcing and Availability											Production is regional, distribution is variable.
Durability and Longevity											
Building Code Compliance											European standards exist and may be used for alternative compliance pathways.
Indoor Air Quality											

CODE COMPLIANCE

Wool insulation is not recognized in most building codes. Many manufacturers have undertaken the testing required showing code equivalency, and the use of tested material should not be problematic in most jurisdictions.

INDOOR AIR QUALITY: *HIGH*

The ability of wool fibers to absorb a great deal of moisture without damage helps to keep wall cavities dry and prevent mold growth.

Wool is naturally nontoxic, but caution should be taken to research the nature of any insect or fire retardants added to the wool, which will vary by manufacturer.

FUTURE DEVELOPMENT

Wool insulation has enough advantages to drive up its market share as green building becomes more popular. The use of batt insulation is a conventional practice and it will be easy for builders to switch to healthier batts as they become available. Manufacturing capacity will need to increase greatly, and the speed at which capacity grows will be dependent on market uptake of wool batts.

Cellulose insulation (wet-sprayed and dry-blown)

What the cheerleaders say...	What the detractors say...
Made with recycled material	Insulation settles (dry type)
Good R-values	Potential insect and pest problems
Easy to install	Potential mold problems

Cellulose. (JEN FEIGIN)

Applications for cellulose insulation

- Wall cavities (wet-sprayed or dry dense-packed only)
- Ceiling and floor cavities (wet-sprayed, dry-blown or dry dense-packed)

Basic materials

- Shredded recycled newsprint
- Borax as a fire retardant (some manufacturers also use ammonium sulfate)
- Proprietary mold-inhibitors (usually chlorine-based) for wet-sprayed cellulose

How the system works

Wet-sprayed cellulose — The cellulose insulation is mixed with a small amount of water as it is sprayed into wall, ceiling and/or floor cavities using a purpose-made sprayer. The mix has similar properties to papier-maché and adheres in cavities to form a semi-solid, dense insulation. The insulation needs to dry for several days after installation; excess insulation is trimmed or shaved before the cavity is closed. **Dry-blown cellulose** — The cellulose insulation is blown through a purpose-made hopper/blower and placed on any horizontal ceiling or floor cavity. Dry-blown cellulose for wall cavities must be dense-packed to at least 55 kg/m³ (3.5 lbs/ft³) to prevent settling and gaps at the tops of walls. It is frequently used in renovations as it is a relatively easy material to insert into existing wall cavities.

Tips for successful walls

1. Professionals with the proper equipment install wet-sprayed cellulose.
2. Homeowners, using a blower rented from the insulation supplier, can install loose, dry-blown

cellulose for attics, but professional equipment is needed for dense packing in wall cavities.

Pros and cons

ENVIRONMENTAL IMPACTS

Harvesting — *Low.* Cellulose insulation is largely composed of shredded recycled newsprint. Much of this material is recycled from industrial sources, though some brands feature high quantities of post-consumer material.

Manufacturing — *Low.* Newsprint is shredded using relatively low-impact mechanical equipment.

The fire retardants used in cellulose insulation are typically borates, which are mineral-based and relatively low in environmental impacts.

The chlorine-based mold inhibitors used in some wet-sprayed brands can be toxic in their manufacture, though they are used in very small quantities.

Transportation — *Low to Moderate.* Sample building uses 1,056 – 1,736 kg of cellulose:

1.6 – 2.6 MJ per km by 15 ton truck
1 – 1.6 MJ per km by 35 ton truck

Cellulose Insulation Embodied Energy

Insulation: Walls = R-30 Ceiling = R-50	Material embodied energy from I.C.E. in MJ/kg	Weight to volume ratio of material*	Volume of material in sample 1000sf/92.9m² building	Sample building embodied energy	Material embodied carbon from I.C.E. in kgCO₂e/kg	Sample building embodied carbon	Notes
Lowest Impact							
Walls @ 200mm (8 in)	0.94	32 kg/m³ loose blown	33 m³ 1056 kg	993 MJ	–	N/A	Lowest EE figure in ICE database.
Ceiling @ 340mm (13.5 in)	0.94	32 kg/m³ loose blown	32 m₃ 1024 kg	963 MJ	–	N/A	
Highest Impact							
Walls @ 190mm (7.5 in)	3.3	56 kg/m³ dense packed	31 m³ 1736 kg	5,729 MJ	–	N/A	Highest EE figure in ICE database.
Ceiling @ 320mm (12.5 in)	3.3	56 kg/m³ dense packed	29.5 m³ 1652 kg	5,452 MJ	–	N/A	Dense packing does not necessarily have highest EE. EE figures depend on recycled content and manufacturing processes.

Transportation: Cellulose transportation by 35 ton truck would equate to 2–3.2 MJ per kilometer of travel to the building site. *Typically from engineeringtoolbox.com

Products are widely produced and should not need to travel far.

Installation — *Moderate.* Cellulose installations tend to be messy and dusty and the blowers require high current electricity.

WASTE: *LOW TO MODERATE*

Recyclable — Plastic packaging.

ENERGY EFFICIENCY

R-value: 3.6–4.0 per inch

Wet-sprayed cellulose provides a reasonable degree of air control in the wall cavity, though it is usually advisable to rely on an additional air control layer to provide a well-sealed wall. Dry-blown cellulose must have an additional air control layer.

Sprayed or blown cellulose are good at filling cavities and conforming to obstacles like plumbing and wiring.

Dry-blown cellulose that is not densely packed will settle over time, which is not problematic on flat surfaces like ceilings but will leave gaps at the tops of wall cavities and cause reductions in thermal performance. For this reason, dense-packing techniques should be used for walls.

MATERIAL COSTS: *LOW*

Cellulose is among the lowest cost insulation materials, often less expensive than other mainstream competitors.

LABOR INPUT: *MODERATE TO HIGH*

A commercial installer must be hired to install wet-blown or dense-packed cellulose. Homeowners can install loose dry-blown varieties, and the process requires two people: one to feed the cellulose bales into the shredder/hopper and the other to manage the blower hose.

Cellulose Insulation Ratings

	Best							Worst			Notes
	1	2	3	4	5	6	7	8	9	10	All insulations require wall/roof structure
Environmental Impacts											Recycled material. Forestry practices not considered.
Embodied Energy											Recycled material. Forestry and virgin paper production not considered.
Waste Generated											Installation can be messy.
Energy Efficiency											
Material Costs											
Labor Inputs											
Skill Level Required by Homeowner		or N/A									Dense packing and wet blowing may require professional equipment and installer.
Sourcing and Availability											
Durability and Longevity											Cellulose has good history, but can be susceptible to moisture damage.
Building Code Compliance											
Indoor Air Quality											Significant dust created during installation.

SKILL LEVEL REQUIRED FOR THE HOMEOWNER: *EASY TO MODERATE*

Dry-blown cellulose requires little training or experience to install. Wet or dense-packed installations must be done by a professional with the proper equipment.

SOURCING/AVAILABILITY: *EASY*

Dry-blown cellulose is widely available and most suppliers of the insulation also supply the installation machinery. The availability of installers for wet-blown cellulose varies widely by region.

DURABILITY: *MODERATE TO HIGH*

Both types of cellulose insulation have been widely used for several decades. The main durability issue comes from excessive wetting of the insulation, which can cause loss of thermal performance, settling and potential for mold growth. Kept dry, cellulose insulation has shown itself to be very durable.

CODE COMPLIANCE

Most building codes accept both wet-sprayed and dry-blown cellulose. Sufficient testing documents exist to show code equivalency where codes do not include cellulose.

INDOOR AIR QUALITY: *MODERATE TO HIGH*

Wet-sprayed cellulose can sometimes contain chlorine-based mold inhibitors. These would be most present in the air during and shortly after installation, but should be avoided if chlorine is on your red list. Check with manufacturers for exact ingredients.

Dry-blown cellulose creates a lot of dust when installed, and the house should be cleaned well before occupancy. If the building's air/vapor control layers are well built, there should be minimal intrusion of dust into the building. However, leaks in these layers could result in cellulose dust being drawn into the building when occupied.

Both types of cellulose insulation are capable of storing a lot of moisture safely, but because the cellulose is a good medium for mold growth, excessive moisture can potentially lead to mold issues.

FUTURE DEVELOPMENT

Wet-sprayed — Despite its many positive aspects, wet-sprayed cellulose has seen a decrease in market share with the recent popularity of spray foam insulation. This is unfortunate, as it has far fewer environmental and health issues and can create a vapor-permeable wall system. The drying time is a drawback for contractors moving quickly to close in buildings. Many installers who now apply spray foam used to apply wet-sprayed cellulose and may still be able to do so, even if they are not advertising the service.

Dry-blown — Due to its user-friendly nature, dry-blown cellulose is very popular for insulating attic spaces and for insulating walls in retrofits. The basic makeup of the material has been the same for decades and is unlikely to change in nature or decrease in popularity. High-pressure dense-packing machinery is relatively new and opens up more possibilities for dry cellulose in new construction.

Both types of cellulose are rare examples of environmentally friendly building materials that are already widely used in the conventional building industry.

Other insulation materials

Mycelium "foam"

The development of a foam-like insulation made from agricultural waste and mycelium (the roots of mushrooms) definitely ranks as one of the most exciting developments in green building.

The material is created by inoculating a blend of agricultural waste fibers (seed hulls, straw, etc) with mycelium. The mixture is placed into forms and allowed to grow until the form is full. The growth process does not require sunlight, water or fertilizers. The fully-grown insulation is then dehydrated and heated slightly to stop the root growth and prevent spore development.

In theory, this is an exceptionally clean and non-toxic way to create an insulation product that has many desirable qualities, including high R-values, rigidity and durability. Each cubic inch of material contains approximately eight miles of mycelium fiber, making it an ideal insulator.

The product can be used to make rigid insulation similar to conventional foam boards, and also to produce structural insulated panels (SIPs).

The product is nearing market-readiness as this book goes to press. Without being able to use it or read reliable reports from users, we could not present it here as a viable option. However, we hope it will soon become a very useful product for sustainable builders and show the way forward for more innovations that create valuable building materials in a more natural, environmentally friendly way.

Follow the development of this product at ecovativedesign.com.

Wood fiber insulation

Wood fiber insulation is quite popular in Europe, and given the immense amount of wood production and manufacturing in North America it is surprising that it has such a small presence in this market. Wood fiber insulation can come in many forms, including cellulose batts (which are similar in appearance and performance to other forms of batt insulation) and rigid or semi-rigid panels used as insulated exterior sheathing boards. Opportunities exist to use recycled pulp and mill waste for these products, but the small market is currently held by European imports. It would be a positive development if these products were to find acceptance in the North American market.

What's not included in this chapter

There are wall and wall insulation materials that are feasible to use but do not meet our sustainability standards for inclusion in this book. Drawing such lines is always controversial, and there will be green building advocates and practitioners who see this as folly. However, we will present our opinion on these materials and readers who disagree will find ample information in other sources to work with if they choose to pursue these options.

Structural insulated panels (SIPs)

The SIP system uses two thin skins of structural sheathing bound to an insulated core to create a wall (or roof) with excellent structural and insulative properties. In theory, these are ideal building materials as they provide structure and insulation with a single installation, and have reduced thermal bridging and unwanted gaps or voids in the thermal control layer. They are relatively quick to install too.

Unfortunately, most SIPs are made from oriented strand board (OSB) as the structural sheathing and some type of foam as the insulated core. Both materials rely heavily on the petrochemical industry for their component parts. The glues used to bind OSB are typically formaldehyde-based and off-gas for a long time after installation. The reliability of these glues is questionable, especially when exposed to water, and life span issues are critical considering these skins provide most of the structural strength of the wall.

Measuring the impacts of the foam insulations used in SIPs will reveal high embodied energy figures and carbon outputs, but these alone are not really reason enough to exclude this category of products. As the foam industry is quick to point out, there is a degree of energy savings from using these products (though the same savings are available with similar amounts of other insulators) that can render the embodied energy less grievous over time. But straight energy analysis, or even life cycle analysis, do not measure the deeper issue as they are typically carried out. Neither of these approaches takes into account the full impact of the petrochemical industry that produce these products. The full "chain of custody" for foam products needs to address the environmentally disastrous processes of this industry (for a fuller discussion of this subject, see the Foam ICF section of Chapter 1: Foundations).

Foam insulations also create vapor-impermeable walls, which are more prone to moisture issues unless continuous mechanical ventilation is provided for the building.

OSB/foam SIPs also represent a problematic disposal issue at the end of their useful life, as neither material is easily recyclable or reusable and the two are bonded together in a way that makes separation difficult and unlikely. The final resting place of a SIP (and all offcuts created during construction) is the landfill.

Not all SIPs are made from OSB and foam, and other options that use the same excellent principle in combination with more environmentally friendly materials have been developed (see Straw Bale SIPs sidebar) and are likely to be developed (see Mycelium foam above).

FOAM INSULATED CONCRETE FORMS

Foam ICFs are described in the foundation section of this book, but are sometimes used to build continuous foundation and wall systems.

Foam ICFs combine all the suspect characteristics of petrochemical insulation (see Foam ICF section of Chapter 1: Foundations) with high concrete and rebar usage, both of which have high embodied energy and carbon output issues.

This combination of materials will also prove very difficult to disassemble and separate at the end of its life, meaning it's most likely headed for landfill and not recycling. The whole system is just too dubious in its environmental impacts to recommend in any way, especially when the alternatives that exist are every bit as feasible and practical.

Chapter title page photo credits. Top left to right.
1. Jen Feigin 2. Chris Magwood 3. Daniel Earle 4. Jen Feigin

3

Floor and roof structure

WE ASK A LOT OF THE FLOOR AND ROOF SYS-
TEMS OF OUR BUILDINGS. They handle all
the loads we impose on them with our activities and
possessions, and all the loads nature sends their way.
The floors and roofs of a home use a lot of structural
material to handle these loads, and therefore represent a good deal of the resources that go into making
a building.

The structural elements of our floors and roofs
are typically hidden behind finishes of many kinds,
so we are often unaware of how they are made and
from what materials. There are not as many choices
as with walls and foundations, but the choices are
important ones as they represent a lot of material
and cost and play a structurally significant role.

Though floors and roofs will have very different
sheathings and finishes, the materials used to create
them are often very similar and are combined in this
chapter to avoid repetition in addressing the various
options.

Building science basics for floor structures

Structurally, a floor transfers live and dead loads
from the building, the occupants and the furnish-
ings to the foundation or the ground. The floor
system will often play a role in providing structural
support to the walls and/or foundation by bracing
these vertical elements and providing diaphragm resistance to racking and twisting.

Floor structures can be divided into two basic
categories:

Grade-based floors — Many floor designs are intended to transfer their loads directly to the ground.
While the floor itself will typically be separated
from the ground by a vapor control layer, a thermal
control layer and compacted fill, there is no open
air space under a grade-based floor. The barriers,
insulation and fill used to create grade-based floors
will vary depending on climate and local codes and
conventions. The focus in this chapter will be on the
material used to create the finished floor and not the
layers beneath or the surface finishes above, unless
the material itself can be the finished floor.

Grade-based floors are the main level floor or the
basement floor. If there are multiple floors, the higher floors will be suspended floors of some type.

Suspended floors — These systems create a floor
that is suspended between the exterior walls and
may also bear on partition walls and leave open,
inhabitable space beneath and above. Suspended

floors will usually have a ceiling finish on the bottom side and a floor finish on the top side. They are not typically insulated as the entire suspended floor is within the insulated building enclosure.

Suspended floors on pier foundations are the exception to this rule, as they are exposed to the exterior and must be insulated to the same degree as the walls of a building.

Mechanical services like plumbing, wiring and ductwork for heating and ventilation are often run in suspended floors.

In residential, low-rise construction both types of floors are viable, and multi-story buildings can combine the two.

Floor structural properties for grade-based floors involve compressive strengths. Fully supported by the ground below, a grade-based floor only needs to resist compression or crushing from the loads imposed on it. Many materials offer the relatively low compressive strengths required to be a grade-based floor.

Suspended floors are typically composed of floor joists, which are structural members carrying the floor loads to the exterior — and sometimes interior — walls. These joists are spaced at regular intervals and are often tied to one another with blocking or bridging at regular intervals. Flooring and ceiling finishes can also provide structural integrity to the system.

Suspended floors must resist bending or deflection when loads are imposed. The amount of structural strength required depends on the spans between points of support. The longer the span, the more strength will be required to resist bending under load. A home can be designed so that the exterior walls are the only supports for the floor system, or interior walls and/or post and beam systems can be used to shorten spans. The depth of joist required gets higher as spans get longer and the spacing between joists may get smaller.

Building codes include span charts that specify the loads a particular floor system must be able to withstand, and offer correlated sizes for floor joists. For proprietary floor joist systems, manufacturers will provide span charts to meet code requirements.

Floor thermal properties are different for grade-based floors than for suspended floors on pier foundations. Grade-based floors are not exposed to outdoor temperatures or wind and the ground below is a constant and fairly moderate temperature; exposed suspended floors are exposed to conditions ranging from extreme heat to extreme cold, as well as wind and varying levels of humidity. The insulation materials and strategies will be very different for these approaches, as will the air and vapor control layers. All the options for insulating and sealing an exposed, suspended floor are covered in Chapter 4: Sheathing and Cladding Materials.

Building science basics for roof structures

A roof structure provides a platform for a weather-resistant sheathing on the outside and a ceiling finish on the inside. A roof must be strong enough to resist the considerable loads of wind, rain and snow and effectively transfer those loads into the walls and foundation. While the roof sheathing provides the protection against water penetration, the roof structure must supply the geometry, support and capacity for the sheathing to be effective.

An almost endless variety of roof shapes are possible, and the structure of the roof will vary depending on the shape chosen. In some scenarios the roof rafters (the sloped members that define the shape of the roof) will act alone, while in other designs they act in conjunction with collar ties or ceiling joists as complementary structural elements.

Roof structural properties are similar to those of suspended floors. Individual rafters are spaced at regular intervals, and are sized to able to handle all expected loads for the given span between points of support. Joist sizing is determined by loads, spans and geometry, and can be found in building codes or supplied by manufacturers of rafter products.

Fasteners, hangers and bracing

To be structurally sound, all suspended floor and roof systems require particular types of fasteners, hangers and/or bracing. We will not address these components in this book, as they will vary between systems and between different designs and installations, but do not change performance parameters significantly.

Wood framing

What the cheerleaders say...	What the detractors say...
Renewable resource	Resource not always harvested responsibly
Reliable, well understood, widely available	Labor intensive
Efficient use of material	Not an efficient use of wood material
Code-approved	Dimensionally unstable; can twist and deform

Floor framing. (Jen Feigin)

Applications for wood framing
- Suspended floor systems
- Roof framing systems

Basic materials
- Dimensional lumber
- Fasteners, hangers and/or bracing

How the system works

Timber is sawn to standard dimensions (2x4, 2x6, 2x8, 2x10, 2x12) and dried to code-approved levels. An appropriate dimension of lumber is chosen to meet specific span requirements. Lumber is cut to suit the application and fastened in place at a specified spacing (usually 12, 16 or 24 inches / 300, 400 or 600 mm on center).

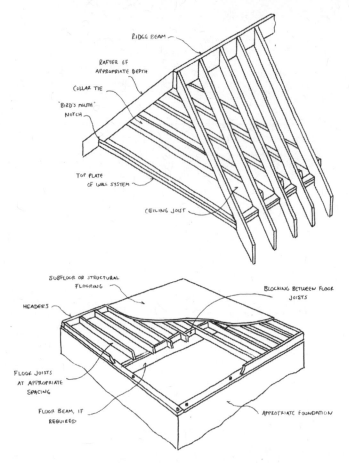

Tips for successful wood framing

1. Choose a good source for framing lumber. Locally, sustainably harvested wood is available in many places, as is third-party certified wood.

2. Choose good quality wood. The effectiveness of the floor or roof system will depend greatly upon the quality of the wood, as will the amount of labor required. Wood that is warped, cupped, split or otherwise flawed will make it harder to do the framing and compromise the results. Many codes require lumber to be "grade stamped" to ensure quality, but this is not always a guarantee of good lumber.

3. Consider the span charts in local codes carefully. Sometimes significant savings can be made in the amount and size of lumber needed by adjusting designs by a small amount.

4. A great deal of excellent literature exists to assist with framing projects and should be referenced before beginning a project.

Pros and cons

ENVIRONMENTAL IMPACTS

Harvesting — *Negligible to High.* Wood harvested from the building site or the local region can have negligible impacts. Unmanaged forestry can have impacts that include significant habitat destruction, soil erosion and ground water contamination. Third-party certification can help to ensure that impacts are minimized.

Metal fasteners may seem like a small component, but dozens of kilograms can go into a frame wall. Ore for steel production is mined in an intensive process with impacts including habitat destruction and soil and water contamination.

Manufacturing — *Negligible to Moderate.* The sawing and planing of structural lumber is a relatively low-impact mechanical process.

Processing raw ore into nails and screws is a multi-stage and intensive process requiring multiple infusions of high heat and fossil fuel use with impacts including air and water pollution.

Transportation — *Negligible to High.* Sample building uses 2,619 kg of lumber for roof and floor:

3.9 MJ per km by 15 ton truck
2.5 MJ per km by 35 ton truck

Timber is a heavy and high-volume material and accrues significant impacts proportional to distance traveled. In most regions it is possible to source lumber a reasonable distance from the building site.

Installation — *Negligible to Moderate.* The number

of offcuts from a wood frame wall can be quite high. Careful cut lists and ordering can minimize this waste.

WASTE: *MODERATE*

Compostable — Wood offcuts.
Recyclable — Metal fasteners.
Landfill — Wood impregnated with fasteners, lumber tarps.

ENERGY EFFICIENCY

A distinct thermal control layer is required for framed roof and floor assemblies. The insulation materials covered in Chapter 2: Walls are all feasible in framed roofs and floors. The depth of the framing members used may determine the amount of insulation that can be added and should be considered carefully. If framing members are not large enough to provide adequate thermal control, consider strapping or furring to provide additional insulation depth and reduce thermal bridging.

MATERIAL COSTS: *LOW TO MODERATE*
LABOR INPUT: *MODERATE*

Floor framing is usually straightforward, with a minimum of cutting and fitting required to complete a floor system.

Roof framing will vary greatly depending on design. A simple shed roof is almost as straightforward to frame as a floor system, but a roof with many pitch

Wood Frame Roof Embodied Energy

Roof type: 6:12 pitch 2x8 rafters @ 400mm (16 in) centers, 2x6 ceiling joists	Material embodied energy from I.C.E. in MJ/kg	Weight to volume ratio of material*	Volume of material in sample 1000sf/92.9m² building	Sample building embodied energy	Material embodied carbon from I.C.E. in kgCO₂e/kg	Sample building embodied carbon	Notes
64 rafters	2.5	450 kg/m³ (spruce lumber)	2.3 m³ 1035 kg	2,588 MJ	0.2	207 kg	Sizing from Ontario Building Code span charts for medium to high snow load zone.
64 ceiling joists	2.5	450 kg/m³ (spruce lumber)	1.31 m³ 589.5 kg	1,474 MJ	0.2	118 kg	
Fasteners (nails, hurricane clips)	20.1 (Steel, general, average recycled content)	7849 kg/m³	30 kg	603 MJ	1.46	44 kg	
Totals				**4,665 MJ**		**369 kg**	

Transportation: Wood transportation by 15 ton truck would equate to 0.9 MJ per kilometer of travel to the building site. *Typically from engineeringtoolbox.com

Wood Frame Floor Embodied Energy

Floor type: 2x10 floor joists at 400mm (16 in) centers	Material embodied energy from I.C.E. in MJ/kg	Weight to volume ratio of material*	Volume of material in sample 1000sf/92.9m² building	Sample building embodied energy	Material embodied carbon from I.C.E. in kgCO₂e/kg	Sample building embodied carbon	Notes
60 joists	2.5	450 kg/m³	2.21 m³ 994.5 kg	2,486 MJ	0.2	199 kg	
Fasteners	20.1 (Steel, general, average recycled content)	7849 kg/m³	10 kg	201 MJ	1.46	15 kg	
Totals				**2,687 MJ**		**214 kg**	

Transportation: Lumber transportation by 15 ton truck would equate to 1.5 MJ per kilometer of travel to the building site. *Typically from engineeringtoolbox.com changes and/or hips and valleys can be very complex. Labor input will depend greatly on design.

SKILL LEVEL REQUIRED FOR THE HOMEOWNER: *MODERATE*

For beginners, a wide range of resources is available to help learn how to frame, from books to hands-on courses. Beginners should be able to undertake simple framing projects, but may want to hire professional help if the project is complex or timelines are tight.

SOURCING/AVAILABILITY: *EASY*

Framing lumber is widely available through major building supply centers. Local mills exist in most areas with forests, but may require effort to locate. Third-party certification programs will have resources available to direct purchasers to outlets for wood bearing their certification.

DURABILITY: *HIGH*

Wood framing has proven itself to be a durable approach over the past hundred and fifty years. Though wood can be prone to rot, mold and insect infestation, strategies to avoid all of these problems are well understood and employed and the majority of wood-framed structures have a long life span.

For roof framing, the quality and condition of the sheathing above will determine the durability of the framing. Leaky roofs will cause rapid deterioration of roof framing components.

CODE COMPLIANCE

Wood frame construction is prescribed in all building codes, which will provide span charts to cover wood usage in most residential flooring and roof systems.

INDOOR AIR QUALITY

Structural roofing systems won't have a direct impact

Wood Framing Ratings

	Best							Worst			Notes
	1	2	3	4	5	6	7	8	9	10	
Environmental Impacts											Forestry practices are highly variable and have a significant impact.
Embodied Energy											
Waste Generated											
Energy Efficiency				N/A							Addition of insulation and sheathing are required.
Material Costs											Addition of insulation and sheathing will add to cost.
Labor Inputs											
Skill Level Required by Homeowner											
Sourcing and Availability											
Durability and Longevity											Frame walls have a generally good durability record, but can be susceptible to moisture damage if poorly constructed.
Building Code Compliance											
Indoor Air Quality											Interior wood framing will not be detrimental to IAQ, though rot and mold can occur if poorly constructed.

on indoor air quality, as the material is outside the living enclosure and separated by air, vapor and thermal control layers as well as finishes.

Interior floor systems, though covered with finishes, occupy space inside the building enclosure. Wood is generally considered to be a natural and benign material with little effect on air quality.

FUTURE DEVELOPMENT

Wood framing has not changed much in the past half century, and is unlikely to undergo any major changes in the future. It is well understood and well used throughout the construction industry.

The greatest change has been the development of third-party sustainability certification programs. Many major timber companies and lumber retailers have been adopting these programs and making certified lumber easier to obtain. While there is debate about the value of some certifications, this movement has been an important development in the greening of the forestry industry.

The development of high-quality, portable sawmills has created a rise in the number of sawyers working on a small scale. Many North American forests have been clear-cut several times, and the regrowth of these forests suits the scale of the small woodlot sawyer. In many regions, growth in the number of small mills will create greater access to this resource.

Resources for further research

Thallon, Rob. *Graphic Guide to Frame Construction: Details for Builders and Designers.* Newtown, CT: Taunton, 2000. Print.

Simpson, Scot. *Complete Book of Framing: An Illustrated Guide for Residential Construction.* Kingston, MA: RSMeans, 2007. Print.

Newman, Morton. *Design and Construction of Wood-Framed Buildings.* New York: McGraw-Hill, 1995. Print.

Burrows, John. *Canadian Wood-Frame House Construction.* Ottawa, ON: Canada Mortgage and Housing Corporation, 2006. Print.

Wooden trusses

What the cheerleaders say...	What the detractors say...
Efficient use of materials	Reliance on plated joints
Lightweight, easy to handle	Potentially problematic in fires
Small dimension lumber	Can't be owner-built
Able to create long spans	
Competitive costs	

Applications for system

- Roof framing systems
- Suspended floor systems

Basic materials

- Dimensional lumber
- Metal plates for truss-style joists
- Fasteners, hangers and/or bracing

How the system works

Timber is sawn to standard dimensions (usually 2x3, 2x4 and 2x6) and dried to code-approved

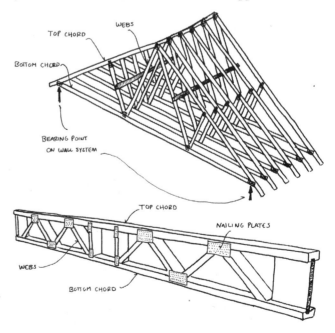

levels. Triangulated joist bracing is used to join top and bottom cords. The members are all connected by the use of metal nailing plates. The trusses are fastened to walls with nails or metal plates at consistent spacings, usually 12, 16 or 24 inches (30, 40 or 60 cm) on center.

Bracing is often nailed perpendicular to the trusses to provide additional strength and tie the trusses together.

Tips for successful installation

1. Find a reputable truss designer/provider in your local area. Truss designs are engineered in-house by the truss company for your building design to meet local code and load conditions.

Roof trusses.

2. Spend some time in discussion with the truss designer early in your design process, as small changes in spans and geometry can make a big difference in the amount of wood required in a truss, as well as cost. The designer will make trusses to work for your design regardless of efficiencies unless he/she is included in the conversation.

3. Third-party certified wood is a better environmental choice, and not all truss manufacturers offer it. Check to be sure that sustainably harvested wood is being used in your trusses.

4. The metal plates connecting truss joints are vulnerable to twisting in fires, causing premature roof collapse. Adding extra gusseting on a number of trusses can provide some added security against this type of failure.

5. Consider using metal "hurricane ties" to fasten roof trusses to the building, even if they are not required. They add little cost or time to the installation and provide a lot of additional durability in high wind conditions.

6. A great deal of excellent literature exists to assist with framing projects and should be referenced before beginning a project.

Pros and cons

ENVIRONMENTAL IMPACTS

Harvesting — *Negligible to High.* Wood sustainably harvested from the local region can have negligible impacts. Unmanaged forestry can have impacts that include significant habitat destruction, soil erosion and ground water contamination. Third-party certification can help to ensure that impacts are minimized.

Metal fasteners may seem like a small component, but dozens of kilograms can go into a frame wall. Ore for steel production is mined in an intensive process with impacts including habitat destruction and soil and water contamination.

Manufacturing — *Negligible to Moderate.* The sawing and planing of structural lumber is a relatively low-impact mechanical process.

Processing raw ore into nails and screws is a multi-stage and intensive process requiring multiple infusions of high heat and fossil fuel use with impacts including air and water pollution.

Transportation — *Negligible to High.* Sample building uses 2,610 kg of wooden trusses:

3.9 MJ per km by 15 ton truck

2.5 MJ per km by 35 ton truck

Timber is a heavy and high-volume material and accrues significant impacts proportional to distance traveled. In most regions it is possible to source lumber a reasonable distance from the building site.

Installation — *Negligible.* The number of offcuts is minimized by truss companies, and no cuts are typically required on-site.

WASTE: *NEGLIGIBLE*

Trusses are built to size, so no offcuts should be generated on-site.

ENERGY EFFICIENCY

Truss roofs and floor joists are typically deeper than their solid lumber counterparts, and this gives more room for insulation. If required, truss roofs can be designed with "raised heels" to ensure that full depth attic insulation can be installed over the walls.

The open spaces in the webbing of a truss will cause less thermal bridging than a solid wood member,

Wood Truss Roof Embodied Energy

Roof type: 6:12 pitch 2x4 trusses @ 600mm (24 in) centers	Material embodied energy from I.C.E. in MJ/kg	Weight to volume ratio of material*	Volume of material in sample 1000sf/92.9m² building	Sample building embodied energy	Material embodied carbon from I.C.E. in kgCO₂e/kg	Sample building embodied carbon	Notes
24 wood trusses	2.5	450 kg/m³ (spruce lumber)	2.36 m³ 1062 kg	2,655 MJ	0.2	212 kg	
Metal plates, 20 per truss plus hurricane ties and nails	20.1 (Steel, general, average recycled content)	7849 kg/m³	0.02 m³ 157 kg	3155 MJ	1.46	229 kg	
Totals				**5,810 MJ**		**441 kg**	

Transportation: Truss transportation by 15 ton truck would equate to 1.8 MJ per kilometer of travel to the building site. *Typically from engineeringtoolbox.com

Wood Truss Floor Embodied Energy

Floor type: 400mm (16 in) deep trusses @ 400mm (16 in) centers, 29 trusses spanning 8m (26.5 ft)	Material embodied energy from I.C.E. in MJ/kg	Weight to volume ratio of material*	Volume of material in sample 1000sf/92.9m² building	Sample building embodied energy	Material embodied carbon from I.C.E. in kgCO₂e/kg	Sample building embodied carbon	Notes
Lowest Impact							
2x4 lumber	2.5	450 kg/m³ (spruce lumber)	3.44 m³ 1548 kg	3,870 MJ	0.2	310 kg	
Steel plates and fasteners	20.1 (Steel, general, average recycled content)	7849 kg/m³	0.04 m³ 314 kg	6,311 MJ	1.46	458 kg	
Totals				**10,181 MJ**		**768 kg**	

Transportation: Truss transportation by 15 ton truck would equate to 3.9 MJ per kilometer of travel to the building site. *Typically from engineeringtoolbox.com but will still contribute to some bridging unless additional steps are taken.

MATERIAL COSTS: *LOW*

Trusses are typically the lowest cost option for roof and floor framing. The use of small dimension lumber and the efficiencies of factory assembly result in low cost assemblies. Simple roofs and floors, as in

the sample building, will see the most cost benefits from truss systems.

LABOR INPUT: *LOW TO MODERATE*

Trusses can lower the amount of labor required to build a floor and especially a roof. The trusses will come sized according to the plans and will require little or no additional cutting or framing, other than

Pallet truss roofs

The use of truss geometries for creating roof structures is not new, and wood has long been used in truss roofs. But

Pallet truss.
(JEN FEIGIN)

the pallet truss roof, developed by Alfred von Bachmayer while working on affordable housing solutions in Mexico, adapts conventional truss geometry for use with a widely available wood resource: slats from wooden shipping pallets. As these pallets are not usually built using conventionally sized lumber, the pallet trusses are made to work with the thinner (usually 25 mm or 1 inch thick) wood and shorter lengths found on pallets.

Using a jig to create a truss of the desired depth and length allows amateur builders to measure and mark all the pieces of the truss accurately. The pieces can be assembled inside the jig as well, ensuring a straight and accurate truss.

The truss geometry and layout should be designed or reviewed by a structural engineer or other competent designer, and the fasteners must be specified to handle anticipated loads and used at the proper points and correct quantities.

Pallet trusses can be made to span distances that work for a wide range of residential settings, both as roof and floor systems. A similar scenario can be adapted to use any available short pieces of wood, including construction site cast-offs and wood from building demolitions.

Resources for further research

Kennedy, Joseph F. *Building Without Borders: Sustainable Construction for the Global Village.* Gabriola Island, BC: New Society, 2004. Print.

temporary and/or permanent bracing to add rigidity to the system. With all the geometry done by the truss manufacturer, the layout and fastening of the trusses is very straightforward and can be done in a relatively short time.

SKILL LEVEL REQUIRED FOR THE HOMEOWNER: *LOW TO MODERATE*

Beginners can do the installation of trusses, especially with some study of resource material in advance. One skilled carpenter can often direct one or two less-skilled laborers in the installation of trusses. Simple designs are very straightforward to complete using trusses, with skill level rising as complexity rises.

SOURCING/AVAILABILITY: *EASY*

In any region where wood-framed houses are common, there will be regional or local truss manufacturers

in operation. Trusses made with third-party certified lumber may be more difficult to source.

DURABILITY: *MODERATE TO HIGH*

Trusses have been in widespread use for over 40 years, with no signs of common durability issues. The system is completely reliant on the metal fastening plates. In normal use, these plates are durable. However, constant exposure to moisture can cause plates to corrode and wood to soften or rot behind the plates and cause failure sooner than with solid lumber. However, with well-maintained sheathing there should be no issues.

The failure of truss roofs in fires is well documented. Modern fire-fighting practices assume the use of truss roofs and the quick failure of roof structures as the metal plates heat up and twist or melt. While it is difficult to plan for durability in fires, trusses do have a poor record in this regard.

Wood Truss Ratings

	Best					Worst					Notes
	1	2	3	4	5	6	7	8	9	10	
Environmental Impacts											Forestry practices are highly variable and have a significant impact.
Embodied Energy											
Waste Generated											
Energy Efficiency				N/A							Addition of insulation and sheathing are required.
Material Costs											
Labor Inputs											Truss building is done off site and not included in labor input.
Skill Level Required by Homeowner											Only installation of trusses is performed by homeowner and will vary depending on complexity of roof shape.
Sourcing and Availability											
Durability and Longevity											Trusses are generally durable but susceptible to failure in fires.
Building Code Compliance											
Indoor Air Quality											Wood framing will not be detrimental to IAQ, though rot and mold can occur if poorly constructed.

CODE COMPLIANCE

Truss manufacturers will engineer floor and roof trusses to comply with local codes. Building departments will typically require a set of the truss drawings stamped by the in-house engineer as part of the building permit submission, and will use these drawings to perform their inspection of the roof and floor framing.

INDOOR AIR QUALITY

Roof trusses exist outside the building enclosure, and so will have little effect on IAQ. Floor trusses will be contained within the living space (although typically covered), but being composed of timber and metal plates, do not create any IAQ issues.

FUTURE DEVELOPMENT

Truss design and construction has been streamlined over the past decades, and are unlikely to change much in the future.

Resources for further research

Metal Plate Connected Wood Truss Handbook. Madison, WI: Wood Truss Council of America, 2002. Print.

————～∿～————

Wooden I-beams

What the cheerleaders say...	What the detractors say...
Use of waste wood products	Glues off-gas
Resource efficiency	Durability questionable
Lightweight, easy to handle	High cost
Able to create long spans	

Applications for system

• Floor and roof framing

Basic materials

• Solid or laminated wood top and bottom cords
• Oriented strand board (OSB)
• Glue to connect OSB to cords

How the system works

An I-beam is created using dimensional lumber or laminated veneer lumber as wide top and bottom cords, slotted to accept a sheet of thin, oriented strand board (OSB) that is glued into the cords to create a deep, thin beam that can be used for floor joists and roof framing. Special fastening brackets and I-joist blocking are used to make connections and bracing in the system.

I-beams are ordered at the appropriate lengths for the project and different depths are available to handle particular spans and loads. I-beam suppliers provide engineering to ensure that appropriate depths and spacing are matched to loads and spans.

Manufactured I-beams do not exhibit the same tendencies to warp, split or otherwise distort that are common with solid timber joists.

Tips for successful installation

Wooden I-beams are proprietary products, and each will have its own installation guidelines that should be followed closely.

Keep I-beams dry once delivered to your job site — the OSB component does not handle wet conditions very well.

Pros and cons

Environmental impacts

Harvesting — *Moderate to High.* Unmanaged forestry can have impacts that include significant habitat destruction, soil erosion and ground water contamination. The use of marginal wood stocks for OSB can help to mitigate impacts. Third-party certification can help to ensure that impacts are minimized.

Glues for binding wood fibers are formaldehyde based, and have significant harvesting impacts.

Metal fasteners may seem like a small component, but dozens of kilograms can go into a frame wall. Ore for steel production is mined in an intensive process with impacts including habitat destruction and soil and water contamination.

Manufacturing — *Negligible to Moderate.* The sawing and planing of structural lumber for I-beam rails is a relatively low-impact mechanical process. Shredding of wood for OSB production has low to moderate impacts.

Glues for binding wood fibers are formaldehyde based, and have significant manufacturing impacts including air and water pollution.

Processing raw ore into nails and screws is a multi-stage and intensive process requiring multiple infusions of high heat and fossil fuel use with impacts including air and water pollution.

Transportation — *Negligible to High.* Sample building uses 2,547 kg of wooden I-beams for roof and floor:

> 3.8 MJ per km by 15 ton truck
> 2.4 MJ per km by 35 ton truck

Timber is a heavy and high-volume material and accrues significant impacts proportional to distance traveled. I-beam manufacturers are relatively well distributed in most regions.

Installation — *Negligible to Moderate.* The number of offcuts from wood I-beams can be quite high.

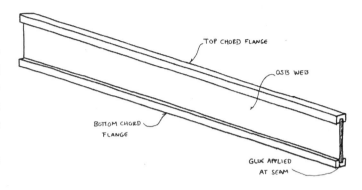

Careful cut lists and ordering can minimize this waste.

Wooden I-beams represent a quandary that is common in green building. On one hand, this product uses wood fibers in the OSB that would not have been suitable for making dimensional lumber, making use of harvested wood that otherwise would not have been useful for construction. On the other hand, the glues used to bond the wood fibers in the OSB are formaldehyde based, raising environmental concerns during their production, off-gassing concerns within the building and trouble with disposal of offcuts and I-beams at the end of the useful life span of the product.

Wooden I-beams can be made from FSC or other third-party certified wood sources, helping to lower environmental impacts.

Waste: *Moderate*

Recyclable — Metal fasteners.
Landfill — I-beam offcuts.

Energy efficiency

Wooden I-beams are typically deeper than comparable solid lumber joists, offering more depth for insulation. The OSB portion of the I-beam is continuous, creating a cold bridge through the insulation though the bridge is very thin. Properly filled with insulation, a roof and/or floor system built with wooden I-beams can be part of an energy-efficient building enclosure.

MATERIAL COSTS: *MODERATE TO HIGH*

I-beams are typically more expensive per lineal meter than comparable solid lumber or truss options.

LABOR INPUT: *LOW TO MODERATE*

One of the main benefits of manufactured joists is that they are lightweight, making it possible for one or two workers to handle very long spans of joist. The ability of the joists to span greater distances can also reduce labor time as it eliminates joints. Longer spans can also reduce the number of load-bearing walls required in a design, eliminating labor throughout the building process, from the foundation upward.

SKILL LEVEL REQUIRED FOR THE HOMEOWNER: *LOW TO MODERATE*

Any builder able to frame a floor or roof with solid lumber will be able to do the same with wooden I-beams. The joists come pre-engineered and will include layout drawings that should be easy for newcomers to follow. Beginners will need to understand basic carpentry skills.

SOURCING/AVAILABILITY: *EASY*

Wooden I-beams are widely available, usually through building supply centers. An in-house designer and/or engineer will work from a set of plans to determine the depth of joist required and a suitable layout.

DURABILITY: *MODERATE TO HIGH*

The weakness of wooden I-beams is their durability. Under normal, dry conditions they can have

Wood I-Beam Roof Embodied Energy

Roof type: 6:12 pitch 400mm (16 in) deep beam @ 600mm (24 in) centers, 44 total rafters	Material embodied energy from I.C.E. in MJ/kg	Weight to volume ratio of material*	Volume of material in sample 1000sf/92.9m² building	Sample building embodied energy	Material embodied carbon from I.C.E. in kgCO₂e/kg	Sample building embodied carbon	Notes
2x4 solid lumber top and bottom cord	2.5	450 kg/m³	1.59 m³ 715.5 kg	1,789 MJ	0.2	143 kg	
OSB I-beam, 11mm (⁷⁄₁₆ in)	15 (OSB)	620 kg/m³	0.87 m³ 539.4 kg	8,091 MJ	0.45	243 kg	
Totals				**9880 MJ**		**386 kg**	Does not include metal brackets or fasteners.

Transportation: I-beam transportation by 15 ton truck would equate to 1.9 MJ per kilometer of travel to the building site. *Typically from engineeringtoolbox.com

Wood I-beam Floor Embodied Energy

Floor type: 400mm (16 in) deep joist @ 400mm (16in) centers, 8m (26.5 ft) span	Material embodied energy from I.C.E. in MJ/kg	Weight to volume ratio of material*	Volume of material in sample 1000sf/92.9m² building	Sample building embodied energy	Material embodied carbon from I.C.E. in kgCO₂e/kg	Sample building embodied carbon	Notes
2x4 solid lumber top and bottom cord	2.5	450 kg/m³ (spruce lumber)	1.59 m³ 715.5 kg	1,789 MJ	0.2	143 kg	
OSB I-beam, 11mm (⁷⁄₁₆ in)	15 (OSB)	620 kg/m³	0.93 m³ 576.6 kg	8,649 MJ	0.45	259 kg	
Totals				**10,438 MJ**		**402 kg**	

Transportation: I-beam transportation by 15 ton truck would equate to 1.9 MJ per kilometer of travel to the building site. *Typically from engineeringtoolbox.com a working life similar to solid wood. However, the OSB portion of the joist does not stand up well to repeated wetting, with the wafers of wood expanding and the glues weakening. Manufacturers insist that the I-beams be kept covered and dry while on the construction site to protect them against this weakening.

Once in a home, these joists should stay dry. However, houses do leak, and when exposed to a constant source of moisture, these joists will deteriorate faster than comparable solid wood options. Because they play a key structural role in a building, deterioration can have major implications.

CODE COMPLIANCE

As a pre-engineered system, wooden I-beams are an accepted solution in most jurisdictions. Building departments will typically want to be provided with a stamped version of the joist drawings as part of the plan submission.

INDOOR AIR QUALITY

The glues used in the OSB portion of the wooden I-beam all contain formaldehyde and will off-gas for a long time. I-beams installed as roof framing will be outside the habitable space and are separated from the indoor air. However, I-beams installed as floor joists will be inside the living space and will contribute to elevated levels of formaldehyde in the air.

FUTURE DEVELOPMENT

A growing number of manufacturers offer FSC or other third-party certified wood sources, and this trend is likely to grow as awareness of certified wood increases. Many manufacturers are working to eliminate or reduce the formaldehyde content in their glues, and a breakthrough in this area would make these products much more attractive from an environmental perspective. Different glues may also resolve water damage issues, further increasing their attractiveness.

Wooden I-beam Ratings

	Best 1 2 3 4 5	6 7	Worst 8 9 10	Notes
Environmental Impacts		▓▓▓▓		Impact of glues/adhesives is difficult to quantify.
Embodied Energy		▓▓		
Waste Generated	▓▓			
Energy Efficiency		N/A		
Material Costs		▓▓▓▓		
Labor Inputs	▓▓▓			
Skill Level Required by Homeowner	▓▓▓			
Sourcing and Availability	▏			
Durability and Longevity	▓▓▓▓	▓		Exposure to moisture can cause rapid deterioration.
Building Code Compliance	▏			
Indoor Air Quality		▓▓▓	▓▓▓	Formaldehyde in glues can have detrimental affect on IAQ when used within the habitable space.

Finger-jointed wood trusses

What the cheerleaders say...	What the detractors say...
Made with small dimension lumber	Glues may not be environmentally friendly
Lighter and more stable than solid wood	Can't be owner-built
No off-gassing from OSB	
Open webs allow for easy installation of mechanical elements	

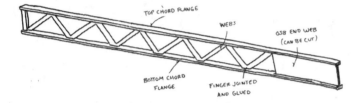

Applications for system

- Floor and roof framing

Basic materials

- Small dimension solid lumber (2x2, 2x3, 2x4) with finger-jointed ends
- Glue at finger-jointed connections
- OSB in some systems

How the system works

An open web joist is created using solid-lumber top and bottom cords that are finger-jointed to accept solid lumber webbing. These open web joists can be customized to a particular length, or can be made with a short section of OSB (identical to the wooden I-beams described earlier) to allow for custom sizing on-site.

Truss joists are ordered at the appropriate lengths for the project and different depths are available to handle particular spans and loads. Suppliers provide engineering to ensure that appropriate depths and spacing are matched to loads and spans.

Truss joists do not exhibit the same tendencies to warp, split or otherwise distort that are common with solid timber joists.

The open webbing of the truss joists allows for easy routing of plumbing, wiring and heating services.

Tips for successful installation

1. Open web joists are proprietary products, and each manufacturer will have its own installation guidelines that should be followed closely.
2. Open web joists cannot be cut or altered except in those places specified by the manufacturer. If site conditions require alteration, ensure that the manufacturer approves any changes.

Pros and cons

ENVIRONMENTAL IMPACTS

Harvesting — *Negligible to High.* Unmanaged forestry can have impacts that include significant habitat destruction, soil erosion and ground water contamination. Third-party certification can help to ensure that impacts are minimized. Finger-jointed wood can make use of marginal wood in short lengths.

Metal fasteners may seem like a small component, but dozens of kilograms can go into a frame wall. Ore for steel production is mined in an intensive process with impacts including habitat destruction and soil and water contamination.

Glues for finger jointing are petrochemical based. **Manufacturing** — *Negligible to Moderate.* The sawing and planing of structural lumber is a relatively low-impact mechanical process.

Processing raw ore into nails and screws is a multi-stage and intensive process requiring multiple infusions of high heat and fossil fuel use with impacts including air and water pollution.

Glues can have impacts including significant air and water pollution.

Transportation — *Negligible to High.* Sample building uses 2,229.4 kg of finger-jointed trusses for roof and floor:

> 3.35 MJ per km by 15 ton truck
> 2.1 MJ per km by 35 ton truck

Timber is a heavy and high-volume material and accrues significant impacts proportional to distance traveled. Regional manufacturers are accessible to many markets.

Installation — *Negligible to Moderate.* The number of offcuts from a truss joist are typically minimal, as joists are ordered to size.

WASTE: *LOW TO MODERATE*

Compostable — Wood offcuts with no glue.

Recyclable — Metal fasteners.

Landfill — Offcuts with glue.

ENERGY EFFICIENCY

Open web wood joists are typically deeper than comparable solid lumber joists, offering more depth for insulation. The webbing in the joists is not continuous, but does create very small cold bridges through the insulation. Properly filled with insulation, a roof and/or floor system built with open web wood joists can be part of an energy-efficient building enclosure.

MATERIAL COSTS: *LOW*

Finger-jointed trusses are not custom-built for each application, but come in standard lengths and are designed to be trimmed to an appropriate length

Finger-Jointed Truss Joist Roof Embodied Energy

Roof type: 6:12 pitch 2x4 trusses @ 600mm (24 in) centers, 44 joists	Material embodied energy from I.C.E. in MJ/kg	Weight to volume ratio of material*	Volume of material in sample 1000sf/92.9m² building	Sample building embodied energy	Material embodied carbon from I.C.E. in kgCO$_2$e/kg	Sample building embodied carbon	Notes
2x4 top and bottom cords	2.5	450 kg/m³	1.59 m³ 715.5 kg	1,789 MJ	0.2	143 kg	
2x3 webs	2.5	450 kg/m³	0.75 m³ 337.5 kg	844 MJ	0.2	68 kg	
OSB end pieces	15 (OSB)	620 kg/m³	0.1 m³ 62 kg	930 MJ	0.45	28 kg	
Totals				3,563 MJ		239 kg	

Transportation: Truss transportation by 15 ton truck would equate to 1.7 MJ per kilometer of travel to the building site. *Typically from engineeringtoolbox.com

Finger-Jointed Truss Joist Floor Embodied Energy

Floor type: 400mm (16 in) deep trusses @ 400mm (16 in) centers, 29 trusses spanning 8m (26.5 ft)	Material embodied energy from I.C.E. in MJ/kg	Weight to volume ratio of material*	Volume of material in sample 1000sf/92.9m² building	Sample building embodied energy	Material embodied carbon from I.C.E. in kgCO$_2$e/kg	Sample building embodied carbon	Notes
2x4 top and bottom cords	2.5	450 kg/m³	1.59 m³ 715.5 kg	1,789 MJ	0.2	141 kg	
2x3 webs	2.5	450 kg/m³	0.79 m³ 355.5 kg	889 MJ	0.2	71 kg	
OSB end pieces	15	620 kg/m³	0.07 m3 43.4 kg	651 MJ	0.45	20 kg	
Totals				3,329 MJ		232 kg	

Transportation: Truss transportation by 15 ton truck would equate to 1.7 MJ per kilometer of travel to the building site. *Typically from engineeringtoolbox.com on site. This allows them to be mass produced and typically provide the lowest cost option for floor and roof framing.

LABOR INPUT: *LOW TO MODERATE*

One of the main benefits of manufactured joists is that they are lightweight, making it possible for one or two workers to handle very long spans of joist. The ability of the joists to span greater distances can

Open floor joist.

also reduce labor time as it eliminates joints. Longer spans can also reduce the number of load-bearing walls required in a design, eliminating labor throughout the building process, from the foundation upward.

Open web joists leave plenty of room for installers to run plumbing, electrical and heating runs, which can help to reduce labor time for these trades.

SKILL LEVEL REQUIRED FOR THE HOMEOWNER: *LOW TO MODERATE*

Any builder able to frame a floor or roof with solid lumber will be able to do the same with truss joists. The joists come pre-engineered, and will include layout drawings that should be easy for newcomers to follow. Beginners will need to understand basic carpentry skills. Often, truss joists are delivered at the required lengths, reducing the number of cuts to be made on-site.

Finger-Jointed Truss Ratings

	Best 1	2	3	4	5	6	7	Worst 8	9	10	Notes
Environmental Impacts				■	■	■	■				Impacts of glues difficult to assess. Forestry practices are highly variable and have a significant impact.
Embodied Energy	■	■	■								EE of glues is difficult to assess.
Waste Generated	■	■	■								
Energy Efficiency					N/A						
Material Costs	■	■									
Labor Inputs	■	■	■								
Skill Level Required by Homeowner	■	■	■	■							
Sourcing and Availability	■	■	■	■							
Durability and Longevity	■	■	■	■	■	■					Lifespan of glues is unproven.
Building Code Compliance	■										
Indoor Air Quality					■	■	■				Glues used at joints are relatively stable, but glues in OSB end sections can affect IAQ.

SOURCING/AVAILABILITY: *EASY TO MODERATE*

Open web wooden joists are widely available, usually through building supply centers. An in-house designer and/or engineer will work from a set of plans to determine the depth of joist required and a suitable layout.

DURABILITY: *MODERATE TO HIGH*

The finger jointed and glued connections of these joists have proven to be very stable, but they have not yet withstood the test of decades. The glues are not susceptible to water in the same way as OSB glues. They achieve suitable fire ratings for residential and commercial use, but may not last as long in a fire as solid lumber.

In regular usage, these joists can be part of a durable structure.

CODE COMPLIANCE

As this is a pre-engineered system, it is a widely accepted solution in most jurisdictions. Building departments will typically want to be provided with a signed, stamped version of the joist drawings as part of the plan submission package.

INDOOR AIR QUALITY

Open web wood joists installed as roof framing are typically outside the building enclosure and should have no effect on IAQ. The IAQ impact of the glues used at the finger joints are difficult to assess without knowing the contents. Several manufacturers claim that their glues are healthy and have no impact on IAQ, but this is not a guarantee, and proprietary recipes make it difficult to assess the glues.

FUTURE DEVELOPMENT

A growing number of manufacturers offer FSC or other third-party certified wood sources, and this trend is likely to grow as awareness of certified wood increases. Many manufacturers are working to make their glues more environmentally sound.

Reciprocal or mandala roof framing

Reciprocal roof systems fall under the category of wood framing, but use a unique geometry to provide free-spanning roofs that do not require central supports. In reciprocal roof framing, overlapping members are used to support one another.

Most reciprocal roof framing systems are used to create round roof structures (though the building below can be square or rectangular), but there are also geometries that allow for linear and complex roof shapes.

Reciprocal roofs can allow a builder to use shorter pieces of lumber and rely less on fasteners while still achieving roof spans that are practical for residential construction. The skill level required can be high, but the results can be visually stunning.

Reciprocal roof.

References for further research

Larsen, Olga Popovic. *Reciprocal Frame Architecture*. Oxford, UK: Architectural, 2008. Print.

Glulam roof and floor framing

What the cheerleaders say...	What the detractors say...
Strong and stable	Heavy to lift and install
Durable	High wood usage
Uses smaller diameter wood	Can't be owner-built
Achieves long spans	

Applications for system

- Floor and roof framing

Basic materials

- Dimensional lumber
- Glue

How the system works

Lengths of dimensional lumber (2x4 and 2x6 are common) are stacked on their flat sides and glued together to create a continuous beam of the desired depth and strength. These glulam beams can be used horizontally as floor and ceiling framing, or in pitched applications — often in truss configuration — for roofs.

Glulams can be made in straight sections, but they can also be curved for vaulted applications, making them more adaptable to creative building shapes than any other structural system.

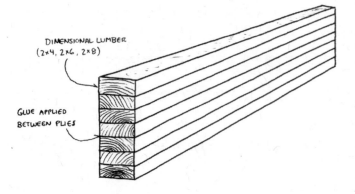

DIMENSIONAL LUMBER
(2x4, 2x6, 2x8)

GLUE APPLIED
BETWEEN PLIES

Tips for successful installations

1. Glulams are proprietary products, and each manufacturer will have its own installation guidelines that should be followed closely.
2. Notching, boring or altering a glulam beam should only be done in a manner approved by the manufacturer.

Pros and cons

ENVIRONMENTAL IMPACTS

Harvesting — *Negligible to High*. Unmanaged forestry can have impacts that include significant habitat destruction, soil erosion and ground water contamination. Third-party certification can help to ensure that impacts are minimized. Smaller diameter trees are required than for similar members of solid timber.

Metal fasteners may seem like a small component, but dozens of kilograms can go into a frame wall. Ore for steel production is mined in an intensive process with impacts including habitat destruction and soil and water contamination.

Glues for laminating are petrochemical based.

Manufacturing — *Negligible to Moderate*. The sawing and planing of structural lumber is a relatively low-impact mechanical process.

Processing raw ore into nails and screws is a multi-stage and intensive process requiring multiple infusions of high heat and fossil fuel use with impacts including air and water pollution.

Glues can have impacts including significant air and water pollution.

Transportation — *Negligible to High*. Sample building uses 2,945.5 kg of glulams for roof and floor framing:

> 4.4 MJ per km by 15 ton truck
> 2.8 MJ per km by 35 ton truck

Timber is a heavy and high-volume material and accrues significant impacts proportional to distance traveled. Regional manufacturers are accessible to many markets.

Installation — *Negligible to Moderate.* The number of offcuts from glulam beams can be quite high. Careful cut lists and ordering can minimize this waste.

WASTE: *LOW TO MODERATE*

Landfill — Glulam offcuts.

ENERGY EFFICIENCY

Glulams are typically used in scenarios where the beams/joists are exposed, and so any insulation strategy is usually accomplished on the outside of the glulam. Careful attention must be paid to keeping the insulation continuous at the roof/wall junction to prevent cold bridges or lesser levels of insulation. As long as the exterior insulation levels are suitable and the roof/wall junction detailed appropriately, the glulam won't have any negative impact on energy efficiency.

However, because they are a solid timber, glulams can constitute a major thermal bridge if they are in contact with both the outside and inside face of the building. This type of use should be avoided, or an insulation strategy to address the bridging must be used.

MATERIAL COSTS: *MODERATE TO HIGH*

Glulams are typically more costly than open web style framing systems, as they use more wood

Glulam. (JEN FEIGIN)

Glulam Roof Framing Embodied Energy

Roof type: 6:12 pitch 80 x 190 mm (3⅛ x 7 ½ in) @ 600mm (24 in) centers	Material embodied energy from I.C.E. in MJ/kg	Weight to volume ratio of material*	Volume of material in sample 1000sf/92.9m² building	Sample building embodied energy	Material embodied carbon from I.C.E. in kgCO₂e/kg	Sample building embodied carbon	Notes
44 rafters	2.5	8.48 kg/m (manufacturer figure)	3.39 m³ 1819.6 kg	4,549 MJ	0.3	546 kg	

Transportation: Glulam transportation by 15 ton truck would equate to 2.7 MJ per kilometer of travel to the building site. *Typically from engineeringtoolbox.com

Glulam Floor Framing Embodied Energy

Floor type: 80 x 150 mm (3⅛ x 6 in) joist @ 600mm (24in) centers, 4m (13.5 ft) span	Material embodied energy from I.C.E. in MJ/kg	Weight to volume ratio of material*	Volume of material in sample 1000sf/92.9m² building	Sample building embodied energy	Material embodied carbon from I.C.E. in kgCO₂e/kg	Sample building embodied carbon	Notes
40 joists	2.5	6.84 kg/m (manufacturer figure)	2 m³ 1125.9 kg	2,815 MJ	0.3	338 kg	

Transportation: Glulam transportation by 15 ton truck would equate to 1.7 MJ per kilometer of travel to the building site. *Typically from engineeringtoolbox.com to achieve high strengths, rather than geometry. However, they are often shallower in depth and this can result in lower building heights, creating savings on other materials in the total building enclosure.

LABOR INPUT: *MODERATE TO HIGH*

Glulam beams and joists tend to be very heavy, and can require many hands and/or mechanical equipment to manage. When used as a roof framing system, cranes are often needed.

Large glulams on wide spacings are often used to replace systems in which smaller, lighter members are used at tighter spacings. By reducing the number of members, some labor savings can be achieved.

Once in place, glulams are usually fastened using prefabricated metal bracketry. This type of fastening can be quite easy to install, but placement needs to be accurate to ensure proper fit for the bracketry.

SKILL LEVEL REQUIRED FOR THE HOMEOWNER: *MODERATE TO HIGH*

Glulams are usually installed as part of a post and beam structure. Post and beam can be challenging for newcomers, and is usually the domain of experienced crews. Large frames require a degree of accuracy that can be challenging for beginners, and the work is often accompished by the use of booms or cranes that can be intimidating for those with no experience.

SOURCING/AVAILABILITY: *EASY TO MODERATE*

There are fewer manufacturers of glulam beams than other manufactured joists, but they are available in most major markets. Some manufacturers offer standard dimensions that will be suitable for a range of projects, and these will be available when needed. Much of the market for glulams is for custom projects where the designer and the glulam

Glulam Ratings

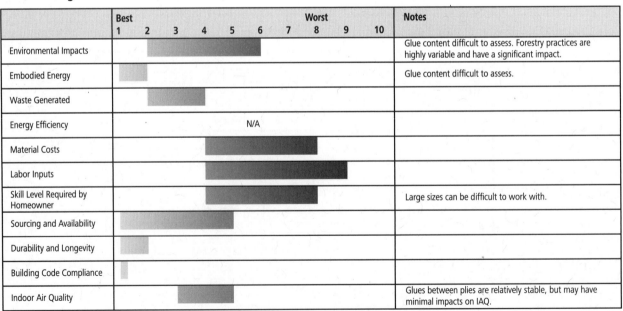

	Best 1	2	3	4	5	6	Worst 7	8	9	10	Notes
Environmental Impacts											Glue content difficult to assess. Forestry practices are highly variable and have a significant impact.
Embodied Energy											Glue content difficult to assess.
Waste Generated											
Energy Efficiency					N/A						
Material Costs											
Labor Inputs											
Skill Level Required by Homeowner											Large sizes can be difficult to work with.
Sourcing and Availability											
Durability and Longevity											
Building Code Compliance											
Indoor Air Quality											Glues between plies are relatively stable, but may have minimal impacts on IAQ.

manufacturer work together to create solutions for a particular need, and in these cases the lead times required must be part of the project planning.

DURABILITY: *HIGH*

Glulams are the oldest type of glued lumber product and have been in use since the 1950s. They

Hyperparabolic or hypar roofs

Roofs on buildings are typically quite complex and material intensive and become very heavy structures to be supported by the walls and foundations.

Hypar roofs are the exception to the norm of heavy, intensive roof systems. Utilizing a minimalist structure — using as few as eight small-dimension pieces of lumber or steel — and a coating of fabric-reinforced latex cement, these roofs are as strong and durable as conventional options while using a fraction of the material.

A hypar roof uses the parabolic geometry created when fabric is stretched over a triangulated frame to create an inherently strong shape for the roof. The fabric is used as a reinforcement mesh for a latex- or acrylic-modified cement that is poured onto the fabric in successive layers, building

up into a remarkably strong and stable roof at thicknesses as little as 10 mm (⅜ inch). These roofs are entirely capable of handling high wind and snow loads.

There are many possible geometries for hypar roofs, including the "hat" style and a quadruple gable that works well for residential construction.

The lightweight structure of a hypar roof does not create a framing depth that can be used to insulate the roof, as with many conventional systems. Building a flat ceiling for insulation under the roof, or a double hypar roof and insulating between the two, could address this. Building an independent framework under the roof is also an option.

While latex and portland cement are not materials that would typically be recommended in a sustainable building book, the amounts of these materials required to build a viable roof are so minimal using this system that negative environmental impacts are offset by the vast reduction in quantity of material required compared to any other roofing system.

Hypar roofs have largely been used in developing countries, where the small amount of framing material is a huge benefit. They have been tested and used in North America, and with the cooperation of a structural engineer they can be a feasible approach within a building code context.

Hypar roofs are an exciting and potentially radical alternative to creating environmentally sound roof structures for a wide range of buildings.

References for further research

Knott, Albert, and George Nez. *Latex Concrete Habitat: A Manual on Construction of Roofs for Recovery from World Poverty.* Victoria, BC: Trafford, 2005. Print.

Hypar roof.

have proven to be very durable over decades of service.

CODE COMPLIANCE

Glulams are a pre-engineered system, and are an accepted solution in most jurisdictions. Building departments will typically want to be provided with a signed, stamped version of the glulam drawings as part of the plan submission.

INDOOR AIR QUALITY

Several companies manufacture glulams using glues that have passed third-party testing by Greenguard, meaning that they meet stringent standards for IAQ. Unlike other glued wood products, the glue between each lamination has very little exposed surface area, minimizing contact between glue and the air or unintentional wetting.

FUTURE DEVELOPMENT

The widespread use of FSC or other third-party certified woods for glulams is likely to continue, making them more environmentally responsible. Glues have already been developed that meet high standards for indoor air quality, and new and better formulations will make glulams an even more attractive option.

Open web steel joists

What the cheerleaders say...	What the detractors say...
Widely available (can be found used)	Requires specialized skills and fasteners
Light weight for long spans	Metal has high embodied energy
Reusable or recyclable at end of life	Can't be owner-built
Open webs simplify mechanical installation	

Applications for system

- Roof framing (typically for flat roofs, but can be used for pitched roofs)
- Floor framing

Basic materials

- Metal top and bottom cords with welded metal webbing

How the system works

Steel top and bottom cords are welded to steel webbing to create a joist capable of handling the required loads and spans.

Typically, these joists are used horizontally, to create floor decks or flat roof decks. Open web steel joists can be custom-ordered to create pitched roofs, vaults or any other geometry. Flat joists are quite cost competitive with wooden competitors, but custom steel joists can be quite expensive.

Common open web steel joists are intended for use in steel-framed buildings. If you are intending to use these joists as part of a frame with wooden posts and beams, check with the manufacturer of the joists to ensure that proper connections and fastening methods are prescribed.

Tips for successful installation

Open web steel joists are proprietary products, and each manufacturer will have its own installation guidelines that should be followed closely.

Cutting, notching or altering an open web steel joist should only be done in a manner approved by the manufacturer.

Pros and cons

ENVIRONMENTAL IMPACTS

Harvesting — High. The extraction of ore for steel production is a high-intensity process, with impacts including habitat destruction and air and water pollution. Recycled content can mitigate these impacts.

Manufacturing — High. Steel production is a high-intensity process, requiring several applications of high heat, with impacts that include fossil fuel use, air and water pollution. These inputs are equally high for recycling steel. It can be difficult to trace the origins of the raw materials that are contained in a manufactured product like an open web joist.

Transportation — Moderate to High. Sample building uses 4,262.8 kg of steel joists for roof and floor:

6.4 MJ per km by 15 ton truck

4 MJ per km by 35 ton truck
1.07 MJ per km by rail

Manufacturers exist in most regions. It is difficult to ascertain the transportation impacts of the material through the whole production cycle, as steel is a multinational industry.

Installation — Negligible.

WASTE: *NEGLIGIBLE*

Recyclable — All metal offcuts.

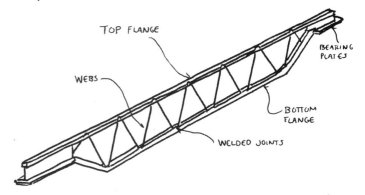

Open Web Steel Roof Joist Embodied Energy

Roof type: 6:12 pitch 355mm (14in) depth @ 600mm (24in) centers, 44 joists	Material embodied energy from I.C.E. in MJ/kg	Weight to volume ratio of material*	Volume of material in sample 1000sf/92.9m² building	Sample building embodied energy	Material embodied carbon from I.C.E. in kgCO₂e/kg	Sample building embodied carbon	Notes
Steel joists	20.1 (Steel, general, average recycled content)	9.5 kg/m (manufacturer figure)	214.5 m 2037.8 kg	40,958 MJ	1.46	2,975 kg	

Transportation: Joist transportation by 35 ton truck would equate to 1.9 MJ per kilometer of travel to the building site. *Typically from engineeringtoolbox.com

Open Web Steel Joist Floor Embodied Energy

Floor type: 355mm (14in) depth @ 400mm (16in) centers, 29 joists	Material embodied energy from I.C.E. in MJ/kg	Weight to volume ratio of material*	Volume of material in sample 1000sf/92.9m² building	Sample building embodied energy	Material embodied carbon from I.C.E. in kgCO₂e/kg	Sample building embodied carbon	Notes
Steel joists	20.1 (Steel, general, average recycled content)	9.5 kg/m (manufacturer figure)	234.2 m 2225 kg	44,720 MJ	1.46	3,249 kg	

Transportation: Joist transportation by 35 ton truck would equate to 2.1 MJ per kilometer of travel to the building site. *Typically from engineeringtoolbox.com

ENERGY EFFICIENCY

Open web steel joists are typically used in scenarios where the beams/joists are inside the building enclosure, so any insulation strategy is usually accomplished on the outside of the joist. As long as the exterior insulation levels are suitable and thermal bridging has been eliminated, the steel joist won't have any impact on energy efficiency.

MATERIAL COSTS: *LOW TO HIGH*

Steel joists for residential construction are not as common as the varieties of wooden options. Steel joists are built to a number of standard sizes, and if a standard size is appropriate then the costs can be quite low. As the joists cannot be modified on site to fit particular spans, custom-sized joists will be fairly expensive.

LABOR INPUT: *MODERATE TO HIGH*

Where open web steel joists are being used as part of a prefabricated steel frame, the labor input can be fairly low as these complete systems have been well designed and refined to minimize labor time.

If the steel joists are being used in a custom context, the amount of labor required will be determined by the complexity of the design, the type of fastening being used and the amount of site-fabrication required. Having a designer who is knowledgeable in the use of steel joists can help to minimize labor input.

Connections between steel joists and other building elements (wooden frames, wooden floor decks) can require specialized fastening systems that can increase labor times.

SKILL LEVEL REQUIRED FOR THE HOMEOWNER: *MODERATE TO HIGH*

Specialized professional crews constructing entire steel frames complete most open web steel joist installations. Most regions have many companies with qualified and competent workers offering this service.

Many open web steel joist installations require on-site welding. If this is the case, the homeowner will need to have the skill and equipment to do that work to the satisfaction of local codes.

An owner-builder can install open web steel joists if the installation is quite straightforward, with simple connections to adjacent materials. If the joists require cutting or welding, only those with the proper tools and training should do the work.

SOURCING/AVAILABILITY: *EASY*

Most regions will have several suppliers of open web steel joists.

DURABILITY: *VERY HIGH*

Open web steel joists should have a long life span. Corrosion due to continuous exposure to moisture is the only thing that can limit life span, and it should

Open web steel joists.

Open web steel joists

be easy to keep joists dry in a properly built and maintained building. Steel joists will often outlive the service life of the commercial buildings in which they are commonly used.

CODE COMPLIANCE

Open web steel joists are a pre-engineered system, and are an accepted solution in most jurisdictions. Building departments will typically want to be provided with a signed, stamped version of the joist drawings as part of the plan submission.

INDOOR AIR QUALITY

The steel joists themselves will have no detrimental effect on indoor air quality, but the coatings on the steel may. The paints used on the steel are applied at the factory, giving the homeowner little choice in the type of paint used. Steel products are sometimes sprayed with oils to further prevent corrosion.

Consultation with the manufacturer or distributor will need to occur to ensure that IAQ will not be detrimentally affected.

It may be possible to coat the steel joists with a healthy paint or sealant on-site to prevent exposure to the factory-applied finishes.

FUTURE DEVELOPMENT

The steel industry has made strides to lower the energy consumption on the production side, and good recycling programs for steel have been well developed. Major changes in the ingredients or manufacturing processes involved in creating steel joists are unlikely.

Open Web Steel Joist Ratings

	Best 1 2 3 4 5 6 7	Worst 8 9 10	Notes
Environmental Impacts			Intensive mining and processing. High carbon output during manufacturing.
Embodied Energy			
Waste Generated			
Energy Efficiency	N/A		
Material Costs			
Labor Inputs			Can require specialized labor force.
Skill Level Required by Homeowner			Can require specialized skills and equipment.
Sourcing and Availability			
Durability and Longevity			
Building Code Compliance			
Indoor Air Quality	N/A		Paints used on steel within the building enclosure may have detrimental IAQ effects.

Timber framing and post and beam

What the cheerleaders say...	What the detractors say...
Renewable resource	Large-diameter wood can be unsustainably harvested
High durability	High cost
Beautiful	High skill level may be required

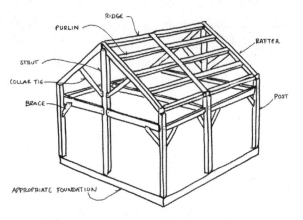

Timber frame.

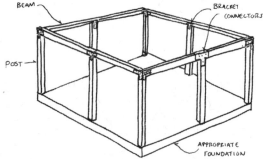

Post and beam.

Applications for system

- Floor and roof framing

Basic materials

- Large timbers
- Metal bracketry and fasteners for post and beam

How the system works

Solid timbers of large dimensions (usually 6x6 inch or greater) are used to create a floor joist system and/or a roof truss system. The spacing of the joists or roof members is determined by the size of the timber and the expected loads.

Traditional timber framing uses wood-to-wood joinery between timbers, typically including the use of wooden pegs to fasten joints. Post and beam systems will use metal bracketry and fasteners to connect members. These metal fasteners can be standard, off-the-shelf materials or can be custom-welded to achieve particular structural and/or aesthetic goals.

Tips for successful installation

1. Large timber structures will typically need to be designed by a professional engineer or a recognized timber designer. Be sure that your designer is able to provide a quality design using all appropriate code guidelines and requirements.
2. Every species of tree has different strength and workability characteristics and appearance, and a timber frame-builder must ensure that the wood used is appropriate for the type of construction chosen.
3. The interface between timber frames and wall and roof enclosures and sheathing must be detailed appropriately to ensure energy efficiency and durability. Cold bridges and proper air sealing are critical considerations at the design and construction phases.
4. Large timbers are heavy and may require special lifting apparatus to install. Whether it is scaffolding and people power, ropes and rigging or cranes, it is important to plan for the lifting of timbers.
5. Timbers can be milled and planed to different degrees of finish, or may be left with a raw wood finish or have a finish applied after installation. Be sure you know what type of finish you want your timbers to have from the outset.

6. The spacing of large timber members is wider than with stick lumber, so the flooring and roof decking must be chosen to suit these wider spacings. Typical plywood subflooring and roof decking is unlikely to be adequate without additional support, and flooring and sheathing are usually visible and part of the overall aesthetic of the building, making these choices an important part of the structural and aesthetic considerations at the design stage.

Pros and cons

ENVIRONMENTAL IMPACTS

Harvesting — *Negligible to High.* Wood harvested from the building site or the local region can have negligible impacts. Unmanaged forestry can have impacts that include significant habitat destruction, soil erosion and ground water contamination. Third-party certification can help to ensure that impacts are minimized.

Metal fasteners and bracketry may be a significant component. Ore for steel production is mined in an intensive process with impacts including habitat destruction and soil and water contamination.

Manufacturing — *Negligible to Moderate.* The sawing and planing of structural lumber is a relatively low-impact mechanical process.

Processing raw ore into nails and screws is a multi-stage and intensive process requiring multiple infusions of high heat and fossil fuel use with impacts including air and water pollution.

Transportation — *Negligible to High.* Sample timber frame building uses 3,222 kg of timber for wall and roof framing:

> 4.8 MJ per km by 15 ton truck
> 3 MJ per km by 35 ton truck

Sample post and beam building uses 1,575 kg of timber for wall framing:

Timber frame. (JEN FEIGIN)

> 2.35 MJ per km by 15 ton truck
> 1.5 MJ per km by 35 ton truck

Timber is a heavy and high-volume material and accrues significant impacts proportional to distance traveled. In most regions it is possible to source lumber a reasonable distance from the building site.

Installation — *Negligible to Moderate.* The number of offcuts from a timber or post and beam frame can be quite high. Careful cut lists and ordering can minimize this waste.

WASTE: *MODERATE*

Compostable — All wood offcuts.
Recyclable — Metal fasteners.

ENERGY EFFICIENCY

Timbers are typically used in scenarios where the beams/joists are exposed, so any insulation strategy is usually accomplished on the outside of the timbers. Careful attention must be paid to keeping the insulation continuous at the roof/wall junction to prevent cold bridges or lesser levels of insulation that will negatively impact thermal performance. As long as the exterior insulation levels are suitable and the roof/wall junction detailed appropriately, the timber framing won't have any impact on energy efficiency.

MATERIAL COSTS: *LOW TO MODERATE*

Timbers can be purchased for a cost that is typically less than for a similar quantity of milled framing lumber, depending on species, dimensions, quality and transportation distance.

The steel connectors for post and beam framing can be quite costly unless it is standard, off-the-shelf connectors. Research is required to accurately cost this element of the frame.

Timber Frame Embodied Energy

	Material embodied energy from I.C.E. in MJ/kg	Weight to volume ratio of material*	Volume of material in sample 1000sf/92.9m² building	Sample building embodied energy	Material embodied carbon from I.C.E. in kgCO₂e/kg	Sample building embodied carbon	Notes
Wall Structure							
4 bents, 3 posts per bent, all 200x200mm (8x8in)	2.5	450 kg/m³ (pine timber)	3.5 m³ 1575 kg	3,938 MJ	0.2	315 kg	
Framing for window and door openings	2.5	450 kg/m³ (spruce lumber)	1.1 m³ 495 kg	1,238 MJ	0.2	99 kg	
Totals				**5,176 MJ**		**414 kg**	
Roof Structure							
4 bents, 1 king post, all 200x200mm (8x8in)	2.5	450 kg/m³ (pine timber)	3.66 m³ 1647 kg	4,118 MJ	0.2	329 kg	
Purlins, 2x6 @ 600mm (24 in) centers	2.5	450 kg/m³ (spruce lumber)	1.2 m³ 540 kg	1,350 MJ	0.2	108 kg	
Totals				**5,468 MJ**		**437 kg**	

Transportation: Timber transportation by 15 ton truck would equate to 6.4 MJ per kilometer of travel to the building site. *Typically from engineeringtoolbox.com

Post and Beam Frame Embodied Energy

	Material embodied energy from I.C.E. in MJ/kg	Weight to volume ratio of material*	Volume of material in sample 1000sf/92.9m² building	Sample building embodied energy	Material embodied carbon from I.C.E. in kgCO₂e/kg	Sample building embodied carbon	Notes
Wall Structure							
4 bents, 3 posts per bent, all 200x200mm (8x8in)	2.5	450 kg/m³ (pine timber)	3.5 m³ 1575 kg	3,938 MJ	0.2	315 kg	
Framing for window and door openings	2.5	450 kg/m³ (spruce lumber)	1.1 m³ 495 kg	1,238 MJ	0.2	99 kg	
Steel connector plates/bolts	20.1 (Steel, general, average recycled content)	7849 kg/m³	1.5 kg per connection 42 kg	844 MJ	1.46	61 kg	
Totals				**6,020 MJ**		**475 kg**	

Transportation: Post and beam transportation by 15 ton truck would equate to 3.2 MJ per kilometer of travel to the building site. *Typically from engineeringtoolbox.com

LABOR INPUT: *MODERATE TO HIGH*

Timber structures have significantly fewer members than stick frame structures, which can lower the amount of labor input. The biggest impact on labor input will be the complexity of the joinery and the time required to complete each joint. This is an issue that can be addressed at the design stage, with joinery specified to meet specific labor requirements.

The metal bracketry of post and beam designs is often chosen to reduce the labor input required to cut traditional joints. However, the reality does not always meet that expectation. Be sure that any bracketry included in the design will indeed save time (and money) on-site. If timbers need to be trimmed or have slots, notches or pre-drilled holes added to fit inside brackets the process could take as much labor time as making timber frame joints.

The method of moving heavy timbers will also impact labor time. Using large work crews to hoist timbers adds more labor hours than using equipment or machinery.

SKILL LEVEL REQUIRED FOR THE HOMEOWNER: *MODERATE TO HIGH*

Traditional timber framing is a highly skilled profession, and it can take many years of experience to cut and assemble a top-notch frame. However, the principles of joining large timbers are quite straightforward, and many beginners will be able to cut and assemble frames that are structurally functional but may lack the refinement and high degree of fit and finish of professionally built frames.

Those with less wood working skills can typically complete post and beam work, as long as the bracketry and fastening system is straightforward. Custom-made bracketry can require welding skills or may need to be hired out.

SOURCING/AVAILABILITY: *MODERATE TO DIFFICULT*

Many regions will have sources of locally and sustainably harvested timbers. If you live in a region without a source of large-diameter timbers, be sure to consider the transportation distances and forestry impacts at the source.

Recycled timbers are relatively common from disassembled barns, homes and factory buildings. If you choose to work with them, it is best to source the timbers first and then base a design around them, as it can be difficult to source recycled timbers to meet predetermined size requirements.

Steel connectors for timber structures will likely need to be special-ordered or custom made.

Specialty tools for timber framing will also need to be sourced.

DURABILITY: *HIGH TO VERY HIGH*

Timber structures have centuries of proven durability. Kept relatively dry and free from damaging insects, a timber frame makes a remarkably durable and adaptable structure.

CODE COMPLIANCE

The long and established history of timber framing makes it a widely acceptable solution familiar to code officials in most jurisdictions. However, most codes do not include specific design standards for timber frames and will require frames to be designed by a structural engineer or other accepted professional.

INDOOR AIR QUALITY

Typically, timber frames will not have a negative impact on IAQ. However, they can be built with a wide variety of wood species, and certain fragrant species may cause reactions for certain occupants.

Recycled timbers should be inspected for potential contamination from their previous use, especially when sourced from factories and barns.

Timber Frame Ratings

	Best 1 – 10 Worst	Notes
Environmental Impacts	(rating ~2–6)	Forestry practices are highly variable and have a significant impact.
Embodied Energy	(rating ~2–5)	
Waste Generated	(rating ~2–4)	
Energy Efficiency	N/A	
Material Costs	(rating ~1–5)	
Labor Inputs	(rating ~5–9)	
Skill Level Required by Homeowner	(rating ~5–9)	
Sourcing and Availability	(rating ~2–5)	
Durability and Longevity	(rating ~1)	
Building Code Compliance	(rating ~1–5)	Guidelines for timber frames exist in codes, but must be applied to custom frames.
Indoor Air Quality	(rating ~1–3)	Timbers generally do not affect IAQ, but can introduce spores and molds in rare circumstances.

Post and Beam Frame Ratings

	Best 1 – 10 Worst	Notes
Environmental Impacts	(rating ~2–7)	Forestry practices are highly variable and have a significant impact. Amount of steel used in connections will raise impacts.
Embodied Energy	(rating ~2–7)	Amount of steel used in connections will raise impacts.
Waste Generated	(rating ~2–4)	
Energy Efficiency	N/A	
Material Costs	(rating ~1–7)	Bracketry used for joints will have variable impact on cost.
Labor Inputs	(rating ~5–8)	
Skill Level Required by Homeowner	(rating ~5–8)	
Sourcing and Availability	(rating ~2–6)	
Durability and Longevity	(rating ~1)	
Building Code Compliance	(rating ~1–5)	Guidelines for timber frames exist in codes, but must be applied to custom frames.
Indoor Air Quality	(rating ~1–3)	Timbers generally do not affect IAQ, but can introduce spores and molds in rare circumstances.

FUTURE DEVELOPMENT

Timber framing has been used for centuries, and it is unlikely that new developments will significantly alter the materials or approach. Dwindling stocks of large-diameter trees make it unlikely that timber framing will ever be a widespread, mainstream solution, but existing commercial and private forests will be able to supply the specialty market for a long time to come.

Resources for further research

Roy, Robert L. *Timber Framing for the Rest of Us.* Gabriola Island, BC: New Society, 2004. Print.

Bensen, Tedd. *The Timber-Frame Home.* London: Taunton, 1997. Print.

Sobon, Jack, and Roger Schroeder. *Timber Frame Construction: All about Post and Beam Building.* Pownal, VT: Storey, 1984. Print.

Stirling, Charles. *Timber Frame Construction: An Introduction.* Garston, UK: BREhop, 2004. Print.

Chappell, Steve. *A Timber Framer's Workshop: Joinery, Design and Construction of Traditional Timber Frames.* Brownfield, ME: Fox Maple, 1998. Print.

Bingham, Wayne J., and Jerod Pfeffer. *Natural Timber Frame Homes: Building with Wood, Stone, Clay, and Straw.* Salt Lake City, UT: Gibbs Smith, 2007. Print.

Beaudry, Michael. *Crafting Frames of Timber.* Montville, ME: Mud Pond Hewing and Framing, 2009. Print.

Law, Ben, and Lloyd Kahn. *Roundwood Timber Framing: Building Naturally Using Local Resources.* East Meon, UK: Permanent Publications, 2010. Print.

Conical grain bin roofs

What the cheerleaders say...	What the detractors say...
Efficient: Structure and sheathing combined	Requires round design
Easy to assemble	Complicated to insulate
Low cost	Difficult to eavestrough

Applications for system

- Roof structure and sheathing for round buildings

Basic materials

- Preformed steel panels
- Bolts and brackets

How the system works

Preformed, ribbed steel panels are bolted together with a compression ring at the top and connection ring at the base of the roof. The ring at the roof base is used to attach the roof to the top of the wall system. Depending on the size of the roof, additional rings may be required mid-span. A hatch or glazed skylight is installed at the peak of the roof.

The roof can be assembled in place on top of the walls, but they are often built on the ground and craned into place.

The roofs are available from manufacturers in a variety of diameters from 4–20 meters (12–60 feet).

The roofs are designed to sit atop round metal grain bins, and will require special adaption to fasten properly to the top of other wall systems and provide adequate overhang.

Tips for successful installation

1. Conical metal roofs are proprietary products, and each manufacturer will have its own installation guidelines that should be followed closely.
2. Modifications to the roof connection system should be designed and approved by a structural

engineer or the manufacturer of the roof system to ensure that loads are properly transferred to the walls and proper uplift resistance is achieved.

3. If a roof overhang is desired, the system must be modified to allow for a wall system of smaller diameter than the roof.

4. An insulation strategy must be designed for the roof system. As the steel roof is the structure, there are no framing members or depth to the system for resting or containing insulation. A secondary framing system is often employed beneath the metal roof to provide the required insulation depth.

5. The manufacturer or a structural engineer must approve modifications to the conical roof such as dormers or skylights.

Pros and cons
ENVIRONMENTAL IMPACTS

Harvesting — *High.* The extraction of ore for steel production is a high-intensity process, with impacts including habitat destruction and air and water pollution. Recycled content can mitigate these impacts.
Manufacturing — *High.* Steel production is a high-intensity process, requiring several applications of high heat, with impacts that include fossil fuel use, air and water pollution. Recycled content incurs the same impacts. It can be difficult to trace

the origins of the raw materials that are contained in a manufactured steel product like a conical grain bin roof.
Transportation — *Moderate to High.* Sample building uses 950 kg of steel and connectors for roof kit:

> 1.43 MJ per km by 15 ton truck
> 0.9 MJ per km by 35 ton truck
> 0.24 MJ per km by rail

Manufacturers exist in most regions. It is difficult to ascertain the transportation impacts of the material through the whole production cycle, as steel is a multinational industry.
Installation — *Negligible.*

WASTE
Prefabricated panels should result in no offcuts or waste.

ENERGY EFFICIENCY
Conical roof systems are not designed to be insulated, so the energy efficiency of a home using a conical roof will depend entirely on the design and execution of an insulation strategy being married to the roof.

Two insulating strategies are possible with this type of roof. Additional framing can be built underneath the steel roof structure, with insulation blown or laid into the cavity between the steel and

Conical Grain Bin Roof Embodied Energy

	Material embodied energy from I.C.E. in MJ/kg	Weight to volume ratio of material*	Volume of material in sample 1000sf/92.9m² building	Sample building embodied energy	Material embodied carbon from I.C.E. in kgCO₂e/kg	Sample building embodied carbon	Notes
11m (36ft) diameter roof for 95m² (1017 ft²)	22.6 (Steel sheet, galvanized, average recycled content)		950 kg**	21,470 MJ	1.54	1,463 kg	**Manufacturer shipping weight for 11 meter roof kit.

Transportation: Grain bin roof transportation by 35 ton truck would equate to 0.9 MJ per kilometer of travel to the building site. *Typically from engineeringtoolbox.com the framing beneath, or a spray-on insulation can be applied directly to the underside of the steel. In both scenarios, some type of finished ceiling will need to be installed to separate and protect the insulation. Performance will vary based on the quantity and thermal value of the chosen insulation. As there is no inherent framing depth in a conical roof, it can be straightforward to design an insulation strategy that is not limited by the depth of structural members, but rather suited to the insulation needs of the building.

MATERIAL COSTS: *HIGH*

The cost of a conical roof kit is higher than any other "framing" system in this chapter, but the system is roof structure and roof sheathing in one assembly. To properly compare costs, a framing system and a sheathing system must be looked at together.

LABOR INPUT: *MODERATE*

Conical roofs are designed to be quick to assemble and install. Most residential builders are likely to be unfamiliar with these systems, so extra time may be required to understand and follow the assembly instructions. As these roofs incorporate structure and sheathing in one assembly, they tend to require less labor time than systems that involve the construction of a frame, decking and then sheathing.

Much of the labor time will be involved in the construction of a system for containing insulation below the roof. The design of this system will have a large impact on labor time.

SKILL LEVEL REQUIRED FOR THE HOMEOWNER: *EASY TO MODERATE*

Conical roofs are straightforward to assemble, and beginners should have no problem following the instructions.

The framing of an insulation layer will potentially involve more skill than the roof assembly. A simple, flat ceiling design in which the conical space is empty attic and insulation is laid on the flat ceiling will be extremely fast and easy to install, though it will sacrifice the use of the conical space as a loft or second storey.

SOURCING/AVAILABILITY: *MODERATE TO DIFFICULT*

There are numerous manufacturers of conical roof systems in North America, and most regions will have available distribution from at least one. As the roofs are designed for agricultural use, they are not available from typical residential construction supply companies.

DURABILITY: *HIGH*

Conical steel roofs rely on the geometry of the steel panels and bolts to maintain their structural integrity, as there are no redundant structural members in the system. Galvanized steel is the most common material for both elements, and will have a long life span. Unlike other roofing systems where the structure is hidden beneath the sheathing and is therefore difficult to monitor, conical roofs can be structurally inspected from the exterior. Rusting will be the telltale sign of deterioration, and should be very visible. Most conical roofs do not show any signs of rust for at least twenty years, and structurally problematic rust may not occur for many decades afterward.

The round shape of the roof spreads loads evenly around the entire roof system and minimizes the effects of wind loads, which can help with durability through extreme weather cycles.

CODE COMPLIANCE

Residential building codes will not include conical steel roofs as an acceptable solution, as they are typically used in agricultural settings. Conical steel roofs are pre-engineered from the manufacturers, and should satisfy the requirements of objective codes. The point of connection between the roof and the wall system will likely be a custom-fabricated arrangement, and a structural engineer's approval may be required to ensure the connection is code-compliant.

INDOOR AIR QUALITY

The conical steel roof will be entirely outside the building enclosure and will have no effect on indoor air quality.

FUTURE DEVELOPMENT

Conical steel roofs have been used for decades in agricultural settings, and the system has been well developed. Since circular designs for residential use are uncommon, it is unlikely that conical steel roof manufacturers will develop prefabricated fastening systems to attach the roofs to typical residential wall systems.

Slab-based floors

What the cheerleaders say...	What the detractors say...
Simple to build	Often require foam insulation
Good thermal mass	Must be thermally separated from ground
Durable	Must have proper moisture control layer
Solid	

Applications for system

- Floor systems for grade-based scenarios

Basic materials

- Vapor/moisture control layer
- Thermal control layer
- Compactable base material (sand/gravel)
- Slab materials are either wet-poured (concrete, clay or other monolithic slabs) or dry-laid (flagstone, earthblock, brick or other masonry units)

Conical Grain Bin Roof Ratings

	Best 1	2	3	4	5	6	Worst 7	8	9	10	Notes
Environmental Impacts							■	■			Intensive mining and processing. High carbon output during manufacturing.
Embodied Energy						■					
Waste Generated	■										
Energy Efficiency											
Material Costs							■	■			Costs include structure and sheathing.
Labor Inputs				■	■						Labor includes structure and sheathing in one process.
Skill Level Required by Homeowner	■	■	■	■	■						
Sourcing and Availability				■	■	■					Must be sourced from specialty distributors.
Durability and Longevity	■										
Building Code Compliance			■	■	■						Pre-engineered, but not to residential standards or specifications.
Indoor Air Quality					N/A						

How the system works

Within the foundation of the building, an appropriate moisture control layer is used to separate the earth from the floor and an appropriate amount of thermal insulation is installed to provide adequate thermal comfort within the building year-round. A level base for the floor is prepared using compactable fill, flattened and tamped to provide a stable surface that will not compress under the expected loads on the floor.

The slab floor material is placed upon the compacted base material. If the floor material is dry — as in flagstone, brick, tile, compressed earth blocks and other masonry-type units — the individual pieces are laid on the base material, which may need to be adjusted for each piece if the sizes vary. A grout or mortar may be used under and around the individual pieces, or they may be dry-laid. If a wet-poured floor is being used, the wet material is poured and leveled on top of the compacted base and brought to the desired height and degree of finish. This may be a single or a multi-step process, depending on the material and chosen finish.

The floor material is typically hard and resilient, and transfers loads directly to the ground under the building.

Similar materials may be used for non-grade-based floors, but they will typically be supported by one of the suspended floor systems outlined in this chapter. A common example is a suspended concrete slab floor supported by open web steel joists.

Tips for successful installation

1. Ensure that an adequate moisture control layer is provided. Even in dry climates, the earth can be very moist and the transfer of that moisture into the building enclosure through a grade-based floor will have negative impacts on the health and durability of the entire building. Various types of plastic sheeting can be used

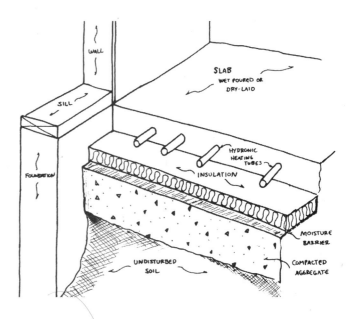

to create a very reliable and complete moisture control layer. Various fill materials can also be used to control rising moisture, though not with the thoroughness of plastic sheeting. Climate and building codes will help to decide what degree of protection is required and what materials will offer this level of protection.

2. Ensure that an adequate thermal control layer is provided. There is a common misconception that it is ideal to couple a floor directly to the earth, as the earth retains a fairly constant temperature year-round. While this is true, ground temperature (usually 8–12°C / 46–54°F) is not necessarily comfortable, especially in the winter. Being coupled to the ground means that the very large mass of the earth will continually take heat away from your building enclosure any time the building temperature is higher than ground temperature.

3. It is a common misconception that "heat rises" and therefore heat loss through a floor will be minimal. Try standing barefoot on a frozen

surface for a couple minutes to experience the effect of heat conduction in a downward direction! Insulation under a slab floor is a must.

4. Levels of thermal protection will not likely need to be as high as for exposed floors, walls and ceilings because the delta-T (temperature difference between the heated and unheated sides of the building enclosure) will be lower between the home and the earth.

5. The chosen insulation must be able to handle being located between the earth and a floor, both in terms of moisture capacity and compressive strength.

6. Slab-style floors require well-compacted bases. Use a suitable base material and ensure that compaction is even throughout the floor area, especially in corners and along the perimeter of the floor, where compaction may be harder to achieve. It is possible for a slab floor to crack or sink if it is not well supported.

7. The grading of the ground for a slab-style foundation must account for all of the various layers that will make up the floor system, and ensure that the finished floor is at the desired height. Be sure the building plans show all the necessary layers with accurate dimensions and that each element is added to the proper thickness.

8. Posts or interior walls that are bearing roof and/or upper floor loads may not be able to bear directly on the floor slab material. In such cases, additional foundation footings will need to be provided in these areas and the floor material will abut the footings. Walls or posts may need to be fastened to the floor, and provision for a means of attachment should be considered at the planning stages.

9. The range of materials included in this section varies widely in hardness, smoothness and strength. Be sure that you have researched your

choices carefully and have chosen materials that suit all your needs.

Pros and cons

ENVIRONMENTAL IMPACTS

Harvesting — *Negligible to High.* Aggregate and binders are mechanically extracted from quarries and can have low to high impacts on habitat and ground and surface water contamination and flow. Earthen materials harvested directly from the site will have negligible impacts.

Manufacturing — *Negligible to High.* Earthen floors from site soils will have negligible processing impacts. Bagged clay is dried using fossil fuel heat, and has moderate impacts.

Hydraulic binders like lime and portland cement are fired at extremely high temperatures and have high impacts including fossil fuel use, air and water pollution and greenhouse gas emissions.

Transportation — *Negligible to High.* Sample building uses 22,005 kg of aggregate for the floor base:

20.7 MJ per km by 35 ton truck

Sample building uses 10,280 – 22,656 kg of slab floor material:

9.7 – 21.3 MJ per km by 35 ton truck

Slab floor materials are all very heavy and accrue impacts proportional to distance traveled.

When assessing the impacts of a grade-based floor, all the components of the floor should be considered, especially the insulation type. Rigid foam insulation is the most common sub-slab insulation, and a floor system built on top of a lot of foam will obviously have higher impacts than one built on a more natural insulation.

Because of the wide range of combinations of vapor control, fill, insulation and floor materials, each complete system will need to be assessed individually.

WASTE

Compostable — All earthen and unmodified aggregates can be left in the environment.
Landfill — Cement and/or lime bags.

ENERGY EFFICIENCY

The insulation beneath a slab floor will have a large impact on the overall energy efficiency of the building. As noted above, conductive heat losses are significant and the earth is a very large mass to try to heat, so adequate thermal control must be used beneath a slab floor of any type.

Insulation below a slab will spend its life span in a damp, humid environment and must be suitable for such conditions. It will also be carrying significant loads and must be able to handle the weight of the floor and the live loads of the building.

A properly insulated slab floor can be very energy efficient, as the temperature of the earth is not as extreme as the temperature of the air surrounding the other sides of the building, and it will not be subjected to wind. Less insulation may be required than on the rest of the building enclosure.

Slab floors can also add significant thermal mass to a building (see sidebar Thermal Mass vs. Insulation) and can be good conductors for hydronic heating systems. While heated slabs are not more energy efficient than other heating systems, some studies have shown that warm slabs (or warm walls) can make people feel warmer in a building, and therefore encourage lower thermostat settings. Where this is the case, energy efficiency will be improved.

Slab Floor Embodied Energy

92.9 m² (1000 ft²) floor	Material embodied energy from I.C.E. in MJ/kg	Weight to volume ratio of material*	Volume of material in sample 1000sf/92.9m² building	Sample building embodied energy	Material embodied carbon from I.C.E. in kgCO₂e/kg	Sample building embodied carbon	Notes
Lowest Impact							
Earth floor							
150mm (6in) aggregate base	0.083 (Aggregate, general)	1554 kg/m³	14.16 m³ 22,005 kg	1,826 MJ	0.0052	114 kg	
100mm (4in) earth floor mix	0.083 (Aggregate, general)	1089 kg/m³	9.44 m³ 10,280 kg	853 MJ	0.0052	53 kg	
Totals				**2,679 MJ**		**167 kg**	
Highest Impact							
Concrete floor							
150mm (6in) aggregate base	0.083 (Aggregate, general)	1554 kg/m³	14.16 m³ 22,005 kg	1,826 MJ	0.0052	114 kg	
100mm (4in) concrete	0.74 (Concrete, general, 20/25mPa)	2400 kg/m³	9.44 m³ 22,656 kg	16,765 MJ	0.107	2,424 kg	
Reinforcing mesh	20.1 (Steel, general, average recycled content)	1.47 kg/m²	92.9 m² 136.6 kg	2,745 MJ	1.46	199 kg	
Totals				**21,336 MJ**		**2,737 kg**	Does not include figures for moisture barriers or insulation.

Transportation: Aggregate transportation by 35 ton truck would equate to 20.7 MJ per kilometer of travel to the building site. Clay transportation by 35 ton truck would equate to 9.7 MJ per kilometer of travel to the building site. Concrete transportation by 35 ton truck would equate to 21.3 MJ per kilometer of travel to the building site. *Typically from engineeringtoolbox.com

MATERIAL COSTS: *LOW TO MODERATE*

The aggregate base for a slab floor is relatively low cost. Slab floor material options range from very low cost (site soil for earthen floors) to moderate cost (concrete).

LABOR INPUT: *HIGH*

Dry Slabs — The size of individual dry fit pieces will have a large impact on labor requirements. More smaller pieces means more time to lay the floor. Regularly sized pieces will be faster to lay than irregular shapes which require careful fitting or cutting. Some dry laid floors will require further treatment of the floor surface, and this step will add additional labor time. Dry laid floors need not be completed under time restraints, so the pace of work can match the abilities and the skills of the labor force.

Wet Slabs — A team of a suitable size will be needed to mix, spread, level and finish a wet slab floor within a fairly limited time frame. Concrete can be ordered from a ready-mix company, easing the workload for site laborers, while earthen mixes are usually made on-site. Both concrete and earthen floors must be

poured, smoothed and finished while they are workable. For concrete, this window can be as little as an hour or two, while earthen slabs may be workable for a day or two. Typically, wet slabs are poured monolithically, but if one is being poured in sections due to labor concerns, the seams will always remain visible. To accomplish this successfully, make definitive divisions and hide the seams under walls if possible, or ensure that they will not interfere with the final look of the floor.

SKILL LEVEL REQUIRED FOR THE HOMEOWNER: *MODERATE TO HIGH*

Dry Slabs — Laying dry slab material is typically quite easy, with the preparation of a stable, level base being the most important element. Practiced hands will have an easier time with this task, but as there are no time restraints with the dry floor elements the work can be done slowly and in stages matching the skill level of the worker(s). Regularly shaped pieces will be simpler to fit together, while irregular shapes and thicknesses require extra time and reward a practiced hand.

Wet Slabs — It is a good idea to have at least one experienced person on a crew to lay a wet slab. There are specific techniques for laying and leveling a large area of wet material to achieve a flat and well-finished floor, and no amount of reading will prepare a novice crew for the work. Wet slabs involve a lot of hard physical work that doesn't require lots of skill, as long as someone knowledgeable is directing it. A practiced team will lay a floor in much less time and with much less drama.

Finishing the surface of a wet slab floor definitely rewards experience. The higher the degree of finish (smoothness and polish) desired, the more experience required. Timing is crucial for the various stages of applying a finish and only experience can tell you when it's time. A beginner can learn from an

Dry laid slab floor.

experienced finisher, while learning on one's own is bound to result in a sound but less than perfect floor.

Sourcing/availability: *Easy to Moderate*

Materials for both dry and wet slab floors are quite common. Earthen materials for compressed blocks, tamped earth or wet slabs are relatively easy to find in most regions. Stone that is suitable for making slabs, flagstone, cobblestone or tiles can be found in many regions, though the ability to properly process the stone may not. If you are using naturally occurring stone from your property, be sure it is suitable for use as flooring. A local quarry will be able to answer questions about sources for appropriate stone.

Concrete is widely available, although it will require contact with the batching plant if you want to use a mix that has a high percentage of recycled material (slag or fly ash).

The used building material market may provide sources for recycled slab flooring options including brick, tile and stone.

Durability: *Moderate to Very High*

Most slab floor materials are quite durable. Dry slabs have the advantage of being repairable/replaceable in small sections should they be damaged, while monolithic floors are more difficult to repair.

Earthen materials are softer and more prone to wear and damage than hard materials like stone and concrete, but are simpler to repair.

Slab floors in general are longwearing and very durable.

Code compliance

Slab floors that are not playing any structural role are usually not prescribed by building codes, meaning that a wide range of feasible materials should be acceptable. Dry laid slabs are not common and may raise eyebrows, but should not face restrictions against their use. Wet laid slabs are commonplace and widely accepted.

Indoor air quality: *Moderate to High*

Due to the large exposed surface area in the building, a slab floor can have a big effect on indoor air quality, and each layer of the floor system can have an effect.

The earth under the slab may contain contaminants that occur naturally (like radon gas or heavy metals) or come from previous site use (agricultural and industrial residues). A proper barrier under the slab floor and/or ventilation under the slab may be enough to prevent such contaminants from entering the building.

Many common sub-slab insulations contain contaminants that may end up airborne in the home, including fire retardants in foam insulation, formaldehyde in mineral wool and asbestos in some mineral insulations. If there is concern about contaminants in the insulation, a different insulation can be chosen or the insulation can be placed under an effective barrier.

The crushed stone and/or sand used as a base for the floor may also contain contaminants. Especially with dry laid floors, there is a good chance that dust from this sub-layer may make its way through the joints in the flooring material and become airborne. To avoid this, joints should be mortared or grouted.

The floor material itself can have a wide range of IAQ impacts. Most of these will come from the final finish (sealants, paints, etc). However, dusting from earthen, stone, brick and even concrete can occur and can contaminate indoor air. Ensure that floor slabs have a relatively smooth finish and that sealants used to bind the surface are nontoxic. If you notice surface dusting of the floor, it is important to deal with the issue by refinishing, resurfacing or covering the floor.

When using recycled flooring, be sure to check the material for potential contamination from previous uses. Clay, brick or stone from old buildings could have absorbed a wide range of contaminants in its previous location, especially if it comes from a factory or industrial building.

FUTURE DEVELOPMENT

As this section covers a wide range of materials and approaches, the potential for development is similarly wide-ranging. More environmentally benign concrete mixtures are likely to be developed, which could potentially make concrete floors a more desirable choice. The development of earthen floor systems also holds plenty of potential, as there is much work being done to stabilize and standardize both wet-poured earthen mixes and compressed earth blocks to make them more user friendly and reliable.

Slab Floor Ratings

	Best 1 2 3 4 5 6 7 Worst 8 9 10	Notes
Environmental Impacts		Impacts vary greatly depending on slab material, with concrete raising impacts significantly.
Embodied Energy		EE varies greatly depending on slab material, with concrete raising EE significantly.
Waste Generated		
Energy Efficiency	N/A	
Material Costs		Slab typically includes finished floor surface, eliminating need for further material.
Labor Inputs		
Skill Level Required by Homeowner		
Sourcing and Availability		
Durability and Longevity		Material of choice will impact durability, with stone/concrete being very durable.
Building Code Compliance		Non-structural floor slabs are not tightly regulated by codes.
Indoor Air Quality		IAQ impacts will vary with slab material, but most choices have minimal impacts.

Chapter title page photo credits. Top left to right.
1. Jen Feigin 2. Chester Rennie 3. Kelly Jacobsen 4. Jen Feigin

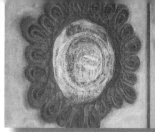

4

Sheathing and cladding materials

S HEATHING AND CLADDING MATERIALS constitute a lot of square footage in a building, covering exterior walls, interior walls and ceilings. They play the defining role in the appearance of the exterior and interior of a building and represent a significant amount of the time, effort and environmental impacts of a building. Multiple choices and combinations are likely in any building, making this an important part of the design process.

In some cases, decisions made earlier in the process regarding wall and roof systems may dictate certain sheathing and cladding choices. Other wall and roof systems will allow for the full range of options presented here. If you are going into the design process with certain options in mind, you may be led toward a particular type of wall or roof choice.

There are a few types of sheathing and cladding presented here that are only appropriate for interior walls and ceilings, and some that are more commonly used on the exterior but which can also be used for interior walls.

The distinction between sheathing and cladding relates to the structural importance of the material. Sheathing materials are fastened directly to the building in such a way as to provide either a primary or secondary structural strength, usually shear strength but sometimes also compressive strength. In contrast, cladding materials are applied in a manner that removes them from playing a key structural role. Some buildings will combine sheathing (such as plywood or plaster) applied directly to the wall with a cladding (such as wood, brick or rainscreen plaster) that is attached to the sheathing via strapping or anchors.

Sheathing and cladding considerations can be two-fold: the material itself and the type of surface finish used to seal and protect it. In some cases, the two can be considered separately with a single material having several options for finishing. In other cases, the material may be left in its raw state with no need for further finishing. Chapter 7: Surface Finishing Materials considers the treatments that may be applied to cladding materials, so the materials in this chapter are considered in their raw form.

Building science basics for exterior sheathing and cladding

Exterior sheathing plays an important structural role in bracing and stabilizing a wall or roof system. The fastening of a sheathing material to a frame or wall substrate creates a stable diaphragm that resists shear and compressive forces. Where sheathing is intended to have a structural role, it must be specified to handle the expected loads and fastened to meet requirements.

Sometimes a structural sheathing will function as a primary air control layer, preventing air from moving into the wall system from the exterior. In these cases, joints and intersections in the sheathing must be made airtight, often using tape, caulking or parging.

In some cases, a structural sheathing will also be the finished surface and be responsible for functioning as a cladding as well.

The primary function of cladding (or siding) is to keep precipitation out of the building. Most cladding materials are applied to the exterior walls in such a way as to create a rainscreen siding. In a rainscreen scenario, the cladding is applied to the wall behind in a manner that leaves a reasonable (20–40-mm or ¾- to 1½-inch) ventilation space and drainage plane between the wall and the cladding. This space should be vertical in orientation to allow for the circulation of air from the bottom of the wall to the top, and to allow for drainage of any water leaking in through the cladding. Air circulation through this space will allow any humidity created by moisture escaping the walls of the building to be equalized with drier outdoor air conditions. In this way, it is possible to prevent moisture buildup on the backside of the siding and/or the exterior face of the wall, which is a key factor in most moisture failures. Vertical channels create entry points for air at both the bottom and the top, following the natural pattern for convective drying.

Horizontal channels suit some kinds of sheathing better than vertical channels, but a horizontal channel doesn't allow for drainage or convective currents with upper and lower entrance points. There may be no actual exit point for horizontal spaces, making moisture buildup more likely.

Rainscreen siding should have adequate ventilation space, but shouldn't be an open channel that allows insects or rodents to take up residence in the building. Screen, mesh or breather strips are available for all types of siding.

Certain wall types, in particular those with plaster finishes, are not designed to have rainscreen sheathing. In these cases of integral sheathing, the plaster is adhered directly to the wall surface and there is no ventilated cavity. For these types of walls, moisture is handled by preventing precipitation from penetrating the plaster (via protection from roof overhangs and sealants or paints that reduce bulk water penetration) and ensuring that the plaster and any sealants are permeable enough to allow moisture to escape to the atmosphere. This strategy has proven to work for many building types and in many regions, but in areas with lots of precipitation (especially wind-driven rain) or for building designs with little roof protection of the walls (especially tall walls), it is prudent to create a rainscreen over the plaster finish. This can be constructed with a different type of sheathing, or by applying another layer of plaster over a breather fabric.

Regardless of the type of siding and manner of installation, all exterior sheathing must have proper consideration and application of flashing at all joints, intersections and openings to prevent water from entering. It is prudent to follow best practices for flashing to match the sheathing type.

Rainscreen cladding is not used as the primary air control layer on the exterior of the wall.

The plaster applied to many natural wall-building systems is often considered an integral part of the structural capacity of the wall. Where this is the case, the type of plaster, method of attachment and application to the wall and potential need for reinforcement must be part of the plan for the building and up to the task of handling the structural requirements.

Building science basics for interior sheathing

Interior sheathing can have an important role in the moisture handling capability of a building. The sheathing can be the primary air control layer, or may require a separate, sheet-style air control layer applied beneath the sheathing. Where the sheathing itself is the primary control layer, it must be installed in such a way as to eliminate cracks and leaks and be properly integrated with other air control layers at all intersections.

Most interior sheathing materials are naturally vapor-permeable, allowing them to be used in wall systems where this characteristic is desirable or required. If permeability is not desired, a sheet-style vapor barrier and/or an impermeable surface coating will need to be used. As a general rule, in heating climates the exterior sheathing should be at least as permeable as the interior sheathing, while in cooling climates the opposite holds true. Otherwise, moisture migrating through the sheathing on the more humid side may accumulate inside the wall at a rate faster than it can leave through the drier side.

In many scenarios the interior sheathing is considered to be playing a structural role, and materials choices and construction methods may need to be made to meet these requirements.

Clay or earthen plaster

What the cheerleaders say...	What the detractors say...
Very low impacts	Durability issues
Widely available materials	Not commercially available
Easy to use, beginner friendly	Labor intensive
Easily repairable	
Nontoxic	

Applications for system

- Structural sheathing
- Exterior cladding
- Interior cladding (walls and ceilings)
- Can be used over natural wall systems or wooden lath

Basic materials

- Clay
- Sand
- Fiber (straw, hemp, or other natural fiber)
- Pigments, if desired
- Admixtures (can include flour paste, natural oil, lime, among others)

How the system works

There are as many different formulations for clay plaster as there are plasterers who work with the material, but all are based on ratios of clay to sand to fiber that create a mixture with the desired characteristics of stickiness and body to suit the needs of the application. In some cases, mixes can resemble conventional cement or lime plasters, with one part of clay to three parts of sand. These mixes are suitable for thin, multi-coat applications over a fairly flat substrate. At the other end of the spectrum are mixes that use one part of clay to as many as three parts of coarse fiber and little to no sand. These mixes are suitable for thick, single-coat applications over uneven substrates. There is a wide range of mixes between these two extremes, which may be chosen for ease of application, desired finish or structural integrity.

Regardless of the type of mix, clay plasters require a substrate with enough "tooth" to give the plaster a good mechanical grip on the wall surface. This surface may be inherent in the wall (as with straw bale, cob, cordwood and other natural wall systems), or may require the use of wooden lath or a mesh material.

The plaster is pressed onto the backing surface using hands and/or trowels, with enough force to create an adequate bond and fill all voids and hollows. The application may require one or several

Clay plaster. (DAVID ELFSTROM)

coats to achieve the intended thickness, with multiple coats requiring drying time and scoring of the surface between applications. The top surface is worked to provide the desired texture and degree of finish.

If clay plaster is playing a structural role, it is typical to require a minimum average thickness of 40–60 mm (1–1½ inch).

Clay plasters must dry thoroughly before a final finish or sealant (if desired) is applied. This can take anywhere from a day or two for very thin coats to several weeks for very thick coats.

Clay plasters do not undergo a chemical change in the mixing or drying process, and are therefore susceptible to damage from excessive wetting that can soften and erode the mixture. These plasters are not as fragile as many believe, and can handle a regular wetting regimen as long as the water does not have a consistent eroding effect. However, unprotected clay plasters are not suitable in areas subject to a lot of rain, where a water-resistant finish and/or roof overhang protection should be considered minimum protection and a rainscreen cladding maximum protection.

Tips for successful installation

1. Understand all structural, control layer and aesthetic requirements of the plaster before committing to the use and formulation of a clay plaster.
2. Source ingredients for clay plasters can come from naturally occurring soils or from manufactured soils, bagged clay or aggregate. If you hope to work with site soil, first ascertain its condition (moisture content, rock/stone content) and the ratio of clay, silt and sand to determine whether it is appropriate. There are many resources available to help determine whether site soils can work for earthen plasters.

3. Work from an established recipe for clay plaster, or prepare test samples to refine a custom mix to best meet the needs of the project.

4. A good plastering job requires properly placed plaster stops or transition considerations at every junction. Many designers and builders will not adequately prepare for the intended thickness of the plaster at the top and bottom of the walls and around door and window openings.

5. Clay plasters will bond well to variegated surfaces but not to smooth surfaces. Even small expanses of flat surface can cause delaminating and/or cracking. Mesh or fiber must bridge all framing and other smooth surfaces.

6. The success of a clay plaster depends largely on the bond it creates with the wall behind. Clay slip coats, mesh, lath or other surface preparations should be done thoroughly. Clay plaster must be applied to the wall surface with sufficient force to ensure it penetrates into all voids and makes strong contact with all surfaces.

7. Give clay plaster adequate time to dry thoroughly before adding sealants or finishes. Even if the surface appears dry, the plaster may still contain significant moisture that may disturb finishes as it dries.

Pros and cons

ENVIRONMENTAL IMPACTS

Harvesting — *Negligible to Moderate.* Clay plasters made from soils found on or near the construction site will have minimal impacts. Bagged clay is extracted from clay pits, and impacts from the pits can include habitat destruction and silting of ground and surface water.

Crushed sand is typically found in every region. Extraction from aggregate pits can have impacts including habitat destruction and silting of ground and surface water.

Fibers used in clay plasters are usually made from waste agricultural fiber and have negligible impacts.

If wood lath is used, the harvesting of the wood will have potential habitat destruction impacts. In general wood lath is cut from undesirable lumber stock and does not involve the harvesting of trees just to create lath.

Manufacturing — *Negligible to Low.* Site soils require no manufacturing process and only low-impact mixing on-site. Manufactured clays are dried and ground to a fine powder, which is a low-impact process.

Sand is a product of the aggregate industry, made from extracting sand and stone from quarries and, when necessary, crushing, washing and screening the sand to the desired size. This is a low-impact process.

Wood lath is milled from lumber that is not of suitable quality for other purposes, and is a low-impact process.

Transportation — *Negligible to High.* Sample building uses 6,751.8 kg of clay soil or bagged clay and aggregate:

> 10.1 MJ per km by 15 ton truck
> 6.35 MJ per km by 35 ton truck

Site soils will need no transportation. Bagged clay is likely to require shipping, as clay processing does not happen in every region. As a heavy material, clay will have significant transportation impacts if it travels long distances.

Sand can be found locally in most regions.

Wood lath can be found locally in most regions.

Installation — *Negligible.*

WASTE: *NEGLIGIBLE*

Compostable — All plaster ingredients may be left in the environment. Plaster is mixed in fairly small batches, so quantities should be minimal.

Recyclable — Packaging of bagged clay.
Landfill — None.

ENERGY *EFFICIENCY*

A well-applied clay plaster can be an effective air control layer and contribute to an energy-efficient enclosure. A poorly applied plaster with cracks and voids at seams will negatively affect energy efficiency. A thick clay plaster (40–160 mm or 1–4 inches) with a lot of fiber content can add some degree of extra thermal protection to a wall system, with values ranging from R 0.5–1.5 per inch.

MATERIAL COSTS: *LOW*

Locally obtained clay soils can be purchased for little more than the price of trucking the material to the building site. If bagged clay is being used, the quantities are relatively small and the costs are still low.

LABOR INPUT: *HIGH*

Clay plasters can be labor intensive. Much of the labor goes into the preparation of the wall for plastering, and may include application of clay slip, lath and plaster stops. Mixing plaster requires a lot of labor input, even when a mechanical mixer is used, as ingredients need to be added by shovel or bucket and mixed plaster must be delivered to the applicator. Hand and trowel application take a similar amount of time. Thick, one-coat applications can save time over multiple thin layers.

Health Warnings — Powdered clay and dry sand can both create a lot of dust that is high in silica content and is dangerous to breathe. Chopped fiber can also be very dusty. Wear proper breathing protection whenever handling dusty materials.

SKILL LEVEL REQUIRED FOR THE HOMEOWNER

Preparation of wall surface — *Easy to Difficult.* The better the surface of the wall is prepared, the easier the plaster application and the more professional-looking the results. At the most basic, plaster can be applied directly to a wall with very little preparation and the results can be functional. At the most complex, preparation for trim, electrical boxes and door and window frames and sills can be time-consuming and require an understanding of how the plaster should finish to all edges.

Installation of sheathing — *Easy to Moderate.* Beginners can apply clay plaster by hand with a relatively good level of finish. It is a forgiving material as the drying times are long and repairs and alterations can be made for several days after application. It can take some experience to achieve a high degree of finish quality, especially at seams and intersections. Troweling a clay plaster can be more difficult for beginners, as it is not as intuitive as using the hands directly.

Clay Plaster Sheathing Embodied Energy

163 m² (1750 ft²), 40mm (1.5 in) coverage	Material embodied energy from I.C.E. in MJ/kg	Weight to volume ratio of material*	Volume of material in sample 1000sf/92.9m² building	Sample building embodied energy	Material embodied carbon from I.C.E. in kgCO₂e/kg	Sample building embodied carbon	Notes
Clay soil	0.083 (Aggregate, general)	1089 kg/m³	6.2 m³ 6751.8 kg	55 MJ	0.0052	35 kg	
Straw (15 bales)	0.24 (Straw)	120 kg/m³	2 m³ 240 kg	58 MJ	0.01	2 kg	
Totals				**113 MJ**		**37 kg**	Does not include mesh or admixtures, if required.

Transportation: Clay soil transportation by 15 ton truck would equate to 10.1 MJ per kilometer of travel to the building site. *Typically from engineeringtoolbox.com

Finishing of sheathing — *Easy.* Clay plasters can be left raw in many cases. Finishes typically involve brushing or sponging a liquid paint of some kind onto the surface.

SOURCING/AVAILABILITY: *EASY TO MODERATE*

All the ingredients for clay plasters are widely available, but there are no commercially available clay or earthen plaster mixes in ready-to-use form. Site soils may require no off-site sourcing. Individual ingredients must be obtained from different sources. Bagged clay typically comes from pottery supply outlets, sand from a local quarry and chopped straw or other fiber from local farms or farm supply outlet. Pigments and admixtures also require separate sourcing.

DURABILITY: *LOW TO HIGH*

Exterior — A well-made, well-applied clay plaster can have a long life span in a well-protected installation, as the ingredients don't decay or degrade unless exposed to enough water to cause erosion. However, erosion can happen quickly under extreme conditions, so proper protection from roof overhangs and/or sealants is important. While clay plaster may, under poor conditions, have durability issues, it is also easy and inexpensive to repair. More clay plaster can be applied over areas with cracks or erosion and create a new, monolithic surface as good as the original plaster. **Interior** — Clay plaster is very durable in any dry interior location, and will not require regular maintenance. Like other mineral-based sheathing, it is prone to denting and chipping when hit with sufficient force.

CODE COMPLIANCE

Clay plaster is not recognized as an exterior or interior sheathing or cladding by any North American building codes. If used as a decorative cladding only (especially on interior walls), there is unlikely to be any resistance from code officials. When used

Clay Plaster Sheathing Ratings

	Best 1	2	3	4	5	6	Worst 7	8	9	10	Notes
Environmental Impacts											
Embodied Energy											
Waste Generated											
Energy Efficiency											Clay plaster can be an effective air control layer.
Material Costs											Local soils will be less expensive than manufactured clay.
Labor Inputs											Degree of mechanization will affect labor inputs.
Skill Level Required by Homeowner											Degree of finish determined by skill level.
Sourcing and Availability											
Durability and Longevity											Durability will depend largely on the quality of the mix and exposure to water erosion.
Building Code Compliance											Use as structural sheathing will require alternative compliance pathways.
Indoor Air Quality											Clay has desirable IAQ effects, but soils can contain contaminants and dust that may have detrimental effects.

structurally as a sheathing/cladding on exterior walls, it is likely to require the approval of a structural engineer or architect.

INDOOR AIR QUALITY: *HIGH*

Clay plaster can have a positive effect on IAQ. Limited testing shows that clay plasters are capable of taking impurities out of the air and storing or transforming them. Clay plasters have a great deal of moisture storage capacity, and can help to mitigate issues of high indoor humidity without resultant mold development.

If a clay plaster is not properly formulated, it can be dusty and contribute fine silica particulate to the air.

FUTURE DEVELOPMENT

Clay plasters offer a remarkably low-impact and high-durability option for sheathing and cladding, especially interiors. The development of bagged, pre-mixed clay plasters or the ability to order local plaster mixes from a ready-mix outlet is very feasible and awaits sufficient consumer demand to become reality. The beauty, simplicity, health benefits and user-friendliness of clay plasters make them an ideal development in sustainable building.

Resources for further research

Guelberth, Cedar Rose, and Daniel D. Chiras. *The Natural Plaster Book: Earth, Lime and Gypsum Plasters for Natural Homes.* Gabriola Island, BC: New Society, 2003. Print.

Meagan, Keely. *Earth Plasters for Straw Bale Homes.* Eureka, CA: Taylor, 2000. Print.

Minke, Gernot. *Building with Earth: Design and Technology of a Sustainable Architecture.* Basel, Switzerland: Birkhäuser, 2006. Print.

Crews, Carole. *Clay Culture: Plasters, Paints and Preservation.* Taos, NM: Gourmet Adobe, 2009. Print.

Weismann, Adam, and Katy Bryce. *Using Natural Finishes: Lime- and Earth-Based Plasters, Renders and Paints: A Step-by-Step Guide.* Totnes, UK: Green, 2008. Print.

Wood plank sheathing and cladding

What the cheerleaders say...	What the detractors say...
Renewable material, widely available	Unstable material (expansion, contraction, cupping)
Durable	Requires regular maintenance
Beautiful	May not be sustainably harvested
Many styles possible	

Applications for system

- Rainscreen cladding (vertical or horizontal orientation)
- Structural sheathing (horizontal orientation, specific nailing pattern required)
- Aesthetic sheathing (vertical or horizontal orientation)

Basic materials

- Softwood plank
- Fasteners
- Surface finish treatment

How the system works

Wood (usually softwood) is milled to a desired size and profile. There is a wide variety of typical wood siding profiles. Wood may be fastened vertically to a series of regularly spaced wooden straps run horizontally, or fastened horizontally to straps run vertically.

Profiles and layouts are designed to overlap or fit together at seams between planks to minimize the possibility of water penetration. Fasteners may be hidden or left exposed depending on profile and aesthetic preference.

Tips for successful installation

1. Wood cladding will have the longest life span if installed as a ventilated rainscreen. Be sure

plans include a vertical air channel behind the siding, with a screened air inlet/outlet at the bottom and top of the wall. For vertical siding, this may require strapping vertically first, then horizontally.

2. If wood cladding is getting a surface treatment, be sure to apply this to all six sides of every piece. Wood that is only treated on the exterior face is prone to cupping and twisting, as well as moisture damage from the backside.

3. Be sure to use fasteners of an appropriate size with the proper kind of head for the particular profile of wood. Fasteners should be galvanized, stainless or made of a non-corroding metal.

4. Design to keep wood cladding at least 30 cm (12 inches) above finished grade, and ensure that wood will not be in the path of constant splashback from the roof.

5. There are many excellent resources available for the installation of every type of wood siding. Be sure to research all applicable strategies and techniques.

Pros and cons

ENVIRONMENTAL IMPACTS

Harvesting — *Negligible to High.* A wide variety of forestry practices are used to harvest wood cladding. At best, impacts are kept to a minimum, but at worst can include habitat destruction, resource depletion, soil erosion and silting and contamination of waterways. Third-party certification can help to ensure that impacts are minimized.

Manufacturing — *Negligible to Low.* Most wood cladding is milled to maximize the potential of each log. There can be as few as one step (rough sawing) and as many as four steps (rough sawing, planing and several steps to mill a profile) to the process, depending on the type of profile and finish being applied.

Vertical wood siding.

Transportation — *Negligible to High.* Sample building uses 1,395 kg of wood siding:

> 2.1 MJ per km by 15 ton truck
> 1.3 MJ per km by 35 ton truck

As a heavy material, wood will have significant transportation impacts if it travels long distances. **Installation** — *Negligible.*

WASTE: *MODERATE TO HIGH*

Compostable — Untreated wood scrap. Quantity may be low or high depending on the application. **Recyclable** — Metal fasteners. Quantity will be low. **Landfill** — Pre-finished wood scrap.

ENERGY EFFICIENCY

Wood sheathing or cladding will not have a large impact on energy efficiency. When used as structural sheathing, the gaps between planks will require the use of a sheet-style air control layer to properly prevent air migration into the wall.

MATERIAL COSTS: *LOW TO HIGH*

There are many types of wood siding and sheathing, from low-cost, rough-cut overlapping options to planed, tongue-and-groove options. Species can vary regionally, which also affects costs. Wood siding is one of the most wide-ranging options in terms of material costs.

Cedar shingles and horizontal wood siding.

LABOR INPUT: *MODERATE TO HIGH.*

The type, quantity and direction of strapping will have a large impact on labor input. Most styles of wood cladding have similar labor inputs for installation. If the wood cladding is being finished on-site, this will add significant time prior to the installation process.

Health Warnings — Avoid breathing sawdust during cutting.

SKILL LEVEL REQUIRED FOR THE HOMEOWNER

Preparation of substrate — *Easy to Moderate.* A homeowner with basic carpentry tools and experience can apply a single or double layer of strapping.

Installation of sheathing — *Easy to Moderate.* A homeowner with basic carpentry tools and experience can apply a wood sheathing/cladding. A good installation requires an understanding of how the cladding is managed at corners and intersections. Trim work for some wood claddings can be moderately difficult.

Finishing of sheathing — *Easy.* Pre-finished siding requires all cut ends to be painted with the same finish. If wood cladding is unfinished, applying treatment is straightforward but can be time-consuming. Raw wood cladding requires no additional finishing time.

Wood Sheathing Embodied Energy

163 m² (1750 ft²)	Material embodied energy from I.C.E. in MJ/kg	Weight to volume ratio of material*	Volume of material in sample 1000sf/92.9m² building	Sample building embodied energy	Material embodied carbon from I.C.E. in kgCO₂e/kg	Sample building embodied carbon	Notes
20mm (¾ in) solid wood siding (shiplap, tongue and groove or board and batten)	2.5	450 kg/m³ (softwood lumber)	3.1 m³ 1395 kg	3,488 MJ	0.2	279 kg	
Nails	20.1 (Steel, general, average recycled content)		20 kg	402 MJ	1.46	29 kg	
Totals				3,890 MJ		308 kg	

Transportation: Wood transportation by 15 ton truck would equate to 2.1 MJ per kilometer of travel to the building site. *Typically from engineeringtoolbox.com

SOURCING/AVAILABILITY: *EASY*

Wood cladding is widely available in many styles from building supply outlets and specialty siding shops.

DURABILITY: *MODERATE*

Raw wood lasts a long time as a cladding if installed properly. It can take seventy-five to a hundred years for raw wood to deteriorate to the point where it is no longer useful, with UV radiation being the most potent agent of decay.

Durability issues are more likely to be caused by finishes and the difficulties involved in refinishing. Paint, especially when applied only to the exterior face of the wood, will often crack and peel, requiring labor-intensive scraping and sanding to refinish. Stains, mineral treatments and washes will fade over time but will not be prone to the same cracking and peeling as paint. Deteriorating finishes will often cause a homeowner to remove and replace wood siding that feasibly had many more years of service life, so choosing a good finish and applying it to all six sides will go a long way toward extending the serviceable life span of wood cladding.

Wood cladding can also cup and warp, becoming visually unappealing. This is often due to improper

Cedar shingle pattern.

Wood Sheathing Ratings

	Best 1	2	3	4	5	6	Worst 7	8	9	10	Notes
Environmental Impacts		██	██	██	██	██					Forestry practices are highly variable and have a significant impact.
Embodied Energy		██									
Waste Generated					██	██	██	██	██	██	
Energy Efficiency					N/A						Wood siding is not an effective air control layer.
Material Costs	██	██	██	██	██	██					
Labor Inputs			██	██	██	██					
Skill Level Required by Homeowner	██	██	██								
Sourcing and Availability	██										
Durability and Longevity		██	██	██	██	██					Wood has a relatively long lifespan, but type of finish will have a large impact on durability and appearance.
Building Code Compliance	██										
Indoor Air Quality	██	██									Used indoors, wood sheathing typically will not have an adverse effect on IAQ. Spores and mold can occur in rare circumstances.

fastening and/or finishing of the wood, and can be avoided by proper installation.

CODE COMPLIANCE

Wood cladding is an acceptable solution in all codes. Regions with termites may have restrictions or regulations to avoid infestation.

INDOOR AIR QUALITY

No impact.

FUTURE DEVELOPMENT

The growth of third-party certification programs is increasing the availability of sustainably harvested wood products, including cladding. Nontoxic finishes are also becoming more widely available.

Resources for further research

Ireton, Kevin. *Exterior Siding, Trim, and Finishes.* Newtown, CT: Taunton, 2004. Print.

DeKorne, Clayton. *The Essential Guide to Exteriors.* Washington, D.C.: Hanley Wood, 2005. Print.

Brumbaugh, James E., and John Leeke. *Complete Siding Handbook: Installation, Maintenance, Repair.* New York: Macmillan, 1992. Print.

Plywood and oriented strand board (OSB) sheathing

What the cheerleaders say...	What the detractors say...
Affordable	Off-gassing from glues
Good structural properties	Little aesthetic appeal, usually needs to be covered
Makes use of marginal and fast-growing wood	Sheet sizing can lead to waste
Fast to install	

Applications for system

- Structural wall sheathing

Basic materials

- Wood veneer (plywood)
- Wood flakes (OSB)
- Adhesive

How the system works

Plywood — Logs are felled, debarked and soaked in hot water. Veneer sheets are peeled from the soaked logs and glued together as plies, with the grain of each ply aligned perpendicular to the adjacent ply. The plies are pressed together with heat. Each ply is typically 3 mm or ⅛ inch thick and sheets for construction are made in 3-, 4-, 5- and 6-ply thicknesses.

OSB — Oriented strand board uses flakes of wood peeled from logs that would not have been suitable for other purposes. The flakes are dried, impregnated with glue, oriented in cross-directional "mats" and then pressed under high heat and pressure to form panels.

Both materials are available in 4x8 ft sheets. In most applications, the sheets are nailed to the studs, sills and headers of a wood frame wall or to roof rafters. Joints between panels are aligned on framing members and blocking. A nailing pattern is specified around the edge and in the field of each panel.

Tips for successful installation

1. If sheet material is to be used as sheathing, plan to make the best use of standard sheathing dimensions. Significant waste can accumulate if many custom cuts are required.
2. Sheet wood can be used as a primary air control layer if all joints are gasketed, caulked or taped appropriately. Typically, these products are used in conjunction with sheet-type barriers, but the barriers are not required if the sheathing itself has been sealed adequately.
3. Plywood and OSB are not very vapor-permeable. As they are usually applied on the exterior of a wall, this dictates the use of low-permeability materials on the interior, or the use of sheet-style vapor barriers.
4. Be sure to follow the nailing pattern recommended by codes and/or manufacturer's instructions and use the specified type and length of nail.

Pros and cons

ENVIRONMENTAL IMPACTS

Harvesting — *Moderate to High.* Logs for sheet materials mainly come from large forestry operations, which can have impacts including habitat destruction, deforestation, soil erosion and silting and contamination of surface water.

Manufacturing — *Moderate to High.* Making sheet materials is a multi-stage process that requires relatively high-energy inputs, in particular the heating of water baths for logs and the heat required when pressing materials into sheets. In plywood manufacturing, between 25 and 50 percent of each log is not usable for creating plies. This used to result in a lot of waste, but much of this material is now used in making OSB.

The glues used for these products are petrochemical based and impacts from their manufacture and use include habitat destruction and air and water pollution.

Transportation — *Low to High.* Sample building uses 1,030 kg of plywood or OSB sheathing for the exterior walls:

> 1.55 MJ per km by 15 ton truck
> 1 MJ per km by 35 ton truck
> 0.25 MJ per km by rail

The vast majority of sheet wood products are manufactured on the midwest coast of North America and shipped across the continent.

Installation — *Low.*

WASTE: *MODERATE TO HIGH*

Compostable — None.

Recyclable — Metal fasteners. Quantities are small.

Landfill — Plywood and OSB offcuts. Quantities can range from small to large, depending on the number of offcuts.

ENERGY EFFICIENCY

Wood sheet materials can contribute to an airtight building enclosure, especially when gasketed, caulked or taped to the framing at all joints. The materials do not directly contribute to thermal performance.

MATERIAL COSTS: *MODERATE*

Sheet materials are produced on a scale that makes them a moderately priced option. Competition between producers and retailers for these high-demand products has created pricing that is not reflective of the relatively high embodied energy of the materials.

LABOR INPUT: *MODERATE*

Sheets cover a large amount of square footage and are sized to correspond to standard framing spacing. When plans make good use of this sizing, labor inputs can be low. The cutting of sheet materials can be time-consuming, so the more custom cuts required the higher the labor input.

Health Warnings — Sawdust contains toxins from glues; wear breathing protection when cutting.

SKILL LEVEL REQUIRED FOR THE HOMEOWNER

Preparation of substrate — *Easy to Moderate.* Sheet wood applies to the studs of a frame wall. A homeowner capable of accurate framing work will create a good backing for sheets.

Installation of sheathing — *Moderate.* Large sheets take some practice to handle, cut and install. A homeowner capable of accurate framing work will also be able to apply sheathing successfully.

Finishing of sheathing — *Easy.* There is typically no finishing applied to sheet wood products. In rare cases where sheet wood is the final finish, surface treatment products are rolled or brushed onto the surface.

SOURCING/AVAILABILITY: *EASY*

Sheet wood is widely available through building supply outlets.

DURABILITY: *MODERATE*

Sheet wood is reasonably durable when kept dry. Though much work has gone into formulating glues that are water-resistant, the surface area of the plies and wood flakes result in a lot of swelling when the products get wet and the swell-shrink cycle can destroy the bond of the glue. OSB in particular is susceptible to degradation from wetting.

The most likely moisture damage to these products comes from condensation on the backside of the sheets due to air leakage from the inside of the walls. As these materials are not very permeable, moisture can accumulate and damage the sheets. This damage won't be seen until the materials are close to or beyond the point of failure because the sheet wood is usually hidden behind cladding.

CODE COMPLIANCE

Sheet wood is an acceptable solution in all jurisdictions.

INDOOR AIR QUALITY

Used on the exterior of the building, these materials

Plywood and OSB Sheathing Embodied Energy

	Material embodied energy from I.C.E. in MJ/kg	Weight to volume ratio of material*	Volume of material in sample 1000sf/92.9m² building	Sample building embodied energy	Material embodied carbon from I.C.E. in kgCO₂e/kg	Sample building embodied carbon	Notes
Exterior walls 163 m² (1750 ft²)							
12mm (½ in) exterior grade	15 (Timber, Plywood and OSB)	500 kg/m³	2.06 m³ 1030 kg	15,450 MJ	0.45	464 kg	
Sub-flooring 92.9m² (1000ft²)							
16 mm (⅝ in) interior grade	15 (Timber, Plywood and OSB)	500 kg/m³	1.49 m³ 743 kg	11,145 MJ	0.45	334 kg	
Roof sheathing 125 m² (1345 ft²)							
12mm (½ in) exterior grade	15 (Timber, Plywood and OSB)	500 kg/m³	1.5 m³ 750 kg	11,250 MJ	0.45	338 kg	Does not include fasteners.

Transportation: Plywood/OSB transportation by 15 ton truck would equate to 1.5 MJ per kilometer of travel to the building site, for exterior walls.
*Typically from engineeringtoolbox.com

will have no effect on IAQ. The glues used in these products are formaldehyde based and can off-gas significantly. They are not recommended for use in any interior applications, as they will have negative IAQ effects.

FUTURE DEVELOPMENT

The growth of third-party certification programs makes it likely that more sustainably harvested sheet wood products will become available. Effort has gone into reducing the amount and type of formaldehyde used in glues, but all exterior-grade sheet wood still contains glues with toxic chemicals. Pressure for more environmentally friendly options is driving R&D developments that may result in more benign adhesives.

The ability to use substandard logs to make OSB means that these products are likely to continue to make up a large and growing portion of the market as the quantity of available high-quality trees continues to shrink. Nontoxic glues would make the use of OSB more environmentally suitable.

Resources for further research

Bramwell, Martyn, editor. *The International Book of Wood*. New York: Simon and Schuster, 1976.

Duncan, S. Blackwell. *The Complete Plywood Handbook*. Blue Ridge Summit, PA: Tab Books, 1981.

Forest Products Laboratory. *Wood Handbook: Wood as an Engineering Material*. United States Department of Agriculture, 1987.

Plywood and OSB Sheathing Ratings

	Best 1	2	3	4	5	6	Worst 7	8	9	10	Notes
Environmental Impacts											Forestry practices are highly variable and have a significant impact. Impacts of glues is difficult to assess.
Embodied Energy											Manufacturing inputs for glues is difficult to assess.
Waste Generated											Sheet goods can accumulate significant off cuts.
Energy Efficiency											Sheet goods can be an effective air control layer.
Material Costs											
Labor Inputs											
Skill Level Required by Homeowner											
Sourcing and Availability											
Durability and Longevity											Exposure to moisture will have negative effect on durability.
Building Code Compliance											
Indoor Air Quality											Used indoors, plywood and OSB will have detrimental effects on IAQ.

Gypsum board, drywall or plasterboard sheathing

What the cheerleaders say...	What the detractors say...
Affordable	Moisture issues can cause mold
Readily available material and expertise	Uniform aesthetic
Relatively low environmental impacts	Can create a lot of waste
Recyclable	Joint compound typically contains toxins

Applications for system

- Interior wall and ceiling sheathing
- Exterior wall sheathing (if specified for exterior purposes)

Basic materials

- Gypsum
- Paper coating (interior uses)
- Fiberglass coating (exterior uses)
- Chemical additives (dependent on type of panel)
- Joint tape or mesh
- Joint compound
- Fasteners
- Corner beads and other trim accessories

How the system works

Gypsum is obtained from quarries or from recycled flue gasses at coal-burning plants. It is dried, ground and heated to alter its chemistry. It is then mixed with water and chemical additives and set between paper or fiberglass sheets. The sheets are oven-cured in a multi-stage process of descending temperatures.

The sheets are made in a variety of thicknesses (¼, ⅜, ½ and ⅝ inch are common) and standard dimensions of 48 and 54 inches by 96, 120 or 144 inches to suit common wall-framing dimensions. Each sheet has two tapered edges that allow for jointing compound to be applied while achieving a smooth finished surface.

The sheets are fastened to wall and ceiling framing with specialty screws, and the screw heads are covered with joint compound.

Joints are bridged with a paper or mesh tape and a gypsum-based jointing compound that is applied in several coats, with sanding to smooth between coats.

Interior gypsum board is commonly painted, but can also be a substrate for finish plasters.

Exterior gypsum products are for sheathing only, and the joints are not covered. These materials are used in conjunction with a variety of cladding options.

Tips for successful installation

1. There are many good resources for homeowners wishing to install drywall. However, there will be a learning curve to achieving good jointing skills. It is good to practice drywall jointing in less obvious areas until results meet expectations.
2. Interior drywall is available in many varieties, including fire code-approved, lightweight and moist-area versions. Be sure you are using the correct product for your specific requirements.
3. The drywall industry is so well established that professional drywall installers have tools, equipment and techniques that allow them to do a job much faster and with much better results than most homeowners. Competition is ubiquitous enough that prices are surprising low, and even a committed DIYer may find it worthwhile to hire out the job.

Pros and cons

ENVIRONMENTAL IMPACTS

Harvesting — *Moderate.* The bulk of the material in the panels is gypsum, a soft rock quarried from surface-based pits, most of which have been long established. Impacts can include habitat destruction and surface and ground water contamination. Some drywall manufacturers use gypsum obtained from industrial chimney flues, reducing the need for virgin gypsum.

Manufacturing — *Moderate.* Heat is applied twice in the manufacturing process, when the raw gypsum is initially calcined and again to dry the panels once they have been formed. The temperatures for these processes are lower than other manufactured mineral and/or sheet products, but still require substantial energy input.

Manufacturing gypsum board requires a lot of water, but effluent levels are not high as the water is dried out of the panels in kilns.

A wide number of additives are mixed with the gypsum in relatively small quantities. These include paper and/or fiberglass fiber, soap-based foaming agents, plasticizers, gypsum crystal, EDTA, starch, mildew resistant agent and wax emulsion for water-resistant drywall. All the additives in drywall will have a range of impacts during their manufacturing processes.

Transportation — *Low to High.* Sample building uses 1,007 – 1,473 kg of drywall for interior wall sheathing:

> 1.5 – 2.2 MJ per km by 15 ton truck
> 0.95 – 1.4 MJ per km by 35 ton truck
> 0.25 – 0.37 MJ per km by rail
> 0.16 – 0.24 MJ per km by ocean freight

Gypsum board production is centralized and manufacturing plants exist close to most population centers in North America. However, complexities in the supply chain does not guarantee that drywall purchased in a region was produced in that region.

Installation — *Moderate to High.* The installation of gypsum board creates a high amount of dust on

Exterior gypsum sheathing.

the building site, especially during the sanding of joints. The dust is extremely fine and can become dispersed throughout the home (including heating and ventilation ductwork) and in the environment around the home. Many joint compounds contain anti-fungal agents and other toxic chemicals that installers will not be able to contain fully.

WASTE: *MODERATE TO HIGH*

Compostable — None.

Recyclable — Drywall offcuts. Drywall recycling programs are starting to become more common. If such programs exist, all scrap will be able to be diverted. Quantities tend to be high.

Landfill — Drywall offcuts. If no recycling program is available, offcuts will go to landfill.

ENERGY EFFICIENCY

Gypsum board products may be used as the primary air control layer on the interior and/or exterior if all seams, penetrations and intersections are properly gasketed and/or caulked. Gypsum board does not contribute to thermal control.

MATERIAL COSTS: *LOW TO MODERATE*

Scale of production and price competition for this widely-used material have led to economies of scale that result in pricing that is lower than embodied energy inputs would typically require.

LABOR INPUT: *HIGH*

Interior gypsum board is a multiple-stage material to install. Sheets must be cut to size and mounted,

Interior drywall mudding.

joints taped/meshed, and joint compound applied in two or three coats with drying time and sanding required between each. Professional tools can greatly reduce labor input.

Health Warnings — Dust from drywall and in particular joint compounds is toxic and proper breathing protection must be worn.

SKILL LEVEL REQUIRED FOR THE HOMEOWNER

Preparation of substrate — *Easy.* Basic framing and carpentry skills.

Installation of sheathing — *Easy to Difficult.* Large sheets are easy to install, level of difficulty increases with quantity and complexity of cuts, penetrations and intersections.

Finishing of sheathing — *Difficult.* Mudding and sanding joints, corner beads and intersections to a good degree of finish requires experience.

Exterior gypsum sheathing does not require jointing.

SOURCING/AVAILABILITY: *EASY*

Gypsum products are widely available through building supply outlets and masonry supply stores.

DURABILITY: *LOW TO HIGH*

Gypsum board is susceptible to moisture damage, and will deteriorate quickly when wet repeatedly or

Drywall Embodied Energy

163 m2 (1750 ft2)	Material embodied energy from I.C.E. in MJ/kg	Weight to volume ratio of material*	Volume of material in sample 1000sf/92.9m² building	Sample building embodied energy	Material embodied carbon from I.C.E. in kgCO₂e/kg	Sample building embodied carbon	Notes
Lowest Impact							
Lightweight drywall/sheetrock	6.75 (Plasterboard)	489 kg/m³	2.06 m³ 1007 kg	6,800 MJ	0.39	393 kg	
Highest Impact							
	6.75 (Plasterboard)	715 kg/m³	2.06 m³ 1473 kg	9,942 MJ	0.39	574 kg	Does not include fasteners or joint compound.

Transportation: Drywall transportation by 15 ton truck would equate to 0.7–2.2 MJ per kilometer of travel to the building site. *Typically from engineeringtoolbox.com continuously. Kept dry, the material is soft and dents and chips relatively easily, but will last a long time.

CODE COMPLIANCE

Acceptable solution in all codes. Particular types of drywall may be required for specific purposes (fire code, moisture resistance).

INDOOR AIR QUALITY: *LOW TO HIGH*

There can be minor to serious issues with gypsum board and IAQ. Synthetic gypsum (which represents a growing percentage of all available gypsum products) is reclaimed from the chimneys of coal-burning installations and may contain contaminants, including sulfur and heavy metals. There are lawsuits currently pending in the United States regarding sulfur gas contamination of homes from drywall sourced from Chinese and American synthetic gypsum. While the number of claims is small in comparison

to the amount of drywall installed, the precautionary principle suggests avoiding synthetic gypsum products.

Non-synthetic gypsum board for interior use is typically faced with paper that is adhered using starch-based glues. This combination is an excellent food source for mold, and drywall in humid or moist conditions can easily become moldy, with dramatic impacts on IAQ.

Pre-mixed joint compound will contain fungicides/biocides that are persistent in the environment. Most wet and dry joint compounds will contain formaldehyde, ethylene vinyl acetate latex and other additives. These will be listed on the product's MSDS sheet.

Complicating the issue is the level of dust created when sanding joint compound. The resulting dust is very fine and pervasive, carrying traces of all the chemical additives as well as silica throughout the

Drywall Sheathing Ratings

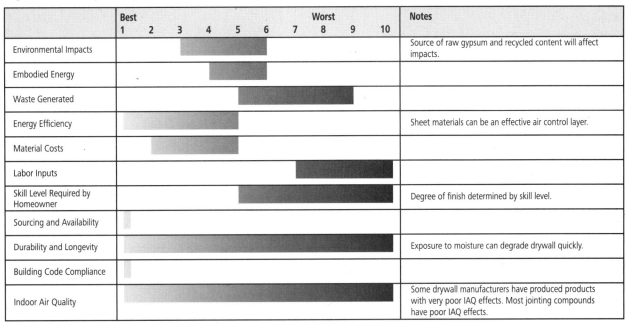

	Best 1	2	3	4	5	6	Worst 7	8	9	10	Notes
Environmental Impacts			███	███	███						Source of raw gypsum and recycled content will affect impacts.
Embodied Energy				███	███						
Waste Generated					███	███	███				
Energy Efficiency	███	███	███								Sheet materials can be an effective air control layer.
Material Costs		███	███								
Labor Inputs							███	███			
Skill Level Required by Homeowner					███	███	███	███			Degree of finish determined by skill level.
Sourcing and Availability	█										
Durability and Longevity	███	███	███	███	███	███	███	███			Exposure to moisture can degrade drywall quickly.
Building Code Compliance	█										
Indoor Air Quality	███	███	███	███	███	███	███	███			Some drywall manufacturers have produced products with very poor IAQ effects. Most jointing compounds have poor IAQ effects.

home. Heating and ventilation ducts are particularly vulnerable to being coated in this dust.

There are a few brands of joint compound that do not contain any chemical additives and are considered hypoallergenic. Note that the dust from these compounds is still high in silica and should not be inhaled.

FUTURE DEVELOPMENT

The amount of potentially dangerous synthetic gypsum being used in the industry is an issue that is currently controversial, and the next decade will see developments that either lead to safer synthetic gypsum or proof that the material is not as dangerous as some currently claim.

Less toxic joint compound will likely make inroads into the industry, with R&D directed toward eliminating toxic chemicals from the material.

Drywall is likely to remain the dominant type of interior wall sheathing as its market acceptance, convenience and aesthetic are key to the majority of construction in North America.

Resources for further research

Ferguson, Myron R. *Drywall: Professional Techniques for Great Results.* Newtown, CT: Taunton, 2002. Print.

Spence, William Perkins. *Installing and Finishing Drywall.* New York: Sterling, 1998. Print.

Magnesium oxide board

What the cheerleaders say...	What the detractors say...
Sustainable drywall alternative	Currently made only in Asia
Not prone to moisture/mold issues	More difficult to cut than drywall
Has structural properties	High cost
Fire and impact resistant	

Applications for system

- Interior wall, ceiling and floor sheathing
- Exterior wall and roof sheathing
- Backer board for tile showers
- Soffit and fascia

Basic materials

- Magnesium oxide
- Fiberglass matt facing
- Paper or mesh tape for joints
- Joint compound
- Fasteners

How the system works

Magnesium carbonite ore is harvested and heated in a kiln at 650°C (1200°F) to form magnesium oxide. This material is ground, made into slurry with water (and sometimes fibers and admixtures) and formed into sheets, usually between two facing mats of fiberglass. The sheets are air-cured into a hard board in standard thicknesses (usually ⅜, ½ and ⅝ inch) and sheet sizes (48 or 54 inches wide and 96, 120 and 144 inches long).

The sheets are fastened to framing using screws. When used as a finish wall cladding, the joints are taped, mudded and sanded in the same manner as drywall. When used as structural sheathing the joints are typically not treated.

The boards are strong enough to be used as structural sheathing in many applications, including exterior walls and floors.

Tips for successful installation

1. In general, the same installation procedures and techniques are used as with drywall. Mag board is harder than drywall, so the scoring and cutting is more difficult and time-consuming. A carbide tipped knife is recommended.
2. Different mag board products are available, each with particular intended uses. Be sure to order the correct product for your application(s).

Pros and cons

ENVIRONMENTAL IMPACTS

Harvesting — *Moderate to High.* Magnesium carbonate is quarried from surface-based pits in Asia (mostly in China). It is difficult to obtain information about these quarries and their impacts, but they will presumably have a similar impact to other surface extraction operations, including habitat destruction and disturbance and/or contamination of ground and surface water.

Manufacturing — *Moderate to High.* Magnesium carbonate converts readily to magnesium oxide at around 650°C (1200°F), a much lower temperature than required to kiln limestone for portland cement, but still requires a substantial amount of energy. Carbon dioxide is emitted from the heated ore, as with portland cement, but that CO_2 is largely reabsorbed by the material during its curing process, making it a much lower carbon alternative to portland cement board products.

The fiberglass matting used on both sides of magnesium board requires high energy input to melt a mixture of silica sand, limestone, kaolin clay, fluorspar, colemanite, dolomite and other minerals to liquid form. The liquid is squeezed through small orifices to make fiber strands that are chemical coated and woven or glued together to make mats. This process yields high carbon and air pollution results.

Transportation — *High.* Sample building uses 1,668.6 kg of magnesium board to sheath interior walls:

> 2.5 MJ per km by 15 ton truck
> 1.57 MJ per km by 35 ton truck
> 0.42 MJ per km by rail
> 0.27 MJ per km by ocean freight

Magnesium board is a heavy material and currently all products are manufactured in China and must be shipped to and distributed throughout North America.

Installation — *Moderate to High.* Dust from magnesium oxide board should not be inhaled, and can be distributed throughout the house, especially when making saw cuts in the material. More problematic is the dust created when sanding jointing compound. This is extremely fine dust and can become dispersed throughout the home (including heating and ventilation ductwork) and in the environment around the home. Many joint compounds contain anti-fungal agents and other toxic chemicals that installers will not be able to contain fully.

WASTE: *MODERATE TO HIGH*

Compostable — None. While the core magnesium oxide could be left in the environment or used as aggregate, it is not easy to separate from the fiberglass matting on both sides.

Recyclable — None. There are currently no programs for magnesium oxide recycling, though in theory the material could be recycled.

Landfill — Magnesium board offcuts. Quantities can be low to high, depending on the requirements of the installation.

ENERGY EFFICIENCY

Magnesium board can be used as an effective primary air control layer on the interior and exterior of the building as long as seams are properly gasketed, caulked or taped. The product has no thermal control properties.

MATERIAL COSTS: *HIGH*

The production of magnesium oxide board is significantly lower in embodied energy than drywall, but limited production and distribution result in significantly higher costs.

LABOR INPUT: *HIGH*

Like drywall, magnesium oxide board is a multiple-stage material to install. Sheets must be cut to size and mounted, joints taped/meshed, and joint compound applied in two or three coats with drying time and sanding required between each. Professional tools can greatly reduce labor input. Cutting will be more labor-intensive than with drywall.

Health Warnings — Dust from mag board and, in particular, joint compounds is toxic and proper breathing protection must be worn.

SKILL LEVEL REQUIRED FOR THE HOMEOWNER

Preparation of substrate — *Easy.* Basic framing and carpentry skills.

Installation of sheathing — *Easy to Difficult.* Large sheets are easy to install, though level of difficulty increases with quantity and complexity of cuts, penetrations and intersections. Cuts require more effort and higher quality tools and blades than with drywall.

Finishing of sheathing — *Difficult.* Mudding and sanding joints, corner beads and intersections to a good degree of finish require experience.

Exterior mag board sheathing does not require jointing.

SOURCING/AVAILABILITY: *MODERATE*

Magnesium oxide board is not regularly stocked at all building material outlets, but can be special ordered from some.

DURABILITY: *HIGH*

Mag board is not affected by water and is very impact-resistant. It is less prone to wear in high-traffic locations than drywall.

Magnesium Oxide Board Embodied Energy

163 m² (1750 ft²)	Material embodied energy from I.C.E. in MJ/kg	Weight to volume ratio of material*	Volume of material in sample 1000sf/92.9m² building	Sample building embodied energy	Material embodied carbon from I.C.E. in kgCO₂e/kg	Sample building embodied carbon	Notes
12mm (½ in) thickness	2.8**	810 kg/m³	2.06 m³ 1668.6 kg	4,672 MJ	N/A	N/A	**EE figure averaged from multiple industry sources for magnesium oxide cement. Does not include fasteners or joint compound.

Transportation: Mag board transportation by 15 ton truck would equate to 2.5 MJ per kilometer of travel to the building site. Mag board transportation by ocean freight would equate to 0.27 MJ per kilometer of travel to the building site. *Typically from engineeringtoolbox.com

CODE COMPLIANCE

Magnesium oxide board may not be recognized directly as an acceptable solution in all jurisdictions, but several manufacturers have done testing to meet ASTM E 136-09 and ASTM E 84 standards for sheathing materials. With this documentation, it should be straightforward to prove equivalence with gypsum board products.

INDOOR AIR QUALITY: *HIGH*

Magnesium oxide board is often the product of choice for sheathing in homes for hypoallergenic homeowners. It does not support mold growth even when continuously damp, and contains no off-gassing compounds.

Pre-mixed joint compound will contain fungicides/biocides that are persistent in the environment. Most wet and dry jointing compounds will contain formaldehyde, ethylene vinyl acetate latex and other additives. These will be listed on the product's MSDS sheet, and all will negatively affect IAQ.

Complicating the issue is the level of dust created when sanding joint compound. The resulting dust is very fine and pervasive, carrying traces of all the chemical additives as well as silica throughout the home. Heating and ventilation ducts are particularly vulnerable to being coated in this dust.

There are a few brands of joint compound that do not contain any chemical additives and are considered hypoallergenic. Note that the dust from these compounds is still high in silica and should not be inhaled.

FUTURE DEVELOPMENT

There are not many significant ore deposits in the USA, though there are several large ones in Canada. Currently, no magnesium oxide board is manufactured in North America, which keeps the price and

Magnesium Oxide Board Ratings

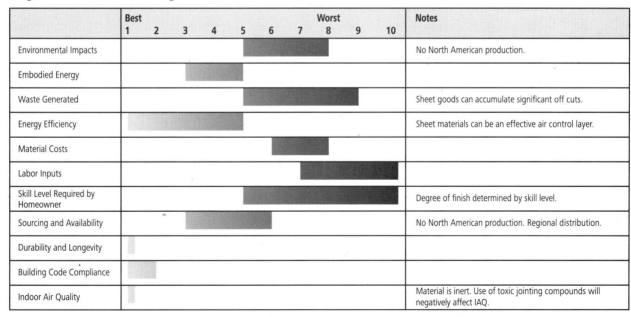

	Best 1	2	3	4	5	6	7	Worst 8	9	10	Notes
Environmental Impacts											No North American production.
Embodied Energy											
Waste Generated											Sheet goods can accumulate significant off cuts.
Energy Efficiency											Sheet materials can be an effective air control layer.
Material Costs											
Labor Inputs											
Skill Level Required by Homeowner											Degree of finish determined by skill level.
Sourcing and Availability											No North American production. Regional distribution.
Durability and Longevity											
Building Code Compliance											
Indoor Air Quality											Material is inert. Use of toxic jointing compounds will negatively affect IAQ.

shipping impacts high. The benefits of this product compared to gypsum board are numerous, in particular its excellent resistance to moisture and its structural properties. As it is so similar to gypsum drywall in sizing and installation procedure, it may start to gain a larger market share. If demand grows sufficiently, North American production could be instituted, helping to drive down costs and shipping impacts.

Currently, the lack of standards for the product can result in widely varying quality between manufacturers. This too may be addressed by increased acceptance in the market and in building codes. North American production would certainly be accompanied by high production standards.

Resources for further research

Baker-Laporte, Paula, Erica Elliott, and John Banta. *Prescriptions for a Healthy House: A Practical Guide for Architects, Builders and Homeowners.* Gabriola Island, BC: New Society, 2008. Print.

Fired clay brick cladding

What the cheerleaders say...	What the detractors say...
Very durable, proven cladding	Expensive
Natural and abundantly available material	Energy intensive
Can be structural	Labor intensive
Good thermal mass, especially interior	

Applications for system

- Exterior cladding
- Exterior and interior structural wall
- Interior cladding
- Decorative/fire-resistant cladding

Basic materials

- Clay
- Sand
- May be small amounts of lime, iron oxide and/or magnesia
- Mortar of clay/sand, lime/sand, or lime/cement/sand

How the system works

Bricks of a typically rectangular shape are cast from a mixture of clay, sand and small amounts of admixture and fired in a kiln at temperatures between 700 and 1100°C (1300 and 2000°F). This heating takes the clay through several stages, including the burn-off of carbon and sulfur, driving off chemically combined water from the clay, quartz inversion, sintering and vitrification. At the end of this firing process, the clay brick is hard and will not soften when it reacts with water.

Bricks are laid in successive courses, bonded by a mortar of clay/sand, lime/sand or lime/cement/sand. There are many different patterns for brickwork, but most feature offset joints between courses. Keystone arches can be formed to create self-supporting openings, or metal reinforcement is used to form straight openings.

When used as cladding, bricks are attached to the structural sheathing by means of metal ties that are nailed to the wall and embedded in the mortar joint, and a space is left between the brick and the sheathing to create a rainscreen. Weeper holes are left at intervals in the top and bottom courses to allow moisture to escape.

When used structurally, brick walls are typically one part of a double masonry wall, with an insulated core between the two wythes. Ties are placed at intervals between the two walls to increase stability. Structural brick walls are also built using a double-wide arrangement of bricks. It is rare for fired clay bricks to be used structurally in modern construction in North America.

Not Cement Brick. Many brick products on the market are actually cement-based and not clay. There are many resources available to make comparisons between cement and clay brick. Cement brick manufacturers often claim that they are "greener" than fired clay because making them doesn't require heat. This, however, ignores the high heat input (and significantly higher carbon release) required to make the cement.

A case can be made for the use of cement brick as a green building product, largely based on its durability. It is not included in this book because of its high carbon footprint and low permeability, and because it is an intensive material to be used non-structurally as a cladding.

Tips for successful installation

1. Building science has brought a good understanding of the porous nature of fired clay brick, which can store large quantities of water during rainfall events, and has reinforced the need for

Brick cladding.

ensuring a properly ventilated air space between brick and wall sheathing.

2. Brick cladding must be designed into the project from the start, as it will require a brick ledge on the foundation and proper detailing for doors, windows and flashing to suit the thickness of the wall and to bridge the air gap between the wall and the brick.

3. There are many excellent resources available to assist in the successful installation of brick cladding. Be sure to seek proper advice and instruction.

4. Clay brick can make an attractive interior wall or wainscoting. For some interior applications, it may be load-bearing and/or self-supporting.

Pros and cons

ENVIRONMENTAL IMPACTS

Harvesting — *Low to moderate.* The clay that forms the bulk of the material in a brick is an abundant resource, with useful deposits in many regions of North America. Clay pits are usually shallow, surface-based harvesting operations that do not use any chemical processes on-site. Disruption to flora and fauna in the immediate region of the pit will be palpable. Many clay pits are in or beside waterways, and pit operations can cause silting of the water and disruptions to flow patterns. In general, clay pits are not considered high-impact mining operations, and are excellent candidates for rehabilitation at the end of their life spans.

Manufacturing — *High*. Clay for bricks requires some mechanical processing. It is ground up and squeezed into a homogeneous mix before being formed. This work is typically all completed by machine in factories, though traditionally it would have been done by hand on or near the building site. The largest impact comes from the firing process, during which the bricks are heated to temperatures of 900 to 1300°C (1650 to 2350°F) for several hours. No toxins are released from the clay during this process, but a lot of fossil fuels are consumed and emissions released into the atmosphere, including sulfur dioxide.

Bricks that are glazed or painted will require additional processes, and these can be more toxic. Paint coatings, in particular, can contain chemicals that are emitted into the atmosphere and/or mixed into water at the factory.

The mortar used between bricks is a significant amount of material. If a cement-based mortar is used, it carries a high carbon footprint. Lime-based mortars have a lower carbon footprint.

Transportation — *Low to High*. Sample building uses 26,192 kg of brick siding for the exterior:

> 24.6 MJ per km by 35 ton truck
> 6.55 MJ per km by rail

Production facilities are typically very close to clay pits, minimizing the transportation of raw materials. Regional manufacturers are close to many major markets, but if this heavy material has to travel long distances it will accumulate high transportation impacts.

Installation — *Negligible*.

WASTE: *LOW*

Compostable — Clay brick offcuts can be left in the environment or used as aggregate or growing medium. Quantities should be low, as partial bricks can be used throughout the wall.

Recyclable — None.

Landfill — Mortar bags.

ENERGY EFFICIENCY

Brick cladding will not have much impact on energy efficiency. As a rainscreen, it can reduce the amount of wind that reaches the wall behind, but will not contribute to air tightness. Bricks add little to no thermal resistance.

Bricks can be used to create thermal mass inside a building. This will not improve energy efficiency, but may help to modulate temperature swings inside the

Clay Brick Sheathing Embodied Energy

163 m² (1750 ft²)	Material energy from I.C.E. in MJ/kg	Weight to embodied material*	Volume of volume ratio of sample 1000sf/92.9m² building	Sample material in embodied energy	Material building carbon from I.C.E. in kgCO$_2$e/kg	Sample embodied embodied carbon	Notes building
100mm (3⅞ in) thick fired clay bricks	3 (Bricks, general, common brick)	1794 kg/m³	14.6 m³ 26,192 kg	78,577 MJ	0.24	6,286 kg	
Mortar, 1 lime: 1 cement: 6 sand	1.11 (Mortar, 1:1:6)	2370 kg/m³	1.4 m³ 3318 kg	3,683 MJ	0.174	577 kg	
Totals				**82,260 MJ**		**6,863 kg**	

Transportation: Brick transportation by 35 ton truck would equate to 24.6 MJ per kilometer of travel to the building site. *Typically from engineeringtoolbox.com building, improving comfort. Brick walls are sometimes used as part of a hydronic heating system.

MATERIAL COSTS: *HIGH*
LABOR INPUT: *HIGH*

Laying brick is very labor-intensive. Each unit is relatively small and requires careful mortar joints on all sides. The material is heavy; mortar is prepared in small batches and must be kept fresh. Brick ties, weepers and headers over windows all add to the labor input. If patterns and/or arches are included in the design, labor input rises further.

Health Warnings — Mortar mixing can cause exposure to high quantities of silica dust, so proper breathing protection is required.

SKILL LEVEL REQUIRED FOR THE HOMEOWNER

Preparation of substrate — *Easy.* Wall framing and sheathing skills are required. The process of measuring and fastening brick ties is straightforward. **Installation of sheathing** — *Moderate to Difficult.* There is a lot to learn in order to successfully install brick cladding. Skills required include marking and measuring for brick courses, mortar mixing, laying mortar and brick and creating appropriate headers/arches for openings. Without prior experience or practice, brick laying may best be left to professionals. **Finishing of sheathing** — *Easy.* Jointing between the bricks is the only finish required once bricks are installed.

SOURCING/AVAILABILITY: *EASY*

Clay bricks are widely available in most regions from masonry supply outlets.

DURABILITY: *HIGH*

Clay bricks provide a very durable cladding that can last for at least a hundred years, and possibly

Clay Brick Sheathing Ratings

	Best 1 2 3 4 5 6	Worst 7 8 9 10	Notes
Environmental Impacts		7–8	
Embodied Energy		9	
Waste Generated	1–2		
Energy Efficiency	N/A		Brick cladding is not an effective air control layer.
Material Costs		7–8	
Labor Inputs		7–8	
Skill Level Required by Homeowner		6–8	
Sourcing and Availability	1		
Durability and Longevity	1		
Building Code Compliance	1		
Indoor Air Quality	1		Used indoors, bricks will not have a detrimental effect on IAQ. Recycled bricks should be inspected for possible IAQ issues.

several centuries. Proper window flashings and an adequate protection from roof splashback will help ensure long life. Bricks that repeatedly absorb a lot of moisture and then freeze (the freeze-thaw cycle) will deteriorate within a decade.

Interior applications of clay brick will be extremely durable.

CODE COMPLIANCE

Acceptable solution in all codes. Be sure to follow local codes for specific requirements.

INDOOR AIR QUALITY

No effect as an exterior cladding.

Interior brick walls should not have a negative impact on IAQ. If using recycled brick, be sure to assess the origin of the brick before using them indoors as they may have been used on a building or in a location where the porous clay may have absorbed toxic materials (e.g., old chimney brick, kiln brick or industrial brick).

FUTURE DEVELOPMENT

It is unlikely that techniques or materials for brick manufacturing will change dramatically. Brick has a long history in building, and will likely continue to have a reasonable portion of the cladding market. Brick is widely perceived to be an "upscale" cladding, used to distinguish a quality home from a cheap home. Rising costs for brick and masons may cause the market to shrink.

Resources for further research

BDA Guide to Successful Brickwork, 3rd Edition. London: Arnold, 2000. Print.

Hendry, A. W., and F. M. Khalaf. Masonry Wall Construction. London: Spon, 2001. Print.

Kelsey, John. Masonry: The DIY Guide to Working with Concrete, Brick, Block, and Stone. East Petersburg, PA: Fox Chapel, 2012. Print.

Lime and lime/cement plaster

What the cheerleaders say...	What the detractors say...
High durability	High embodied energy
Works with any wall system	Materials are corrosive to skin during application
Wide variety of aesthetic possibilities	Cracks may need regular repair
Combines structure, airtightness and finishing in one material	

Applications for system

- Exterior sheathing, as a rainscreen or directly applied to wall substrate
- Interior sheathing
- Ceiling sheathing

Basic materials

- Hydrated lime (for air-curing lime plaster)
- Hydraulic lime (for hydraulic-curing lime plaster)
- Portland cement (for lime/cement mixtures)
- Pozzolanic material (fired clay, gypsum, slag, fly ash; for hydraulic-curing lime plaster)
- Sand
- Fibers (if required)
- Lath and/or mesh

How the system works

All of the plasters covered in this section are similar, in that they take a processed mineral material, mix it with sand and water and apply it to a surface where it chemically cures to closely resemble the original rock from which it was sourced. In substrate preparation, application method, finished texture and appearance and durability, the plasters are close to identical. However, in processing, curing process and environmental impacts, they differ enough to be considered separately.

Hydrated Lime Plaster. Also known as "air lime," this type of plaster is based on limestone that has been heated to 900–1100°C (1650–2000°F) to form "quicklime." The powdered quicklime is then combined with water (a process that is highly reactive and generates a substantial amount of heat) to form a stable hydrated lime. Many people are surprised to find that "hydrated" lime is most often sold as a dry powder, but the hydration refers to the chemical absorption of water and not to the state of the final product.

The hydrated lime is mixed on-site with water and sand aggregate (and fibers, if required for additional tensile strength) and applied to the substrate, usually by trowel.

The plaster on the wall will dry, losing water content to the air and the substrate (and this must be mitigated by continually moistening the plaster during the curing process), but the actual setting of the plaster is a chemical reaction involving the lime ingredients, water and air, during which the hydrated lime carbonizes. The carbonization process is long and slow. The plaster will become hard to the touch within a few days or weeks (depending on conditions) but will continue to cure and harden for decades as airborne carbon reacts with the lime.

Hydrated lime plasters are best suited for application in thin coats, building up thickness slowly. If the plaster is too thick, the deep areas will not carbonize for a long time. These plasters require careful application and tending during the early stages of curing. They can mature into strong, durable and beautiful plasters.

Hydraulic Lime Plaster. This type of lime plaster contains fired limestone and also some amount of a pozzolanic material, which can be naturally occurring in the limestone (as with natural hydraulic lime or NHL) or added to the lime at the time of mixing (as with fired clay, gypsum, slag, fly ash or other pozzolans). Regardless of the source of the pozzolan, its addition in the mix creates a chemical reactivity

with water that provides some setting action in the plaster. In hydraulic lime plasters, the limestone continues to carbonize over the long term as with "air limes," but there is a fast, initial setting that occurs due to the pozzolanic reaction. The amount of water reactivity can vary depending on the type of pozzolan in the mix and its reactivity. NHL is rated based on its reactivity; site-mixed hydraulic limes can be adjusted by adding more or less of the pozzolan material to the mix. Pozzolans may be as low in volume as 5 percent and as much as 50 percent of the binder content.

Hydraulic lime plasters are similar to hydrated lime plasters in regards to the care required during curing (well protected from sun, wind and continuously moistened) and the need for relatively thin, even coats to encourage carbonization. These plasters will harden to the touch within hours, rather than days.

Lime/Cement Plaster. In this type of plaster, the portland cement content acts as the pozzolan, allowing the plaster to cure quickly in a water reaction. The difference is that portland cement is a very powerful pozzolan and, depending on the proportions used in

Lime plaster.

Decorative plaster.

the mix, the plaster will take on characteristics that are more cement-like than lime-like. Lime plasters are relatively soft and permeable, while cement plaster is harder, more brittle and less permeable. In the right combination (25%–50% cement), a lime/cement plaster can have fast set times (2–6 hours) and cure to be hard and durable yet still be sufficiently permeable to be part of a vapor flow-through wall system. Too high a cement content and the plaster may become too brittle and impermeable.

These lime/cement mixes are commonly available as preformulated mortar mixes for laying brick and block.

Lime/cement plasters have two advantages over straight lime plasters. Rapid set times allow for the application of successive coats within short periods of time (1–2 days) and the hydraulic set allows

for the application of thicker (and therefore fewer) coats, reducing labor input.

Tips for successful installation

1. Substrate preparation is important for all lime-based plasters. The smoother the surface, the less likely the plaster will have varying thicknesses that can cause cracking or soft spots. If the surface to be plastered is uneven, lime plasters can be built up in low spots over one or more applications, to create a level surface for the first full coat of plaster. Alternatively, the plaster can be applied at a consistent thickness to follow the contours of the wall.

2. Lime plasters require a substrate with adequate mechanical adherence. If plastering over smooth substrates, a mesh of some type will be required and must be firmly adhered to the surface.

3. Each successive coat of lime plaster requires the previous coat to be scratched or roughened to provide mechanical grip for the subsequent coat, to avoid potential delamination.

4. Lime plaster has good permeability qualities, but is not very resistant to water penetration. Its open pore structure allows water to soak into the plaster relatively easily. While this will not affect the plaster itself, it may be problematic for the wall surface behind if repeated wetting is experienced. Rainscreen applications will leave a ventilation space behind the plaster to assist with drying. If the lime plaster is adhered directly to the wall, consider coatings that will repel bulk water in vulnerable areas.

5. Lime plaster requires care during its curing process. In particular, it is important with all lime-based plasters to maintain an adequate level of moisture in the curing plaster. Direct exposure to sunlight and wind can rob the plaster of moisture very quickly, resulting in

poor curing and cracking. The plaster will need regular misting for about a week in addition to protection from excessive drying.

6. There are many excellent resources to aid with the successful mixing and application of lime plaster. Be sure to research thoroughly before application.

Pros and cons

ENVIRONMENTAL IMPACTS

Harvesting — *Moderate.* Limestone is a non-renewable but abundantly available material. It is mechanically extracted from quarries. Impacts can include habitat destruction, surface and ground water interference and contamination.

Manufacturing — *High.* Limestone is mechanically crushed and heated (900–1100°C / 1650–2000°F for lime and 1400–1600°C / 2500–2900°F for cement). This is an energy-intensive process during which large amounts of fossil fuels are burned, contributing to habitat destruction and air and water pollution and high carbon emissions. During the kilning process, large amounts of CO_2 are driven out of the rock (approximately 1 kg of CO_2 for every 1 kg of lime or cement). In the case of cement, this CO_2 stays in the atmosphere. In the case of lime, it is slowly recombined with the lime through the carbonization process. In theory, the carbon uptake for lime can be close to 100 percent but in practice it is less because not all of the lime will have adequate exposure to the atmosphere.

Sand is mechanically extracted from quarries and mechanically crushed. Impacts can include habitat destruction and surface and ground water contamination.

Transportation — *Moderate to High.* Sample building uses 9,787 kg of plaster for exterior:

14.7 MJ per km by 15 ton truck
9.2 MJ per km by 35 ton truck
1.56 MJ per km by ocean freight

Limestone is available in many regions, but is not necessarily harvested and processed in all regions. Impacts for this heavy material will vary depending on distance from the site. Natural hydraulic lime (NHL) most commonly comes from France or Portugal, carrying high transportation impacts for use in North America.

Sand is locally harvested in nearly every region, and should have minimal transportation impacts.

Installation — *Negligible.*

WASTE: *Low*

Compostable — Lime plaster can be left in the environment or crushed to make aggregate. Hydrated lime plaster can be kept wet indefinitely and doesn't need to be disposed of. Quantities should be low, as it is mixed in small batches.

Recyclable — None.

Landfill — Packaging (usually paper and/or plastic bags) from lime and cement.

Lime and Lime/Cement Plaster Embodied Energy

163 m² (1750 ft²)	Material embodied energy from I.C.E. in MJ/kg	Weight to volume ratio of material*	Volume of material in sample 1000sf/92.9m² building	Sample building embodied energy	Material embodied carbon from I.C.E. in kgCO₂e/kg	Sample building embodied carbon	Notes
1 lime: 1 cement: 6 sand mix, 25mm (1 in) thickness	1.11	2370 kg/m³	4.13 m³ 9787 kg	10,864 MJ	0.174	1,703 kg	Does not include mesh, if required.

Transportation: Mortar mix transportation by 35 ton truck would equate to 9.2 MJ per kilometer of travel to the building site. *Typically from engineeringtoolbox.com

ENERGY EFFICIENCY

Lime plaster can be the primary air control layer on the exterior and/or interior of walls and the interior of ceilings. Properly applied and detailed, the plaster can be airtight and contribute to a high level of energy efficiency. Poorly applied plaster can allow leakage through cracks and shrinkage gaps around edges and at intersections with other materials, greatly reducing efficiency.

Lime plaster adds no thermal resistance to the enclosure.

MATERIAL COSTS: *MODERATE*

Source and quality of ingredients can influence costs. Standard lime/cement mortar mixes are widely produced and available and are relatively low cost. Specialty lime products can be more expensive, and are often imported from Europe.

LABOR INPUT: *HIGH*

Lime plaster requires significant labor input. Substrate preparation, mixing and application are all labor-intensive processes. The need for multiple thin coats (3–4 for lime, 2–3 for lime/cement) stretches labor time.

Health Warnings — Lime, cement and sand are high in silica content and are dangerous to inhale. Lime and cement are caustic when wet and can cause irritation of the skin that can range from mildly uncomfortable to painful chemical burns.

SKILL LEVEL REQUIRED FOR THE HOMEOWNER

Preparation of substrate — *Moderate to Difficult.* Lime plasters are only as good as the substrate preparation, making attention to detail very important. Extensive mesh and plaster stops may be required, as is the masking of all intersecting materials and the protection of floors.

Installation of sheathing — *Moderate to Difficult.* The basics of trowel application of wet plaster can be learned quickly, and an inexperienced homeowner can apply a functional plaster. Instructions for the curing of the plaster must be followed carefully to obtain a good result. Quality of finish will improve dramatically with experience.

Finishing of sheathing — *Easy to Difficult.* The final coat of plaster can be the final finish, and as long as it is functionally sound no further treatment may be necessary. Particular textures and degrees of finish will vary with skill and experience. In some applications, a final surface treatment may be brushed, rolled or troweled onto the plaster surface.

SOURCING/AVAILABILITY: *EASY TO DIFFICULT*

Lime/cement mixes are widely available as type-N mortar from building supply outlets and masonry supply shops. Hydrated lime is fairly widely available from masonry supply shops. Agricultural lime, available through farm supply shops, is not suitable for lime plastering. Hydraulic lime is a specialty product that will likely need to be special ordered from a regional distributor.

DURABILITY: *HIGH*

All forms of lime plaster can have a long life span of at least a hundred years, and potentially much longer. Proper maintenance will have a lot of impact on durability. Repair of cracks and reapplication of protective coatings (where required) will help to maximize life span.

CODE COMPLIANCE

Acceptable solution in all codes. ASTM and other standards exist for lime and lime/cement plaster and are referenced by codes.

INDOOR AIR QUALITY: *HIGH*

Used as an interior sheathing or cladding, lime plaster should have no negative impact on IAQ. The antiseptic nature of lime can discourage mold growth, helping to maintain good IAQ in damp areas. Lime plasters have excellent moisture-handling qualities and will absorb excess interior moisture rather than having condensation form on the plaster surface.

The dust from mixing lime plaster and from cleanup after plastering is high in silica content and can be pervasive. Be sure to protect air ducts and other vulnerable areas during plastering and clean up to avoid contamination.

FUTURE DEVELOPMENT

The practice of harvesting and manufacturing lime plaster is thousands of years old. Modern practices are efficient and the results very consistent compared to historical practices. It is unlikely that developments in the production of lime will change much. Greater efficiency in kilns and use of waste heat may reduce embodied energy as fuel costs rise.

Lime plastering may grow in popularity as the understanding of vapor-permeable wall systems increases, but it is unlikely that lime plaster will return to its once dominant place as a sheathing/cladding material.

Resources for further research

Holmes, Stafford, and Michael Wingate. *Building with Lime: A Practical Introduction.* London: Intermediate Technology, 1997. Print.

Guelberth, Cedar Rose, and Daniel D. Chiras. *The Natural Plaster Book: Earth, Lime and Gypsum Plasters for Natural Homes.* Gabriola, BC: New Society, 2003. Print.

Eckel, Edwin C. *Cements, Limes, and Plasters: Their Materials, Manufacture, and Properties.* New York: Wiley, 1922. Print.

Nordmeyer, Herb. *The Stucco Book: The Basics.* San Antonio, TX: Nordmeyer, 2012. Print.

Schwartz, Max, and Walter F. Pruter. *Builder's Guide to Stucco, Lath and Plaster.* Canoga Park, CA: Builder's Book, 2007. Print.

Lime and Lime/Cement Plaster Ratings

	Best 1–10 Worst	Notes
Environmental Impacts	6–8	
Embodied Energy	5–6	
Waste Generated	1	
Energy Efficiency	1–5	Plaster can be an effective air control layer.
Material Costs	3–6	
Labor Inputs	6–8	
Skill Level Required by Homeowner	4–7	Degree of finish determined by skill level.
Sourcing and Availability	1–6	Specialty lime products may be difficult to source.
Durability and Longevity	1–2	
Building Code Compliance	1	
Indoor Air Quality	1	

Stone cladding

What the cheerleaders say...	What the detractors say...
Very durable	Labor intensive
Locally available in many regions	Expensive
Beautiful	
Excellent thermal mass properties	

Applications for system

- Exterior cladding (rainscreen)
- Interior cladding
- Solid interior or exterior walls

Basic materials

- Natural stone
- Mortar (lime, sand, cement if required)

How the system works

Stone of a suitable composition is harvested and either used in an unmodified form or cut/shaped to a desired dimension and profile. The stone is laid in successive courses, bonded by a mortar of lime/sand or lime/cement/sand. There are many different patterns for stonework, but most feature offset joints between courses. Keystone arches can be formed to create self-supporting openings, or metal reinforcement is used to form straight openings.

When used as cladding, stone is attached to the structural sheathing by means of metal ties that are nailed to the wall and embedded in the mortar joint, and a space is left between the stone and the sheathing to create a rainscreen. Weeper holes are left at intervals in the top and bottom courses to allow moisture to escape.

When used structurally, stone walls are typically one part of a double wall, with an insulated core between the two wythes. Ties are placed at intervals between the two walls to increase stability. It is rare for stone to be used structurally in modern construction in North America.

Not Manufactured Stone. A great deal of stone cladding used in modern building is not natural stone, but a cement product manufactured to look like stone. Manufactured stone can have a wide range of appearances and qualities, and is typically less expensive than natural stone. It has the high impacts associated with cement products. A case can be made for the use of manufactured stone as a green building product, largely based on its durability. It is not included in this book because of its high carbon footprint and because it is an intensive material to be used non-structurally as a cladding.

Tips for successful installation

1. Before using a natural stone, especially site-harvested stone, ensure it has suitable properties for use as a cladding. Some natural stone is prone to cracking due to moisture absorption and freeze/thaw cycles.
2. Stone cladding must be designed into the project from the start, as it will require a ledge on the foundation and proper detailing for doors, windows and flashing to suit the thickness of the wall.
3. There are many excellent resources available to assist in the successful installation of stone cladding. Be sure to seek proper advice and instruction.
4. Stone can make an attractive interior wall or wainscoting. For some interior applications, it may be load-bearing and/or self-supporting.

Pros and cons

ENVIRONMENTAL IMPACTS

Harvesting — *Negligible to Moderate.* Stone is a non-renewable but abundant resource. Some naturally occurring stone can be harvested directly from the surface of the ground on the building site. Most commercially available stone is quarried from established pits, where it is mechanically extracted.

Impacts may include habitat destruction and ground and surface water contamination. Stone may be usable directly from the quarry, or may require further cutting and shaping.

Lime and/or cement for mortars are made from quarried limestone. Impacts can include habitat destruction and surface and ground water contamination.

Sand for mortars is quarried with low impacts.

Manufacturing — *Negligible to Moderate.* Stone may require little to no manufacturing after harvesting, as some stone will be suitable for building walls in its naturally occurring state. Other stone will be quarried in large pieces and then sawn or split into shapes that are suitable for cladding. These processes are not very energy intensive and typically have minimal impacts that can include release of silica dust and water contamination.

Mortar ingredients require heating of limestone to high temperature, with resultant high fossil fuel use and emissions and impacts including air and water pollution.

Transportation — *Negligible to High.* Sample building uses 35,944 kg of stone for exterior cladding:

33.8 MJ per km by 35 ton truck.

As a heavy material, the transportation impacts of stone will increase with distance from harvesting and manufacturing source.

Installation — *Negligible.*

Waste: *Low*

Compostable — Stone may be left in the environment or used as aggregate or fill.

Recyclable — None.

Landfill — Bags for mortar ingredients.

Energy efficiency

Stone is most commonly a rainscreen cladding and does not act as the primary air control layer. The thermal mass properties of stone walls may help to moderate temperature swings, especially in indoor applications, but stone walls have no appreciable thermal control benefits.

If stone is being used as a structural wall, it may be difficult to make the wall air tight due to the number of joints and the variegated surface of the stone. Another form of primary air barrier (plaster coating, sheet material) may be necessary to make the wall airtight and efficient.

Stone and wood cladding.
(Jen Feigin)

Stone Cladding Embodied Energy

163 m² (1750 ft²)	Material embodied energy from I.C.E. in MJ/kg	Weight to volume ratio of material*	Volume of material in sample 1000sf/92.9m² building	Sample building embodied energy	Material embodied carbon from I.C.E. in kgCO₂e/kg	Sample building embodied carbon	Notes
Cut limestone, 100mm (4 in) thick	1.5 (Stone, limestone)	2723 kg/m³	13.2 m³ 35,944 kg	53,915 MJ	0.09	3,235 kg	
Mortar, 1 lime: 1 cement: 6 sand	1.11 (Mortar, 1:1:6)	2370 kg/m³	3.3 m³ 7821 kg	8,681 MJ	0.174	1,361 kg	
Totals				62,596 MJ		4,596 kg	

Transportation: Stone transportation by 35 ton truck would equate to 33.8 MJ per kilometer of travel to the building site. *Typically from engineeringtoolbox.com

MATERIAL COSTS: *LOW TO HIGH*

The source of stone and the degree of manufacture to shape the stone will greatly influence the price.

LABOR INPUT: *HIGH*

Site-harvested stone can be very labor intensive, including the digging, lifting and sorting of a heavy material. The wall requires preparation including the fastening of ties. Laying the walls requires the mixing of mortar, laying of stone and finishing of joints.

Health Warnings — Stone cutting and mortar mixing can cause exposure to high quantities of silica dust, so proper breathing protection is required.

SKILL LEVEL REQUIRED FOR THE HOMEOWNER

Preparation of substrate — *Easy.* Wall framing and sheathing skills are required. The process of measuring and fastening stone ties is straightforward.

Installation of sheathing — *Difficult.* There is a lot to learn in order to successfully install stone cladding. Skills required include marking and measuring for courses, mortar mixing, laying mortar and stone and creating appropriate headers/arches for openings. The varied nature of stone requires aesthetic decisions while laying stone. Without prior experience or practice, stone masonry may best be left to professionals.

Finishing of sheathing — *Easy.* Jointing between the stones is the only finish required once stone is installed.

SOURCING/AVAILABILITY: *EASY TO MODERATE*

Natural stone is available directly from quarries and through masonry supply stores. Mortar materials are available from building supply centers and masonry supply stores.

DURABILITY: *VERY HIGH*

Stone cladding and walls will last for hundreds of years, with the mortar joints being the weakest

Stone Cladding Ratings

	Best 1	2	3	4	5	6	Worst 7	8	9	10	Notes
Environmental Impacts											Source of stone and degree of processing will affect impacts.
Embodied Energy											
Waste Generated											
Energy Efficiency					N/A						Stone cladding is not an effective air control layer.
Material Costs											Source of stone will have significant impact on cost.
Labor Inputs											
Skill Level Required by Homeowner											
Sourcing and Availability											Production/availability is regional.
Durability and Longevity											
Building Code Compliance											
Indoor Air Quality											Used indoors, stone cladding will have no detrimental effect on IAQ.

element. Proper attention to maintenance of mortar joints (every ten to twenty years) will greatly extend the life span of a stone wall.

CODE COMPLIANCE

Stone is an acceptable solution in some codes. Though stone construction has a lot of historical precedent, the use of natural stone in modern construction is rare enough that some codes no longer directly reference it as an acceptable solution. There are sufficient published standards to make a reasonable case for its acceptance as an alternative solution in these jurisdictions.

INDOOR AIR QUALITY: *HIGH*

Used indoors, natural stone is unlikely to have a negative effect on IAQ. The exception would be stone that emits radon gas, a naturally occurring radioactive gas associated with some types of granite and limestone in some regions. Radon gas is a serious contaminant with carcinogenic properties.

FUTURE DEVELOPMENT

Stone wall construction is unlikely to experience major changes or innovations, as the system has been refined over centuries and the raw materials are largely unrefined. In regions where appropriate stone is available, the costs of natural stone may become more favorable compared to manufactured alternatives as the price of fuel rises. However, the high amount of labor and skill required are likely to keep stone wall construction to a small portion of the overall market.

Resources for further research

See Stone Foundation resources

Roof sheathing materials as wall sheathing

In addition to all of the choices outlined in this chapter, walls and sometimes ceilings can be clad with the same materials outlined in Chapter 5: Roof Sheathing. Any material that is suitable for roofing will be able to function, usually with increased durability, as wall sheathing. These include:

- Metal sheet and tiles
- Cedar shake and shingle
- Thatch
- Slate
- Composite shingles
- Clay tiles
- Green or living walls

Roof sheathing materials are applied to walls as rainscreens, using the same type of strapping and fasteners as would be used on the roof. None of the roofing materials would be able to act as a primary air control layer for a wall or ceiling, so the system would need to have such a layer designed to operate separately from the cladding material.

Some roofing materials may not be desirable as interior cladding due to potential off-gassing (composite shingles, cedar shingles, paints on some metal products). Permeability issues may need to be addressed if using metal sheets or tiles as an interior cladding. Green walls are constructed similarly to green roofs, with additional consideration for retaining soil on a vertical surface.

Considering roofing options as cladding greatly increases the number of viable choices and aesthetic combinations available to a homeowner.

5

Roof sheathing

THE PALETTE OF PRACTICAL, DURABLE ROOF SHEATHING MATERIALS has not changed a great deal in the past century, with rubber membranes and asphalt shingles being the newcomers (and the least environmentally-friendly). It's not a long list of options to consider, and often price and availability will shrink the list to the point where an owner is choosing between a very limited range of materials.

Making the right choice for roof sheathing material is very important, as the roof plays a critical role in the durability of a building. A building with a weak, leaky roof will have a very short life span, regardless of the rest of the materials used.

Many of the conventional roofing options are also reasonably sustainable, making it possible to choose a material that is widely available, affordable, has a proven history and still meets high environmental standards.

More than any other element of a building, roof sheathing requires not just a good choice of material but also a very high quality of workmanship. The best roofing material laid in a poor manner will be leaky. This is one area in particular where quality of installation is every bit as important as quality of material. This factor must be weighed carefully when choosing a particular roofing material, as an owner needs to be able to source not just the material but the right person or thorough instructions for installation. Material warranties and workmanship guarantees are important considerations in the selection process.

Another important consideration when assessing the environmental and cost impacts of a particular roofing choice is the type of strapping or sheathing that is required underneath the sheathing. Some roofing types are installed over minimal wooden strapping, while others require a solid deck of plywood or lumber that can significantly raise costs and impacts. Certain roof types will require specific underlayment membranes, and these too can add to the environmental and financial tally. Be sure to understand the requirements of the full roof sheathing system before making decisions.

Building science basics for roof sheathing

It is the job of roof sheathing to keep water out of our buildings and to resist any forces that might deter the sheathing from keeping water out. While it is only one task, it's a difficult one.

The roof's job is made more difficult by design choices we make to change pitches and add ridges, hips, valleys and dormers to the roof shape. The situation is further complicated by the need to add penetrations through the roof sheathing for things like chimneys, vents and plumbing stacks. The simpler the roof design and the less penetrations through the roof, the easier it will be to provide reliable, long-term protection with the roof sheathing. A simple shed roof with a minimum pitch of 3:12 with no penetrations is not difficult to keep leak-free for decades. Every seam added to the roof sheathing increases the chances of leakage.

Successful roof sheathing is all about providing positive lapping wherever there is a seam and ensuring that water and snow have as free a path as possible to leave the roof with the help of gravity. Each roof sheathing material will have specific means of lapping and flashing at intersections, and care must be taken during the installation to ensure that all seams have been properly detailed. It is wise to avoid strategies that rely on caulking to provide the primary protection against leakage. Proper lapping of sheathing materials and flashing should be the primary protection, with caulking used as a backup defense under extreme conditions. Don't skimp on the width or depth of ridge, hip or valley flashings and be sure to specify the highest quality flashing kits for penetrations like chimneys and plumbing stacks where they absolutely must go through the roof.

Ice damming on roofs in cold climates was one of the issues that initiated the study of building science, as the issue causes many premature roof failures. Ice damming is usually caused by heat leaking from the house into the attic space under the roof, which causes snow to melt. At the edge of the roof where warm air no longer leaks from the house, this runoff refreezes and builds up along the edge of the roof and potentially sends water under the sheathing. Most building codes enforce design regulations intended to prevent ice damming, including sufficient attic insulation and air and vapor control layers at the ceiling so that heat and moisture do not leak into the attic space, as well as ventilation strategies to encourage outside air to move under the roof sheathing to maintain a similar temperature on the top and bottom sides of the sheathing. If you live in a cold climate, be sure to detail your attic space according to codes and/or best practices.

In warm weather and under direct sunlight, a roof can get very warm. This heat can be transmitted into the building and result in much higher cooling loads. The solar reflectance index (SRI) of a roofing product is defined by ASTM Standard E1980-01 and is a calculation that uses solar reflectance and thermal emittance. The US Environmental Protection Agency summarizes SRI as "the relative steady-state surface temperature with respect to the standard white (SRI=100) and standard black (SRI=0) under the standard solar and ambient conditions." The color of a roof product has a larger effect on SRI than the material used, though certain roof types will have better SRI ratings than others. The Cool Roof Rating Council maintains a database of products in the full range of available colors to help homeowners choose cooler roofs that will help to reduce cooling loads and improve energy efficiency.

Resources for further research

coolroofs.org
epa.gov/heatisld/resources/pdf/CoolRoofs
   Compendium.pdf

Metal roofing

What the cheerleaders say...	What the detractors say...
Very long lifespan and reliability	Expensive
Easy to install	High embodied energy
Widely available	Difficult to flash at penetrations
Recyclable at end of use	

Applications for system

- Roof sheathing

Basic materials

- Metal sheets or tiles
- Strapping over roof framing on 16- or 24-inch centers
- Some codes require a sheet membrane under steel roofs

How the system works

Metal roofing is a very broad category of products, with many variations and styles available. The key variations between different products are:

Types of metal — The two most common types of metal roofing are steel and aluminum. Copper, stainless steel and zinc alloys are also available at premium prices. Every metal has a different environmental impact, but all should be fully recyclable. Manufacturers offer varying levels of recycled material in their roofing products, and this can have a large impact on the environmental costs.

Gauge of thickness — Different thickness gauges of metal are widely available, typically ranging from 29 gauge at the thinnest, 26 gauge in the mid-range and 24 gauge at the thickest. In some jurisdictions, codes may indicate a minimum gauge requirement. Cost rises with thickness, as does weight and difficulty of installation with the trade-off being increased durability.

Steel roof. (CHESTER RENNIE)

Coatings — Paints, powder coatings, alloy coatings and stone chip coatings are among the options available. From an environmental point of view, the coatings on metal roofing are often the least environmentally friendly element of the roof. In particular, chemical compounds including Teflon, polyurethanes, acrylics and paints can contain elements that are environmentally detrimental during their production and are spread from the roof to the ground as the coatings wear. It is very important to thoroughly research the coatings used on any metal roofing you are considering purchasing, especially if you intend to collect and use rainwater from the metal roof.

Fastening systems — Metal roofs use either exposed fasteners (usually screws with an integral rubber or neoprene washer) or hidden fasteners. Exposed fasteners tend to be less expensive and easier to install, but can have a shorter life span.

Closures and Flashings — Each roofing company will tend to offer its own version of the basic ridge, hip and valley flashings, as well as different trim options, drip edges and chimney flashings. Raised rib roofs also come with foam closure strips to prevent water and pests from entering the area under the raised sections of roofing. Look for flashing systems that have generous widths and logical fastening, overlapping and drainage provisions.

Among these variations, there are also three basic types of metal roofing:

Sheet-style metal roofing — Sheets of metal with a pattern of ribs are ordered to match the lengths required for the particular roof. There are many rib styles, and the sheets can vary in width and gauge of thickness. The sheets are installed with the last rib of one sheet overlapping the first rib of the adjacent sheet. The sheets are typically fastened using roofing screws that have a rubber or neoprene washer under the head. The screws are used on the raised ribs or on the flat sections of roof, depending on manufacturer recommendations and installer preference. The ribs in sheet-style metal roofing offer strength to the sheets and allow for the use of simple and cost-effective strapping systems to support the sheathing. In general, sheet-style metal roofs will be the least expensive, fastest to install option.

Sheet-style metal roofs can also come in versions that mimic the appearance of shingles, clay tiles or other types of roofing; these are usually higher in cost and slightly more time-intensive to install.

Standing seam metal roofing — Sheets of metal are ordered to match the lengths required for the particular roof. The sheets will have steep, sharp ribs along both edges and a completely or relatively flat profile elsewhere. Fastening systems vary by manufacturer, but the ribs will overlap and be attached to the roof deck in a manner that does not leave the fasteners visible nor penetrate the surface of the roof with the fastener. For this reason, these roofs can have greater durability but can be slower to install and are often more expensive. Depending on the manufacturer, a solid roof decking must be provided

for standing seam metal roofs, raising the costs compared to ribbed sheets. Standing seam roofs are typically installed by professionals.

Metal roofing tiles — Tiles or shingles are fastened to the roof decking (usually a solid deck and not strapping) in a manner common to other shingle products. Fasteners are used along the top edge of the shingle or tile and covered by the next course of shingles or tiles. Some products use an interlocking system as well as fasteners to join the individual shingles or tiles, and these will tend to have a longer life span and be slightly slower to install. The size, shape and profile of shingles and tiles can vary widely between manufacturers. This type of roofing will usually take longer to install than either of the sheet-style roofs.

Tips for successful installation

1. Be sure to understand and follow the manufacturer's installation instructions. Every product will have different procedures, and these should be carried out accurately.
2. Leaks in metal roofs happen predominately at seams, particularly hip, valley and other flashing seams. The cost difference between different metal roofing systems is often based on the quality of the flashing and trim components, and it is worth using high-quality options. Generous positive lapping and clear drainage paths are critical, as are proper use of closure strips and well-applied caulking where required.
3. Sheet-style products with exposed fasteners must have the fasteners secured at the proper torque. If the fastener is driven too deeply, it can dent the metal and cause leaks; if it is not driven deeply enough, water will be able to get under the integral washer.
4. Sheet-style products require careful squaring of the roof surface before installation. It is difficult to make corrections in the sheets once

the installation has begun, and angled sheets will create a jagged roof edge that looks untidy. Strapping or roof decking can be used to create a decent, square surface for the roofing.

5. Sheet-style products can be long and awkward to work with. Be sure to have a work crew capable of handling the full-length sheets without excessive bending that might damage the ribs.

6. Metal roofs are slippery to work on. Be sure that workers have adequate training and safety equipment. Avoid walking on the metal roof once it is in place, and be sure that if people are going to walk on it, they do so safely and without damaging the roof.

Pros and cons

ENVIRONMENTAL IMPACTS

The category of metal roofing covers a wide variety of products. There are three main components to consider when weighing the environmental impacts of a metal roofing system:

1) **Type of metal and recycled content** — Each type of metal will have its own footprint at the mining and processing stages. Be sure to consider the regional source of the ore and the amount and intensity of the processing required to transform it into roofing. Recycled content makes a meaningful difference in the intensity of metal roofing products, making high-percentage recycled roofs an environmental imperative.

2) **Decking and underlayment requirements** — A large portion of the impact of a metal roofing system will be the supporting elements of the decking and underlayment. Some metal roofs require only thin wooden strapping on 16- or 24-inch centers, while others call for a solid plywood or lumber deck, which significantly raises the amount of material required and the environmental impacts. Systems that require a membrane material to be laid under the whole roof will also raise impacts, and these membranes are often made from plastics that can have serious implications in their creation, use and disposal. Be sure to consider the impacts of the whole system.

3) **Coatings** — The coatings on a particular metal roof may far outweigh the environmental impacts of the metal itself. Coatings can range from metallic alloys like galvanizing to paints, epoxies, polymers and other chemical coatings. Depending on the type of coating, the impacts may be negligible or considerable, making research a very important part of selecting a metal roof. It can be difficult to assess the impacts of paints and other coatings, as most manufacturers do not release the chemical composition of their coatings.

The coatings will have two types of environmental impact. At the time of mixing and application, varying amounts of toxins will be released into the environment, and a certain amount of the coating will also get dispersed into the air and water around the building during the roofing's life span. This second environmental impact is especially important if water is being collected from the roof. The NSF rating agency offers advice on roof coating products that have been tested for use in rainwater systems.

Harvesting — *High.* While different types of metals have varying impacts at the harvesting stage, they are all degrees of high impact. The extraction of ore is a high-intensity activity that is accompanied by major impacts on the immediate environment. Destruction of flora and fauna, contamination of soil and water from runoff and tailings ponds and the need to build access roads are all part of mining ore. Harvested ore is heavy, and incurs high transportation impacts, especially considering it is often transported long distances from source to production facility.

Manufacturing — *High.* The process of transforming raw ore into finished metal roofing product is energy intensive, and is responsible for significant greenhouse gas emissions, contaminated water, toxic dust, airborne dioxins and other impacts. It is often completed in distinct processes with transportation of heavy materials between facilities in the process.

The manufacturing and application of the coatings for steel roof products, in particular paints and powder coatings, is responsible for significant quantities of airborne pollutants, VOCs and contaminated water. Petrochemical underlayment materials can carry similar negative impacts.

Metal roofs with recycled content can have significantly lowered impacts. With many common roofing metals, energy input can be reduced by a factor of as much as ten. Some products come with as much 65 percent post-consumer recycled content, and these choices mitigate harvesting and manufacturing impacts considerably.

Transportation — *Moderate to High.* Sample building uses 1600 kg of metal roofing:

> 2.4 MJ per km by 15 ton truck
>
> 1.5 MJ per km by 35 ton truck
>
> 0.4 MJ per km by rail

Impacts will be based on the distance traveled from manufacturing plant to distributor, retailer and finally the job site. Roofing materials are heavy, and large trucks are used to move even fairly small quantities.

Installation — *Low.* On-site, the installation of a steel roof is not very energy intensive. Hand tools and small power tools are used. Sheets and tiles are individually quite lightweight and are usually moved into place manually.

WASTE: *LOW TO HIGH*

Recycleable — Metal offcuts. Quantities can be negligible for simple roofs, but can be significant if there are multiple hips and valleys.

Landfill — Empty caulking tubes, offcuts of foam adhesive strips, membrane or underlayment offcuts. Quantities will be low.

ENERGY EFFICIENCY

Steel roofing lies outside the building enclosure, and may seem at first glance to have little impact on energy efficiency. However, the color of the roofing can make quite a difference on cooling loads within the building in warm weather. Light-colored roofs reflect more sunlight than dark roofs, and the resultant heating of the roof surface on dark roofs has an impact on temperatures within the building. The more cooling days in your climate, the more important it is to choose a roof with a light color.

Metal Roof Embodied Energy

125 m² (1345 ft²) roof area	Material embodied energy from I.C.E. in MJ/kg	Weight to volume ratio of material*	Volume of material in sample 1000sf/92.9m² building	Sample building embodied energy	Material embodied carbon from I.C.E. in kgCO₂e/kg	Sample building embodied carbon	Notes
29 gauge galvanized steel	22.6 (Steel sheet, galvanized, average recycled content)	12.8 kg/m²**	125 m² 1600 kg	36,160 MJ	1.54	2,464 kg	**Average of manufacturer's data. Does not include paint, fasteners or underlayment.

Transportation: Steel roofing transportation by 35 ton truck would equate to 1.5 MJ per kilometer of travel to the building site. *Typically from engineeringtoolbox.com

MATERIAL COSTS: *MODERATE TO HIGH*

There are many kinds of metal roofing, covering a wide range of price points. Sheet versions will tend to be less expensive than shingle or patterned versions, and price will rise with gauge of steel, paints/coatings and trim details.

LABOR INPUT: *EASY TO MODERATE*

Working at heights to install roofing has inherent dangers. Proper setup and safety precautions should always be taken when working on a roof.

Sheet-style metal roofs are among the least labor-intensive roofs to install if the design is fairly simple. The more hips and valleys involved, the more installation times will increase. Sheet roofing usually comes cut to the desired length from the factory, and if the roof is simple there may be no cuts required during installation. If there are many hips and/or valleys, many sheets may need cutting, adding significant time to the installation. Sheet-style roofing is best installed with a crew of at least two and as many as four people, as long sheets can be difficult to handle and cut.

Shingle-style products take longer to install than sheets, but are easier to cut and manage on complicated roofs, so labor inputs will be more favorable on more complex roofs.

SKILL LEVEL REQUIRED FOR THE HOMEOWNER

Decking — *Easy.* A homeowner capable of the carpentry skills to frame a roof will be able to install the required strapping or decking for a steel roof.

Underlayment (if required) — *Easy.* Underlayment products are typically sheet products that come in rolls and are straightforward to install.

Steel sheets or tiles — *Easy to Moderate.* The cutting and installation of metal roofing products takes some practice, and a beginner would do well to try a

Metal Roof Ratings

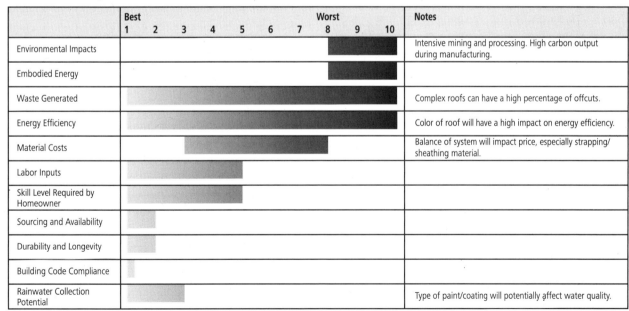

	Best 1 2 3 4 5 6 7	Worst 8 9 10	Notes
Environmental Impacts		■	Intensive mining and processing. High carbon output during manufacturing.
Embodied Energy		■	
Waste Generated			Complex roofs can have a high percentage of offcuts.
Energy Efficiency			Color of roof will have a high impact on energy efficiency.
Material Costs			Balance of system will impact price, especially strapping/sheathing material.
Labor Inputs			
Skill Level Required by Homeowner			
Sourcing and Availability			
Durability and Longevity			
Building Code Compliance			
Rainwater Collection Potential			Type of paint/coating will potentially affect water quality.

small roofing job before tackling a whole house project. The basic process of squaring and preparing the roof is important, especially with sheet-style roofing, as it is easy to have sheets begin to run crooked and look sloppy. Each manufacturer will have particular instructions for their products, which should be followed.

Caps and Flashings — *Easy to Difficult.* Typical ridge and hip caps and perimeter flashing are quite simple to install. Intersections and penetrations through steel roofing can be tricky to flash properly, and the more of these that exist on a roof the harder the job of keeping them watertight. Some experience or the ability to carefully follow written directions is important.

SOURCING/AVAILABILITY: *EASY*

Metal roofing products are widely available everywhere in North America.

DURABILITY: *VERY HIGH*

Metal roofing is among the most durable roofing choices. If it is installed in a way that prevents leakage from the start, it will typically last 40 to 80 years, and often carries long (15–25 year) warranties.

CODE COMPLIANCE

Metal roofing is an acceptable solution in all building codes. Requirements for gauge of metal, roof decking and membranes will vary by region, so be sure to know the local requirements for metal roofs.

RAIN WATER COLLECTION CAPABILITY: *HIGH*

Steel roofs are among the best options for collecting clean, uncontaminated rain water for use in the building. Some paints and coatings may not be appropriate. NSF ratings exist for numerous types of metal roofing if the rain water is to be used for human consumption.

FUTURE DEVELOPMENT

The basic metals and alloys and the formats for metal roofing are well established and unlikely to change much. What may improve is the environmental friendliness of the coatings, or access to useful information about coatings and their impacts. A wider variety of light-colored roofing is also likely to become available as the value of reflective roof surfaces is better understood. Recycled content may also increase as consumer awareness drives the market toward more environmentally friendly products.

Resources for further research

Harrison, H. W. *BRE Building Elements: Roofs and Roofing: Performance, Diagnosis, Maintenance, Repair and the Avoidance of Defects.* London: Construction Research Communications, 2000. Print.

Scharff, Robert, and Terry Kennedy. *Roofing Handbook.* New York: McGraw-Hill, 2001. Print.

Fine Home Building. *Roofing: The Best of Fine Homebuilding.* Newtown, CT: Taunton, 1996. Print.

Cedar shake and shingle

What the cheerleaders say...	What the detractors say...
Renewable resource	High cost
Long lifespan	Flammability
Long, proven history	Can require environmentally unfriendly underlayments
No landfill waste	

Applications for system

- Roof sheathing for roofs with a minimum pitch of 3:12 or 4:12
- Siding

Basic materials

- Cedar shakes or shingles
- Strapping
- Nails
- Underlayment may be required in some installations

How the system works

The terms "shake" and "shingle" refer to how the roofing is made from the original cedar log. Shingles are milled (saw cut) from the log, while shakes are split from the log. Shingles are much more common in this era. Most of the products called shakes today are saw-milled, but done so at varying thicknesses to reproduce the more random thicknesses associated with old hand-split shakes. The more "authentic" modern shakes are textured on one side to further replicate a hand-split appearance.

Regardless of whether shakes or shingles are used, the system for installation is the same, and is similar to any shingle-style product. Horizontal courses of shingles are laid side by side (with a small gap to allow for expansion when wet), with the next course laid over top of the preceding one such that a set amount of the lower course is left exposed. The seams between shingles are offset between courses, and the "reveal" exposed on each course is such that a cross section of the roof would show three layers of shingle at any point in the roof. The shingles come in varying widths, making it easy to stagger the joints between courses.

Shingles can be installed in even courses or staggered slightly to create a variegated pattern at each course. Sometimes shingles are cut into patterns on the exposed edge, creating patterns across a single course or over multiple courses.

Older cedar shingle installations were fastened to roof strapping laid at centers that corresponded to the length of the shingles and the desired reveal. This allowed for air circulation behind the shingles, which aided in helping them dry out between rainfalls. The move to solid plywood decking in the 1950s resulted in shorter life spans for cedar shingles, as water would remain trapped between the shingles and plywood, where they were in constant contact. The same issue can arise when products like tar paper or other membranes are placed directly behind the shingles.

Today, strapping is often added on top of plywood decking to provide ventilation, or plastic

Cedar shingles.

mesh products are used to create airspace between plywood and shingles. However, the old style of installation over simple strapping works very well, as it minimizes material use, costs and labor time.

Shingles are overlapped to create ridge and hip caps and metal flashings are typically used in valleys, with the shingles cut to leave the flashing exposed.

Cedar shingles are a unique roofing material in that they actually absorb a large amount of the water that strikes them and then release this moisture to the air after the rainfall. They swell as they absorb water and if properly spaced, the gaps between them will close.

Cedar shingles are often made from western red cedar and exported across the continent. However, eastern white cedar can be used to make long-lasting shingles, reducing shipping for the eastern half of the continent.

Tips for successful installation

1. Whether using simple strapping or a synthetic breather layer, ensure that shingles have an air space behind them. Attaching shingles directly to a solid decking will dramatically reduce life span. The type of decking and/or spacer used will affect costs, installation time and environmental impact, so be sure to consider the roofing as a whole system.

2. Shingles can be prone to splitting when being nailed in place. Using the proper-sized nail or staple is critical. Any split shingle should be removed, or treated as two shingles each with its own fastener.

3. Don't overtighten the fasteners. Drive each fastener deep enough that its head makes only light contact with the surface of the shingle, to prevent splitting when the shingle swells when wet.

4. The first course of shingle is a double course to provide the "three-thick" shingle profile at the edge of the roof. Many installers place the first layer "upside down," with the thicker end pointing up the roof to prevent the double layer from changing the pitch at the end of the roof. Overlapping seams between the doubled first courses is important.

5. The location of a cedar shingle roof will have an impact on its life span. Cedar roofs do best when they can go through complete drying cycles between wettings, so cedar roofs in highly shaded areas will often sprout moss and deteriorate at an accelerated rate.

6. Do not put cedar shingles at too shallow a pitch. This type of roofing requires the assistance of gravity to prevent water from making its way underneath the courses and causing leaks. Systems with solid underlayment and/or membranes will specify a minimum 3:12 pitch, while the minimum for shingles over strapping is 4:12.

7. Shingle suppliers may offer as many as four grades of shingle. Only A-grade shingles with no imperfections should be used for roofing. High-quality B-grade may be suitable for steeper pitches. C- or D-grade should not be used.

8. Some shingle suppliers will chemically treat shingles to extend life span or maintain appearance. Many of these treatments involve toxic chemicals, and should be well researched before purchasing.

Pros and cons

ENVIRONMENTAL IMPACTS

Harvesting — *Negligible to High.* A cedar log cut locally and wisely and split into shake by hand will have dramatically lower impacts than a cedar log that is clear-cut from sensitive ecosystems far away from the building site. The use of FSC or other third-party certified wood will go a long way to ensuring minimal impacts.

Manufacturing — *Negligible to Moderate.* The processing of cedar logs into shingles is not particularly energy intensive and is often done at local, small-scale mills.

Chemical treatments may be applied to shingles, including trisodium phosphate, bleach, zinc or copper sulfate, zinc chloride and proprietary biocides. To minimize the air- and water-borne impacts of these chemicals during manufacturing and application, specify shingles that are not treated.

The balance of the roofing system will also affect impacts. Simple strapping over roof framing will have the lowest manufacturing impacts (especially if local and/or third-party certified wood is used). Solid plywood decking with a plastic breather product and/or waterproofing membrane will raise the impacts significantly. Determining all the components of the system is important in assessing the choice of cedar as a roofing material, especially when introducing petrochemicals to an otherwise natural system.

Transportation — *Negligible to Moderate.* Sample building uses 475 kg of cedar shingles/shakes:

> 0.71 MJ per km by 15 ton truck
>
> 0.45 MJ per km by 35 ton truck
>
> 0.12 MJ per km by rail

Distance from point of harvest to point of manufacture to final building site can vary from nothing to cross-continent truck journeys. Sourcing locally lowers impacts significantly.

Installation — *Negligible to Low.* Putting cedar shingles on a roof is a low-intensity job which can be completed entirely with hand tools with very little penalty in labor input. Shingles are light to move onto the roof and can be cut with a sharp blade and nailed into place, eliminating or minimizing power tool use.

Waste: *Negligible to Low*

Compostable — All cedar and strapping offcuts. Quantities will vary from negligible to moderate, depending on the complexity of the roof.

Recycleable — Metal fasteners. Quantities will be negligible.

Landfill — Plywood offcuts, membrane or underlayment offcuts, caulking tubes. Quantities will be low.

Energy efficiency

The use of cedar shingle roofing will have little impact on the overall energy efficiency of the building. The reflectivity of cedar shingles is better than even the lightest-colored asphalt shingles, though less than white roofs of other materials*.

Cedar Shingle Roof Embodied Energy

125 m² (1345 ft²) roof area	Material embodied energy from I.C.E. in MJ/kg	Weight to volume ratio of material*	Volume of material in sample 1000sf/92.9m² building	Sample building embodied energy	Material embodied carbon from I.C.E. in kgCO₂e/kg	Sample building embodied carbon	Notes
Factory sawn cedar shingles	2.0**	380 kg/m³	1.25 m³ 475 kg	950 MJ	0.2	95 kg	**Figure not from ICE. Average of industry figures.
Nails	20.1(Steel, general, average recycled content)		20kg	402 MJ	1.46	29 kg	
Totals				1,352 MJ		124 kg	Does not include strapping, sheathing or underlayment.

Transportation: Cedar shingle transportation by 15 ton truck would equate to 0.7 MJ per kilometer of travel to the building site. *Typically from engineeringtoolbox.com

MATERIAL COSTS: *MODERATE TO HIGH*

Areas where cedar is a common roofing option will have lower costs.

LABOR INPUT: *MODERATE TO HIGH*

Working at heights to install roofing has inherent dangers. Proper setup and safety precautions should always be taken when working on a roof.

A cedar shingle roof is relatively labor intensive to install. If strapping is being used, it will be on much closer centers (typically 5–8 inch / 12–20 cm OC) than required for other sheathings, increasing installation time. Using solid decking and/or underlayment or waterproofing membranes will also increase installation time.

The laying of the shingles is fairly straightforward and comparable to other styles of shingles except that the cedar will come in a variety of widths that must be selected for each space, and each shingle should be inspected for imperfections before being installed.

Ridge and hip caps are time-consuming to install, as the overlapping must be done carefully to ensure a long, leak-free life span.

SKILL LEVEL REQUIRED FOR THE HOMEOWNER

Decking — *Easy.* Homeowners possessing the carpentry skills to create the roof structure will have no difficulty decking the roof for cedar shingles.

Underlayment (if required) — *Easy.* Underlayment materials are lightweight and typically come in rolls that are straightforward to place.

Shingles — *Easy.* The basic laying of shingles is quite straightforward and beginners should be able to follow instruction manuals for a successful installation. A solo builder or a small crew can lay cedar shingles, albeit at a slower pace. Adding cut patterns to a roof requires careful planning and pre-cutting of shingles, but is not overly difficult to execute.

Caps and Flashing — *Moderate to Difficult.* Capping and flashing details can also be learned from manuals, but may be better understood by examining existing roofs or consulting with a professional. Metal ridge and hip flashing can be used over cedar shingles if a beginner is uncertain about installing these elements of the roof in cedar.

SOURCING/AVAILABILITY: *EASY TO MODERATE*

As both western red cedar and eastern white are viable options, any builder in a region where these trees exist should be able to source quality shingles. Western red cedar is exported across the continent, though it may be a special order item in some regions.

DURABILITY: *MODERATE TO HIGH*

Properly installed with adequate ventilation below the shingles, a proper pitch and adequate drying potential, a cedar shingle roof can have a life span of 30 to 40 years. Assess the life span of existing cedar shingle roofs in your region, as climate will have a definite impact on longevity.

CODE COMPLIANCE

Cedar shingle roofs have a long history in North America, but are not always directly recognized in modern building codes. Many code jurisdictions accept cedar shingle roofs based on technical documents from lumber groups and manufacturers, and these will often mandate the use of a synthetic breather layer, plywood decking and a membrane product. Those wishing to use the simpler, low-impact method of shingles over strapping may have to work harder to convince code officials of the viability.

Some urban areas will not allow cedar shingle roofs due to concerns about fire, so be sure to check fire codes as well as building codes before choosing a cedar shingle roof.

RAINWATER COLLECTION CAPABILITY: *Low*

Water caught from a cedar shingle roof will be heavily loaded with cedar tannins and oils that will render the rainwater harvested unfit for potable uses and potentially problematic for irrigation purposes. Treated shingles will also leach embedded chemicals into the water.

FUTURE DEVELOPMENT

It is unlikely that the method of producing or installing cedar will undergo much change. The availability and cost of cedar will fluctuate based on supply and demand. The wider use of third-party certification for harvesting cedar will likely have a positive impact over time.

*Laboratory Testing of the Reflectance Properties of Roofing Materials. D.S. Parker, J.E.R. McIlvaine, S.F. Barkaszi, D.J. Beal, M.T. Anello. Florida Solar Energy Center (FSEC), FSEC-CR-670-00.

Reagan and Acklam (1979) measured the solar reflectance of new unoiled and unpainted cedar shake wood shingles at 32%. Oiled shakes had a total solar reflectance of 28%.

Resources for further research

Cedar Shake and Shingle Bureau, *New Roof Construction Manual,* cedarbureau.org/cms-assets/documents/30985-306719.roof-manual-011.pdf

Red Cedar Shingle and Shake Design and Application Manual for New Roof Construction. Bellevue, WA: Red Cedar Shingle and Handsplit Shake Bureau, 1990. Print.

Harrison, H. W. *BRE Building Elements: Roofs and Roofing: Performance, Diagnosis, Maintenance, Repair and the Avoidance of Defects.* London: Construction Research Communications, 2000. Print.

Roofing: *The Best of Fine Homebuilding.* Newtown, CT: Taunton, 1996. Print.

Scharff, Robert, and Terry Kennedy. *Roofing Handbook.* New York: McGraw-Hill, 2001. Print.

Cedar Shingle Ratings

	Best 1	2	3	4	5	6	7	Worst 8	9	10	Notes
Environmental Impacts											Forestry practices are highly variable and have a significant impact.
Embodied Energy											
Waste Generated											
Energy Efficiency											Natural colour reasonably light and reflective.
Material Costs											
Labor Inputs											
Skill Level Required by Homeowner											
Sourcing and Availability											Production is regional.
Durability and Longevity											Proper slope and exposure to sunlight will affect durability.
Building Code Compliance											Accepted solution in some codes, but may be disallowed by fire codes in some urban areas.
Rainwater Collection Potential											Tannins will affect chemistry of water. May be suitable for some irrigation purposes.

Thatch roofs

What the cheerleaders say...	What the detractors say...
The only rapidly renewable roofing	Potential fire hazards
Very low environmental impacts	High amount of labor input required
Long lifespan	No established source for materials
Fully compostable at end of lifespan	Very little expertise available

Applications for system

- Roof sheathing for roofs with a minimum pitch of 10:12
- Wall sheathing

Basic materials

- Long-stemmed reeds or straw
- Strapping
- Twine or wire to fasten thatch to strapping

How the system works

While it may seem strange for modern builders to think that a bunch of dried grass stems can provide a thoroughly water-resistant and long-lasting roof, thatch roofs have a long and successful history across a wide range of climatic zones. Thatching techniques have been developed worldwide, adapting the basic principle to suit available materials and to work in specific climates. Modern thatched roofs are installed in almost every region of the world, though in relatively small numbers.

The system of thatching used in many wet and/ or cold climates involves fastening bundles of long, thick reeds or straw to the roof strapping in successive courses, each overlapping the preceding course. The thatch is laid at a thickness (which can range from 8–20 cm / 3–8 inch) that prevents water from working its way through the layers. Thatched roofs have very steep pitches to aid in this drainage.

Traditional thatch was hand-tied to the roof strapping using twine or rope. Modern thatchers often use screws and wire to provide attachment. Regardless of regional variations in material and technique, the thatch is held in place by securing a horizontal member across the thatch and tying that member back to the strapping through the thatch. The next course of thatch then covers the tie point as the roof is built upward. At the edges of the roof, the thatch is laid at a slight angle to encourage runoff to leave the edge of the roof and to provide a consistent appearance.

Thatching on flat sections of roof is relatively straightforward, but the same cannot be said for ridge, hip and valley sections. These areas take considerable knowledge and experience to execute in a weather-tight and long-lasting manner.

Many modern installations use a fire-resistant (often fiberglass) membrane under the roof strapping to prevent the spread of a fire from inside the building to the roof. Eavestroughing is not used with thatched roofs, making them incompatible with rainwater harvesting.

Tips for successful installation

1. Thatching methods vary widely with the type of thatch material being used and the tradition of thatching used in the region. Ensure that the reed or straw being used is compatible with the climate and the installation technique.
2. Be sure you are able to obtain the material and expertise required to create a thatched roof. It is a rare type of roofing in North America, and must be well researched before deciding to proceed.
3. Plans for a thatched roof must be properly detailed before construction. The uncommon thickness of the roofing, the steep pitch required and the particular details at hips and valleys

must be incorporated into the drawings to ensure the roof will work when built.

Pros and cons

ENVIRONMENTAL IMPACTS

Harvesting — *Negligible to Low.* Thatch that is harvested regionally will have the lowest environmental impact of any roofing material. The plants that produce useful thatch are annual grasses, making it the only annually renewable roofing. Some reeds that are suitable for thatching do not need to be manually seeded, but occur naturally on marginal lands that are otherwise not suitable for agriculture and aren't sprayed or treated in any way. Most modern grain plants have been bred to have much shorter, narrower stalks than their genetic ancestors and are not suitable for thatch, but less common grains (spelt, rye, etc) still have stalk lengths and diameters that may work for thatch. Farmed grains may have environmental impacts associated with the use of herbicides and/or pesticides.

Manufacturing — *Negligible to Low.* Thatch requires little to no processing other than cutting, cleaning and bundling. These processes are done on a small scale and with minimal machinery and fossil fuel input. There are no toxic by-products created.

At the most intensive, a thatch roof will use a small amount of metal wire and screws and a layer of fiberglass matting that has high energy input and some toxic by-products. At the least intensive, round wood strapping and natural fiber twine is used.

Transportation — *Negligible to High.* Sample building uses 2,250 kg of thatch:

> 3.4 MJ per km by 15 ton truck
> 0.9 MJ per km by 35 ton truck
> 0.36 MJ per km by ocean freight

Some thatch projects in North America are completed using thatch imported from Europe, because there are no commercial suppliers on this continent. This adds high transportation impacts to an otherwise low-impact roof. Many thatch roofs are made with locally, manually harvested material, keeping impacts very low.

Installation — *Negligible.* Thatch is largely installed without the use of power tools and does not create any problematic waste or by-products.

WASTE: *NEGLIGIBLE*

Compostable — All reed or straw thatching, natural fiber twine.

Recyclable — Polypropylene twine, metal wire.

Landfill — Fiberglass matt offcuts, if used. Quantities can be negligible to low.

Thatch roof and materials.

ENERGY EFFICIENCY

Historically, thatched buildings relied on the fairly significant amount of air trapped in the thatch to insulate the roof of the building. However, thatch allows for a lot of air infiltration and would not be considered adequate insulation or airtight enough to meet codes or modern comfort levels on its own. Modern buildings with thatched roofs rely on an insulation layer independent from the roof sheathing.

A thatch roof can have some beneficial effects by reducing summertime warming of the attic space quite significantly. Thatch roofs will also eliminate the issue of condensation on the back side of the roof sheathing as the material will not have the low surface temperatures of more dense sheathing and is able to adsorb and absorb moisture without condensation.

MATERIAL COSTS: *VERY LOW TO HIGH*

Suitable material for thatching can be harvested locally in many parts of North America for no cost, but material is often harvested and processed far from the building site in low quantities as a "boutique" material with high costs.

LABOR INPUT: *HIGH*

Working at heights to install roofing has inherent dangers. Proper setup and safety precautions should always be taken when working on a roof.

Thatch roofing is unique in that, for most North American builders, harvesting the material is likely to be a necessary preliminary step. While suitable materials are widely available, harvesting and preparing them can be a very labor-intensive process, easily requiring more hours than the installation itself. In areas of the world where thatch material is harvested commercially and available for delivery to a job site, the labor input is obviously much lower.

Thatching is the most labor-intensive form of roofing. An experienced thatch crew can move at a speed that approaches that of an experienced cedar shingle crew. Beginners will move a great deal slower, as the process of laying thatch is very particular and must be done accurately and correctly.

SKILL LEVEL REQUIRED FOR THE HOMEOWNER: *MODERATE TO HIGH*

Thatching requires a good deal of skill. In European countries, it takes many years of apprenticeship and experience to obtain the title of "Master Thatcher." Beginners are advised to start with a very small roof, such as a small shed, and to keep roof shapes to simple gables or sheds. Hips and valleys add a lot of complexity to the thatching process, and should be left to those with plenty of experience.

SOURCING/AVAILABILITY: *DIFFICULT*

Both the material and the expertise to build a thatch roof can be difficult to source in North America. A few master thatchers practice in the U.S. and they tend to import their thatch material from Europe.

Thatch Roof Embodied Energy

125 m² (1345 ft²) roof area	Material embodied energy from I.C.E. in MJ/kg	Weight to volume ratio of material*	Volume of material in sample 1000sf/92.9m² building	Sample building embodied energy	Material embodied carbon from I.C.E. in kgCO₂e/kg	Sample building embodied carbon	Notes
150mm (6in) depth	0.24 (Straw)	120 kg/m³	18.75 m³ 2250 kg	540 MJ	0.01	23 kg	Does not include strapping, fasteners or underlayment.

Transportation: Thatch transportation by 15 ton truck would equate to 3.4 MJ per kilometer of travel to the building site. Thatch transportation by ocean freight would equate to 0.36 MJ per kilometer of travel to the building site. *Typically from engineeringtoolbox.com

A homeowner wishing to attempt a thatch roof may have to resort to harvesting thatch material locally and learn from books or by taking workshops with experienced thatchers and bringing the skill back home.

DURABILITY: *MODERATE TO HIGH*

Thatch roofs are surprisingly durable. In northern European climates, they can last for 40 to 80 years. Depending on the style of ridge cap used, the ridge may need repair or replacing every 10 to 20 years. A thatched roof at the end of its life span is not typically replaced; rather new thatch is built over top of the existing thatch.

CODE COMPLIANCE

No building codes in North America address the use of thatch roofs. Proposing a thatch roof will likely require a fair bit of documentation and persuasion, as there are few examples of thatched roofs on which a code official can base an assessment. The historical and modern use of thatch in Europe means that a lot of code-related testing and documentation exists to support it. A building department may be willing to consider a thatch roof with the right amount of documentation and some assurance that the installation is being done properly. The few master thatchers working in North America have been able to have their work approved, as have a small number of owner-builders.

RAINWATER COLLECTION CAPABILITY: *LOW TO MODERATE*

It is possible to filter rain water from a thatch roof, but not without issues. Thatch roofs can be difficult to mount with gutters suitable for collecting rain water. Even with functioning gutters, the thatch is capable of holding onto a considerable amount of

Thatch Roof Ratings

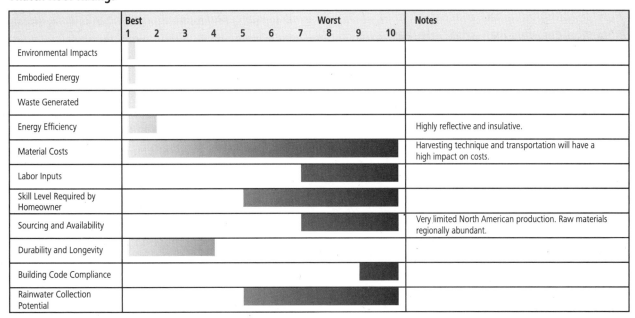

	Best 1	2	3	4	5	6	7	Worst 8	9	10	Notes
Environmental Impacts											
Embodied Energy											
Waste Generated											
Energy Efficiency											Highly reflective and insulative.
Material Costs											Harvesting technique and transportation will have a high impact on costs.
Labor Inputs											
Skill Level Required by Homeowner											
Sourcing and Availability											Very limited North American production. Raw materials regionally abundant.
Durability and Longevity											
Building Code Compliance											
Rainwater Collection Potential											

biological material that can come out in the rain water, requiring additional filtration.

FUTURE DEVELOPMENT

There is no reason for thatch to be disregarded in North America, as it is a viable, durable roofing option that is remarkably environmentally friendly. As the costs of conventional roofing materials rise with the price of fuel to make them, thatch will start to look better and better. The machinery required to mechanically harvest and bundle thatch is not complicated or expensive, and viable thatch material grows in many places on the continent. There will always be limitations to the use of thatch roofing in urban areas, as fire safety concerns would limit the density of thatched roofs. But there are many locations where thatched roofs are feasible, appropriate and the best possible environmental choice. It will take many dedicated homeowners willing to push the boundaries and create a market in which thatch may start to take the kind of foothold where it creates a viable niche market, similar to cedar shingles.

Resources for further research

Billett, Michael. *The Complete Guide to Living with Thatch*. London: Robert Hale, 2003. Print.

Fearn, Jacqueline. *Thatch and Thatching*. Aylesbury, UK: Shire Publications, 1976. Print.

Sanders, Marjorie, and Roger Angold. *Thatches and Thatching: A Handbook for Owners, Thatchers and Conservators*. Ramsbury, UK: Crowood, 2012. Print.

Slate

What the cheerleaders say...	What the detractors say...
Naturally occurring material	Very heavy, requires extra framing
Very durable	Source of material limited
Beautiful	High installation costs
	Requires regular maintenance

Applications for system

- Roof sheathing
- Wall sheathing

Basic materials

- Slate tiles
- Ceramic or metal ridge and hip caps, in some cases
- Roofing nails
- Wooden strapping

How the system works

Slate roofing uses wide, flat pieces of quarried slate in a manner similar to all other shingle-style roofing systems. The slate is quarried to a predetermined thickness, length and width, with holes drilled at the top edge to accept nails. The slates are nailed to a solid roof deck or appropriately spaced strapping. The weight of slate often necessitates additional strength in the roof framing and decking.

As with most shingles, a double row is laid at the edge of the roof with the next course laid over top of the preceding one such that a set amount of the lower course is left exposed. The seams between shingles are offset between courses, and the "reveal" exposed on each course is such that a cross section of the roof would show three layers of slate at any point in the roof. The slates come in varying widths, making it easy to stagger the joints between courses.

Ridge and hip capping is often achieved by

careful overlapping the slates to provide positive lapping and drainage. In some cases, ceramic or metal capping is mortared onto the slate at hips and ridges. Valley flashing is usually a metal flashing with the slate cut to leave the metal exposed in the valley.

Tips for successful installation

1. Be sure to size roof framing members and decking to be compatible with the weight of slate tiles.
2. The use of the proper non-corroding nails is essential. It is important to drive the nail deeply enough that the head sits fully in the countersunk hole or else it will rub on the underside of the slate above and potentially cause cracking; at the same time it is important not to drive the nail too deeply such that it exerts pressure on the slate that might cause it to crack. Careful installation is the key.
3. Roofers must be kept from stepping on slates. While slate is very durable, it is prone to cracking when point loaded with foot traffic. Roofing ladders, scaffolding or other means of keeping workers off of slates must be used.
4. Be sure the slate you are using is intended for roofing purposes. Many types of slate that are used for interior flooring applications are not suitable for roofing, as freeze/thaw cycles on a roof can destroy them.

Pros and cons

ENVIRONMENTAL IMPACTS

Harvesting — *Low to Moderate.* Slate is only quarried in a few regions and the quarries have been established for a very long time, so the immediate effects on local ecosystems took place many decades (sometimes centuries) ago.

Manufacturing — *Low.* The cutting of slate uses basic machinery and is not energy intensive. The final stages of cutting are still done by hand in most facilities.

Transportation — *Low to High.* Sample building uses 9,202 kg of slate:

> 13.8 MJ per km by 15 ton truck
> 8.65 MJ per km by 35 ton truck
> 2.3 MJ per km by rail

Slate only occurs naturally in certain regions in North America, largely in the northeast, and is a very heavy material. Shipping will accrue significant impacts the further the material is moved from the point of production.

Installation — *Negligible to Low.* Most of the work of laying slate is manual labor, with no or minimal use of power tools.

Slate Roof Embodied Energy

125 m² (1345 ft²) roof area	Material embodied energy from I.C.E. in MJ/kg	Weight to volume ratio of material*	Volume of material in sample 1000sf/92.9m² building	Sample building embodied energy	Material embodied carbon from I.C.E. in kgCO$_2$e/kg	Sample building embodied carbon	Notes
Slate shingles @ 25mm total thickness	0.5**	2940 kg/m³	3.13 m³ 9202 kg	4,601 MJ	0.03	276 kg	**Middle of data range from ICE.
Nails	20.1 Steel, (general, average recycled content)		20 kg	402 MJ	1.46	29 kg	
Totals				**5,003 MJ**		**305 kg**	Does not include strapping sheathing or underlayment.

Transportation: Slate transportation by 35 ton truck would equate to 8.6 MJ per kilometer of travel to the building site. *Typically from engineeringtoolbox.com

Slate

WASTE: *LOW*

Compostable — All slate offcuts can be left in the environment. Quantities will vary from negligible to moderate, depending on the complexity of the roof.
Recyclable — Metal fasteners and flashing. Quantities will be negligible to low.
Landfill — Underlayment (if required). Quantities will be negligible to low.

ENERGY EFFICIENCY

A slate roof will not have a large impact on energy efficiency. Dark-colored slate will create heat build-up in the summer that can add to air-conditioning loads.

MATERIAL COSTS: *HIGH*

Slate tiles are a specialty roofing option produced in comparatively small quantities, putting them at a cost premium.

LABOR INPUT: *HIGH*

Working at heights to install roofing has inherent dangers. Proper setup and safety precautions should always be taken when working on a roof.

Slate tiles are fastened to the roof with only one or two nails per tile, and the layout of the roof is the same as with other shingle or tile systems. Slate is heavy, and additional labor time is accrued in the moving of the material from ground to roof. The necessity of avoiding walking on the roof once slate is in place also adds some preparation time not required with other roofing styles.

Shaping the slate decoratively will add significantly to the labor time.

SKILL LEVEL REQUIRED FOR THE HOMEOWNER

Decking — *Easy.* A homeowner with the ability to frame a roof will be able to lay the required decking for a slate roof.

Slate Roof Ratings

	Best 1 2 3 4 5	Worst 6 7 8 9 10	Notes
Environmental Impacts			
Embodied Energy			
Waste Generated			
Energy Efficiency			Color of slate will impact heat gain.
Material Costs			
Labor Inputs			
Skill Level Required by Homeowner			
Sourcing and Availability			Production is regional.
Durability and Longevity			
Building Code Compliance			Accepted solution in some codes. Historical precedent assists with alternative compliance.
Rainwater Collection Potential			

Underlayment (if required) — *Easy.* Underlayment is lightweight and comes in rolls that are straightforward to apply.

Shingles — *Easy to Moderate.* Slate roofing skills can be learned and successfully applied by beginners. The premise is the same as any shingle or tile roof system, and the basic dos and don'ts can be found in accessible resources. There are workshops available to help acquire some experience.

Caps and Flashing — *Moderate to Difficult.* Beginners working from written manuals or instructions will be able to manage simple slate roofs. More complex ridge and hip caps and valley and penetration flashings require some experience, input from a professional or excellent instruction to complete successfully.

SOURCING/AVAILABILITY: *MODERATE TO DIFFICULT*

Access to slate materials and expertise will vary widely by region. The closer one is to slate quarries, the easier it will be to locate slate, installers and learning opportunities. The northeastern United States and southeastern Canada are the main roofing slate-producing regions in North America.

DURABILITY: *VERY HIGH*

A properly installed slate roof can be exceptionally durable, with some roofs still in serviceable condition after 150 years. Slate that is stressed by foot traffic or other point loads can crack and fall from the roof, but otherwise the material does not deteriorate, corrode, wear or break down from UV radiation.

CODE COMPLIANCE

Building codes in regions where slate roofs have been used traditionally are likely to still have provisions to accept slate roofs in a modern context. There is a very thorough ASTM standard written for slate roofing that will be referenced in codes or acceptable to code officials. Where slate roofs do not have historical precedent, it may be more difficult to persuade code officials, but the ASTM standard should help.

RAINWATER COLLECTION CAPABILITY: *HIGH*

Water from slate roofs is typically of high quality and would be suitable for use inside the building with regular filtration strategies.

FUTURE DEVELOPMENT

The methods for quarrying or installing slate are not likely to change. The high cost of slate will likely see it remain a less popular option.

Resources for further research

ASTM C406 / C406M — 10: Standard Specification for Roofing Slate

Jenkins, Joseph C. *The Slate Roof Bible: Understanding, Installing and Restoring the World's Finest Roof.* White River Junction, VT: Chelsea Green, 2003. Print.

Stearns, Brian, Alan Stearns, and John Meyer. *The Slate Book: How to Design, Specify, Install, and Repair a Slate Roof.* Stowe, VT: Vermont Slate and Copper Services, 1998. Print.

Composite shingles

What the cheerleaders say...	What the detractors say...
Recycling of waste stream materials	Lifespan unproven
Potentially long-lasting	Often require membranes/underlayment
Aesthetic matching of other roof styles	Must check "green" credentials

Applications for system

- Roof sheathing
- Wall sheathing

Basic materials

There are many different composite shingle products available, each using different materials. They typically use the following types of ingredients:

- Recycled plastic or rubber
- Agricultural, wood or paper fiber
- Roofing nails
- Wooden strapping or solid decking
- Waterproof membrane or underlayment may be required

How the system works

While each proprietary composite shingle product is different from its competitors, they all share a fairly similar approach. The shingles are made from a recycled plastic or rubber material reinforced with some kind of fiber. As with all shingle roofing, the individual shingles are nailed to the roof surface side by side in consecutive courses, with a specified amount of reveal left on each course. The shingles are usually installed such that a section through any point on the roof would reveal three layers of shingle everywhere on the roof surface.

As proprietary products, each shingle will come with manufacturer's instructions for installation. These instructions should be followed carefully, and should be examined in advance to understand all of the requirements of the roofing system.

Tips for successful installation

1. As these products constitute a relatively new category of roof sheathing, it is wise to contact people who have had a particular product installed and get firsthand references.
2. Many companies offer training workshops or have online video training resources. Take advantage of any such offers to ensure correct installation.
3. Ascertain what kind of roof decking is required for a particular system, and whether or not any kind of roof membrane is required, as this will affect cost, installation time and environmental impacts.
4. If possible, decide to use a composite product at the design phase of the building, so that any particular details required by the roofing can be incorporated into the drawings.

Pros and cons

ENVIRONMENTAL IMPACTS

Harvesting — *Low to High.* Each composite shingle product has a different formulation with greatly varying quantities of recycled content. Post-consumer recycled content usually carries greater reductions in impact than post-industrial recycling. Determining overall quantity of recycled material is important, as many of the virgin materials in composite shingles are petrochemicals with all the associated extractive impacts, including greenhouse gases, air and water contamination and habitat destruction.

Fibers can come from low-impact or recycled sources, or may have moderate impacts in their growing and harvesting cycle, especially if they involve heavy pesticide and herbicide usage.

Manufacturing — *Moderate to High.* The use of recycled petrochemicals typically involves some degree of air and water pollution. Manufacturing processes can range from moderately to highly energy intensive. Research carefully regarding toxins or harmful by-products generated during manufacturing. If possible, try to find third-party verification of company claims.

Transportation — *Low to High.* Composite shingle production facilities tend to be small and regional. Transportation distances can vary from short and factory-direct to cross-continent and via many sub-distributors.

Installation — *Low to Moderate.* Most composite shingle products are installed with a minimum of power tools. Saw cuts can create toxic "sawdust" and release airborne toxins. Shingles cut with a sharp blade leave less waste on-site and in the air.

EMBODIED ENERGY

Composite shingles are manufactured from many source materials, and each particular brand of shingle must be considered individually where embodied energy is concerned. Third party data is not available for most of the products in this category, leaving homeowners to figure out approximate values based on source materials and processes.

WASTE: *MODERATE TO HIGH*

Composite products are often not recyclable because of the mix of ingredients used. Check to see if the product is accepted in local recycling streams or if the manufacturer accepts offcuts and leftover product for recycling at the factory. Otherwise, all offcuts will need to go to landfill. Quantities will vary from negligible to high, depending on the complexity of the roof.

Recyclable — Metal fasteners. Quantities will be negligible.

Landfill — Shingle offcuts, membrane or underlayment offcuts, caulking tubes. Quantities will vary from negligible to high, depending on the complexity of the roof.

ENERGY EFFICIENCY

Composite shingles can have an effect on energy efficiency depending on their color and density, with darker and heavier products having a greater negative impact on cooling requirements.

MATERIAL COSTS: *MODERATE TO HIGH*

This category covers a wide range of different products, with price points that span over the range of prices for other manufactured materials in this chapter. Quotations should be obtained for any composite shingle to compare individual brands directly with other options.

LABOR INPUT: *EASY TO MODERATE*

Each product will have specific requirements that determine labor input, but in general the labor required will be similar to other shingle roofing systems.

SKILL LEVEL REQUIRED FOR THE HOMEOWNER

Decking — *Easy.* A homeowner with the ability to create a roof frame will be able to deck the roof for composite shingles.

Underlayment (if required) — *Easy.* Underlayment is lightweight and comes in rolls that are straightforward to apply.

Shingles — *Easy to Moderate.* As proprietary products, some shingle manufacturers may require that an approved installer is hired and may not sell directly to homeowners, while others may be willing to sell product directly to a homeowner for self-installation. If the product is available to homeowners, there is likely to be installation support in the form of written and/or video installation instructions aimed at first-time installers. The process is similar to that of any shingle-style roofing.

Caps and Flashing — *Easy to Moderate.* Composite shingle companies that support homeowner installation will have products and instructions to make cap and flashing installation as straightforward as possible.

SOURCING/AVAILABILITY: *MODERATE*

Most of the companies producing composite shingles are fairly small, and their distribution networks may be limited. Check for availability direct from the factory or for a local distributor in your area.

DURABILITY: *MODERATE*

Most composite shingle manufacturers advertise lengthy warranties for their products, making this one of their main sales pitches. In theory, products made from recycled plastic or rubber should have a long life span. However, most of these products are less than a decade old so there is no historical data to back up these claims.

CODE COMPLIANCE

Most manufacturers will have data to show code compliance for their product. Check with the company to see what documentation they have available and get the building department's opinion on the documentation before purchasing the product. If a company has met appropriate ASTM, CSA or other code-referenced standards, then the product is likely to be accepted. However, if there is only in-house data from the company, there may be hurdles to getting it accepted. Some companies will work directly with building departments to address concerns, which can alleviate some effort on the homeowner's behalf.

Composite Shingle Roofing Ratings

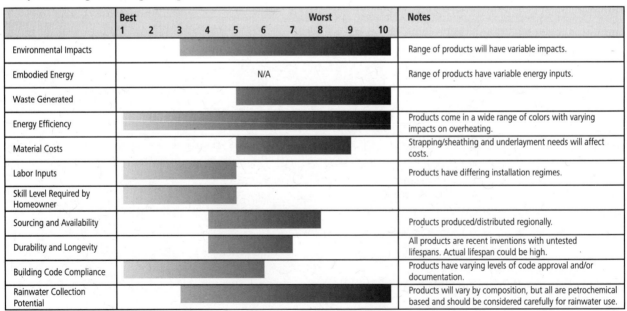

	Best 1	2	3	4	5	6	7	Worst 8	9	10	Notes
Environmental Impacts											Range of products will have variable impacts.
Embodied Energy					N/A						Range of products have variable energy inputs.
Waste Generated											
Energy Efficiency											Products come in a wide range of colors with varying impacts on overheating.
Material Costs											Strapping/sheathing and underlayment needs will affect costs.
Labor Inputs											Products have differing installation regimes.
Skill Level Required by Homeowner											
Sourcing and Availability											Products produced/distributed regionally.
Durability and Longevity											All products are recent inventions with untested lifespans. Actual lifespan could be high.
Building Code Compliance											Products have varying levels of code approval and/or documentation.
Rainwater Collection Potential											Products will vary by composition, but all are petrochemical based and should be considered carefully for rainwater use.

RAINWATER COLLECTION CAPABILITY:
LOW TO HIGH

Not all composite shingles are suitable for rainwater collection. Check with manufacturers to see if their product has detrimental effects on rainwater. Some plastic and rubber materials may leach into rain water and be difficult to filter.

FUTURE DEVELOPMENT

Composite shingles are likely to become a larger part of the roofing market, especially as asphalt shingles rise in price. As with any new product category, there will be a time during which numerous start-ups enter the market and offer a variety of options. Over the next decade, some of these will take hold and grow a wider acceptance and distribution network, while others are likely to fail and disappear. A decade will also give a better indication if the projected life span of the products is realistic or not. At this time, homeowners using composite shingles are taking the risks of early adopters. This can be a great opportunity to work with and support deserving companies as they establish excellent products in the marketplace, or it can be problematic if the product does not live up to expectations and the company doesn't survive. Do your research well!

Resources for further research

enviroshake.com
ecostarllc.com/index.aspx
penfoldsroofing.com/our-roofing-products/
    ecoroof-rubber-shakes
titanroofsystems.com/roof-tile/shake-roof.htm
euroshieldroofing.com
Harrison, H. W. *BRE Building Elements: Roofs and Roofing: Performance, Diagnosis, Maintenance, Repair and the Avoidance of Defects.* London: Construction Research Communications, 2000. Print.

Green roofs/living roofs

What the cheerleaders say...	What the detractors say...
Aesthetically pleasing	Expensive
Can provide agricultural space	Uses environmentally unfriendly membrane products
Helps reduce cooling loads	Requires maintenance
Helps reduce heat island effect on large buildings	Rainwater is not usable for collection
Restores habitat disturbed by building	Heavy, requires substantial structure
Reduces storm water runoff	

Applications for system

- Roof sheathing, typically on low-slope roofs (3:12 or less)

Basic materials

- Growing medium and plants
- Root barrier membrane
- Drainage plane membrane
- Waterproofing membrane
- Solid roof decking

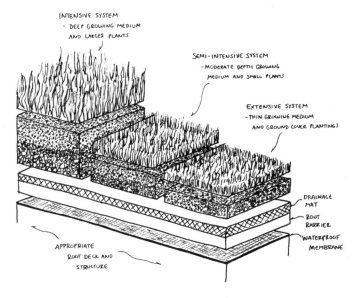

INTENSIVE SYSTEM
- DEEP GROWING MEDIUM AND LARGER PLANTS

SEMI-INTENSIVE SYSTEM
- MODERATE DEPTH GROWING MEDIUM AND SMALL PLANTS

EXTENSIVE SYSTEM
- THIN GROWING MEDIUM AND GROUND COVER PLANTINGS

DRAINAGE MAT
ROOT BARRIER
WATERPROOF MEMBRANE

APPROPRIATE ROOF DECK AND STRUCTURE

Planting a green roof.

How the system works

There are many different green roofing systems, ranging from simple homemade versions to pre-manufactured snap-together systems with plants already established.

There are three basic categories of green roofing, based on the depth of the growing medium, the types of plants grown and the amount of maintenance expected.

Extensive: These roofs use a thin layer of growing medium (usually not a soil but a mix of lightweight growing medium and/or lightweight aggregate enriched with compost), with 10–25 pounds per square foot (psf) (0.5–1.2 kPa) of weight and 5–15 cm (2–6 inches) of depth. These roofs are usually designed to have low maintenance requirements and are often not accessible. Low-growing plants with shallow root systems and an ability to tolerate drought are usually installed.

Intensive: These roofs use a thick layer of growing medium that is more like regular soil than extensive mixes, in typical depths of 15–90 cm (6–36 inches) and weights of 80–150 psf (3.8–7 kPa). These roofs can have fairly high maintenance requirements as they are often used to grow food, flowers or decorative gardens. They are usually designed to have regular foot traffic. Plantings can include grasses, flowers, vegetables, perennials, shrubs and small trees. Pathways, benches and other human elements can also be designed into the roof.

Semi-intensive: As the name indicates, this type of green roof is designed for weights, plants and uses that lie somewhere between the extensive and intensive.

Roofs can combine zones of extensive, semi-intensive and intensive use. Regardless of the type of green roof, the basic elements are quite similar:

- A roof structure that is designed to handle the expected loads of the green roof, which can require substantially larger roof members than for other roof sheathings.
- A low pitch is common for green roofs, though it is possible to build green roofs on steeper pitches by including retaining systems to prevent growing medium from sliding off the roof when wet and heavy. Most common is a "flat" roof, which has only a very minimal pitch (less than 1:12).
- Solid decking is used to help support the weight; depending on the type of green roof the decking may need to be doubled.
- A waterproof membrane is the key to the green roof. These membranes are usually made from synthetic rubber compounds. EPDM (ethylene propylene diene monomer), HDPE (high-density polyethylene), PVC (polyvinylchloride) and

butyl rubber are common. The membrane is laid on the roof decking either as continuous sheets or as large sections that are glued or welded together.

- A drainage membrane and/or a root barrier membrane (some products combine the two in one layer) are used to provide a means for excess water to leave the roof without the growing medium getting waterlogged, and to prevent tap roots from growing down and puncturing the waterproofing membrane and causing leaks. Manufactured tray systems can incorporate drainage and root barrier in a planting tray that can come pre-grown and be lain directly on the roof.
- Growing medium can vary widely in composition and depth, depending on the intent for the roof. These range from dirt excavated from the foundation of the building to specially graded lightweight mediums.
- Plants are chosen to meet the intent of the roof design, work in the type of growing medium provided and suit the climate and irrigation levels.
- Some living roofs incorporate irrigation systems to ensure plants are kept watered.

Tips for successful installation

1. Be clear on the reasons for installing a living roof. The design of the system depends on intended uses, which can range from low-maintenance, no-foot-traffic scenarios to food production or gardening areas with high foot traffic. It is difficult and in some cases structurally prohibitive to change from one type of use to another after the roof is built.
2. Green roofs are definitely an entire roofing system, and may require more than one designer and installer to complete the whole project. Be sure that you are researching and getting

quotes on the full scope of work for decking, membrane, drainage/root barrier layers, growing medium (including lifting onto the roof), plantings, parapets, railings and access points.
3. The waterproofing membrane is the heart of the roofing system, and must be installed correctly. This process is best done by experienced professionals who warranty their work.
4. Be sure the plants intended for the roof are suitable for the chosen growing medium and the likely conditions on the roof. Because the growing medium on a living roof is disconnected from the earth, the roof will dry out faster than the ground during periods of drought and may need to be irrigated more than anticipated.

Pros and cons

ENVIRONMENTAL IMPACTS

It is difficult to measure the impacts of a green roof, especially on a small, residential scale. This type of roof uses more resources in its construction than any other roofing system, from extra structural elements to the membrane layers to the growing mediums. A green roof that produces food or has other direct environmental benefits can to some degree balance out these higher initial impacts, and that can only be decided on a case-by-case basis. If keeping environmental impacts low is a project priority, be sure to weigh up the impacts versus the benefits before choosing this type of roof.

Harvesting — *High*. The roofing membrane and the products used to seal and caulk it are materials containing petrochemicals that have a wide range of impacts at the harvesting stage, including habitat destruction, greenhouse gas emissions and water and air pollution.

The root barrier and/or drainage layer membranes can be sourced from recycled materials, but any virgin petrochemical content will carry the same impacts as the membrane.

Growing mediums can range from site soil to specially formulated soil and aggregate mixes. Some soil mixes contain topsoil and/or peat that may not be harvested in a sustainable manner. Be sure to verify the source of the growing medium.

The required increase in roof strength will carry greater harvesting impacts for whatever materials are used for the roof structure.

Manufacturing — *High.* The petrochemical elements of the green roof will have a variety of air and water pollution impacts during manufacturing, and may continue to off-gas and leach toxins in the roof assembly.

The high number of products required for a green roof raises the impacts by sheer volume, but vary based on the choices for each.

Transportation — *Moderate to High.* The different layers of a green roof will typically come from different sources, each transported separately. Membrane and growing medium materials are heavy, with correspondingly high transportation impacts.

Installation — *Moderate to High.* Mechanical equipment is typically used for several stages of the construction of a green roof. Petrochemical products used to weld or caulk the membrane will off-gas. The larger the green roof, the more likely it is to have high impacts due to the sheer amount of material that needs to be moved into place.

WASTE: *MODERATE TO HIGH*

Compostable — Growing medium. Quantities should be negligible if proper calculations are done at the estimate stage.

Recyclable — Some drainage and/or root barrier membranes. Quantities can be moderate to high, as roll sizes do not always correspond well with actual roof size.

Landfill — Waterproofing membrane offcuts, some drainage mat/root barrier, caulking tubes. Quantities can be moderate to high, as roll sizes do not always correspond well with actual roof size.

ENERGY EFFICIENCY

The combination of evaporative cooling, thickness and shade provided by plants will help to reduce cooling loads for buildings with green roofs, in some cases quite dramatically. Some studies have shown benefits during the heating season as well, but this

Green Roof Embodied Energy

125 m² (1345 ft²) roof area	Material embodied energy from I.C.E. in MJ/kg	Weight to volume ratio of material*	Volume of material in sample 1000sf/92.9m² building	Sample building embodied energy	Material embodied carbon from I.C.E. in kgCO₂e/kg	Sample building embodied carbon	Notes
EPDM roofing membrane, 1.5mm	91 (Rubber)	1522 kg/m³	0.19 m³ 289.2 kg	26,315 MJ	2.85	824 kg	
Root barrier, LDPE (low density polyethylene)	78.1 (LDPE resin)	1 kg/m²	125 m² 125 kg	9,763 MJ	2.08	260 kg	
100mm (4in) lightweight growing medium	0.083 (Aggregate, general)	420 kg/m³	12.5 m³ 5250 kg	436 MJ	0.0052	27 kg	
Totals				**36,514 MJ**		**1,111 kg**	Does not include sheathing (sometimes doubled).

Transportation: EPDM transportation by 15 ton truck would equate to 0.4 MJ per kilometer of travel to the building site. LDPE transportation by 15 ton truck would equate to 0.2 MJ per kilometer of travel to the building site. Growing medium transportation by 15 ton truck would equate to 7.9 MJ per kilometer of travel to the building site.
*Typically from engineeringtoolbox.com

would only be for roof systems in which the roof insulation and green roof layers are in direct contact, and will be more pronounced on intensive roofs with taller plants that fall over and provide trapped air as an additional insulation blanket.

MATERIAL COSTS: *HIGH*

LABOR INPUT: *HIGH*

The multiple layers of a green roof make it the most labor-intensive form of roof sheathing. Large, heavy items must be lifted onto the roof, including rolls of waterproofing membrane, drainage/root barrier membrane, growing medium and plants. This is typically done mechanically, by crane and soil-blower, but can be done manually, though a fairly large crew and good scaffolding setup will be needed. Pre-manufactured systems that combine drainage, root barrier and plants in ready-made trays can reduce the amount of labor required, and are typically used for extensive green roofs.

SKILL LEVEL REQUIRED FOR THE HOMEOWNER

Roof Decking — *Easy.* Homeowners able to do carpentry, including roof framing, will be able to handle the requirements for decking the roof.

Waterproof Membrane — *Difficult.* It is recommended that the laying of waterproofing membrane be done by an experienced professional, especially if the roof has penetrations through the membrane that require sealing or welding. A homeowner may be willing to undertake this task if the roof is simple and the membrane doesn't require special equipment to join sections together. The weight and volume of this material can present challenges and is often lifted mechanically.

Drainage/Root Barrier Layers — *Easy.* Homeowners able to follow manufacturer's instructions will be able to install these layers. The weight and volume of the materials may present some challenges,

but can typically be handled manually with a good scaffolding or lift setup.

Growing Medium — *Moderate.* The weight and volume of this material is high, and is usually placed on the roof with mechanical assistance. Companies with soil blowing equipment can be hired, and the work overseen by a homeowner. Lifting growing medium onto a roof manually is a very large and heavy task, suitable only for small roofs or large crews organized in a "bucket brigade."

Planting — *Easy.* Homeowners with gardening experience or with good instructions can handle the planting of a green roof, though research or consultation with a professional regarding plant selection and maintenance is recommended.

SOURCING/AVAILABILITY: *MODERATE*

The base waterproofing membrane of a green roof is the same as any conventional flat roof, and this means there are many companies that specialize in this type of roofing, and sourcing competitive quotes or even the materials to do it yourself should be easy in all developed regions.

There is a rapidly growing industry building up around green roofs, though it is mainly focused on very large commercial buildings rather than residential applications. Most major urban centers will have companies that specialize in the design and construction of green roofs, where commercial projects are driving the industry, but such services and materials may be more difficult to source in smaller centers.

Resources and courses about green roofs are widely available.

DURABILITY: *HIGH*

The waterproofing membrane is the key to keeping a green roof from leaking, and the multiple layers of a green roof tend to provide excellent protection for the membrane. By shielding it from UV radiation and direct exposure to the elements, most estimates for life span are in the 50-year range.

The success of the plantings on a green roof are not necessarily important to the life span of the waterproofing membrane, but are likely to be important to the homeowner or client wishing to see greenery on their green roof. Durability in the plantings will depend on the type of growing medium and plants selected, and of course the climate. Drought is the biggest issue with green roofs, as the thinner soil levels on a roof tend to retain less water than soils on the ground. A green roof may need watering or permanent irrigation to remain green year-round, and will be susceptible to all the ups and downs associated with gardening on the ground, including weeds, pests and disease among the plantings. Appropriate plants and due care and diligence in caring for them should result in a green roof that remains green for the long term.

CODE COMPLIANCE

Code prescriptions for flat roofs using waterproofing membranes exist in all jurisdictions, and a green roof is really just a variation on conventional membrane roofing. Many urban jurisdictions have been quick to write or adopt codes for green roofs specifically, and some jurisdictions are actively promoting them. Smaller jurisdictions may not have green roof provisions, but it should not prove difficult to prove compliance using existing codes for membrane roofs and the ample resources written to cover green roofs.

RAINWATER COLLECTION CAPABILITY: *Low*

Rainwater is held by a green roof in the porous growing medium, limiting roof run off. While this is an advantage in many ways, it limits the amount of useful rain water that can be harvested. Rainwater collected from a living roof will be difficult to treat to

Green Roof Ratings

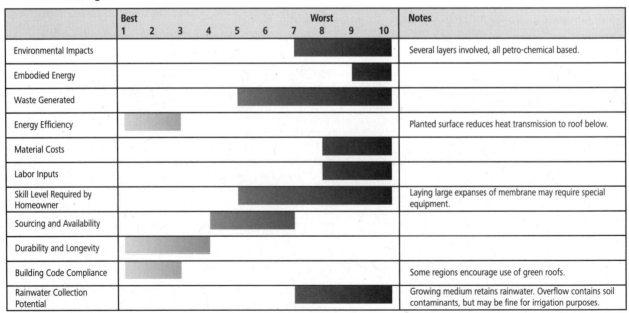

	Best 1	2	3	4	5	6	7	Worst 8	9	10	Notes
Environmental Impacts							█	█	█		Several layers involved, all petro-chemical based.
Embodied Energy								█	█		
Waste Generated					█	█	█	█	█	█	
Energy Efficiency	█	█									Planted surface reduces heat transmission to roof below.
Material Costs							█	█	█		
Labor Inputs							█	█	█		
Skill Level Required by Homeowner					█	█	█	█			Laying large expanses of membrane may require special equipment.
Sourcing and Availability			█	█	█	█					
Durability and Longevity	█	█	█								
Building Code Compliance	█	█	█								Some regions encourage use of green roofs.
Rainwater Collection Potential							█	█	█	█	Growing medium retains rainwater. Overflow contains soil contaminants, but may be fine for irrigation purposes.

a quality appropriate for indoor uses due to potential contaminants in the growing medium, but can be collected and stored for irrigation purposes.

FUTURE DEVELOPMENT

Green roofing, though it has existed in some forms for centuries, is a relatively recent development in modern building. There is a great deal of research and development occurring now, driven by the benefits of green roofing in urban centers where vast, flat roofs cause heat island effect, loss of natural habitat and storm water management issues. This is leading to a rapid development of standards, designs, products and procedures that will continue to be refined over the next decade or so. Green roofs will likely lower in price and complexity as systems are developed and become more widely accepted by codes and homeowners. Hopefully, membrane products with less chemical content and environmental impacts will be part of the development. However, issues of weight and plant maintenance will always be part of choosing a green roof.

Resources for further research

Youngman, Angela. *Green Roofs: A Guide to Their Design and Installation.* Ramsbury, UK: Crowood, 2011. Print.

Hanson, Beth, and Sarah Schmidt. *Green Roofs and Rooftop Gardens.* Brooklyn, NY: Brooklyn Botanic Garden, 2012. Print.

Dunnett, Nigel. *Small Green Roofs: Low-Tech Options for Greener Living.* Portland, OR: Timber Press, 2011. Print.

Dakin, Karla, Lisa Lee Benjamin, and Mindy Pantiel. *The Professional Design Guide to Green Roofs.* Portland, OR: Timber Press, 2013. Print.

Snodgrass, Edmund C., and Linda McIntyre. *The Green Roof Manual: A Professional Guide to Design, Installation, and Maintenance.* Portland, OR: Timber Press, 2010. Print.

Clay tile roofing

What the cheerleaders say...	What the detractors say...
Long lifespan	Heavy
Proven history	May not hold up to freeze/thaw cycles
Beautiful	Expensive
Natural materials	Not easily accessible in all regions

Applications for system

- Roof sheathing

Basic materials

- Fired clay tiles
- Solid roof decking or strapping
- Fasteners

How the system works

Clay roofing tiles are made from naturally occurring clay and sand, fired in a kiln at high temperature. Some tile manufacturers will add fluorite, quartz, feldspar or other fluxes to reduce porosity. The tiles are formed when the clay mixture is wet, using a variety of form shapes to meet a desired appearance. The color of the tile depends on the color of the clay, with shades of red being the most common. Tints can be added to provide a range of color options.

While there are a multitude of different clay tile profiles available, the system is essentially like all other shingle-style roofing materials. A solid roof deck or appropriate strapping is placed over the framing, along with any required membrane or underlayment. Overlapping courses are fastened to the roof such that there are no exposed seams or joints. The type of overlap and/or interlock on clay tiles will vary depending on the profile of the tile. The tile will have one or more holes cast into the top edge for nailing (using galvanized or copper nails) and some form of interlocking between neighbouring tiles. Some systems use metal clips that slip into the tile and are tacked to the roof deck.

At hips and ridges, tiles cast with an appropriate profile are mortared in place, typically with a cement-based mortar. Penetrations through the roof like vents or chimneys are handled with cast tile pieces and/or metal flashing. Cuts are made in tiles at hip and valley with a tile cropper or a wet saw.

In northern climates, clay roof tiles gained a poor reputation when European-style tiles were prone to cracking due to water absorption and freeze/thaw cycles. Higher firing temperatures and the addition of mineral-based fluxes have reduced porosity to the point where clay tiles are suitable for harsher climates, but the poor reputation lingers.

Tips for successful installation

1. Include the significant dead weight of clay roofing tiles in calculations for the roof structure beneath.
2. At the design stage, be certain that details for the chosen profile of clay tile are incorporated. Some clay tiles are thicker than other roofing choices, so intersections with other building elements need to account for this depth. Chimneys and vent pipes should also be appropriately detailed.
3. In northern climates, select roof tiles that are made to ASTM Grade 1 standards (or equivalent). These tiles are made to have low porosity and to be able to handle repeated freeze/thaw cycles.
4. Installation must be done such that workers do not stand on finished sections of roofing, as this is the primary cause of failure of clay tiles. Roofing ladders, scaffolding or other work platforms must be used.

5. Care must be taken when nailing clay tiles. If the nail is left proud of the top of the tile, it could prevent the next tile from interlocking properly and can create a pressure point where a crack could occur. However, if the nail is driven too deeply (or the hammer misses it), the tile can crack.
6. Cutting clay roof tiles takes practice and appropriate tools. A tile cropper or a wet saw can be used to shape tile at hips and valleys, but first-timers are likely to break a few tiles while getting the hang of the process.
7. The mortaring of ridge and hip caps is done with a cement-based mortar formulated specifically for clay roof tiles. There will be mortaring procedures particular to each manufacturer's tiles.

Pros and cons

ENVIRONMENTAL IMPACTS

Harvesting — *Low to Moderate.* The clay that forms the bulk of the material in a roof tile is an abundant resource, with useful deposits in many regions of North America. Clay pits are usually shallow, surface-based harvesting operations that do not use any chemical processes on-site. Many clay pits are in or beside waterways, and pit operations can silt the water and disrupt flow patterns. In general, clay pits are not considered high-impact mining operations, and are excellent candidates for rehabilitation at the end of the pit's life span.

Manufacturing — *Moderate to High.* Clay for tiles requires very little mechanical processing. It is ground up and squeezed into a homogeneous mix before being formed. This work is typically all completed by machine in factories, though traditionally it would have been done by hand on or near the building site. The largest impact from clay tiles comes from the firing process, during which the tiles are heated to temperatures of 900 to 1300°C (1650 to 2350°F) for several hours. No toxins are released from the clay during this process, but a lot of fossil fuels are consumed and emissions released into the atmosphere.

Tiles that are glazed or painted will require additional processes, and these can be more toxic. Paint coatings, in particular, can contain chemicals that are emitted into the atmosphere and/or mixed into water at the factory.

The mortar used at ridges and hips is a very small amount of material, but as it is cement based, it carries a high carbon footprint.

Transportation — *Moderate to High.* Sample building uses 5,125 kg of clay tiles:

> 7.7 MJ per km by 15 ton truck
> 4.8 MJ per km by 35 ton truck
> 1.3 MJ per km by rail
> 0.82 MJ per km by ocean freight

Production facilities are typically located very close to clay pits, minimizing the transportation of raw materials. With only a few manufacturers supplying the entire continent, this heavy material may have to travel long distances to reach some regions, accumulating high transportation impacts.

Installation — Clay tiles require the use of power tools for cutting. Chemical products used in mortar, caulking and flashing will be the items with the highest impact, as the tiles themselves are inert.

WASTE: *MODERATE TO HIGH*

Compostable — Clay tile offcuts can be left in the environment or crushed to make aggregate or growing medium. Quantities will be negligible for simple roofs, but can be quite high if there are numerous hips and valleys.

Recyclable — Metal flashing offcuts and fasteners, wood strapping scrap. Quantities will be negligible for simple roofs, but can be moderate if there are numerous hips and valleys.

Landfill — Mortar bags, plywood decking. Quantities will be negligible for simple roofs, but can be moderate if there are numerous hips and valleys.

ENERGY EFFICIENCY

A tile roof has a moderate effect on cooling loads in hot weather, with most common tile colors certified as Cool Roof by the Cool Roof Rating Council, with a SRI value greater than 29.

MATERIAL COSTS: *HIGH*

While clay tile roofing is quite cost competitive in other parts of the world, in North America it is much less common and therefore prices are comparatively high.

LABOR INPUT: *HIGH*

A clay tile roof is quite labor intensive. The labor input will depend on the size of tile, with larger tiles requiring less time to be laid. Clay tiles are heavy and fragile, so they take longer to move on-site than more flexible and lighter materials. Cutting custom tiles is slower than with most other shingles, and the mortaring of ridge and hip caps also takes additional

Clay Tile Roof Embodied Energy

125 m² (1345 ft²) roof area	Material embodied energy from I.C.E. in MJ/kg	Weight to volume ratio of material*	Volume of material in sample 1000sf/92.9m² building	Sample building embodied energy	Material embodied carbon from I.C.E. in kgCO₂e/kg	Sample building embodied carbon	Notes
Fired clay tiles, unglazed	6.5 (Clay tile)	41 kg/m²**	125 m² 5125 kg	33,313 MJ	0.24	1,230 kg	**Average figure from manufacturers.

Transportation: Clay tile transportation by 35 ton truck would equate to 4.8 MJ per kilometer of travel to the building site. *Typically from engineeringtoolbox.com time. The requirement to do the roofing without standing on the finished tiles will be an additional labor factor.

SKILL LEVEL REQUIRED FOR THE HOMEOWNER

Decking — *Easy.* Homeowners able to perform the general carpentry required to frame a roof would be able to deck the roof with strapping and/or sheet materials as required.

Membrane (if required) — *Easy.* If membranes must be used, they will typically be roll-type products that are straightforward to install.

Tiling — *Moderate.* A homeowner with some training, workshop experience or good written instruction can place the tiles on a simple roof. Practice is required for the cutting of tiles and to be able to nail quickly and accurately without damaging tiles.

Capping and Flashing — *Difficult.* Mortaring ceramic caps and creating flashing for valleys and roof penetrations requires experience or training from a professional. A workshop or practice on a small structure is recommended.

SOURCING/AVAILABILITY: *MODERATE TO DIFFICULT*

Clay tiles are not widely manufactured and distributed in North America, with only a handful of plants responsible for the production of the vast majority of tiles on the market. In regions where clay tiles are a common option, sources and competitive quotes for installation will be readily available. In many regions, clay tiles will be difficult to come by, and experienced installers rare.

DURABILITY: *MODERATE TO HIGH*

Clay tile roofs can last from 75 to 150 years. Cracked or broken tiles will need to be replaced as part of a regular maintenance schedule to keep the entire roof

Clay Tile Roof Ratings

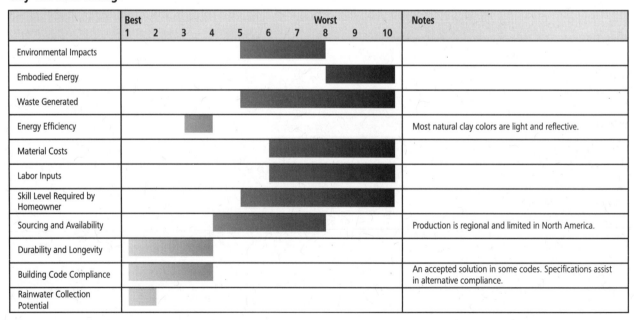

	Best 1	2	3	4	5	6	7	Worst 8	9	10	Notes
Environmental Impacts											
Embodied Energy											
Waste Generated											
Energy Efficiency											Most natural clay colors are light and reflective.
Material Costs											
Labor Inputs											
Skill Level Required by Homeowner											
Sourcing and Availability											Production is regional and limited in North America.
Durability and Longevity											
Building Code Compliance											An accepted solution in some codes. Specifications assist in alternative compliance.
Rainwater Collection Potential											

healthy. Annual checks of the roof and immediate replacement of damaged tiles is important.

CODE COMPLIANCE

Many building codes will recognize clay tiles as an accepted solution. Code officials will want to ensure that the roof structure has been designed to accept the weight of the tiles, and may insist on the need for an experienced installer. In jurisdictions where clay tiles are not part of the accepted solutions, adequate standards, documentation and historical precedent exist to make a reasonable case for their acceptance.

RAINWATER COLLECTION CAPABILITY: *HIGH*

Clay tiles are generally accepted to be a good solution for rainwater collection for indoor applications.

FUTURE DEVELOPMENT

Clay tiles are a dominant roofing choice in much of the world, but much less so in North America.

Aesthetics and a reputation for being unreliable in cold climates are two factors that have limited their acceptance. As a very small part of the market in most regions, the cost of clay tiles and installation has also kept the system from becoming more widely accepted. With the development of tiles that meet cold-climate standards, there is no practical reason to avoid clay tile roofing. As a roofing product made from natural materials with a long life span and the ability to be recycled into useful growing medium at the end of its life, there is much to recommend clay tiles for sustainable buildings. It remains to be seen if these benefits will move the system into more widespread acceptance.

Resources for further research

ASTM C1167 astm.org/Standards/C1167.htm

Scharff, Robert, and Terry Kennedy. *Roofing Handbook*. New York: McGraw-Hill, 2001. Print.

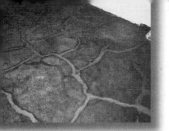

6

Flooring

FLOORING PLAYS A DEFINING VISUAL AND VISCERAL ROLE in a building, as we see it and touch it constantly. The homebuilder is faced with a wide range of options when making flooring choices, and these choices represent a substantial financial investment. They are not decisions that are easy or inexpensive to change.

Flooring obviously receives a great deal of wear and tear, and durability is of utmost importance. Patterns of wear, aesthetic preference and type of construction may all dictate that a home has more than one type of flooring, so the decision-making process may include multiple choices each of which suits a particular need in a particular part of the home.

Flooring considerations are actually twofold: the flooring material itself and the type of surface finish used to seal and protect it. In some cases, the two can be considered separately, with a single flooring product having several options for finishing. In other cases, the materials come pre-finished and the choice for material and finish must be made together. However, in many of the categories of comparison in this book, the flooring material and the finish may have very different ratings. We will attempt to clarify the choices and differences for each option discussed.

Building science basics for flooring

Flooring choices will have few impacts on the performance of the building in the parameters examined by building science.

If an in-floor heating system is used, then the conductive properties of the flooring will have an impact on how quickly heat transfers from the source to the space (and the toes!) above it. Assuming proper insulation levels have been installed under the floor, the conductive properties of the floor will not affect the overall performance of the heating system, but it will have an effect on response-time and perceived sensation of heat in the floor. The greater the density of the flooring material, the better heat will transfer through it and the "warmer" it will feel to feet in contact with it. More dense types of flooring will also require longer periods of heat input to reach a set temperature and will cool down over a longer period of time, potentially resulting in less "cycling" of the heating system.

Concerns that wooden flooring is not suitable for in-floor heating systems are not fact-based. Wood does not shrink or swell to any problematic degree through temperature change; it is changes in moisture content that cause expansion and contraction issues in solid wood flooring. As long as humidity levels are relatively constant and changes in humidity do not occur rapidly, a solid wood floor (or any other flooring type examined in this chapter) over in-floor heating is not a problematic choice.

Some flooring choices can introduce a large amount of moisture into the building at the construction phase, and some will continue to do so for as long as a full year after occupation. Floors that are wet-poured, such as earthen and concrete slabs, bring high quantities of moisture into the building that will not have long-term implications but may affect humidity levels in the early stages of home occupation. Wood and stone floors will carry less moisture, but may contain enough to be noticeable after occupation.

Resources for further research

Dutfield, Andrew, Jo Mundy, and Jane Anderson. *Environmental Impact of Materials: Floor Finishes*. London: Routledge, 2011. Print.

Clay or earthen floors

What the cheerleaders say...	What the detractors say...
Very low environmental impact	May not wear well
Unparalleled "feel"	Materials not commercially available
Healthy	Long drying time
Beautiful	
Durable and easily repairable	

Applications for system

- Finished flooring. Suitable for installation over wet-poured floor and wooden floor systems.

Basic materials

Floor Materials

- Clay, sand and gravel aggregate. *Clay floors* tend to refer to those that are made with commercially prepared clay and aggregate, while *earthen floors* refer to those based on naturally occurring site soils that contain an appropriate mix of clay and aggregate. The terms are often used interchangeably.
- Admixtures, including flour paste, casein, hydrated lime, blood and other regional formulations
- Fiber, including chopped straw, hemp, poly fiber
- Pigments, if desired

Finish Material Options

- Natural oils, including linseed, hemp, tung and walnut oil
- Natural wax (usually applied over oil finishes)
- Commercial floor finishing products (see Chapter 7: Surface Finishing Materials)

How the system works

People have used earthen floors in their dwellings since we first started making shelters. They have ranged from the soil that was already underfoot to well-mixed and finely finished clay floors. There is certainly a long history to draw upon when considering earthen floors, and many examples of very durable floors. The experience of walking on a well-made clay floor often convinces homeowners they want one!

A clay or earthen floor requires a very stable sub-floor base, as too much flex in the sub-floor may cause the finished floor to crack. Any type of sub-flooring can work, as long as it is constructed to minimize or eliminate deflection under typical conditions.

An appropriate mixture of clay, aggregate and water (along with any admixtures, fiber and/or pigments) are mixed to the desired consistency and poured onto the sub-floor. The material is worked to the desired level and surface texture, usually with trowels. The thickness of this type of flooring can vary greatly, from a thin skim coat to as much as 150 mm (6 inches), though with thick floors it is common to do a thin finish coat separately. In general, the final finished floor is applied 12–25 mm (½–1 inch) thick.

The final surface texture may be achieved during the initial installation, but it is more common to re-trowel the surface at least one time as the floor begins to dry. Some clay floor installers will trowel or rub in a very fine clay mixture at this stage.

Once the desired surface texture has been achieved, the floor is allowed to dry fully (from one week to several months, depending on thickness and climatic conditions). A clay floor must be protected from wear while it is drying. It may be left untouched, or may be covered or planked if work must continue around it.

With the floor suitably dry, the surface treatment is applied. This can range from cold or hot oil applications, waxes or commercial floor-finishing products. Number of coats and time between applications will vary based on the type of treatment used. Natural oils are usually applied in numerous

Earth floor. (CHESTER RENNIE)

coats, until the floor reaches saturation. Commercial products will have manufacturer's instructions to guide their application.

Tips for successful installation

1. While earthen floors have a long and proven history, they are not common in modern construction. Enough excellent examples exist to prove their feasibility, but they are rare enough that anyone choosing this type of flooring is definitely an "early adopter" engaging in an experiment. With proper research and construction, a clay floor is a low-risk experiment, but must be approached with awareness that a successful floor is not guaranteed.

2. Be sure that the construction schedule allows for the drying times required for clay floors. These can range from a week to a month, during which it is best to avoid all traffic on the floor surface.

3. The sourcing of materials for a clay floor is critical, and finding appropriate ingredients will be up to the homeowner and/or installer. Off-the-shelf clay floor mixes are next to non-existent (see Claylin sidebar).

Earthen floor.

4. Unless the installer is experienced, it is best to create test samples, made on the same type of base as the intended sub-floor and at the intended thickness. Different clay type, aggregate grading and quantities of admixture can have very different results. Time spent refining the formulation will help to achieve a beautiful, durable finished floor.

5. The knowledge base for how to pour, level and trowel a concrete floor can be useful to a clay floor builder. The two materials share enough commonalities that a person capable of working concrete can usually figure out how to work a clay floor.

6. Finishing a clay floor properly is as important as getting the mix right and laying it well. A good deal of the durability comes from the finish, and achieving best results here can take some experimentation.

7. In northern climates, clay floors and finishes are not appropriate for entryways, where wet and salty boot traffic will be problematic for natural oil finishes.

8. North Americans tend to be obsessed with perfectly flat floors, and while clay floors can be made perfectly flat they are an excellent medium for introducing gentle undulations underfoot, to which many people take an instant liking.

Pros and cons

Environmental impacts

Harvesting — *Negligible to Low.* The basic clay and aggregate materials are widely available in many regions, and small-scale extraction has minimal impacts. If sub-soil conditions on-site are suitable for making the floor, enough material is likely to be extracted in preparing the foundation. You may be able to be find small quantities of suitable material from local excavators or at local stone quarries. When manufactured clay and aggregates are used, impacts go up slightly, but commercial extraction is not a toxic process, though it will disturb the immediate ecosystem. Long-established clay pits and aggregate quarries are common, and local ecosystems will have adapted to their presence in many cases.

The finishing products can have a wide variation in impact. Carefully research the origins of "natural" oils, as they can range from locally and organically produced to GMO, factory-farmed oils with toxic chemical additives (in particular, "double-boiled" linseed oil is a highly toxic product). Raw oils are preferable. Waxes, too, can range in impact from locally sourced beeswax to petrochemical wax products.

If you choose commercial finish products, find out what is in them and where they are made to help you assess their environmental impacts.

Manufacturing — *Negligible to Low.* Processing dry, bagged clay products is a relatively low-energy and nontoxic process, as is aggregate extraction. Clay floors do not require intensive processing. All mixing is typically done on-site by hand or small mechanical mixer. If dry ingredients are being mixed, breathing protection should be worn as airborne silica and other mineral dusts are dangerous to inhale.

There are no toxic by-products created during the mixing process.

The manufacturing processes for finishing products vary widely in impact, ranging from low-impact, cold pressing of oil to high-impact petrochemical mixtures.

Transportation — *Negligible to Moderate.* Sample building uses 1,927.5 kg of clay flooring:

> 2.9 MJ per km by 15 ton truck
> 1.8 MJ per km by 35 ton truck

Clay floor ingredients are heavy, and moving them over long distances incurs large transportation impacts. However, most regions will have accessible ingredients within a reasonable radius.

Finishing products are used in quite small quantities and will not incur significant impacts even if they travel long distances, though it's always preferable to source locally when possible.

Installation — *Negligible.*

WASTE: *NEGLIGIBLE*

Compostable — All leftover clay floor mix can be left in the environment on-site. Quantities will tend to be minimal, as small-batch mixes are the norm.

Recyclable — Containers of finishing products, unless disallowed by recycling programs. Quantities will be minimal.

Landfill — Containers of finishing products if not recyclable. Quantities minimal.

Toxic Waste — Remnants and containers of finishing products if labeled toxic. Quantities minimal.

ENERGY EFFICIENCY

A clay floor will not have a direct impact on energy efficiency.

MATERIAL COSTS: *LOW*

Mixes using local clay soils will be very low cost, while those using dried, bagged clay will cost more but still be at the low end of the spectrum.

LABOR INPUT: *MODERATE*

A clay floor has a similar degree of labor input to other flooring options, though the labor is likely to be spread out over a longer period of time to allow for drying of floor mixes and finishing products.

SKILL LEVEL REQUIRED FOR THE HOMEOWNER

Preparation of sub-floor — *Easy.* If the sub-floor is suitable stiff, very little needs to be done in advance of pouring the floor. Mesh or fasteners are sometimes used to reinforce the floor and minimize movement.

Installation of floor — *Moderate to Difficult.* Once a suitable mix has been established, the mixing process is straightforward and the equipment simple to operate. Laying the floor requires some basic understanding of leveling and troweling wet mixtures (similar to working with concrete or plasters), with undulating surfaces being easy to achieve and perfectly smooth and flat surfaces requiring more practice.

Clay Floor Embodied Energy

92.9 m² (1000 ft²) floor area	Material embodied energy from I.C.E. in MJ/kg	Weight to volume ratio of material*	Volume of material in sample 1000sf/92.9m² building	Sample building embodied energy	Material embodied carbon from I.C.E. in kgCO₂e/kg	Sample building embodied carbon	Notes
Clay floor mix @ 20mm (¾ in) thickness	0.083 (Aggregate, general)	1089 kg/m³	1.77 m³ 1927.5 kg	160 MJ	0.0052	10 kg	Does not include surface treatment.

Transportation: Clay mix transportation by 15 ton truck would equate to 2.9 MJ per kilometer of travel to the building site. *Typically from engineeringtoolbox.com

Clay or earthen floors

Finishing of floor — *Easy*. Finishing products are generally easy to apply, being brushed or rolled onto the floor and sometimes wiped back with a cloth.

SOURCING/AVAILABILITY: *MODERATE*

While the raw materials needed to make a clay floor are widely available, they may not come from conventional building supply sources. Clay soils, if not evident on the building site, can be located locally by talking with excavators and/or aggregate pit operators. Bagged clay is easiest to source from pottery supply outlets. The finishing products may need to be sourced from specialty suppliers.

DURABILITY: *MODERATE*

Each clay floor is made with a custom mix of ingredients, installed with varying techniques and degrees of experience and finished with different products, so durability can range from low to high. Well-mixed,

-applied and -finished clay floors can match the durability of commercial flooring options, with a life span of 10 to 40 years. Depending on the type of finish used, maintenance may be required at intervals between one to five years.

CODE COMPLIANCE

Most codes are not prescriptive when it comes to finished flooring materials, as long as the sub-floor has been constructed to code and in a manner intended to support the dead load imposed by the flooring. While it may raise eyebrows, it is unlikely that there will be code restrictions against installing a clay finshed floor.

INDOOR AIR QUALITY: *HIGH*

The clay floor itself will only have a negative impact on IAQ if the soil, clay and/or aggregate contain toxins. This can happen if the ingredients happen

Clay Floor Ratings

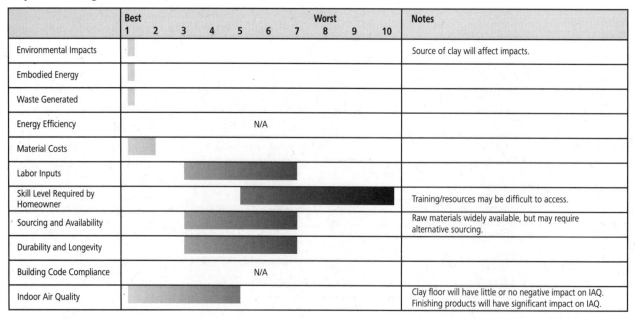

	Best 1	2	3	4	5	6	7	Worst 8	9	10	Notes
Environmental Impacts											Source of clay will affect impacts.
Embodied Energy											
Waste Generated											
Energy Efficiency				N/A							
Material Costs											
Labor Inputs											
Skill Level Required by Homeowner											Training/resources may be difficult to access.
Sourcing and Availability											Raw materials widely available, but may require alternative sourcing.
Durability and Longevity											
Building Code Compliance				N/A							
Indoor Air Quality											Clay floor will have little or no negative impact on IAQ. Finishing products will have significant impact on IAQ.

to come from a contaminated source, with contaminants ranging from naturally occurring substances like radon gas and arsenic to those resulting from human activities, like gasoline and oil. These contaminants can be wide-ranging and difficult to detect. Samples can be sent to a laboratory if research into sources shows reason for concern. In general, clay floor ingredients are quite inert and unlikely to be problematic, but shouldn't be assumed to be so.

The larger IAQ impact is likely to come from the finishing products. Even natural finishes can have high levels of VOCs and other contaminants. Linseed oil, in particular, is a common finish used on clay floors and can have impacts ranging from long-lasting odor to heavy metals from "double-boiled" products. Homeowners with allergies should be certain that any oil product does not cause a reaction before applying it to the floor. Commercial finishing products meeting Greenguard or similar certification will have reliably low impacts on air quality.

FUTURE DEVELOPMENT

Clay floors are a remarkably environmentally friendly option, with a great deal of potential for development. It would not require very much R&D to be able to formulate reliable clay floor mixes from bagged clay and manufactured aggregates, and the equipment required to harvest, mix and deliver such a product already exists to serve other industries, such as the concrete industry. It would be wonderful to see creative and forward-thinking builders and manufacturers move in this direction, helping to create a wider market for this low-impact, low-cost, no-waste flooring option. Only consumer demand will drive this movement.

Resources for Further Research

www.naturalbuildingblog.com/ten-earth-floor-methods

Crimmel, Sukita Reay and Thomson, James. *Earthen Floors: A Modern Approach to an Ancient Practice.* Gabriola Island, BC. New Society Publishers, 2014. Print.

Claylin floors

Claylin is the first North American producer of a manufactured clay floor mixture. Based in Portland, Oregon, the company developed a formulation for the mixture based on many years of laying clay floors using site soils and/or bagged clays. They market their mix for DIY installers wishing to have the benefits of a clay floor without the need to source raw materials and experiment with mixes and finishes.

The clay floor material is augmented with finishing products ideally suited for use on clay floors, including pigments, oils and waxes.

While clay floor materials are too heavy to be shipped long distances, the development of a product like Claylin bodes well for similar developments in other regions, making clay floors more accessible to homeowners. claylin.com

Claylin floor.

Hardwood flooring

What the cheerleaders say...	What the detractors say...
Durable	Wood may not be sustainably harvested
Renewable	Finishes can be toxic
Beautiful	

Applications for system

- Finished flooring. Can be applied on wooden sub-floors. May require strapping or sheathing if applied over slab floors.

Basic materials

- Hardwood planks, milled with a tongue-and-groove profile to a variety of widths
- Finishes can range from natural oils and waxes to petrochemical products

How the system works

Strips of hardwood with typical widths varying from 40–150mm (1½–6 inches) are laid in successive rows, interlocked by the tongue-and-groove fit and fastened with nails or staples driven through the tongue or groove to remain invisible on the finished floor surface.

Tips for successful installation

Hardwood flooring should be stored in the home where it is to be installed for a minimum of one week prior to installation, to give the wood a chance to balance with the ambient humidity of the home. Hardwood will expand or contract noticeably as it gains or loses moisture, and must be allowed to arrive at the size that matches the humidity level of the home. If conditions are unusually dry or moist, the flooring may shrink or swell when conditions return to normal.

There are many resources available to explain the proper procedure for installing hardwood flooring, including manufacturer's instructions.

Pros and cons

ENVIRONMENTAL IMPACTS

Harvesting — *Low to High.* Priority should be placed on sustainably harvested hardwood in order to minimize impacts. Locally produced wood allows the homeowner to speak directly to the forester to ascertain practices. Third-party certifications should be sought whenever buying from a supplier with whom personal connection cannot be made.

Finishing products may have impacts ranging from low for some natural oils and waxes to very high for petrochemical-based finishes.

Manufacturing — *Low to Moderate.* The process of milling wood into flooring has relatively low impacts. The narrow profile of hardwood flooring allows for good use of logs, and many third-party certification programs ensure that manufacturing processes meet high environmental standards.

The manufacturing of finishing products has impacts ranging from low for some natural oils and waxes to very high for petrochemical-based finishes.

Transportation — *Negligible to High.* Sample building uses 1,218.8 kg of hardwood flooring:

> 1.8 MJ per km by 15 ton truck
> 1.15 MJ per km by 35 ton truck
> 0.3 MJ per km by rail

Hardwood is a very heavy material with correspondingly high transportation impact dependent upon distance traveled. Most regions will have hardwoods suitable for flooring available locally.

Installation — *Negligible to Low.* There are no significant impacts resulting from the installation of hardwood flooring.

WASTE: *MODERATE*

Compostable — Untreated wood offcuts. Quantity can be low to high, depending on the requirements of the installation.

Recyclable — Metal fasteners. Quantities will be negligible.

Landfill — Treated wood offcuts. Quantity can be low to high, depending on the requirements of the installation.

ENERGY EFFICIENCY

There will be no energy efficiency effect from hardwood flooring.

MATERIAL COSTS: *MODERATE TO HIGH*

Species of wood and transportation distance will affect costs, as will degree and type of finish.

Prefinished costs eliminate additional labor and material costs after installation.

LABOR INPUT: *MODERATE TO HIGH*

Hardwood floors have a similar amount of labor input as other finished flooring materials. Prefinished options will have much lower labor input than site-finished floors.

SKILL LEVEL REQUIRED FOR THE HOMEOWNER

Preparation of sub-floor — *Easy.*

Installation of floor — *Easy to Moderate.* A homeowner with the carpentry skills to build a wooden sub-floor structure will be able to install hardwood flooring. The installation usually requires a pneumatic nailer, which can be rented.

Finishing of floor — *Easy.* Pre-finished floors require no effort. Finishing raw wood involves the straightforward brush or roller application of a liquid product according to manufacturer's instructions.

SOURCING/AVAILABILITY: *EASY*

Hardwood flooring is widely available, though sustainably harvested wood with nontoxic finishes may be more difficult to source.

DURABILITY: *HIGH*

Hardwood flooring is very durable, with life span ranging from 40 to 150 years. Quality of finish will have an impact on durability, and finishes can

Hardwood Flooring Embodied Energy

92.9 m² (1000 ft²) floor area	Material embodied energy from I.C.E. in MJ/kg	Weight to volume ratio of material*	Volume of material in sample 1000sf/92.9m² building	Sample building embodied energy	Material embodied carbon from I.C.E. in kgCO₂e/kg	Sample building embodied carbon	Notes
Hardwood							
20mm (¾ in) thickness	2.5	688 kg/m³ (hardwood lumber)	1.77 m³ 1,218.8 kg	3,044 MJ	0.2	244 kg	Does not include fasteners or surface finishes.

Transportation: Wood flooring transportation by 35 ton truck would equate to 0.7–1.1 MJ per kilometer of travel to the building site. *Typically from engineeringtoolbox.com require maintenance or re-application on a cycle of one to twenty years, depending on the finish.

CODE COMPLIANCE

Most codes are not prescriptive when it comes to finished flooring materials, as long as the sub-floor has been constructed to code and in a manner intended to support the dead load imposed by the flooring.

INDOOR AIR QUALITY: *LOW TO HIGH*

Hardwood flooring generally has little to no negative impact on IAQ. Certain species of hardwoods may contain natural oils that are allergens to some people.

Finishes will have a range of impacts from negligible to high, depending on the type of finish. It is common to find low-VOC finishes for hardwood flooring, but this does not guarantee that there are no toxins contaminating the air. Look for Greenguard or similar certifications for petrochemical finishes to ensure minimal impacts.

FUTURE DEVELOPMENT

The growth of third-party certification programs for forest products will likely increase the availability of sustainably harvested hardwood flooring. Similar programs for the chemical content of finishes seem to be spurring R&D into less toxic products.

Resources for further research

Peterson, Charles. *Wood Flooring: A Complete Guide to Layout, Installation and Finishing*. Newtown, CT: Taunton, 2010. Print.

The Complete Guide to Flooring. Minneapolis, MN: Creative Publishing International, 2010. Print.

Bollinger, Don. *Hardwood Floors: Laying, Sanding and Finishing*. Newtown, CT: Taunton, 1990. Print.

Hardwood Flooring Ratings

	Best 1 2 3 4 5 6 7	Worst 8 9 10	Notes
Environmental Impacts			Species of hardwood and harvesting techniques will affect impacts.
Embodied Energy			
Waste Generated			
Energy Efficiency	N/A		
Material Costs			
Labor Inputs			
Skill Level Required by Homeowner			
Sourcing and Availability			
Durability and Longevity			Finishing products will affect durability.
Building Code Compliance	N/A		
Indoor Air Quality			IAQ is high for most hardwood species. Finishing products will have significant impact on IAQ.

Softwood flooring

What the cheerleaders say...	What the detractors say...
Renewable resource	Wood may not be harvested sustainably
Low cost	Finishes may be toxic
Durable	Shows wear, marks easily
Beautiful	

Applications for system

- Finished flooring. Can be applied on wooden sub-floors. May require strapping or sheathing if applied on wet-poured floors.
- At greater thicknesses (40 mm or 1½ inch), can be sub-floor and finished floor in one layer.

Basic materials

- Softwood planks, milled with a tongue-and-groove profile to a variety of widths
- Finishes can range from natural oils and waxes to petrochemical products

How the system works

Strips of softwood with typical widths varying from 40–150 mm (1½–6 inches) are laid in successive rows, interlocked by the tongue-and-groove fit between pieces and fastened with nails or staples driven through the tongue or groove to remain invisible on the finished floor surface.

Tips for successful installation

1. Softwood flooring should be stored in the home where it is to be installed for a minimum of one week prior to installation, to give the wood a chance to come to balance with the ambient humidity of the home. Softwood expands or contracts less than hardwood as it gains or loses moisture, but should still be allowed to arrive at the size that matches the humidity level of the home. If conditions are unusually dry or moist, the flooring may shrink or swell when conditions return to normal.
2. Softwood flooring is not as widely available through commercial flooring sources as hardwood. As it is more likely to come from smaller, local mills it may not come with installation instructions. Homeowners may need advice from experienced installers or other resources for instructions.
3. Narrower strips of softwood will be less likely to expand, contract or cup than wider boards.
4. If thick softwood is to be both the structural sub-floor and the finished floor, be sure the thickness of wood selected is appropriate for the intended loads and for the floor joist spacing.

Pros and cons

ENVIRONMENTAL IMPACTS

Harvesting — *Negligible to High.* Priority should be placed on sustainably harvested softwood in order to minimize impacts. Locally produced wood allows the homeowner to speak directly to the

Softwood floor. (DAVID ELFSTROM)

forester to ascertain practices. Third-party certifications should be sought whenever buying from a supplier with whom personal connection cannot be made. It is possible to have softwood trees from the building site turned into flooring locally, resulting in the lowest possible impacts.

Softwoods are typically faster-growing species than hardwood, and are therefore renewable on a shorter timeframe than hardwoods.

Finishing products may have impacts ranging from low for some natural oils and waxes to very high for petrochemical-based finishes.

Manufacturing — *Low to Moderate.* The process of milling wood into flooring has relatively low impacts, and many third-party certification programs ensure that manufacturing processes meet high environmental standards.

The manufacturing of finishing products has impacts ranging from low for some natural oils and waxes to very high for petrochemical-based finishes.

Transportation — *Negligible to High.* Sample building uses 796.5 kg of softwood flooring:

> 1.2 MJ per km by 15 ton truck
> 0.75 MJ per km by 35 ton truck

Softwood is a heavy material with a correspondingly high transportation impact dependent upon distance traveled. Most regions will have softwoods suitable for flooring locally available.

Installation — *Negligible.*

WASTE: *MODERATE*

Compostable — Untreated wood offcuts. Quantity can be low to high, depending on the requirements of the installation.

Recyclable — Metal fasteners. Quantities will be negligible.

Landfill — Treated wood offcuts. Quantity can be low to high, depending on the requirements of the installation.

ENERGY EFFICIENCY

There will be no energy efficiency effect from softwood flooring.

MATERIAL COSTS: *LOW TO MODERATE*

LABOR INPUT: *MODERATE TO HIGH*

Softwood floors have a similar amount of labor input as other finished flooring materials. Prefinished options will have much lower labor inputs than site-finished floors.

SKILL LEVEL REQUIRED FOR THE HOMEOWNER

Preparation of sub-floor — *Easy.*

Installation of floor — *Easy to Moderate.* A homeowner with the carpentry skills to build a wooden sub-floor structure will be able to install softwood flooring. The installation usually requires a pneumatic nailer, which can be rented.

Finishing of floor — *Easy.* Pre-finished floors require no effort. Finishing raw wood involves the

Softwood Flooring Embodied Energy

92.9 m² (1000 ft²) floor area	Material embodied energy from I.C.E. in MJ/kg	Weight to volume ratio of material*	Volume of material in sample 1000sf/92.9m² building	Sample building embodied energy	Material embodied carbon from I.C.E. in kgCO₂e/kg	Sample building embodied carbon	Notes
Softwood							
20mm (¾ in) thickness	2.5	450 kg/m³ (softwood lumber)	796.5 kg	1,991 MJ	0.2	159 kg	Does not include fasteners or surface finishes.

Transportation: Wood flooring transportation by 35 ton truck would equate to 0.7–1.1 MJ per kilometer of travel to the building site. *Typically from engineeringtoolbox.com straightforward brush or roller application of a liquid product according to manufacturer's instructions.

SOURCING/AVAILABILITY: *EASY*

Softwood flooring is not widely available through conventional flooring suppliers. Local saw mills tend to be the best source for this type of material, though building supply centers can often special order softwood flooring. Sustainably harvested wood with nontoxic finishes may be more difficult to source.

DURABILITY: *MODERATE*

Softwood flooring is very durable, with life span ranging from 40 to 100 years. It will not maintain a pristine surface, but the wood itself will last a very long time. Quality of finish will have an impact on durability, and finishes can require maintenance or reapplication on a cycle of one to twenty years, depending on the finish.

CODE COMPLIANCE

Most codes are not prescriptive when it comes to finished flooring materials, as long as the sub-floor has been constructed to code and in a manner intended to support the dead load imposed by the flooring.

INDOOR AIR QUALITY: *LOW TO HIGH*

Softwood flooring generally has little to no negative impact on IAQ. Certain species of softwoods may contain natural oils that are allergens to some people.

Finishes will have a range of impacts from negligible to high, depending on the type. It is uncommon to find pre-finished softwood flooring, so the installer or homeowner will be responsible for choosing and applying the finish in most cases. Look for Greenguard or similar certifications for petrochemical finishes to ensure minimal impacts.

Softwood Flooring Ratings

	Best 1	2	3	4	5	6	Worst 7 8	9	10	Notes
Environmental Impacts										Species of softwood and harvesting techniques will affect impacts.
Embodied Energy										
Waste Generated										
Energy Efficiency					N/A					
Material Costs										
Labor Inputs										
Skill Level Required by Homeowner										
Sourcing and Availability										
Durability and Longevity										Finishing products will affect durability.
Building Code Compliance					N/A					
Indoor Air Quality										IAQ is high for most softwood species. Finishing products will have significant impact on IAQ.

FUTURE DEVELOPMENT

Softwood floors were common historically in North America, and there is some indication that acceptance of softwood floors may be returning. The wear patterns that show on softwood floors give a home much sought after character, an antidote to a too-pristine new home appearance.

The use of thick softwood planks that act as both sub-floor and finished floor may rise in popularity as a low cost option that minimizes the number of steps and different materials required.

The growth of third-party certification programs for forest products will likely increase the availability of sustainably harvested softwood flooring. Similar programs for the chemical content of finishes seem to be spurring R&D into less toxic products.

Resources for further research

Jeffries, Dennis. *The Flooring Handbook: The Complete Guide to Choosing and Installing Floors.* Toronto, ON: Firefly, 2004. Print.

Engineered wood floors

What the cheerleaders say...	What the detractors say...
Renewable resource	Glues may be toxic
More stable than solid wood	Finishes may be toxic
Beauty of real wood	
Faster installation time	

Applications for system

- Finished flooring. Can be applied on wooden sub-floors. May require strapping or sheathing if applied over wet-poured floors.

Basic materials

- Hardwood or softwood veneer
- Plywood base
- Finishing product
- Underlayment layer (if required)

How the system works

A veneer layer of the desired type of wood for the surface of the floor is bonded to a plywood base with a tongue-and-groove or other interlocking edge pattern milled into it. This system has two advantages over solid wood flooring: it allows the value and beauty of a particular wood to be the visible element of the floor without requiring the use of valuable species of wood for the entire depth of the floor; and the plywood base is much less susceptible to expansion, contraction and fit issues. The drawback is higher processing energy input and the use of glues between the plies that are likely to contain toxic chemicals unless sourced to minimize or avoid chemical exposure.

Underlayment material may be required for some products. Be sure to investigate the costs and environmental impacts of this part of the system if it is an integral part of the chosen flooring.

Tips for successful installation

Engineered flooring products are proprietary, and will be supplied with manufacturer's installation instructions.

Pros and cons

ENVIRONMENTAL IMPACTS

Harvesting — *Low to High*. Appropriate sourcing for both the veneer and the base plies will determine the harvesting impact. Using third-party certified products will help to minimize impacts.

In some cases, engineered flooring is a means to make exotic hardwoods more affordable, using just a thin veneer of the expensive wood over a base of less expensive wood. Avoid exotic species that may be having large harvesting impacts in other parts of the world, and be especially aware of products that claim to be third-party certified without ensuring that the exotic wood is also certified.

Manufacturing — *Moderate to High*. Making an engineered wood floor is similar to manufacturing plywood. Veneer sheets are peeled from raw logs and glued together (usually with 2, 3 or 5 plies) to form the floor planks. Some type of interlocking connection is milled into the edges of the planks. Modern, efficient plywood factories have made strides to minimize waste, water use and effluent discharge, while older plants can be major sources of pollution.

Transportation — *Moderate to High*. Sample building uses 885 kg of engineered wood flooring:

1.3 MJ per km by 15 ton truck

0.8 MJ per km by 35 ton truck

Some engineered wood plants are located close to wood sources, while others must import wood over long distances. Some plants do all the work required to make the flooring in-house, while others will import veneer sheets, sometimes over long distances. Exotic hardwood products will usually involve shipping either logs or veneer over long distances.

Installation — *Low*.

WASTE: *MODERATE*

Recyclable — Metal fasteners. Quantities will be negligible. Boxes and packaging. Quantities will be moderate to high.

Landfill — Flooring offcuts. Quantities will be low to high, depending on the requirements of the installation. Underlayment offcuts. Quantities will be low to high, depending on the requirements of the installation.

ENERGY EFFICIENCY

Engineered wood flooring will have no impact on energy efficiency.

MATERIAL COSTS: *LOW TO HIGH*

Engineered wood flooring is a large product category with a wide range of price points.

LABOR INPUT: *MODERATE TO HIGH*

Some types of engineered wood flooring are designed to "float," with no need to attach with nails

Engineered Wood Flooring Embodied Energy

92.9 m² (1000 ft²) floor area	Material embodied energy from I.C.E. in MJ/kg	Weight to volume ratio of material*	Volume of material in sample 1000sf/92.9m² building	Sample building embodied energy	Material embodied carbon from I.C.E. in kgCO₂e/kg	Sample building embodied carbon	Notes
20mm (¾ in) thickness	15 (Timber, plywood)	500 kg/m³	1.77 m³ 885 kg	13,275 MJ	0.45	398 kg	Does not include fasteners or surface treatment.

Transportation Engineered flooring transportation by 35 ton truck would equate to 0.8 MJ per kilometer of travel to the building site. *Typically from engineeringtoolbox.com or staples, and these will be among the fastest floors to install. Products that require fastening will be comparable with other types of wood flooring. Engineered wood flooring is typically prefinished.

SKILL LEVEL REQUIRED FOR THE HOMEOWNER

Preparation of sub-floor — *Easy.*

Installation of floor — *Easy to Moderate.* A homeowner with the carpentry skills to build a wooden sub-floor structure will be able to install engineered wood flooring. Some installations require a pneumatic nailer, others are "click-down" systems requiring no fastening.

Finishing of floor — *Easy.* Pre-finished floors require no effort.

SOURCING/AVAILABILITY: *EASY*

Engineered wood floors are widely available through building material supply outlets and specialty flooring shops. It will take more effort to source third-party certified wood products and glues.

DURABILITY: *HIGH*

The quality of the glue used to bond the plies together will be the determining factor of longevity, as the wood itself will be long-lasting. The surface finish will also have a large impact on durability.

CODE COMPLIANCE

Most codes are not prescriptive when it comes to finished flooring materials, as long as the sub-floor has been constructed to code and in a manner intended to support the dead load imposed by the flooring.

INDOOR AIR QUALITY: *MODERATE*

The wood content in engineered flooring is unlikely to have a negative impact on IAQ, though certain wood species can be allergens for some people. The

Engineered Wood Flooring Ratings

	Best 1 2 3 4 5 6 7	Worst 8 9 10	Notes
Environmental Impacts			Forestry practices will affect impacts. Manufacturing of glues difficult to assess.
Embodied Energy			Manufacturing of glues difficult to assess.
Waste Generated			
Energy Efficiency	N/A		
Material Costs			
Labor Inputs			
Skill Level Required by Homeowner			
Sourcing and Availability			
Durability and Longevity			
Building Code Compliance	N/A		
Indoor Air Quality			Glues in engineered wood and finishing products can have a large impact on IAQ.

biggest issue will be the glue used between the plies and the surface treatment product. It is possible to find engineered flooring with Greenguard or similar certification, to ensure minimal impacts.

FUTURE DEVELOPMENT

The use of third-party certified wood, glues and finishes is likely to increase with greater consumer demand for eco-friendly materials.

Resources for further research

Jeffries, Dennis. *The Flooring Handbook: The Complete Guide to Choosing and Installing Floors.* Toronto, ON: Firefly, 2004. Print.

Tile flooring

What the cheerleaders say...	What the detractors say...
Durable, proven history, even in wet areas	High embodied energy
Wide variety of materials	Very little North American manufacturing
Wide variety of finishes	Often use toxic materials in installation
Beautiful	

Stone tile floor.
(JEN FEIGIN)

Applications for system

- Finished flooring. Can be applied on wooden sub-floors, but may require underlayment. Can be applied directly over slab floors.

Basic materials

- Natural tiles are made from stone or slate
- Manufactured clay tiles are made from earthenware, stoneware or porcelain
- Manufactured terrazzo tiles are made from aggregate and concrete
- Manufactured tiles are sometimes made from glass and binders

- Adhesives for tiles include cement mortar, modified cement mortar and glue adhesives
- Underlayment includes plywood, cement board and/or sheet barrier materials
- Grout between tiles is made from cement or modified cement

How the system works

Natural stone tiles are cut or quarried from deposits of a stone that is suitable for flooring. They may be left relatively rough and matte in finish, honed perfectly smooth or polished to a high gloss. They are cut into tiles of a desired size for a particular installation.

Clay tiles are made from clay, aggregates, pigments or dyes and sometimes mineral fluxes. These are fired at a high temperature; the higher the temperature, the harder and less porous the finished tile. Many tiles are then glazed using mineral and/or petrochemical glazes, which are fired onto the surface of the tile during a second trip to the kiln.

Terrazzo tiles are made by mixing a cement-based binder with aggregate and honing and polishing the resulting tile to expose a pattern of aggregate and binder in the finished surface.

Each type of tile is laid in a similar way. Individual tiles are set into a bed of adhesive on the sub-floor in a chosen pattern. Once set in the adhesive, the gaps between the tiles are filled with grout to the desired level.

Tips for successful installation

1. Tile flooring must be placed on a very stable sub-floor, as deflection in the floor can cause cracking of the grout or the tile.
2. Each type of tile may require a particular type of underlayment and adhesive. Follow manufacturer's instructions or the advice of an experienced tile installer.
3. Be aware of the different surfaces on tiles. Some will become very slippery when wet, and shouldn't be used in areas where water can be expected to accumulate.
4. It is possible to be very creative with tile installation. A variety of patterns will be possible using the same size tiles, and tiles can be ordered in different sizes or cut on-site to further increase the possibilities. Whenever a creative tile pattern is being used, carefully lay out the pattern before beginning the installation.
5. The gaps between tiles can be set with spacers (or chalk lines) to a variety of widths. Be sure to consider the aesthetics of the gaps when creating a tile surface. Choose grout material and color to suit the width of the gaps.

Pros and cons

ENVIRONMENTAL IMPACTS

Harvesting — *Moderate.* Natural stone, clay and terrazzo ingredients are non-renewable but abundant resources that are widely available. They are quarried or dug from geological deposits. Most quarries and pits have been long established, so are not responsible for the disturbance of untouched ecosystems. Impact at the quarry tends to be low, and can include interference with and silting of ground and surface water and the creation of airborne dust. Little to no contaminated effluent is created and no chemicals are used in obtaining these materials.

The balance of materials required for tiling can have moderate to high impacts. Grout and mortar are often cement based, and require quarrying to harvest. Petrochemical additives to mortars and grouts, in particular chemical adhesives, often require intensive and polluting processes to harvest raw materials.

Manufacturing

Natural Stone — *Low.* Stone is mechanically cut and/or split into tiles in a process that uses relatively little energy and produces little to no effluent or pollution. Honing and polishing are mechanical procedures that are also low-intensity.

Clay Tiles — *Moderate to Very High.* The production and forming of raw clay into tiles uses relatively little energy and produces little to no effluent or pollution. The kilns used to fire tiles are very energy-intensive. Fuels used include natural gas, oil, coal and wood, in large quantities, with significant pollution and greenhouse gas emissions. The harder the tile, the higher the firing temperature and the longer the time spent in the kiln. Soft tiles, like "Mexican" clay tiles, are at the low end of the spectrum, with porcelain tiles at the high end. The addition of a second firing for glazing adds further to the energy input and the pollution output. The addition of glazes can introduce toxic chemicals into the process (depending on the type of glaze) and increase quantities of air pollution and effluent.

Terrazzo Tiles — *High.* Terrazzo is a type of concrete, using portland cement to bind a mixture of aggregates. The creation of portland cement is high intensity, with limestone being fired in kilns to very high sustained temperatures. Fuels used include natural gas, oil, landfill waste and coal, in large quantities, with significant pollution and very significant greenhouse gas emissions. Once formed and cured, the polishing process is mechanical and of relatively low intensity, with airborne particulate as the main waste.

Balance of Materials — *Moderate to Very High.* Mortar and grout carry the same impacts as any cement-based material, though the quantities are relatively small. Chemical additives to mortar and grout, in particular tile adhesives, tend to be very intensive in their production and can produce high levels of toxic emissions and byproducts during production.

Transportation — *Moderate to Very High.* Sample building uses 1,406 – 2,035 kg of floor tile:

2.1 – 3.1 MJ per km by 15 ton truck
1.3 – 1.9 MJ per km by 35 ton truck
0.22 – 0.33 MJ per km by ocean freight

All tile products are very heavy, and incur significant transportation impacts based on distance traveled. If raw materials are shipped long distances to point of manufacture, this will add to the total impacts.

Tile Floor Embodied Energy

92.9 m² (1000 ft²) floor area	Material embodied energy from I.C.E. in MJ/kg	Weight to volume ratio of material*	Volume of material in sample 1000sf/92.9m² building	Sample building embodied energy	Material embodied carbon from I.C.E. in kgCO₂e/kg	Sample building embodied carbon	Notes
Lowest Impact							
Clay tile, 8mm (⁵/₁₆ in) thick	6.5 (Clay, tile)	1900 kg/m³	0.74 m³ 1406 kg	9,139 MJ	0.48	675 kg	
Mortar, 6mm (¼ in) thick	1.11 (Mortar, 1:1:6)	2370 kg/m³	0.59 m³ 1393.3 kg	1,552 MJ	0.174	242 kg	
Totals				**10,691 MJ**		**917 kg**	
Highest Impact							
Ceramic tile, 8mm (⁵/₁₆ in) thick	12 (Ceramics, tile)	2750 kg/m³	0.74 m³ 2035 kg	24,420 MJ	0.78	1,587 kg	
Mortar, 6mm (¼ in) thick	1.11 (Mortar, 1:1:6)	2370 kg/m³	0.59 m³ 1393.3 kg	1,552 MJ	0.174	242 kg	
Totals				**25,972 MJ**		**1,829 kg**	

Transportation: Tile flooring transportation by 35 ton truck would equate to 1.3–1.9 MJ per kilometer of travel to the building site. Tile flooring transportation by ocean freight would equate to 0.2-0.3 MJ per kilometer of travel to the building site. *Typically from engineeringtoolbox.com

The majority of clay tile sold in North America is manufactured in Europe or Asia, and has significant transportation impacts.

Installation — *Low to Moderate.* Tile is often cut with a grinder or saw, and if done while dry can create a significant amount of airborne dust that is high in silica content.

WASTE: *HIGH*

Compostable — Unglazed tile offcuts can be left in the environment as aggregate.

Landfill — Glazed tile offcuts, containers from adhesives and grout. Quantities low to high.

ENERGY EFFICIENCY

A tile floor will have no effect on energy efficiency.

MATERIAL COSTS: *LOW TO HIGH*

Floor tiles include a wide range of products with highly variable price points.

LABOR INPUT: *HIGH*

Tiling is a multi-stage process involving a high amount of labor. In many cases, work must be done to prepare the substrate for tiling. Then comes layout, which must be performed carefully; tile cutting, a time-consuming task; and the actual laying of the tiles, which must also be done carefully. Complicated patterns are especially intensive. Grouting is a separate process and requires significant cleanup time, and a sealant is often applied to the grout or the whole floor, adding another step.

A number of specific tools will need to be purchased for a tile job, including a mechanical or manual tile cutter, nibblers, mortar trowel and sponge float.

SKILL LEVEL REQUIRED FOR THE HOMEOWNER

Preparation of sub-floor — *Easy to Difficult.* Tile adhesive/mortar can be applied directly to some slab floors. Wooden sub-floors may be able to accept tile directly, or may require one or more layers of underlayment to ensure a crack-free installation. The more complex the underlayment, the more difficult the preparation for tiling. Preparation for waterproof tile installations in showers and baths adds a degree of difficulty.

Installation of floor — *Easy to Difficult.* The size, shape and layout of the tiles will determine the ease of the installation. Complex layouts and the need for lots of cutting and fitting will raise the level of difficulty, as will the need to make a waterproof installation.

Finishing of floor — *Easy to Moderate.* Grouting is fairly simple, but may need to be done in a few stages and must be done carefully to get even results. Understanding the timing for grouting can take some practice, as sponging too soon can remove too much grout from the cracks but waiting too long can result in grout that is too high or uneven.

SOURCING/AVAILABILITY: *EASY*

Tile and all that is required to install it is available widely, through building supply outlets and specialty tile shops.

DURABILITY: *VERY HIGH*

Well-installed tile has a very long life span. The tile itself will last for hundreds of years, with the life span of the mortar or adhesive determining the serviceable life of the floor. Modern mortars and adhesives can typically be relied upon for 30 to 60 years or more. Uncracked tile can be relaid with new mortar or adhesive to continue the life of the floor.

CODE COMPLIANCE

Most codes are not prescriptive when it comes to finished flooring materials, as long as the sub-floor has been constructed to code and in a manner intended to support the dead load imposed by the flooring.

INDOOR AIR QUALITY: *HIGH*

Tile is unlikely to have a negative impact on IAQ, but the mortars and/or adhesives can be mildly to extremely toxic. In particular, chemical adhesives often carry serious warnings about the inhalation of vapors, with potential cancer-causing and birth defect-causing effects. Be sure to select mortars or adhesives that have been formulated to have the least possible impact on IAQ.

FUTURE DEVELOPMENT

Tiling has been around for thousands of years, and some installations are still intact. Recent changes in tiling have come in the form of new ways to color tile (including inexpensive screen printing) and chemical additives for grout, mortar and adhesives.

These modern additions to tiling are also the more high-impact elements, and a homeowner looking to minimize environmental impacts will choose to tile the old-fashioned way, with a lime-based mortar and grout that is chemical free. It takes longer for this mortar to set, but it's an excellent example of a return to past methods being the best direction for the future.

There is work being done on making less-toxic adhesives. If using chemical adhesives, look for those that have third-party certification for air quality and off-gassing.

Resources for further research

The Complete Guide to Ceramic Tile. Minneapolis, MN: Creative Publishing International, 2010. Print.
The Complete Guide to Flooring. Minneapolis, MN: Creative Publishing International, 2010. Print.

Tile Floor Ratings

	Best							Worst			Notes
	1	2	3	4	5	6	7	8	9	10	
Environmental Impacts					▓	▓	▓	▓			Harvesting and manufacturing processes vary among tile types.
Embodied Energy						▓	▓	▓			
Waste Generated					▓	▓	▓	▓			
Energy Efficiency					N/A						
Material Costs			▓	▓	▓	▓	▓	▓			
Labor Inputs					▓	▓	▓	▓			
Skill Level Required by Homeowner					▓	▓	▓	▓			
Sourcing and Availability	▓										
Durability and Longevity	▓										
Building Code Compliance					N/A						
Indoor Air Quality	▓										Adhesives, grout and sealant can have significant impact on IAQ.

Linoleum

What the cheerleaders say...	What the detractors say...
Natural, renewable materials	Little North American production
Durable, proven history	Often use toxic materials in installation
Many aesthetic possibilities	
Beautiful	

Applications for system

- Finish flooring. Can be applied directly to wooden sub-floors and wet-poured floors with adhesive, or over wooden and wet-poured floors in laminate-style planks or tiles.

Basic materials

- Oxidized linseed oil (pressed from flax seed) or other polymerizing oil (soya bean or menhaden oil)
- Resin (often pine resin, or ester or kauri gum)
- Calcium carbonate (ground limestone)
- Wood powder (ground sawdust) and/or cork powder
- Pigment for coloring
- Jute or other natural fiber for backing
- Laminated wood or fiberboard for backing, when applicable
- Adhesive, when applicable

How the system works

Linoleum glue is formed by blending oxidized linseed oil and pine resin, into which powered limestone, wood and cork are mixed, along with any desired pigment. This mixture is added over a wide-woven natural fabric, such as jute or burlap backer. The linoleum is then cured in a kiln or drying room for a number of days to complete the polymerization of the oils and harden the mixture.

Rolls of sheet material or individual tiles are cut from the cured linoleum. This material can be applied directly to sub-floors by means of an adhesive.

Tiles or planks of linoleum may also be adhered to laminate wood or fiberboard backing to make a "click-down" form of interlocking tiles.

Tips for successful installation

1. Sheet-style, tile or click-down options require different installation procedures. Be sure you know which kind of linoleum you'd like to install at the planning stage, as final floor thickness and appearance vary considerably between the options. Sheet linoleum can cover large areas with no seams, or can be cut into patterns that would be difficult to match with any other flooring style. Adhesive tiles and click-down will create patterns similar to other tile or plank floors.
2. Sheet-style linoleum installations should be done by a professional. Tools and techniques are quite specific, in particular the welding of seams, and typically not appropriate for homeowners.
3. Linoleum that requires adhesive connection may require special treatment and glues for different sub-floor types.
4. Linoleum of all types will come with manufacturer's instructions for installation, which should be followed carefully.

Pros and cons

ENVIRONMENTAL IMPACTS

Harvesting — *Low to Moderate.* There are many components to linoleum, but none are high intensity at the harvesting stage. The oils come from agricultural production, and will carry whatever impacts created by the style of farming used, which can include pesticide and herbicide use, groundwater contamination and destruction of habitat for farming. Oil harvesting and pressing is not considered a high-impact process. Pine resin can be harvested sustainably by tapping appropriate pine trees and collecting the raw resin, and is not generally considered a high-impact process. The wood and cork dust is typically derived from waste material from other manufacturing processes, keeping it from burning or landfill. Calcium carbonate, used in small quantities, is harvested from limestone quarries. Impacts include groundwater disruption and contamination. Jute is made from the fibers of plants in the genus Corchorus. This type of plant is rain-fed in monsoon areas and typically needs little or no herbicides, pesticides or fertilizer, and is considered a low-impact material to harvest.

Harvesting the ingredients for chemical adhesives can have impacts including air and water pollution, habitat destruction and greenhouse gas emissions.

Manufacturing — *Moderate.* Creating linoleum is a multi-stage process, but it is not highly energy intensive. The largest energy inputs are used to heat the oil early in the process and again to provide warm drying rooms for the product to cure. VOC emissions are released during manufacture, but are typically controlled against release to the atmosphere.

Transportation — *High.* Sample building uses 272.5 – 741.6 kg of linoleum flooring:

  0.4 – 1.1 MJ per km by 15 ton truck
  0.25 – 0.7 MJ per km by 35 ton truck
  0.04 – 0.12 MJ per km by ocean freight

The ingredients for linoleum come from different parts of the world and must be transported to the factory, incurring high transportation impacts. The only commercial linoleum producers are based in Europe, and all North American linoleum is imported, incurring a second round of transportation impacts.

Installation — *Moderate.* The welding of seams for sheet-style installations releases VOCs as the linoleum welding rods are melted. Chemical adhesives will also off-gas during construction.

WASTE: *MODERATE TO HIGH*

Compostable — Sheet and tile linoleum off-cuts. In theory, linoleum is compostable, as all the

Linoleum Flooring Embodied Energy

92.9 m² (1000 ft²) floor area	Material embodied energy from I.C.E. in MJ/kg	Weight to volume ratio of material*	Volume of material in sample 1000sf/92.9m² building	Sample building embodied energy	Material embodied carbon from I.C.E. in kgCO₂e/kg	Sample building embodied carbon	Notes
Lowest Impact							
2.5mm (⅛ in) thick sheet material	11**	1185 kg/m³	0.23 m³ 272.5 kg	2,998 MJ	N/A	N/A	**ICE figure is 25. Industry figures average 11.
Highest Impact — Click tiles or boards							
2.0mm (³⁄₃₂ in) thick sheet	11**	1185 kg/m³	0.19 m³ 225 kg	2,477 MJ	N/A	N/A	
6.8mm (¼ in) High Density Fiberboard (HDF)	16 (Timber, hardboard)	820 kg/m³	0.63 m³ 516.6 kg	8,266 MJ	1.09	563 kg	
Totals				**10,743 MJ**			Does not include fasteners, adhesive or surface treatment.

Transportation: Linoleum transportation by 35 ton truck would equate to 0.3–0.5 MJ per kilometer of travel to the building site. Linoleum transportation by ocean freight would equate to 0.04–0.08 MJ per kilometer of travel to the building site. *Typically from engineeringtoolbox.com ingredients are biodegradable. However, it will take a long time for the polymerized oil to break down in the environment and it may not be feasible to send the material to compost. Quantities can vary from low to high, depending on the installation.

Landfill — Sheet and tile linoleum offcuts. If the material cannot be sent to an appropriate composting facility, they will likely end up in landfill. Quantities can vary from low to high, depending on the installation.

Click-down linoleum offcuts. The composite of linoleum and wood-fiber backer will not be easily separable and is typically sent to landfill. Quantities can vary from low to high, depending on the installation.

ENERGY EFFICIENCY

Linoleum flooring will have no impact on energy efficiency.

MATERIAL COSTS: *MODERATE TO HIGH*

Natural linoleum occupies a small percentage of the market and is typically aimed at high-end uses, with attendant high costs.

LABOR INPUT: *MODERATE*

Linoleum flooring requires a similar amount of labor as other flooring options. Click-down versions are at the low end and sheet-style at the higher end.

SKILL LEVEL REQUIRED FOR THE HOMEOWNER

Preparation of sub-floor — *Easy.* Click-down versions will require little to no preparation, while adhesive versions may require a surface preparation that is typically rolled or brushed onto the sub-floor.

Installation of floor — *Easy to Difficult.* Click-down versions are straightforward to install, and require simple layout and saw-cutting skills. Adhesive tiles are similarly easy, with cuts made with a sharp

Linoleum Flooring Ratings

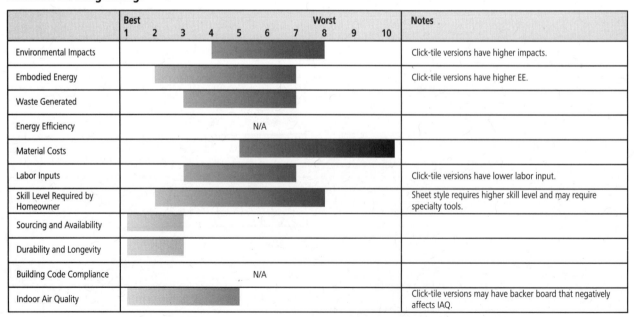

	Best 1 2 3 4 5 6 7 8 9 10		Worst		Notes
Environmental Impacts					Click-tile versions have higher impacts.
Embodied Energy					Click-tile versions have higher EE.
Waste Generated					
Energy Efficiency	N/A				
Material Costs					
Labor Inputs					Click-tile versions have lower labor input.
Skill Level Required by Homeowner					Sheet style requires higher skill level and may require specialty tools.
Sourcing and Availability					
Durability and Longevity					
Building Code Compliance	N/A				
Indoor Air Quality					Click-tile versions may have backer board that negatively affects IAQ.

blade and tiles laid directly onto the floor. Sheet-style installations are difficult, as it takes practice to handle and cut large rolls to size. Adhesive needs to be applied evenly to a large area of floor and the sheet laid carefully to avoid bubbling. Welding seams requires special tools and training.

Finishing of floor — *Easy.* Most linoleum products are pre-finished and will require no additional work.

SOURCING/AVAILABILITY: *EASY*

Linoleum is becoming more widely available, with versions available at many building supply outlets and specialty flooring shops.

DURABILITY: *HIGH*

Old linoleum has been known to last 30 to 50 years, and estimates for modern versions range from 15 to 50. Proper maintenance of linoleum is a key part of longevity, with periodic application of a sealing product recommended by the manufacturer helping to extend life span. Most modern linoleum is designed for and installed in high-traffic public buildings, and will do well in residential scenarios with lower wear.

CODE COMPLIANCE

Most codes are not prescriptive when it comes to finished flooring materials, as long as the sub-floor has been constructed to code and in a manner intended to support the dead load imposed by the flooring.

INDOOR AIR QUALITY: *HIGH*

Linoleum itself is quite inert and should have little to no detrimental effect on IAQ. Some people may have sensitivities to linseed oil and may want to see if exposure to linoleum has an effect on them.

The adhesives used for some installations often carry serious warnings about the inhalation of vapors, with potential cancer-causing and birth defect-causing effects. There may be residual and lingering off-gassing from these products. Be sure to select adhesives that have been formulated to have the least possible impact on IAQ, preferably those with third-party certification.

FUTURE DEVELOPMENT

The basic recipe for linoleum was developed in the 1800s, and has changed very little. Linoleum has seen a real resurgence over the past decade, as this once-popular type of flooring has made a comeback largely due to its generally strong environmental characteristics. It would be ideal if demand led to the re-establishment of North American production facilities, reducing the need to import all linoleum products from Europe.

Development is likely to lead to simpler installation methods and less toxic adhesive options. The use of linoleum in public buildings, especially hospitals and schools, is likely to raise its profile among homeowners and continue to grow demand.

Resources for further research

The Complete Guide to Flooring. Minneapolis, MN: Creative Publishing International, 2010. Print.

———~~~———

Bamboo flooring

What the cheerleaders say...	What the detractors say...
Rapidly renewable resource	Material may not be sustainably harvested
Durable	Work conditions in factories may not be appropriate
Beautiful	Requires shipping from Asia

Applications for system

- Finished flooring. Can be applied on wooden sub-floors. May require strapping or sheathing if applied on wet-poured floors.

Basic materials

- Bamboo strips or bamboo fiber
- Adhesive to bond bamboo
- Surface finishes, typically petrochemical

How the system works

Bamboo is processed into strips or into fiber, and then pressed and bonded with adhesive to form planks with a tongue-and-groove profile milled into them. The planks are pre-finished with a petrochemical product.

The bamboo planks (with typical widths varying from 40–150 mm / 1½–6 inches) are laid in successive rows, interlocked by the tongue-and-groove fit between pieces and fastened with nails or staples driven through the tongue or groove to remain invisible on the finished floor surface.

Tips for successful installation

1. Bamboo shares much in common with hardwood flooring, and construction details and installation methods are very similar.
2. Manufacturer instructions for installation should be followed.

Pros and cons

ENVIRONMENTAL IMPACTS

Harvesting — *Low to High*. As with forest products in North America, harvesting practices vary widely in Asia's bamboo forests. Bamboo production can lead to monoculture planting and habitat destruction, clear-cutting, soil erosion and water contamination. Labor practices may also be substandard. There are third-party certification programs similar to those used for forest products, and bamboo sourced with these certifications will contribute to lower impacts.

All bamboo flooring products rely on adhesives to bind the bamboo fibers together, and impacts from harvesting materials for glues and finishes can include habitat destruction, air and water pollution and greenhouse gas emissions.

Manufacturing — *High*. Bamboo flooring requires a multi-stage manufacturing process, which includes the input of high amounts of processing energy. The raw bamboo is milled and steam-treated. The bamboo strips are then kiln-dried before the milled bamboo is combined with adhesives and again heat-treated. These three stages of high heat input require high quantities of fossil fuels and result in air pollution and greenhouse gas emissions.

The manufacturing of the adhesives and finishes also results in significant air and water pollution.

Transportation — *Moderate to High*. Sample building uses approximately 1,500 kg of bamboo flooring:

> 2.25 MJ per km by 15 ton truck
> 1.4 MJ per km by 35 ton truck
> 0.24 MJ per km by ocean freight

All bamboo flooring is harvested and most is manufactured in Asia, and requires shipping to North American markets. The flooring may make many stops between point of production and the building site.

Installation — *Negligible*.

EMBODIED ENERGY

Third party embodied energy figures are not currently available for bamboo flooring. Homeowners must consider the harvesting techniques and equipment, type of process used and source for the glues and adhesives in order to judge approximate embodied energy for comparison.

WASTE: *MODERATE*

Landfill — Bamboo flooring offcuts. The high quantity of adhesives in bamboo flooring renders the material non-compostable. Quantities can be low to high, depending upon the installation.

ENERGY EFFICIENCY

Bamboo flooring will have no impact on energy efficiency.

MATERIAL COSTS: *MODERATE*

The recent expansion of bamboo flooring in the market has put pricing on par with many other options. However, bamboo flooring with sustainable harvesting certification and nontoxic binders and finishes will tend to be at the high end of the price scale.

LABOR INPUT: *MODERATE TO HIGH*

Bamboo flooring has a similar amount of labor input as other flooring options. The majority of bamboo flooring comes prefinished.

SKILL LEVEL REQUIRED FOR THE HOMEOWNER

Preparation of sub-floor — *Easy.*

Installation of floor — *Easy to Moderate.* A homeowner with the carpentry skills to build a wooden sub-floor structure will be able to install bamboo flooring. The installation usually requires a pneumatic nailer, which can be rented.

Finishing of floor — *Easy.* Pre-finished bamboo requires no effort.

Bamboo Flooring Ratings

	Best							Worst			Notes
	1	2	3	4	5	6	7	8	9	10	
Environmental Impacts											No North American production. Harvesting practices can vary widely.
Embodied Energy					N/A						No reliable data available.
Waste Generated											
Energy Efficiency					N/A						
Material Costs											
Labor Inputs											
Skill Level Required by Homeowner											
Sourcing and Availability											
Durability and Longevity											
Building Code Compliance					N/A						
Indoor Air Quality											Glues and finishing products will have significant impact on IAQ.

SOURCING/AVAILABILITY: *EASY*

Bamboo flooring has quickly gained a foothold in the North American market, with versions widely available through most building supply outlets and flooring supply shops. Sourcing bamboo from sustainable sources and with nontoxic finishes is possible, but requires research.

DURABILITY: *MODERATE TO HIGH*

There is no historical precedent for laminated bamboo flooring, but manufacturers typically state an expected life expectancy of 30 to 50 years. The surface of many brands can be refinished, which can extend life span further.

CODE COMPLIANCE

Most codes are not prescriptive when it comes to finished flooring materials, as long as the sub-floor has been constructed to code and in a manner intended to support the dead load imposed by the flooring.

INDOOR AIR QUALITY: *MODERATE TO HIGH*

As all bamboo flooring is made with adhesives and comes pre-finished with petrochemical products, it is the quality of these components that will determine the flooring's impact on IAQ. Products can range from high levels of VOCs and other toxic emissions to those that are third-party certified for low emissions. In general, the lower the cost of bamboo flooring, the higher the emissions are likely to be. Careful research should be done to verify the impacts a bamboo floor may have on IAQ.

FUTURE DEVELOPMENT

Bamboo flooring has made rapid inroads in the North American flooring market in the past decade. At least some of this expansion has been due to the perceived "greenness" of using a rapidly renewable resource to replace solid wood, which has a much longer regeneration cycle. While this is true, it is difficult to ascertain if the energy intensity of the production process and the shipping impacts offset the renewability. Further factors to consider are the quantity and quality of adhesives and finish used in the products and the forestry and labor practices that go into making particular bamboo flooring. Third-party certification programs are starting to appear in the bamboo market, and these can give homeowners some certainty that impacts are being minimized.

The future of bamboo flooring will depend greatly on the price of fossil fuels, which are used extensively in the production process, and the economic relationship between China and North America. If bamboo remains cost-competitive with other flooring options, it will continue to grow its market share. Developments in the use of lower-energy production methods and healthier adhesives will hopefully result in more sustainable options.

Resources for further research

Jeffries, Dennis. *The Flooring Handbook: The Complete Guide to Choosing and Installing Floors.* Toronto, ON: Firefly, 2004. Print.

Cork flooring

What the cheerleaders say...	What the detractors say...
Renewable resource	Limited resource
Comfortable surface	Raw materials not grown in North America
Durable	
Beautiful	

Applications for system

- Finished flooring. Can be applied on wooden sub-floors. May require strapping or sheathing if applied on wet-poured floors.

Basic materials

- Cork (bark layer from cork oak tree)
- Wood fiber base (for some products)
- Adhesive (for some products)
- Surface finish

How the system works

The bark of the cork oak tree is harvested (on cycles of seven to twelve years) and air-dried into sheets. Wine corks are punched from the sheets, and the remainder is ground, boiled and formed with adhesives into sheets for cork flooring. Some flooring types use cork sheets that are directly adhered to the sub-floor, while some adhere the cork sheets to a wood fiber backer that forms interlocking planks or tiles. Some forms of interlocking cork require nails or staples to fasten them, while others operate as a floating floor.

Tips for successful installation

1. Sheet cork and laminated cork have different thicknesses and application processes, and a decision to use one or the other should be made at the planning stage in order to ensure proper detailing.
2. Cork flooring is only available as proprietary systems, with manufacturers supplying installation instructions that should be followed carefully.

Pros and cons

ENVIRONMENTAL IMPACTS

Harvesting — *Low to Moderate*. Cork is harvested in a sustainable manner, with the same trees bearing

Cork Flooring Embodied Energy

92.9 m² (1000 ft²) floor area	Material embodied energy from I.C.E. in MJ/kg	Weight to volume ratio of material*	Volume of material in sample 1000sf/92.9m² building	Sample building embodied energy	Material embodied carbon from I.C.E. in kgCO₂e/kg	Sample building embodied carbon	Notes
Lowest Impact							
5mm (³/₁₆ in) thick sheet	4 (Insulation, cork)	240 kg/m³	0.44 m³ 105.6 kg	422 MJ	0.19	20 kg	
Highest Impact, click tiles or boards							
5mm (³/₁₆ in) thick sheet	4 (Insulation, cork)	240 kg/m³	0.44 m³ 105.6 kg	422 MJ	0.19	20 kg	
6.8mm (¼ in) High Density Fiberboard	16 (Timber, hardboard)	820 kg/m³	0.63 m³ 516.6 kg	8,266 MJ	1.09	563 kg	
Totals				8,688 MJ		583 kg	Does not include fasteners, adhesive or surface treatment.

Transportation: Cork flooring transportation by 35 ton truck would equate to 0.09–0.5 MJ per kilometer of travel to the building site. Cork flooring transportation by ocean freight would equate to 0.015–0.08 MJ per kilometer of travel to the building site. *Typically from engineeringtoolbox.com a crop of new bark every seven to twelve years. The harvesting work is still largely done by hand, with little to no impact on the land, water and air.

Cork is made into sheets using binders. The binders can be based on natural resins (like pine resin) that are relatively low-impact in harvesting, but can also be chemical binders such as urea melamine and phenol formaldehyde, which have higher impacts.

Manufacturing — *Low to Moderate.* Flooring cork is made from the leftover material from bottle stopper manufacturing. Some manufacturers claim that all cork is "recycled" from industrial waste, but the volume of cork used for flooring is equivalent to that used for bottle stoppers and manufacturers do not see the leftover cork as waste but plan equally for its use as flooring and other products. The cork is boiled during processing, which is a relatively high-energy operation, using a lot of water that becomes contaminated. The remainder of the manufacturing process, including grinding and forming sheets with adhesives, is relatively low-energy.

The manufacturing of the adhesives used to bind cork will often involve petrochemicals and will carry high impacts, including air and water pollution and habitat destruction. These adhesives are used in fairly small quantities.

A small amount of cork flooring is made from recycled bottle stoppers, reducing the initial processing impacts of virgin cork.

Transportation — *Low to High.* Sample building uses 105 – 622.2 kg of cork flooring:

> 0.15 – 0.9 MJ per km by 15 ton truck
> 0.1 – 0.6 MJ per km by 35 ton truck
> 0.02 – 0.1 MJ per km by ocean freight

Cork is only grown around the Mediterranean region and the vast majority of cork flooring is manufactured in that region, keeping initial transportation impacts low. However, cork flooring used in North America must be shipped from this region, carrying high levels of impact.

Installation — *Negligible.*

Waste: *Moderate*

Compostable — In theory, cork is compostable, though the adhesives binding it may not break down and/or leave chemical traces in compost. Most cork flooring is adhered to a wood composite backer and the combined product is not compostable.

Recyclable — Packaging. Quantities can be high, as flooring is often boxed in cardboard and wrapped in plastic in fairly small bundles.

Landfill — Cork flooring offcuts. Quantities can be low to high, depending on the requirements of the installation.

Energy efficiency

While cork has the highest R-value of all the flooring products in this book, at approximately R-3 per inch, the actual thickness of the cork component of the flooring is usually 5–10 mm ($\frac{3}{16}$–$\frac{3}{8}$ inch), so it will only be adding ~R-1, which is negligible.

Cork flooring does offer the advantage of "feeling" warm underfoot because it does not conduct heat very well, and so can contribute to a space that doesn't require as high a thermostat setting because occupants feel warmer.

Material costs: *Moderate to High*

Type of backing and finish will have a large impact on cost.

Labor input: *Moderate to High*

Similar to other prefinished floorings.

Skill level required for the homeowner

Preparation of sub-floor — *Easy.*
Installation of floor — *Easy to Moderate.* Click-down flooring requires minimal tools and experience.

Flooring that is fastened with nails or staples requires slightly more skill.

Finishing of floor — *Easy.* Pre-finished.

SOURCING/AVAILABILITY: *EASY*

Cork flooring has seen a significant growth in popularity, to some degree because of its environmental benefits. It can be obtained from most building supply outlets and specialty flooring shops.

DURABILITY: *MODERATE*

The soft, pliable nature of cork means this type of flooring is prone to wear issues. Properly maintained and used in areas that are not high-traffic and/or subjected to regular wetting, cork flooring can last from ten to fifty years.

There are several issues that affect the life span of cork. Abrasion can wear down cork flooring, making it inappropriate for muddy, sandy or otherwise dirty locations where dirt can abrade the surface. Cork is also negatively affected by UV light, causing color changes and degradation of the surface over time. While there are naturally occurring water repellents in cork, the flooring is not durable under consistently wet conditions that can affect the surface finish and the wood-fiber backing material.

Most manufacturers recommend refinishing cork floors occasionally, depending on wear patterns.

CODE COMPLIANCE

Most codes are not prescriptive when it comes to finished flooring materials, as long as the sub-floor has been constructed to code and in a manner intended to support the dead load imposed by the flooring.

INDOOR AIR QUALITY: *MODERATE TO HIGH*

Cork itself is relatively benign for IAQ, but a number of the products associated with the cork flooring

Cork Flooring Ratings

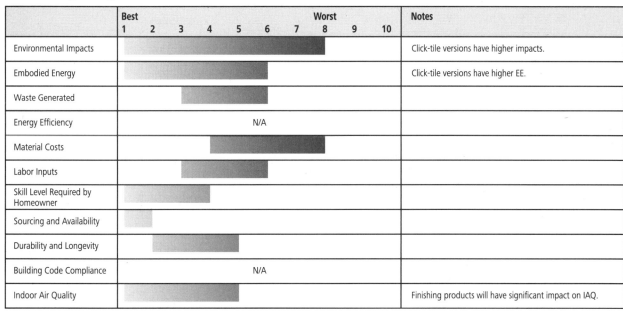

	Best 1 2 3 4 5 6 7 Worst 8 9 10	Notes
Environmental Impacts		Click-tile versions have higher impacts.
Embodied Energy		Click-tile versions have higher EE.
Waste Generated		
Energy Efficiency	N/A	
Material Costs		
Labor Inputs		
Skill Level Required by Homeowner		
Sourcing and Availability		
Durability and Longevity		
Building Code Compliance	N/A	
Indoor Air Quality		Finishing products will have significant impact on IAQ.

system may have negative impacts that range from negligible to high. Wood-fiber backing boards are typically made with formaldehyde glues, and surface finishing products are typically petrochemical based and may off-gas over the short and/or long term. In addition, most manufacturers recommend fairly frequent refinishing of the surface, and the majority of products are petrochemical based.

There are third-party certified versions of cork flooring, which should be sought if IAQ is of concern.

FUTURE DEVELOPMENT

The world's cork supply is limited, as the cork oak only grows in particular climatic and soil conditions in a small region of the world. Trees take 25 years to reach maturity for harvesting, and may only be harvested on seven- to twelve-year cycles. This means that there can never be enough cork to supply more than a small portion of the world's flooring needs, and as pressure increases on the limited supply the price will remain high or climb higher. While it may be feasible to make a very sustainable building using well-sourced cork flooring, it is not a solution that will serve more than a small number of homeowners.

Resources for further research

Jeffries, Dennis. *The Flooring Handbook: The Complete Guide to Choosing and Installing Floors.* Toronto, ON: Firefly, 2004. Print.

———————

Concrete flooring

What the cheerleaders say...	What the detractors say...
Very durable	High embodied energy
Can be structural and finished floor	High greenhouse gas emissions
Can be beautiful	Uncomfortable/unhealthy for feet

Applications for system

- Floor slabs. Can be a skim coat finish floor or a finish can be applied to a slab that is serving a structural role.

Basic materials

- Portland cement
- Aggregate
- Admixtures (including slag, fly ash and other pozzolans to offset portland cement content)
- Metal reinforcing mesh and/or reinforcement fibers
- Pigment (can be dispersed through concrete or used as a surface treatment)
- Sealants and/or finishes

How the system works

Concrete is a mixture of portand cement, aggregate and admixtures. Most slab floors are made from ready-mixed concrete, which is prepared at a batching plant and delivered to the building site mixed and ready to pour. Smaller slabs can be made by site-mixing the ingredients with water. In both cases, formwork is created to shape the slab, filled with wet concrete and leveled. As the concrete sets (a chemical process, not a matter of drying) several stages of finishing occur as the concrete stiffens.

Slab floor. Some buildings will be designed to have a concrete slab floor, and in these cases the most sustainable choice for flooring may be to use the concrete surface as the finished floor.

Concrete Skim Floor. In some cases, concrete may be applied over an existing sub-floor in a relatively thin layer to provide a finished floor surface. Often, this is done as a means of covering hydronic tubing for radiant floor heating systems built on joist floors.

Concrete can be finished to a wide variety of surfaces, from roughly textured to highly polished. Concrete surfaces can also be stamped in a wide variety of patterns, using rubber mats with the pattern molded in that are applied to the surface when the concrete is still soft. Choices about surface texture will be based on practicality (slippery vs. grippy), aesthetic preferences and the skill and ability of the concrete finisher. It should be made clear to the person in charge of doing the concrete work if the surface is intended to be the finished surface.

Concrete can be poured with pigment mixed in, or the pigment may be cast onto the wet surface of the slab and worked into the concrete during finishing. Concrete can also be poured and finished with no color, or have a color finish applied to the surface after the slab is cured. Some homeowners may choose to have the natural color of the concrete be the finish, whether unsealed or sealed.

Tips for successful installation

1. To minimize environmental impacts, be sure to specify a concrete mix with the highest possible amount of portland cement replacement material (such as slag or fly ash) and recycled aggregate (crushed concrete). It may take some research to find a batching plant and a concrete finisher willing to do this.

2. Plan for the type of finish desired prior to ordering and installing the concrete. Be sure both the batching plant and the finisher understand the intent and tailor the mix and their finishing efforts to suit. This is especially the case if using pigments in the concrete or on the surface.

Concrete slab being laid.

3. Large slab areas are difficult to install for beginners. From creating and properly bracing forms to mixing, laying and finishing, there is a lot to know before pouring your own concrete. There is a lot of good resource information about working with concrete; research well before proceeding.

Pros and cons

ENVIRONMENTAL IMPACTS

Harvesting — *Moderate to High.* Portland cement and aggregate ingredients are non-renewable but abundant resources that are widely available. They are quarried or dug from geological deposits. Most limestone quarries have been long established, so are not responsible for the disturbance of untouched ecosystems. Impact at existing quarries tends to be low, and can include interference with and silting of ground and surface water and the creation of airborne dust. Little to no contaminated effluent is created and no chemicals are used in obtaining these materials. Pressure for ever-increasing quantities of aggregate means new pits are being opened, usually close to urban centers and often on or near prime agricultural lands, resulting in serious impacts including loss of arable land, natural habitat disturbance and contamination of ground and surface water.

The balance of materials required for concrete are mainly mined or quarried (including gypsum, calcium sulfate and bauxite, among others), and make up a very small percentage of the mix. These will all have harvesting impacts similar to other quarried materials.

Mining ore to make steel for reinforcement bars or mesh is a high-intensity activity, resulting in serious impacts including habitat destruction and air and water pollution. Depending on the specifications for the slab, the amount of steel used can be low to high.

Manufacturing — *High*. Portland cement is made by crushing the raw limestone and heating it in a kiln to a high temperature (1300–1500°C / 2350–2750°F). This is an energy-intensive process and uses fuels such as natural gas, oil, coal and landfill waste, with resulting air and water pollution and habitat destruction. During the heating process, the limestone releases a large amount of carbon dioxide, contributing significantly to greenhouse gas emissions.

Aggregate is relatively low in manufacturing energy inputs and resulting effects.

Admixtures for concrete are often industrial by-products, like blast furnace slag (from ore smelting) and fly ash (from coal burning). While these activities have high impacts, the by-products are not typically attributed with the effects.

The making of steel for reinforcement bars and mesh is a high-intensity activity, including high-energy inputs for melting ore. Impacts include significant air and water pollution.

Transportation — *Moderate to High*. Sample building uses 5,664 – 14,047 kg of concrete flooring:

5.3 – 21.3 MJ per km by 35 ton truck

Most of the processes involved in making concrete happen relatively close to the source of raw materials, to minimize transportation costs for these heavy materials. Distances from point of harvesting to batching plant may be small or large, depending on the region.

Steel for reinforcement will have varying transportation impacts, depending on the origin of the steel and the number of steps it takes from manufacture to site delivery.

Installation — *Moderate to High*. The mixing and delivery of cement involves mechanical mixing

Concrete Floor Embodied Energy

92.9 m² (1000 ft²) floor area	Material embodied energy from I.C.E. in MJ/kg	Weight to volume ratio of material*	Volume of material in sample 1000sf/92.9m² building	Sample building embodied energy	Material embodied carbon from I.C.E. in kgCO$_2$e/kg	Sample building embodied carbon	Notes
Lowest Impact							
25 mm (1 in) skim coat	0.62 (20/25mPa with blast furnace slag at 50%)	2400 kg/m³	2.36 m³ 5664 kg	3,512 MJ	0.077	436 kg	
Highest Impact							
100 mm (4 in) slab floor	0.62 (20/25mPa with blast furnace slag at 50%)	2400 kg/m³	9.44 m³ 22,656 kg	14,047 MJ	0.077	1,745 kg	

Transportation: Concrete transportation by 35 ton truck would equate to 5.3 – 21.3 MJ per kilometer of travel to the building site. *Typically from engineeringtoolbox.com equipment, with the delivery truck typically doing the mixing as it travels to the site. Some installations require the use of pumper trucks, adding to the impacts. Finishing equipment is often gasoline-powered, further adding to impacts.

WASTE: *LOW*

Compostable — Excess concrete. Can be left in the environment if crushed into aggregate. Quantities can vary depending on the accuracy of the material take-off for ordering.

Landfill — Excess concrete. Bags from site-mixed concrete ingredients. Quantities can vary from low to high.

ENERGY EFFICIENCY

A concrete floor will have little impact on energy efficiency. When used as a slab floor on grade, an adequate amount of insulation must be used to isolate the slab from cold ground temperatures and in particular any edges of the slab that are exposed to the cold exterior. A concrete floor is very conductive, and feet in contact with concrete may feel colder than the actual temperature indicates, resulting in higher thermostat settings to maintain comfort levels.

MATERIAL COSTS: *MODERATE*
LABOR INPUT: *MODERATE*

Pouring a concrete slab is a labor-intensive activity, and includes the construction and bracing of formwork, laying of reinforcement bars and/or mesh, mixing/pouring/leveling of concrete and multiple steps of finishing.

Pouring a thin finished floor will not usually require any formwork to be constructed, eliminating one labor-intensive step.

SKILL LEVEL REQUIRED FOR THE HOMEOWNER

Preparation of sub-floor — *Moderate to Difficult.* If formwork is needed, carpentry skills will be required. An aggregate base must be laid, leveled and tamped, then a grid work of reinforcing steel laid. The perimeter of the formwork must be leveled, and all required drains, water lines and electrical conduits installed, braced and leveled.

Skim coat floors will not require as much preparation in terms of formwork, but reinforcement and floor penetrations must still be handled.

Installation of floor — *Moderate to Difficult.* The placement and leveling of wet concrete is a skill that requires some experience to master, and as the size of the pour increases so does the level of difficulty. Creating a level floor requires careful preparation and screeding and troweling skills. Finishing concrete requires an understanding of the stages of the curing process and troweling or power-troweling experience. Concrete has a limited working time due to its chemical curing process, so there is no time for mistakes or slow work.

Finishing of floor — *Easy to Difficult.* If a homeowner is intending to trowel off the finished surface, it can be difficult to achieve a smooth, even floor. Particular finishes (stamping, pigmenting, high gloss) are very difficult to achieve without prior experience. If a fairly level, fairly smooth surface is acceptable, this can be achieved with a moderate level of difficulty. If the homeowner is only applying a finish treatment to the surface of the concrete, then it is a relatively simple process that typically involves brushing or rolling a product onto the floor surface as per manufacturer's instructions.

SOURCING/AVAILABILITY: *EASY*

Concrete and concrete finishing are available in every region. Premixed concrete is ordered from a local batching plant, or ingredients can be ordered from building supply outlets or masonry supply stores. Concrete finishing is a common trade, and competitive quotes should be obtainable in most regions.

DURABILITY: *VERY HIGH*

A concrete floor can last for at least 100 years, and possibly longer.

CODE COMPLIANCE

A concrete slab must be designed and installed to meet the structural requirements of local codes, which all recognize this type of floor. If the concrete floor is only a finish, the sub-floor will have to be designed to meet the loads imposed by the concrete.

INDOOR AIR QUALITY: *HIGH*

Cured concrete is quite benign, and will have little effect on IAQ. Some products used to color and seal concrete can be extremely toxic. Acid stains will carry warnings for cancer, reproductive system damage and miscarriages for pregnant women. Sealants are often petrochemical based, and many off-gas dangerously in the short and/or long term. Using third-party certified finishes will help to ensure minimal impacts on IAQ.

FUTURE DEVELOPMENT

There is a lot of R&D work into making more environmentally friendly concrete. Currently, concrete manufacturers tout the long life span of concrete as an adequate offset for its high environmental impacts, but this is difficult to support in any balanced analysis. Before concrete becomes a sustainable choice, the high energy inputs and high greenhouse gas emissions must be addressed. While it is likely that developments in these regards will occur, for now the best argument for concrete is in its combined use as a structural floor material and a finished floor. By reducing the need for additional flooring materials, some of its impacts may be balanced. Should it become feasible to create a concrete with much lower impacts that can still serve the double functions of structure and finish, it would be a revolutionary development.

Chapter title page photo credits. Top left to right.
1. Chris Magwood 2. Chester Rennie 3. Jen Feigin
4. Chris Magwood

Concrete Floor Ratings

	Best 1	2	3	4	5	6	7	Worst 8	9	10	Notes
Environmental Impacts											Intensive manufacturing process and high carbon output.
Embodied Energy											Thickness of concrete floor has significant impacts on EE.
Waste Generated											
Energy Efficiency					N/A						
Material Costs											
Labor Inputs											
Skill Level Required by Homeowner											Degree of finish determined by skill level.
Sourcing and Availability											
Durability and Longevity											
Building Code Compliance					N/A						
Indoor Air Quality											Finishing products will have significant impact on IAQ.

7

Surface finishing materials

T HERE IS A WIDE RANGE OF SURFACES in a building that require a surface finish to protect the material and/or add an aesthetic dimension to the material. Even a small home may have thousands of square feet of surfaces that require treatment, and choices in finishes visually define the building as well as influence longevity. It is rare that one type or one color of finish is chosen for the whole home, leading to multiple finishing decisions that must all work together, both aesthetically and practically.

In many cases, the surface finish is a key element in the durability of the material it is protecting. We ask a lot of our finishes, which take the brunt of exposure to the elements, wear and tear and cleaning. Modern science has succeeded in creating finishing products that offer excellent durability, color choice and fastness, ease of application and adhesion. Unfortunately, in the pursuit of such qualities these products have become proprietary chemical soups. Even the "greenest" petrochemical finishes rely on extraction and manufacture of chemical components that have a wide variety of problematic environmental impacts. There have been excellent developments in reducing the impacts on the end user of such products, but this does not take into account impacts that happen throughout the entire chain of production.

The majority of the finishes described in this chapter fit under the heading of "natural finishes." They use naturally occurring and minimally processed ingredients that are entirely free of petrochemical products. They are viable on a wide range of surfaces and materials, and offer low impacts and low or no toxins from raw material acquisition through to final application. In some cases, the products may not offer quite the same degree of color choice and fastness, ease of application, durability and adhesion as their petrochemical counterparts; a small trade-off for vastly reduced environmental impacts. And in many cases, the natural finishes offer a beauty and richness that cannot be matched by petrochemical finishes.

The one exception to the focus on all-natural finishes is the section on nontoxic latex paints. While almost every paint company offers a low- or no-VOC version of their latex paint, this alone is not enough to warrant inclusion in this book. These paints may not emit volatile organic compounds, but they still include many dangerous substances, many of which are known carcinogens, endocrine disruptors or other health-adverse chemicals. These can include (but are not limited to): ethyl acrylate, zinc pyrithione, benzisothiazolin, triclosan, methylchloroisothiazolin, hexanoic acid, tetraethylene glycol, nepheline syenite, ethylene-vinyl acetate and an array of antimicrobials. There are a few paint companies making an attempt to create actual nontoxic latex paints, and while these are a vast improvement over petrochemical paints of the past, even they are not entirely clean and free of toxins, nor can the chain of production be guaranteed to be clean and nontoxic. However, in the hope of increasing interest in truly nontoxic latex paints, we include them as a category in this chapter. They will offer homeowners the same level of performance expected from commercial paints with greatly lowered impacts.

Building science basics for finishes

Surface finishes can alter the moisture-handling characteristics of the materials to which they are applied, and this is an important building science consideration when selecting finishes.

We often desire a finish that is "waterproof," and for good reason. If a finish can completely repel all liquid water from penetrating the material it is protecting, the life span of that material can theoretically be extended. However, a truly waterproof coating can often cause as many moisture problems as it alleviates. Moisture will inevitably penetrate building materials; even the best waterproof coating can only delay the process. Depending on the position of the material on the building, restricting the passage of water can also prevent the passage of vapor, robbing the material of the ability to dry out properly and perhaps causing moisture to accumulate in the material or in adjacent materials, causing more harm than a porous finish might suffer.

As an example, a coat of latex paint on the exterior plaster skin of a permeable natural wall system will cause moisture that would have harmlessly passed through the wall and been released to the atmosphere to be trapped in the wall, first saturating the plaster and then the material behind the plaster. Rot and mold will follow.

The most versatile coatings are those that discourage the entry of bulk water via a very tight pore structure, but that still have pores to allow vapor to pass through the finish. This ability to allow moisture to transpire is measured in "perms," and many finishes have published perm ratings. Many natural finishes do not necessarily have quantified perm ratings, but we can extrapolate from successful applications in a wide variety of climates and over long periods of time that they have a range of permeability that is suitable for long-term durability.

It is never a good strategy to rely on a finish to do a job that the material it is covering cannot do, at least to some reasonable degree, on its own. Finishes should be an enhancement, but not an integral part of, a building science strategy. Paints should not be considered a primary air or vapor control layer, and should not be relied upon to make otherwise vulnerable materials "durable."

FINISHES

Accurate data for the embodied energy of finish materials is not widely available or consistent between sources. Gross quantities of finishing materials also tend to be small, and many are mixtures of numerous materials that must each be quantified, making accurate embodied energy figures too uncertain to be valuable or meaningful — so they are not included.

Extrapolations for comparison purposes can be made by examining the harvesting and manufacturing impacts listed for each finish.

CODE COMPLIANCE AND FINISHES

Building codes will rarely prescribe finishes for residential construction, except in rare cases in which a particular finish is required by a material in order to be successfully used in a building. For this reason, code compliance is not rated for the products in this chapter.

Clay or earthen finish plaster

What the cheerleaders say...	What the detractors say...
Very low impacts	Durability issues
Widely available materials	Not suitable for wet areas
Easy to use, beginner friendly	Labor intensive
Easily repairable	Formulas too variable
Nontoxic and permeable	

Applications for system

- Finish coat for application over most interior substrates, including plaster, drywall, magnesium oxide board, brick, stone, concrete and sheet wood materials

Basic materials

- Clay
- Fine sand
- Fiber (straw, hemp or other natural fiber)
- Pigments, if desired
- Admixtures (can include flour paste, natural oil, hydrated lime, among others)
- Adhesion coat, if required

How the system works

Clay finish plasters are very similar to the clay sheathing plaster described in the previous chapter, but applied as a very thin skim coat. The thinness of the coating requires finer grades of aggregate, but the general mix ratios remain similar, with one part of clay to two to three parts of fine aggregate. Admixtures are common to add strength and abrasion resistance to the plaster.

For application over smooth, unplastered substrates, an adhesion coat is typically used to help the plaster to bond to flat surfaces. This coat is a mixture of sand and glue (natural flour paste or casein glue) that is brushed or rolled onto the wall, creating a textured surface.

Many different finishing techniques are used on clay finish plasters, from a highly polished surface to a rough trowel or skip trowel look. The choices in surface texture are almost limitless.

Most natural pigments take very well to clay plaster, giving rich colors and a sense of depth that is quite unlike painted surfaces.

Tips for successful installation

1. Ingredients for clay plasters can come from naturally occurring local soils or from manufactured bagged clay or aggregate. If you hope to work with site soil, first ascertain its condition (moisture content, rock/stone content) and the ratio of clay, silt and sand to determine whether it is appropriate. Finish coats require very fine particle sizes, and site soil mixes may require more preparation than those used for bulk coats due to the screening of larger particles.

2. Work from an established recipe for clay plaster, or prepare test samples to refine a custom mix to best meet the needs of the project. Create samples with the same surface finish intended for use.

Clay plaster mixing.

Clay plaster carving.

3. A good plastering job requires properly placed plaster stops or transition considerations at every junction. Careful masking/preparation of all edges will produce a professional appearance. Pull tape before plaster hardens to avoid uneven edges.

4. Clay plasters can develop a "cold edge" while being applied. These seams will be apparent in the finished appearance, so be sure to start and finish sections of wall that can be completed in one continuous application.

Pros and cons

ENVIRONMENTAL IMPACTS

Harvesting — *Negligible to Moderate.* Clay plasters made from soils found on or near the construction site will have minimal impacts. Bagged clay is extracted from clay pits, and impacts from the pits can include habitat destruction and silting of ground- and surface-water.

Crushed sand is typically found in every region, and extraction from aggregate pits can have impacts including habitat destruction and silting of ground- and surface-water.

Manufacturing — *Negligible to Low.* Site soils require no manufacturing process and only low impact if mixed on-site. Manufactured clays are dried and ground to fine powder, which is a low-impact process. Some bagged clays are heated to dry them, adding appreciable embodied energy.

Sand is a product of the aggregate industry, made from extracting sand and stone from quarries and, when necessary, crushing, washing and screening the sand to the desired size. This is a low-impact process.

Transportation — *Negligible to High.* Site soils will need no transportation. Bagged clay is likely to require shipping, as clay is not processed in every region. As a heavy material, clay will have significant transportation impacts if it travels long distances.

Sand can be found locally in most regions.

Installation — *Negligible.*

WASTE: *NEGLIGIBLE*

Biodegradable/Compostable — All plaster ingredients may be left in the environment. Plaster is mixed in fairly small batches, so quantities should be minimal.

Recyclable — Packaging of bagged clay. Quantities can be low to high, depending on the amount of bagged clay required.

Landfill — None.

MATERIAL COSTS: *LOW TO HIGH*

Ingredients for clay plaster are relatively low cost, but some natural pigment colors can add significantly to the cost. Manufactured products are significantly more expensive than homemade versions.

LABOR INPUT: *MODERATE TO HIGH*

Clay plasters can be labor intensive. The wall surface may need an adhesion coat, which must be mixed and applied. Clay plaster ingredients must be mixed with water in advance of application. Clay finish plaster is applied in one or two coats, as required by the desired appearance. Single-coat finishes are typically less expensive.

Health Warnings — Powdered clay and dry sand can both create a lot of dust that is high in silica content, and is dangerous to breathe. Chopped fiber can also be very dusty. Wear proper breathing protection whenever handling dusty materials.

SKILL LEVEL REQUIRED FOR THE HOMEOWNER

Preparation of wall surface — *Moderate.* Masking of edges must be done carefully, as the tapelines will translate directly to the quality of the finished appearance. The adhesion coat must be site-mixed and is brushed and/or rolled onto the wall. This step will not be required if the plaster is being applied to an existing clay plaster base or a textured, porous surface.

Application of finish — *Moderate to Difficult.* Experience with skim coat plaster is recommended, as the troweling skills and techniques for a fine finish take some practice to acquire.

Clay skim plaster can be the final finish, or a variety of paints and sealants may be applied over a clay finish plaster for added visual effect, or to provide a color change in the future.

SOURCING/AVAILABILITY: *EASY TO DIFFICULT*

All the ingredients for clay plasters are widely available. Site soils may require no off-site sourcing. Individual ingredients must be obtained from different sources. Bagged clay typically comes from pottery supply outlets, sand from a local quarry and chopped straw or other fiber from local farms or farm supply outlets. Pigments and admixtures also require separate sourcing.

There are several sources for manufactured clay finishing products, which can be bought from manufacturers or from specialty sustainable building shops.

Clay Finish Plaster Ratings

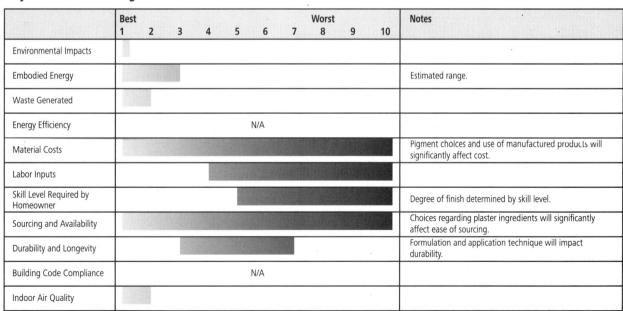

	Best 1	2	3	4	5	6	7	Worst 8	9	10	Notes
Environmental Impacts											
Embodied Energy											Estimated range.
Waste Generated											
Energy Efficiency				N/A							
Material Costs											Pigment choices and use of manufactured products will significantly affect cost.
Labor Inputs											
Skill Level Required by Homeowner											Degree of finish determined by skill level.
Sourcing and Availability											Choices regarding plaster ingredients will significantly affect ease of sourcing.
Durability and Longevity											Formulation and application technique will impact durability.
Building Code Compliance				N/A							
Indoor Air Quality											

DURABILITY: *MODERATE*

Clay plasters are very durable in any dry interior location, and should not require regular maintenance. Like other mineral-based sheathing, they are prone to denting and chipping when hit with sufficient force. Constant abrasion can be problematic if the mix does not contain adequate binder.

INDOOR AIR QUALITY: *HIGH*

Clay plasters can have a positive effect on IAQ. Limited testing shows that they are capable of taking impurities out of the air and storing or transforming them. Clay can be a source of beneficial negative ions in the home.

If a clay plaster is not properly formulated, it can be dusty and contribute problematic fine silica particulate to the air.

FUTURE DEVELOPMENT

Clay plasters offer a remarkably low-impact, high-durability and uniquely beautiful option for interior finishing. Bagged, pre-mixed versions are being developed and are just beginning to gain a foothold in the market. The beauty, simplicity and user-friendliness of clay plasters make them an ideal development in sustainable building.

Resources for further research

Guelberth, Cedar Rose. and Daniel D. Chiras. *The Natural Plaster Book: Earth, Lime and Gypsum Plasters for Natural Homes.* Gabriola Island, BC: New Society, 2003. Print.

Crews, Carole. *Clay Culture: Plasters, Paints and Preservation.* Taos, NM: Gourmet Adobe, 2009. Print.

Weismann, Adam, and Katy Bryce. *Using Natural Finishes: Lime- and Earth-Based Plasters, Renders and Paints: A Step-by-Step Guide.* Totnes, UK: Green, 2008. Print.

Lime finish plaster

What the cheerleaders say...	What the detractors say...
High durability	High embodied energy
Interior and exterior applications	Materials are corrosive to skin during application
Wide variety of aesthetic possibilities	Requires skilled application
Materials widely available	
Permeable	

Applications for system

- Finish coat for application over most interior substrates, including plaster, drywall, magnesium oxide board, brick and sheet wood materials
- Finish coat for application over plaster or masonry exterior substrates

Basic materials

- Hydrated lime (for air-curing lime plaster)
- Hydraulic lime (for hydraulic-curing lime plaster)
- Pozzolanic material (if required to create hydraulic curing of hydrated lime, including fired clay, gypsum, slag, fly ash)
- Sand
- Fibers (if required)
- Pigment (if required)

How the system works

Lime finish plasters have a long history, with centuries of development and artistry resulting in a range of recipes and application techniques.

Lime finish plasters can be made with either hydrated lime or hydraulic lime (see previous chapter) and finely graded aggregate to allow for a very thin skim coat.

For application over smooth substrates, an adhesion coat is used to help the plaster to bond to flat surfaces. This coat is typically a mixture of sand and glue (natural flour paste or casein glue) that is brushed or rolled onto the wall, creating a textured surface.

Many different finishing techniques are used on lime finish plasters, from a highly polished surface (marmorino and tadelakt, see sidebar) to a rough trowel or skip trowel look.

Tips for successful installation

1. If plastering over smooth, unplastered substrates, an adherence coat of glue and sand is required.
2. A good plastering job requires properly placed plaster stops or transition considerations at every junction. Careful masking of all edges will produce a professional appearance. Pull tape before plaster hardens to avoid uneven edges.
3. Lime plaster requires attention during the curing process. In particular, it is important with all lime-based plasters to maintain an adequate level of moisture in the curing plaster. Direct exposure to sunlight or wind can rob the plaster of moisture very quickly, resulting in poor curing and cracking. The plaster will also need regular misting for a few days to keep it properly hydrated.
4. Lime plasters can develop a "cold edge" while being applied. These seams will be apparent in the finished appearance, so be sure to start and finish sections of wall that can be completed in one application.
5. There are many excellent resources to aid with the successful mixing and application of lime plaster. Be sure to research thoroughly before application.

Pros and cons

ENVIRONMENTAL IMPACTS

Harvesting — *Moderate.* Limestone is a non-renewable but abundantly available material. It is mechanically extracted from quarries. Impacts can

Finish plaster samples.

include habitat destruction, surface and ground water interference and contamination.

Manufacturing — *High.* Limestone is mechanically crushed and heated (900–1100°C / 1650–2000°F for lime and 1400–1600°C / 2500–2900°F for cement). This is an energy-intensive process during which large amounts of fossil fuels are burned, contributing to habitat destruction and air and water pollution and carbon emissions. During the kilning process, large amounts of CO_2 are emitted (approximately 1 kg of CO_2 for every 1 kg of lime or cement). In the case of lime, it is slowly recombined with the lime through the carbonization process. Thin finish coats of lime plaster are likely to reabsorb the majority of the CO_2 as the surface area to thickness ratio is quite high.

Sand is mechanically extracted from quarries and mechanically crushed. Impacts can include habitat destruction and surface and ground water contamination.

Transportation — *Moderate to High.* Limestone is available in many regions, but is not necessarily harvested and processed in all regions. Impacts for this heavy material will vary depending on distance from the site. Natural hydraulic lime (NHL) most commonly comes from France or Portugal, carrying high transportation impacts for use in North America.

Sand is locally harvested in nearly every region, and should have minimal transportation impacts. **Installation** — *Negligible.*

WASTE: *NEGLIGIBLE*

Compostable — Lime plaster can be left in the environment or crushed to make aggregate. Hydrated lime plaster can be kept wet indefinitely and doesn't need to be disposed. Quantities should be low, as it is mixed in small batches.

Landfill — Packaging (usually paper and/or plastic bags) from lime. Quantities depend on the size of the job.

MATERIAL COSTS: *MODERATE TO HIGH*

The basic ingredients for lime plaster are moderately priced, but pigments can add significantly to costs. Manufactured products are more costly than homemade versions.

LABOR INPUT: *MODERATE TO HIGH*

Lime plaster requires significant labor input. Substrate preparation, mixing and application are all labor-intensive processes. Single-coat applications will

Tadelakt

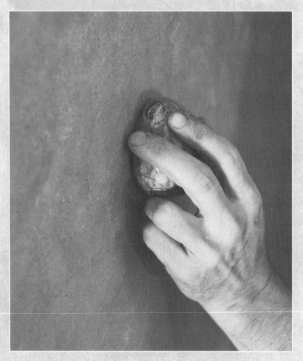

Tadelakt is a lime plastering technique that originates in Morocco. While it resembles other lime plasters in its basic materials (hydrated lime and limestone aggregate), the surface of the plaster is highly polished, first with a trowel and then with a hard stone. During the polishing process, olive oil soap is added to the surface and polished into the curing lime. The soap and the lime create calcium stearate, a naturally waterproof substance. Tadelakt is, therefore, one of the few naturally "waterproof" coatings, which makes it possible to use tadelakt plasters in showers, sinks, tubs and other high-moisture areas in a home. Though it requires some skill and practice to master the polishing technique, the reward is a beautiful, glassy surface that is stunning to look at and touch while holding up to constant direct wetting.

Resources for further research

Ochs, Michael Johannes. *Tadelakt.* New York: Norton, 2010. Print.
Weismann, Adam, and Katy Bryce. *Using Natural Finishes: Lime- and Earth-Based Plasters, Renders and Paints: A Step-by-Step Guide.* Totnes, UK: Green, 2008. Print.

typically require less labor time than multiple coats.

Health Warnings — Lime and sand are high in silica content and are dangerous to inhale. Lime is caustic when wet and can cause irritation of the skin that ranges from mildly uncomfortable to painful chemical burns.

SKILL LEVEL REQUIRED FOR THE HOMEOWNER

Preparation of substrate — *Moderate.* On smooth surfaces, an adherence coat will need to be painted or rolled. Accurate masking of all intersections is an important step with a strong influence on the final appearance.

Application of Finish — *Moderate to Difficult.* The basics of trowel application of finish coat plaster require some practice. Quality of finish will improve dramatically with experience. High-gloss finishes like marmorino or tadelakt (see sidebar) can require a fair bit of practice.

SOURCING/AVAILABILITY: *EASY TO DIFFICULT*

The materials to mix lime finish plaster are widely available from masonry supply outlets. Prepared mixes, especially those intended to create a particular kind of finish, are commercially available but may require sourcing from manufacturers or specialty plaster distributors.

DURABILITY: *HIGH*

All forms of lime plaster can have a long life span of at least 100 years, and potentially longer. Proper maintenance will have a lot of impact on durability. Repair of cracks and reapplication of protective coatings (where required) will help to maximize life span.

INDOOR AIR QUALITY: *HIGH*

Lime finish plaster should have no negative impact on IAQ. The antiseptic nature of lime can discourage

Lime Finish Plaster Ratings

	Best						Worst				Notes
	1	2	3	4	5	6	7	8	9	10	
Environmental Impacts											
Embodied Energy											Estimated range.
Waste Generated											
Energy Efficiency					N/A						
Material Costs											Pigment choices and use of manufactured products will significantly affect cost.
Labor Inputs											
Skill Level Required by Homeowner											Degree of finish determined by skill level.
Sourcing and Availability											Choices regarding plaster ingredients will significantly affect ease of sourcing.
Durability and Longevity											Formulation and application will affect durability.
Building Code Compliance					N/A						
Indoor Air Quality											

mold growth, helping to maintain good IAQ in damp areas.

The dust from mixing lime plaster and from cleanup after plastering is high in silica content and can be pervasive. Be sure to protect air ducts and other vulnerable areas during plastering and clean up to avoid contamination.

FUTURE DEVELOPMENT

The practice of harvesting and manufacturing lime plaster is thousands of years old. Modern practices are efficient and the results very consistent compared to historical ones. It is unlikely that developments in the production of lime will change much, though greater efficiency in kilns and use of waste heat may reduce embodied energy as fuel costs rise.

Lime plastering may grow in popularity as the understanding of vapor-permeable wall systems increases, but it is unlikely that lime plaster will return to its once dominant place as a very common and an artisanal finish.

Resources for further research

Guelberth, Cedar Rose, and Daniel D. Chiras. *The Natural Plaster Book: Earth, Lime and Gypsum Plasters for Natural Homes.* Gabriola Island, BC: New Society, 2003. Print.

Weismann, Adam, and Katy Bryce. *Using Natural Finishes: Lime- and Earth-Based Plasters, Renders and Paints: A Step-by-Step Guide.* Totnes, UK: Green, 2008. Print.

Milk paint

What the cheerleaders say...	What the detractors say...
Natural and abundant ingredients	Matt surface difficult to wash
Can be used on many surfaces	Requires porous surface or surface preparation
No dangerous VOCs or petrochemicals	Mixing from dry powder can give varying results
Can be homemade	Paint cannot be kept wet without spoiling
Permeable finish	

Applications for finish

- Wood (interior and exterior)
- Plaster (interior)
- Drywall (interior)

Not Suitable for:

- Floors, unless treated with oil or sealant
- Previously painted surfaces (require additional binder)
- Metal (requires additional binder)
- Plastic

Basic materials

- Casein (milk protein)
- Lime or borax
- Clay and/or calcium carbonate
- Pigment
- Microfibers (if required)
- Admixtures (if required)

How the system works

The homeowner can purchase milk paint as ready-made dry powder from a number of manufacturers, or mix it from the basic ingredients.

The effectiveness of milk paint is based on the properties of casein molecules, which contain a glue-like substance. In the presence of a base chemical like lime or borax, the casein molecule is opened and the glue (calcium caseinate) made soluble in the mixture. Powdered fillers like clay and/or calcium carbonate give the paint "body" and pigments add the color. Microfibers (such as cellulose) can add further body, and a number of natural or chemical admixtures may be added to give particular properties to the paint.

Once mixed with water, the paint requires a short amount of time (20–60 minutes) for the reaction between the casein and lime to occur. It is then applied by brush or roller, typically in two or three coats for fully opaque coverage. Additional water can be added to the mix to create a stain or wash effect. The largest use for milk paint is on furniture, where it is used to accurately replicate historic milk paint finishes and colors and where the many potential wash and antiquing effects it can create are most desired.

Milk paints are reasonable permeable, but there are no published test results or standards at this time to give an accurate indication of how permeable and in what conditions.

In areas where high wear or water exposure is expected, an oil or wax finish can be applied over the milk paint to add a further degree of protection. These coatings will reduce permeability while increasing water repellency.

Tips for successful installation

1. Measure dry ingredients and water ingredients carefully and mix thoroughly. Small variations in water quantity can affect appearance noticeably, especially with darker colors.
2. Mechanical mixing (hand blender or food processor) helps to ensure even distribution of dry ingredients and pigment. Let mixed paint sit for at least twenty minutes prior to use, to allow the calcium caseinate to form.

Milk paint rolling on clay plaster substrate.

3. Milk paint can often develop a foamy layer when mixed, and careful brushing may be required to eliminate bubbles from the finished surface.
4. There can be noticeable differences in color between batches of milk paint. Use a "continuous mixing" process in which one batch is used until it is half finished, and then half of the next batch is added to the remaining half of the previous batch. This will help to ensure that there are no dramatic shifts in color in one area.
5. Once mixed with water, milk paint can spoil, especially in hot weather. Unused paint will last 7–10 days if kept refrigerated.

Pros and cons

Environmental impacts

Harvesting — *Moderate.* Cow's milk is the raw ingredient for casein production. Harvesting techniques vary greatly, but dairy farming can have impacts that include habitat destruction, methane release from cows and potential water contamination from manure.

Milk paint on wood fascia.

Lime is quarried from pits, with attendant habitat destruction and potential surface and groundwater contamination.

Clay and pigments are harvested from surface pits with relatively low impacts.

Manufacturing — *Moderate to High.* Casein is extracted from raw milk through a multi-stage process that includes pasteurization (requiring heat), filtering, incubation, decanting, drying (requiring heat) and crushing. There are several useful by-products created during this process, mitigating the energy inputs.

Lime is crushed and heated to very high temperatures with significant carbon emissions and air pollution.

Transportation — *Moderate to High.* The ingredients for milk paint will have been assembled from different points of manufacture. Casein production for commercial use is based in Eastern Europe.
Installation — *Negligible.*

WASTE: *LOW TO MODERATE*

Compostable — Leftover milk paint can be added to a compost pile or sent down the drain.
Recyclable — Paint containers.

MATERIAL COSTS: *MODERATE TO HIGH*

Raw ingredients for homemade milk paint are moderately priced, with some pigments adding significant costs. Manufactured versions are more costly.

LABOR INPUT: *MODERATE*

Milk paint must be mixed with water prior to applying, and allowed to sit for at least twenty minutes before use. This adds a small amount of additional labor time. Otherwise, the application process is the same as any type of paint.

If a natural oil will be used to protect the milk paint, this will add another step, taking the same length of time as another coat to apply.

Health Warnings — Powdered milk paint contains silica dust, and breathing protection should be worn while handling dry powder. The lime content of the paint makes it mildly caustic to skin; wearing gloves and eye protection is recommended.

SKILL LEVEL REQUIRED FOR THE HOMEOWNER

Preparation of substrate — *Easy.* Porous substrates require no preparation. Painted surfaces may require a coat of acrylic binder or an amount of acrylic binder added to the milk paint.
Application of finish — *Easy to Moderate.* Brush and/or roller application. Careful brushing may be required to avoid bubbles on the surface.

SOURCING/AVAILABILITY: *EASY TO MODERATE*

The raw ingredients to mix milk paint are widely available. While casein powder may be difficult to locate in small quantities, skim milk powder can be used in its place to make milk paint. Lime, calcium carbonate and some types of pigment are available at masonry supply stores. Artist supply stores will have more types of pigment and are more likely to carry natural pigment if desired.

Several companies in North America manufacture high-quality milk paint with consistent coloration and formulation. Some have distribution through paint and green building supply stores; all will ship directly to homeowners.

DURABILITY: *LOW TO MODERATE*

Milk paint was very widely used in the pre-petrochemical age. It takes around 30 days to fully cure, and in this time is vulnerable to water. Once dry to the touch, milk paint will not be removed easily with water, but may show spotting within the first month if splashed.

Milk paint has the qualities of both stain and paint. On porous surfaces, it will soak into the substrate and bond with the material to provide protection and pigmentation. The more coats that are added, the more the paint acts like a coating, offering additional protection but also becoming vulnerable to cracking and peeling over time.

Used indoors in relatively dry areas, milk paint has a lifetime from 15 to 50 years. It is possible to add additional coats of milk paint over time.

Used outdoors, milk paint will help to protect wood and will remain quite colorfast for about ten years. Over time, it will fade and wear. Many old barns were treated with milk paint, and it's possible to see the faded colors on those that haven't been treated with modern paints.

Milk Paint Ratings

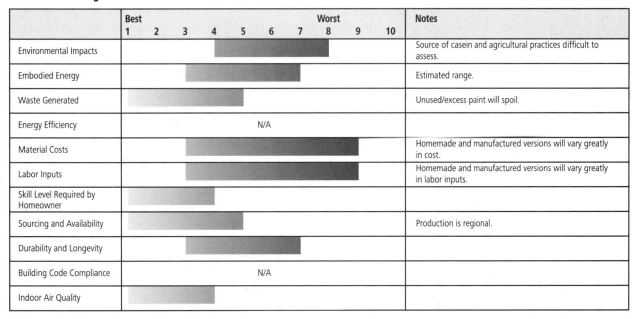

	Best 1	2	3	4	5	6	Worst 7	8	9	10	Notes
Environmental Impacts											Source of casein and agricultural practices difficult to assess.
Embodied Energy											Estimated range.
Waste Generated											Unused/excess paint will spoil.
Energy Efficiency					N/A						
Material Costs											Homemade and manufactured versions will vary greatly in cost.
Labor Inputs											Homemade and manufactured versions will vary greatly in labor inputs.
Skill Level Required by Homeowner											
Sourcing and Availability											Production is regional.
Durability and Longevity											
Building Code Compliance					N/A						
Indoor Air Quality											

It is possible to extend the life span and water-resistance of milk paints by treating them with natural oil (see section below).

INDOOR AIR QUALITY: *HIGH*

Milk paint will have no adverse effect on IAQ.

FUTURE DEVELOPMENT

Milk paint formulas have been used for centuries. Modern processing of casein and lime can result in much more consistent products. It is possible that advances in natural chemistry may result in improvements in milk paint.

Consumer demand for nontoxic finishes seems to be increasing, and milk paint could certainly fill some of that demand. Users need to be willing to commit to the additional step of mixing the dry ingredients with water to get the beneficial trade-off of a beautiful, nontoxic finish.

Resources for further research

Weismann, Adam, and Katy Bryce. *Using Natural Finishes: Lime- and Earth-Based Plasters, Renders and Paints: A Step-by-Step Guide.* Totnes, UK: Green, 2008. Print.

Edwards, Lynn, and Julia Lawless. *The Natural Paint Book: A Complete Guide to Natural Paints, Recipes, and Finishes.* Emmaus, PA: Rodale, 2002. Print.

Clay paint and alise

What the cheerleaders say...	What the detractors say...
Natural, nontoxic, abundant	Durability issues
Vapor permeable	Color consistency difficult to achieve
Beautiful, many aesthetic possibilities	Can be dusty and affect indoor air quality
Infinitely repairable	
Easy to use	

Applications for finish

- Interior wall and ceiling
- Porous surfaces

Not suitable for use on:

- Exterior surfaces
- Floors
- Metal or plastic

Basic materials

- Clay
- Aggregate (including sand, silica, mica, calcium carbonate)
- Pigment
- Binder (including flour paste and casein)
- Fibers (if required)

How the system works

Clay paints are as old as human civilization, as they can be made with materials that occur naturally in most regions. Complementary mineral ingredients have been combined in ways that have lasted tens of thousands of years in the form of cave paintings.

Ingredients can be proportioned and mixed by the homeowner/applicator, or pre-manufactured mixtures can be purchased and mixed with water. Small variations in the mix can have noticeable impacts on the resulting finish, allowing for a wide range of aesthetic possibilities.

Clay paint and alise do not undergo a chemical change when mixed and applied to the wall. If a binder is used, it is typically a water-soluble binder that does not change the chemistry of the paint. The mixture is applied by brush, roller, sponge and/or trowel, depending on the consistency and the desired appearance of the finish. Once applied, the mixture dries and hardens, but is susceptible to damage if wetted.

Clay paint and alise allow a wide range of finishes. Variation in the type, size and quantity of aggregate produce finishes from grainy, heavily textured surfaces to polished, glass-like ones; the finer the aggregate, the smoother the texture. Qualities of the aggregate can become part of the finish, with colored or sparkling sands able to show through the surface. Application techniques such as rubbing, sponging and trowel burnishing will lend the finish different appearances.

Tips for successful installation

1. The range of potential mixtures for making a successful clay paint or alise is extremely wide. This allows for many possible finishes, but also opens the door to mixes that are less than ideal. If mixing your own clay paint, experimentation will lead to feasible recipes and application techniques.
2. While clay paints can be durable and very colorfast, they are not appropriate in wet areas where they can soften and erode.
3. Finish techniques that result in shinier, denser surfaces will be more durable in areas of high wear.
4. Clay paints require a porous substrate, and cannot be successfully applied over glossy, non-porous surfaces.
5. Clay paints invite a sense of play and adventurousness. While it is possible to mix and apply them in a manner that gives very even,

consistent results akin to more conventional paints, the beauty of the material is in its variation, whether subtle or intentional.

Pros and cons
ENVIRONMENTAL IMPACTS
Harvesting — *Negligible to Moderate.* Clay, aggregate and other ingredients can be obtained from local soils and sources, making these paints a potentially no-impact finish. If clay, aggregate and other ingredients are purchased commercially, they will have been dug or quarried, with impacts that may include habitat destruction and ground and surface water disruption or contamination.
Manufacturing — *Negligible to Low.* Commercial ingredients will have been minimally processed. None of the common materials in clay paint require heat input or chemical processes.
Transportation — *Negligible to High.* Clay and aggregate are heavy materials, and may need to travel long distances.
Installation — *Negligible.*

WASTE: *NEGLIGIBLE*
Compostable — All ingredients.
Recyclable — Containers for ingredients.

MATERIAL COSTS: *LOW*
LABOR INPUT: *LOW TO HIGH*

The wide variety of preparations and application techniques make for widely varying amounts of labor input. At the simplest, the ingredients can be mixed together with water and immediately applied with a brush or roller, comparable to commercial paint. Other mixes and techniques can take substantially longer, involving multiple steps, coats and burnishing.

Health Warnings — Clay, sand and pigment are all high in silica dust. Breathing protection should be worn when working with dry ingredients.

SKILL LEVEL REQUIRED FOR THE HOMEOWNER

Preparation of substrate — *Easy.* On porous surfaces, no preparation may be needed. In some cases, a base of natural glue and aggregate may be desirable.

Application of finish — *Easy to Moderate.* A simple clay paint can be applied with the same skill level and technique required to apply conventional paint. More elaborate applications require practice and/or a willingness to experiment.

SOURCING/AVAILABILITY: *EASY TO DIFFICULT*

Feasible clay paint can be made from site- or locally-harvested materials. Bagged clay can be obtained from pottery supply outlets. Different types and grades of aggregate and pigment can be found at pottery supply outlets and masonry supply stores. Pigments can be obtained from artist supply shops.

DURABILITY: *LOW TO MODERATE*

Clay paints are stable and UV resistant, and can last for hundreds of years. They are prone to softening and erosion in very humid conditions or when exposed to moderate quantities of liquid water.

Polished, burnished surfaces will wear better than rough, porous ones where the paint will be exposed to a lot of contact.

INDOOR AIR QUALITY: *HIGH*

Clay paints should not have a negative impact on IAQ. Some testing shows that clay paint may have properties that helps to improve indoor air.

Some clays, pigments and aggregates can be contaminated with radon and other radioactive elements, heavy metals and other earth-bound elements. Know the source of all ingredients and research to ensure they are clean.

Clay Paint Ratings

	Best 1	2	3	4	5	6	7	Worst 8	9	10	Notes
Environmental Impacts											
Embodied Energy											Estimated range.
Waste Generated											
Energy Efficiency					N/A						
Material Costs											
Labor Inputs											
Skill Level Required by Homeowner											
Sourcing and Availability											Choices regarding paint ingredients will significantly affect ease of sourcing.
Durability and Longevity											Formulation and application will affect durability.
Building Code Compliance					N/A						
Indoor Air Quality											

A number of commercially made clay paints have come to market in the past decade, and these formulations are consistent, durable and easy to apply. Improvements in natural chemistry may help the number of products and their effectiveness to continue to improve.

Consumer demand for nontoxic finishes may help clay paints achieve a larger share of the market.

Clay paints create custom finishes, and for owners looking to make a uniquely beautiful home, they offer many possibilities that may make them more popular.

Resources for further research

Weismann, Adam, and Katy Bryce. *Using Natural Finishes: Lime- and Earth-Based Plasters, Renders and Paints: A Step-by-Step Guide.* Totnes, UK: Green, 2008. Print.

Edwards, Lynn, and Julia Lawless. *The Natural Paint Book: A Complete Guide to Natural Paints, Recipes, and Finishes.* Emmaus, PA: Rodale, 2002. Print.

Crews, Carole. *Clay Culture: Plasters, Paints and Preservation.* Taos, NM: Gourmet Adobe, 2009. Print.

Lime wash and lime paint

What the cheerleaders say...	What the detractors say...
Natural and abundant material	Can be dusty
Antiseptic qualities	Durability issues
Vapor permeable	Caustic material when wet
Beautiful, many aesthetic possibilities	Limited color palette
Infinitely repairable	

Lime paint.

Applications for finish

- Interior walls and ceilings
- Exterior walls
- Porous surfaces

Not suitable for use on:

- Floors
- Non-porous surfaces

Basic materials

- Hydrated or hydraulic lime
- Aggregate
- Binder (usually casein)
- Pigment
- Fiber (if required)

How the system works

Lime wash and paint are based on the ability of powdered, fired limestone to be mixed with water, applied to a surface and then chemically re-carbonize into a durable material that resembles the original stone. Both are vapor permeable and highly UV resistant, and will not soften or erode when exposed to water. The lime will reach its working strength in thirty days, and continue to strengthen over time. Multiple coats require curing time between applications of at least 24 hours, to allow time for carbonization to begin. For thicker coats, longer curing time between coats is recommended.

Lime Wash. In a lime wash, the only materials are lime and water (and pigment, if desired). The materials are mixed to a paint-like consistency and applied to the porous substrate, usually with a special heavy-bristle whitewash brush. Anything from one thin coat to multiple heavy coats may be applied, depending on the desired opacity of the finish and the degree of protection desired for the substrate. A lime wash gives a bright white finish unless pigmented.

Lime Paint. Lime paint can include a wide variety of combinations of aggregate, binder and fiber along with the lime, water and pigment. Some binders work chemically to bring desired properties to the paint (pozzolanic reactions, chemical binding), others help give the paint a desired consistency and body. Binders can add a degree of water repellency not found in a straight whitewash, and may add a reasonable amount of protection for the substrate material. The addition of casein to lime paint creates the calcium caseinate found in milk paint. There is a blurry line where casein-lime paint stops and milk paint starts.

The addition of aggregate and/or fiber in the mix gives lime paint enough body to create thicker coats than is possible with lime wash. Lime paint can fully cover a substrate, filling small cracks and pores and surface irregularities that would show through lime wash.

Untinted lime paint will be white, but the brightness will be affected by the type and quantity of aggregate.

Tips for successful installation

1. The high pH of lime will affect the coloration of most pigments, tending to make them lighter in tone. Be sure to experiment with pigments and allow the wash or paint to cure for at least 24 hours to see what the finished color will look like.
2. While highly resistant to degradation from wetting, lime wash offers little resistance to water penetration, while some lime paint formulations can be very water repellent. Be sure to match the desired level of water protection with the appropriate mixture.
3. Lime wash and paint will tend to have a matte finish and slightly rough texture, unless admixtures are used to give a smoother, shinier surface.
4. Lime finishes will often be different in appearance on wood surfaces than on plaster or other masonry.

Pros and cons

ENVIRONMENTAL IMPACTS

Harvesting — *Moderate to High.* Limestone is a non-renewable but abundantly available material. It is mechanically extracted from quarries. Impacts can include habitat destruction, surface and ground water interference and contamination.

Manufacturing — *High.* Limestone is mechanically crushed and heated (900–1100°C / 1650–2000°F). This is an energy-intensive process during which large amounts of fossil fuels are burned, contributing to habitat destruction and air and water pollution and carbon emissions.

Transportation — *Moderate to High.* Limestone is available in many regions, but is not necessarily harvested and processed in all regions. Impacts for this heavy material will vary depending on distance from the site. Natural hydraulic lime (NHL) most commonly comes from France or Portugal, carrying high transportation impacts for use in North America. **Installation** — *Negligible.*

WASTE: *NEGLIGIBLE*

Compostable — Lime wash and paint can be placed in compost. Straight lime mixes are very basic, and may change the pH of compost or soil.
Recyclable — Bags for lime.

MATERIAL COSTS: *LOW*

LABOR INPUT: *MODERATE*

The mixing process may be very straightforward or require multiple steps. Application time will be similar to conventional paint.

Health Warnings — Lime and aggregate have high silica content. Breathing protection should be worn when working with powdered materials. Wet lime is caustic to skin, and gloves and eye protection should be worn.

SKILL LEVEL REQUIRED FOR THE HOMEOWNER

Preparation of substrate — *Easy.* No preparation is required for suitable substrates.
Application of finish — *Easy to Moderate.* Brush or roller application.

SOURCING/AVAILABILITY: *EASY TO DIFFICULT*

Ingredients are widely available from masonry supply stores. Pigment may be found at artist supply outlets. Casein, if used, must be sought from industrial suppliers or skim milk powder may be used.

Commercial lime paint mixes are available from sustainable building supply stores or directly from manufacturers.

Lime Wash and Paint Ratings

	Best (1–5)	Worst (6–10)	Notes
Environmental Impacts	3–6		
Embodied Energy	5–6		Estimated range.
Waste Generated	1		
Energy Efficiency	N/A		
Material Costs	3–6		Pigment choices and use of manufactured products will significantly affect cost.
Labor Inputs	3–6		
Skill Level Required by Homeowner	1–5		
Sourcing and Availability	1–9		Choices regarding paint ingredients will significantly affect ease of sourcing.
Durability and Longevity	2–6		Formulation and application will have significant impacts.
Building Code Compliance	N/A		
Indoor Air Quality	1–2		

DURABILITY: *MODERATE*

Lime paints are very durable, as they form a mineral coating that is not prone to deterioration from moisture or sunlight. However, as lime coatings don't typically provide much protection from water penetration, the main cause of deterioration is from water damage to the substrate behind the lime finish. Expansion, contraction and freeze/thaw issues can cause the lime finish to spall and flake in very wet locations, depending on the vulnerability of the substrate to water.

Lime coatings can be reapplied indefinitely. If re-coating a flaking lime coating, sand or brush away any loose lime before reapplying.

INDOOR AIR QUALITY: *HIGH*

Lime paints will have no negative impact on IAQ. However, if the finish is very dusty on the surface it will be a source of fine silica dust in the home. If an interior lime finish is dusting, recoat or apply a sealant.

The basic nature of lime makes it antiseptic and unlikely to support mold or mildew growth.

FUTURE DEVELOPMENT

Lime finishes have been used for thousands of years, and the basic recipes have not changed much over time. Modern manufacturing processes have made lime more consistent in quality and properties.

Natural chemistry may provide new formulations of lime-based paints that will retain the positive qualities and increase adhesion and water repellency. The desire for nontoxic finishes may result in a wider demand for lime-based paints.

Resources for further research

Weismann, Adam, and Katy Bryce. *Using Natural Finishes: Lime- and Earth-Based Plasters, Renders and Paints: A Step-by-Step Guide.* Totnes, UK: Green, 2008. Print.

Edwards, Lynn, and Julia Lawless. *The Natural Paint Book: A Complete Guide to Natural Paints, Recipes, and Finishes.* Emmaus, PA: Rodale, 2002. Print.

Silicate paint

What the cheerleaders say...	What the detractors say...
Ideal moisture handling properties	Only works on mineral surfaces
Durable and colorfast	Not widely available
Simple to apply	
Wide range of colors available, including clear coat	

Applications for finish

- Interior and exterior mineral surfaces (clay, lime, cement, gypsum)

Not suitable for use on:

- Floors
- Wood
- Metal

Basic materials

- Sodium silicate or potassium silicate
- Water
- Alkaline-resistant pigment

How the system works

Silicate paints are also known as water glass, silicate dispersion paint, silicate mineral paint or silicate emulsion paint.

Sodium and potassium silicate are water soluble, and when dispersed onto a mineral surface such as clay, lime or cement plaster will bind with silicates in the substrate, petrifying into a micro-crystalline structure. These tiny pores are ideal for repelling liquid water but do not restrict the passage of vapor, giving this paint the ideal balance of moisture-handling properties. Exterior surfaces are protected against the entry of rain but allow migrating humidity to leave the wall. Interior surfaces are washable, so the paint can be used in kitchens and bathrooms.

Application of silicate paint is usually a two-step process, with a primer/binder going on as a first coat and the paint as a second and, if necessary, third coat.

Tips for successful installation

1. Silicate paints are proprietary products. Follow the manufacturer's instructions for successful application.
2. Silicate paint will reduce the carbonization that occurs in lime plasters. Avoid painting for at least thirty days after applying the plaster.

Pros and cons

ENVIRONMENTAL IMPACTS

Harvesting — *Moderate.* Sodium silicate is made by combining silica and sodium hydroxide.

Industrial silica comes from quartz deposits. Quartz, the second most common mineral on the planet, is an abundant, non-renewable resource. Silica sand deposits are most commonly surface-mined in open-pit operations, but dredging and underground mining are also common methods of extraction. Impacts include habitat destruction and water contamination.

Sodium hydroxide (also known as lye), derived from sodium chloride (brine, or salt water), is a common compound used in everything from food to drain cleaner. Impacts are relatively low.

Manufacturing — *Moderate to High.* Quartz ore undergoes considerable processing to increase the silica content by reducing impurities. It is then dried and sized to produce the optimum particle size distribution for the intended application. Impacts include air and water pollution and greenhouse gas emissions.

The manufacture of sodium hydroxide from sodium chloride requires high energy input, with chlorine gas a by-product. Impacts include air and water pollution and greenhouse gas emissions.

Silicate Paint Ratings

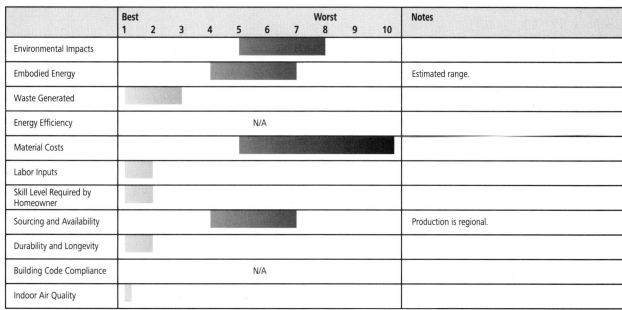

	Best 1	2	3	4	5	6	7	Worst 8	9	10	Notes
Environmental Impacts					▓	▓	▓				
Embodied Energy				▓	▓	▓					Estimated range.
Waste Generated	▓										
Energy Efficiency					N/A						
Material Costs				▓	▓	▓	▓	▓			
Labor Inputs	▓										
Skill Level Required by Homeowner	▓										
Sourcing and Availability				▓	▓	▓					Production is regional.
Durability and Longevity	▓										
Building Code Compliance					N/A						
Indoor Air Quality	▓										

Transportation — *Low to High.* Silicate paint is not widely manufactured, and is shipped as a heavy liquid. It may incur significant transportation impacts depending on distance traveled.
Installation — *Negligible.*

WASTE: *NEGLIGIBLE*

Compostable/Biodegradable — Silicate paint can be put in compost or on the ground.
Recyclable — Paint containers.

MATERIAL COSTS: *HIGH*

These manufactured products are produced on a limited scale and tend to be priced higher than other commercially available paints.

LABOR INPUT: *LOW*

Silicate paint is comparable to other paint types, and can be applied by brush and/or roller.
   Health Warnings — None.

SKILL LEVEL REQUIRED FOR THE HOMEOWNER

Preparation of substrate — *Easy.* In most cases, a silicate primer coat is required.
Application of finish — *Easy.* Brushing or rolling.

SOURCING/AVAILABILITY: *MODERATE*

There are only a few manufacturers of silicate paints in North America, and their products are not typically available through paint stores or building supply outlets. Silicate paints can be ordered directly from the manufacturer or through specialty retailers.

DURABILITY: *HIGH*

Silicate paint mineralizes on the substrate, forming a chemical bond that is very different from film-type coatings. These paints become part of the substrate and do not flake or crack, providing a very long-lasting finish. Inorganic pigments resist fading due to UV exposure. Additional coats may be added directly over old paint.

INDOOR AIR QUALITY: *HIGH*

Silicate paint will have no negative effect on IAQ. There are no toxins and no off-gassing from these paints. They are anti-bacterial due to their alkaline nature.

FUTURE DEVELOPMENT

Silicate paint is gaining a foothold in the market for the refurbishment of older concrete, brick and stone structures. As its popularity and availability increases, its benefits may be applied to new construction as well. These paints are widely recognized in the natural building world as an ideal coating for walls that have integral plaster skins with no rainscreen, as they provide a lot of protection from rain without restricting vapor permeability.

Acrylic (latex) paint

What the cheerleaders say...	What the detractors say...
Durable	Typically contains dangerous chemicals
Washable	Impermeable, can cause moisture issues
Predictable performance	Cleanup contaminates water/soil
Wide color range	Manufacturing process creates pollution
Widely available	

Applications for finish

• Interior and exterior surfaces

Not suitable for use on:

• Surfaces requiring vapor permeability

Basic materials

• Water
• Binder (a blend of acrylic, vinyl and/or polyvinyl acetate)
• Filler (including calcium carbonate, clay, barite and/or cellulose)
• Additives (proprietary recipes protect many additives from being named)
• Pigment (titanium dioxide in most paints, other pigments and dyes as required by color formulation)

How the system works

While "latex" is the common name for water-based acrylic paints, naturally derived latex (a milky substance found in certain flowering plants) is not used in the vast majority of household paint. The binder portions of the paint tend to be blends (dispersions) of acrylic (polymethyl methacrylate or PMMA), styrene-acrylic, vinyl and polyvinyl acetate (PVA), with different proportions of those three ingredients based on the paint's intended use and cost. Fillers, which are inert bulking agents, are used to create a desired viscosity and texture. Pigment almost always includes titanium dioxide to create a white base, and natural or synthetic pigments or dyes to achieve the intended color.

There are different formulations of acrylic paint to suit particular applications. The higher the quality and durability of the paint, the higher the percentage of acrylic. Cheaper, less durable paints have more vinyl and polyvinyl acetate.

Due to a generally high level of environmental impacts and toxicity, this category of finishes would not be included in this book if not for the concerted efforts of a small number of acrylic paint manufacturers making serious attempts to reduce the toxic content of their products and clean up the manufacturing process. A sustainable builder should not consider using acrylic paint unless it is sourced from manufacturers with the highest verifiable standards.

Tips for successful installation

Acrylic paints are proprietary products. Follow the manufacturer's instructions for successful application.

Pros and cons

ENVIRONMENTAL IMPACTS

Harvesting and Manufacturing — *High.* Accurately assessing the environmental impacts of acrylic paint is difficult. A large number of elements go into any particular paint formulation, and it is beyond the scope of this book to trace each element from harvesting through manufacturing for such a wide product category.

The US Environmental Protection Agency states "Paint and coating manufacturing operations can produce hazardous air pollutants, including heavy metals. Mixing and cleaning operations can release some toxic air pollutants and volatile organic compounds (VOC). Chemicals in these substances can react in the air to form ground-level ozone (smog), which has been linked to a number of respiratory effects. Pigment grinding and milling emits particle pollution (dust), which can contain heavy metals and other toxic air pollutants."

Each stage in the harvesting and production of individual elements of an acrylic paint can have wide-ranging impacts, in particular air and water pollution. While North American regulations have stiffened in the past decade, the industries involved in providing materials for acrylic paint manufacturing and the paint manufacturers themselves are responsible for a wide array of toxic emissions that have serious environmental impacts.

A concerted focus has been placed on reducing the quantity of volatile organic compounds (VOCs) in the final paint product, but high volumes of VOCs are still emitted during production. At each stage of harvesting and production, air and water pollution may be created through off-gassing, cleaning and creation of by-products.

The recent trend toward low- or no-VOC acrylic paint is encouraging, but VOCs are not the only toxins in these paints. Even in "eco-friendly" paints, other dangerous compounds include, but are not limited to, ethyl acrylate, zinc pyrithione, benzisothiazolin, hexanoic acid, tetraethylene glycol, acticide, triclosan, nepheline syenite, methylchloroisothiazolinone and vanadium pentoxide.

It is incumbent upon homeowners making an attempt to purchase acrylic paints with the smallest environmental impacts to do thorough research and distinguish between the claims of manufacturers that are greenwashing and those that are making real efforts to minimize impacts.

Transportation — *Low to High.* Check manufacturer proximity to job site and distribution network to ascertain impacts.

Installation — *Moderate to High.* Although acrylic paints are water-soluble, cleanup from application will have environmental impacts. Wash water sent to municipal wastewater facilities or septic systems can contaminate large volumes of water, requiring significant cleaning efforts or resulting in the dispersion of chemicals into the environment. In some municipalities, discharging paint-contaminated water into the sewage system is illegal, and in others it is encouraged as an alternative to dumping in storm sewers or the ground. In either case, contamination is likely to end up in the environment.

WASTE: *HIGH*

Hazardous Waste — All empty containers and used brushes, rollers and cleanup water should be taken to a hazardous waste recovery site.

MATERIAL COSTS: *MODERATE TO HIGH*

LABOR INPUT: *LOW*

Most acrylic paint requires a two-coat application, with application labor similar to other brushed or rolled coatings.

Health Warnings — No-VOC paints greatly reduce health effects for applicators. See manufacturer labels and MSDS sheets for specific product information.

SKILL LEVEL REQUIRED FOR THE HOMEOWNER

Preparation of substrate — *Easy.* None typically required.

Application of finish — *Easy.* Brushed and/or rolled application.

SOURCING/AVAILABILITY: *EASY*

Acrylic paints are widely available from paint specialty shops and building supply outlets. Nontoxic acrylics are not widely available, and may be sourced directly from the manufacturer or from sustainable building supply outlets.

DURABILITY: *HIGH*

Formulations for acrylic paints make them the industry standard against which other finishes are compared. Life span can be 15 to 40 years. Additional coats can be applied.

INDOOR AIR QUALITY: *LOW TO HIGH*

Any quantity of VOCs in acrylic paint will have a negative effect on IAQ, and for this reason only no-VOC paints should be chosen. Be aware that even a no-VOC designation does not mean there are absolutely no VOCs being released in the home. VOCs are not the only compounds that may off-gas from acrylic paint, and it is in the area of these potential air contaminants that the new breed of acrylic paints will have varying impacts depending on manufacturer. A homeowner concerned about IAQ will need to carefully research each brand of paint to determine what toxins may be in it and what risk of air contamination from those toxins may exist.

Nontoxic acrylic paint

While most paint manufacturers now offer a no-VOC (volatile organic compounds) formulation, this alone does not guarantee that a paint is not toxic. There are currently only a few companies that make paints comparable to conventional "latex" paints without using any toxic chemicals.

AFM Safecoat, Mythic and Yolo all offer paints that are free from reproductive toxins, mutagens, hazardous air pollutants, ozone-depleting compounds, formaldehyde and phthalates. These paints are not yet as widely available as their still-toxic counterparts, but the cost and application quality are comparable. They are well worth seeking out if you are committed to making a healthy building.

Nontoxic Acrylic Paint Ratings

	Best						Worst				Notes
	1	2	3	4	5	6	7	8	9	10	
Environmental Impacts							███████				
Embodied Energy								████			Estimated range.
Waste Generated							██████				
Energy Efficiency						N/A					
Material Costs						████████████					
Labor Inputs	██										
Skill Level Required by Homeowner	██										
Sourcing and Availability	███										
Durability and Longevity	████										
Building Code Compliance						N/A					
Indoor Air Quality	████████████████████										Nontoxic acrylics should not affect IAQ, but ingredients should be carefully researched.

FUTURE DEVELOPMENT

Acrylic paints and manufacturing processes have been improved quite dramatically in the past decade, and efforts continue to be made by some manufacturers to work toward ever-cleaner paints. The result may eventually be acrylic paints that contain no harmful chemicals and are safely biodegradable, but it is equally possible that dangerous content can be minimized but never fully eliminated. Natural chemistry may provide solutions that are new formulations of existing sustainable finishes. This is an area in which the near future is likely to see a significant amount of change.

Resources for further research

Pharos Project database, see pharosproject.net

Fact sheets on reducing air pollution from paint and coating manufacturing issued by the US Environmental Protection Agency, see epa.gov/oaqps001/community/details/paint_manuf.html#4

Natural oil paint

What the cheerleaders say...	What the detractors say...
Renewable materials	Can be slow-drying
Durable, flexible	Expensive
Colorfast	Can have high VOC output
Simple application	
Can be nontoxic	

Applications for finish

- Wood
- Porous surfaces (including plaster)

Not suitable for use on:

- Metal
- Previously painted surfaces
- Surfaces requiring high vapor permeability

Basic materials

- Natural, siccative (oxidizing) oil (typically cold-pressed linseed, but can be semi-siccative oil like walnut, hemp, poppy, tung, sunflower, safflower, soya and even fish oil)
- Solvent thinner (typically citrus thinner or natural alcohol)
- Pigment
- Admixtures, as required (may include pine resin, drying agents and polymerizing compounds)

How the system works

The household paints that are commonly referred to as "oil paints" are actually alkyd paints. Drying alkyd resins are a type of polyester that is modified with fatty acids. The polyester base is derived from polyols (typically based on glycerin, sucrose, ethylene glycol or pentaerythritol) and dicarboxylic acid or carboxylic acid anhydride.

Natural oil paints are those in which the resin is natural oil. While many oils are suitable for creating paint, linseed oil (pressed from flax seed) is by far the most common. Natural oils are extremely slow to dry (some never dry completely) and require a solvent to dry sufficiently for use as paint. Natural turpentine and citrus solvent are the two most common drying agents for natural oil paint. Solvent content in oil paint can be very high, and even natural solvents contain volatile organic compounds (VOCs) that can have ill effects on health. Synthetic solvents tend to have worse health impacts, but proper ventilation is a necessity and those with chemical sensitivities should be sure that natural solvents are not a trigger.

During the drying process for oil paints (though dry to the touch in a matter of days, full drying can take months), the oil undergoes a natural polymerization. In recent years, advances in polymerizing natural oils have resulted in oil paints that dry faster and harder without requiring as much solvent. Some of these processes are natural, while others are chemical.

Pigments must be oil-soluble in order to work in this type of paint, which can limit the available color palette.

Tips for successful installation

1. Ensure that drying time for natural oil paint does not interfere with construction schedule. Some paints may require 2–7 days to dry, and while wet will trap airborne dust and be vulnerable to water and direct contact. Commercially produced natural oil paints tend to have shorter drying times.
2. Natural oil paints are often stickier than other coatings, and may require attention to detail to eliminate brush marks and overlap marks.
3. Manufactured natural oil paints are proprietary products. Follow the manufacturer's instructions for successful application.

Pros and cons
ENVIRONMENTAL IMPACTS
Harvesting — *Low to Moderate.* Natural oils are pressed from seeds. Seed crops are grown in a wide variety of manners all over the world, from small-scale organic to factory farms. Some oil-bearing seed crops (flax and hemp, in particular) also bear useful fibers in their stems, resulting in a harvest with very little waste. Impacts will vary greatly, and can include habitat destruction, pesticide and herbicide runoff and soil depletion.

The two most common types of natural solvents are turpentine and citrus solvent. Turpentine is distilled from pine resin, with relatively low impacts from harvesting. Products called citrus thinners can have a range of ingredients, from pure citrus oil (extracted from lemon, orange and/or grapefruit rind) to blends of citrus oil and mineral oil and herbal essential oils. Citrus growing can have significant impacts, including high pesticide, fungicide and herbicide use. However, the fruit rind is a secondary product of citrus farming, and its use helps to reduce waste.

Manufacturing — *Low.* Cold-pressing of seed oils is a low-energy and low-impact mechanical process.

The distillation of turpentine and extraction of citrus oil are both low-energy, low-impact processes. Most manufacturers now recapture emitted VOCs, which are the most detrimental impact.

Transportation — *Low to High.* Check manufacturer proximity to job site and distribution network to ascertain impacts.

Installation — *Low to Moderate.* Cleanup from oil painting requires the use of additional solvent to remove paint from brushes and rollers. Significant volumes of used solvent can be highly impactful if sent down drains or spread on the soil.

WASTE: *HIGH*

Biodegradable/Compostable — Natural oil paints

are made with all-natural ingredients, but they are not well suited to biodegradation at a household level. The oils will remain sticky and persistent for a very long time, creating problems in compost piles or in the soil.

Recyclable — Paint containers.

Hazardous Waste — Oil paint that cannot otherwise be used should be sent to a hazardous waste facility.

MATERIAL COSTS: *MODERATE TO HIGH*

A variety of price points are available from a range of manufacturers.

LABOR INPUT: *LOW*

Natural oil paints are similar in application time to conventional paints, with two coats normally required.

Health Warnings — Natural solvents are not non-toxic. Turpentine, in particular, can be dangerous

to work with. Citrus solvent is much preferable to turpentine, but read the product label for handling instructions.

SKILL LEVEL REQUIRED FOR THE HOMEOWNER

Preparation of substrate — *Easy.* No preparation required.

Application of finish — *Easy to Moderate.* Conventional brush and/or roller application is used. Thick paint may take additional care to achieve a high degree of finish.

SOURCING/AVAILABILITY: *MODERATE*

All the ingredients for natural oil paint are available from artist supply outlets. Bulk quantities of natural, cold-pressed oils may require specialty sourcing.

Commercial oil paints are produced and can be obtained from specialty sustainable building suppliers.

Natural Oil Paint Ratings

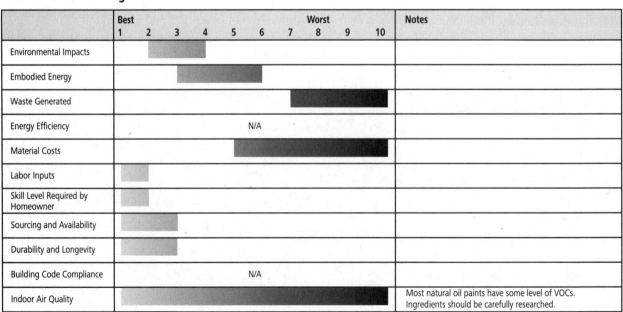

	Best 1	2	3	4	5	6	7	Worst 8	9	10	Notes
Environmental Impacts											
Embodied Energy											
Waste Generated											
Energy Efficiency					N/A						
Material Costs											
Labor Inputs											
Skill Level Required by Homeowner											
Sourcing and Availability											
Durability and Longevity											
Building Code Compliance					N/A						
Indoor Air Quality											Most natural oil paints have some level of VOCs. Ingredients should be carefully researched.

DURABILITY: *HIGH*

Natural oil paints create a very flexible coating, able to expand and contract with the substrate material. This makes them ideal for coating plaster and drywall, and they provide a durable finish for interior and exterior wood. They are water repellent and can be washed. They are easier to scratch than chemical-based paints, and will not retain a high degree of gloss if touched or rubbed. This does not affect life span, only appearance.

INDOOR AIR QUALITY: *LOW TO HIGH*

Some natural oil paints may have a negative impact on IAQ. Paints using turpentine or chemical solvent should be avoided, as these will emit high quantities of VOCs over a long period of time. Paints using citrus solvents will also emit VOCs, though there is evidence that these emissions are not as dangerous to human health. The chemically sensitive should research reactivity to citrus oil before using these paints.

Natural oils themselves also emit VOCs. Each oil type is different in this regard, and reactivity to various types of oil should be researched. Some people find the fragrance of natural oil paints to be pleasing, while others find it distracting or distressing. All paint manufacturers will disclose their VOC content, with some paints qualifying as no-VOC.

FUTURE DEVELOPMENT

Natural oil paints have been used for thousands of years, only losing their place in the market in the past half century, and they have been seeing a slow but growing resurgence in recent years. Advances in the availability of citrus-based solvents and oil production and polymerization have created a new breed of oil paints that avoid many of the drawbacks of traditional versions. Advances in natural chemistry may further improve on the qualities of these paints, and consumer demand for environmentally friendly coatings may increase the market share for natural oil paint.

Resources for further research

Weismann, Adam, and Katy Bryce. *Using Natural Finishes: Lime- and Earth-Based Plasters, Renders and Paints: A Step-by-Step Guide.* Totnes, UK: Green, 2008. Print.

Edwards, Lynn, and Julia Lawless. *The Natural Paint Book: A Complete Guide to Natural Paints, Recipes, and Finishes.* Emmaus, PA: Rodale, 2002. Print.

Safecoat AFM Naturals, see afmsafecoat.com/products.php?page =4

Allbäck linseed oil paints, see linoljeprodukter.se/eng

Natural oils and waxes

What the cheerleaders say...	What the detractors say...
Renewable materials	Slow-drying
Durable, flexible	Expensive
Colorfast	Limited color range
Can be nontoxic	Can have high VOC output

Applications for finish

- Raw wood, plaster, concrete
- Walls, floors, countertops, windowsills, furniture

Not suitable for use on:

- Drywall
- Metal

Basic materials

- Natural, siccative (oxidizing) oil (typically cold-pressed linseed, but can be semi-siccative oil like walnut, hemp, poppy, tung, sunflower, safflower, soya and even fish oil)
- Solvent thinner (typically citrus thinner or natural alcohol)
- Admixtures, as required (may include pine resin, drying agents and polymerizing compounds)
- Beeswax, carnauba or other natural wax

How the system works

Natural oil finishes are very similar to natural oil paints (see page 310), but do not contain pigments or bulking agents to add opaqueness to the finish. They are typically a clear coat used to enhance the natural color of the substrate, or are lightly tinted to accent the substrate color.

Oils for finishes may be pure oil or a blend of oils and waxes formulated to provide desired characteristics. There are many such blends, and their intended use should be researched before committing to use of a particular blend.

Some oil finishes are referred to as "hard oils." This refers to a lack of solvents or thinners in the mix, and not necessarily to a more solid or durable surface.

Raw oils used on surfaces will take a very long time to dry, and if applied too thickly may never completely harden. Most oils are blended for best drying characteristics, or are polymerized during production to speed curing times.

Oils are sometimes blended with waxes in a single product, but more often wax is applied to an oiled surface. In both cases, wax helps provide water repellency, shine and flexibility to the finish. There are many types of natural waxes, but the majority of commercially available waxes are either blends of natural wax and petrochemical wax, or fully petrochemical.

Tips for successful installation

1. Natural oils and waxes are formulated for many specific uses. Species of wood or [other type of substrate], interior or exterior use, degree of surface glossiness and tint are among the differences between products. Be sure to choose an appropriate finish for the desired result.
2. The decision to use a wax finish should be made carefully. While waxes can add luster and durability to a surface, the addition of wax makes it very difficult to change the finish in the future, as the wax will repel any new coating (except more wax). Wax finishes require maintenance to keep them buffed and lustrous.
3. Many natural oils and waxes are proprietary products. Follow the manufacturer's instructions for successful application.

Pros and cons

ENVIRONMENTAL IMPACTS

Harvesting — *Low to Moderate.* Natural oils are pressed from seeds. Seed crops are grown in a wide variety of manners all over the world, from small-scale organic to factory farms. Some oil-bearing seed crops (flax and hemp, in particular) also bear useful fibers in their stems, resulting in a harvest with very little waste. Impacts will vary greatly, and can include habitat destruction, pesticide and herbicide runoff and soil depletion.

Natural wax harvesting, whether from bees or from plants, is a relatively low-impact process. Beehives and wax-bearing plants are not typically destroyed in harvesting, as they can continuously regenerate wax.

The two most common types of natural solvents are turpentine and citrus solvent. Turpentine is distilled from pine resin, with relatively low impacts from harvesting. Products called citrus thinners can have a range of ingredients, from pure citrus oil (extracted from lemon, orange and/or grapefruit rind) to blends of citrus oil, mineral oil and herbal essential oils. Citrus growing can have significant impacts, including high pesticide, fungicide and herbicide use. However, the fruit rind is a secondary product of citrus farming, and its use helps to reduce waste.

Manufacturing — *Low.* Cold-pressing of seed oils is a low-energy and low-impact mechanical process.

Natural wax manufacturing involves the use of very low amounts of heat input and is otherwise a very low-impact process.

The distillation of turpentine and extraction of citrus oil are both low-energy, low-impact processes. Most manufacturers now recapture emitted VOCs, which are the most detrimental impact.

Transportation — *Low to High.* Oil-bearing crops grow in almost every region, but centralized production may mean that oils have traveled long distances. Beeswax is produced in many places around the world, and wax may be imported from regions with low wages. Carnauba wax is harvested only in Brazil.

Natural oil floor treatment.

Installation — *Negligible.* Oily rags from application or cleanup can be combustible and must be treated with care to prevent fire.

WASTE: *NEGLIGIBLE*

Biodegradable/Compostable — Natural oil finishes are made with all-natural ingredients, but they are not well suited to biodegradation at a household level. The oils will remain sticky and persistent for a very long time, creating problems in compost piles or in the soil.

Recyclable — Containers.

Hazardous Waste — Oil finishes that cannot otherwise be used should be sent to a hazardous waste facility.

MATERIAL COSTS: *LOW TO HIGH*

A wide range of products are manufactured at different price points.

LABOR INPUT: *LOW TO HIGH*

Application procedures and number of required coats will vary by product. Typically, application labor will be similar to painting. Wax applications require application and an intensive buffing process.

Health Warnings — Solvents in some oil finishes can be toxic. Read labels carefully for warnings.

SKILL LEVEL REQUIRED FOR THE HOMEOWNER

Mixing of finish — *Easy to Moderate.* A simple oil finish may require no mixing. More complicated formulations may require heating and special blending techniques.

Preparation of substrate — *Easy.*

Application of finish — *Easy to Moderate.* Oils are typically brushed onto a surface and then wiped back with a lint-free cloth to avoid pooling. Anywhere from one to three coats is common. Wax

is typically applied with a lint-free cloth and then buffed or polished after some curing time.

SOURCING/AVAILABILITY: *MODERATE*

The individual ingredients for oil and wax finishes are reasonably easy to acquire, though they may require individual sourcing.

Commercial oil finishing products are widely available through building supply stores and furniture finishing specialty shops. All-natural formulations may be more difficult to source from manufacturers or sustainable building supply outlets.

DURABILITY: *MODERATE*

Natural oil finishes create very flexible coatings that can expand and contract with the substrate material. This makes them ideal for coating wood, and they provide a very durable finish for both interior and exterior wood. They are water repellent and can

Natural Oils and Waxes Ratings

	Best 1	2	3	4	5	6	7	Worst 8	9	10	Notes
Environmental Impacts											
Embodied Energy											Estimated range.
Waste Generated											
Energy Efficiency				N/A							
Material Costs											Wide range of products covers full range of price points.
Labor Inputs											Products vary greatly. Multiple coats and buffing will add significantly to labor input.
Skill Level Required by Homeowner											
Sourcing and Availability											
Durability and Longevity											
Building Code Compliance				N/A							
Indoor Air Quality											Ingredients should be carefully researched.

be washed. They are easier to scratch than chemical-based paints, and will not retain a high degree of gloss if touched or rubbed. This does not affect life span, only appearance.

Natural oils do not resist UV light very well, and the substrate material (especially wood) can deteriorate and cause the finish to fail.

Wax is very water resistant, and can keep substrate materials well protected. Wax finishes have a low melting temperature, and can deteriorate in direct sunlight.

Additional coats of oil or wax can be applied to surfaces to maintain protection.

INDOOR AIR QUALITY: *LOW TO HIGH*

Natural oil finishes may have a negative impact on IAQ. Those using turpentine or chemical solvents should be avoided, as these will emit high quantities of VOCs over a long period of time. Finishes using citrus solvents will also emit VOCs, though there is evidence that these emissions are not as dangerous to human health. The chemically sensitive should research reactivity to citrus oil before using these paints.

Natural oils themselves also emit VOCs. Each oil type is different in this regard, and reactivity to various types of oil should be researched. Some people find the fragrance of natural oil paints to be pleasing, while others find it distracting or distressing.

FUTURE DEVELOPMENT

Natural oil finishes have been used for thousands of years, especially on wood, and only lost their place in the market in the past half century. There has been a slow but growing resurgence of these finishes in recent years. Advances in the availability of citrus-based solvents and oil production and polymerization have created a new breed of oil paints that don't have many of the drawbacks of traditional versions. Advances in natural chemistry may further improve on the qualities of these finishes, and consumer demand for environmentally friendly coatings and the natural beauty of oiled wood may increase the market share.

Resources for further research

Weismann, Adam, and Katy Bryce. *Using Natural Finishes: Lime- and Earth-Based Plasters, Renders and Paints: A Step-by-Step Guide.* Totnes, UK: Green, 2008. Print.

Edwards, Lynn, and Julia Lawless. *The Natural Paint Book: A Complete Guide to Natural Paints, Recipes, and Finishes.* Emmaus, PA: Rodale, 2002. Print.

Safecoat AFM Naturals, see afmsafecoat.com/products.php?page=4

Natural wallpaper and wall covering

What the cheerleaders say...	What the detractors say...
Nontoxic, renewable resources	Glues may be toxic or grow mold
Wide variety of aesthetic possibilities	Difficult to remodel
Vapor permeable	Labor-intensive to install
Easy to install	

Applications for finish

- Interior wall covering
- Interior ceilings

Not suitable for use on:

- Exterior walls

Basic materials

- Coated and/or embossed paper
- Woven grasses or fibers
- Stitching, if required (nylon, cotton, polyester)
- Adhesive to attach to wall

How the system works

Decorative papers are printed and/or embossed. Grass or fiber wall coverings are woven and/or stitched. Both are made in rolls and applied to the substrate using an adhesive. Rolls are made in regular widths and are applied side by side to cover a desired area.

Many conventional wallpapers and coverings are made or surface-treated with polyvinylchloride (PVC), acrylic, polyurethane and toxic inks, and are adhered to walls with adhesives that are high in VOCs, fungicides, fire-retardants and other toxic ingredients.

In order to be considered a sustainable finish, the products must not contain any dangerous substances. There are many manufacturers whose wall coverings meet sustainable criteria, but many more that do not. Homeowners must research thoroughly to ensure that products meet all expectations.

Tips for successful installation

1. Wall coverings and adhesives are proprietary products. Follow the manufacturer's instructions for successful installation.
2. Wall coverings can be difficult to remove and the process may damage the substrate so it needs repair or replacement.

Pros and cons

ENVIRONMENTAL IMPACTS

Harvesting — *Low to Moderate.* All-natural wall coverings are made with renewable materials. Harvesting techniques can range from environmentally benign to highly impactful. Chose products with third-party certification to help ensure minimal impacts. Recycled paper products reduce the burden on forests. The forestry industry can have impacts that include habitat destruction, soil erosion and water pollution. The harvesting of jute, hemp, bamboo and other fiber materials is centered in developing countries where it can be difficult to discern harvesting techniques or working conditions. Some third-party certification programs exist for these materials, but homeowners may need to research individual company claims.

Manufacturing — *Low to Moderate.* Sustainable wall coverings are typically manufactured in a highly mechanized manner but without high heat or chemical input. Homeowners must research to ensure that this is the case, and that no petrochemical additives are added to coverings or adhesives.

Transportation — *Low to High.* Check manufacturer proximity to job site and distribution network to ascertain impacts.

Installation — *Negligible.*

WASTE: *HIGH*

Biodegadable/Compostable — Wallpaper and woven wall coverings. Ensure that inks and dyes are suitable for biodegradation.

Recyclable — Wallpaper. Containers for adhesive.

Landfill — Stitched wall coverings with synthetic stitching material.

MATERIAL COSTS: *MODERATE TO HIGH*

A wide range of products are manufactured at different price points. Natural wallpapers tend toward the higher end of the cost scale.

LABOR INPUT: *HIGH*

Applying wall coverings is a labor-intensive finish. Rolled material must be measured, cut and test-fitted before applying adhesive and hanging material.

Health Warnings — Check for warnings on adhesive containers.

SKILL LEVEL REQUIRED FOR THE HOMEOWNER

Preparation of substrate — *Easy.* Some adhesives require a two-part process, with adhesive applied to the wall and to the roll of wall covering.

Application of finish — *Moderate to Difficult.* Wall covering requires accurate measuring and cutting, and often involves lining up patterns on adjacent sheets to minimize the appearance of seams. The adhesive has a limited working time, requiring sheets to be hung relatively quickly and accurately. Coverings need to be applied in a way that avoids bubbling or crinkling. Particular care must be taken if the wall covering wraps around an inside or outside corner.

SOURCING/AVAILABILITY: *MODERATE*

While conventional wall coverings are widely available at building supply outlets and paint/wallpaper stores, those made with sustainable materials and using nontoxic adhesives may require sourcing

Natural Wallpaper Ratings

	Best 1 2 3 4 5 6 7	Worst 8 9 10	Notes
Environmental Impacts	▓ (4–7)		Forestry and manufacturing practices will have a significant impact.
Embodied Energy	▓ (4–8)		Estimated range.
Waste Generated	▓ (6–7)		
Energy Efficiency	N/A		
Material Costs	▓ (5–7)		
Labor Inputs	▓ (6–7)		
Skill Level Required by Homeowner	▓ (5–7)		
Sourcing and Availability	▓ (4–5)		Production is limited.
Durability and Longevity	▓ (4–5)		
Building Code Compliance	N/A		
Indoor Air Quality	▓ (4–7)		Glues and paper ingredients will affect IAQ and should be researched.

directly from the manufacturer or specialty sustainable building stores.

DURABILITY: *MODERATE*

The durability of wall coverings is largely dependent on the quality of the adhesive and the bond it forms with the substrate and the covering. Installation quality will also impact durability. The coverings themselves range in durability, but will typically last 15 to 50 years. High levels of moisture can shorten the life span by encouraging deterioration of natural fibers (and possibly encouraging mold growth) and weakening adhesives.

INDOOR AIR QUALITY: *LOW TO MODERATE*

A natural wall covering with a nontoxic adhesive should have no negative effect on IAQ. Many wall coverings are treated with fire retardants that are highly toxic, and should be avoided completely. Biocides and fungicides are sometimes added to wall coverings and adhesives to prevent mold growth, and these too should be avoided.

FUTURE DEVELOPMENT

Natural wall coverings are beginning to gain market share. The unique textures, colors and patterns available with these materials are difficult to achieve with other finishes. The development of nontoxic adhesives and the move toward recycled paper content and third-party certification programs for wood and fiber products will make it easier for homeowners to make sustainable choices.

8

Windows

THE MOST ENERGY-EFFICIENT AND INEXPENSIVE HOUSE TO BUILD would be a box with a single door and no windows. Windows are the weak link in the thermal performance of any building, as even the most expensive units are many times less thermally efficient than a regularly insulated wall. Windows are usually the main source of air leakage, both in the window unit and in the sealing details around the window. Window openings are often the places where water leaks into the enclosure as well.

Of course, we wouldn't dream of having a home with no windows. For all the compromises they force on a building, the natural light, views, ventilation and connection to the outdoors are priceless.

There aren't the same kinds of widely varying options available to homeowners when it comes to windows as there are for other elements of the home. All windows operate on the same principle and differ only in a few important areas.

Frame material — Retailers and consumers tend to differentiate windows mainly by the material out of which the frame and casings are made, see table below.

Frame Material Ratings

1 – Worst 3 – Best

	Fiberglass	Wood	Wood with aluminum casing	Vinyl	Aluminum
Durability	3	1	2–3	2	3
UV resistance	3	1	3	2	3
Dimensional stability	3	2	2	1	1
Thermal properties	3	3	3	2	0
Embodied energy	2	3	2	1	1
Manufacturing impacts	1	2 (3 with third-party certified wood)	2	1	1
Maintenance	3	1	3	3	3
Cost	1–2 (varies by manufacturer)	2–3	2	3	2
Availability	1–3 (varies by region)	3	3	3	3
IAQ	3	3 (depending on paint/finish type)	3 (depending on paint/finish type	1 (PVC off-gassing, especially in UV)	3

Operational style — Fixed, casement, awning, hopper, slider, single hung, double hung, tilt-and-turn or dual action

Window units can be ordered that have combinations of the different operational styles. Units can be side-by-side and/or vertically stacked to achieve a desired mix of ventilation and performance.

Glazing layers — Single-pane windows are not accepted by codes for new construction. Double,

triple and quadruple glazing layers are available, with cost, energy efficiency and weight increasing with each additional layer. Some triple- and quadruple-pane units use a clear plastic sheet as one of the central panes to reduce weight and increase thermal performance.

Glazing coatings — The term "Low-E" glass indicates that a low-emissivity coating has been applied to the glazing. The metallic coating reflects a percentage of the long-wave heat radiation striking the glass, helping to improve energy efficiency. There are actually two kinds of Low-E coating:

Operational Style Ratings
1 – Worst 3 – Best

	Seal/energy efficiency	Ventilation properties	Cleanability	Cost
Fixed	3	0	1	3
Casement	3	3	3	2
Awning	3	2	1	2
Hopper	3	2	1	2
Slider	1	1–2	2	3
Single hung	1	1	2	3
Double hung	1	1–2	3	2
Tilt-and-turn or dual action	3	3	3	1

Hard-coat Low-E glass is made by pouring a very thin layer of molten tin over the glass while it is still slightly molten. The liquid tin welds to the molten glass, creating a coating that is very strong and scratch resistant. It has an R-value equivalent of 2.75.

Soft-coat Low-E glass has tin, silver or zinc applied to it in a vacuum chamber filled with an electrically charged inert gas. Atoms of the coating metal are sputtered on the surface of the glass. This coating is not very scratch resistant, and is always applied to an inward-facing pane. It has an R-value equivalent of 4.35.

Window units can be ordered with different coatings on different faces of the glazing, depending on whether they need to resist heat gain from the outside or heat loss from the inside.

The addition of Low-E coatings reduces the amount of light transmitted through the glass. For this reason, it is often omitted on windows where maximum solar gain is desired.

Exterior and interior arched window. (Jen Feigin)

Spacer material — The spacers that separate the panes of glazing around the edges of the unit can be made from aluminum or from a variety of rubber or foam compounds. The more conductive the spacer material, the lower the thermal performance. Good "warm edge" spacers make a substantial difference in performance.

Gas fill — The space between glazing panes can be filled with an inert gas, either argon or krypton. These gasses are less conductive than air and help to minimize heat loss.

Thermally broken frame — Very efficient windows have "thermally-broken" frames, ensuring that there is no part of the window unit that is continuous from the interior side to the exterior. The separation is usually made with rigid foam insulation.

Exterior trim — A wide variety of exterior trim components can be attached to windows to suit different window depths, trim details, siding types and aesthetics.

Interior trim — Windows can be ordered with drywall return slots or wooden jamb extensions built in. These can speed up the finishing and trimming of the window opening.

WINDOW LABELING

The Energy Star program provides a standardized window labeling program in the US and Canada, giving buyers key information for comparison between brands and models.

U-factor is the thermal resistance of the window. The lower the number, the better the thermal performance.

Solar heat gain coefficient is the amount of warming solar radiation that will make it through the glazing. The higher the number, the more solar heat will penetrate into the building.

Visible transmittance is the amount of the visible light spectrum that penetrates the window into the building. The higher the number, the more natural light.

Air leakage is tested by depressurizing the area behind the window to see how much air will infiltrate the unit. The smaller the number, the better the thermal performance.

Canadian windows will give these figures in metric measurements, and US windows in imperial. Be sure to convert if comparing between units from the different countries.

Choosing the best possible windows is a critical step in making an energy-efficient building. While it is not quite true to say that the more expensive the window the better its performance, it is true that high-performance windows will not be the cheapest option.

Consider glazing decisions at the design phase of the building, and discuss options with the window

Triple pane, two section window.

Solar Light Tubes

Bringing light into a building from the side walls is not the only strategy to provide adequate daylighting. While roof-mounted glazing in the form of skylights has been an option for many decades, the inherent energy-efficiency flaws of too much solar gain in the summer and too much heat loss in the winter makes skylights a poor choice in many conditions.

Solar light tubes use a roof-mounted dome and reflector plates to gather unobstructed sunlight and send those rays of light down a highly reflective tube and into a room below. The amount of light available through a solar light tube is impressive, equaling that of a relatively large wall-mounted window. As the light entering the tube is often available all day, light levels in the room aren't dependent on the time of day.

Light tubes can run impressively long distances, able to direct light into a room as many as three stories below the roof, and with up to 90 degrees of cumulative bends in the tube.

A lens on the ceiling mount prevents air leakage from the heated space into the tube, and the sealed dome at the top keeps cold air out, making light tubes much more energy efficient than skylights.

This type of day lighting is a great option for an energy-conscious homeowner.

manufacturer. Good window design considers the type and placement of Low-E coatings, solar heat gain coefficient, visible transmittance, energy performance and ventilation requirements. A "one size/type fits every opening" approach is never the most efficient option.

Resources for further research

Consumer's Guide to Buying Energy-efficient Windows and Doors. Ottawa, ON: Office of Energy Efficiency, 2004. Print.

Fisette, Paul. "Understanding Energy Efficient Windows." *Fine Homebuilding* 114 (1998): 68–73. Print.

The Efficient Windows Collaborative, see efficientwindows. org/index.php

NFRC

National Fenestration Rating Council ®

CERTIFIED

World's Best Window Co.

Millennium 2000+

Vinyl-Clad Wood Frame
Double Glazing • Argon Fill • Low E
Product Type: **Vertical Slider**

ENERGY PERFORMANCE RATINGS

U-Factor (U.S./I-P)	Solar Heat Gain Coefficient
0.30	**0.30**

ADDITIONAL PERFORMANCE RATINGS

Visible Transmittance	Air Leakage (U.S./I-P)
0.51	**0.2**

Manufacturer stipulates that these ratings conform to applicable NFRC procedures for determining whole product performance. NFRC ratings are determined for a fixed set of environmental conditions and a specific product size. NFRC does not recommend any product and does not warrant the suitability of any product for any specific use. Consult manufacturer's literature for other product performance information. www.nfrc.org

Mechanical systems

THE MODERN HOME is as much about its mechanical systems as its structure. Electrical generation and distribution, water collection and distribution, wastewater removal and treatment, heating, cooling and ventilation are all key components of any residential construction project. Though in many cases these systems are well hidden, their functionality is what makes a modern home so comfortable.

These systems are also what cost homeowners and the planet so dearly. The ongoing financial and environmental costs of keeping every home serviced in the manner to which we've become accustomed is not sustainable, and the choices we make today about mechanical systems in buildings will have a huge influence on our collective sustainability and resilience in the future.

The life cycle analysis of buildings shows that the "operating energy" used to make our mechanical systems function is by far the largest contributor to a building's energy footprint. Beyond measures of energy, our mechanical systems dictate our impact on water resources, air pollution and greenhouse gas emissions.

There are many points along the line between our current energy-intensive practices and the no-energy option of eliminating all mechanical systems. The following chapters are intended to give an overview of the options that exist and their potential for reducing impacts while maintaining comfort.

Resources for further research

Wing, Charles. *How Your House Works: A Visual Guide to Understanding and Maintaining Your Home.* Kingston, MA: RS Means, 2007. Print.

 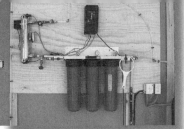  

9

Water systems

For most of human history, we have spent a huge amount of our time collecting, moving and storing water, mostly with manual labor. There are still many places in the world where turning a tap to receive an endless supply of potable water is not the norm. And there is good reason that we should no longer consider water to be the cheap, disposable resource we've come to expect at every faucet.

Water issues are complex. In the simplest terms, we tend to consider the source, quality and quantity of water that comes out of taps and faucets in the home. These are obviously very important issues, and there are significant concerns on all three counts that help to direct more sustainable choices.

What we rarely consider are the high energy costs that accompany water. Figures for the province of Ontario, Canada, for instance, show that "water and wastewater services together represent a third to a half of a municipality's total electricity consumption," and that "municipalities, largely responsible for the provision of water in Ontario, have been reported to consume more electricity than any industrial sector outside Pulp and Paper."[1] This does not take into account the energy used for private residential and commercial wells or industrial water pumping. Conserving water, when seen in this light, is about more than reducing the use of a valuable natural resource — it is also inherently about energy conservation.

In combination, these issues make smart thinking about water systems a must for anybody interested in more sustainable building, as the dividends for lowering water use are double. The good news is that there is still a lot of "low hanging fruit" available, making significant water savings relatively easy.

Water systems are highly regulated in our building industry. Sources of water are subject to many levels of government jurisdiction that will regulate how, when and where water is extracted. All components of a drinking water system must meet the requirements of codes. In some regions, a drinking water system may need to be designed by a licensed professional, with each component specified and inspected.

What follows is an overview of available options when it comes to water systems. All are feasible, but not all are prescribed by building codes. They may be combined in different ways to meet specific situations, according to need, climate, personal preference and local regulations.

Water sources

Water systems begin with a source of water that can be accessed for use in the home. There are really only four options for sourcing water; depending on your location you may be lucky enough to be able to choose from more than one, but often there are only one or two feasible possibilities.

Individual vs. municipal supply

All water sources may be used for a single-family residence, a neighbourhood or an entire region. If your home is located in an area that is serviced by a municipal water system you may not have any choice regarding the source of the water. Some municipalities will not allow private water systems to be used within their boundaries, so be sure to check local codes before pursuing any alternative to the municipal supply.

Note

Greenhouse Gas and Energy Co-Benefits of Water Conservation, by Carol Mass, POLIS Research Report 09-01, March 2009

Resources for further research

Ingram, Colin. *The Drinking Water Book: How to Eliminate Harmful Toxins from Your Water.* Berkeley, CA: Celestial Arts, 2006. Print.

Lewis, Scott. *The Sierra Club Guide to Safe Drinking Water.* San Francisco: Sierra Club, 1996. Print.

Stauffer, Julie. *Safe to Drink? The Quality of Your Water.* Machynlleth, Powys, UK: Centre for Alternative Technology Publications, 1996. Print.

Kuhuna Kupua Aó, Lono. *Don't Drink the Water Without Reading This Book: The Essential Guide to Our Contaminated Drinking Water and What You Can Do About It.* Pagosa Spring, CO: Kali, 1996. Print.

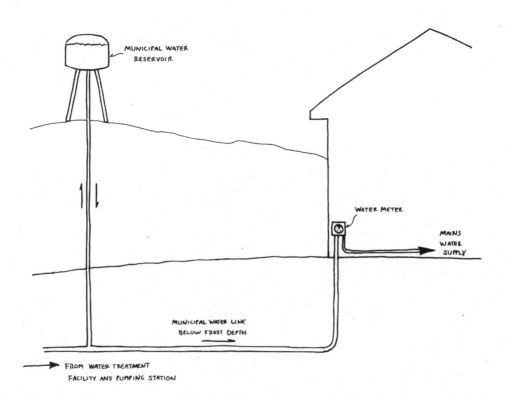

MUNICIPAL WATER RESERVOIR

WATER METER

MAINS WATER SUPPLY

MUNICIPAL WATER LINE BELOW FROST DEPTH

FROM WATER TREATMENT FACILITY AND PUMPING STATION

Surface water

What the cheerleaders say...	What the detractors say...
Abundant in many locations	Sources often contaminated
Minimal invasiveness for access	Extensive treatment may be required
Water levels easy to monitor	
Low-energy pumping	

System components

- Foot valve and screened intake
- Tubing, buried to avoid freezing where applicable
- Land-based or submersible pump
- Pressure tank, if required
- Filtration as required

How the system works

Water is drawn directly from a lake, river, stream or pond. This system is used for individual residences and entire municipalities.

Water is drawn from the source as required, using the natural capacity of the water body as a storage medium.

WATER QUALITY ISSUES

Surface water is vulnerable to a wide range of natural and human contamination, and will almost certainly need extensive treatment in order to be potable.

Assessing water quality can be difficult, as the water will vary greatly in quality depending on season, weather events, human influence and natural cycles and issues. Before choosing to use a surface water source, determine the origin of the water body and find out what kinds of activities happen upstream from your intake, in particular industries, sewage treatment facilities and major highways, any of which can introduce contaminants. If the water body is subject to seasonal flooding and/or drought, this will also affect quality by introducing new contaminants or concentrating existing contaminants.

Surface water should be tested regularly, as levels and types of contamination will change.

PUMP OPTIONS

Submersible, jet, diaphragm and hand pumps can all work with the low heads that are typical with surface

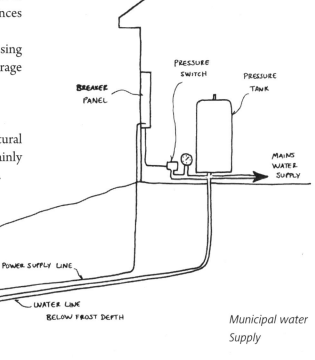

Municipal water Supply

water collection. Certain rivers and streams may be suitable for the installations of a ram pump.

Tips for successful installation

1. Choose an inlet point that is not too close to the bottom or the top surface of the water body, where contaminants tend to be more concentrated. Keep the inlet in a position where plant growth will not interfere with intake.
2. Attach the inlet securely so it is not dislodged by fast-moving water or human or animal activity.
3. In regions with freezing conditions, the inlet must be below the expected depth of ice coverage, and must be routed to the house in a way that will prevent exposure to freezing.
4. Be sure that the installation does not interfere with existing fish or animal habitat.

Pros and cons

ENVIRONMENTAL IMPACTS: *LOW TO HIGH.*

Residential use of surface water does not typically have negative impacts on surface water sources. Large municipal systems can draw quantities significant enough to change overall water levels in some surface sources and create changes to ecosystems.

MATERIAL COSTS: *LOW TO MODERATE*

Systems rarely require deep digging, but distance from water source will affect cost. Low heads require less expensive pumping options.

LABOR INPUT: *LOW TO MODERATE*

Surface water systems are relatively easy to set up. In cold climates, water lines will need to be dug below the frost line.

SKILL LEVEL REQUIRED FOR THE HOMEOWNER

Use — *Easy.* Once installed, most surface water systems operate automatically. Proper inlet positioning should ensure a supply of water as long as levels remain within expected norms.

Maintenance — *Easy to Moderate.* Inlets should be inspected and cleaned on an annual basis at minimum. Pumps have a finite life span and will eventually need replacing. Pumps positioned and plumbed for easy access and removal will greatly reduce labor time when issues arise.

SOURCING/AVAILABILITY: *EASY*

Surface water collection systems are common, and components and installation professionals will be easy to access.

FUTURE DEVELOPMENT

Long established as a viable water source, the components of a surface water system have been well developed and are unlikely to change dramatically.

RESILIENCE

Surface water sources are susceptible to climate change, which can raise or lower water levels. Changes are likely to happen at a pace that will not catch the owner of a surface water system by surprise, but may require adaptation.

It is possible to operate a surface water system with little or no energy using hand- or bicycle-powered pumps.

Resources for further research

Burns, Max. *Country and Cottage Water Systems: A Complete Out-of-the-City Guide to On-Site Water and Sewage Systems including Pumps, Plumbing, Water Purification and Alternative Toilets.* Toronto, ON: Cottage Life, 2010. Print.

Hyde, Nicholas. *Harvesting H2O: A Prepper's Guide to the Collection, Treatment, and Storage of Drinking Water While Living off the Grid.* N.p.: CreateSpace Independent, 2012. Print.

Well water

What the cheerleaders say...	What the detractors say...
Accessible by many	Uncertainty regarding source
Less prone to surface contamination	Expensive
Water may not need treatment	Difficult to monitor water level

System components

- Well casing (concrete for shallow wells, metal for deep wells)
- Submersible pump
- Tubing, buried to avoid freezing where needed
- Pressure tank
- Filtration as required

How the system works

There are two types of wells, but both operate on the same principle. An underground aquifer is accessed by digging or drilling an intake point into an area with sufficient flow to provide the required quantity of water.

Dug Wells — These wells tend to be shallow, from 3–12 meters (10–40 feet). A hole is excavated (by hand or machine) and the sides shored up and retained by sidewalls. Water in the ground collects inside the well and is pumped or lifted from this reservoir.

Drilled Wells — Used to access deep aquifers from 12–120 meters (40–400 feet), these wells are mechanically drilled (through any type of soil or rock) until sufficient water has been reached. A metal well pipe is then fitted into the hole and water from the aquifer fills some portion of this pipe. A submersible pump is lowered into the pipe and sits in the water.

WATER QUALITY ISSUES

Drilled wells may supply potable water with no need for treatment. Deeper wells tend to have fewer issues with bacterial contamination, but are often rich in mineral content. Depending on its composition, the rock around the aquifer can affect the odor and taste of the water and the interior of the piping can suffer buildup of mineral scale. Treatment may be required to remove mineral content.

Drilled wells may be contaminated by sources far from the intake, especially as the movement of underground aquifers is not well mapped and water can travel long and circuitous paths. On the plus side, deep wells tend not to be affected by seasonal changes, and a well that provides clean water is likely to continue to do so unless new human activity somehow affects it.

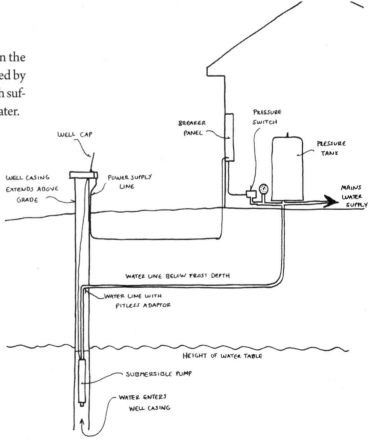

PUMP OPTIONS

Submersible pumps are used for all deep wells. Shallower wells (under 30 meters / 100 feet) may be fitted with submersibles, or with land-based jet, diaphragm or hand pumps.

Tips for successful installation

Sub-surface water can be difficult to locate. In some regions, a well may be dug or drilled anywhere with a high probability of finding water, but in many areas there is no guarantee that water will be found. In some cases, several attempts may need to be made to locate a suitable aquifer. Dowsers and experienced well-drillers can help, but finding water can still be a matter of chance.

Pros and cons

ENVIRONMENTAL IMPACTS: *LOW TO HIGH*

Single-family dwellings are unlikely to affect water levels in underground aquifers, but municipal wells with heavy draws can have serious impacts on the quantity and quality of water.

MATERIAL COSTS: *MODERATE TO HIGH*

A significant amount of digging or drilling is typically required. Cost will be directly proportional to well depth. More expensive pumps are required to overcome high heads.

LABOR INPUT: *MODERATE*

Digging a well by hand is extremely hard work and is rarely done today. Backhoes are used to dig shallow wells and purpose-built well-drilling rigs are used for deep wells.

SKILL LEVEL REQUIRED FOR THE HOMEOWNER

Use — *Easy.* Once installed, most well water systems operate automatically.

Maintenance — *Easy to Moderate.* Wells may need maintenance to break up mineral scale that can affect water flow into the well. Frequency will depend on the mineral content of the water. Pumps have a finite life span and will eventually need replacing. Removing a deep well pump can be difficult.

SOURCING/AVAILABILITY: *EASY*

Wells are common, and components and installation professionals will be easy to access.

FUTURE DEVELOPMENT

Long established as a viable water source, the components of a well water system have been well developed and are unlikely to change dramatically.

RESILIENCE

Groundwater sources are less susceptible to climate change than those on the surface, but it is difficult to predict potential changes to any given aquifer.

It is possible to operate a well water system with little or no energy using hand- or bicycle-powered pumps, but only possible to dig shallow wells by hand.

Resources for further research

Burns, Max. *Country and Cottage Water Systems: A Complete Out-of-the-City Guide to On-Site Water and Sewage Systems including Pumps, Plumbing, Water Purification and Alternative Toilets.* Toronto, ON: Cottage Life, 2010. Print.

Hyde, Nicholas. *Harvesting H2O: A Prepper's Guide to the Collection, Treatment, and Storage of Drinking Water While Living off the Grid.* N.p.: CreateSpace Independent, 2012. Print.

Woodson, R. Dodge. *Audel Water Well Pumps and Systems Mini-ref.* Hoboken, NJ: Wiley, 2012. Print.

Rainwater catchment

What the cheerleaders say...	What the detractors say...
Can be an abundant supply of water	Water supply intermittent
Not prone to contamination from unknown sources	Requires maintenance
Can be operated with little or no energy	Water has no mineral content

System components

- Roofing of suitable material for collecting potable water
- Eavestroughs/gutters with screen covering
- Downspouts
- First flush diverter
- Storage tank
- Land-based or submersible pump
- Filtration as required

How the system works

The roof area of a building is used to capture rainwater via eavestroughing. Downspouts typically carry the water to a first-flush diverter, which directs a quantity of water from the beginning of a rain event away from the tank to prevent contaminants on the roof from entering the tank. The water is directed to a storage tank where it is held until required for use.

Pump options

The storage tank may be fitted with a submersible, jet, diaphragm or hand pump.

Water quality issues

Rainwater is typically very clean, unless contaminated by particularly heavy air pollution or toxic dust on the roof. Rainwater is distilled water and therefore has very low mineral content. Unless re-mineralized, it can have long-term health effects if it is the main source of drinking water. Low mineral content in the water can also cause leaching of mineral content from piping, which is of special concern if the

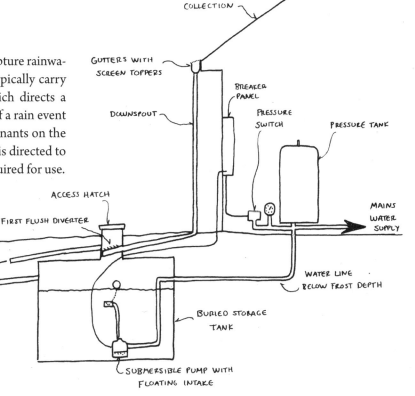

APPROPRIATE ROOFING FOR WATER COLLECTION

GUTTERS WITH SCREEN TOPPERS

DOWNSPOUT

BREAKER PANEL

PRESSURE SWITCH

PRESSURE TANK

ACCESS HATCH

FIRST FLUSH DIVERTER

OVERFLOW

MAINS WATER SUPPLY

WATER LINE BELOW FROST DEPTH

BURIED STORAGE TANK

SUBMERSIBLE PUMP WITH FLOATING INTAKE

piping contains fittings that may have lead and/or zinc content.

Re-mineralizing of rainwater can be achieved using a simple sand filter, or by partially filling the storage tank with sand and gravel.

The storage tank is susceptible to algae growth under the right temperature and light conditions. Dark, cold tanks are unlikely to support algae.

Tips for successful installation

1. Install a roof sheathing that is suitable for rainwater harvesting. It should be an inert surface that does not impart any chemical content to the water.
2. High-quality eavestrough is crucial. Leaks in the eavestrough or downspouts will rob the system of water and may introduce contaminants.

Rain water tank installed.

3. An eavestrough mesh should be installed, and the finer the mesh the more contaminants it will keep out of the system. High-quality stainless steel mesh is ideal.
4. A good first-flush diverter helps to keep contaminants out of the tank. In cold climates, be sure the diverter is not prone to damage from freezing.
5. Install a tank that may be accessed for occasional cleaning.
6. With properly sized storage tanks, most regions that can support human habitation can have functional rainwater harvesting. In dry areas, it is important that catchment area and storage capacity be sized to take advantage of all seasonal rainfall events, so that the maximum amount of water can be stored.
7. There are established formulas for estimating average annual rainfall and calculating catchment from a roof area that can be used when sizing storage tanks and roof size.

Pros and cons

Environmental impacts: *Negligible*

Rainwater catchment systems are a very low-impact means of collecting water, making use of natural rainfall events in a way that has very little impact on surface and groundwater levels and quality.

Material costs: *Low to Moderate*

A storage tank will be the most expensive component of the system, and prices vary depending on tank material and capacity. NSF certified gutters, downspouts and other accessories may be more expensive than uncertified versions.

Labor input: *Moderate to High*

All the components of a rainwater harvesting system are straightforward, but there are more components to install than with other systems.

SKILL LEVEL REQUIRED FOR THE HOMEOWNER

Use — *Easy to Moderate.* Once installed, most rainwater systems operate automatically. Homeowners will need to monitor water level to ensure use does not outstrip supply.

Maintenance — *Moderate.* Eavestrough, mesh covering and first-flush diverters need to be inspected regularly to ensure there are no leaks or blockages. The storage tank should be inspected at least annually to ensure it is clean and operating properly. Pumps have a finite life span, but are easy to access in most systems.

SOURCING/AVAILABILITY: *MODERATE TO DIFFICULT*

While there are some commercially-packaged rainwater harvesting systems, many systems are composed of individually sourced components. All components are available from standard plumbing supply outlets.

FUTURE DEVELOPMENT

Rainwater harvesting is growing in popularity. In some areas it is the most feasible means of collecting water, and codes and standards being developed in these jurisdictions are helping to make systems more acceptable elsewhere. The low-impact, low-energy nature of these systems will increase their market share as water security issues become more prevalent.

RESILIENCE

Climate change may make rainfall levels unpredictable, with some areas receiving more than normal and others experiencing longer periods of drought. The feasibility of rainwater harvesting will depend on these factors, though any area that can support human habitation can use rainwater catchment.

It is possible to construct and operate a rainwater harvesting system in a low- or no-energy manner.

Resources for further research

Banks, Suzy, and Richard Heinichen. *Rainwater Collection for the Mechanically Challenged.* Dripping Springs, TX: Tank Town, 2004. Print.

Krishna, J. H. *The Texas Manual on Rainwater Harvesting.* Austin, TX: Texas Water Development Board, 2005. Print.

Fryer, Julie. *The Complete Guide to Water Storage: How to Use Gray Water and Rainwater Systems, Rain Barrels, Tanks, and Other Water Storage Techniques for Household and Emergency Use.* Ocala, FL: Atlantic, 2012. Print.

Kinkade-Levario, Heather. *Design for Water: Rainwater Harvesting, Stormwater Catchment, and Alternate Water Reuse.* Gabriola Island, BC: New Society, 2007. Print.

Desalinated water

What the cheerleaders say...	What the detractors say...
Uses most accessible, abundant water supply	Expensive
High water quality	Energy intensive
Much of world's population lives near salt water	

How the system works

There are several methods for desalinating seawater or brackish groundwater:

Distillation methods

- Vapor compression
- Multi-stage flash distillation
- Multiple-effect distillation

These methods use high amounts of heat to separate salt content from the water.

Membrane processes

- Reverse osmosis
- Electrodialysis reversal
- Nanofiltration
- Membrane distillation

These methods use pressure and a membrane capable of capturing salt while allowing water to pass through.

Solar desalination

There are many variations of solar desalination, but most rely on evaporative processes using the sun's energy.

Desalination can be undertaken at a residential level, which would favor membrane or solar technologies, while municipal facilities use large-scale distillation or membrane plants.

In 2009, 14,451 desalination plants operated worldwide, producing 59.9 million cubic meters of potable water per day.[1]

There is a great deal of research and development going into improvements in existing technologies and exploring new ways of achieving desalination. Low-temperature thermal desalination and thermo-ionic technologies are both promising. Many low-tech, homemade or small-scale systems have been invented and are in use around the world at a residential scale. Small desalinators typically work by slowly processing water, which is then stored for use. A storage tank is therefore an integral part of the system.

PUMP OPTIONS

Most desalination methods are surface-based, requiring low-head submersible, jet, diaphragm or hand pumps.

WATER QUALITY ISSUES

Desalination can provide high-quality water requiring no further treatment.

Tips for successful installation

1. Each commercial desalination method will have its own particular requirements. Follow manufacturer's installation instructions.
2. For homemade systems, carefully consider the water needs of the home and the cycle of use and size storage capacity and output of the desalination system to meet those needs.

Pros and cons

ENVIRONMENTAL IMPACTS: *HIGH*

Desalination offers a great deal of promise as a way to reduce demand on the planet's limited fresh water resources, especially in the world's densely populated coastal regions. However, current technologies use a lot of energy in the desalination process, either to produce heat or pressure, and are currently a strain on fossil fuel resources and a significant contributor to greenhouse gas emissions. A lot of effort is going into reducing the energy costs associated with desalination, and large plants are often being twinned with other industrial processes to make use of waste heat (nuclear power plants can be used in this way) to help reduce these impacts. Unless some of the promising new technologies are brought to market affordably or significant technological advances are made, increasing demand will offset any minor improvements in efficiency and will not reduce impacts.

On a small, residential scale in a sunny climate, solar energy can often be used to desalinate enough water for a household via both low- and hi-tech means. These can be all solar, or a combination of solar and other sources of energy.

Regardless of the scale of a desalination system, the resulting brine can have environmental impacts. The highly concentrated levels of salt that are the by-product of desalination cannot be returned directly to water or soil without having potentially serious implications, as raising the salt level in the ground or in a water body can alter pH and kill off plant and animal life.

MATERIAL COSTS: *HIGH*

LABOR INPUT: *MODERATE TO HIGH*

Installing a home-scale desalination system may involve the on-site creation of an appropriate solution, and may take time to assemble and fine-tune.

Over-the-counter systems have relatively short installation times.

SKILL LEVEL REQUIRED FOR THE HOMEOWNER

Use — *Moderate.* Once installed, most desalination systems operate automatically. Homeowners will need to monitor water level to ensure use does not outstrip supply.

Maintenance — *Moderate to Difficult.* There is regular maintenance to do on a desalination system,

including checking and cleaning intake point, cleaning pipes, filters and membranes (where used) and properly disposing of brine.

Commercial systems will have a prescribed maintenance cycle that should be adhered to.

SOURCING/AVAILABILITY: *MODERATE TO DIFFICULT*

Commercially produced desalination systems are relatively easy to source, especially through marine supply outlets and directly from water purification manufacturers.

There are instruction manuals and online resources for those wishing to build their own desalinator. Most or all of the parts required will be available through plumbing supply stores or water purification outlets.

FUTURE DEVELOPMENT

Large-scale desalination is the subject of a great deal of research and development by nations that rely on this method to provide water to their citizens. With water security a national priority in many parts of the world, expect rapid development and deployment of this technology.

If large-scale developments provide new solutions that are appropriate for small-scale desalination, the trickle-down effect will help homeowners. A lot of experimentation is happening among those using homemade desalinators, and this may also bring refinements and developments that make for better owner-builder solutions and home-scale commercial systems.

RESILIENCE

For anybody living in a coastal region with a limited or uncertain fresh water supply, a desalination system is an important element in being resilient. Home setups that require little or no energy will ensure clean water supply independent of fossil fuels or climate changes.

Note:

1. Henthorne, Lisa. *The Current State of Desalination.* International Desalination Association World Congress on Desalination and Water Reuse, 2011

Resources for further research

Hyde, Nicholas. *Harvesting H₂O: A Prepper's Guide to the Collection, Treatment, and Storage of Drinking Water While Living off the Grid.* N.p.: CreateSpace Independent, 2012. Print.

Cipollina, Andrea, Giorgio Micale, and Lucio Rizzuti. *Seawater Desalination: Conventional and Renewable Energy Processes.* Heidelberg, Germany: Springer, 2009. Print.

Pumps

The heart of all water systems is the pump that makes the water flow. In most cases, the type of water system will dictate the style and size of pump required. Head (the height water must be moved), flow (volume of water moved) and pressure (force of the water) are the variables, and must be matched to meet the water needs of the users. Most pumps have electronic or mechanical pressure switches that turn the motor on or off as required.

SUBMERSIBLE PUMPS

These pumps can range from tiny recirculation pumps to very large pressure pumps. As the name implies, the pump is submerged directly into the water source, whether it be a natural water body, a tank or

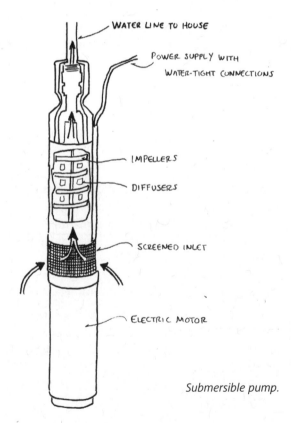

Submersible pump.

a shallow or deep well. These pumps use a positive displacement pumping mechanism to move water, typically a rotary vane or screw pump. Lobe and gear pumps are also available, though not as common.

The advantage of submerging the pump is the elimination of any inlet piping and the need for the pump to have a "sucking" action to pull water in and a "blowing" action to push the water through a supply pipe. Because it sits in the water, there is no danger of the pump losing its "prime" and not being able to draw water.

On the down side, submersibles can be difficult to inspect and maintain as they are often in locations that require some effort to physically remove the pump. The majority of submersibles have the electric motor in the water as well, and rely on excellent seals and a housing (usually oil-filled) to keep this from getting wet. Should these seals fail, the motor will short-circuit and cease working, and may suffer permanent damage.

SOLAR SLOW PUMPS

A subcategory of submersible pumps is the solar slow pump, which has its electric motor directly wired to a photovoltaic panel and moves water any time the sun is shining, at a speed proportional to the amount of sunlight available. These pumps do not produce the kind of pressure and volume required to directly supply fixtures in the home, but are used to slowly and steadily move water to a storage container, from where it can be used when needed. They do not require battery storage or any other components used in a household solar electric system, making them simple to install and use.

Solar slow pumps are often used to lift water to a storage tank at a high point in the home, from which the water can use gravity to produce usable pressure. They can also be used to pump water from deep wells to a storage tank in or near the house, from which a small electric or hand pump can provide pressure.

JET PUMPS

These pumps are positioned close to the water source. The electric motor powers a centrifugal pump that provides flow and pressure to the output line supplying the home. A small amount of the water exiting the pump is siphoned away and sent down to the well, where it is pushed through a venturi. The pressure difference at the venturi draws more water up to the centrifugal pump. For shallow (0–12 meters /0–40 feet) wells, the venturi may be located at the pump, while for deep wells (12–30 meters /40–100 feet) it will be at the bottom of the well. Jet pumps are limited to about 30 meters (100 feet) of depth.

The chief advantage of the jet pump is that it does not rely on a tight seal to move water, and so requires less precise machining and is less prone to loss of

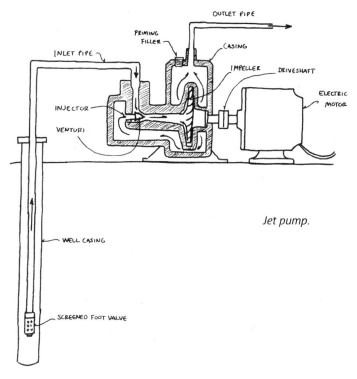

Jet pump.

performance due to wear than other pumps. In an era when metallurgy and seal technology was not as refined, this was the preferred way to pump water.

Jet pumps are less common now because of their main disadvantage, the need to be primed and maintain a prime. This means the reservoir at the pump and the jet and intake lines must be filled with water before the pump will work. A spring-loaded foot valve keeps water in the system when the pump is not running, but any leak in the system will mean manually priming again.

DIAPHRAGM PUMPS

A diaphragm pump uses a flexible membrane to exert positive and negative pressure on a chamber. In the state of negative pressure, water is drawn into the chamber through a one-way check valve. In the state of positive pressure, water is pushed out of the chamber through another one-way valve. Rapidly pushing and pulling on the diaphragm draws water into the pump and through the outlet pipe to the home.

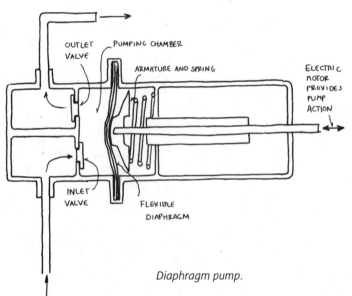

Diaphragm pump.

Advances in rubber and plastic membrane quality now make these pumps very reliable. As there are no moving parts in direct contact with the water, diaphragm pumps are not prone to corrosion or seal and bearing failure. They can also move water with particulate without causing damage to the pump.

Diaphragm pumps with good-quality valves can be self-priming, as the pump will displace air and create a low-pressure area that draws water into the pump body. Pumps will specify the amount of head that can be overcome by the self-priming action, with ranges from 0–150 meters (0–500 feet).

These pumps tend to cost less, but will not provide flow and pressure rates as high as other options. However, many models on the market will easily provide standard household water pressure. The diaphragm is prone to wear and fails more frequently than other pumps, but can also be replaced quickly and affordably on some models. Ensure that the diaphragm can be replaced before purchasing a unit.

HUMAN-POWERED PUMPS

One of the important unrecognized technical revolutions came with the invention of the piston or siphon pump in ancient Greece. The ability to move water mechanically while remaining stationary eliminated the labor-intensive need to carry water in vessels from a source to a point of use, especially where there are large changes in elevation. This freed a huge amount of labor to be put to other uses. Until the invention of the electric motor, hand (or foot) pumping of water was common and effective.

Human-powered pumps can use almost any type of positive displacement pump action. They type of action is chosen based on anticipated speed of the pump, the length of the displacement stroke and the head to be overcome.

Regardless of the type of pump, the propelling force comes from human action. A pump exists to match any type of human movement, from the raising and lowering of the arm on an "old-fashioned" bucket pump to high-efficiency "bicycle" units to those driven by rowing machines, oscillating exercise equipment or a foot-powered diaphragm.

In most cases, human-powered pumps are used to move water to a storage vessel from which fixtures are supplied with gravity pressure. Hand or foot pumps can provide on-demand flow, but with at least one limb busy pumping, it can be difficult to simultaneously use the water!

Human-powered pumps have benefitted from the same advances in seal technology and metallurgy as electric pumps. It is possible to move 5–10 liters (1.25–2.5 gallons) per minute (lpm) at heads of 6–12 meters (20–40 feet), and as much as 40 lpm (10 gallons per minute) at low heads. Even at the low end of that range, 10–20 minutes of cycling could provide enough water for a full day's use.

Typically, human-powered pumps are used as backups so that water can still be supplied when there is no electrical power.

RAM PUMPS

The ram pump is a positive displacement pump that uses the kinetic energy of moving water to provide the power to lift water. Water entering the pump from the flow of the stream pushes against a one-way valve, closing it. The resulting shock wave provides a moment of flow in the opposite direction. This back flow is directed to the pump's outlet hose, which has another one-way valve that allows the water to push into the outlet but not return. This process is repeated in rapid cycles, depending on the speed of flow and the volume. The output side of the pump is able to lift water approximately six times higher

than the head of the river or stream providing the flow. Water is ejected from the pump between shock cycles, which is fine when using the run of a stream or river, where the ejected water rejoins the flow.

Ram pumps for a household would be coupled to a storage tank, as the pump produces a continuous low flow at relatively low pressure. Water would accumulate in the tank and a small electric pump or gravity would provide the delivery pressure.

If all the conditions are right, a ram pump is an excellent, no-energy means of moving water. In areas where the driving water would freeze in the winter, this type of pump provides only a seasonal option.

Commercial ram pumps may be purchased, or the parts to make one are available from any plumbing supply store. The costs are very low and the number of moving parts very limited, making ram pumps very reliable.

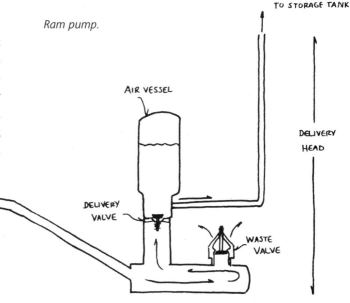

Ram pump.

Filters

The treatment of water to potable quality is extremely important, and qualified professionals should design filtration and treatment systems if there is any concern that the water source may have harmful contaminants.

Where municipal water supply is available to residents, most jurisdictions require that the service be used. Special permission may be required to use a private water collection and treatment system.

Local municipalities or health authorities regulate privately owned water systems in most jurisdictions. There may be minimal requirements specifying only that a suitable water system be installed, or prescriptive regulations and requirements for testing of water to meet established standards.

A homeowner's selection of filters and/or treatment systems will vary greatly depending on the quality of the source water. It is important to remember that standards for "safe" drinking water

Filtration centre.

change over time, and that only a small number of thousands of potential contaminants are covered by regulations and detected in testing. Whether a municipal or private water source is being used, filters and treatments may be needed or desired to address issues ranging from taste to concern about particular minerals or contaminants.

All water systems should be subjected to regular testing, whether mandated by law or not. It is in the homeowner's interest to ensure that their water supply is as clean as it can be. When sending water for testing, request the most comprehensive test available. Basic testing may only be detecting bacteria (coliform and *E. coli*), and not addressing minerals and heavy metals, VOCs, pesticides and herbicides, PCBs and organic and inorganic chemicals of many types, including those that may be derived from components of the water system itself.

Once thorough testing has been completed, the proper types of filters and/or treatment can be installed.

Filters are rated by pore dimension, measured in microns, or thousandths of a millimeter. The "micron size" of a filter is determined by one of two testing standards that can give different results for filters with the same nominal micron size.

Nominal Micron Rating (NMR) indicates the filter can capture a given percentage of particles of the stated size. For example, a filter might be said to have a nominal rating of 90 percent at 5 micron.

Absolute Micron Rating (AMR) results are obtained by making a single pass of fluid containing particles through a flat sheet of filter material and capturing and measuring the particles in the passed fluid.

Cryptosporidium and *Giardia* are two common water-borne microorganisms that can reliably be removed by a 1 absolute micron filter. When using filters to remove microorganisms, be sure to get "absolute micron" filters, as the nominal rating means that some percentage will be getting through.

It is not uncommon to use multiple particle filters of descending micron size, to stop large particles from clogging up the finer filters. Screen filtration typically covers sizes 5 microns and larger; micro filtration covers the 0.1 to 1 micron range and ultra filtration from 0.01 to 0.1 micron. Nano filtration is used for anything finer than 0.01 micron, and is rarely used in household water filtration.

Whole house filtration uses one set of filters through which all water used at every fixture in the home will pass.

Point of use filtration uses specific filters at chosen fixtures.

Filters require regular inspection and replacement. It can require a good deal of pressure to force water through very fine filters, and some drop in the quantity and pressure of water may be experienced. Clogged filters can seriously restrict water flow.

The material that is caught in a water filter may be biologically active, and may colonize in the filter. If a water system is dormant for a long time or has a high degree of biological activity, change the filters frequently.

Backwash capability in a filter system allows a reverse flow of water to unclog surfaces and flush the freed particulate out of the system. These systems will be more expensive to install but will reduce the cost of filter replacement over the life span of the system.

PARTICLE OR SEDIMENT FILTERS

The most basic type of filtration removes particulate from the water. These filters may be screen, mesh, woven fabric, string or filaments of various materials. They are most commonly used as the first filters in a series, as they are less expensive and will remove large particles, extending the life span of the finer, more expensive filters downstream.

In cases where water is free of microorganisms and other health issues, a sediment filter may be all that is required to remove particulate and suspended solids.

ACTIVATED CARBON OR "CHARCOAL" FILTERS

Carbon filters are a common component of many home water filtration systems. The filter contains "activated" carbon (typically derived from coconut husk), which has been given a positive electrical charge and is good at removing sediment, chlorine and VOCs. The carbon, in either block or granular form, has a large amount of surface area (as much as 80 hectares in 1 kg), and is able to adsorb a great deal of material. These types of filters are not effective at removing salts or minerals.

Carbon filters may be sold at particular micron ratings, and can take the place of sediment filters in some systems. They are more expensive than sediment filters, so if there is a high volume of particulate it would be beneficial to use a less expensive sediment filter in advance of the carbon filter.

Some carbon filters are impregnated with activated silver to stop bacteria from growing in them.

CERAMIC FILTERS

Ceramic filters use a core of diatomaceous earth, a matrix of microscopic shells. This type of filter can remove particles as small as 0.2 micron, providing very effective filtration that can be considered bacteriologically safe.

Ceramic filters have less surface area than carbon filters, and will typically reduce flow rates more than other filter types. They are cleanable and can be washed and reused many times, reducing waste and saving money.

Some ceramic filters are impregnated with activated silver to prevent bacterial growth within the filter.

BIOSAND FILTERS

These filters have been used to clean water for hundreds of years, but have only recently been the focus of a great deal of study. They can offer an inexpensive and accessible form of water filtration that is highly effective.

A biosand filter is a container filled with clean drainage gravel topped with clean sand. A diffuser is used above the sand to prevent incoming water from agitating the sand.

The small pore sizes between the grains of sand work to mechanically trap particles and pathogens as gravity carries the water through the deep sand bed. In a relatively short period of time, an active biosand layer develops in the top 5–10 centimeters (2–4 inches) of the filter. Microorganisms colonize the sand in the upper layers and consume pathogens as they pass through. Pathogens that are not consumed will often complete their life cycle within the sand bed, where they die because of lack of food or oxygen. By the time water reaches the gravel layer and exits the filter to a storage container, it has been significantly cleaned.

Biosand filters are widely used in the developing world, where they provide a low-cost option that can be made with locally available materials to provide filtration on a household or village scale. A growing number of peer-reviewed field and laboratory tests attest to the potential of this type of filtration. These filters do not remove most salts or metals.

Biosand filters cannot process pressurized water on demand. Water must be allowed to move through the filter at a slow rate, and there must be pause time between dousing. Filtered water trickles into a separate storage container for later use. Some commercial systems mechanize the dousing process to ensure maximum output, while others require the owner to fill the filter as required.

The biosand layer requires some maintenance. If it gets too thick, flow rates will be drastically reduced. Agitating and skimming the surface will restore flow.

There are commercial manufacturers in North America that offer biosand filters in a range of different sizes and flow rates. To date, authorities do not approve these filters as a potable water solution, but they may be used as highly effective "pre-filters" to help extend the life span of other filters.

Water treatment systems

Water may require more than filtration in order to meet high standards. There are several types of treatment systems that subject source water to a process that removes or sterilizes pathogens. There are two main categories of water treatment: those that introduce chemicals to the water and those that use an energy input. Chemical treatment systems, while effective, have too many environmental and health issues to be considered sustainable. Energy input systems also carry impacts that must be considered in the production of the required energy, but as this energy can be provided in renewable, non-polluting ways, these treatments are given consideration.

Most water treatment systems are used in conjunction with filters, as they do not remove particulate, metals or VOCs.

ULTRAVIOLET TREATMENT

Concentrated amounts of ultraviolet (UV) light is effective at sterilizing pathogens, killing their DNA. These treatment systems employ a UV light bulb in a flow chamber. When water passes through the chamber it is exposed to the light for enough time to ensure all pathogens are rendered sterile.

UV systems require the bulb to be lit at all times, bringing an energy cost that can be considerable. Bulbs for whole-house systems range from 60–100 watts, consuming 1.4–2.4 kilowatt hours daily. This is not prohibitively expensive at today's low electricity rates, but adds a significant burden to renewable energy systems and used widely would increase overall energy demand noticeably.

One of the advantages of UV filters is that they can process water in "real time" as the water passes through the filter at regular flow and pressure rates. The water does not need to be stored, pumped or regulated.

UV filters require relatively clean water, as particulate could provide shading that may allow some

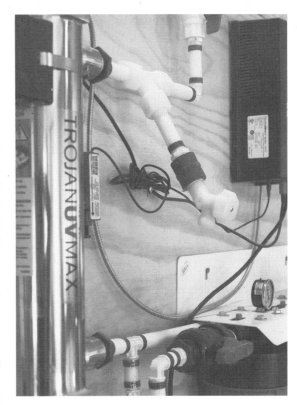

UV filter.

pathogens to pass through the light chamber without enough exposure to sterilize them.

Bulbs in UV filters need to be replaced fairly frequently, with most manufacturers recommending annual changing. Some regulations require an alarm system to be built into the filter as the light is not visible from the outside, making it impossible to verify functionality.

REVERSE OSMOSIS TREATMENT

Reverse osmosis technology uses several layers of a thin, semi-permeable membrane with tiny pores. Water is put under pressure (0.35–0.48 MPa / 50–70 psi for most household systems) to force it through this membrane, catching any molecules larger than water on the filter while relatively pure water passes straight through.

These systems cannot treat water on demand, and work with a pressure tank that is filled with filtered water, ensuring supply at expected pressure and flow.

Reverse osmosis units keep the membrane clear of built-up minerals by washing water over it. The amount of wash water required can be quite high, with ratios of two parts wash water to one part filtered water not uncommon, so be sure to check efficiency rates before purchasing. In some systems, this wash water is sent to sewer, wasting a lot of water; there are others systems that send wash water to the hot water tank or other uses, helping reduce overall water consumption. In systems where inline water pressure is not sufficient to force water through the membrane, additional pumping capacity will need to be added.

Reverse osmosis filters require thorough pre-filtration to prevent excess clogging of the fine membrane.

In general, reverse osmosis is used on a household scale as a point-source filter for drinking water. A large system would be needed to provide filtered water for high-flow uses like showering or dishwashing.

OZONE TREATMENT

Ozone is trioxygen, an unstable grouping of three oxygen atoms. It is a powerful and highly reactive oxidant, as one of the oxygen atoms is ready to break away and combine with other atoms. As a water treatment system, ozone is generated with an electrical arc or high-UV light in the presence of oxygen. The resultant ozone bubbles are released into water, where their oxidizing effect is used to react with and kill pathogens and alter or precipitate metals and other contaminants.

The systems use a pump to compress air, which is exposed to the UV or the electrical arc. The resulting ozone enters a water reservoir through a diffuser tube that causes the ozone to break into small bubbles that rise through the water and react with contaminants. The process is very effective and thorough, removing or neutralizing the majority of water-borne contaminants.

The systems do not purify water on demand, relying instead on a storage tank to hold the water as it is purified. Pre-filtration is recommended, and particle filtration is also used after the ozone treatment to remove precipitate caused by oxidation. There are no filters or membranes that need cleaning or replacing, but the air compressor has moving parts and the UV light or "spark plug" will need occasional replacement.

The power consumption of ozone systems is the main drawback, with household units consuming from 55–200 watts continuously, or 1.3–4.8 kilowatt hours per day. This is not prohibitively expensive at today's low electricity rates, but adds a significant burden to renewable energy systems and used widely would increase overall energy demand noticeably.

Resources for further research

Burns, Max. *Country and Cottage Water Systems: A Complete Out-of-the-City Guide to On-Site Water and Sewage Systems including Pumps, Plumbing, Water Purification and Alternative Toilets.* Toronto, ON: Cottage Life, 2010. Print.

Dean, Tamara. *The Human-Powered Home: Choosing Muscles over Motors.* Gabriola Island, BC: New Society, 2008. Print.

Ingram, Colin. *The Drinking Water Book: How to Eliminate Harmful Toxins from Your Water.* Berkeley, CA: Celestial Arts, 2006. Print.

Kuhuna Kupua Aó, Lono. *Don't Drink the Water Without Reading This Book: The Essential Guide to Our Contaminated Drinking Water and What You Can Do About It.* Pagosa Spring, CO: Kali, 1996. Print.

Campbell, Stu. *The Home Water Supply: How to Find, Filter, Store, and Conserve It.* Charlotte, VT: Garden Way, 1983. Print.

Piping

Piping is an essential element of any water system, and includes supply lines and waste lines. These elements of a building are among the least sustainable, with high environmental impacts in their manufacture and serious questions about their effects on occupant health.

Copper piping

Rigid copper pipe has been the industry standard for supply-side plumbing for many decades, and is only in the past decade beginning to lose market share to plastic alternatives.

How the system works

Sections of copper pipe are connected with various elbows and couplings to move water from the source to fixtures. The joints are made watertight by soldering, which requires heat, a flux paste and solder, a metal alloy with a low melting point. The melted solder is drawn into the joint between two pieces of copper by the presence of the flux. When it cools, the joint is fused solidly and able to withstand pressure.

INDOOR ENVIRONMENT QUALITY: *LOW TO MODERATE*

Every element in a copper piping system is potentially toxic to humans. Copper is recognized as having toxic effects, and governments regulate the allowable amount of copper in drinking water (EPA limit: 1.3 ppm). Known effects include gastrointestinal distress and liver or kidney damage. Copper piping can be corroded by the water flowing through it, resulting in copper leaching into household water.

Most flux paste formulations are labeled as toxic, and can include ammonium chloride, petrolatum and zinc chloride. Vapor created while heating is dangerous for installers, and residual flux paste is

Copper pipe assembly.

water-repellent and can coat the interior of piping joints and contaminate water over a long period of time.

Solder used to contain a high amount of lead, but this has been banned from use in residential plumbing for a long time. Current formulations include tin, silver and copper. While all three metals can be toxic to humans, the quantity in contact with water in pipes is minimal.

ENVIRONMENTAL IMPACTS: *HIGH*

Copper has high environmental impacts from harvesting, including habitat destruction, surface and groundwater contamination and air pollution. Copper mines also have a long history of poor working conditions and safety records.

Manufacturing requires very high heat input and attendant fossil fuel use and pollution.

EMBODIED ENERGY: *VERY HIGH*

WASTE: *HIGH*

All leftover copper is recyclable.

COST: *HIGH*

The price of copper has risen dramatically in the past decade, making copper piping the most expensive option for home plumbing. The metal's ability to handle very high temperatures ensures that it is still the tubing of choice for connections at hot water heaters, and for solar hot water applications.

LABOR INPUT: *HIGH*

Copper piping is more labor-intensive than the plastic alternatives, as it must be cut and soldered at every change in direction.

DURABILITY: *HIGH*

Copper piping is very reliable, and once properly soldered will last for decades with no maintenance or issues.

PEX tubing

Tubing made from PEX, or cross-linked polyethylene, has quickly become the norm in residential construction.

How the system works

A flexible tubing, PEX is joined using brass or plastic elbows and tees that are made watertight with a copper compression ring that is squeezed over the joint.

INDOOR ENVIRONMENT QUALITY

There were many concerns about potential health effects from PEX piping when it was launched, and it was not allowed for use in potable water systems in some jurisdictions until the early 2000s. A number of studies since have found no direct health effects from the use of PEX tubing in potable water systems, but there are claims that standard testing does not necessarily include elements or compounds that may be unique to PEX. Some types of PEX are made with bisphenol A (BPA), a controversial organic compound that may pose health risks. PEX tubing is nonetheless considered safe by all national, state and provincial governments and standards associations in North America.

ENVIRONMENTAL IMPACTS: *HIGH*

The petrochemicals used to make high-density polyethylene have a wide range of impacts from harvesting, including habitat destruction, ground and surface water contamination and air pollution.

The manufacturing process requires significant amounts of heat and the use of toxic compounds, with impacts including air pollution and water contamination.

EMBODIED ENERGY: *HIGH*

WASTE: *MODERATE TO HIGH*

PEX offcuts are not recyclable and must be sent to landfill. Offcuts can be minimal, because the material comes in long rolls and can be cut exactly to required lengths.

Cost: *Low*

PEX is by far the most affordable option for supply-side plumbing.

Labor input: *Low*

The ability of PEX to bend around corners without requiring joints greatly reduces labor time, as single runs of pipe can be used between fixtures and trunk lines. Where joints are required, the compression rings are fast to install and require little skill and no heating equipment.

Durability: *Moderate*

PEX is expected to be quite durable, though it has not been in use long enough to have proven itself in the field over decades. It is prone to degradation in sunlight, and must not be run in exposed locations. There were early issues with failures of brass fittings at joints, and of damage from contact between certain brass formulations and PEX. These issues have been addressed in recent years.

PEX has an upper temperature limit of 90–140°C (195–285°F), depending on the type of tubing. It is typically not used to attach directly to hot water tanks, flash heaters or solar hot water systems.

Polypropylene tubing

Polypropylene tubing is not nearly as common as PEX, and many types of polypropylene are not rated for potable use. However, some manufacturers produce certified plumbing tubing from polypropylene, a type of thermoplastic polymer resin. It has been more widely adopted in Europe over the past few decades, and is only just finding its way into the North American market.

How the system works

High-grade polypropylene is formed into lengths of tubing. Elbows and tees are also polypropylene, and are joined using heat fusion. This process uses relatively low heat on both sides of the joint and pressure to bond the two sides together, resulting in joints that are solid and continuous, with no unlike materials or weak points.

Polypropylene tubing may also be used on the waste/drain side of the plumbing system, where it is by far the most sustainable option.

Indoor environment quality: *Moderate to High*

Polypropylene is considered a non-leaching plastic, with approvals for potable use. It is considered the least toxic of the food-grade plastics and does not contain bisphenol A (BPA). Its high melting point makes it stable even for hot water piping.

Some green building programs recognize polypropylene piping as the least toxic option available and will reward its use with points in scoring systems.

Environmental impacts: *Moderate to High*

The petrochemicals used to make polypropylene have a wide range of impacts from harvesting, including habitat destruction, ground and surface water contamination and air pollution.

The manufacturing process requires less heat input and chemical processes than other plastics, but still contributes to air and water pollution.

EMBODIED ENERGY: *MODERATE*

WASTE: *MODERATE*

The tubing and connectors are fully recyclable, even once fused.

COST: *HIGH*

As a relative newcomer to the North American market, polypropylene is more expensive than other potable plastic pipe. This is likely to change as it is more widely adopted.

The fusing tools required for joints are an investment that must be made in order to use polypropylene pipe.

LABOR INPUT: *MODERATE TO HIGH*

Polypropylene pipe is faster to install than copper but slower than PEX, as it is not flexible enough to turn sharp corners and requires more fittings, with each fitting taking longer to install.

DURABILITY: *MODERATE TO HIGH*

Over the past three decades in Europe, polypropylene pipe has proven itself to be very durable. Its main marketing angle is increased durability over metal and other plastic pipe, due in large part to the fused joints.

Drain-waste-vent pipe

The pipe used to create the drain-waste-vent (DWV) system in a home is often one of the least sustainable elements, and it is difficult to reduce impacts in this area.

The two most common and affordable options are ABS and PVC plastic tubing. Cast iron and galvanized steel pipe are also accepted solutions in most jurisdictions.

ABS — Acrylonitrile butadiene styrene (ABS) pipe is used widely in DWV systems. This plastic is rigid, impact-resistant and biologically and chemically resistant. However, it is very sensitive to UV light and cannot be used where it will be exposed to sunlight.

The manufacturing process for ABS is intensive and all of its basic ingredients are environmentally problematic. Numerous toxic by-products are also created.

On the job site, ABS piping is joined using a glue that is highly toxic to installers, containing methyl ethyl ketone and acetone. The vapors disperse relatively quickly, but in manufacturing, use and disposal of this product is very problematic.

ABS is not accepted by most plastic recycling programs, and ABS offcuts are therefore sent to landfill.

PVC — Polyvinyl chloride (PVC) pipe is used widely in DWV and septic systems. This plastic is rigid, slightly brittle and is biologically and chemically resistant. It is more UV-resistant than many other plastics.

The manufacturing process for PVC is intensive, and it is singled out by many environmental organizations as the most problematic plastic due to its high chlorine content and the dangerous by-products that result from its manufacture and degradation. Vinyl chloride is a known carcinogen, and high levels of cancer among workers involved in PVC manufacturing are attributed to exposure.

On the job site, PVC piping is joined using a glue that is highly toxic to installers, containing tetrahydrofuran, methyl ethyl ketone and cyclohexanone. The vapors disperse relatively quickly, but in manufacturing, use and disposal of this product is very problematic.

PVC recycling programs exist, and will often accept piping offcuts.

Polypropylene — Polypropylene pipe is a relatively recent option in North America, gaining acceptance in many codes in the past decade. See supply-side pipe description above.

Polypropylene is the best choice among the plastic piping options for DWV, as it is the least problematic and does not require the use of toxic glues during assembly.

Cast Iron — Most of what is still commonly called cast iron pipe is actually ductile iron pipe, which largely replaced cast iron in the 1970s and '80s. This type of pipe usually has a polyurethane or cement mortar lining on the inside to help resist corrosion. The exterior of the pipe may be coated as well (often with plastic) when the pipe is buried. This type of pipe is not typically used in residential DWV systems, but is an accepted solution in most codes. It may not be available in some of the smaller diameters commonly used in residential plumbing.

Iron pipe is manufactured from largely recycled metal content, but the process is still energy-intensive, requiring high heat input. The cement and/or plastic linings and coatings are also high-impact materials.

Iron pipe is fit together on-site using flanges and bolts or spigot and socket connections. Both rely on an elastomeric gasket and/or sealant to prevent leakage. Pipes come in pre-determined lengths with flanges or sockets cast in, making on-site fitting clumsy and time-consuming.

The cost and weight of iron pipe, the slow fitting process and the potential for leakage at joints are all drawbacks for this option. For a homeowner attempting to make a plastic-free home, the nature of the gaskets, sealant and pipe linings must be considered.

Iron pipe is recyclable.

Galvanized Steel — Galvanized steel pipe with threaded joints and fittings is an accepted solution in most codes for DWV uses in a building, but not for buried lines. This type of pipe was commonly used on supply-side plumbing for many decades, but is no longer supported by codes because of corrosion issues.

Steel pipe is manufactured from largely recycled metal content, but the process is still energy-intensive, requiring high heat input. The galvanization process typically involves dipping the steel pipe and fittings into molten zinc, a second heat-intensive process. The zinc coating helps to inhibit corrosion.

Galvanized steel pipe is fit together on-site using threaded couplings, elbows and tees. Pipe comes in standard lengths, but can be cut and threaded on-site where custom sizing is required. This is a labor-intensive process, and is avoided whenever possible. Threads are wrapped in Teflon tape or "pipe dope" to prevent leakage.

The cost and weight of steel pipe, the slow fitting process and the potential for leakage are all drawbacks for this option. For a homeowner attempting to make a plastic-free home, it is nonetheless the best option available.

Steel pipe is recyclable.

Clay — Vitrified clay pipe (VCP) is allowable by some codes for use as a drainage pipe for sewage systems and weeping beds, but not as a DWV solution.

10

Wastewater systems

THE DEVELOPMENT OF MODERN WASTEWATER SYSTEMS has been intent on only one objective: ensuring that the user doesn't have to think about wastewater. It is an issue we collectively don't want to consider and we certainly haven't wanted to be directly involved in any part of our own wastewater treatment.

Wastewater issues are a critical part of creating a sustainable building, and any home built to the status quo in this regard is contributing to environmental issues, including water resource depletion; surface, groundwater and soil contamination; and high costs for municipalities and homeowners. These impacts affect us in more tangible ways than those involving material extraction and processing, many of which happen outside our bioregion, as they impact our immediate environment. Our watersheds are contaminated, unfit for drinking and often even swimming because of the mismanagement of our wastewater. Drinking water sources, crops and soils can similarly be rendered toxic due to wastewater disposal. Wastewater treatment typically represents 15–35 percent of the overall budget of municipal governments, and many municipalities are facing issues with aging sewer infrastructure that will require even larger capital expenditure.

The very concept of "waste" water is at the root of this issue. The majority of what goes down our drains need not be considered waste, and if there are things going down the drain that require intensive processes to separate from the water and safely reuse, they shouldn't be going down the drain in the first place. Certainly the water itself should not be considered waste; it is one of our most valuable resources.

The regulatory framework for dealing with wastewater is the most restrictive and prescriptive aspect of most codes and many homeowners are dissuaded from attempting to employ more sustainable strategies in the face of government resistance. The impetus for these regulations is understandable: a desire to minimize the harm caused by improper wastewater disposal and/or inadequate treatment. Unfortunately, many of the acceptable solutions in current codes reinforce practices that are responsible for much of this harm, and discourage the use of alternative solutions that attempt to address these issues.

There are signs of positive change in this area. Rainwater catchment, grey water recycling and composting toilets are beginning to find acceptance in some codes, and the majority of codes will likely follow in the next decade or two.

Homeowners wishing to pursue sustainable wastewater strategies should familiarize themselves with local regulations and, if proposing an alternative solution, be prepared to absorb extra time and possibly extra cost in the planning and construction process.

What follows is an overview of available options when it comes to wastewater systems. All are feasible, but not all are prescribed by building codes. They may be combined in different ways to meet specific needs, according to need, climate, personal preference and local regulations.

Municipal wastewater treatment

What the cheerleaders say...	What the detractors say...
Elected government responsible for effective treatment system	Systems have proven to be ineffective and responsible for much contamination
Collective resource sharing	High costs
	Mixing of low-risk residential effluent with high-risk industrial effluent
	Quantities and concentrations of contaminants difficult to treat

How the system works

A building's drain system empties into a publicly maintained sewer system, a network of subterranean pipes that flow (or is pumped) to a centralized wastewater treatment facility. These facilities are typically located close to a natural body of water, as a natural low-elevation point and a place to discharge treated water.

The operations and processes at wastewater treatment facilities vary depending on local practices, regulations and environmental conditions, but all follow a similar overall procedure:

Primary treatment — Wastewater is collected in holding tanks or settling ponds so that "scum" (grease, oil, soaps) can rise to the surface and solids settle to the bottom. Scum is removed for separate treatment or landfill disposal. Solids, or "sludge," is typically sent to a digester, where anaerobic activity helps to break down dangerous pathogens.

Secondary treatment — En route from primary to secondary treatment water is aerated. Secondary treatment processes vary widely between facilities. In some cases, additional settling and mechanical filtration are the only remaining steps before the water is discharged into waterways. Sometimes it is given adequate conditions to allow microorganisms to treat dissolved and suspended biological matter.

Tertiary treatment — There are a variety of possible tertiary treatments, including biological processes, chemical treatment and microfiltration. After tertiary treatment, water is released to the environment, or may be directed toward other uses such as irrigation or industry.

Sludge treatment — In every cubic meter of wastewater, there is 80 to 220 grams of solids[1]. This aspect of treatment facilities is often overlooked when volumes of treated water are discussed. Sludge is subjected to different treatment processes, from landfill disposal to digestion, drying and finishing. It is often highly contaminated and only partially treated before being used as fertilizer, resulting in contaminated surface water and soil.

Any discussion of public wastewater treatment must be preceded by a reminder that many municipalities provide little or no treatment of wastewater before it is ejected into waterways. According to Environment Canada, in 2009, the water used by 18 percent of the population has only primary treatment or less[2]. The Clean Water Act (1972) and supporting grants in the U.S. eliminated raw sewage discharge by the 1980s, but according to the EPA ten million people are still served by systems that provide only primary treatment. In both countries, the number of people served by systems that include some form of tertiary treatment prior to discharge of wastewater is remarkably small.

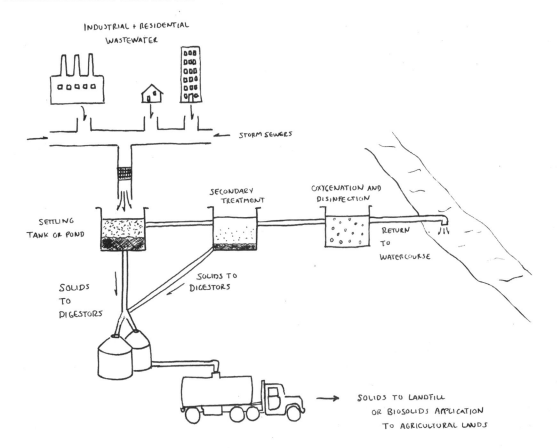

Types of waste handled

- Black water
- Grey water

Tips for successful installation

Connecting a home to an available city sewer service is not complicated. Be sure to determine the location and depth of the service, and follow local regulations for applying for hookup.

Pros and cons

ENVIRONMENTAL IMPACTS: *VERY HIGH*

Issues with municipal wastewater treatment are numerous. The largest problem is that many municipalities have twinned sewage and stormwater management systems. During rainfall events the flow of stormwater can overwhelm the holding capacity at the treatment facility, resulting in the direct discharge of combined stormwater and sewage into waterways. Billions of liters of raw sewage enter the ecosystem every year in this manner, even from those municipalities that have good-quality tertiary treatment systems. The Sierra Legal Defense Fund's Sewage Report Card for Canada[3] says, "Over one trillion liters of primary or untreated sewage is collectively dumped into our waters every year by cities evaluated in this report. This volume would cover the entire 7800 kilometer length of the TransCanada Highway to a depth of nearly 20 meters — six stories high."

Beyond the release of raw sewage, the output from waste treatment facilities can be high in nitrogen and phosphorous, which affect aquatic life. Temperature differentials, chlorine and high bacterial levels can all cause issues in natural waterways. These subjects have been well documented and homeowners can research particular issues with local wastewater treatment effluent quite easily.

MATERIAL COSTS: *VERY HIGH*

There are two elements to the costs of municipal sewer systems. Initial hookup costs will vary by municipality, but are usually lower than the cost of installing most on-site treatment systems.

The larger costs include the public maintenance and capital investment required to operate the system. A high percentage of most municipalities' budget, all citizens bear the high cost of these systems through local taxation.

LABOR INPUT: *VERY HIGH*

The labor required to make an initial hookup to a municipal sewer system is quite low. Digging to the required hookup point and a small amount of pipe fitting are all that is required.

On the municipal side, many employees are needed to build, operate and maintain a wastewater treatment system, constituting a relatively high percentage of municipal or utility company employees.

SKILL LEVEL REQUIRED FOR THE HOMEOWNER

Installation — *Easy.*
Use — *Easy.*
Maintenance — *Easy.*

CODE COMPLIANCE

Hookup to a municipal sewage system is an acceptable solution in all codes. Where the service is available, hookup may be a requirement and other options may be disallowed.

SOURCING/AVAILABILITY: *EASY*

Municipal sewage facilities are available in the majority of towns and cities.

DURABILITY: *LOW TO MODERATE*

The portion of the system for which the homeowner is responsible is very durable. The publicly owned balance of the system requires constant maintenance and updating.

FUTURE DEVELOPMENT

Pressure is growing on all levels of government to address wastewater effluent issues. A growing number of municipalities are investing in better secondary and tertiary treatment systems, and many of these are using technologies pioneered by sustainable builders, including constructed wetlands and lagoons, in which biological processes are managed to add a significant degree of cleaning to effluent.

Current improvements in municipal wastewater treatment are motivated by concern about the pollution of waterways. A movement toward seeing the nutrients in "waste" water as valuable resources could provide further motivation for improvement and help turn a revenue-losing activity into a generative process.

RESILIENCE

Wastewater treatment infrastructure depends entirely on fossil fuel energy. From pumping stations to move effluent to the plant-to-plant operations and hauling of treatment products and departing solids, there is no part of the system that can operate with little or no energy.

Notes

1   *Solids Inventory Control for Wastewater Treatment Plant Optimization*, Issue No. 1.0, March 2004, © 2004 Federation of Canadian Municipalities and National Research Council, ISBN 1–897094–60–4

2   See ec.gc.ca/indicateurs-indicators/default.asp?lang=en&n=2647AF7D-1

3   See georgiastrait.org/files/share/PDF/sewage_report_card_2.pdf

Septic systems

What the cheerleaders say...	What the detractors say...
Code compliant	Does not deal with sludge
Well understood and accessible	Can contaminate ground water
Reasonable treatment of effluent	Requires maintenance that is often ignored
	Expensive

Septic tank buried.

How the system works

Sewage discharge from the home is carried to a septic tank equipped with one or two chambers. The inlet to the tank is equipped with a baffle that forces incoming solids to the bottom of the tank. Further baffles keep floating scum from clogging the exit pipe. After initially filling, every incoming quantity of sewage forces an equal amount of effluent out the exit pipe and into a series of perforated pipes known as the weeping bed. Here the effluent is discharged into the ground, where it percolates in the soil and is remediated to whatever degree the biological conditions in the soil can provide.

Tanks and weeping beds are sized to meet standard flow rates for the number of bedrooms in the home.

The soil around the weeping bed area needs to be tested regularly to ensure adequate percolation rates.

Some anaerobic secondary treatment takes place within the tank, but the majority of treatment occurs in the biolayer of the soil in the weeping bed. Solids are not broken down very much in the tank and slowly accumulate, requiring removal. These solids are often taken to municipal wastewater treatment facilities or to landfill.

Many alternative wastewater treatment systems — including constructed wetland, peat beds, aerobic tanks, soil air injection and biofilters, among others — are extensions of this basic septic system. They use the same type of tank and weeping bed setup, but introduce a tertiary treatment element between the tank and the bed, helping to deposit cleaner water into the soil.

Types of waste handled

- Black water
- Grey water

Tips for successful installation

1. Have the system designed by a qualified professional, working from proper soil tests performed in the weeping bed area.
2. Consider using a tertiary treatment element in the system. Though this will add cost, it will also greatly improve the cleanliness of the effluent and reduce environmental impacts.

Pros and cons

ENVIRONMENTAL IMPACTS: *VERY HIGH*

The largest impact from most septic systems is not the effluent discharge but the high volume of untreated solids that must be removed from the system and treated off-site. Even systems with high-performance tertiary treatment, such as constructed wetlands and biofilters, produce the same volume of untreated solids. Options for dealing with large quantities of these solids are limited, and few are environmentally sound.

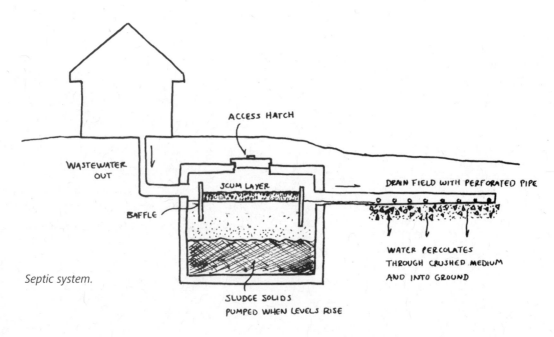

Septic system.

As very little effective treatment of effluent takes place within the septic tank, the discharge from the home winds up in the soil directly outside the home. A properly maintained system draining into a well-graded and biologically active soil is unlikely to cause soil or groundwater contamination. However, any conditions that can disrupt the ecological balance in the soil can cause the system to fail, allowing contaminated water into the ground. Harsh chemical cleaners (including many off-the-shelf products) in the system, too large a volume of flow, too little flow, deep frost penetration, high volumes of grease or oil and saturation of the weeping bed due to high rains or flooding are examples of conditions that cause failure.

Impacts from septic systems are multiplied if numerous systems are in close proximity to one another, such as happens in subdivisions where municipal services are not available.

MATERIAL COSTS: *MODERATE TO VERY HIGH*

The components for a conventional septic system are relatively expensive, but are easy to price. Fully installed costs can vary dramatically depending on soil conditions in the weeping bed area. High clay content, shallow bedrock, a lot of large rock or soils that are too sandy can all create poor percolation conditions, which can only be addressed by excavating and removing large amounts of soil and replacing it with better imported soil. This can raise costs dramatically, to the point where, in areas with poor soil conditions for a conventional weeping bed, the costs of alternative systems may become favorable.

Costs for alternative systems can also vary dramatically. Some are commercially produced systems that require professional installation, while others can be built and installed by homeowners.

Recurrent costs for pumping of solids should be taken into account when considering the life cycle costs of the system.

LABOR INPUT: *LOW TO HIGH*

Excavation equipment is required to install a septic system, and many jurisdictions require installers to be licensed professionals.

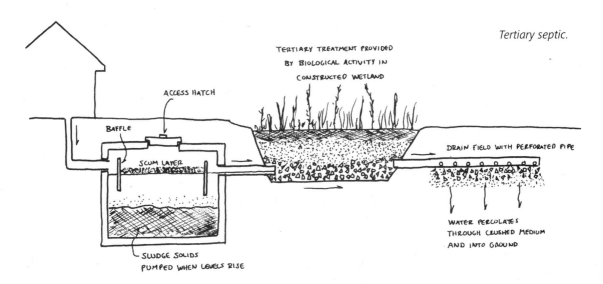

Tertiary septic.

TERTIARY TREATMENT PROVIDED BY BIOLOGICAL ACTIVITY IN CONSTRUCTED WETLAND

ACCESS HATCH

BAFFLE

SCUM LAYER

DRAIN FIELD WITH PERFORATED PIPE

WATER PERCOLATES THROUGH CRUSHED MEDIUM AND INTO GROUND

SLUDGE SOLIDS PUMPED WHEN LEVELS RISE

SKILL LEVEL REQUIRED FOR THE HOMEOWNER

Installation — *Difficult.* The equipment and knowledge required to install a septic system are substantial. Where it is legal for a homeowner to perform the installation, adequate training and/or research should be sought.

Use — *Easy.* Regular usage requires no effort.

Maintenance — *Moderate to Difficult.* Annual septic inspections should be performed, requiring the opening of the lid on the tank (an unpleasant task due to high levels of hydrogen sulfide). A professional with the proper equipment must pump solids from the tank and clean weeping tiles as required. Solids removal is usually scheduled on a biannual basis.

SOURCING/AVAILABILITY: *EASY*

The components and expertise to install a conventional septic system will be widely available in any region where such systems are an accepted solution.

Alternative tertiary treatment systems will require research to find qualified designers/installers.

DURABILITY: *MODERATE*

Twenty to thirty years is an average life span for a septic system, at which point the soil in the weeping field will no longer be able to process effluent and/or the weeping tiles will become clogged with solids and/or the roots of plants.

There are no moving parts in a septic system (unless a sewage pump is required due to elevation issues), but cleaning issues can shorten the life span if the tank overfills with solids and/or the weeping tiles become clogged with grease or solids.

FUTURE DEVELOPMENT

Tertiary treatment systems for septic systems have been the subject of a lot of research and development and commercializing, with many more types of systems available. Many of these have been approved as accepted solutions in certain codes, though few systems are universally accepted at this point. More movement in this direction is likely to happen as wastewater treatment issues are taken more seriously.

Rapid changes in regulations dealing with solids removed from septic systems have raised the costs of the process, as waste in many jurisdictions must now be taken to approved facilities and not spread directly on the land.

Stricter regulations regarding the design and installation of septic systems are likely to come into effect as policy makers take water quality issues more seriously.

RESILIENCE

An owner can build a basic septic system, or a septic system with tertiary treatment components, with little or no energy input. The legality and functionality of homemade systems can be questionable, but there is no reason a well-made system cannot perform on par with commercial systems. However, a composting toilet system will take less effort to create and be more effective.

Resources for further research

Parten, Susan M. *Planning and Installing Sustainable Onsite Wastewater Systems: A Detailed Guide to Sustainable Decentralized Wastewater Systems.* New York: McGraw-Hill, 2010. Print.

Kahn, Lloyd. *The Septic System Owner's Manual.* Bolinas, CA: Shelter, 2007. Print.

Composting toilets

What the cheerleaders say...	What the detractors say...
Conserves fresh water	Requires maintenance
Creates compost instead of waste	Can produce odors
Completes natural nutrient cycle	Can be breeding ground for insects
Only sustainable way to deal with human waste	Potential release of pathogens into soil

How the system works

Composting toilets collect urine and feces — referred to as humanure in the rest of this chapter — and treat it completely on-site, until it is transformed into useful compost or humus.

This category of treatment system does not include common pit outhouses, which do not provide ideal conditions for the conversion of humanure to compost, though given enough time the material in a pit toilet can undergo this transformation.

There are three common types of composting toilet:

Bucket toilet — This low-tech version of the composting toilet uses a bucket or similar portable receptacle placed under a seat/container to receive humanure deposits. Sawdust, wood shavings, chopped straw or another form of cellulose material is used to cover each deposit in the toilet, helping to reduce odor, absorb urine and provide aeration. Once full, the bucket is emptied into an outdoor compost heap. Here the material is layered and mixed and covered with more cellulose material, providing the right conditions for the natural conversion to compost/humus.

The indoor toilet construction is usually provided with passive or active ventilation, but no water connection or flushing action is used.

Self-contained toilet — These units provide a seat over an integral composting tray in a single, self-contained structure. Humanure deposits are received in the tray and provided with the appropriate conditions for composting action within the unit. These toilets all use some form of mechanical ventilation

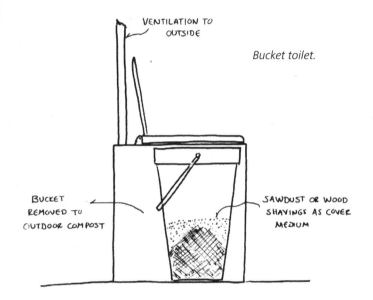

Bucket toilet.

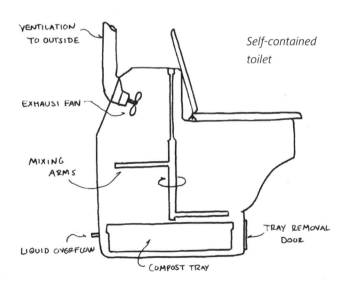

Self-contained toilet

Public washroom with composting toilet.

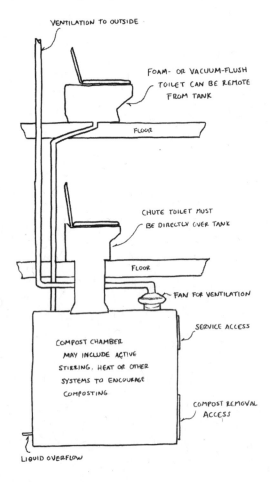

VENTILATION TO OUTSIDE

FOAM- OR VACUUM-FLUSH TOILET CAN BE REMOTE FROM TANK

FLOOR

CHUTE TOILET MUST BE DIRECTLY OVER TANK

FLOOR

FAN FOR VENTILATION

SERVICE ACCESS

COMPOST CHAMBER MAY INCLUDE ACTIVE STIRRING, HEAT OR OTHER SYSTEMS TO ENCOURAGE COMPOSTING

COMPOST REMOVAL ACCESS

Remote chamber toilet.

LIQUID OVERFLOW

to reduce odor. Excess urine may require a separate handling system, or heat may be used to speed evaporation. Due to limited storage capacity, these toilets normally use some form of mechanical action and/or acceleration for the composting process and are only suitable for low numbers of users or for intermittent use.

The compost tray is removed from the unit when processing is complete or when the tray is full. It is often necessary to have an outdoor compost heap to receive material from these units, as it can prove difficult to complete the composting process within the unit.

Some models of self-contained toilet use chemicals or high heat to "cook" the humanure into a benign state. The material from these toilets is not useful compost, as the biological activity that creates rich, useful soil has been killed off.

Remote chamber toilet — A toilet (dry chute or low-water flush) sits above a large, enclosed chamber that receives humanure. The chamber is of sufficient capacity and design to contain and process a high volume of completed compost.

Units handle humanure in various ways. Some use heat and/or evaporation to rid the chamber of excess urine and water and speed the composting process, while others retain and process all material. Mixing or stirring capabilities, misting sprayers and rotating trays are options offered by certain manufacturers. Vacuum flush, allowing the toilet to be level with or below the height of the chamber, is also available.

Some units gather excess urine after it has passed through the bulk material in the chamber and retain this liquid as a high-quality fertilizer. This makes best use of the potential value of all material entering the toilet, as up to 80 percent of the nutrient value in toilet waste is in the urine. Once transformed into nitrites and nitrates after passing through the biologically active compost solids, the liquid can be a safe and low-odor fertilizer.

All chamber-style toilets provide humanure with enough time and adequate conditions to fully convert to compost before being removed from the unit. These are the only units that do not require additional outdoor composting capacity.

Types of waste handled

- Black water (though most systems are waterless)

Tips for successful installation

1. Understand the maintenance requirements of any type of composting toilet before committing to installation. All require some maintenance, and dealing with humanure is not for everybody. Some units require infrequent maintenance, others daily.
2. Check local codes before planning for a composting toilet. They are an accepted solution in some codes but not in others.
3. Check local codes for the legal status of composted humanure. Though a good deal of documentation exists to show the material is biologically benign, some jurisdictions require compost to be treated as hazardous waste.
4. Some types of composting toilets require specific layout arrangements that must become part of the home design.
5. Mechanical ventilation is part of most composting toilets, requiring an exit tube that passes through the roof of the building with as straight a run as possible.
6. Plan for an easily accessible route from the point of removal to the outdoors, to facilitate emptying of the toilet or chamber.
7. Be sure there is sufficient provision on the property for units requiring outdoor composting facilities, and that the process of

Remote chamber toilet.

finishing humanure compost outdoors is well understood.
8. When using commercially produced units, follow the manufacturer's instructions for successful installation.

Pros and cons

ENVIRONMENTAL IMPACTS: *Low*

Composting toilets are the only form of toilet that does not treat human excrement as waste, and rather as a potentially regenerative material for amending soils and fertilizing plants. A large environmental problem is thereby transformed into a solution to soil depletion, creating more robust growing environments.

The composting of humanure is not without issues, and untreated or partially treated material can be contaminated with pathogens that are potentially dangerous to humans and animals and can contaminate soil and ground water. There is a growing body of evidence that complete composting of humanure is relatively easy to accomplish reliably, but the correct conditions must be understood and created.

MATERIAL COSTS: *LOW TO HIGH*

Simple bucket toilets and appropriate outdoor composters can be built for as little as a hundred dollars. Complete remote chamber toilet systems can cost between four and eight thousand dollars.

LABOR INPUT: *MODERATE TO HIGH*

Depending on the type of composting toilet, labor input can vary greatly. Other toilets do not require direct ventilation, and even the simplest composting toilet has more components and longer installation times than a conventional flush toilet.

SKILL LEVEL REQUIRED FOR THE HOMEOWNER

Installation — *Moderate to Difficult.* Multiple components and connections can complicate installation.

Use — *Easy.*

Maintenance — *Moderate to Difficult.* Some form of regular maintenance is inevitable with composting toilets. Bucket toilets can require daily maintenance to transfer full buckets to the compost pile. Chamber units may only need monthly inspections and annual emptying.

SOURCING/AVAILABILITY: *EASY TO MODERATE*

There are many commercially available self-contained and remote chamber toilets. These are typically sold directly from the manufacturer or in specialty shops. Bucket toilets are homemade, with plans readily available online or in books.

Plumbing for any composting toilet system are standard components available through any plumbing supply outlet.

DURABILITY: *MODERATE*

The simpler the toilet system, the greater the durability. Units with heaters and moving parts are more prone to durability issues. Consider the accessibility of parts that may need repair or replacement; if they are in difficult locations (especially if they require emptying of the toilet's contents) they will be unpleasant to service.

FUTURE DEVELOPMENT

Interest in composting toilets is just beginning to grow, and the technology is likely to develop rapidly in coming decades. There has been a significant shift in understanding about humanure, from a sense of revulsion and the certainty of contamination and illness to an appreciation of the simplicity and value of composting. It will be some time before this shift affects a broad constituency of builders and homeowners, but the research and experience currently being gained in this field by early adopters will be valuable contributions to a technology that is potentially transformative. There is little else in home-building practice that could so radically improve the environmental impacts of our homes.

RESILIENCE

Build and operating a composting toilet system in a low- or no-energy scenario is straightforward. The bucket toilet is an excellent example of resilient technology, as it not only replaces an energy- and resource-intensive practice, but does so in a way that gives back valuable nutrients to the ecosystem.

Resources for further research

Jenkins, Joseph C. *The Humanure Handbook: A Guide to Composting Human Manure.* Grove City, PA: Joseph Jenkins, 2005. Print.

Del Porto, David, and Carol Steinfeld. *The Composting Toilet System Book: A Practical Guide to Choosing, Planning and Maintaining Composting Toilet Systems, an Alternative to Septic Systems and Sewers.* Concord, MA: Center for Ecological Pollution Prevention, 2007. Print.

Darby, Dave. *Compost Toilets: A Practical DIY Guide.* Winslow, UK: Low-Impact Living Initiative, 2012. Print.

11

Heating and cooling systems

OUR ABILITY TO EMPLOY MECHANICAL SYSTEMS to automatically modulate the temperature (and often, humidity) of our homes is a radical change from the previous millenia of human habitation. Our heating and cooling systems are complex, high-performance devices that give us fingertip control over indoor climate that would have been unthinkable less than a century ago. Until quite recently, the devices we used to achieve stable temperatures were functional but inefficient, using large quantities of fuel to meet our thermostat settings. A lot of development has gone into increasing efficiency, and in many cases this has come with increased complexity and cost.

Though most heating devices are intricate systems, it is quite easy to understand the basic technology behind them. As a homeowner, it is worth understanding these systems and not leaving it to company reps or installers to provide selling points.

It is easiest to think of heating and cooling systems as falling into categories of means of heat production and means of heat delivery. From this understanding, it is possible to narrow down the pool of options to those that suit a project's needs.

Means of heat production

Despite all the competing products in the heating and cooling market, there are just four kinds of heat production. Details for each system are provided individually later in the chapter.

1) SOLAR HEAT

In effect, all sources of heat are based on solar energy, as the fuels used in every heating system are the result of captured and stored solar energy. However, this classification of heating systems is based on direct harvesting of solar energy in real time. Heat from the sun can be collected (and sometimes concentrated) in, on or near the building and distributed for use throughout the building.

There are three basic types of solar heat, which may be used in any combination.

Passive solar — A building may be designed with sufficient glazing on the sunny side of the building to allow for a measurable increase of indoor temperature when the sun is shining.

Active solar air — Collector units are used to gather and concentrate the sun's heat in a flow of air that is supplied to a heat exchanger or directly to the building.

Active solar water — Collector units are used to gather and concentrate the sun's heat in a flow of liquid that is supplied to a heat exchanger or directly to the building.

This category of heating devices does not include photovoltaic cells, which use solar energy to generate electrical current and not directly to produce heat. Heat created by solar electric current is considered in the category of electric resistance heating.

Solar energy systems may appear to have low efficiency rates, with figures ranging from 10 to 70 percent depending on ambient temperatures and type of collector, among other factors. These figures represent the percentage of available potential energy from the sun: approximately 1000 watts per meter squared (W/m^2) for a surface perpendicular to the sun's rays at sea level on a clear day. A reduced figure of 800 W/m^2 is often used in generating comparative figures for solar devices. While it is beneficial to increase efficiency rates to produce more heat from less collector area, the efficiency rates aren't directly comparable to those of combustion devices as no sunlight is actually "wasted" and no harmful by-products are generated by the solar energy that is not absorbed by the collector.

Solar heating systems do not generate emissions, fuel extraction or transportation impacts or air pollution, with the exception of those systems that use non-solar energy to drive small pumps or fans.

2) COMBUSTION DEVICES

This category of equipment is by far the most prevalent. Regardless of the type of system and fuel used, all combustion devices burn a fuel and extract heat from the flame. All these devices rely on a supply of oxygen to react with the fuel and create the flame; an exhaust to allow spent combustion gasses to exit the unit and the building; and a heat exchanger that passes the heat from the flame to the delivery system that supplies heat to the home. There are two broad categories of combustion devices:

Gas/Liquid fuel combustion — These are the dominant players in the market, and include all the various forms of fossil fuel such as natural gas, propane and oil, as well as biofuels like biodiesel and vegetable oil.
Solid fuel combustion — This group includes wood-burning devices as well as devices that use other forms of biomass such as compressed pellets.

Combustion devices have efficiencies that range from 50 percent for some wood-burning models to 98 percent for some new gas-burning ones. This means that almost all the heat potential of the fuel is captured and used to supply the building.

Exhaust gasses from combustion devices differ depending on the fuel, the combustion efficiency and the conditions, but all release CO_2 and a host of other by-products with environmental effects (see Ranking Fuel Sources sidebar).

3) HEAT PUMPS

This category of equipment is already widely used in the form of air conditioners, and has started to capture a larger portion of the heating market. Heat pumps use the refrigerant cycle to transfer latent heat from a source and deliver it to a destination or heat sink. How this works exactly can be difficult to understand, but it is worth figuring out the principle at play in order to decipher manufacturer claims. Heat pumps can seem like they magically make heat from no heat if the refrigerant cycle is unclear.

Mechanical energy (usually from an electric motor) is used to cycle a volatile refrigerant that is chemically designed to boil and condense in the expected operating temperature range of the heat

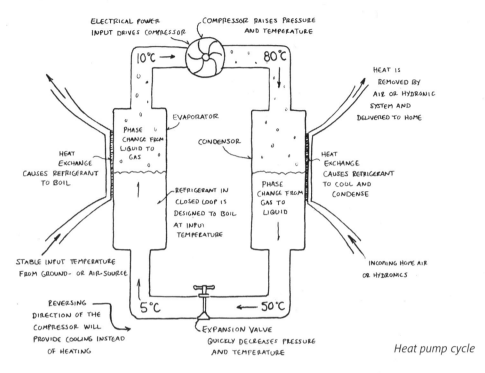

ELECTRICAL POWER
INPUT DRIVES COMPRESSOR

COMPRESSOR RAISES PRESSURE
AND TEMPERATURE

10°C →

80°C

HEAT IS
REMOVED BY
AIR OR HYDRONIC
SYSTEM AND
DELIVERED TO HOME

EVAPORATOR

PHASE
CHANGE FROM
LIQUID TO
GAS

CONDENSOR

HEAT
EXCHANGE
CAUSES REFRIGERANT
TO BOIL

HEAT
EXCHANGE
CAUSES REFRIGERANT
TO COOL AND
CONDENSE

REFRIGERANT IN
CLOSED LOOP IS
DESIGNED TO BOIL
AT INPUT
TEMPERATURE

PHASE
CHANGE FROM
GAS TO
LIQUID

STABLE INPUT TEMPERATURE
FROM GROUND- OR AIR-SOURCE

INCOMING HOME AIR
OR HYDRONICS

REVERSING
DIRECTION OF THE
COMPRESSOR WILL
PROVIDE COOLING INSTEAD
OF HEATING

5°C

← 50°C

EXPANSION VALVE
QUICKLY DECREASES PRESSURE
AND TEMPERATURE

Heat pump cycle

pump. The refrigerant is in its liquid state when it absorbs latent heat from a source (air, ground or water for most residential purposes). *This heat does not need to be in a temperature range that feels warm or hot to the touch,* as the refrigerant's chemical properties will ensure its boiling point is at or near to the source temperature. Once the refrigerant has passed through the heat collection exchanger, the electric compressor pressurizes the warmed refrigerant, which is at or close to its boiling point. The pressurization causes the refrigerant to become a hot vapor. This vapor passes through a heat exchanger where the heat generated from pressurization is dispersed. The refrigerant condenses as the heat is removed. Condensed refrigerant now passes through an expansion valve where the pressure is released; the refrigerant then returns to its liquid state, goes back to the exchanger and repeats the cycle until a thermostat indicates the proper room temperature has been reached.

It is the process of boiling and condensing a refrigerant under different pressures that creates the heat exchange. Useful heat exists in this boiling/condensing cycle, regardless of the actual boiling point of the refrigerant. As long as the heat collection side is above absolute zero, there will be heat to extract. Consider the home refrigerator: the freezer does not generate cold; rather, heat is extracted from the freezer and released via the heat coils on the back of the fridge.

The refrigerant cycle can happen in either direction, and some types of heat pumps are designed to work as both heating and air-conditioning units by reversing the direction of flow of the refrigerant.

There are three broad categories of heat pumps for residential use:

Ground source heat pumps (GSHP) — The source of heat is the stable temperature of the ground (below the frost line in cold climates). Base ground temperature is very reliable and steady, and the ground provides a large surface area and capacity for heat exchange. Most GSHPs are reversible and can provide heat and cooling.

Air source heat pumps (ASHP) — The source of heat is the ambient air temperature outside the building. As this temperature can be quite variable, different refrigerants and/or pumps are used to continuously extract useful heat from changing air temperature. Most ASHPs are reversible and can provide heat and cooling.

Air conditioners (AC) — The source of heat is the uncomfortably warm air that is affecting comfort. These units provide cooling only.

Efficiencies for heat pumps far exceed those of combustion devices. The amount of energy needed to compress the refrigerant is significantly lower than the amount of heat energy that is extracted from the process, and this is how manufacturers claim efficiencies ranging from 200 to 500 percent. But the heat is not "free" as some claim — for every one unit of electrical energy applied to the system, two to four units of heat are returned. The systems don't work without the electric motors, but they are much more efficient than combustion devices.

While there is no combustion and therefore no exhaust gasses from heat pumps, environmental impacts will vary depending on the source of the electricity used to power the system. The refrigerants used can also be powerful greenhouse gasses, though stricter regulations are resulting in less damaging formulations.

4) ELECTRIC RESISTANCE HEAT

Electrical current can be passed through a resistive conductor to produce heat. This is known as resistive, Joule or ohmic heating. The heat produced is proportional to the square of the current multiplied by the electrical resistance of the wire or element. The amount of current supplied can be adjusted to vary the heat output. Heat energy may be supplied through convection and/or infrared radiation, depending on the kind of heating element used.

Efficiency of electrical resistance heating is considered to be 100 percent, as all the potential energy in the current is converted to heat. However, many sources of electrical power are less than 100 percent efficient, so overall system performance must take into account the type of generation used to supply the electricity.

The type of generation will also determine the environmental impacts, which can range from high for coal-fired power plants (with delivered power efficiencies as low as 35 percent) to negligible for renewable energy streams like solar, wind and microhydro.

Means of heat delivery

Heat always flows from a warmer object to a colder one. Heat flow can occur in three ways:

Conduction — Heat energy is transferred from a warmer object to a colder one by direct contact.

Convection — Heat energy is transferred from a warmer object to the air surrounding the object and then to cooler objects in contact with the warmed air. Warmed air become less dense and rises, creating convection currents that affect objects in the path of the current.

Radiation — Heat energy is transferred from a warmer object to a cooler object by electromagnetic waves, caused by energy released by excited atoms.

These neat categorizations do not adequately describe heat delivery systems in buildings, as any heating system will warm a space in all three ways to varying degrees. Consider the element on an electric range: anything that touches the hot element will be heated by conduction. At the same time, air near the element will be warmed and become buoyant and warm objects near the range by convection. And the heated element will radiate heat to nearby cooler objects, warming the surface of the range and nearby utensils that are not touching the element nor in the path of heated air.

Certain heating systems will rely on one of these methods of heat flow more than others, but cannot be categorized by a particular kind of heat flow. Instead it is more useful to consider heating systems in regard to the medium of delivery, of which there are two. Almost any kind of heat production can be twinned with any kind of delivery system.

1) Air delivery

Passive air delivery — These systems rely only on natural convection currents to move heat from a source to the desired locations in the building. No fans or ducts are used to direct warmed air.

Active air delivery (forced air) — These systems use some form of mechanical energy to force air movement in a desired direction. Ductwork is often used to deliver a concentrated stream of warmed air to a particular location.

Air can be an effective medium for delivering heat in some circumstances. It is not very dense, and it is therefore easy to change the temperature of a large volume of air quite quickly. The energy required to move air from one location to another is low, as it flows and changes direction easily and large volumes can be moved quickly. Natural convection loops of rising warmed air and falling cool air can be exploited to good effect to contribute some or all of the required flow.

Occupants in buildings will feel heated air against

their skin and have an immediate awareness of warmth and perceived comfort.

These advantages of air as a heating medium are also the disadvantages. The low density of air means that it loses its heat very quickly to denser objects; raising the temperature of objects in a building via air flow can take a long time, and often objects and the surfaces of the building remain significantly cooler than the ambient air temperature. This can lead to discomfort as the warm occupants in the home will unwittingly be trying to heat the building's surfaces radiantly, one of the reasons it's possible to feel a "chill" even in a warm building.

The convection loops associated with air delivery ensure that the warmest area of the building is at the ceiling and the coolest is at the floor. Since occupants reside on the lower side of this balance, some heat is "wasted" by being concentrated outside the contact zone for occupants. Convection loops can also make cool air move against occupants in some areas of the building, causing the feeling of chilly drafts even in an airtight building.

In forced-air systems with ductwork and fans, the layout must be done carefully if it is going to be efficient. Limiting the number of bends and restrictions increases flow, and proper positioning of outlets can reduce unwanted convection loops and create a relatively even distribution of heat.

Air heating systems will move a significant amount of dust and allergens as they flow. In forced-air systems, inline filtration is highly recommended. For natural convection systems, an active filtration system is worth considering.

2) Hydronic delivery

Using a fluid (typically water) to transfer heat from a source to a destination is a strategy with a long history. Water has a high capacity for absorbing and releasing heat in the range of temperatures used in

Biomass as a heat source

Wood- and pellet-fired boilers are the subject of much debate in regard to environmental impacts. Proponents tout the abundance and renewability of biomass fuel and the carbon neutrality of burning biomass, which is part of the regular carbon cycle of the planet regardless of whether it is burnt or decomposes naturally. Opponents point out that biomass may not be a feasible fuel source for a high percentage of the population as need could outstrip supply and the renewability cycle. Burning biomass contributes particulate and other polluting gasses to the air, even if it is carbon neutral.

All of these points are valid, and as with most options for sustainable building, there is no one right or wrong approach. Context is everything, and both choices can be environmentally sound in the right circumstances.

Wood-fired — Boilers fired by cordwood or stick wood have traditionally been very inefficient, with fuel to heat conversion rates of 35–60 percent. New technologies, including gasification boilers, can raise efficiency into the 75–85 percent range, although often at increased cost and complexity.

There are inherent inefficiencies to cordwood burning that limit the upper range of efficiency. Stick wood fires take a relatively long time to reach an efficient ignition temperature, during which time they are releasing unburnt gasses and essentially wasting fuel potential and releasing toxic smoke. With an efficient fire in the burn chamber a wood boiler will likely be producing many more Btus than required for residential heating, but to avoid the hassle (and inefficiency) of having to put out and relight a fire to match demand needs, overproduction of heat is normal. Older wood boiler technology choked oxygen supply to the fire when heat demands were met, allowing the fire to smolder wastefully and dirtily until the damper was opened to reignite the flame. Properly sized storage can mitigate this

issue, but is difficult to do accurately and requires careful monitoring and input by the homeowner.

Cordwood is not a feasible fuel for vast urban populations, but it is a reasonable and often ecologically sound choice in areas where wood lots can provide adequate fuel for a certain population in a completely sustainable way. In forested areas of Canada, "an area of ~3.5 ha of woodlot or forest would provide an indefinite supply" of firewood for a single family dwelling[1]. The work involved in the collecting, splitting, stacking, fire-building and maintaining such systems limits the feasibility of this fuel source.

Cordwood fuel offers a degree of self-sufficiency and resilience to a certain population that is not available from any other fuel source, but one that would be short-lived if a high percentage of the population attempted to make use of it.

Pellet-fired — Compressed biomass pellets are a relatively new fuel source, especially in North America. A wide range of biomass stock, much of it currently waste material from the lumber and food industries, can be pelletized. High-yield grass crops as well as urban and agricultural waste can also be turned into pellets. The process is relatively low-energy, with an average input of energy required to manufacture and transport pellets that represents less than two percent of the energy content of the pellets[2]. That compares very favorably with widely accepted estimates that crude oil requires an energy investment of 20–33 percent of its energy content (and more still to process into usable fuel stock).

The many potential biomass feedstocks make pellets a suitable fuel source in almost all regions. Pelletization can be accomplished on a micro- or macro-scale with equal effectiveness, encouraging the development of small-scale, local production close to feedstocks and end users. Estimates of the amount of feasible biomass stock are only just ☛

starting to be made and vary widely, but even the most conservative estimates show that biomass could practically become a significant percentage of our fuel economy.

Beyond their widespread availability, pellets have many advantages over solid wood fuel. Their density and moisture content can be easily regulated, allowing Btu output to be calculated and consistent. The compact form allows for efficient transportation, storage and movement.

Their burn characteristics are far superior to cordwood. The small size allows for fast ignition times and very complete combustion. Combined with automatic ignition and feeding systems, it is easy to modulate the output of a pellet-fuelled device, ensuring that only the required amount of heat is generated.

Pellet-burning devices require more maintenance than fossil fuel equivalents, as a certain amount of ash

Fuel Characteristics

	Average	Unit	Moisture	Sources		Average	Unit	Moisture	Sources
Fossil Fuels					**Agricultural Crop Waste**				
Fuel oil	18,015	Btu/lb	-	2	Straw chopped	6,234	Btu/lb	15	2
Coal	10,749	Btu/lb	-	2	Straw big bales	6,234	Btu/lb	15	2
Oil	18,355	Btu/lb	-	1	Grass pellets	6,879	Btu/lb	8	10, 11
Natural gas	100,000	Btu/therm	-	1	Corn stalks/stover	7,777	Btu/lb	-	12, 13,17
Propane	91,600	Btu/gal	-	1	Sugarcane bagasse	7,900	Btu/lb	-	12, 13, 17
Lignite coal	6,578	Btu/lb	-	1	Wheat straw	7, 556	Btu/lb	-	12, 13, 17
Wood					Hulls, shells, pruning	7,825	Btu/lb	-	13, 14
Pellets	7,524	Btu/lb	8	2	Fruit pits	9,475	Btu/lb	-	13, 14
Pile wood	4,084	Btu/lb	-	2	**Herbaceous Crops**				
Hardwood wood	8,469	Btu/lb	-	14, 18	Miscanthus	8,100	Btu/lb	-	17
Softwood wood	8,560	Btu/lb	-	12-17	Switchgrass	7,994	Btu/lb	-	12, 13, 17
Softwood chips	4,084	Btu/lb	50	2	Switchgrass dry	7,750	Btu/lb	-	9
Softwood chips	6,535	Btu/lb	20	2	Other grasses	7,901	Btu/lb	-	17
Forest S. chips	5,718	Btu/lb	30	2	Bamboo	8,330	Btu/lb	-	17
Forest H. chips	5,718	Btu/lb	30	2	**Woody Crops**				
Sawdust dry	8,000	Btu/lb	0	3, 4	Black Locust	8,496	Btu/lb	-	12, 17
Sawdust green	4,500	Btu/lb	50	5	Eucalyptus	8,303	Btu/lb	-	12, 13, 17
Animal Waste					Hybrid poplar	8,337	Btu/lb	-	12, 14, 17
Manure	8,500	Btu/lb	0	6	Willow	8,240	Btu/lb	-	13, 14, 17
Manure	4,200	Btu/lb	50	6	**Urban Residues**				
Poultry litter	5,000	Btu/lb	25	7, 8	MSW	7,093	Btu/lb	-	13, 17
					Newspaper	9,014	Btu/lb	-	13, 17
					Corrugated paper	7,684	Btu/lb	-	13, 17
					Waxed cartons	11,732	Btu/lb	-	13

Adapted from Daniel Lepp Friesen, *Minnesota Biomass Heating Feasibility Guide,* Agricultural Utilization Research Institute, 2012.

remains and must be removed and disposed of. New devices are making this a simpler, less frequent requirement, but it will always be necessary.

Pellet fuel is likely to play an increasingly prominent role in the North American energy market, and the technology and devices will see a steep improvement curve in the coming years.

Notes

1. D. Barto, J. Cziraky, S. Geerts, J. Hack, S. Langford, R. Nesbitt, S. Park, N. Willie, J. Xu, and P. Grogan, "An Integrated Analysis of the Use of Woodstoves to Supplement Fossil Fuel–Fired Domestic Heating," *Journal of Natural Resources and Life Sciences Education* 38: 87–92, 2009.
2. Manomet Center for Conservation Science, "Biomass Sustainability and Carbon Policy Study: Report to the Commonwealth of Massachusetts Department of Energy Resources," 2010.

buildings, and its high density means it can store a lot of heat.

Hydronic heating systems are often called "radiant" heating systems, especially when the heat is delivered to an entire floor area, but this is not an accurate description. Floor heat is conducted through feet, and a very even and useful form of convection accompanies the radiant transfer of heat.

Hydronic heat delivery can be achieved via a radiator with a large surface area. Such radiators can be the floor, walls and/or ceilings of the building, or purpose-built radiator systems. Water-to-air systems use a radiator inside forced-air ductwork to create a hybrid system.

In all of these systems, produced heat is absorbed into the transfer fluid and moved through pipes by a mechanical pump. The fluid is delivered through branch pipes to the point(s) of delivery where the heat is released, before being recirculated to the heat source again.

Hydronic heating systems take longer to deliver perceptible heat than air systems, as the water requires more heat input to reach a perceptible temperature change. Once delivered to the radiator, the quantity of heat in the mass of the water and radiator creates much slower release times. The mass of air (and in some systems, even people) in the building will be lower than the heated mass, and all will rapidly be warmed to the radiator's temperature without "draining" the radiator of its stored heat, resulting in longer but less frequent cycling of the heating system compared to air systems.

The design of hydronic systems needs to account for the surface area and distribution of the radiator(s), the length of piping and head, and the temperatures required to provide comfort based on the radiator layout. Systems can be quite simple, with a single pump and just a few radiator loops, or complex, with multiple pumps and valves responding to individual thermostats in each radiator zone.

HEATING SYSTEM DESIGN: HEAT LOSS CALCULATION

Regardless of type of heat production and means of delivery, the design of an effective heating system starts with an accurate assessment of the expected heating needs for the building. This is achieved through a heat loss calculation. Many building codes now require such a calculation, and even if it is not a legal requirement it is recommended. Oversized or undersized heating systems are not efficient, and will cost a lot more than the calculation.

There are free, simple spreadsheets that can be used for heat loss calculations. These involve gathering dimensions for wall, floor, ceiling, window and door surface areas from the building plans and assigning each its expected heat loss rate (U-value or R-value). These figures are tallied and factored with the number of degree days and minimum anticipated temperature. The results include the hourly heat loss for the coldest expected day (expressed as Btu/hr) and total yearly heat loss (in millions of Btu).

More complex and comprehensive computer modeling programs will include more variables in the calculation, giving consideration to solar gain, thermal bridging in the building enclosure, anticipated air leakage rates and occupant behavior, among other factors. The more detailed the calculation, the more useful the resulting figures for sizing heating systems.

The hourly heat loss figure determines the maximum required output of the heating system, and the total yearly heat loss helps to anticipate energy requirements and costs. Figures from a good heat loss calculation also allow the design of the building to be tweaked for maximum efficiency at the design stage, as variables can be adjusted to determine ideal levels of insulation, window size and quality and air tightness.

Once you've used the results of the heat loss calculation to establish the parameters, you can design the particulars of the system to meet these needs in the most efficient and comfortable way.

Resources for further research

Pahl, Greg. *Natural Home Heating: The Complete Guide to Renewable Energy Options*. White River Junction, VT: Chelsea Green, 2003. Print.

Powers, Chase M. *Heating Handbook*. New York: McGraw-Hill, 1999. Print.

Passive solar heating

What the cheerleaders say...	What the detractors say...
Free and accessible	Unlikely to supply all required heat
Low-tech	Not practical for all designs on all sites
Reliable	
Provides reasonably high solar fraction	

Heat production and delivery
- Solar heat production
- Passive heat transfer
- Passive air delivery

System components
- South-facing glazing
- Thermal mass, as required

How the system works
Passive solar heating is not really a heating system, rather it is a design approach that has space heating benefits. Windows are arranged on the south-facing side of the building such that they are 10–30 percent of the floor area of the room behind. They are positioned to receive the full penetration of the low winter sun, and provided with static or active shading to prevent penetration of the high summer sun.

Solar radiation enters the windows and warms the air and the mass in the room.

System output
Output can vary greatly depending on a number of factors:

- Available solar radiation
- Latitude
- Transmission rating of glazing
- Climatic conditions (hours of clear sunlight)

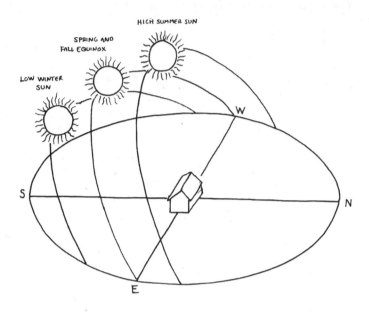

HIGH SUMMER SUN

SPRING AND
FALL EQUINOX

LOW WINTER
SUN

W

S

N

E

Path of sun for passive solar consideration.

In northern climate studies, effective passive solar design has been shown to provide a solar heating fraction of 10–35 percent. While this is far from the full heating load, it is entirely free and significantly reduces the requirement for other heating systems.

Tips for successful installation

1. There are many resources available for calculating ideal passive solar attributes in different latitude and climatic zones. Use these to create the most advantageous design. Good computer modeling software can be very helpful in this regard.

2. In many climates, cold and warm alike, the shading aspects of passive solar design can produce more energy savings by reducing cooling needs than heat gains in the winter. This is an oft-ignored element of passive solar design that has significant benefits.

3. Passive solar design is not an all-or-nothing proposition. Even when site conditions may not be conducive to best-case passive solar design, any amount of solar fraction (or summer shading benefit) that can be gained will be worthwhile. Passive solar optimization can be done on any building on any site.

4. Be conscious about choosing the correct window glazing and coatings for windows. A reasonable degree of solar gain and solar reflectance can be achieved with glazing selected for each exposure of the building.

5. Don't over-glaze or overdo the amount of thermal mass used. More is not always better. A balance must be struck between gains received from windows when the sun is shining and losses through the windows when it is not. Too much thermal mass can make it impossible for a day's worth of solar radiation to raise the temperature of the mass noticeably.

Pros and cons

ENVIRONMENTAL IMPACTS: *NONE*

Passive solar is a benign approach.

MATERIAL COSTS: *NEGLIGIBLE TO MODERATE*

Adjustments to window sizes and glazing types will have minimal impact on costs. Active window shading will add costs, but a great deal more passive solar benefit.

LABOR INPUT: *NEGLIGIBLE*

No additional labor is required, unless active window shades are installed.

SKILL LEVEL REQUIRED FOR THE HOMEOWNER

Installation — *Easy.*
Use — *Easy.*
Maintenance — *Easy.*

SOURCING/AVAILABILITY: EASY

As long as the building site has some access to the sun, passive solar approaches are freely available.

CODE COMPLIANCE

Building codes do not address passive solar design. Some codes may restrict the amount of glazing on a particular face of the building, depending on proximity to other structures.

DURABILITY: *HIGH*

There are no durability issues with passive solar, unless active window shades are used.

Annualized geo solar (AGS)

In most northern climates, the drawback to using solar energy for heating is that there is not enough solar radiation available to provide the Btus required in winter; in the summer, however, solar radiation is abundant. Many people have put their minds to figuring how to capture those summertime Btus in a way that makes them accessible in the winter, when they are needed.

Any such scheme requires a form of thermal storage, where summertime heat can be "banked" and then withdrawn in the winter. Air and water are the most common mediums for moving solar heat, with water tanks and the earth being the most common storage banks.

While the idea makes sense in theory, it can be difficult to put into practice. It has been implemented on a small scale for single-family homes and famously on a large scale at the 52-home Drake Landing Solar Community in Okotoks, Alberta, where AGS has provided over 90 percent of the community's heating needs since 2008.

Implementing a successful AGS system requires an accurate calculation of the amount of solar energy that can be reliably collected during the summer and the capacity and holding potential of the storage medium. The insulation of the storage medium is critical, as the heat must be retained for a long period of time before it is used.

The simplest systems use solar hot air collection to transfer heat to the ground deep enough beneath a building that by the time the full mass is charged with heat it is winter and the heat is wanted in the building. An insulation blanket skirts the perimeter of the building to prevent heat loss to frozen ground in the winter.

More complex systems use solar hydronics to heat a large mass of water in an insulated tank. If enough summer temperature can be held in enough water, the available Btus can be enough to provide heating through the winter.

There are not enough AGS systems in use to provide sound design guidelines. It is a radical experiment for a homeowner to invest in a system that can involve unusual design and construction requirements and will not provide a guaranteed return on that investment.

Computer modeling for AGS systems is not well developed, and most strictly mathematical analysis shows such systems coming up short in providing all the heating requirements of a northern home. However, simple AGS systems can be installed for little cost and can provide a reasonable enough return of free, renewable, non-polluting heat to offset the use of other fuels. This system is worthy of further exploration and research.

Resources for further research

Hait, John N. *Passive Annual Heat Storage: Improving the Design of Earth Shelters, Or, How to Store Summer's Sunshine to Keep Your Wigwam Warm All Winter.* Missoula, MT: Rocky Mountain Research Center, 1983. Print.

INDOOR AIR QUALITY: *HIGH*

Passive solar will not have a direct effect on indoor air quality. If a reasonable amount of heat is generated in this way, it will reduce the need for the use of other heating systems, many of which do have IAQ issues.

FUTURE DEVELOPMENT

Better computer models for calculating passive solar are being developed, and this will help to refine designs and make passive solar easier for all designers to employ. The more accurate the computer model, the easier it becomes to make small changes that have real-world energy results.

RESILIENCE

Passive solar is a highly resilient approach, requiring no energy input to receive benefits.

Resources for further research

Chiras, Daniel D. *The Solar House: Passive Heating and Cooling.* White River Junction, VT: Chelsea Green, 2002. Print.

Kachadorian, James. *The Passive Solar House: Using Solar Design to Heat and Cool Your Home.* White River Junction, VT: Chelsea Green, 1997. Print.

Bainbridge, David A., and Kenneth L. Haggard. *Passive Solar Architecture: Heating, Cooling, Ventilation, Daylighting, and More Using Natural Flows.* White River Junction, VT: Chelsea Green, 2011. Print.

Solar hydronic heating

What the cheerleaders say...	What the detractors say...
Free, renewable energy source	Adequate amount of winter sunshine required
No emissions	Systems can be expensive and complex
Comfortable hydronic delivery	Large storage capacity may be required
	Design parameters uncertain

Heat production and delivery

- Solar heat production
- Active or passive heat transfer
- Hydronic or forced-air delivery
- Can be used for domestic hot water heating

System components

- Solar thermal collector (flat plate or evacuated tube)
- Circulation pump and controls
- Storage vessel
- Heat exchanger for delivery system

How the system works

The sun's energy is gathered in the collector, a system of tubing with a solid connection to a flat metal collector plate or fin with a large surface area. The absorbed heat is then transferred to the hydronic fluid, which is pumped (or sometimes moved by convection alone) to a storage vessel, where it deposits its heat via a heat exchanger. A thermostatically controlled pump circulates the hot fluid in the tank directly to the delivery system or through a second heat exchanger.

There are two types of collectors: flat plate and evacuated tube. Each has advantages and disadvantages, and they should be compared carefully to ensure the choice best suits the needs of the particular system.

There are numerous configurations for such systems, including closed loop, drain back and thermosyphon options. Different types of storage tanks and heat exchangers also exist.

Solar energy is stored in an insulated tank or vessel, allowing for use of the heat when required, and not only when the sun is shining. Tank capacity and insulation levels must be designed to provide an adequate storage-to-production ratio so that heat is available when required.

A careful design process must be used to determine how much heat can be reliably delivered via a solar hydronic system. This is the "solar fraction," which can range from 100 percent in some climates to as low as 25 percent in others. The cost-effectiveness of the system must be compared to the solar fraction and the cost of backup or complementary heating.

Solar hydronic heating systems will overproduce heat during the summer months. If there is no adequate "dump" for this heat, they will need to be drained and/or shuttered in the warmer months.

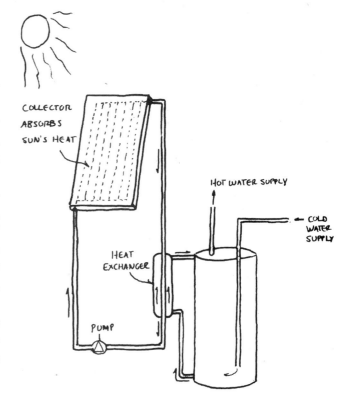

System output

A typical solar thermal collector is rated at 20,000 – 50,000 Btu per square foot of collector per day. The lower figure corresponds to cloudy days and the higher figure to sunny days. Actual outputs are dependent on collector type, solar angle and exposure. Proper estimates can be prepared for particular locations to help with system design.

Tips for successful installation

1. Careful system sizing will determine the amount of collector area required. The collectors must be given a south-facing position on the building (usually on the roof, but sometimes on walls) or on the site close to the building. Roof- or wall-mounted systems must account for the collector weight and wind uplift forces.

2. Solar hydronic systems are quite complex, and require temperature and pressure relief valves and air release valves in specific locations and properly positioned drain and fill points for the fluid to ensure proper function and maintenance.

3. Consider using photovoltaic (PV) panels to provide power to pumps and controls, as they will be producing electricity when the sun is shining and the system requires power. Interruptions in power supply can cause the system to fail and need to be refilled.

4. Creating suitable plumbing chases in the home during construction will make it simpler to run pipes to the solar collector during installation.

5. Try to keep the system as simple as possible. It is possible to end up with multiple heat

Solar hot water collectors.

Solar hot water heat exchanger and storage tank.

exchangers, thermostats, pumps and valves, all of which are potential maintenance issues.

Pros and cons

ENVIRONMENTAL IMPACTS: *LOW*

Solar hydronic systems have very minimal impacts, with no extraction, transportation, delivery, emissions or by-products from the fuel source. Electrical consumption for pumps and controls is very low, and can be affordably supplied by on-site photovoltaic (PV) panels.

MATERIAL COSTS: *MODERATE TO HIGH*

Type of collector and the components used in the balance of the system will affect price.

LABOR INPUT: *HIGH*

Installing a solar hydronic system involves assembling and connecting numerous separate components, including collectors, pumps, heat exchangers, tanks and controls, and filling and bleeding at least two closed hydronic loops. The heat delivery system also needs to be installed and connected to the solar heat supply. Commissioning the system may require revisiting several times to fine-tune all the various elements.

SKILL LEVEL REQUIRED FOR THE HOMEOWNER

Installation — *Difficult.* Construction, plumbing and electrical skills and tools are required. Experience with heating systems and solar hydronics is recommended.

Use — *Easy.* If properly installed and commissioned, the system should run automatically. A power failure during a sunny period may require recommissioning.

Maintenance — *Moderate to Difficult.* The pH level of the antifreeze solution in the solar system needs annual testing, and it is wise to inspect the entire system at the same time.

SOURCING/AVAILABILITY: *EASY*

Every major component of a solar hydronic heating system is available from commercial suppliers, but there are few off-the-shelf systems that include all components and connections. Collectors, pumps and controls can be purchased directly from manufacturers or solar specialty distributors, who may also sell tanks, heat exchangers and controls. The balance of the system can be sourced from plumbing supply outlets.

CODE COMPLIANCE

Solar hydronic heating is not an accepted solution in most codes. It is likely to be accepted as an alternative solution if a licensed professional completes the design and any expected shortfall in heat output is addressed with a code-compliant backup system.

DURABILITY: *LOW TO MODERATE*

The collectors, tanks and heat exchangers are all simple pieces of equipment with no moving parts, and will be very durable. Circulating pumps and controls have an expected life span of five to fifteen years. Hydronic fluid has a limited life span of about five years.

INDOOR AIR QUALITY: *HIGH*

Hydronic heat delivery lends itself well to good IAQ, as air flow and convection currents in the building are slower and gentler, moving less dust and allergens. There are no combustion products with solar heating, removing another source of irritants.

Adequate ventilation is required in any well-sealed home. Whether provided actively or passively, ensure that pre-warmed fresh air is introduced and circulated in the home during seasons when windows are closed.

FUTURE DEVELOPMENT

More energy-efficient homes and better components are making solar hydronic systems more practical, by raising the solar fraction so it can be a significant contributor to the overall heating system. The rising cost of fuel can make the investment in a reasonably high solar fraction system a good financial decision.

The development of commercially packaged, integrated systems will greatly expand the market for solar hydronic heating. The current need to blend the expertise of solar installers, plumbers and heating technicians to create a custom system inhibits uptake. A plug-and-play approach designed for a particular climate zone would lower costs and increase reliability.

The rising cost of fuel is going to make a technology that greatly reduces or even eliminates future fuel costs more and more desirable.

RESILIENCE

A simple solar hydronic heating system can be assembled by an owner from readily available used materials, and be designed and built in a low-energy manner. The system may lack the refined controls of a commercially produced installation, but it will successfully provide useful, fuel-free heat.

Resources for further research

Ramlow, Bob, and Benjamin Nusz. *Solar Water Heating: A Comprehensive Guide to Solar Water and Space Heating Systems.* Gabriola Island, BC: New Society, 2006. Print.

Rose, Lee. *Solar Hot Water: Choosing, Fitting and Using a System.* Winslow, UK: Low-Impact Living Initiative (LILI), 2012. Print.

Solar hot air heating

What the cheerleaders say...	What the detractors say...
Low-tech, low cost	Low temperature output
Low maintenance	Heat only available during sunlight hours
Simple to install	

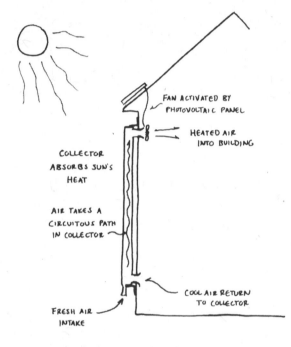

Heat production and delivery

- Solar heat production
- Active or passive heat transfer
- Passive or forced-air delivery

System components

- Solar thermal collector (glazed or unglazed)
- Ductwork
- Controls and fans, as required

How the system works

Solar radiation is collected in glazed or unglazed collectors in which air is heated in a plenum, often employing a circuitous or perforated pathway, and ducted into the building. Some systems use simple convection principles while others use a fan and ductwork to move air to a desired location in the building.

The air being heated in the panels can be fresh air from outdoors or recirculated indoor air. It is possible to create a system where the air source can be selected on demand. Heated outdoor air is likely to enter the building at lower temperatures than recirculated air, but can provide much-needed fresh air in a tightly closed home in the winter without adding any strain to the heating system.

Most systems are designed to be inexpensive and simple. Solar fraction may be relatively low, but so are cost and complication.

System output

There is a wide range of solar hot air collector designs, and output rates are highly variable.

Tips for successful installation

1. Solar hot air systems give reasonable returns when they are simple and low-cost. Avoid complexity and systems that will require maintenance.
2. Be sure that all penetrations made in the building enclosure during the installation are well sealed and that the system has some means of preventing thermosyphoning of heated indoor air to the outside when the collector is not producing heat. These kinds of losses could negate the heat gains from the collector.

Pros and cons

ENVIRONMENTAL IMPACTS: *NEGLIGIBLE*

If solar energy is used to run any fans required, there will be no impacts from the operation of a solar hot air collector.

MATERIAL COSTS: *LOW*

The majority of hot air collectors are home made from simple and widely available materials. Manufactured systems will have high costs, but are still comparatively low in overall cost.

LABOR INPUT: *LOW TO MODERATE*

Systems and controls can vary in complexity.

SKILL LEVEL REQUIRED FOR THE HOMEOWNER

Installation — *Moderate.* There are many types of DIY solar hot air panels that homeowners can build. Installing a pre-built unit requires fastening the collector to the building and creating a penetration in the building for the input tube.

Use — *Easy.*

Maintenance — *Easy.*

SOURCING/AVAILABILITY: *EASY TO MODERATE*

There are many commercially available solar hot air systems. Most must be sourced directly from the manufacturer. A large percentage of solar hot air installations are homemade from widely available materials.

CODE COMPLIANCE

Solar air heating is not an accepted solution in most codes. It is likely to be accepted as an alternative solution if a licensed professional completes the design and any expected shortfall in heat output is addressed with a code-compliant backup system.

DURABILITY: *HIGH*

There are few or no moving parts in a solar hot air system, and they are typically very durable.

INDOOR AIR QUALITY: *HIGH*

Solar hot air systems can be used to warm incoming fresh air during the winter, and can be an important part of a good ventilation system.

Solar hot air collector.

Whether a solar hot air system introduces fresh air or recirculates indoor air, it will move dust and allergens. Introduce a good filter into the system and clean it regularly.

Be sure to consider the types of materials — especially paints and caulking — used in solar hot air systems, as these can off-gas and be directed into the home.

FUTURE DEVELOPMENT

The commercial development of solar hot air collectors is relatively recent and the systems are likely to improve dramatically in the coming decade. Though solar hot air cannot provide all the heat required for a building in most climates, the production of inexpensive, building-integrated collectors will make gaining this solar fraction easier and less expensive. With a lot of square footage of exterior surface area receiving sunlight, high fuel costs will make it practical to make the best advantage of this free heating input.

RESILIENCE

Solar hot air technology can be constructed and used by an owner in a no- or low-energy scenario.

Resources for further research

Kornher, Steve, and Andy Zaugg. *The Complete Handbook of Solar Air Heating Systems: How to Design and Build Efficient, Economical Systems for Heating Your Home.* Emmaus, PA: Rodale, 1984. Print.

Hastings, S. R. *Solar Air Systems: Built Examples.* London: James and James, 1999. Print.

Ground source heat pumps (GSHP)

What the cheerleaders say...	What the detractors say...
Free energy from the earth	Intensive installation
Zero emissions	High initial costs
Can be used for heating and cooling	Complex machinery
	Environmentally unfriendly refrigerants

Heat production and delivery

- Heat pump production
- Air or hydronic delivery
- Can be used for domestic hot water heating

System components

- Ground loops (buried horizontally in deep trenches or vertically in drilled wells) and circulation pump
- Heat pump unit with compressor
- Air or hydronic delivery system
- Controls as required

How the system works

There are two basic arrangements for GSHPs:

Horizontal Ground Loop — The collection loop for the heat pump is placed in trenches dug to a depth below the frost line. Horizontal loops can also be submerged in bodies of water below the expected ice depth.

Vertical Ground Loop — The collection loop for the heat pump is placed in one or more vertically drilled wells that are capped and grouted to protect ground water.

The ground loops collect or disperse heat (depending on whether the GSHP is in heating or cooling mode) in the ground. The length of the tubes is designed to ensure that the fluid in the pipes has enough contact time with the ground that input temperatures will be constant. The more Btus required of the system, the longer the ground loops. These can be closed loops that circulate a heat exchange fluid, direct exchange loops in which refrigerant from the heat pump is sent through the ground loop or, more rarely, open loops that draw ground water in and then discharge it in a different well or location in a body of surface water.

Fluid from the ground loops imparts its temperature to the refrigerant on one side of the heat pump, and the compressor puts the refrigerant through the heat pump cycle to either create or extract heat for the home.

The output side of the heat pump has a heat exchanger that transfers temperature to an air or hydronic delivery system, as required by the home's thermostat.

SYSTEM OUTPUT

Independent testing of ground source heat pump units by Natural Resources Canada showed output for a wide array of residential units ranged from 8.7 to 12.8 Btu/hr/watt,[1] or a coefficient of performance (COP) of 2.6 to 3.8.

When considering COP figures for heat pumps, it is important to note that the electrical energy required to run the pump is often excluded, making the figures look much more positive than the reality in use.

In North America, GSHPs are often rated by "tons" of output. A ton is 12,000 Btu/hr, and residential units typically range from 0.75–5 tons (9,000 – 60,000 Btu/hour) of output.

Tips for successful installation

1. A GSHP must be designed based on an accurate heat loss calculation. If they are too large or too small, the units will operate outside of their most efficient range and performance can be disappointing.

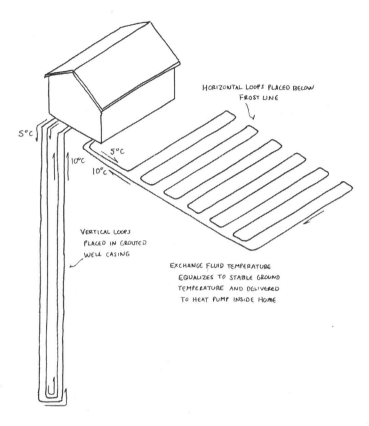

Vertical and horizontal ground source heat pump loops.

2. Excavation for horizontal loops can be very destructive to the building site. Assess the site's ecosystem and ensure that the digging will not cause irreparable harm.
3. The heat pump unit can be very loud. Be sure to separate it from the living space to sufficiently muffle the sound.
4. Some models of GSHP can help to heat domestic hot water, a cost-efficient option.
5. Output temperatures of GSHPs are lower than those of combustion devices. Heat delivery systems must be quite efficient to ensure delivered temperatures are high enough for comfort.

Pros and cons

ENVIRONMENTAL IMPACTS: *MODERATE TO HIGH*

There are benefits to the efficiencies enjoyed by GSHPs, reducing overall energy use and emissions. If the electrical energy is supplied by renewable sources, the systems can be emission free.

The refrigerants used in the heat pumps are significant greenhouse gasses, with impacts much higher (as much as a hundred times) than that of CO_2. The most dangerous refrigerants have been or are in the process of being phased out, but the current compounds still have significant impacts during manufacturing, commissioning, repairs and if or when leaks occur in the system. Currently, refrigerants like R-410A are touted as being environmentally friendly, but only compared to the extremely unfriendly versions they replace.

Digging of ground loop trenches is highly disruptive to the immediate ecosystem, and drilling wells can affect ground water.

Geothermal exchange tubing in trench.

Ground source heat pump unit.

MATERIAL COSTS: *VERY HIGH*
LABOR INPUT: *HIGH*

The installation has several distinct phases, all of which require a lot of labor.

SKILL LEVEL REQUIRED FOR THE HOMEOWNER

Installation — *Difficult.* Only licensed installers can perform a GSHP installation, due to the need to charge the system with refrigerant.

Use — *Easy.*

Maintenance — *Moderate to Difficult.* Leaks in any part of the system can be very hard to trace and repair. Professionals must address issues with the hardworking compressor pump or any aspect of the system that requires charging/discharging of refrigerant.

SOURCING/AVAILABILITY: *EASY TO MODERATE*

There are sufficient numbers of GSHP designers, suppliers and installers that competitive quotes should be available in most regions.

CODE COMPLIANCE

GSHPs are an accepted solution in many codes. If not directly recognized, a properly designed system should be accepted as an alternative solution.

DURABILITY: *MODERATE*

Residential GSHPs are relative newcomers to the market that have not proven themselves over decades, but are anticipated to have a life expectancy of 15 to 20 years. Manufacturers will offer warranties of five to ten years on compressors.

INDOOR AIR QUALITY

A GSHP will not have any direct effect on IAQ, except in the rare case of a refrigerant leak.

Hydronic delivery systems result in gentle air movement and minimal circulation of dust and allergens.

Forced-air delivery systems can circulate a lot of dust and allergens. Use the best filters possible to help reduce issues.

Adequate ventilation is required in any well-sealed home. Whether provided actively or passively, ensure that pre-warmed fresh air is introduced and circulated in the home during seasons when windows are closed.

FUTURE DEVELOPMENT

Rapid and significant improvements have been made to GSHPs over the past decade, and while dramatic changes are unlikely there will be continued gains in efficiency and lowering of costs. The most important development from an environmental perspective would be a move to more benign refrigerants. CO_2 is being used as a refrigerant in some new units, and other natural compounds are being researched. All natural refrigerants require design changes to heat pumps that currently raise electrical demand and have durability issues, but growing pressure to phase out all damaging refrigerants will likely lead to positive developments.

RESILIENCE

There is no way to build, install or operate a GSHP in a low- or no-energy scenario.

Notes

1. See oee.nrcan.gc.ca/publications/residential/heating-heat-pump/7158

Resources for further research

Lloyd, Donal Blaise. *The Smart Guide to Geothermal: How to Harvest Earth's Free Energy for Heating and Cooling.* Masonville, CO: PixyJack, 2011. Print.

Egg, Jay, and Brian C. Howard. *Geothermal HVAC: Green Heating and Cooling.* New York: McGraw-Hill, 2011. Print.

Stojanowski, John. *Residential Geothermal Systems: Heating and Cooling Using the Ground Below.* Staten Island, NY: Pangea Publications, 2010. Print.

Air source heat pumps (ASHP)

What the cheerleaders say...	What the detractors say...
More affordable than GSHP	Less efficient than GSHP
No damage to ecosystem for installation	Noisy units immediately outside home
Simpler installation	Expensive
Provide heating and cooling	

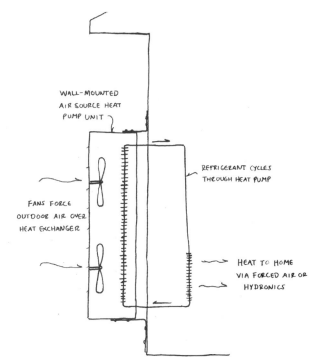

WALL-MOUNTED AIR SOURCE HEAT PUMP UNIT

REFRIGERANT CYCLES THROUGH HEAT PUMP

FANS FORCE OUTDOOR AIR OVER HEAT EXCHANGER

HEAT TO HOME VIA FORCED AIR OR HYDRONICS

Heat production and delivery

- Heat pump production
- Air delivery (hydronic delivery beginning to be available)

System components

- Heat pump (placed outside the home)
- Heat exchanger/plenum (inside the home)
- Air or hydronic delivery system
- Controls as required

How the system works

A heat pump unit is mounted outside the home. This includes one or more large fans to move outdoor air over the heat exchanger coil, to transfer air temperature to the refrigerant. The condenser/heat exchanger is contained in a plenum in the ductwork of the home, where the heat is delivered via forced air. The cycle is reversed to provide cooling in the summer.

A subset of ASHPs called ductless mini-splits operate on the same heat pump principle, with outdoor pumps absorbing heat from the ambient air. However, instead of supplying heat to a plenum in a central forced-air system, they send the heated refrigerant to one or more (up to six, for some models) independent condenser "heads" or cassettes placed in a room; room air is then blown over the heated refrigerant. This option eliminates the need for central ductwork and can provide well-distributed heat in an energy-efficient home for a lower cost.

SYSTEM OUTPUT

ASHPs and ductless mini-splits can be purchased with output ranging from 9,000 – 40,000 Btu/hour (0.75–3 ton).

Most systems will advertise a coefficient of performance (COP) from 3.0–4.0. Due to the highly variable temperature differences in outdoor air, this figure is usually a best-case scenario. Reviewing a graph of COP based on outdoor temperature will usually show a COP ranging from 1.0 (the same as electric resistance heating) at the coldest outdoor temperatures up to 3.0–4.0 in more moderate temperatures.

Tips for successful installation

1. The fans and compressor in the outdoor portion of the heat pump can be quite noisy. Be sure to locate units where the sound will not disturb occupants or neighbours.
2. In locations with very low winter temperatures, be sure the ASHP can produce enough heat at those temperatures; if it can't, a back-up heat source will be required.
3. When using ducted systems, ensure that the ductwork design is very efficient, as temperatures from ASHPs are lower than those of combustion systems.

Pros and cons

ENVIRONMENTAL IMPACTS: *MODERATE TO HIGH*

There are benefits to the efficiencies enjoyed by ASHPs, reducing overall energy use and emissions compared to combustion and electric resistance devices. If the electrical energy is supplied by renewable sources, the systems can be emission free.

The refrigerants used in the heat pumps are significant greenhouse gasses, with impacts much higher (as much as hundred times) than that of CO_2. The most dangerous refrigerants have been or are in the process of being phased out, but the current compounds still have significant impacts during manufacturing, commissioning, repair and if or when leaks occur in the system. Currently, refrigerants like R-410A are touted as being environmentally friendly, but only compared to the extremely unfriendly versions they replace.

Air source heat pump outdoor unit.

MATERIAL COSTS: *MODERATE TO HIGH*

ASHP units vary in cost by output and by useful operating temperature range. Less expensive models will tend to have lower output and function in a narrower temperature range.

LABOR INPUT: *MODERATE*

The installation of ASHP units is straightforward. For ducted systems, the ductwork will require more labor than the ASHP.

SKILL LEVEL REQUIRED FOR THE HOMEOWNER

Installation — *Difficult.* Only licensed professionals can perform an ASHP installation, due to the need to charge the system with refrigerant.
Use — *Easy.*
Maintenance — *Easy to Moderate.* Units are typically easily accessible for inspection and maintenance.

SOURCING/AVAILABILITY: *EASY TO MODERATE*

There are sufficient numbers of ASHP designers, suppliers and installers that competitive quotes should be available in most regions.

CODE COMPLIANCE

ASHPs are an accepted solution in many codes, though regions in colder climates may not yet consider them an acceptable solution without backup heat. In these cases, a properly designed system based on an accurate heat loss calculation should be accepted as an alternative solution.

DURABILITY: *MODERATE*

ASHPs have shown themselves to be relatively durable within their expected service life of 15 to 20 years. Many manufacturers warranty compressors for five to ten years.

INDOOR AIR QUALITY

An ASHP will not have any direct effect on IAQ, except in the rare case of a refrigerant leak.

Forced-air delivery systems can circulate a lot of dust and allergens. Use the best filters possible to help reduce issues.

Adequate ventilation is required in any well-sealed home. Whether provided actively or passively, ensure that pre-warmed fresh air is introduced and circulated in the home during seasons when windows are closed.

FUTURE DEVELOPMENT

Rapid and significant improvements have been made to ASHPs for cold climates over the past few years, and while dramatic changes are unlikely, there will be continued gains in efficiency and lowering of costs.

The most important development from an environmental perspective would be a move to more benign refrigerants. CO_2 is being used as a refrigerant in some new units, and other natural compounds are being researched. All natural refrigerants require design changes to heat pumps that currently raise electrical demand and have durability issues, but growing pressure to phase out all damaging refrigerants will likely lead to positive developments.

ASHPs designed to supply heat for hydronic systems are nearing widespread introduction, opening the technology to homeowners who wish to combine this means of heat production with hydronic delivery.

RESILIENCE

There is no way to build, install or operate a GSHP in a low- or no-energy scenario.

Resources for further research

Petit, Randy F., and Turner L. Collins. *Heat Pumps: Operation, Installation, Service.* Mount Prospect, IL: ESCO, 2011. Print.

Boilers and condensing boilers

What the cheerleaders say...	What the detractors say...
Time-tested technology	Most units use fossil fuels
Efficient	Expensive
Easy to modulate	

Heat production and delivery

- Biomass heat production (wood- and pellet-fired)
- Fossil fuel heat production (gas- and oil-fired)
- Biofuel heat production (biodiesel- and vegetable oil-fired)
- Electric resistance heat production
- Hydronic heat delivery (can supply an air delivery system)
- Can be used for domestic hot water heating

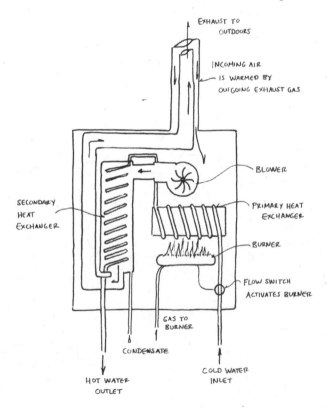

EXHAUST TO OUTDOORS

INCOMING AIR IS WARMED BY OUTGOING EXHAUST GAS

BLOWER

SECONDARY HEAT EXCHANGER

PRIMARY HEAT EXCHANGER

BURNER

FLOW SWITCH ACTIVATES BURNER

GAS TO BURNER

CONDENSATE

HOT WATER OUTLET

COLD WATER INLET

System components

- Combustion chamber (or resistance elements for electric units)
- Exhaust chimney (not required for electric units)
- Heat exchanger
- Direct vent (sealed) intake and exhaust (for combustion units)
- Circulation pump
- Temperature and pressure relief valve, expansion tank, air bleeder as required
- Controls as required

How the system works

When heat is required, a burner ignites (or electric elements are powered). A water jacket heat exchanger places water in the path of the heat in a configuration for optimal heat absorption. When the water has reached the desired temperature, a circulating pump moves it through the system, providing a constant flow of heated output water.

Direct heat — The heated water from the boiler is provided directly to the heating system. The boiler cycles on every time there is a call for heat. This system is common for space heating systems.

Indirect heat — The heated water from the boiler is supplied to one or more storage tanks with a capacity based on expected heat requirements, and the storage tank is maintained at a set temperature by the boiler. When heat is called for it is drawn from this tank rather than directly from the boiler. This system is common if the boiler is supplying both the space heating and domestic hot water systems, multiple units or domestic hot water alone. These systems do not require the boiler to cycle on each time there is a call for heat.

Condensing boiler — Many newer combustion units (both direct and indirect) are condensing boilers. Exhaust gasses carrying waste heat are used to warm incoming water, putting more of the heat generated to use. The incoming pipes are carrying cooler water, and condensation can form on the pipes in the presence of the hot exhaust gasses. Condensate is removed through a drain. This type of boiler is more efficient than non-condensing models.

SYSTEM OUTPUT

Residential boilers have outputs that range from 50,000–300,000 Btu/hr. Efficiency rates for condensing boilers range from 90–98 percent, with many units at 95–96 percent.

In most cases, the expressed efficiency is not the "true" thermal efficiency, which could be measured at an ideal steady state and not reflect real world performance. The accepted standard of efficiency is "annual fuel utilization efficiency" (AFUE). The method for determining the AFUE for residential furnaces is the subject of ASHRAE Standard 103. Ensure that rated output for comparison between units is the AFUE.

Tips for successful installation

1. Many boilers have output capacities and temperatures that far exceed the needs of an energy-efficient home. Be sure to choose a unit that matches your heat loss calculation and required temperature closely.
2. Units with stainless steel or aluminum/silicon alloy heat exchangers can be a worthwhile investment, inhibiting corrosion of vulnerable components.
3. Boilers are proprietary units and each will have unique installation instructions that should be followed.

Pros and cons

ENVIRONMENTAL IMPACTS: HIGH

The impacts for boilers are directly linked to the fuel source used to fire them. When considering

Boiler unit.

the impacts of a fuel source, it is important to be as thorough as possible. Calculations for impacts must consider the entire life cycle, from extraction to processing, transportation, combustion and by-products. Effects on habitat, social fabric, geopolitical and financial systems and resilience must be taken into account, along with more easily quantifiable (though likely controversial) numerical assessments such as carbon contributions and air pollutants (see Ranking Fuel Sources sidebar).

MATERIAL COSTS: *MODERATE TO HIGH*

Unit type and output will affect costs.

LABOR INPUT: *MODERATE*

Boilers are relatively straightforward to install for trained professionals.

SKILL LEVEL REQUIRED FOR THE HOMEOWNER

Installation — *Difficult.* Most boiler installations require a qualified professional.
Use — *Easy.*

Maintenance — *Easy to Moderate*. Annual inspection of temperature and pressure readings, burner flame (if required) and water pH.

SOURCING/AVAILABILITY: *EASY*

There are sufficient numbers of boiler system designers, suppliers and installers that competitive quotes should be available in most regions.

CODE COMPLIANCE

Boiler systems are an accepted solution in all codes. New technologies like pellet and biofuel boilers may require alternative compliance efforts.

INDOOR AIR QUALITY

All combustion devices can create IAQ issues, as they consume air and produce exhaust. Modern, code-approved devices have "sealed" combustion, meaning that combustion air is drawn directly from outside and exhausted back to the outside, and usually drawn by a fan to ensure proper flow. There are many possible points of leakage in these systems; be sure to check installations for issues. The combustion chamber is never completely sealed from indoors, and some amount of indoor air will be drawn into the unit.

Solid fuel-burning devices will generate ash as a by-product, and in most cases the ash is stored in the unit and will need to be manually emptied. This can introduce a lot of dust into the home. The movement of firewood and, to a lesser degree, pellet fuel will also introduce dust and allergens.

Hydronic delivery systems result in gentle air movement and minimal circulation of dust and allergens.

Forced-air delivery systems can circulate a lot of dust and allergens. Use the best filters possible to help reduce issues.

Adequate ventilation is required in any well-sealed home. Whether provided actively or passively,

Ranking fuel sources

It is beyond the scope of this book (and likely beyond the ability of any researcher) to definitively calculate the environmental impacts of all the common energy sources, and provide a scientifically accurate ranking from best to worst.

That said, having spent many hours over the course of many years thinking about and researching these issues, here is my own ranking of fuel sources, from best to worst:

1. Solar thermal (including passive, hydronic and air systems)
2. Micro hydro (assuming little or no damage is inflicted on the waterway and its inhabitants)
3. Photovoltaic
4. Wind

5. Biomass (typically pellets, local sources and processing are ideal)
6. Biofuel (typically vegetable oil or biodiesel, local sources and processing are ideal)
7. Natural gas (from non-fracked sources)
8. Oil and oil derivatives

Numbers 2–4 can generate electrical energy to power a wide range of heating systems with low impacts.

Numbers 7 and 8 cannot be considered sustainable in my estimation. While they may represent reasonable and practical choices for homeowners, for anybody designing a place to live with high environmental goals, they do not reflect best possible practices.

ensure that pre-warmed fresh air is introduced and circulated in the home during seasons when windows are closed.

DURABILITY: *MODERATE*

Modern boilers can last 15 to 40 years, depending on use and maintenance. Manufacturers offer warranties of five to ten years on heat exchangers and pumps.

FUTURE DEVELOPMENT

Efficiency levels for boilers are approaching 100 percent, beyond which there is no further improvement. Refinement of controls and pumps will likely lead to small gains for entire systems.

A possible avenue for improvement is the incorporation of solar thermal heating systems that work in conjunction with boilers, resulting in systems that seamlessly use the least amount of non-solar energy possible.

RESILIENCE

Boilers can be operated in a low-energy scenario, but the entire system could not be manufactured and installed without significant energy input.

Resources for further research

Woodson, Roger Dodge. *Radiant Floor Heating.* New York: McGraw-Hill, 2010. Print.

Tankless or on-demand heaters

What the cheerleaders say...	What the detractors say...
Produce heat only when needed	Complicated technology
Instant delivery of heat	Limited output
No need for storage tanks with attendant heat losses	Most units require fossil fuels

Heat production and delivery

- Fossil fuel heat production (gas- and oil-fired)
- Electric resistance heat production
- Hydronic heat delivery (can supply an air delivery system)
- Can be used for domestic hot water heating

System components

- Combustion chamber (or resistance elements for electric units)
- Exhaust chimney (not required for electric units)
- Heat exchanger
- Direct vent (sealed) intake and exhaust (for combustion units)
- Circulation pump
- Temperature and pressure relief valve, expansion tank, air bleeder and balance of system as required
- Controls as required

How the system works

Tankless or on-demand heaters are very similar to direct heat boilers. The difference is in the design of the heat exchanger, which can heat a relatively small amount of water quickly. This can provide benefits for the production of domestic hot water, but is of dubious value for space heating systems.

A flow detector triggers the heater when water begins to move in the supply pipe. Advanced models also sense the temperature of incoming water and modulate the amount of heat accordingly.

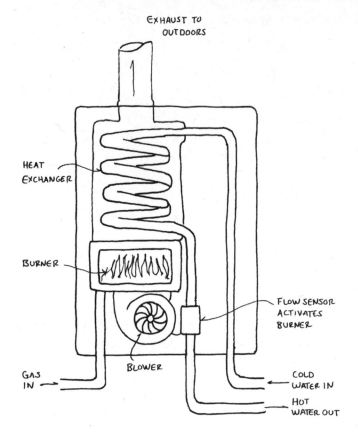

EXHAUST TO
OUTDOORS

HEAT
EXCHANGER

BURNER

FLOW SENSOR
ACTIVATES
BURNER

BLOWER

GAS
IN

COLD
WATER IN

HOT
WATER OUT

SYSTEM OUTPUT

Residential tankless heaters have outputs that range from 10,000–300,000 Btu/hr. Efficiency rates for condensing boilers range from 90–98 percent, with many units at 95–96 percent. Electric units are 100-percent efficient.

In most cases, the expressed efficiency is not the "true" thermal efficiency, which could be measured at an ideal steady state and not reflect real world performance. The accepted standard of efficiency is "annual fuel utilization efficiency" (AFUE). The method for determining the AFUE for residential furnaces is the subject of ASHRAE Standard 103. Ensure that rated output for comparison between units is the AFUE.

Tips for successful installation

1. Many boilers have output capacities and temperatures that far exceed the needs of an energy-efficient home. Be sure to choose a unit that matches your heat loss calculation and required temperature closely.
2. Units with stainless steel or aluminum/silicon alloy heat exchangers can be a worthwhile investment, inhibiting corrosion of vulnerable components.
3. Boilers are proprietary units and each will have unique installation instructions that should be followed.

Pros and cons

ENVIRONMENTAL IMPACTS: *HIGH*

The impacts for tankless heaters are directly linked to the fuel source used to produce the heat. When considering the impacts of a fuel source, it is important to be as thorough as possible. Calculations for impacts must consider the entire life cycle, from extraction to processing, transportation, combustion and by-products. Effects on habitat, social fabric, geopolitical and financial systems and resilience must be taken into account along with more easily quantifiable (though likely controversial) numerical assessments such as carbon contributions and air pollutants (see Ranking Fuel Sources sidebar).

MATERIAL COSTS: *MODERATE*

Unit type and output will affect cost.

LABOR INPUT: *MODERATE*

SKILL LEVEL REQUIRED FOR THE HOMEOWNER

Installation — *Difficult.* Most boiler installations require a qualified professional.
Use — *Easy.*
Maintenance — *Easy to Moderate.* Annual inspection of burner flame (if required).

SOURCING/AVAILABILITY: *EASY*

There are sufficient numbers of tankless system designers, suppliers and installers that competitive quotes should be available in most regions.

CODE COMPLIANCE

Tankless systems are an accepted solution in all codes.

DURABILITY: *MODERATE*

Tankless heaters are relatively new to the North American market, but are expected to last 15 to 30 years, depending on use and maintenance. Manufacturers offer warranties of five to ten years on heat exchangers.

INDOOR AIR QUALITY

All combustion devices can create IAQ issues, as they consume air and produce exhaust. Modern, code-approved devices have "sealed" combustion, meaning that combustion air is drawn directly from outside and exhausted back to the outside, and usually drawn by a fan to ensure proper flow. There are many possible points of leakage in these systems; be sure to check installations for issues. The combustion chamber is never completely sealed from indoors, and some amount of indoor air will be drawn into the unit.

Hydronic delivery systems result in gentle air movement and minimal circulation of dust and allergens.

Forced-air delivery systems can circulate a lot of dust and allergens. Use the best filters possible to help reduce issues.

Adequate ventilation is required in any well-sealed home. Whether provided actively or passively, ensure that pre-warmed fresh air is introduced and circulated in the home during seasons when windows are closed.

FUTURE DEVELOPMENT

Efficiency levels for condensing tankless heater are approaching 100 percent, beyond which there is no further improvement. Refinement of controls and pumps will likely lead to small gains for entire systems.

A possible avenue for improvement is the incorporation of solar thermal heating systems that work in conjunction with tankless heaters, resulting in systems that seamlessly use the least amount of non-solar energy possible.

RESILIENCE

Some tankless heaters can be operated in a low-energy scenario, but entire systems are very difficult to build and install without hi-tech components.

Tank or batch heaters

What the cheerleaders say...	What the detractors say...
Simple technology, well-proven	Tanks experience significant heat losses
Low cost	
Easily combined with solar hydronics	

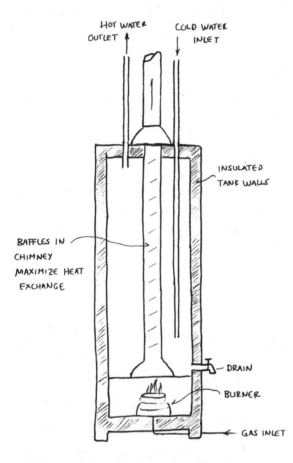

Heat production and delivery

- Biomass heat production (pellet-fired)
- Fossil fuel heat production (gas- and oil-fired)
- Biofuel heat production (biodiesel- and vegetable oil-fired)

- Electric resistance heat production
- Hydronic heat delivery (can supply an air delivery system)
- Can be used for domestic hot water heating

System components

- Metal or glass-lined metal tank with required inlet and outlet ports
- Tank insulation
- Integrated heat exchanger(s) if required
- Direct vent (sealed) intake and exhaust (for combustion units)
- Pressure and temperature relief valve, pumps, expansion tank and balance of system as required
- Controls as required

How the system works

A tank of the desired size (75–1100 liters / 20–300 gallons is common for residential purposes) holds water, which is heated from inside the tank. Combustion-fired units have a burner and exhaust inside the tank, and heat is absorbed into the water through contact with the chimney. Electric units have resistance heating elements inside the tank. Water is raised to and maintained at the desired temperature, and drawn from the tank as use requires.

Some units have integrated heat exchanger(s) to allow for combined use of space heating and domestic hot water and/or combining the tank with solar hydronic input.

SYSTEM OUTPUT

Residential water heater tanks have outputs that range from 10,000–200,000 Btu/hr, depending on their volume capacity and type of burner or electric element. Efficiency rates for combustion boilers range from 90–98 percent. Electric units are 100-percent efficient.

Tips for successful installation

1. Heat loss is the largest drawback for water tanks. Choose a tank with the best possible insulation value, and consider adding extra insulation to the tank once it is installed.
2. Position the tank in a conditioned space to prevent heat losses that will occur in colder, unconditioned parts of the home.

Pros and cons

ENVIRONMENTAL IMPACTS: *HIGH*

The impacts for water heater tanks are directly linked to the fuel source used to generate the heat. When considering the impacts of a fuel source, it is important to be as thorough as possible. Calculations for impacts must consider the entire life cycle, from extraction to processing, transportation, combustion and by-products. Effects on habitat, social fabric, geopolitical and financial systems and resilience must be taken into account along with more easily quantifiable (though likely controversial) numerical assessments such as carbon contributions and air pollutants (see Ranking Fuel Sources sidebar).

MATERIAL COSTS: *LOW*

LABOR INPUT: *LOW*

Tank batch heaters are simple to install.

SKILL LEVEL REQUIRED FOR THE HOMEOWNER

Installation — *Easy.*

Use — *Easy.*

Maintenance — *Easy.* Annual flushing will help prevent build up of sediment.

SOURCING/AVAILABILITY: *EASY*

Competitive quotes will be available in all regions.

CODE COMPLIANCE

Hot water tanks are an accepted solution in all building codes. It is not common to use a hot water tank as the main heat supply for a home, but if the Btu output matches the heat loss calculation it will be acceptable.

DURABILITY: *MODERATE TO HIGH*

Tanks are very durable, and elements and burners can be replaced without changing the whole tank. Sedimentation and scaling are the biggest issues, but can be addressed with regular maintenance. Glass-lined tanks will not corrode, but metal tanks will eventually corrode over decades.

INDOOR AIR QUALITY

Any combustion device can create IAQ issues, as they consume air and produce exhaust. Modern, code-approved devices have "sealed" combustion, meaning that combustion air is drawn directly from outside and exhausted back to the outside, and usually drawn by a fan to ensure proper flow. There are many possible points of leakage in these systems; be sure to check installations for issues. The combustion chamber is never completely sealed from indoors, and some amount of indoor air will be drawn into the unit.

Hydronic delivery systems result in gentle air movement and minimal circulation of dust and allergens.

Forced-air delivery systems can circulate a lot of dust and allergens. Use the best filters possible to help reduce issues.

Adequate ventilation is required in any well-sealed home. Whether provided actively or passively, ensure that pre-warmed fresh air is introduced and circulated in the home during seasons when windows are closed.

FUTURE DEVELOPMENT

The hot water tank is a simple device that has not changed much in the past decade, and is unlikely to develop in the future. More and better insulation is starting to be used on tanks, and improvements in this area would help reduce heat loss.

RESILIENCE

Hot water tanks can function in some low-energy scenarios. The tanks are simple to adapt to home-made solar hydronic collectors.

———

Forced-air furnaces

What the cheerleaders say...	What the detractors say...
Time-tested technology	Most units use fossil fuels
Efficient	Expensive
Easy to modulate	Ductwork is costly
	Dust and allergens circulated

Heat production and delivery

- Biomass heat production (wood- and pellet-fired)
- Fossil fuel heat production (gas- and oil-fired)
- Biofuel heat production (biodiesel- and vegetable oil-fired)
- Electric resistance heat production
- Forced-air delivery

System components

- Combustion chamber (or resistance elements for electric units)
- Heat exchanger and plenum
- Direct vent (sealed) intake and exhaust (for combustion units)
- Circulation fan
- Controls as required

How the system works

When heat is required, a burner ignites (or electric elements are powered). A heat exchanger plate absorbs heat from the flame/element and transfers it to the air being blown through the plenum.

The ductwork has both heat supply ducts and cold air return ducts. The cold air return ducts congregate at the plenum, where the air is reheated and forced through the supply ducts to outlets throughout the home. A filter is situated near the plenum to remove dust and allergens as the air is circulated.

SYSTEM OUTPUT

Residential furnaces typically have outputs that range from 40,000–150,000 Btu/hr. Efficiency rates range from 89–96 percent.

In most cases, the expressed efficiency is not the "true" thermal efficiency, which could be measured at an ideal steady state and not reflect real world performance. The accepted standard of efficiency is "annual fuel utilization efficiency" (AFUE). The method for determining the AFUE for residential furnaces is the subject of ASHRAE Standard 103. Ensure that rated output for comparison between units is the AFUE.

Tips for successful installation

1. Be sure the furnace is sized appropriately, based on an accurate heat loss calculation.
2. A variable speed fan can increase efficiency by turning at a speed best suited to the heating requirements, rather than being on or off.
3. Consider integrating a mechanical ventilation system into the ductwork for the furnace, rather than having two separate systems.
4. Keep ductwork within the building enclosure and be sure the ductwork layout is as efficient as possible.
5. Carefully consider the positioning of ductwork outlets. Common practice places outlets blowing upwards beneath windows, but this is not necessary in an airtight, efficient home with high-quality windows. Try to place outlets where they won't be blocked by furniture, and aimed so they blow horizontally across the floor instead of pumping hot air at the ceiling.
6. Invest in the highest quality filters available for the furnace.
7. Be sure to have the system balanced at commissioning. Fine-tuning the output of each outlet will result in greater comfort and efficiency.

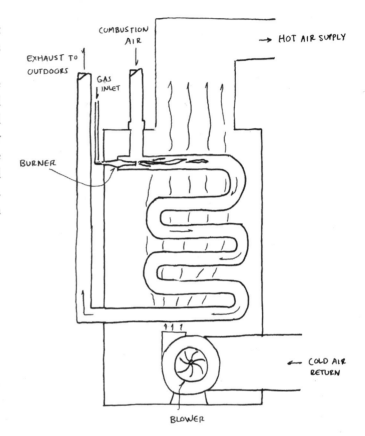

Pros and cons

ENVIRONMENTAL IMPACTS: *HIGH*

The impacts for furnaces are directly linked to the fuel source used to fire the furnace. When considering the impacts of a fuel source, it is important to be as thorough as possible. Calculations for impacts must consider the entire life cycle, from extraction to processing, transportation, combustion and by-products. Effects on habitat, social fabric, geopolitical and financial systems and resilience must be taken into account along with more easily quantifiable (though likely controversial) numerical assessments such as carbon contributions and air pollutants (see Ranking Fuel Sources sidebar).

MATERIAL COSTS: *MODERATE*

LABOR INPUT: *MODERATE*

Installing a furnace is fairly straightforward, but the ductwork can add a great deal of time and complexity.

SKILL LEVEL REQUIRED FOR THE HOMEOWNER

Installation — *Difficult.* Most furnace and ductwork installations require a qualified professional.

Use — *Easy.*

Maintenance — *Easy to Moderate.* Monthly inspection of filter. Annual inspection of burner flame (if required).

SOURCING/AVAILABILITY: *EASY*

Competitive quotes for furnace system designers, suppliers and installers will be available in all regions.

CODE COMPLIANCE

Furnace systems are an accepted solution in all codes. New technologies like pellet and biofuel boilers may require alternative compliance efforts.

INDOOR AIR QUALITY

Any combustion device can create IAQ issues, as they consume air and produce exhaust. Modern, code-approved devices have "sealed" combustion, meaning that combustion air is drawn directly from outside and exhausted back to the outside, and usually drawn by a fan to ensure proper flow. There are many possible points of leakage in these systems; be sure to check installations for issues. The combustion chamber is never completely sealed from indoors, and some amount of indoor air will be drawn into the unit.

Solid fuel burning devices will generate ash as a by-product, and in most cases the ash is stored in the unit and will need to be manually emptied. This can introduce a lot of dust into the home. The movement of firewood and, to a lesser degree, pellet fuel will also introduce dust and allergens.

Hydronic delivery systems result in gentle air movement and minimal circulation of dust and allergens.

Forced-air delivery systems can circulate a lot of dust and allergens. Use the best filters possible to help reduce issues.

Adequate ventilation is required in any well-sealed home. Whether provided actively or passively, ensure that pre-warmed fresh air is introduced and circulated in the home during seasons when windows are closed.

DURABILITY: *MODERATE TO HIGH*

Modern furnaces can last 20 to 50 years, depending on use and maintenance. Manufacturers offer warranties of five to ten years on heat exchangers and fans.

FUTURE DEVELOPMENT

Efficiency levels for furnaces are approaching 100 percent, beyond which there is no further improvement. Refinement of controls and especially variable speed fans will likely lead to some gains for entire systems.

The integration of ventilation systems with furnaces offers an opportunity to make both systems more efficient and improve the air quality in the home.

RESILIENCE

Furnaces can be operated in a low-energy scenario, but the entire system could not be manufactured and installed without significant energy input.

Resources for further research

Vizi, Roger. *Forced Hot Air Furnaces: Troubleshooting and Repair.* New York: McGraw-Hill, 1999. Print.

Wood and pellet stoves

What the cheerleaders say...	What the detractors say...
Local, sustainable fuel source	High maintenance, manual input
Creates pleasant heat and ambiance	Potentially high air pollution
Simple and affordable	Not code compliant as primary heat source in many jurisdictions
Resilient, no fossil fuels	Dangers due to open flame and chimney creosote

Heat production and delivery

- Biomass heat production (wood- and pellet-fired)
- Passive air/radiant delivery system
- Hydronic heat delivery available for some systems
- Forced-air delivery available for some systems
- Can be used for domestic hot water heating

System components

- Burn chamber and ash pan
- Air inlet and controls
- Exhaust outlet and controls
- Fuel delivery system (pellet stoves)
- Blower fan (some units)
- Water-heating coil or tank (some units)

How the system works

A freestanding unit is placed, usually centrally, in the home. The unit has a burn chamber where a fire is lit and burns, heating a combination of masonry and metal around the chamber.

Combustion air is introduced through a manually or mechanically controlled inlet. Ideally, this air enters through a sealed inlet directly from outdoors. This is nearly always the case with pellet-burning units, but not as common with woodstoves.

Exhaust is vented through a chimney. This is accomplished passively in some units (mostly woodstoves), relying on the warm temperature of spent exhaust gas to provide an upward draft. In some units (mostly pellet stoves), a fan is used to draw combustion gasses out of the burn chamber and through the chimney.

The heat from the fire makes the metal surface of the unit hot, and the heat is transferred radiantly and also through significant convection loops formed as air is heated by the stove and rises with some force. As warmed air moves along the ceiling it cools and falls. Room shape and the location of door and window openings will help determine the paths of convection loops.

A fan may be incorporated to actively move heat from the stove into the room. Minimal ductwork is incorporated in some units.

Rare models feature the ability to heat water within the stove. This can be a contribution to hydronic space heating and/or domestic hot water.

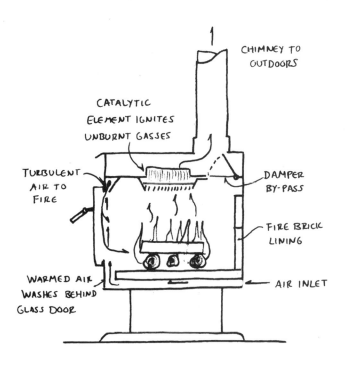

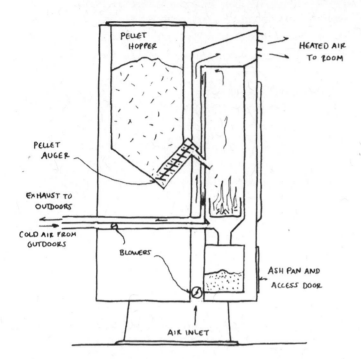

Labels in diagram: PELLET HOPPER, HEATED AIR TO ROOM, PELLET AUGER, EXHAUST TO OUTDOORS, COLD AIR FROM OUTDOORS, BLOWERS, ASH PAN AND ACCESS DOOR, AIR INLET

Fuel for woodstoves is manually input directly into the firebox through an opening door. Pellet stoves use an auger to automatically deliver fuel for combustion from a supply hopper. This hopper must be filled with pellets as required. Large hoppers can be used to ensure long periods of unattended operation.

SYSTEM OUTPUT

Rated outputs for woodstoves are estimations, and actual output will be dependent upon combustion air supply, chimney draft and the species and dryness of firewood. Typical residential models range from 50,000–200,000 Btu/hr. Burn efficiency is also difficult to accurately establish, but manufacturer claims range from 65–80 percent.

Pellet stoves have more accurate ratings, as pellets have relatively uniform density and moisture properties. Typical residential models range from

30,000–160,000 Btu/hr. Manufacturers claim burn efficiencies ranging from 70–90 percent.

Tips for successful installation

1. The positioning of the unit in the home will affect performance, especially where heat transfer is entirely passive. Central positioning is usually considered ideal, but placement should correspond to areas where more or less heat is desired in the home.
2. Chimney installation often has to be done by a licensed professional. Chimney position should ensure proper clearances, lengths, minimal bends and proper height.
3. The need to bring fuel to the stove and remove ash should be considered when deciding upon placement.
4. Every stove will have specifications for minimum clearances from all sides of the unit, and for chimney placement and floor protection. Be sure to follow these guidelines accurately.

Pros and cons

ENVIRONMENTAL IMPACTS

See Biomass as a Heat Source sidebar.

MATERIAL COSTS: *LOW TO MODERATE*
LABOR INPUT: *LOW TO MODERATE*

Chimney installation is the largest labor component with solid fuel devices. Woodstoves require an extensive chimney that must exit the building through the roof, adding complexity and cost. Pellet devices are typically direct-vented, using fan-driven air and chimneys that can exit the building directly through the wall, a simpler solution requiring lower labor input.

SKILL LEVEL REQUIRED FOR THE HOMEOWNER

Installation — *Moderate to Difficult.* In many jurisdictions, a licensed professional must install stoves.

Owner installation requires making penetrations through wall and/or ceiling/roof for the chimney and inlet air.

Use — *Moderate to Difficult*. Stoves must be monitored regularly for temperature regulation, and fuel added as required. Pellet stoves typically have automatic ignition, removing the need to light fires when needed.

Maintenance — *Moderate to Difficult*. Ash pans must be emptied regularly, and combustion chambers cleaned. Chimney inspections should be performed at least twice a year.

Sourcing/availability: *Easy to Moderate*

Competitive quotes for supplying and installing wood and pellet stoves are available in all regions with a heating season.

Code compliance

Woodstoves are an acceptable solution in all codes, but many codes will not accept them as a "primary" heat source, requiring some form of automated heating system to ensure the home can be heated if the stove is not running. This does not mean that the homeowner cannot use the woodstove as the main source of heat, but another form of heat must be included.

Pellet stoves are a more recent addition, and are an accepted solution in most codes. They currently occupy a "grey area" in regards to their use as a primary heat source, as they can be fed automatically for a length of time that corresponds to the storage capacity of the hopper.

Durability: *Moderate to High*

Woodstoves are very durable. Most have no or only simple moving parts and can be expected to last for the lifetime of the building.

Pellet stoves have more mechanical components, but have shown themselves to be quite durable.

Expected life span is 15 to 40 years, with manufacturers offering warranties from five to ten years.

Indoor air quality

Wood and pellet burning devices will have a negative impact on IAQ.

Woodstoves — The movement of cordwood through the home and its storage in the home can introduce large quantities of mold spores, dust and other outdoor allergens. The collection and movement of ash will result in some amount of the material being spread in the air. As the woodstove is opened to feed the fire, combustion gasses and

Woodstove.

Pellet stove.

ash will enter the room, and this process is repeated many times a day.

Pellet stoves — Filling the hopper with pellets and emptying the ashes will introduce significant quantities of dust into the air. Hoppers can be placed outside the building to significantly eliminate this source of dust.

The high surface temperature of the stoves can cause large convection currents that circulate dust and allergens. Dust can also be burnt as it touches the stove body, resulting in combustion by-products from a wide variety of particles.

The use of wood- or pellet-burning devices should be accompanied by the use of a good quality active air filtration system if indoor air quality is a priority.

Adequate ventilation is required in any well-sealed home. Whether provided actively or passively, ensure that pre-warmed fresh air is introduced and circulated in the home during seasons when windows are closed.

FUTURE DEVELOPMENT

Woodstoves — Developments in wood-burning technology in the past couple of decades have seen the widespread adoption of secondary combustion systems that help to burn unspent gasses before they exit the unit. Without a move toward more active systems, including gasification and other fan-driven technologies, woodstoves are unlikely to see substantial change.

Pellet stoves — Residential pellet stoves are relative newcomers, and large improvements have been made over the past couple of product generations. Efficiency rates have risen and reliability and controls are better and more accurate. There are likely to be several more generations of improvement before the technology becomes more widespread and stable.

RESILIENCE

Wood and pellet stoves are ideal heating systems for low- or no-energy scenarios, where fuel stocks are readily accessible.

Resources for further research

Thomas, Dirk. *The Harrowsmith Country Life Guide to Wood Heat.* Charlotte, VT: Camden House, 1992. Print.

Thomas, Dirk. *The Woodburner's Companion: Practical Ways of Heating with Wood.* Chambersburg, PA: Alan C. Hood, 2006. Print.

Jenkins, Dilwyn. *Wood Pellet Heating Systems: The Earthscan Expert Handbook on Planning, Design and Installation.* London: Earthscan, 2010. Print.

Masonry heaters

What the cheerleaders say...	What the detractors say...
Very efficient wood burning	Expensive
Even temperatures compared to woodstoves	Heavy
No chimney fire issues	High maintenance, manual input
Easily used for cooking and water heating	

Heat production and delivery

- Biomass heat production (wood-fired)
- Passive air/radiant delivery system
- Hydronic heat delivery available for some systems
- Can be used for domestic hot water heating

System components

- Burn chamber and ash pan
- Masonry chimney with non-linear pathway
- Masonry shroud (can be any kind of masonry, including clay)
- Air inlet and controls
- Cooking oven space (some units)
- Water heating coil or tank (some units)

How the system works

A freestanding unit is placed, usually centrally, in the home. The weight of the unit often requires special foundation considerations for adequate support. The unit has a burn chamber where a fire is lit and burns.

Combustion air is introduced through a manually or mechanically controlled inlet. Ideally, this air enters through a sealed inlet directly from outdoors. Masonry heaters do not use dampers on the air inlet, as the fire is burned at the highest possible temperature, requiring a significant column of air.

Exhaust gasses do not exit directly into a straight chimney, as with woodstoves. Instead, a masonry chimney with a non-linear path receives the gasses. Once the combustion chamber and chimney have become heated, the entire chimney pathway acts as a secondary burn chamber. At full temperature, practically 100 percent of the gasses are combusted within the chimney. These units are not limited in their burn temperatures by any metal components, and can burn at 1200–1800°C (2200–2900°F).

Heat is absorbed by the masonry of the combustion chamber and chimney and radiated to an outer sheathing of masonry separated from the core by an air space. In this way, the interior of the home is not exposed to the very high temperatures, but the majority of the stored heat is slowly released to the room at comfortable temperatures. The outer sheathing can be made from a wide range of materials, from stone or brick to clay or tile. Spent

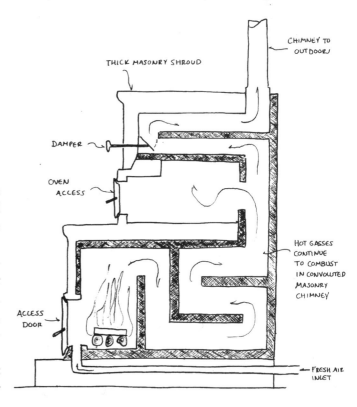

gasses leave the building via a straight run of metal or masonry chimney.

A fire is built in the masonry heater as often as is required to keep the whole unit at a comfortable temperature. The large amount of fuel requires a long time to reach operating temperature, and then takes a long time to cool down. The units are at their most efficient when burning hot, and timing of fires is important to keep the heaters in the proper temperature range. The burn time is usually much shorter than with less efficient woodstoves.

Rare models feature the ability to heat water within the stove. This can contribute to hydronic space heating and/or domestic hot water.

Fuel for woodstoves is manually input directly into the firebox through an opening door, and ash is removed as required.

SYSTEM OUTPUT

There are no third-party ratings for masonry heaters, but estimates based on the volume of wood typically burned in an hour of operation range from 10,000–30,000 Btu/hr.

At proper operating temperature, combustion is 100-percent efficient. It will be less than that when starting from cold temperatures.

Tips for successful installation

1. Be sure the masonry heater is "lifestyle appropriate" before deciding to install one. These heaters require an even schedule of firing, and are not suitable for quickly taking the chill off a room. A cold stove can take long hours to reach comfortable temperatures.
2. Foundations must be designed to carry the weight of a masonry heater.
3. Central placement in the home is usually recommended. The mild surface temperature and passive heat delivery are most evenly distributed from the middle of the building.

4. A suitable column of outdoor air should be available to the stove, and must be included in the building plans.
5. The need to bring fuel to the stove and remove ash should be considered when deciding upon placement.
6. Many masonry heaters come as Precast kits, in which a properly designed combustion chamber and chimney are prefabricated and assembled on-site. Follow all installation instructions when using a kit.

Pros and cons

ENVIRONMENTAL IMPACTS: *Low*

Masonry heaters make efficient use of wood fuel, extracting the full heat value and leaving only minute traces of gasses in the atmosphere. See Biomass as a Heat Source sidebar.

MATERIAL COSTS: *MODERATE TO HIGH*
LABOR INPUT: *MODERATE TO HIGH*

The assembly of a masonry core and shroud is quite labor intensive. A bigger heater and the addition of features like ovens and water heating jackets will increase labor.

SKILL LEVEL REQUIRED FOR THE HOMEOWNER

Installation — *Difficult.* Precast kits make it possible for owners to build a masonry heater, but some degree of experience with masonry work is recommended.

Use — *Moderate.* Firings must be made on a regular schedule.

Maintenance — *Easy to Moderate.* Ash removal must be performed regularly.

SOURCING/AVAILABILITY: *MODERATE*

Several manufacturers in North America specialize in making precast kits for masonry heater cores, and a small number of masons build units from scratch. Any experienced mason should be able to build a kit unit and a custom shroud.

CODE COMPLIANCE

Masonry heaters are not an accepted solution in any codes in North America. Provisions exist for the construction of masonry fireplaces, which are of quite different construction but present a useful framework. A standard has been developed, ASTM 1602 E–01 "Standard Guide for Construction of Solid Fuel Burning Masonry Heaters," and this document is helpful for achieving alternative compliance.

DURABILITY: *VERY HIGH*

A well-built masonry heater can last for centuries.

INDOOR AIR QUALITY

The movement of cordwood through the home and its storage in the home can introduce large quantities of mold spores, dust and other outdoor allergens. The collection and movement of ash will result in some amount of the material being spread in the air. As the woodstove is opened to feed the fire, combustion gasses and ash will enter the room and this process is repeated many times a day.

The use of wood-burning devices should be accompanied by the use of a good quality active air filtration system if indoor air quality is a priority.

Adequate ventilation is required in any well-sealed home. Whether provided actively or passively, ensure that pre-warmed fresh air is introduced and circulated in the home during seasons when windows are closed.

FUTURE DEVELOPMENT

Masonry heater technology can be traced back thousands of years, with a variety of approaches having been developed in most northern climates. The advent of commercially produced core kits was a major development over the past couple of decades, allowing homeowners and masons to build heaters that perform well without the potential problems of site-built designs. Combustion technology continues to inform and refine these designs.

The coupling of masonry heater design with pellet fuel systems would combine the benefits of masonry heaters with automatic ignition and feed convenience.

The further integration of water heating and cooking into heater designs will help to offset the high initial costs by absorbing several functions.

The weight and permanence of masonry heaters makes it unlikely that they will ever be a major part of the market, but their efficiency and comfort deserves to win them a larger presence than they currently maintain.

RESILIENCE

It is possible to build and operate a masonry heater in a no- or low-energy scenario. They are the most efficient and practical option for a homeowner with access to fuel stock.

Resources for further research

Matesz, Ken. *Masonry Heaters: Designing, Building, and Living with a Piece of the Sun.* White River Junction, VT: Chelsea Green, 2010. Print.

Lyle, David. *The Book of Masonry Stoves: Rediscovering an Old Way of Warming.* Andover, MA: Brick House, 1984. Print.

Rocket mass heaters

Rocket stoves are a type of wood burner that can provide intense, concentrated heat from a small amount of wood. They were initially conceived to assist people in developing countries maximize the cooking potential of scarce fuel stocks. The system utilizes a similar principle as masonry stoves, with the fire being fed as much air as required for complete combustion.

Rocket stoves vary in design, but typically feature an open combustion chamber leading into a vertical (often insulated) chimney section into which additional air is supplied. The secondary burn in the vertical chimney section reaches high temperatures and combusts most of the wood gasses. The heat from the secondary burn is absorbed in a masonry (usually clay) mass and allowed to radiate into the home in a manner similar to the masonry heater. A masonry chimney ducts the spent gasses out of the home, absorbing most of the remaining heat.

There are many challenges to incorporating a rocket mass heater into a home. Most are built with an open combustion chamber, which can allow smoke to backdraft into the home. This can happen when the fire is first being lit and proper updraft has not been established, or if pressure changes outside the house cause blowback. Rocket heaters use small-diameter wood, which is quick to ignite and burn and is easier to collect than large-diameter cordwood. However, thinner pieces burn quickly and the stoves can require fairly constant attention and feeding.

The principle of the rocket mass heater has a lot of promise, and early adopters will likely continue to develop and refine the approach until it becomes a feasible heating option for a wider number of homeowners. It is likely that commercialized versions of the rocket stove will make their way onto the market in the next few years.

There is currently no building code or standards recognition of rocket mass heaters, but this too is likely to change as the design is commercialized and standardized.

Resources for further research

Evans, Ianto, and Leslie Jackson. *Rocket Mass Heaters: Superefficient Woodstoves You Can Build.* Coquille, OR: Cob Cottage, 2006. Print.

Chapter title page photo credits. Top left to right. 1, 3 & 4. Chris Magwood 2. Dan Earle

12

Electrical generation

IN THE SHORT SPACE OF A CENTURY, electrical energy has gone from a rare novelty to an absolute necessity. Rare is the homeowner that does not envision some form of electrical power in their building. For lighting, heating, refrigeration, communications or work reducing appliances, electrical energy is ubiquitous in our homes. It has proven to be an abundant and affordable source of power, the likes of which have never been experienced on the planet.

Homeowners wishing to make use of electrical energy have three major sourcing options to meet their power needs.

Grid power — Most homeowners receive their energy from public or private utility companies, whose large, centralized generating stations produce high volumes of energy that are distributed through a network of transmission lines that connect almost every home and business in North America and has come to be known as "the grid."

The infrastructure of the electrical grid is vast. It is a rare and uninhabited place in North America where some visual sign of the electrical grid is not present. The energy on the grid is carefully monitored and controlled from point of generation to end user.

There are many kinds of electrical generation on the grid, including:

Hydroelectric — The power of falling water is used to spin turbines that generate electricity.

Fossil fuel plants — Heat from the burning of fossil fuels (including coal and natural gas) is used to create steam that is used to spin turbines that generate electricity.

Nuclear plants — Heat from the fission of atoms is used to create steam that is used to spin turbines that generate electricity.

2009 US Electricity Generation by Source

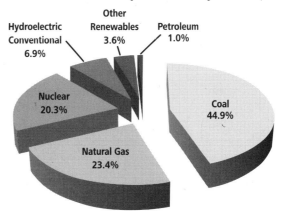

Hydroelectric Conventional 6.9%
Other Renewables 3.6%
Petroleum 1.0%
Nuclear 20.3%
Natural Gas 23.4%
Coal 44.9%

Wind turbines — The power of wind is used to spin turbines that generate electricity.

Solar thermal — The heat of the sun is concentrated and used to create steam that is used to spin turbines that generate electricity.

Photovoltaic — Photons from the sun are used to displace free electrons on a silicon wafer to generate electrical current.

Regionally, different balances of these sources make up the overall available energy. It is impossible for a homeowner to know the exact source of the electrical energy being used in the home. Proximity to a particular generating station is some indication, but it is the nature of the grid that it is impossible for the homeowner to predict power flow.

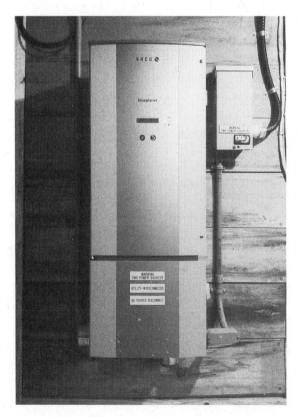

Grid tie inverter.

Most of the electrical power on the grid is generated by means that have major, well-documented environmental impacts. Centralized production is also extremely inefficient, with overall losses in production ranging from 30–70 percent and transmission losses around 8 percent, which means that only a fraction of the energy value of the fuel being used is actually making it to the end user.

A small number of private utility companies offer homeowners a means of "purchasing" 100 percent renewable energy from the grid. Under these programs, the amount of electricity used by a homeowner is put onto the grid by the private utility, offsetting the need for that amount of "dirty" power to be generated.

Grid-Tied — The grid has always been a two-way power highway; electrons will move from a point of generation to a point of consumption in either direction along a wire. Until quite recently, utility companies treated the grid like a one-way street running from central production facilities to end users. In recent years, the value of "distributed generation" has become evident and many utilities have begun to allow for small-scale production by homeowners and businesses, often under direction from governments.

"Grid-tied" homeowners and businesses produce power (typically with renewable sources like photovoltaic, wind and small-scale hydro) under a variety of different contracts and terms. Generated power is put onto the grid and the owner of the generator receives money or credit for that power. If the owner also requires electrical power, it is supplied from the grid. In this way, a homeowner can become a "net-zero" electricity user, generating as much power as he or she uses.

These grid-tied systems offer numerous benefits to both homeowners and utility companies. Homeowners can provide for a desired portion of their own electrical needs (from a small percentage to overproduction for profit), yet not be reliant on having to store and manage their own power supply, as would be necessary for off-grid systems. Renewable sources like solar and wind produce a lot of power sometimes and no power at other times. With the grid as a "buffer" the home is never without power when needed. Utility companies benefit from having homeowners and businesses put out the investment for new production that can collectively offset the need for expensive new large-scale generating capacity and increase the percentage of clean renewable energy in their mix.

Distributed generation helps to reduce the high production and transmission losses associated with centralized power plants by reducing the distance from point of production to point of use, and creates a more resilient grid less susceptible to massive outages when a large power plant goes offline.

Dual gang meter for grid tie.

Off-Grid — A much smaller number of homeowners generate and manage their own electrical energy, functioning independently in "off-grid" homes. These systems typically rely on a bank of batteries that provide chemical storage of electrical energy, which can be charged by the home energy system as power is available and drained when power is required in the home.

Off-grid systems reward energy-efficient home design and conservative power use within the home. If energy demands are low, this type of system can be affordable and reliable. As demands rise (and most North Americans demand much more power than is practical to supply in an off-grid system), the systems grow in size, complexity and cost.

The addition of battery storage, off-grid systems require the homeowner to house and maintain batteries and associated controls and ensure the balance of power in and out of the system.

Inverter and off grid solar controls.

Off-grid systems are typically much larger than grid-tied systems, to accommodate the variable nature of renewable energy, where daily and seasonal swings in generation can require overproduction and large storage capacity of power is to be available through times of low or no production.

Off-grid systems provide a high degree of independence and resilience, with little or no reliance on outside sources of production or delivery.

For the purposes of this book, only renewable forms of electrical power generation will be considered.

Photovoltaic power

What the cheerleaders say...	What the detractors say...
Clean, non-polluting	Limited hours of production
Abundantly renewable	Expensive
Reliable	
Affordable	

Energy source
- Solar radiation

System components
- Photovoltaic panels
- DC to AC inverter
- Connectors, junctions and balance of system components
- Storage batteries (if required)

How the system works

The photovoltaic effect describes the ability of photons of light (predominantly from the sun) to excite electrons into a higher state of energy, allowing them to act as charge carriers for an electric current.

Most photovoltaic systems use flat cells of silicon that have been "doped" with an additional electron on one side and one less electron on the other. Photons strike and excite the extra electron, causing it to "jump" to conductors embedded in the cell, where it completes whatever circuit has been wired to the cell. Multiple cells are linked together as modules (panels), which are protected by a glass covering and typically installed in an aluminum frame. Multiple panels can be wired together to provide a desired output.

PV modules produce direct current (DC). In most systems, an inverter is employed to change DC to alternating current (AC), the type of current used for grid power and household appliances.

SYSTEM OUTPUT

Modules from different manufacturers will have

varying output depending on the size, number and efficiency of the cells. Modules are rated for their output in watts in peak sun conditions. Typical output for current photovoltaic technology is in the range of 1000kWh per year per 1kW peak module sizing, or an average continuous output of 114W.

Current PV technology converts 13–18 percent of the available solar energy to electric energy.

Tips for successful installation

1. Modules must face the sun as squarely as possible. For fixed installations, this means facing south at a tilt angle that is the best average of the sun's height above the horizon.
2. Any amount of shading of the modules will greatly reduce output. Ensure that trees, buildings and other potential obstructions will not shade the modules at any time of day, year round.
3. Follow all local electrical code requirements for the installation of PV modules and equipment.

Pros and cons

ENVIRONMENTAL IMPACTS: *Low*

PV emits no carbon or other pollutants to produce power. The US Department of Energy and the National Renewable Energy Laboratory both estimate that a PV module generates as much energy as the input required to manufacture the module in about two years. Given life expectancy that exceeds 30 years, the overall energy output far exceeds the embodied energy.

As PV only produces power in the presence of direct sunlight, no power is produced at night and output is reduced in cloudy weather and at around dusk and dawn. Environmental impacts can arise from the need to either store the PV power or use other, less clean forms of power when PV is not producing.

Photovoltaics. (CHESTER RENNIE)

MATERIAL COSTS: *MODERATE TO HIGH*

LABOR INPUT: *MODERATE TO HIGH*

Racks and mounts are prefabricated for straightforward installation. Labor requirements will be based on the placement of the mounts. Roof mounts may require additional bracing of the roof framing, and care must be taken while making multiple penetrations through the roof to avoid creating leaks. Ground mounts can require substantial anchors.

SKILL LEVEL REQUIRED FOR THE HOMEOWNER

Installation — *Moderate to Difficult.* An understanding of basic wiring and PV configuration is required. Roof mounting may require special equipment.

Use — *Easy.*

Maintenance — *Easy.* Panels should be kept clean for maximum output.

SOURCING/AVAILABILITY: *EASY*

PV has become widely available in the past decade, with sufficient suppliers and installers to ensure competitive quotes.

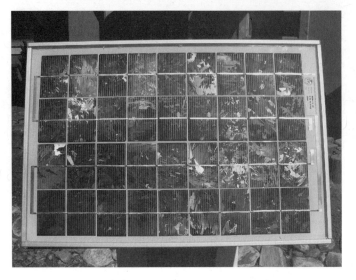

PV panel.

In the meantime, existing PV technology has experienced a cost revolution, with increased demand and production lowering prices dramatically in the past five years, and little sign of imminent decline. Per watt PV prices are approaching parity with other, dirtier forms of power.

The number of utilities and governments offering incentives to homeowners and businesses for PV installations are making the technology familiar and common in many regions.

RESILIENCE

PV panels cannot be manufactured in a low-energy scenario, but can be operated for decades with no further input.

Resources for further research

Boxwell, Michael. *Solar Electricity Handbook: A Simple, Practical Guide to Solar Energy — Designing and Installing Photovoltaic Solar Electric Systems*. Ryton-on-Dunsmore, UK: Greenstream, 2010. Print.

Mayfield, Ryan. *Photovoltaic Design and Installation for Dummies*. Hoboken, NJ: Wiley, 2010. Print.

Chiras, Daniel D., Robert Aram, and Kurt Nelson. *Solar Electricity Basics*. Gabriola Island, BC: New Society, 2010. Print.

CODE COMPLIANCE

All North American electrical codes now address PV installations. Building codes may offer accepted solutions for roof mounting systems, or may require engineered designs.

DURABILITY: *VERY HIGH*

PV manufacturers offer a standard 25-year output warranty. Inverters are typically warrantied for five to ten years.

FUTURE DEVELOPMENT

A huge amount of research and development work is being applied to improving the efficiency of current PV technologies and experimenting with new approaches. Hardly a week goes by when the news media doesn't trumpet a laboratory "breakthrough" in solar technology. We will likely see improvements and perhaps even major advances in this field in the upcoming decades.

Wind turbines

What the cheerleaders say...	What the detractors say...
Clean, non-polluting	Unreliable output
Abundantly renewable	Complex
Affordable	Requires ideal conditions
	Towers are intrusive

Energy source

- Wind movement

System components

- Airfoil blades
- Generator
- Directional tail
- Tower base
- Balance of system as required

How the system works

Airfoil blades are attached to the shaft of a generator. The force of moving air causes the blades to spin and the generator to produce current.

The blades and generator are mounted on a pivot at the top of a tower that places the unit in clean air flow, undisturbed by obstructions that cause turbulence in the wind.

Most residential units produce "wild" power, with output levels that vary based on wind speed. Controllers even out the power delivery. Power may be produced in either AC or DC current, depending on the design of the unit.

Some form of wind speed limiter will be used for every turbine, as extreme wind conditions can severely damage the unit.

SYSTEM OUTPUT

Wind generators are rated according to their output at a particular wind speed. The wattage advertised is not a static output, and manufacturers do not all use the same wind speed for their ratings. This makes direct comparisons difficult.

More important than any advertised rating is the power curve for the unit, which shows how much power is produced at any given wind speed. Choose a unit that has the best possible output at the average wind speed at the installation site.

Tips for successful installation

1. Lack of obstruction is critical for residential-scale wind turbines. In general, the turbine must be twice as tall as any obstruction within ten times its height. Otherwise it will be in turbulent air and produce much less power.
2. Follow the manufacturer's instructions for tower assembly and turbine installation.

Wind power.

Pros and cons

Environmental impacts: *Low*

Wind power emits no carbon or other pollutants to produce power. The units will produce many times more power than was used in their creation.

Environmental issues that are sometimes raised for large-scale turbine installations do not typically apply to small residential units.

Material costs: *Moderate to High*
Labor input: *High*

Raising a tall tower can be a labor-intensive process, and typically represents the majority of the labor time for a wind installation.

Skill level required for the homeowner

Installation — *Moderate to Difficult.* Raising a tall tower can require experience and special equipment.
Use — *Easy.*
Maintenance — *Moderate to Difficult.* The turbine will need to be inspected on an annual basis, which can require bringing down or climbing the tower.

Sourcing/availability: *Moderate to Difficult*

Numerous companies manufacture residential wind turbines, and experienced installers can be found in most regions with viable wind resources.

Code compliance

All electrical codes address the wiring of residential wind turbines. Building codes and/or municipal by-laws may govern the construction of towers.

Durability: *Low to Moderate*

Wind turbines are often subjected to extreme conditions, and can experience durability issues. High wind speeds and buffeting, freezing rain and lightning strikes can all cause failure. In reasonable conditions, key components like blades, bearings and generator should last five to ten years and can be replaced to keep the unit functional for much longer.

Future development

Wind power is limited by two key factors that cannot be overcome by technological advancements: average wind speed and height above obstructions.

There is no magic way to make more power than the average wind speed can produce. Refinements in blade design and innovations in vertical shaft technology have raised outputs minimally, but most turbines do not produce useful power in wind speeds lower than 13–16 km/h (8–10 mph).

Turbines must be placed in clear air flow, at least twice as high as the tallest obstruction within ten times the tower height.

Mechanical energy from wind power

The generation of electrical current requires high revolutions per minute (rpm) to make useful power. In many cases, low wind speed and high tower heights make it impractical to generate electrical power with residential wind turbines.

However, there are many applications for torque-based, mechanical energy that can be derived from wind energy at much lower speeds. These include powering belt-driven appliances, water pumps, compressor motors and pond aerators.

Many of these wind power applications can be bought or built for a lot less money than turbines and are worth investigating.

If wind speed and height conditions exist to make an installation feasible, wind power is a feasible option and improvements in controls, aerodynamics and durability will be appreciated.

RESILIENCE

It is possible to build and install a wind turbine in a low- or no-energy scenario.

Resources for further research

Shea, Kevin, and Brian C. Howard. *Build Your Own Small Wind Power System*. New York: McGraw-Hill, 2012. Print.

Chiras, Daniel D., Mick Sagrillo, and Ian Woofenden. *Wind Power Basics*. Gabriola Island, BC: New Society, 2010. Print.

Micro-hydro turbines

What the cheerleaders say...	What the detractors say...
Clean, non-polluting	Conditions for installation are rare
Abundantly renewable	Permits may be difficult to obtain
Affordable	Freezing issues in winter
Consistent, reliable output	

Energy source

- Flowing water

System components

- Turbine (many styles to suit different conditions)
- Generator
- Penstock (water intake)
- Tailrace (water release)
- Valves and controls as required

How the system works

A turbine converts the flow and pressure of falling water to mechanical energy, which turns a generator to produce electrical current.

A waterway must have a suitable amount of head (elevation between inlet and outlet points) and flow (quantity of water) to make a useful amount of power.

A penstock diverts some water from the high point in the system and directs it to the turbine. The pressurized water is passed through the turbine, causing it to spin and turn the generator to produce current. The water leaves the turbine and rejoins the flow of the river or creek.

There are numerous styles of turbine, each one suited to particular head and flow characteristics.

Valves are installed to shut off flow for servicing.

SYSTEM OUTPUT

Output figures are based on available head and flow and the efficiencies of the piping and turbine. Very

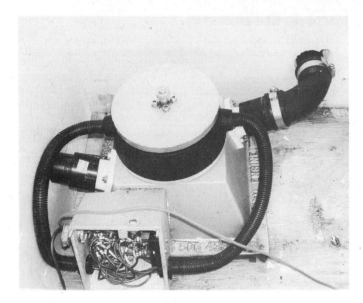

Microhydro generator.

low head, low flow systems can generate as little as 20 watts, while the upper limit of micro-hydro is generally accepted to be 100 kilowatts. Larger output systems are considered to be full-scale hydro electric projects.

A water turbine system produces power constantly, unlike solar and wind systems. Even relatively low output can add up to a significant amount of power.

Tips for successful installation

1. Accurate measurements of head and flow are critical for system design.
2. Permits from a variety of government agencies may be required.
3. Consider annual high and low water levels and ice depth when assessing a site.
4. Size power cables properly to account for the distance between generator and point of power use.
5. Place the turbine where it can be easily accessed for servicing in high and low water conditions.

6. Provide adequate screening at the intake to prevent debris from clogging or damaging the turbine.
7. Install control valves at the top and bottom of the penstock to isolate the turbine for servicing.

Pros and cons

Environmental impacts: *Low*

Micro hydro emits no carbon or other pollutants to produce power. The units will produce many times more power than was used in their creation.

Proper design should ensure that a small scale Run of River (ROR) system does not have a detrimental impact on the ecology of the waterway. Intake pipe(s) do not require damming or altering of the watercourse, and the tailrace can be designed to prevent erosion.

Material costs: *Low to Moderate*
Labor input: *High*

The amount of modification required to the water source, in addition to the amount of piping and controls, will determine the labor input for a micro-hydro installation.

Skill level required for the homeowner

Installation — *Moderate to Difficult.* Even small amounts of flowing water can produce forces that are difficult to manage. Cold climates will require special considerations to avoid having the system freeze.

Use — *Easy.*

Maintenance — *Moderate to Difficult.* Monthly inspections of turbine, intake, tailrace and valves.

Sourcing/availability: *Moderate to Difficult*

There are a limited number of system designers and manufacturers, and it can require diligent research to find the right people and equipment for a successful installation.

CODE COMPLIANCE

Electrical codes will cover the wiring of a system. Building codes will not apply to micro hydro systems unless a powerhouse of sufficient size as to be covered by codes must be built. Conservation authorities and environment and fisheries ministries may need to issue permits to allow the use of a river or stream for micro hydro.

DURABILITY: *MODERATE*

A properly maintained micro hydro system will be very durable. The turbine bearings will need scheduled replacement, but the balance of the system should last for decades.

Waterways are subject to intense flooding, which can cause damage to systems.

FUTURE DEVELOPMENT

Water turbine technology is well developed, and unlikely to change dramatically. Utility companies are showing renewed interest in the many hydro installations that exist along rivers in many parts of the continent, and that used to power mills and small industries. This infrastructure of dams and penstocks represents a large amount of potential green energy that is likely to be redeveloped.

RESILIENCE

Water turbines can be created in a low- or no-energy scenario, and are a valuable resource for resilient living.

Resources for further research

Harvey, Adam. *Micro-Hydro Design Manual: A Guide to Small-Scale Water Power Schemes.* London: Intermediate Technology, 1993. Print.

Rodríguez, Luis, and Teodoro Sánchez. *Designing and Building Mini and Micro Hydropower Schemes: A Practical Guide.* Rugby, UK: Practical Action, 2011. Print.

Davis, Scott. *Microhydro: Clean Power from Water.* Gabriola Island, B.C. New Society, 2003. Print.

Conclusion

No book can prepare you for the emotional rollercoaster of a major building project. The unexpected raises its head on a daily basis and you need to readjust schedules and expectations constantly. This is true regardless of the building materials and systems you choose. If you don't want hassles, don't build anything. Taking on a project using more sustainable materials and methods doesn't guarantee more turbulence, but it definitely doesn't guarantee less! Any time you attempt something for the first time, the learning curve is steep and the potential for slowdowns and the unforeseen is great. It's best to go into such projects with a flexible timeline and an accepting attitude.

People make better buildings

One may get the impression from this book that a building is a collection of materials and systems. But it's not the materials that make the building; that's the job of people.

Creating a building is based on a lot of relationships. Designers, tradespeople, authors and researchers, manufacturers and retailers and family and community members all contribute their knowledge, time, passion and skills to assemble a building.

Any choice made as a result of reading this book requires the accompanying choice of a person who can make that option viable. It is a mistake to prioritize a material or a system over a person who is willing and able to help you meet your goals; the right person is much more important than any particular building component. With the right team of people working together, you will inevitably make a better building. Keeping these relationships sustainable is as important as any of the technical considerations in this book. It is best to go about making friends as well as making buildings.

Making better buildings is a collective act because the lessons learned — both positive and negative — inform all future builders. We can make the kinds of buildings we do today because of the hundreds of generations who have steadily built that pool of experience and passed it along to us. Be generous with your knowledge, and be respectful of the knowledge of others. This knowledge is the most valuable commodity in the construction world. Keep aside a small portion of your budget to pay for knowledge in the form of books and consultations. Of the tens or even hundreds of thousands of dollars you will spend while building, paying for knowledge will represent a tiny fraction of the overall cost, but is definitely your wisest investment. Remember that knowledgeable people have spent years or decades learning what they know, and this knowledge is worth your investment.

The title of this book is *Making Better Buildings*, not *Make the Best Building*. We will never make the best possible building. No matter how good a job we do, there will always be room for improvement. But aiming to make the best building possible in a particular place, today, is a great goal, and hopefully this book has helped you in achieving that goal!

Appendix

<table>
<tr><th colspan="5">INVENTORY OF CARBON & ENERGY (ICE) SUMMARY</th></tr>
<tr><th>Materials</th><th colspan="3">Embodied Energy & Carbon Coefficients</th><th>Comments</th></tr>
<tr><th></th><th>EE - MJ/kg</th><th>EC - kgCO2/kg</th><th>EC - kgCO2e/kg</th><th>EE = Embodied Energy, EC = Embodied Carbon</th></tr>
<tr><td colspan="5">Aggregate</td></tr>
<tr><td>General (Gravel or Crushed Rock)</td><td>0.083</td><td>0.0048</td><td>0.0052</td><td>Estimated from measured UK industrial fuel consumption data</td></tr>
<tr><td colspan="5">Aluminium</td></tr>
<tr><td></td><td colspan="4">Main data source: International Aluminium Institute (IAI) LCA studies (www.world-aluminium.org)</td></tr>
<tr><td>General</td><td>155</td><td>8.24</td><td>9.16</td><td>Assumed (UK) ratio of 25.6% extrusions, 55.7% Rolled & 18.7% castings. Worldwide average recycled content of 33%.</td></tr>
<tr><td>Virgin</td><td>218</td><td>11.46</td><td>12.79</td><td></td></tr>
<tr><td>Recycled</td><td>29.0</td><td>1.69</td><td>1.81</td><td></td></tr>
<tr><td>Cast Products</td><td>159</td><td>8.28</td><td>9.22</td><td>Worldwide average recycled content of 33%.</td></tr>
<tr><td>Virgin</td><td>226</td><td>11.70</td><td>13.10</td><td></td></tr>
<tr><td>Recycled</td><td>25.0</td><td>1.35</td><td>1.45</td><td></td></tr>
<tr><td>Extruded</td><td>154</td><td>8.16</td><td>9.08</td><td>Worldwide average recycled content of 33%.</td></tr>
<tr><td>Virgin</td><td>214</td><td>11.20</td><td>12.50</td><td></td></tr>
<tr><td>Recycled</td><td>34.0</td><td>1.98</td><td>2.12</td><td></td></tr>
<tr><td>Rolled</td><td>155</td><td>8.26</td><td>9.18</td><td>Worldwide average recycled content of 33%.</td></tr>
<tr><td>Virgin</td><td>217</td><td>11.50</td><td>12.80</td><td></td></tr>
<tr><td>Recycled</td><td>28</td><td>1.67</td><td>1.79</td><td></td></tr>
<tr><td colspan="5">Asphalt</td></tr>
<tr><td>Asphalt, 4% (bitumen) binder content (by mass)</td><td>2.86</td><td>0.059</td><td>0.066</td><td>1.68 MJ/kg Feedstock Energy (Included). Modelled from the bitumen binder content. The fuel consumption of asphalt mixing operations was taken from the Mineral Products Association (MPA). It represents typical UK industrial data. Feedstock energy is from the bitumen content.</td></tr>
<tr><td>Asphalt, 5% binder content</td><td>3.39</td><td>0.064</td><td>0.071</td><td>2.10 MJ/kg Feedstock Energy (Included). Comments from 4% mix also apply.</td></tr>
<tr><td>Asphalt, 6% binder content</td><td>3.93</td><td>0.068</td><td>0.076</td><td>2.52 MJ/kg Feedstock Energy (Included). Comments from 4% mix also apply.</td></tr>
<tr><td>Asphalt, 7% binder content</td><td>4.46</td><td>0.072</td><td>0.081</td><td>2.94 MJ/kg Feedstock Energy (Included). Comments from 4% mix also apply.</td></tr>
<tr><td>Asphalt, 8% binder content</td><td>5.00</td><td>0.076</td><td>0.086</td><td>3.36 MJ/kg Feedstock Energy (Included). Comments from 4% mix also apply.</td></tr>
<tr><td colspan="5">Bitumen</td></tr>
<tr><td>General</td><td>51</td><td>0.38 - 0.43 (?)</td><td>0.43 - 0.55 (?)</td><td>42 MJ/kg Feedstock Energy (Included). Feedstock assumed to be typical energy content of Bitumen. Carbon dioxide emissions are particularly difficult to estimate, range given.</td></tr>
<tr><td colspan="5">Brass</td></tr>
<tr><td>General</td><td>44.00</td><td>2.46 (?)</td><td>2.64 (?)</td><td>Poor data availability. It is believed that the data may be largely dependent upon ore grade. Poor carbon data, making estimate of embodied carbon difficult.</td></tr>
<tr><td>Virgin</td><td>80.00</td><td>4.47 (?)</td><td>4.80 (?)</td><td></td></tr>
<tr><td>Recycled</td><td>20.00</td><td>1.12 (?)</td><td>1.20 (?)</td><td></td></tr>
<tr><td colspan="5">Bricks</td></tr>
<tr><td>General (Common Brick)</td><td>3.00</td><td>0.23</td><td>0.24</td><td></td></tr>
<tr><td>EXAMPLE: Single Brick</td><td>6.9 MJ per brick</td><td>0.53 kgCO2 per brick</td><td>0.55</td><td>Assuming 2.3 kg per brick.</td></tr>
<tr><td>Limestone</td><td>0.85</td><td>?</td><td>-</td><td></td></tr>
</table>

INVENTORY OF CARBON & ENERGY (ICE) SUMMARY

Materials	Embodied Energy & Carbon Coefficients			Comments
	EE - MJ/kg	EC - kgCO2/kg	EC - kgCO2e/kg	EE = Embodied Energy, EC = Embodied Carbon
Bronze				
General	69.0 (?)	3.73 (?)	4.0 (?)	Average of the only two references
Carpet				
General Carpet	74 (187 per sqm)	3.9 (9.8 per sqm)	-	For per square meter estimates see material profile. Difficult to estimate, taken from Ref. 94.
Felt (Hair and Jute) Underlay	19.00	0.97	-	Ref. 94.
Nylon (Polyamide), pile weight 300 g/m2	130 MJ per sqm	6.7 (GWP) per sqm	6.7 (GWP) per sqm	Total weight of this carpet 1,477 g/m2. See Refs. 277 & 279. These carpets (inc. below) are a tufted surface pile made of 100% nylon (polyamide) with a woven textile backing and flame proofed on the basis of aluminium hydroxide.
Nylon (Polyamide), pile weight 500 g/m2	180 MJ per sqm	9.7 (GWP) per sqm	9.7 (GWP) per sqm	Total weight of this carpet 1,837 g/m2. See Refs. 277 & 279.
Nylon (Polyamide), pile weight 700 g/m2	230 MJ per sqm	12.7 (GWP) per sqm	12.7 (GWP) per sqm	Total weight of this carpet 2,147 g/m2. See Refs. 277 & 279.
Nylon (Polyamide), pile weight 900 g/m2	277 MJ per sqm	15.6 (GWP) per sqm	15.6 (GWP) per sqm	Total weight of this carpet 2,427 g/m2. See Refs. 277 & 279.
Nylon (Polyamide), pile weight 1100 g/m2	327 MJ per sqm	18.4 (GWP) per sqm	18.4 (GWP) per sqm	Total weight of this carpet 2,677 g/m2. See Refs. 277 & 279.
Carpet tiles, nylon (Polyamide), pile weight 300 g/m2	178 MJ per sqm	7.75 (GWP) per sqm	7.75 (GWP) per sqm	Total weight of this carpet 4,123 g/m2. See Refs 277 & 279. These carpet tiles (inc. below) are a tufted surface pile made of 100% nylon (polyamide) fleece-covered bitumen backing and flame-proofed on the basis of aluminium hydroxide
Carpet tiles, nylon (Polyamide), pile weight 500 g/m2	229 MJ per sqm	10.7 (GWP) per sqm	10.7 (GWP) per sqm	Total weight of this carpet 4,373 g/m2. See Refs. 277 & 279.
Carpet tiles, nylon (Polyamide), pile weight 700 g/m2	279 MJ per sqm	13.7 (GWP) per sqm	13.7 (GWP) per sqm	Total weight of this carpet 4,623 g/m2. See Refs. 277 & 279.
Carpet tiles, nylon (Polyamide), pile weight 900 g/m2	328 MJ per sqm	16.7 (GWP) per sqm	16.7 (GWP) per sqm	Total weight of this carpet 4,873 g/m2. See Refs. 277 & 279.
Carpet tiles, nylon (Polyamide), pile weight 1100 g/m2	378 MJ per sqm	19.7 (GWP) per sqm	19.7 (GWP) per sqm	Total weight of this carpet 5,123 g/m2. See Refs. 277 & 279.
Polyethylterepthalate (PET)	106.50	5.56	-	Includes feedstock energy
Polypropylene	95.40	4.98	-	Includes feedstock energy, for per square meter see material profile
Polyurethane	72.10	3.76	-	Includes feedstock energy
Rubber	67.5 to 140	3.61 to 7.48	-	
Saturated Felt Underlay (impregnated with Asphalt or tar)	31.70	1.65	-	Ref. 94.
Wool	106.00	5.53	-	For per square meter see material profile. See Refs. 63, 201, 202 & 281 (Same author).
Cement				
General (UK weighted average)	4.5	0.73	0.74	Weighted average of all cement consumed within the UK. This includes all factory made cements (CEM I, CEM II, CEM III, CEM IV) and further blending of fly ash and ground granulated blast furnace slag. This data has been estimated from the British Cement Association's factsheets (see Ref. 59). 23% cementitious additions on average.
Average CEM I Portland Cement, 94% Clinker	5.50	0.93	0.95	This is a standard cement with no cementitious additions (i.e. fly ash or blast furnace slag). Composition 94% clinker, 5% gypsum, 1% minor additional constituents (mac's). This data has been estimated from the British Cement Association's factsheets (see Ref. 59.).
6-20% Fly Ash (CEM II/A-V)	5.28 to 4.51	0.88 (@ 6%) to 0.75 (@ 20%)	0.89 to 0.76	
21-35% Fly Ash (CEM II/B-V)	4.45 to 3.68	0.74 to 0.61	0.75 to 0.62	See material profile for further details.
21-35% GGBS (CEM II/B-S)	4.77 to 4.21	0.76 to 0.64	0.77 to 0.65	
36-65% GGBS (CEM III/A)	4.17 to 3.0	0.63 to 0.38	0.64 to 0.39	
66-80% GGBS (CEM II/B)	2.96 to 2.4	0.37 to 0.25	0.38 to 0.26	
Fibre Cement Panels - Uncoated	10.40	1.09	-	Few data points. Selected data modified from Ref. 107.
Fibre Cement Panels - (Colour) Coated	15.30	1.28	-	
Mortar (1:3 cement:sand mix)	1.33	0.208	0.221	
Mortar (1:4)	1.11	0.171	0.182	
Mortar (1:5)	0.97	0.146	0.156	
Mortar (1:6)	0.85	0.127	0.136	Values estimated from the ICE Cement, Mortar & Concrete Model
Mortar (1:½:4½ Cement:Lime:Sand	1.34	0.200	0.213	
Mortar (1:1:6 Cement:Lime:Sand mix)	1.11	0.163	0.174	
Mortar (1:2:9 Cement:Lime:Sand mix)	1.03	0.145	0.155	
Cement stabilised soil @ 5%	0.68	0.060	0.061	Assumed 5% cement content.
Cement stabilised soil @ 8%	0.83	0.082	0.084	Assumed 8% stabiliser contents (6% cement and 2% quicklime)

INVENTORY OF CARBON & ENERGY (ICE) SUMMARY

Materials	Embodied Energy & Carbon Coefficients			Comments
	EE - MJ/kg	EC - kgCO2/kg	EC - kgCO2e/kg	EE = Embodied Energy, EC = Embodied Carbon
Ceramics				
General	10.00	0.66	0.70	Very large data range, difficult to select values for general ceramics.
Fittings	20.00	1.07	1.14	Ref. 1.
Sanitary Products	29.00	1.51	1.61	Limited data.
Tiles and Cladding Panels	12.00	0.74	0.78	Difficult to select, large range, limited data. See Ref. 292.
Clay				
General (Simple Baked Products)	3.00	0.23	0.24	General simple baked clay products (inc. terracotta and
Tile	6.50	0.45	0.48	
Vitrified clay pipe DN 100 & DN 150	6.20	0.44	0.46	
Vitrified clay pipe DN 200 & DN 300	7.00	0.48	0.50	
Vitrified clay pipe DN 500	7.90	0.52	0.55	
Concrete				
General	0.75	0.100	0.107	It is strongly recommended to avoid selecting a 'general value for concrete. Selecting data for a specific concrete type (often a ready mix concrete) will give greater accuracy, please see material profile. Assumed cement content 12% by
16/20 Mpa	0.70	0.093	0.100	
20/25 MPa	0.74	0.100	0.107	
25/30 MPa	0.78	0.106	0.113	Using UK weighted average cement (more representative of 'typical' concrete mixtures).
28/35 MPa	0.82	0.112	0.120	
32/40 MPa	0.88	0.123	0.132	
40/50 MPa	1.00	0.141	0.151	

% Cement Replacement - Fly Ash	EE - MJ/kg			EC - kgCO2/kg			EC - kgCO2e/kg			Note 0% is a concrete using a CEM I cement (not typical)
	0%	15%	30%	0%	15%	30%	0%	15%	30%	
GEN 0 (6/8 MPa)	0.55	0.52	0.47	0.071	0.065	0.057	0.076	0.069	0.061	Compressive strength designation C6/8 Mpa. 28 day compressive strength under British cube method of 8 MPa, under European cylinder method 6 MPa. Possible uses: Kerb bedding and backing. Data is only cradle to factory gate but beyond this the average delivery distance of ready mix concrete is 8.3 km by road (see Ref. 244).
GEN 1 (8/10 MPa)	0.70	0.65	0.59	0.097	0.088	0.077	0.104	0.094	0.082	Possible uses: mass concrete, mass fill, mass foundations, trench foundations, blinding, strip footing.
GEN 2 (12/15 MPa)	0.76	0.71	0.64	0.106	0.098	0.087	0.114	0.105	0.093	-
GEN 3 (16/20 MPa)	0.81	0.75	0.68	0.115	0.105	0.093	0.123	0.112	0.100	Possible uses: garage floors.
RC 20/25 (20/25 MPa)	0.86	0.81	0.73	0.124	0.114	0.101	0.132	0.122	0.108	-
RC 25/30 (25/30 MPa)	0.91	0.85	0.77	0.131	0.121	0.107	0.140	0.130	0.115	Possible uses: reinforced foundations.
RC 28/35 (28/35 MPa)	0.95	0.90	0.82	0.139	0.129	0.116	0.148	0.138	0.124	Possible uses: reinforced foundations, ground floors.
RC 32/40 (32/40 MPa)	1.03	0.97	0.89	0.153	0.143	0.128	0.163	0.152	0.136	Possible uses: structural purposes, in situ floors, walls, superstructure.
RC 40/50 (40/50 MPa)	1.17	1.10	0.99	0.176	0.164	0.146	0.188	0.174	0.155	Possible uses: high strength applications, precasting.
PAV1	0.95	0.89	0.81	0.139	0.129	0.115	0.148	0.138	0.123	Possible uses: domestic parking and outdoor paving.
PAV2	1.03	0.97	0.89	0.153	0.143	0.128	0.163	0.152	0.137	Possible uses: heavy duty outdoor paving.

% Cement Replacement - Blast Furnace Slag	EE - MJ/kg			EC - kgCO2/kg			EC - kgCO2e/kg			Note 0% is a concrete using a CEM I cement
	0%	25%	50%	0%	25%	50%	0%	15%	30%	
GEN 0 (6/8 MPa)	0.55	0.48	0.41	0.071	0.056	0.042	0.076	0.060	0.045	
GEN 1 (8/10 MPa)	0.70	0.60	0.50	0.097	0.075	0.054	0.104	0.080	0.058	
GEN 2 (12/15 MPa)	0.76	0.62	0.55	0.106	0.082	0.061	0.114	0.088	0.065	
GEN 3 (16/20 MPa)	0.81	0.69	0.57	0.115	0.090	0.065	0.123	0.096	0.070	
RC 20/25 (20/25 MPa)	0.86	0.74	0.62	0.124	0.097	0.072	0.132	0.104	0.077	
RC 25/30 (25/30 MPa)	0.91	0.78	0.65	0.131	0.104	0.076	0.140	0.111	0.081	See fly ash mixtures
RC 28/35 (28/35 MPa)	0.95	0.83	0.69	0.139	0.111	0.082	0.148	0.119	0.088	
RC 32/40 (32/40 MPa)	1.03	0.91	0.78	0.153	0.125	0.094	0.163	0.133	0.100	

INVENTORY OF CARBON & ENERGY (ICE) SUMMARY

Materials	Embodied Energy & Carbon Coefficients								Comments
	EE - MJ/kg			EC - kgCO2/kg			EC - kgCO2e/kg		EE = Embodied Energy, EC = Embodied Carbon
RC 40/50 (40/50 MPa)	**1.17**	1.03	0.87	**0.176**	0.144	0.108	**0.188**	0.153	0.115	
PAV1	**0.95**	0.82	0.70	**0.139**	0.111	0.083	**0.148**	0.118	0.088	
PAV2	**1.03**	0.91	0.77	**0.153**	0.125	0.094	**0.163**	0.133	0.100	

COMMENTS

The first column represents standard concrete, created with a CEM I Portland cement. The other columns are estimates based on a direct substitution of fly ash or blast furnace slag in place of the cement content. The ICE Cement, Mortar & Concrete Model was applied. **Please see important notes in the concrete material profile.**

REINFORCED CONCRETE - Modification Factors

For reinforcement add this value to the appropriate concrete coefficient for each 100 kg of rebar per m3 of concrete	1.04	0.072	0.077	Add for each 100 kg steel rebar per m3 concrete. Use multiple of this value, i.e. for 150 kg steel use a factor of 1.5 times these values.
EXAMPLE: Reinforced RC 25/30 MPa (with 110 kg per m3 concrete)	1.92 MJ/kg (0.78 + 1.04 * 1.1)	0.185 kgCO2/kg (0.106 + 0.072 * 1.1)	0.198 kgCO2/kg (0.113 + 0.077 * 1.1)	with 110 kg rebar per m3 concrete. UK weighted average cement. This assumes the UK typical steel scenario (59% recycled content). Please consider if this is in line with the rest of your study (goal and scope) or the requirements of a predefined method.

PRECAST (PREFABRICATED) CONCRETE - Modification Factors

For precast add this value to the selected coefficient of the appropriate concrete mix	0.45	0.027	0.029	For each 1 kg precast concrete. This example is using a RC 40/50 strength class and is not necessarily indicative of an average precast product. Includes UK recorded plant operations and estimated transportation of the constituents to the factory gate (38km aggregates, estimated 100km cement). Data is only cradle to factory gate but beyond this the average delivery distance of precast is 155km by road (see Ref. 244). UK weighted average cement. See also the new report on precast concrete pipes (Ref 300).
EXAMPLE: Precast RC 40/50 MPa	1.50 MJ/kg (1.00 + 0.50)	0.168 kgCO2/kg (0.141 + 0.027)	0.180 kgCO2/kg (0.151 + 0.029)	
EXAMPLE: Precast RC 40/50 with reinforcement (with 80kg per m³)	2.33 MJ/kg (1.50 + 1.04 * 0.8)	0.229 kgCO2/kg (0.171 + 0.072 * 0.8)	0.242 kgCO2/kg (0.180 + 0.077 * 0.8)	

CONCRETE BLOCKS (ICE CMC Model Values)

Block - 8 MPa Compressive Strength	0.59	0.059	0.063	Estimated from the concrete block mix proportions, plus an allowance for concrete block curing, plant operations and transport of materials to factory gate.
Block - 10 MPa	0.67	0.073	0.078	
Block -12 MPa	0.72	0.082	0.088	
Block -13 MPa	0.83	0.100	0.107	
Autoclaved Aerated Blocks (AAC's)	3.50	0.24 to 0.375	-	Not ICE CMC model results.

NOMINAL PROPORTIONS METHOD (Volume), Proportions from BS 8500:2006 (ICE Cement, Mortar & Concrete Model Calculations)

1:1:2 Cement:Sand:Aggregate	1.28	0.194	0.206	High strength concrete. All of these values were estimated assuming the **UK average content of cementitious additions** (i.e. fly ash, GGBS) for **factory supplied cements** in the UK, see Ref. 59, plus the proportions of other constituents.
1:1.5:3	0.99	0.145	0.155	Often used in floor slab, columns & load bearing structure.
1:2:4	0.82	0.116	0.124	Often used in construction of buildings under 3 storeys.
1:2.5:5	0.71	0.097	0.104	
1:3:6	0.63	0.084	0.090	Non-structural mass concrete.
1:4:8	0.54	0.069	0.074	

BY CEM I CEMENT CONTENT - kg CEM I cement content per cubic meter concrete (ICE CMC Model Results)

120 kg / m³ concrete	0.49	0.060	0.064	Assumed density of 2,350 kg/m3. Interpolation of the CEM I cement content is possible. These numbers assume the **CEM I cement content (not the total cementitious content**, i.e. they do not include cementitious additions). They may also be used for fly ash mixtures without modification, but they are likely to slightly underestimate mixtures that have additional GGBS due to the higher embodied energy and carbon of GGBS (in comparison to aggregates and fly ash).
200 kg / m³ concrete	0.67	0.091	0.097	
300 kg / m³ concrete	0.91	0.131	0.140	
400kg / m³ concrete	1.14	0.170	0.181	
500 kg / m³ concrete	1.37	0.211	0.224	

MISCELLANEOUS VALUES

Fibre-Reinforced	7.75 (?)	0.45 (?)	-	Literature estimate, likely to vary widely. High uncertainty.
Very High GGBS Mix	0.66	0.049	0.050	Data based on Lafarge 'Envirocrete', which is a C28/35 MPa, very high GGBS replacement value concrete

INVENTORY OF CARBON & ENERGY (ICE) SUMMARY

Materials	Embodied Energy & Carbon Coefficients			Comments
	EE - MJ/kg	EC - kgCO2/kg	EC - kgCO2e/kg	EE = Embodied Energy, EC = Embodied Carbon
Copper				
EU Tube & Sheet	42.00	2.60	2.71	EU production data, estimated from Kupfer Institut LCI data. 37% recycled content (the 3 year world average). World average data is expected to be higher than these values.
Virgin	57.00	3.65	3.81	
Recycled	16.50	0.80	0.84	
Recycled from high grade scrap	18 (?)	1.1 (?)		Uncertain, difficult to estimate with the data available.
Recycled from low grade scrap	50 (?)	3.1 (?)		
Glass				
Primary Glass	15.00	0.86	0.91	Includes process CO2 emissions from primary glass manufacture.
Secondary Glass	11.50	0.55	0.59	EE estimated from Ref 115.
Fibreglass (Glasswool)	28.00	1.54	-	Large data range, but the selected value is inside a small band of frequently quoted values.
Toughened	23.50	1.27	1.35	Only three data sources
Insulation				
General Insulation	45.00	1.86	-	Estimated from typical market shares. Feedstock Energy 16.5 MJ/kg (Included)
Cellular Glass	27.00	-	-	Ref. 54.
Cellulose	0.94 to 3.3	-	-	
Cork	4.00	0.19	-	Ref. 55.
Fibreglass (Glasswool)	28.00	1.35	-	Poor data difficult to select appropriate value
Flax (Insulation)	39.50	1.70	-	Ref. 2. 5.97 MJ/kg Feedstock Energy (Included)
Mineral wool	16.60	1.20	1.28	
Paper wool	20.17	0.63	-	Ref. 2
Polystyrene	See Plastics	See Plastics	-	see plastics
Polyurethane	See Plastics	See Plastics	-	see plastics
Rockwool	16.80	1.05	1.12	Cradle to Grave
Woodwool (loose)	10.80	-	-	Ref. 205.
Woodwool (Board)	20.00	0.98	-	Ref. 55.
Wool (Recycled)	20.90	-	-	Refs. 63, 201, 202 & 281.
Iron				
General	25.00	1.91 (?)	2.03	It was difficult to estimate the embodied energy and carbon of iron with the data available.
Lead				
General	25.21	1.57	1.67	Allocated (divided) on a mass basis, assumes recycling rate of 61%
Virgin	49.00	3.18	3.37	
Recycled	10.00	0.54	0.58	Scrap batteries are a main feedstock for recycled lead
Lime				
General	5.30	0.76	0.78	Embodied carbon was difficult to estimate
Linoleum				
General	25.00	1.21	-	Data difficult to select, large data range.
Miscellaneous				
Asbestos	7.40	-	-	Ref. 4.
Calcium Silicate Sheet	2.00	0.13	-	Ref. 55.
Chromium	83	5.39	-	Ref. 22.
Cotton, Padding	27.10	1.28	-	Ref. 38.
Cotton, Fabric	143	6.78	-	Ref. 38.
Damp Proof Course/Membrane	134 (?)	4.2 (?)	-	Uncertain estimate.
Felt General	36	-	-	
Flax	33.50	1.70	-	Ref. 2.
Fly Ash	0.10	0.008	-	No allocation from fly ash producing system.

INVENTORY OF CARBON & ENERGY (ICE) SUMMARY

Materials	Embodied Energy & Carbon Coefficients			Comments
	EE - MJ/kg	EC - kgCO2/kg	EC - kgCO2e/kg	EE = Embodied Energy, EC = Embodied Carbon
Grit	0.12	0.01	-	Ref. 114.
Ground Limestone	0.62	0.032	-	
Carpet Grout	30.80	-	-	Ref. 169.
Glass Reinforced Plastic - GRP - Fibreglass	100	8.10	-	Ref. 1.
Lithium	853	5.30	-	Ref. 22.
Mandolite	63	1.40	-	Ref. 1.
Mineral Fibre Tile (Roofing)	37	2.70	-	Ref. 1.
Manganese	52	3.50	-	Ref. 22.
Mercury	87	4.94	-	Ref. 22.
Molybedenum	378	30.30	-	Ref. 22.
Nickel	164	12.40	-	Ref. 114.
Perlite - Expanded	10.00	0.52	-	Ref. 114.
Perlite - Natural	0.66	0.03	-	Ref. 114.
Quartz powder	0.85	0.02	-	Ref. 114.
Shingle	11.30	0.30	-	Ref. 70.
Silicon	2355	-	-	Ref. 167.
Slag (GGBS)	1.60	0.083	-	Ground Granulated Blast Furnace Slag (GGBS), economic allocation.
Silver	128.20	6.31	-	Ref. 148.
Straw	0.24	0.01	-	Refs. 63, 201, 202 & 281.
Terrazzo Tiles	1.40	0.12	-	Ref. 1.
Vanadium	3710	228	-	Ref. 22.
Vermiculite - Expanded	7.20	0.52	-	Ref. 114.
Vermiculite - Natural	0.72	0.03	-	Ref. 114.
Vicuclad	70.00	-	-	Ref. 1.
Water	0.01	0.001	-	
Wax	52.00	-	-	Ref. 169.
Wood stain/Varnish	50.00	5.35	-	Ref. 1.
Yttrium	1470	84.00	-	Ref. 22.
Zirconium	1610	97.20	-	Ref. 22.
Paint				
General	70.00	2.42	2.91	Large variations in data, especially for embodied carbon. Includes feedstock energy. Water based paints have a 70% market share. Water based paint has a lower embodied energy than solvent based paint.
EXAMPLE: Single Coat	10.5 MJ/Sqm	0.36 kgCO2/Sqm	0.44	Assuming 6.66 Sqm Coverage per kg
EXAMPLE: Double Coat	21.0 MJ/Sqm	0.73 kgCO2/Sqm	0.87	Assuming 3.33 Sqm Coverage per kg
EXAMPLE: Triple Coat	31.5 MJ/Sqm	1.09 kgCO2/Sqm	1.31	Assuming 2.22 Sqm Coverage per kg
Waterborne Paint	59.00	2.12	2.54	Waterborne paint has a 70% of market share. Includes feedstock energy.
Solventborne Paint	97.00	3.13	3.76	Solventborne paint has a 30% share of the market. Includes feedstock energy. It was difficult to estimate carbon emissions for Solventborne paint.
Paper				
Paperboard (General for construction use)	24.80	1.29	-	Excluding calorific value (CV) of wood, excludes carbon sequestration/biogenic carbon storage.
Fine Paper	28.20	1.49	-	Excluding CV of wood, excludes carbon sequestration
EXAMPLE: 1 packet A4 paper	70.50	3.73	-	Standard 80g/sqm printing paper, 500 sheets a pack. Doesn't include printing.
Wallpaper	36.40	1.93	-	
Plaster				
General (Gypsum)	1.80	0.12	0.13	Problems selecting good value, inconsistent figures, West et al believe this is because of past aggregation of EE with
Plasterboard	6.75	0.38	0.39	See Ref [WRAP] for further info on GWP data, including disposal impacts which are significant for Plasterboard.

INVENTORY OF CARBON & ENERGY (ICE) SUMMARY

Materials	Embodied Energy & Carbon Coefficients			Comments
	EE - MJ/kg	EC - kgCO2/kg	EC - kgCO2e/kg	EE = Embodied Energy, EC = Embodied Carbon
Plastics		Main data source: Plastics Europe (www.plasticseurope.org) ecoprofiles		
General	80.50	2.73	3.31	35.6 MJ/kg Feedstock Energy (Included). Determined by the average use of each type of plastic used in the European construction industry.
ABS	95.30	3.05	3.76	48.6 MJ/kg Feedstock Energy (Included)
General Polyethylene	83.10	2.04	2.54	54.4 MJ/kg Feedstock Energy (Included). Based on average consumption of types of polyethylene in European
High Density Polyethylene (HDPE) Resin	76.70	1.57	1.93	54.3 MJ/kg Feedstock Energy (Included). Doesn't include the final fabrication.
HDPE Pipe	84.40	2.02	2.52	55.1 MJ/kg Feedstock Energy (Included)
Low Density Polyethylene (LDPE) Resin	78.10	1.69	2.08	51.6 MJ/kg Feedstock Energy (Included). Doesn't include final fabrication
LDPE Film	89.30	2.13	2.60	55.2 MJ/kg Feedstock Energy (Included)
Nylon (Polyamide) 6 Polymer	120.50	5.47	9.14	38.6 MJ/kg Feedstock Energy (Included). Doesn't include final fabrication. Plastics Europe state that two thirds of nylon is used as fibres (textiles, carpets…etc) in Europe and that most of the remainder as injection mouldings. Dinitrogen monoxide and methane emissions are very significant contributors to GWP.
Nylon (polyamide) 6,6 Polymer	138.60	6.54	7.92	50.7 MJ/kg Feedstock Energy (Included). Doesn't include final fabrication (i.e. injection moulding). See comments for Nylon 6 polymer.
Polycarbonate	112.90	6.03	7.62	36.7 MJ/kg Feedstock Energy (Included). Doesn't include final fabrication.
Polypropylene, Orientated Film	99.20	2.97	3.43	55.7 MJ/kg Feedstock Energy (Included).
Polypropylene, Injection Moulding	115.10	3.93	4.49	54 MJ/kg Feedstock Energy (Included). If biomass benefits are included the CO2 may reduce to 3.85 kgCO2/kg, and GWP down to 4.41 kg CO2e/kg.
Expanded Polystyrene	88.60	2.55	3.29	46.2 MJ/kg Feedstock Energy (Included)
General Purpose Polystyrene	86.40	2.71	3.43	46.3 MJ/kg Feedstock Energy (Included)
High Impact Polystyrene	87.40	2.76	3.42	46.4 MJ/kg Feedstock Energy (Included)
Thermoformed Expanded Polystyrene	109.20	3.45	4.39	49.7 MJ/kg Feedstock Energy (Included)
Polyurethane Flexible Foam	102.10	4.06	4.84	33.47 MJ/kg Feedstock Energy (Included). Poor data availability for feedstock energy
Polyurethane Rigid Foam	101.50	3.48	4.26	37.07 MJ/kg Feedstock Energy (Included). Poor data availability for feedstock energy
PVC General	77.20	2.61	3.10	28.1 MJ/kg Feedstock Energy (Included). Based on market average consumption of types of PVC in the European construction industry
PVC Pipe	67.50	2.56	3.23	24.4 MJ/kg Feedstock Energy (Included). If biomass benefits are included the CO2 may reduce to 2.51 kgCO2/kg, and GWP down to 3.23 kg CO2e/kg.
Calendered Sheet PVC	68.60	2.61	3.19	24.4 MJ/kg Feedstock Energy (Included). If biomass benefits are included the CO2 may reduce to 2.56 kgCO2/kg, and GWP down to 3.15 kg CO2e/kg.
PVC Injection Moulding	95.10	2.69	3.30	35.1 MJ/kg Feedstock Energy (Included). If biomass benefits are included the CO2 may reduce to 2.23 kgCO2/kg, and GWP down to 2.84 kg CO2e/kg.
UPVC Film	69.40	2.57	3.16	25.3 MJ/kg Feedstock Energy (Included)
Rubber				
General	91.00	2.66	2.85	40 MJ/kg Feedstock Energy (Included)
Sand				
General	0.081	0.0048	0.0051	Estimated from real UK industrial fuel consumption data
Sealants and adhesives				
Epoxide Resin	137.00	5.70	-	42.6 MJ/kg Feedstock Energy (Included). Source: www.plasticseurope.org
Mastic Sealant	62 to 200	-	-	
Melamine Resin	97.00	4.19	-	Feedstock energy 18 MJ/kg - estimated from Ref 34.
Phenol Formaldehyde	88.00	2.98	-	Feedstock energy 32 MJ/kg - estimated from Ref 34.
Urea Formaldehyde	70.00	2.76	-	Feedstock energy 18 MJ/kg - estimated from Ref 34.
Soil				
General (Rammed Soil)	0.45	0.023	0.024	
Cement stabilised soil @ 5%	0.68	0.060	0.061	Assumed 5% cement content.
Cement stabilised soil @ 8%	0.83	0.082	0.084	Assumed 8% stabiliser content (6% cement and 2% lime).
GGBS stabilised soil	0.65	0.045	0.047	Assumed 8% stabiliser content (8% GGBS and 2% lime).
Fly ash stabilised soil	0.56	0.039	0.041	Assumed 10% stabiliser content (8% fly ash and 2% lime).

INVENTORY OF CARBON & ENERGY (ICE) SUMMARY

Materials	Embodied Energy & Carbon Coefficients			Comments
	EE - MJ/kg	EC - kgCO2/kg	EC - kgCO2e/kg	EE = Embodied Energy, EC = Embodied Carbon
Steel	Main data source: International Iron & Steel Institute (IISI) LCA studies (www.worldsteel.org)			
UK (EU) STEEL DATA - EU average recycled content - See material profile (and Annex on recycling methods) for usage guide				
General - UK (EU) Average Recycled Content	20.10	1.37	1.46	EU 3-average recycled content of 59%. Estimated from UK's consumption mixture of types of steel (excluding stainless). **All data doesn't include the final cutting of the steel** products to the specified dimensions or further fabrication activities. Estimated from World Steel Association (Worldsteel) LCA data.
Virgin	35.40	2.71	2.89	
Recycled	9.40	0.44	0.47	Could not collect strong statistics on consumption mix of recycled steel.
Bar & rod - UK (EU) Average Recycled Content	17.40	1.31	1.40	EU 3-average recycled content of 59%
Virgin	29.20	2.59	2.77	
Recycled	8.80	0.42	0.45	
Coil (Sheet) - UK (EU) Average Recycled Content	18.80	1.30	1.38	Effective recycled content because recycling route is not typical. EU 3-average recycled content of 59%
Virgin	32.80	2.58	2.74	
Recycled		Not Typical Production Route		
Coil (Sheet), Galvanised - UK (EU) Average Recycled Content	22.60	1.45	1.54	Effective recycled content because recycling route is not typical. EU 3-average recycled content of 59%
Virgin	40.00	2.84	3.01	
Engineering steel - Recycled	13.10	0.68	0.72	
Pipe- UK (EU) Average Recycled Content	19.80	1.37	1.45	Effective recycled content because recycling route is not typical. EU 3-average recycled content of 59%
Virgin	34.70	2.71	2.87	
Recycled		Not Typical Production Route		
Plate- UK (EU) Average Recycled Content	25.10	1.55	1.66	Effective recycled content because recycling route is not typical. EU 3-average recycled content of 59%
Virgin	45.40	3.05	3.27	
Recycled		Not Typical Production Route		
Section- UK (EU) Average Recycled Content	21.50	1.42	1.53	
Virgin	38.00	2.82	3.03	
Recycled	10.00	0.44	0.47	
Wire - Virgin	36.00 (?)	2.83 (?)	3.02	
Stainless	56.70	6.15		World average data from the Institute of Stainless Steel Forum (ISSF) life cycle inventory data. Selected data is for the most popular grade (304). Stainless steel does not have separate primary and recycled material production routes.
OTHER STEEL DATA - 'R.O.W' and 'World' average recycled contents - See material profile (and Annex on recycling methods) for usage guide				
General - R.O.W. Avg. Recy. Cont.	26.20	1.90	2.03	Rest of World (non-E.U.) consumption of steel. 3 year average recycled content of 35.5%.
General - World Avg. Recy. Cont.	25.30	1.82	1.95	Whole world 3 year average recycled content of 39%.
Bar & rod- R.O.W. Avg. Recy. Cont.	22.30	1.82	1.95	
Bar & rod - World Avg. Recy. Cont.	21.60	1.74	1.86	
Coil - R.O.W. Avg. Recy. Cont.	24.40	1.81	1.92	
Coil - World Avg. Recy. Cont.	23.50	1.74	1.85	
Coil, Galvanised - R.O.W. Avg. Recy. Cont.	29.50	2.00	2.12	
Coil, Galvanised - World Avg. Recy.	28.50	1.92	2.03	Comments above apply. See material profile for further information

INVENTORY OF CARBON & ENERGY (ICE) SUMMARY

Materials	Embodied Energy & Carbon Coefficients			Comments
	EE - MJ/kg	EC - kgCO2/kg	EC - kgCO2e/kg	EE = Embodied Energy, EC = Embodied Carbon
Pipe - R.O.W. Avg. Recy. Cont.	25.80	1.90	2.01	
Pipe - World Avg. Recy. Cont.	24.90	1.83	1.94	
Plate - R.O.W. Avg. Recy. Cont.	33.20	2.15	2.31	
Plate - World Avg. Recy. Cont.	32.00	2.06	2.21	
Section - R.O.W. Avg. Recy. Cont.	28.10	1.97	2.12	
Section - World Avg. Recy. Cont.	27.10	1.89	2.03	
Stone	*Data on stone was difficult to select, with high standard deviations and data ranges.*			
General	1.26 (?)	0.073 (?)	0.079	ICE database average (statistic), uncertain. See material profile.
Granite	11.00	0.64	0.70	Estimated from Ref 116.
Limestone	1.50	0.087	0.09	Estimated from Ref 188.
Marble	2.00	0.116	0.13	
Marble tile	3.33	0.192	0.21	Ref. 40.
Sandstone	1.00 (?)	0.058 (?)	0.06	Uncertain estimate based on Ref. 262.
Shale	0.03	0.002	0.002	
Slate	0.1 to 1.0	0.006 to 0.058	0.007 to 0.063	Large data range
Timber	*Note: These values were difficult to estimate because timber has a high data variability. These values exclude the energy content of the wooden product (the Calorific Value (CV) from burning). See the material profile for guidance on the new data structure for embodied carbon (i.e. split into foss and bio)*			
General	10.00	$0.30_{fos}+0.41_{bio}$	$0.31_{fos}+0.41_{bio}$	Estimated from UK consumption mixture of timber products in 2007 (Timber Trade Federation statistics). Includes 4.3 MJ bio-energy. All values do not include the CV of timber product and exclude carbon storage.
Glue Laminated timber	12.00	$0.39_{fos}+0.45_{bio}$	$0.42_{fos}+0.45_{bio}$	Includes 4.9 MJ bio-energy.
Hardboard	16.00	$0.54_{fos}+0.51_{bio}$	$0.58_{fos}+0.51_{bio}$	Hardboard is a type of fibreboard with a density above 800 kg/m3. Includes 5.6 MJ bio-energy.
Laminated Veneer Lumber	9.50	$0.31_{fos}+0.32_{bio}$	$0.33_{fos}+0.32_{bio}$	Ref 150. Includes 3.5 MJ bio-energy.
MDF	11 (?)	$0.37_{fos}+0.35_{bio}$	$0.39_{fos}+0.35_{bio}$	Wide density range (350-800 kg/m3). Includes 3.8 MJ bio-energy.
Oriented Strand Board (OSB)	15.00	$0.42_{fos}+0.54_{bio}$	$0.45_{fos}+0.54_{bio}$	Estimated from Refs. 103 and 150. Includes 5.9 MJ bio-energy.
Particle Board	14.50	$0.52_{fos}+0.32_{bio}$	$0.54_{fos}+0.32_{bio}$	Very large data range, difficult to select appropriate values. Modified from CORRIM reports. Includes 3.2 MJ bio-energy (uncertain estimate).
Plywood	15.00	$0.42_{fos}+0.65_{bio}$	$0.45_{fos}+0.65_{bio}$	Includes 7.1 MJ bio-energy.
Sawn Hardwood	10.40	$0.23_{fos}+0.63_{bio}$	$0.24_{fos}+0.63_{bio}$	It was difficult to select values for hardwood, the data was estimated from the CORRIM studies (Ref. 88). Includes 6.3 MJ bio-energy.
Sawn Softwood	7.40	$0.19_{fos}+0.39_{bio}$	$0.20_{fos}+0.39_{bio}$	Includes 4.2 MJ bio-energy.
Veneer Particleboard (Furniture)	$23_{(fos + bio)}$	(?)	(?)	Unknown split of fossil based and biogenic fuels.
Tin				
Tin Coated Plate (Steel)	19.2 to 54.7	1.04 to 2.95	-	
Tin	250.00	13.50	14.47	lack of modern data, large data range
Titanium				
Virgin	361 to 745	19.2 to 39.6 (??)	20.6 to 42.5 (??)	lack of modern data, large data range, small sample size
Recycled	258.00	13.7 (??)	14.7 (??)	lack of modern data, large data range, small sample size
Vinyl Flooring				
General	68.60	2.61	3.19	23.58 MJ/kg Feedstock Energy (Included), Same value as PVC calendered sheet. *Note: the book version of ICE contains the wrong values. These values are up to date*
Vinyl Composite Tiles (VCT)	13.70	-	-	Ref. 94.
Zinc				
General	53.10	2.88	3.09	Uncertain carbon estimates, currently estimated from typical UK industrial fuel mix. Recycled content of general Zinc 30%.
Virgin	72.00	3.90	4.18	
Recycled	9.00	0.49	0.52	

INVENTORY OF CARBON & ENERGY (ICE) SUMMARY

Materials	Embodied Energy & Carbon Coefficients			Comments
	EE - MJ/kg	EC - kgCO2/kg	EC - kgCO2e/kg	EE = Embodied Energy, EC = Embodied Carbon
Miscellaneous (No material profiles):				
	Embodied Energy - MJ	**Embodied Carbon - Kg CO2**		
PV Modules	**MJ/sqm**	**Kg CO2/sqm**		
Monocrystalline	4750 (2590 to 8640)	242 (132 to 440)	-	Embodied carbon estimated from typical UK industrial fuel mix. This is not an ideal method.
Polycrystalline	4070 (1945 to 5660)	208 (99 to 289)	-	
Thin Film	1305 (775 to 1805)	67 (40 to 92)	-	
Roads			Main data source: ICE reference number 147	
Asphalt road - Hot construction method - 40 yrs	2,509 MJ/Sqm	93 KgCO2/Sqm	99 KgCO2/Sqm	730 MJ/Sqm Feedstock Energy (Included). For more detailed data see reference 147. (Swedish study). The data in this report was modified to fit within the ICE framework. Includes all sub-base layers to construct a road. Sum of construction, maintenance, operation.
Construction	1,069 MJ/Sqm	30.9 KgCO2/Sqm	32.8 KgCO2/Sqm	480 MJ/Sqm Feedstock Energy (Included)
Maintenance - 40 yrs	471 MJ/Sqm	11.6 KgCO2/Sqm	12.3 KgCO2/Sqm	250 MJ/Sqm Feedstock Energy (Included)
Operation - 40 yrs	969 MJ/Sqm	50.8 KgCO2/Sqm	54.0 KgCO2/Sqm	Swedish scenario of typical road operation, includes street and traffic lights (95% of total energy), road clearing, sweeping, gritting and snow clearing.
Asphalt road - Cold construction method - 40 yrs	3,030 MJ/Sqm	91 KgCO2/Sqm	97 KgCO2/Sqm	1,290 MJ/kg Feedstock Energy (Included). Sum of construction, maintenance, operation.
Construction	825 MJ/Sqm	26.5 KgCO2/Sqm	28.2 KgCO2/Sqm	320 MJ/Sqm Feedstock Energy (Included)
Maintenance - 40 yrs	1,556 MJ/Sqm	13.9 KgCO2/Sqm	14.8 KgCO2/Sqm	970 MJ/Sqm Feedstock Energy (Included)
Operation - 40 yrs	969 MJ/Sqm	50.8 KgCO2/Sqm	54.0 KgCO2/Sqm	See hot rolled asphalt.
Concrete road - 40 yrs	2,084 MJ/Sqm	142 KgCO2/Sqm	-	Sum of construction, maintenance, operation.
Construction	885 MJ/Sqm	77 KgCO2/Sqm		
Maintenance - 40 yrs	230 MJ/Sqm	14.7 KgCO2/Sqm		
Operation - 40 yrs	969 MJ/Sqm	50.8 KgCO2/Sqm	-	Swedish scenario of typical road operation, includes street and traffic lights (95% of total energy), and also road clearing, sweeping, gritting and snow clearing.

Note: *The above data for roads were based on a single reference (ref 145). There were other references available but it was not possible to process the reports into useful units (per sqm). One of the other references indicates a larger difference between concrete and asphalt roads than the data above. If there is a particular interest in roads the reader is recommended to review the literature in further detail.*

Windows	MJ per Window			
1.2mx1.2m Single Glazed Timber Framed Unit	286 (?)	14.6 (?)	-	Embodied carbon estimated from typical UK industrial fuel mix
1.2mx1.2m Double Glazed (Air or Argon Filled):	--	--	-	--
Aluminium Framed	5470	279		
PVC Framed	2150 to 2470	110 to 126		
Aluminium -Clad Timber Framed	950 to 1460	48 to 75	-	
Timber Framed	230 to 490	12 to 25	-	
Krypton Filled Add:	510	26	-	
Xenon Filled Add:	4500	229	-	

NOTE: Not all of the data could be converted to full GHG's. It was estimated from the fuel use only (i.e. Not including any process related emissions) the full CO2e is approximately 6 percent higher than the CO2 only value of embodied carbon. This is for the average mixture of fuels used in the UK industry.

Index

About the author

CHRIS MAGWOOD HAS DESIGNED AND BUILT some of the most innovative, sustainable buildings in North America, including the first off-grid, straw bale home in Ontario which became a fifteen-year research project into the implementation of sustainable building materials and technologies. He created the Sustainable Building Design and Construction program at Fleming College in 2005, and together with Jen Feigin founded and directs the Endeavour Centre for Innovative Building and Living. Chris is the author of 3 previous books on sustainable building including Straw Bale Details and More Straw Bale Building.

If you have enjoyed *Making Better Buildings* you might also enjoy other

BOOKS TO BUILD A NEW SOCIETY

Our books provide positive solutions for people who want to make a difference. We specialize in:

**Sustainable Living • Green Building • Peak Oil
Renewable Energy • Environment & Economy
Natural Building & Appropriate Technology
Progressive Leadership • Resistance and Community
Educational & Parenting Resources**

New Society Publishers

ENVIRONMENTAL BENEFITS STATEMENT

New Society Publishers has chosen to produce this book on recycled paper made with **100% post consumer waste,** processed chlorine free, and old growth free.

For every 5,000 books printed, New Society saves the following resources:[1]

64	Trees
5,780	Pounds of Solid Waste
6,359	Gallons of Water
8,295	Kilowatt Hours of Electricity
10,506	Pounds of Greenhouse Gases
45	Pounds of HAPs, VOCs, and AOX Combined
16	Cubic Yards of Landfill Space

[1]Environmental benefits are calculated based on research done by the Environmental Defense Fund and other members of the Paper Task Force who study the environmental impacts of the paper industry.

For a full list of NSP's titles, please call 1-800-567-6772 *or check out our website* at:

www.newsociety.com